EVERYMAN,
I WILL GO WITH THEE,
AND BE THY GUIDE,
IN THY MOST NEED
TO GO BY THY SIDE

CYNTHIA OZICK

IN A YELLOW WOOD

WOOD

SELECTED STORIES
AND ESSAYS

WITH AN INTRODUCTION
BY THE AUTHOR

EVERYMAN'S LIBRARY
Alfred A. Knopf New York London Toronto

431

THIS IS A BORZOI BOOK
PUBLISHED BY ALFRED A. KNOPF

First included in Everyman's Library, 2025
Compilation copyright © 2025 by Cynthia Ozick
Introduction copyright © 2025 by Cynthia Ozick
Bibliography and Chronology copyright © 2025 by Everyman's Library

This edition is published by arrangement with Melanie Jackson
Agency, RCW Literary Agency, HarperCollins Publishers, Weidenfeld
& Nicolson, and Atlantic Books Ltd. Details can be found in the
bibliographical note at the end of this volume which constitutes an
extension to this copyright page.

All rights reserved. Published in the United States by Alfred A. Knopf,
a division of Penguin Random House LLC, New York, and distributed
in Canada by Penguin Random House Canada Limited, Toronto.
Distributed by Penguin Random House LLC, New York. Published
in the United Kingdom by Everyman's Library, 50 Albemarle Street,
London W1S 4BD and distributed by Penguin Random House UK,
20 Vauxhall Bridge Road, London SW1V 2SA.

everymanslibrary.com
www.everymanslibrary.co.uk

ISBN: 978-0-593-99220-3 (US)
978-1-84159-431-6 (UK)

A CIP catalogue reference for this book is available from
the British Library

Typography by Peter B. Willberg

Book design by Barbara de Wilde and Carol Devine Carson

Typeset in the UK by Input Data Services Ltd, Bridgwater, Somerset

Printed and bound in Germany by GGP Media GmbH, Pössneck

CONTENTS

v

CYNTHIA OZICK

INTRODUCTION

Two roads diverged in a yellow wood,
And sorry I could not travel both
And be one traveler, long I stood . . .
I took the one less traveled by,
And that has made all the difference.
—Robert Frost

What is to be expected when a writer is asked to introduce a sampling of a lifetime's progression from yearning youth to skeptical old age, and from ink to typewriter to computer, while at the same time zigzagging from fiction to essays and back again? And these two prose-ridden roads: are they less the divergence of separate genres than a unitary mode of metaphysical merging? If the writer's decision—or, rather, her indecision, her unresisted fate—is that of being one traveler on two roads, does this signify that she will be stuck forever in that autumnally yellow wood? And what, after all, is the meaning of the yellow wood? Does it hint at autobiography half-hidden in the undergrowth?

The ink-bottle years had a longhand intent of their own: the inescapably physical. A fountain pen induces the most acutely felt source of *writing*: out of the three fingers gripping its neck, close to the nib, it mainly seeps, but also can gallop. It is conscious of the outermost reach of somatic self-knowledge, even as it denies the nature of body. The silken streaming of ink is kin to how thinking is dreaming. But afterward: nevermore. The muscular reign of the typewriter brought industrial-mechanical noise, and back ache and shoulder strain and wrist tremor. The computer restores something like silence (with a background of tapping like the steady drip of water), but is less efficient than the typewriter, which, unlike the strict separation of a Mac, could combine printing with typing—traveling two roads while still one traveler.

I can, if pressed, devise many reasons for the double presence of stories and essays—but they would be inventions, transparent alibis, made-up stories about non-identical twins. In the past,

I have too often spoken of Intellect and Imagination, claiming that both are present in each of the two byways, but with different proportions: more Intellect in essays, more Imagination in fiction. "An essay," I would say, "begins with something—a subject—already in hand, while fiction is all empty pockets, obliged to search and discover." True enough, but irrelevant. Essays on occasion grow out of reviews, and reviews are, if you are lucky, solicited by editors at periodicals, whatever their format. Or they are responses to some current eruption in the culture, or an irritant arising from history, or memory, or mood. At bottom, who really knows where essays come from? And fiction is even more elusive: from childhood on, the urge toward Story begins with an inexplicable *feeling*, a palpable sensation, an irrepressible desire, a need for a species of wilderness, a naked appetite; and it is always linked to the drive to read, read, read, *so that* you will write.

But—for the sake of honesty—where does all this leave ambition? Again in the past, I would distinguish between ambition, which strives for some self-gratifying scepter of power, and aspiration, which I could perhaps disingenuously define (as in the very first sentence of the first paragraph above) as "yearning." Aspiration is redolent of virtue, and of a kind of gauzy egoless nobility. Ambition is ruthless and machiavellian; it carries clout, it reaches for nothing less forceful than brute fame. Yet there can also be a third face to hungering wishfulness, one that skirts both the ravenous and the rapturous: the hope for recognition. No written work can be regarded as consummated until it attains print—until it admits to its private precincts a public readership, however minuscule it may be. The word itself, concept unclothed in alphabet, is not enough. Nor is recognition the same as success, or just deserts, or vindication. Veracity must own a name. Sequestered in the yellow wood, Melville will sprout, Emily Dickinson will germinate. Some mute inglorious Milton? Likely not. As a cobbler can't be called a cobbler without ever having sold a shoe, in the same way a writer can't claim to be a writer in the absence of assurance that her words may one day come into the hands of a stranger.

And it is from one or another such stranger—happenstance reader or unsparing critic—that I have been given a verdict: in the hierarchy of the kingdom of prose, the essays in this volume, and beyond, are deemed better—more welcoming—than the fiction. But like the forlornly impassioned character in Lionel Trilling's abandoned mid-century novel, I cling to the cry of *novel or nothing*, and to the supremacy of the short story as a corridor to human verity. If the novel has lost its dominance (as the half-forgotten critic Trilling has lost his) in the electronic seas of film and streaming and song, and the short story even more so, how can I gainsay this judgment? In the contest between Make-Believe and an essay declaring itself to be Thought and Idea—and setting aside the quality of the practitioner's skills, or lack of it—viable Thought will nearly always win, Idea will almost always prosper, and Make-Believe will forever go where it must. If an essay fails to persuade, if its theme rots on the vine, it will vanish, unmourned: because even when it has predecessors, it is tethered to a singularity. But Make-Believe is itself the vine, infinitely fructifying; there will always be a living tale somewhere in the making, if not by one writer, then by another. An essay, then, is canny. It knows things, or purports to know them. A story begins by knowing nothing, and is compelled to unearth its own meaning; it has the uncanny power, besides, to beget newer stories, from Odysseus to Leopold Bloom, from Elizabeth Bennet to Isabel Archer.

All the foregoing touches on the *how* of writing. But what of the *why?* In an essay bluntly titled "Why I Write," George Orwell stresses the aesthetic pressure of language, but ties it to citizenly purpose: "What I have most wanted to do . . . is to make political writing into an art." Of his two most influential novels, and also his most lasting, *Animal Farm* and *Nineteen Eighty-four*, one is crafted from Aesopian metaphor and the other from dystopian futurism, and both are steeped in allegory. Under the same heading, but leaving purposefulness behind, Karl Ove Knausgaard defines why he writes as "the ability to hit upon something inadvertently, to regard it from a position of defenselessness and unknowing." Joan Didion, in her own reflections on writing (while admitting that she stole her title from George Orwell), speaks of "pictures in my mind." She tells how they "shimmer for me. Look hard enough, and you can't miss the shimmer. It's there. You can't think too much about these pictures that

shimmer. You just lie low and let them develop. You stay quiet."
A passiveness, an openness to the unpremeditated. The picture,
she concludes, alluding apparently to both fiction and essays,
"tells you. You don't tell it."

In a probing interview, Rachel Cusk interrogates the motives embedded in her novel *Second Place*: "What felt important
to me . . . was to sever certain links with reality and to try to
. . . destabilize the book from its narrative or linear foundations
and to suggest some unreality, some kind of other realm . . . the
question of . . . time and linearity felt unbelievably oppressive."
In musing on "one's own female history," she searches for a
"directionless non-state of non-being, this difficult-to-grasp
phase of femininity." And again: "The question is very, very
bound to the whole idea of the female voice and what that is—
what it really is." Her culminating motif comes as a statement
of crux. "Character is a very difficult thing to believe in or to
assert the existence of in anything other than a very static set of
circumstances."

*Defenseless and unknowing. It tells you, you don't tell it. Some unreality,
some kind of other realm.*

These are tendrils of the tenets of Story's credo.

Yet here is a particle of a Knausgaard paragraph, excavated
from *My Struggle: Book 1*:

As your perspective of the world increases not only is the pain it inflicts
on you less but also its meaning. Understanding the world requires you
to take a certain distance from it. Things that are too small to see with
the naked eye, such as molecules and atoms, we magnify. Things that
are too large, such as cloud formations, river deltas, constellations, we
reduce. At length we bring it within the scope of our senses and we
stabilize it with fixer. When it has been fixed we call it knowledge.

From Rachel Cusk's *Outline*:

I felt that I could swim for miles, out into the ocean: a desire for freedom, an impulse to move, tugged at me as though it were a thread
fastened to my chest. It was an impulse I knew well, and I had learned
that it was not the summons from a larger world I used to believe it
to be. It was simply a desire to escape from what I had. . . . Yet this

impulse, this desire to be free, was still compelling to me: I still, somehow, believed in it, despite having proved that everything about it was illusory.

And from *The Last Thing He Wanted*, by Joan Didion:

Moving fast. Get the big suite, the multiline telephones, get room service on one, get the valet on two, premium service, out by nine back by one. Download all data. . . . Plug into this news cycle, get the wires raw, nod out the noise. *Get me audio,* someone was always saying in the nod where we were. *Agence Presse* is moving this story. Somewhere in the nod we were dropping cargo. . . . Weightlessness seemed at the time the safer mode. Weightlessness seemed at the time the mode in which we could beat both the clock and affect itself, but I see now that it was not. I see now that the clock was ticking.

Each of these first-person ruminative passages is cited, let us recall, not from a writer's memoir, or autobiography, but—perhaps surprisingly—from a novel. In each instance the voice we hear is directly that of the author or, as with Didion, indirectly as the author's stand-in. Nor is this in any way an anomaly in the history of invented narrative: *David Copperfield* is written in the first person, and represents much of Dickens's own experience. *Robinson Crusoe, Jane Eyre, The Catcher in the Rye, Lolita, Huckleberry Finn, The Great Gatsby, The Sound and the Fury,* are all fictions posing as real-life accounts. Still, even if they may pause here and there for an essaylike discursus, not one of these earlier novels turns away from the primacy of character and the explicitly imagined situation.

Didion's salient repute is that of an illustrious journalist: her novels reflect her worldly/political preoccupations; her jazzy staccato sentences are attuned to the au courant. But Knausgaard and Cusk pursue what has come to be called autofiction, a phrase that I believe is less a harmless deceit than an artful trick. If *novel or nothing* continues ascendant as chief among literary goals—as every young writer attests—then the source and the hidden aim of autofiction is to wrest the almost mystical prestige of the novel for the essayist's purpose, not far from George Orwell's hope to make art of politics. Knausgaard and

Cusk show no overt proclivity for political thought, though they are attached to it willy-nilly, Cusk through "the whole idea of the female voice and what that is," and Knausgaard inevitably, however determinedly he and his readers may shun it, by *Min Kamp*, the chosen Norwegian title of his massive work. Didion in her why-I-write manifesto declares outright that she was "no legitimate resident in any world of ideas. I knew I couldn't think," but Knausgaard and Cusk are genuine thinkers. They think ideationally, philosophically, sometimes nearly solipsistically— what is the nature of the self? And when Cusk argues that character "is a very difficult thing to believe in" except when it appears in "a very static set of circumstances" (undefined), she is repudiating not merely the novel in its traditional and modernist forms, but the raison d'être of storytelling itself.

Book I of Knausgaard's *My Struggle* opens with a lengthy meditative essay on human mortality, an objective textbook recounting of the process of the corpse's decay by "enormous hordes of bacteria" in hospitals "hidden away in discrete, inaccessible rooms . . . the dead bodies being wheeled by are always covered." While in "The Death of Ivan Ilyich" Tolstoy is similarly unafraid of confronting the merciless conditions of death and dying, there is no trace of Knausgaard's minutely accumulated clinical abstractions of social institutions, or his microscopic examination of the elemental motes of existence—impressive though these may be. Instead, we are thrust into the destitute aloneness of the moribund Ivan, as he lies in his sickroom only steps away from the superficial chatter of the indifferent living. Ivan gives off the heat of human despair; character seizes belief.

Fifty years ago, in mid-century France, and soon afterward in faddishly vulnerable America, it was the author whom it was difficult to believe in. The leading author of the author-is-dead theorists was the philosopher Roland Barthes, but it was the novel-erasing novelists Nathalie Sarraute and Alain Robbe-Grillet who rose to be household names in the most advanced literary publications of the period. The nouveau roman, as it was dubbed, expunged character, chronology, plot, omniscience, the concept of narrative itself. What remained was a kind of pointillist procession of objects and observations, the world seen less as an encompassment than as a conglomerate of disparate perceptions; it scattered the broken vertebrae of the novel's expectations like wanton dice. "Not only," Robbe-Grillet insisted, "do we no longer consider the world as our very own, our private property, designed according to our needs and readily domesticated, but we no longer believe in its 'depth.'" Susan Sontag, the champion of the American branch of what had become a movement, in 1963 published *The Benefactor*, subtitled *A Novel*, a conscious embodiment of its thesis. From then on, her personal glamor and growing critical authority reshaped a literary era—until the unbridled assumption of the novel's death itself died, and by her own hand. Her repudiation of what she had promulgated in essay after essay came in the form of two late-life novels, *The Volcano Lover* and *In America*. The first is a historical romance, the second an adventure tale about nineteenth-century actors who establish a utopian commune in California. There is character, there is chronology, there is plot in abundance, there is (or hopes to be) storyteller's suspense; there is, above all, the authorial drive not to fulfill an innovative literary manifesto, but to tell a living human story. In an interview in 2000, Sontag in effect sent theory packing: "Writing fiction seems to me a way of being in the world, of paying attention to the world, without imprisoning yourself in yourself." So much for the nouveau roman.

This last phrase—"imprisoning yourself in yourself"—may apply as well to so-called autofiction; but autofiction may not yet be a broadly recognized movement with a roster of named attributes and a webbed history of metaphysical theorists. Nor can two acclaimed adepts be enough to count even as a trend. For all that, Knausgaard and Cusk, though each is distinct from the other, do have something in common; and in common also with the abolished nouveau roman—the obliteration of character and its interpenetration of the world. For both, the self is its own world. As Cusk puts it, "I don't think character exists any more." Or else: character is replaced by self-perception, by the analytical eye of the "I." To acknowledge this is to acknowledge a departure from what we take to be the novel in all its period guises, whether by Fielding, or George Eliot, or Henry James, or the modernists. The analytical eye is the essayist's eye; and to deprive the novel of character is to admit to being, after all, essentially an essayist.

To make this distinction is not to be hostile to the essay or essayists. Essays too can discover, reveal, and astonish, and are writers whose subject is subjectivity to be faulted for eliciting, as they often can, the selfsame stirrings as stories? And more: essays have changed the struts and ramparts and conscience and judgment of whole societies—*Common Sense*, *The Origin of Species*, the *Communist Manifesto*, *Mein Kampf*, Justice Robert Jackson's speech at Nuremberg. But so have novels—*Uncle Tom's Cabin*, Chinua Achebe's *Things Fall Apart*, Elie Wiesel's *Night*, Theodor Herzl's *The Jewish State*, George Orwell's *Nineteen Eighty-four*, Alexander Solzhenitsyn's *The Gulag Archipelago*. In this arena, essay and fiction stand shoulder to shoulder.

Yet by and large, in the less expository and far more intimate corner of the private writer, essays and fiction remain two diverging roads. Few will choose to linger for long in the yellow wood, undecided. As for the stories and essays herein: they carry the Himalayan camel's double hump, and that too has made all the difference. So I ask, is one traveler on two roads afflicted by writerly fever, or has it been little more than hubris and folly?

Cynthia Ozick

SELECT BIBLIOGRAPHY

NOVELS

Trust, New American Library (New York, 1966).
The Cannibal Galaxy, Alfred A. Knopf (New York, 1983).
The Messiah of Stockholm, Alfred A. Knopf (New York, 1987).
The Shawl, Alfred A. Knopf (New York, 1989).
The Puttermesser Papers, Alfred A. Knopf (New York, 1997).
Heir to the Glimmering World, Houghton Mifflin Harcourt (New York, 2004) .
Foreign Bodies, Houghton Mifflin Harcourt (New York, 2010).

STORY COLLECTIONS

The Pagan Rabbi and Other Stories, Alfred A. Knopf (New York, 1971).
Bloodshed and Three Novellas, Random House (New York, 1976).
Levitation: Five Fictions, Alfred A. Knopf (New York, 1982).
Collected Stories, Weidenfeld & Nicolson (London, 2006).
Dictation: A Quartet (novellas), Houghton Mifflin Harcourt (New York, 2008).
Antiquities and Other Stories, Alfred A. Knopf (New York, 2022).

ESSAY COLLECTIONS

Art & Ardor, Alfred A. Knopf (New York, 1983).
Metaphor & Memory, Alfred A. Knopf (New York, 1989).
What Henry James Knew and Other Essays on Writers (London, 1993).
Portrait of the Artist as a Bad Character, Pimlico (London, 1996).
Fame & Folly, Alfred A. Knopf (New York, 1996).
The Cynthia Ozick Reader, ed. Elaine Kauvar, Indiana University Press (1996).
Quarrel & Quandary, Alfred A. Knopf (New York, 2000).
The Din in the Head, Houghton Mifflin Harcourt (New York, 2006).
Critics, Monsters, Fanatics, and Other Literary Essays, Houghton Mifflin Harcourt (New York, 2016).
Letters of Intent: Selected Essays, ed. David Miller, Atlantic Books (London, 2017).

POETRY

Epodes: First Poems, with woodcuts by Sidney Chafetz, Logan Elm Press and Ohio State University (Columbus, 1992).

PLAY

Blue Light, based on (and a sequel to) *The Shawl*. Producers: Kathy Levin, David Brown. Staged reading, Playwrights Horizons, October 1993. Director, Don Scardino (Artistic Director, Playwrights Horizons). Première production, Bay Street Theater, Sag Harbor, Long Island, August 1994. Director, Sidney Lumet. New York production, retitled *The Shawl*, Playhouse 91, Summer 1996. Director, Sidney Lumet.

CRITICISM

BLOOM, HAROLD, ed., *Cynthia Ozick: Modern Critical Views*, Facts on File, 1986.
COHEN, SARAH BLACHER, *Cynthia Ozick's Comic Art: From Levity to Liturgy*, Indiana University Press, 1994.
KAUVAR, ELAINE M., *Cynthia Ozick's Fiction: Tradition and Invention*, Indiana University Press, 1993.
LOWIN, JOSEPH, *Cynthia Ozick*, Twayne Publishers, 1988.
PINSKER, SANFORD, *The Uncompromising Fictions of Cynthia Ozick*, University of Missouri Press, 1987.
STATLANDER-SLOTE, JANE, *Roots of Passion: Essays on Cynthia Ozick*, Aeon Publishing, 2016.

SELECTED INTERVIEWS AND FEATURE ARTICLES

The Guardian, "A Life in Writing: Cynthia Ozick," by Emma Brockes, July 4, 2011.
The New York Times Magazine, "Cynthia Ozick's Long Crusade," by Giles Harvey, June 23, 2016.
The Paris Review, "Cynthia Ozick: The Art of Fiction," by Tom Teicholz, Spring 1987.
The Center for Fiction, Interview by Alessandra Farkas (originally in *Corriere della Sera*, Italy), 2009.
Hadassah Magazine, "Profile: Cynthia Ozick," by Rahel Musleah, February/March 2012.

SELECT BIBLIOGRAPHY

Soundings: An Interdisciplinary Journal, "Cynthia Ozick as the Jewish T. S. Eliot," by Mark Krupnick, Fall/Winter 1991.

Jewish Review of Books, "Cynthia Ozick's Art and Ardor," by Allegra Goodman, Spring 2021.

Studies in American Jewish Literature, Cynthia Ozick and the Art of Nonfiction, Volume 43, Number 1 (special issue), 2024.

CHRONOLOGY

DATE	AUTHOR'S LIFE	LITERARY CONTEXT
1928	Born in New York City (Manhattan), April 17. The second of two children, Ozick is raised in the Bronx by her parents, Celia (née Regelson) and William Ozick, Jewish immigrants from Russia and proprietors of the Park View Pharmacy.	Lawrence: *Lady Chatterley's Lover.* Remarque: *All Quiet on the Western Front.* Woolf: *Orlando.* Yeats: *The Tower.*
1929		Faulkner: *The Sound and the Fury.* Hammett: *The Maltese Falcon.* Hemingway: *A Farewell to Arms.* Larsen: *Passing.* Woolf: *A Room of One's Own*
1930		Eliot: *Selected Poems.* Hughes: *Not Without Laughter.* Waugh: *Vile Bodies.*
1931		Buck: *House of Earth Trilogy* (to 1935). Cather: *Shadows on the Rock.*
1932		Huxley: *Brave New World.*
1933		Hammett: *The Thin Man.* Orwell: *Down and Out in Paris and London.*
1934		Scott Fitzgerald: *Tender Is the Night.* Miller: *Tropic of Cancer.* H. Roth: *Call It Sleep.* Waugh: *A Handful of Dust.*
1935		Du Bois: *Black Reconstruction in America.* Isherwood: *Mr. Norris Changes Trains.* Lewis: *It Can't Happen Here.* Steinbeck: *Tortilla Flat.* Wolfe: *Of Time and the River.*
1936		Faulkner: *Absalom, Absalom!* Mitchell: *Gone with the Wind.*

Hoover elected US president. Fleming discovers penicillin.
USSR: Stalin *de facto* dictator. First Five-Year Plan (to 1932).

Wall Street Crash and beginning of world depression. Trotsky expelled from USSR.

Gandhi begins civil disobedience movement in India.
USSR: Collectivization program accelerated, 25,000 industrial workers dispatched into countryside to enforce it, met with widespread resistance.

Election of Roosevelt in the US. Nazis become largest party in German Reichstag. Stalin's policies result in Great Famine, principally in Ukraine; Moscow refuses relief.
Roosevelt announces New Deal. Hitler becomes Reichskanzler (Chancellor). Concentration camps start in Germany. US recognizes Soviet government.
USSR: Second Five-Year Plan (to 1937).
USSR joins League of Nations. Hitler German Führer.

Nuremberg Laws in Germany deprive Jewish people of citizenship and rights.

Outbreak of Spanish Civil War (to 1939). Hitler and Mussolini form Rome–Berlin Axis.

DATE	AUTHOR'S LIFE	LITERARY CONTEXT
1937		Hurston: *Their Eyes Were Watching God.*
		Steinbeck: *Of Mice and Men.*
		Woolf: *The Years.*
1938		Beckett: *Murphy.*
		Bowen: *The Death of the Heart.*
		Du Maurier: *Rebecca.*
		Orwell: *Homage to Catalonia.*
		Woolf: *Three Guineas.*
1939		Joyce: *Finnegans Wake.*
		Isherwood: *Goodbye to Berlin.*
		Miller: *Tropic of Capricorn.*
		Porter: *Pale Horse, Pale Rider.*
		Rhys: *Good Morning, Midnight.*
		Steinbeck: *The Grapes of Wrath.*
1940		Greene: *The Power and the Glory.*
		Hemingway: *For Whom the Bell Tolls.*
		Stead: *The Man Who Loved Children.*
		Wright: *Native Son.*
1941		Fitzgerald: *The Last Tycoon.*
		Welty: *A Curtain of Green.*
		Woolf: *Between the Acts.*
1942	Attends Hunter College High School in Manhattan (to 1946).	Camus: *The Outsider.*
		M. McCarthy: *The Company She Keeps.*
		Steinbeck: *The Moon Is Down.*
1943		
1944		Bellow: *Dangling Man.*
		Borges: *Ficciones.*
1945		Orwell: *Animal Farm.*
		Waugh: *Brideshead Revisited.*
1946		Frankl: *Man's Search for Meaning.*
		Orwell: *Why I Write.*

CHRONOLOGY

Japanese invasion of China. Stalin's "Great Purge" of the Communist Party (from summer of 1937 to November 1938 approximately 1.6 million people are arrested and 700,000 shot. "Ex-kulaks" and ethnic minorities targeted).

"Kristallnacht" in Germany: Nazis terrorize Jewish community. Germany annexes Austria. Munich Crisis. USSR: Third Five-Year Plan (to 1942).

Nazi-Soviet Pact; Hitler invades Poland. Outbreak of World War II.

Italy enters war as a German ally. German occupation of Belgium, Netherlands, France (part), Norway and Denmark. Battle of Britain. Warsaw ghetto opened. Trotsky assassinated in Mexico.

Japanese attack Pearl Harbor; US enters war. Hitler invades USSR; Siege of Leningrad begins (to 1944). Holocaust in western USSR where around 2 million Jewish people are shot by the Germans (to 1942). In Poland (to 1944) some two-and-a-half million Polish Jews are killed in extermination camps.
Wannsee Conference co-ordinates Hitler's "Final Solution" for the annihilation of the European Jewish population. Russian victory at Stalingrad. Rommel defeated at El-Alamein.

Allied invasions of Italy. Fall of Mussolini. New government under Badoglio declares war on Germany. Further Red Army victories west and south of Stalingrad. Germans surrender in North Africa. Meeting of Churchill, Roosevelt and Stalin in Tehran.
Allied landings in Normandy.

Death of Roosevelt; Truman president. Mussolini shot by Partisans. Fall of Berlin and suicide of Hitler. VE Day: Germany surrenders. End of World War II. US drops atomic bombs on Hiroshima and Nagasaki. Foundation of the United Nations. Nuremberg Trials (to 1946).
USSR extends influence in Eastern Europe. Beginning of Cold War.

CYNTHIA OZICK

DATE	AUTHOR'S LIFE	LITERARY CONTEXT
1947		*The Diary of Anne Frank.* Camus: *The Plague.* Levi: *If This Is a Man.* Williams: *A Streetcar Named Desire.*
1948		Mailer: *The Naked and the Dead.*
1949	B.A. *cum laude*, with honors in English, Phi Beta Kappa, New York University.	de Beauvoir: *The Second Sex.* Miller: *Death of a Salesman.* Orwell: *Nineteen Eighty-Four.*
1950	M.A. in English literature from Ohio State University, focusing on the work of Henry James.	Lessing: *The Grass Is Singing.*
1951		Asimov: *Foundation Trilogy* (1953). Bradbury: *The Illustrated Man.* Forster: *Two Cheers for Democracy.* Salinger: *The Catcher in the Rye.*
1952	Marries Bernard Hallote, a lawyer.	Beckett: *Waiting for Godot.* Ellison: *The Invisible Man.* Hemingway: *The Old Man and the Sea.* Malamud: *The Natural.* O'Connor: *Wise Blood.* Steinbeck: *East of Eden.*
1953		Baldwin: *Go Tell It on the Mountain.* Bellow: *The Adventures of Augie March.* Bradbury: *Fahrenheit 451.* Salinger: *Nine Stories.*
1954		Amis: *Lucky Jim.* Golding: *Lord of the Flies.* Murdoch: *Under the Net.*
1955		Baldwin: *Notes of a Native Son.* Nabokov: *Lolita.*
1956		Baldwin: *Giovanni's Room.* Camus: *The Fall.* Osborne: *Look Back in Anger.*
1957		Cheever: *The Wapshot Chronicle.* Kerouac: *On the Road.* Mailer: *The White Negro.* Malamud: *The Assistant.* Nabokov: *Pnin.* Pasternak: *Doctor Zhivago.*

CHRONOLOGY

DATE	AUTHOR'S LIFE	LITERARY CONTEXT
1958		Achebe: *Things Fall Apart.*
		Capote: *Breakfast at Tiffany's.*
		Lampedusa: *The Leopard.*
		Wiesel: *The Night Trilogy*
		(to 1961).
1959		Bellow: *Henderson the Rain King.*
		Burroughs: *Naked Lunch.*
		Grass: *The Tin Drum.*
1960		Bashevis Singer: *The Magician of Lublin.*
		Lee: *To Kill a Mockingbird.*
		O'Connor: *The Violent Bear It Away.*
		Updike: *Rabbit Angstrom* (to 1981).
1961		Heller: *Catch-22.*
		Naipaul: *A House for Mr. Biswas.*
		Salinger: *Franny and Zooey.*
		Spark: *The Prime of Miss Jean Brodie.*
		Yates: *Revolutionary Road.*
1962		Bashevis Singer: *The Slave.*
		Bassani: *The Garden of the Finzi-Continis.*
		Borges: *Labyrinths.*
		Nabokov: *Pale Fire.*
		Solzhenitsyn: *One Day in the Life of Ivan Denisovich.*
1963		Arendt: *Eichmann in Jerusalem.*
		Baldwin: *The Fire Next Time.*
		Cortázar: *Hopscotch.*
		M. McCarthy: *The Group.*
		Plath: *The Bell Jar.*
		Pynchon: *V.*
1964		Bellow: *Herzog.*
		Selby: *Last Exit to Brooklyn.*
1965	Daughter Rachel is born.	Capote: *In Cold Blood.*
		Mailer: *An American Dream.*
		Pynchon: *The Crying of Lot 49.*
		Wolfe: *The Kandy-Kolored Tangerine-Flake Streamline Baby.*

CHRONOLOGY

HISTORICAL EVENTS

NASA created. US launches Explorer 1 satellite, USSR launches Sputnik 3.

Castro comes to power in Cuba. US vice-president Nixon and USSR premier Khrushchev engage in the impromptu "Kitchen Debate" arguing the merits of capitalism and communism.

Kennedy elected US president. Vietcong formed in Hanoi.

China formally denounces Soviet communism. Erection of Berlin Wall.

Cuban Missile Crisis.

Assassination of President Kennedy. Johnson becomes US president. Protest march on Washington; Martin Luther King Jr.'s "I have a dream" speech.

Civil Rights Act prohibits discrimination in US. Brezhnev becomes Communist Party General Secretary in USSR. Nelson Mandela jailed for life, South Africa (released 1990).
Indo-Pakistani War following Pakistan's Operation Gibraltar.

DATE	AUTHOR'S LIFE	LITERARY CONTEXT
1966	First novel, *Trust*, published.	Asimov: *Fantastic Voyage.* Barth: *Giles Goat-Boy.* Malamud: *The Fixer.* Rhys: *Wide Sargasso Sea.* Solzhenitsyn: *Cancer Ward.* Sontag: *Against Interpretation and Other Essays.*
1967		Bulgakov: *The Master and Margarita.* Kundera: *The Joke.* Márquez: *One Hundred Years of Solitude.* Potok: *The Chosen.* Styron: *The Confessions of Nat Turner.*
1968	Awarded a National Endowment for the Arts Fellowship.	Dick: *Do Androids Dream of Electric Sheep?* Didion: *Slouching Towards Bethlehem.* Mailer: *The Armies of the Night.* Oates: *Expensive People.* Updike: *Couples.*
1969		Angelou: *I Know Why the Caged Bird Sings.* Atwood: *The Edible Woman.* Bradbury: *I Sing the Body Electric.* Oates: *Them.* P. Roth: *Portnoy's Complaint.* Sontag: *Styles of Radical Will.*
1970		Bellow: *Mr. Sammler's Planet.* Didion: *Play It as It Lays.* Morrison: *The Bluest Eye.*
1971	First story collection, *The Pagan Rabbi and Other Stories*, published.	M. McCarthy: *Birds of America.* Munro: *Lives of Girls and Women.* O'Connor: *The Complete Stories.* Stegner: *Angle of Repose.* Thompson: *Fear and Loathing in Las Vegas.*
1972	Finalist for National Book Award, winner of Edward Lewis Wallant Award for Fiction.	Calvino: *Invisible Cities.* Trunk: *Judenrat.* Welty: *The Optimist's Daughter.*

CHRONOLOGY

DATE	AUTHOR'S LIFE	LITERARY CONTEXT
1973	Wins American Academy of Arts and Letters Award for Literature.	Algren: *The Last Carousel.* Morrison: *Sula.* Pynchon: *Gravity's Rainbow.* Solzhenitsyn: *The Gulag Archipelago 1918–1956.*
1974		Baldwin: *If Beale Street Could Talk.* Heller: *Something Happened.*
1975		Bellow: *Humboldt's Gift.* Doctorow: *Ragtime.* Levi: *The Periodic Table.*
1976	*Bloodshed and Three Novellas* published.	Alther: *Kinflicks.* Carver: *Will You Please Be Quiet, Please?* Haley: *Roots.* Kingston: *The Woman Warrior.*
1977		Cheever: *Falconer.* Herr: *Dispatches.* Morrison: *Song of Solomon.*
1978		Cheever: *The Stories of John Cheever.* Greene: *The Human Factor.* Irving: *The World According to Garp.* Kundera: *The Book of Laughter and Forgetting.* Lessing: *Collected Stories.* Murdoch: *The Sea, The Sea.*
1979		Butler: *Kindred.* Calvino: *If on a winter's night a traveler.* Didion: *The White Album.* Mailer: *The Executioner's Song.*
1980	Short story "The Shawl" published in *The New Yorker*; later published as part of a longer work.	Bowen: *Collected Stories.* Eco: *The Name of the Rose.* Grossman: *Life and Fate.* Robinson: *Housekeeping.* Welty: *Collected Stories.*
1981		Carver: *What We Talk About When We Talk About Love.* Márquez: *Chronicle of a Death Foretold.* Plath: *The Collected Poems.* Rushdie: *Midnight's Children.*

CHRONOLOGY

Military coup in Chile: General Pinochet comes to power.
Arab–Israeli War. Supreme Court in US rules that abortion is legal and
suspends capital punishment (until 1976). Mobile phones first marketed.

Nixon resigns after Watergate scandal; Ford becomes US president.

Vietnam War ends. Bill Gates and Paul Allen found Microsoft. Western
powers and USSR sign Helsinki Agreement.

Chairman Mao dies. Carter elected US president. First Apple computer.
Lilith, the Jewish feminist magazine, begins publication.

Camp David Agreement signed by Egyptian president Sadat and Israeli
prime minister Begin.

Soviet troops occupy Afghanistan. Carter and Brezhnev sign SALT II. Shah
of Iran forced into exile; Ayatollah Khomeini establishes an Islamic state;
American embassy siege in Tehran. Margaret Thatcher becomes the UK's
first woman prime minister.

Reagan elected US president. Iran–Iraq War begins (to 1988).

Assassination attempt on Reagan, Washington. Maiden voyage of Space
Shuttle. Egypt: Sadat killed by Islamic fundamentalists.

DATE	AUTHOR'S LIFE	LITERARY CONTEXT
1982	Finalist, National Book Critics Circle Award; awarded Guggenheim Fellowship and American Academy of Arts and Letters Strauss Living Award; *Levitation: Five Fictions* published.	Allende: *The House of the Spirits*. Levi: *If Not Now, When?* Mason: *Shiloh and Other Stories*. Walker: *The Color Purple*.
1983	Finalist, National Book Critics Circle Award; *The Cannibal Galaxy* published; *Art & Ardor* published.	Carver: *Cathedral*. Updike: *Hugging the Shore*. Welty: *One Writer's Beginnings*.
1984	Finalist, PEN/Faulkner Award; Distinguished Service in Jewish Letters Award, Jewish Theological Seminary. Awarded first of many honorary degrees.	Brookner: *Hotel du Lac*. Cisneros: *The House on Mango Street*. Kundera: *The Unbearable Lightness of Being*. Duras: *The Lover*. Updike: *The Witches of Eastwick*.
1985		Atwood: *The Handmaid's Tale*. Auster: *The New York Trilogy* (to 1986). DeLillo: *White Noise*. Márquez: *Love in the Time of Cholera*. Murakami: *Hard-Boiled Wonderland and the End of the World*. Tyler: *The Accidental Tourist*.
1986	Rea Award for the Short Story.	Davis: *Break It Down*. Munro: *The Progress of Love*. Spiegelman: *Maus: A Survivor's Tale* (second volume 1991).
1987	*The Messiah of Stockholm* published.	Ellroy: *L.A. Quartet* (to 1992). Didion: *Miami*. Morrison: *Beloved*. Murakami: *Norwegian Wood*. Wolfe: *The Bonfire of the Vanities*.
1988	Finalist, PEN/Faulkner Award. Elected to American Academy of Arts and Letters.	Atwood: *Cat's Eye*. Carey: *Oscar and Lucinda*. Carver: *Where I'm Calling From*. Rushdie: *The Satanic Verses*. Tyler: *Breathing Lessons*.
1989	*Metaphor & Memory* published; *The Shawl* published.	Auster: *Moon Palace*. Irving: *A Prayer for Owen Meany*. Ishiguro: *The Remains of the Day*. Tan: *The Joy Luck Club*.

CHRONOLOGY

Equal Rights Amendment does not meet requirement of thirty-eight state ratifications and is not adopted as a constitutional amendment. Beginning of 1980s stock market boom in US. Lebanese Civil War: multinational force lands in Beirut to oversee the PLO withdrawal from Lebanon. Falklands War between Argentina and UK. IBM Personal Computer launched.

US troops invade Grenada after government overthrown. Famine in Ethiopia.

Reagan re-elected in landslide. Indian prime minister Indira Gandhi assassinated.

Reform begins in USSR under Gorbachev, new General Secretary of the Communist Party.

US bombs Libya. Gorbachev–Reagan summit. Nuclear explosion in Chernobyl, USSR. Elie Wiesel wins Nobel Peace Prize.

Reagan makes Berlin Wall speech. World population reaches five billion.

George H. W. Bush elected US president. Soviet troops withdrawn in large numbers from Afghanistan.

Berlin Wall dismantled. Communism collapses in Eastern Europe. Tiananmen Square massacre in China. USSR holds first democratic elections. US troops invade Panama. Tim Berners-Lee publishes research paper proposing World Wide Web.

DATE	AUTHOR'S LIFE	LITERARY CONTEXT
1990	Finalist, National Book Critics Circle Award.	Byatt: *Possession*.
1991		Pynchon: *Vineland*.
		Chang: *Wild Swans: Three Daughters of China*.
		Okri: *The Famished Road*.
		Smiley: *A Thousand Acres*.
1992	Founding member of Académie Universelle des Cultures, Paris (Elie Wiesel, president); *Epodes: First Poems* published.	C. McCarthy: *The Border Trilogy* (to 1998).
		Oates: *Black Water*.
		Ondaatje: *The English Patient*.
		Tartt: *The Secret History*.
1993	*What Henry James Knew and Other Essays on Writers* published in London.	Eugenides: *The Virgin Suicides*.
		Proulx: *The Shipping News*.
		Vikram Seth: *A Suitable Boy*.
1994	*Blue Light*, play based on (and sequel to) *The Shawl*, première production with Dianne Wiest, directed by Sidney Lumet, Bay Street Theater, Sag Harbor, N.Y.	Gurnah: *Paradise*.
		Guterson: *Snow Falling on Cedars*.
		Heller: *Closing Time*.
		Márquez: *Of Love and Other Demons*.
		Murakami: *The Wind-Up Bird Chronicle*.
		Oates: *What I Lived For*.
1995		P. Roth: *Sabbath's Theater*.
1996	*Fame & Folly* published; *Portrait of the Artist as a Bad Character* published in London; *The Cynthia Ozick Reader*, edited by Elaine Kauvar, published; *The Shawl*, New York production, directed by Sidney Lumet, Playhouse 91, New York, N.Y.	Atwood: *Alias Grace*.
		Updike: *In the Beauty of the Lilies*.
		Wallace: *Infinite Jest*.
1997	Finalist for Pulitzer Prize (*Fame & Folly*); *The Puttermesser Papers* published (finalist for National Book Award); PEN/Spiegel-Diamondstein Award for the Art of the Essay; Harold Washington City of Chicago Literary Award; National Jewish Book Council Award for Distinguished Literary Contribution.	Bellow: *The Actual*.
		De Lillo: *Underworld*.
		Frazier: *Cold Mountain*.
		Morrison: *Paradise*.
		Pynchon: *Mason & Dixon*.
		P. Roth: *American Pastoral*.
1998	National Magazine Award for Essays and Criticism.	Pamuk: *My Name Is Red*.
1999	John Cheever Award; finalist, International IMPAC Dublin Literary Award.	Coetzee: *Disgrace*.
		Lahiri: *Interpreter of Maladies*.
		Lethem: *Motherless Brooklyn*.

CHRONOLOGY

Gulf War begins. Nelson Mandela released in South Africa. Boris Yeltsin becomes president of Russia. NASA deploys Hubble Space Telescope. Bush and Gorbachev sign START arms reduction treaty.

Bill Clinton elected US president. War in Bosnia.

Palestinian leader Arafat signs peace agreement with Israeli prime minister Rabin. World Trade Center bombing.

Apartheid ends in South Africa. Mandela's ANC takes power after South African elections. Civil war in Rwanda. Jordan and Israel sign peace treaty.

Rabin assassinated in Israel. Oklahoma City bombing. Launch of eBay. Clinton re-elected US president. UN adopts Comprehensive Nuclear Test Ban Treaty.

Hong Kong: transfer of sovereignty to China by the UK. Economic crisis: stock markets around the world crash, Dow Jones Industrial Average plummets. Death of Princess Diana in Paris. First public use of WiFi.

Clinton impeached over sex scandal (acquitted 1999). Good Friday peace agreement in Northern Ireland. Google founded.
Ethnic Albanians attacked by Serbs in Kosovo; US leads NATO in bombing of Belgrade.

DATE	AUTHOR'S LIFE	LITERARY CONTEXT
1999 *cont.*		Sontag: *In America*. Whitehead: *The Intuitionist*.
2000	Lannan Foundation Award for Fiction; *Quarrel & Quandary* published.	Atwood: *The Blind Assassin*. Bellow: *Ravelstein*. Chabon: *The Amazing Adventures of Kavalier & Clay*. P. Roth: *The Human Stain*. Smith: *White Teeth*.
2001	National Book Critics Circle Award for Criticism.	Franzen: *The Corrections*. Gordimer: *The Pickup*. Martel: *Life of Pi*. McEwan: *Atonement*. Munro: *Hateship, Friendship, Courtship, Loveship, Marriage*. Russo: *Empire Falls*.
2002		Eugenides: *Middlesex*. Safran Foer: *Everything Is Illuminated*. Krauss: *Man Walks into a Room*. Shields: *Unless*. Pamuk: *Snow*.
2003		Atwood: *Oryx and Crake*. Hosseini: *The Kite Runner*. DeLillo: *Cosmopolis*.
2004	*Heir to the Glimmering World* published.	Mitchell: *Cloud Atlas*. Robinson: *Gilead Series* (to 2020). P. Roth: *The Plot Against America*.
2005	Finalist, International Man-Booker Award.	Didion: *The Year of Magical Thinking*. Ishiguro: *Never Let Me Go*. Krauss: *The History of Love*.
2006	*The Din in the Head* published; hardcover *Collected Stories* published in London.	Adichie: *Half of a Yellow Sun*. C. McCarthy: *The Road*. Munro: *The View from Castle Rock*. Pynchon: *Against the Day*. Updike: *Terrorist*.
2007	*The Shawl* is selected in the US for the nation-wide Big Read project of the National Endowment for the Arts; awarded Presidential Medal for the Humanities.	Chabon: *The Yiddish Policemen's Union*. J. Díaz: *The Brief Wondrous Life of Oscar Wao*. Russo: *Bridge of Sighs*.

CHRONOLOGY

George W. Bush elected US president. Putin succeeds Yeltsin as Russian president. Milosevic's regime collapses in former Yugoslavia.

Al-Qaeda attacks New York's World Trade Center; US and allies take action against Taliban in Afghanistan.

Bush creates Department of Homeland Security. Moscow theater hostage crisis.

US and British troops invade Iraq; Saddam Hussein captured.

Bush re-elected US president. Terrorist bombings in Madrid. Tsunami in Indian Ocean. Facebook launched.

Hurricane Katrina floods New Orleans. Terrorist bombings in London. YouTube founded.

Iran joins "nuclear club." North Korea tests nuclear weapon. Saddam Hussein sentenced to death.

Virginia Tech shooting. Bush reduces US forces in Iraq. Al Gore and UN climate scientists win Nobel Peace Prize. Nancy Pelosi elected first woman Speaker of US Congress. iPhone introduced.

DATE	AUTHOR'S LIFE	LITERARY CONTEXT
2008	PEN/Nabokov Award; PEN/Malamud Award; *Maison des écrivaines étrangers* (Institute of Foreign Writers) prize, France; *Dictation: A Quartet* published.	Auster: *Man in the Dark*. Lahiri: *Unaccustomed Earth*. Oates: *My Sister, My Love*.
2009		Kingsolver: *The Lacuna*. Moore: *The Gate at the Stairs*. Munro: *Too Much Happiness*. Murakami: *1Q84*. P. Roth: *The Humbling*. Tóibín: *Brooklyn*.
2010	*Foreign Bodies* published.	Auster: *Sunset Park*. Egan: *A Visit from the Goon Squad*. Franzen: *Freedom*.
2011	National Jewish Book Center Lifetime Achievement Award.	Eugenides: *The Marriage Plot*. Ferrante: *My Brilliant Friend*. Patchett: *State of Wonder*. Wallace: *The Pale King*.
2012	Shortlisted for Orange Prize.	Morrison: *Home*. Munro: *Dear Life*. Tyler: *The Beginner's Goodbye*.
2013	*Foreign Bodies* shortlisted for Wingate Book Prize, London.	Adichie: *Americanah*. Tartt: *The Goldfinch*.
2014		Atwood: *Stone Mattress*. Oates: *Lovely, Dark, Deep*. Smiley: *The Last Hundred Years Trilogy* (to 2015).
2015		Beatty: *The Sellout*. Franzen: *Purity*. Hannaham: *Delicious Foods*. Lee: *Go Set a Watchman*. Morrison: *God Help the Child*. Rushdie: *Two Years Eight Months & Twenty-Eight Nights*. Yanagihara: *A Little Life*.
2016	*Critics, Monsters, Fanatics, and Other Literary Essays* published.	Whitehead: *The Underground Railroad*. Gyasi: *Homegoing*.
2017	Husband Bernard dies. *Letters of Intent: Selected Essays* published in London.	Auster: *4 3 2 1*. Egan: *Manhattan Beach*. Strout: *Anything is Possible*.
2018		Burns: *Milkman*. Moshfegh: *My Year of Rest and Relaxation*.

CHRONOLOGY

Barack Obama, Democratic Senator from Illinois, elected first Black president of the US. Collapse of Lehman Brothers triggers world financial crisis.

Ongoing world financial crisis. H1N1 ("swine flu") global pandemic. Obama awarded Nobel Peace Prize.

Healthcare Reform Bill passed by President Obama. Deepwater Horizon (BP rig) oil spill in Gulf of Mexico. US combat mission ends in Iraq. iPad introduced.
"Arab Spring": protests and rebellions against repressive regimes across Middle East. Syrian Civil War begins. Osama Bin Laden killed by US Navy Seals.

Obama re-elected US president. Mars Science Laboratory "Curiosity Rover" lands on Mars. Xi Jinping becomes General Secretary of Chinese Communist Party (CCP).
Edward Snowden leaks classified documents revealing mass surveillance by the US National Security Agency. Boston Marathon bombing. Black Lives Matter movement begins.
Russia annexes Crimea. ISIS declares Islamic Caliphate.

Iran agrees deal on nuclear program with world powers. Paris Climate Accord commits majority of countries to reducing greenhouse gas emissions. Islamic terror attacks in Paris. Refugee crisis in Europe. US Supreme Court rules that all states must recognize same-sex marriage.

Trump wins US presidential election. UK referendum on EU membership results in "Leave" vote. Missile and nuclear testing in North Korea. Coup in Turkey fails.
Trump takes up office of president, promising to "make America great again." Xi Jinping granted second term as General Secretary of CCP. North Korean crisis (to 2018).
"Trade War": Trump imposes tariffs on imports from China. Trump announces his intention to withdraw the US from the Iranian nuclear agreement but negotiates with North Korea's Kim Jong-un over denuclearization. #MeToo movement goes global.

DATE	AUTHOR'S LIFE	LITERARY CONTEXT
2019		Atwood: *The Testaments.*
		Whitehead: *The Nickel Boys.*
2020		DeLillo: *The Silence.*
		Offill: *Weather.*
		Yu: *Interior Chinatown.*
2021	Paperback *Collected Stories* published in London.	Didion: *Let Me Tell You What I Mean.*
		Everett: *The Trees.*
		Franzen: *Crossroads.*
		Ishiguro: *Klara and the Sun.*
2022	*Antiquities and Other Stories* published.	H. Diaz: *Trust.*
		Egan: *The Candy House.*
		C. McCarthy: *The Passenger.*
		Yanagihara: *To Paradise.*

CHRONOLOGY

Hong Kong protests (to 2020). President Trump impeached. Amazon rainforest wildfires. First COVID-19 case in Wuhan, China.

COVID-19 declared a pandemic by World Health Organization. Climate disasters continue: Australia fire season, US wildfires, droughts and tropical storms. George Floyd killed by police in Minneapolis, triggering worldwide Black Lives Matter protests. Biden elected as president; Kamala Harris elected first Black vice president.

Trump supporters storm the Capitol building in protest of election results. US commits to rejoin Paris Climate Agreement. COVID-19 vaccine created. Last US troops withdraw from Afghanistan; Taliban take over the country.

Russia invades Ukraine. Roe v Wade overturned by US Supreme Court; constitutional protections for abortion severed. Inflation rises worldwide. Protesters in Iran march against the country's treatment of women. Pakistan flooding crisis. Death of Queen Elizabeth II.

STORIES

The Coast of New Zealand

To burn always with this hard, gemlike flame,
to maintain this ecstasy, is success in life.
——WALTER PATER

THE LAST TIME George and the three women met, it was
on a warm October afternoon in that same small Greek restaurant, with bluish fluorescent lights overhead, in Stamford,
Connecticut. Their knees were crowded under the tablecloth,
and inadvertently rubbed one against another. Though they
all wore glasses (Ruby was seriously myopic), even so it was
difficult to read the menu.

"Nice," George said. "Gives the place the feel of a modest
bordello." And only Evangeline laughed; Olive made a face,
and Ruby sighed in disgust, but it was merely to tease. Not
that it escaped him that behind the ribbing was an old and
avid jealousy; they adored what they could not attain. He had
decided on Stamford as the geographical midpoint of their
reunion, he told them, because it was equidistant from wherever their fates might eventually drive them. It was the very
center of the planet's fragile equilibrium. But why, they asked,
this unprepossessing eatery smelling of fried eggplant? Because,
he said, the eggplant is earth's most beautifully sculptured fruit.

The four of them had been at library school together, and
had exchanged clandestine notes in a course on the history
of books, which George, one of three males in the class, had
named Spinsters 101. The two others he called Mouse One and
Mouse Two. The notes were all about George, and George
wrote notes about himself: *six feet two*, *brainy*, *unusual*. Or else:
early balding, *doomed to success*. And once, nastily: *Lady librarians
never marry*.

By the time they graduated, he had slept with all of them.

They had long ago forgiven him, and also one another. And
they had all agreed to abide by the Pact—George's invention.

Its terms were simple enough: once a year they were to gather at this very spot, if possible at their usual table (but they must insist on this), the one closest to the kitchen. All correspondence, any exchange of any kind in the long intervals between meetings, was forbidden. Tales of dailiness and its intimacies, their cluttered lives, their tiny news and parochial views were never to be the object of their coming together. Consensus was forbidden; the Pact was a treaty of solitary will. "Our interest," he explained, "lies in extremes. Abhor the mundane, shun the pedestrian. Cause the natural to become unnatural." And then this: "What is our object? To live in the whirlpool of the extraordinary. To aspire to the ultimate stage of fanaticism. To know that eventuality is always inevitability, that the implausible is the true authenticity." He spoke these words with the portentousness of Laurence Olivier as Henry V rallying the troops on St. Crispin's Day.

They were sensible women, and took it as the joke they believed it was meant to be: to live life as a witticism. As a feat. As an opera. But it was also an Idea, and George was a master of ideas. They had their Idea too: they were committed feminists, despised patriarchy, and loathed what they could instantly sense was male domination. George was exempted from such despicable categories. He was a schemer of witchcraft. His brain was neither male nor female. It was, they understood, a vessel of daring, and they had only to climb aboard to feel its oceanic sweep. They were not four, or three, or two. They were, counting George, One.

He had been drawn to them, lured by those dusty old curios—their preposterous names. It was as if they had been situated together the way artifacts similar in the taste of an era are collected in the same museum vitrine. It must mean something, he said, that you are all named for grandmothers or great-grandmothers.

"Well, what does it mean?" Ruby asked.

"He thinks we're ghosts," Evangeline said.

But Olive said, "It was just the way the schedule worked out. We were assigned to the same class in the same room at the same time. It was bound to happen."

"What a pedant you are," Evangeline said.

Evangeline's grandmother's name was, in fact, Bella, but she let the misapprehension stand. She had no wish to admit that she was stuck with Evangeline because it was her grandmother's favorite poem. Still, nothing could prevent George from declaiming the first twenty-two lines of it, which he had, in hoarse and secretive breaths, by heart. The rest of them could remember only the opening words: *This is the forest primeval.* Nowadays nobody quoted Longfellow, or even knew who he was. And they were all dumbstruck by George's acrobatic memory. This alone set him apart.

It lasted—the Pact—four years. Or it might have been four, had the Greek restaurant with the bluish fluorescent lights not in the interim been replaced by a used-car lot.

On that fourth year, only Evangeline showed up.

"It can't be a Pact if it's only the two of us," Evangeline said. "A Pact has to have several parties, like the Kellogg-Briand Pact, or the Triple Entente. It can't be just us."

They walked around the block, looking for a coffee shop. It was a shabby neighborhood, battered stucco houses with high stoops, noisy ragamuffins with their sticks and balls.

Ragamuffins was George's word. Evangeline noticed that he had taken on something like a British accent, though not quite. He looked different. Not that old student outfit, sweatshirt and jeans and no socks. He wore an actual suit, with a surprising vest that had a little pocket for an old-fashioned watch on a chain. The jacket was a showy tweed, with outmoded leather patches on the elbows and pimpled all over with forest-green nubbles. The patches were a bright orange worthy of parrots. His tie was diagonally striped, and it too had the look of obsolescence. He'd acquired the suit in New Zealand, he said, to look more like the New Zealanders. They were notorious swimmers, and in summer went about half naked, but otherwise they dressed like peacocks.

In the end, they found a dirty little park, more concrete than leafy, and sat on a bench sticky with bird droppings. But it could not be avoided: they spoke of the mundane and the pedestrian and the parochial—what had become of the

defectors. Ruby had found a job as the librarian of an elementary school in an obscure Ohio town (population 1,396).
Olive, who had settled in Chesapeake, Virginia, was already
the mother of two little boys, and worked part-time in the
local branch of the public library. She was no longer Olive; she
had changed her name to Susan—talk of the mundane! And
even Evangeline, who hadn't defected and remained loyal to
the Pact, had to acknowledge that she was more chauffeur than
librarian. She drove a green truck outfitted with bookshelves to
a far weedy corner of the Bronx, on the odorous edge of rusted
railroad tracks.

But George had emigrated to New Zealand. His position
there, he said, had a future. Though he was now on the middle
rung of a great university library in Auckland, in five years, he
predicted, he would be its director. It was an ingenuity of fore-
sight that had landed him in the very first library to digitize, not
only in New Zealand but in the world at large. New Zealand
was a model, and it was in connection with this revolutionary
transition that he had been sent as a liaison to New York on an
errand that required discretion. His value was recognized. The
director had arranged for him to stay at the Waldorf, certainly
to facilitate meetings but also for his personal comfort.

Evangeline herself had an unexpected story to tell. In that
forlorn neighborhood, where on Friday afternoons the clusters of children and their mothers were congregated under
umbrellas (it seemed always to be raining), waiting for the
green truck and its cargo, she too beheld her imminent good
fortune. She had seen surveyors' chalkings on the pavements
around a disused old comfort station marked for renovation. It
was a low handsome concrete building in the style of a Greek
temple; weathered carvings of Hygeia, the goddess of health,
and Amphitrite, the goddess of waters, ran across the frieze
below its pediment. From the look of it, you couldn't imagine
that it had once housed public toilets. What it promised for
Evangeline was that the truck with its dented fenders and its
rain-damaged books would be cashiered, and she would soon
be permitted to come indoors.

"An anointment," George said. "From bottom-feeder to

kingfish." It meant, Evangeline knew, that he didn't think much of her prospects. She was letting down her solitary will.

They abandoned the bench and walked together to the train station. According to the Pact, its adherents were obliged to disperse immediately after the completion of the proceedings of the reunion; no one was to spy on the destination of the others. But it couldn't be helped: they had to board the same train, and because of the rush-hour crowding had to sit in the same car. George was heading for Grand Central in Manhattan to get to the Waldorf, and Evangeline for the Fordham stop in the Bronx. They had even found seats directly across the aisle.

Leaning over, Evangeline asked, "But we still haven't decided where to meet next time. Or when."

"Same date as always."

"How do you know you'll be able to come? Supposing the university doesn't send you?"

"As it happens, I have another reason. A family reason. I've told you about my uncle."

He had. He had told all three of them at their very first meeting in the Greek restaurant; he had told them every jot and tittle of what he called his blighted yet colorful bloodline. His parents were suicides. Side by side, like Stefan Zweig and his wife Lotte in Petrópolis, they had taken poison. He was then a child of two. He knew nothing about it for years, only that his mother and father weren't really his mother and father: they were his great-aunt and his great-uncle. They were both very old, and his aunt was dead. In their prime, they had been vaudevillians. Their closets were packed with stage apparel. George often had his dinners in the wings. The Waldorf was agreeable, he admitted, but he'd much prefer to stay with his unregenerate uncle, at ninety-nine still hankering after a gig.

None of the others knew where Petrópolis was. Olive guessed Greece, but Evangeline said, "Two suicides? One would be excessive, but two is exorbitant."

Ruby asked, "Is that Oscar Wilde?"

"Evangeline, how heartless you are," Olive said. Still, George didn't mind: the uncommon was his legacy. It was what he sought. He knew he was a sport, a daring mutation. He took his stand on the precipice of life, and if Evangeline wanted to mock, it was all right with him. He knew it was out of envy.

"Fine," Evangeline said, "same date, but where?"

"Same place."

"But there's nothing there!" she called as she stepped out of the car.

"There will be," he yelled back.

The newly constructed library had a laboratory look, sleek and metallic. It betrayed everything library school remembered. Gone were the wood-paneled walls, gone were the wooden drawers with their rows of handwritten index cards. Gone were the pencils with those overworked rubber date stamps on their tails. And gone were the footprints of winter boots (here they left no marks on the all-weather carpet), and, in summer, gone was the staccato creak of antique fans as they turned their necks from side to side. Instead: rows of computers with their cold faces, air-conditioners and their goosepimpling blasts. Polite young men with research degrees—Mouse One and Mouse Two—behind steel desks. Because of the double-glazed windows you could never smell the rain.

Evangeline blamed Hygeia and Amphitrite for permitting this invasion; they had since been removed as unfit for contemporary taste. The plumbing was new, the temple bare of its goddesses. Its visitors were called, condescendingly, customers, as if they were coming to argue over the cost of tomatoes in a market. The children's room was located in what had been the women's toilets, far from the hushed center. And unlike the shrieks and the tumult that had greeted the green truck when it veered into view, here it was disconcertingly quiet. Many of the customers seemed to be hobbyists, or half-insane cranks catching up on their sleep, or lonely browsers searching for spiritual succor.

The more typical customers came and went with their emptied plastic grocery bags newly loaded, but the hobbyists were the most persistent. They would arrive at ten in the morning and sit at the reading tables until four in the afternoon. They were mostly elderly widows copying needlepoint patterns, or genealogical enthusiasts hoping to find a royal ancestor, or backyard farmers who grew potatoes in pots and were looking into the possibility of beekeeping.

But one of these oddities appeared to be a generation younger than the rest, and turned up only one day a week, generally not long before closing. He was of middling height and habitually carried a worn canvas portfolio. He wore a seaman's cap—an affectation, Evangeline decided, meant to counteract mediocrity. He would spend no more than half an hour with a writing pad and—this was notable—a child's box of crayons, gazing at colorful photographs in sizable volumes and making notes. His subject was birds, she saw, each time a different bird. His drawings were moderately talented. He used every crayon in the box. Though he always arrived late in the day, he rarely overstayed; but once, hurrying to pack up when the lights were already switched off, he left behind one of his papers. It had slipped from the table to the floor, unnoticed.

Evangeline picked it up. It was a picture of a bird with pink legs and yellow breast feathers, and under it, in capital letters, SMALL-HEADED FLYCATCHER.

"I saved this for you," she told him the next time he came. "I thought you might be missing it."

"It's extinct," he said, "so it's really missing. You can only see it in Audubon."

"Are you an artist?" she asked, though she doubted it. He didn't have the look of an artist. He said he was interested in bird-watching, and it was only his amateur's illusion that he might someday spot an actual small-headed flycatcher. It turned out that he was a math teacher in a nearby high school. She asked him, politely, what subjects he taught. Elementary algebra, he said, intermediate algebra, geometry, trigonometry, spherical trigonometry, and, for the advanced students, introduction to calculus. His recitation was insistently precise.

After that she dismissed him as intolerably earnest. Even his drawings of each minute nostril hole in each beak testified to dogged monotony: beak after beak after beak, all with those tiny black specks. But he began arriving earlier, and lingered on, and now and then he approached her desk to display his latest work.

"This one," he explained, "is a blue mountain warbler, and look at this eastern pinnated grouse, it's really a species of prairie chicken. They're both extinct. Did you know what a butcher Audubon was? He killed thousands of birds to lay out their carcasses to paint."

And then he invited her to go bird-watching on the coming Sunday.

Looking up from her keyboard (Evangeline too was now digitized), she choked down a laugh. Was this middle-sized fellow in a seaman's cap courting her?

"I have an excellent pair of binoculars," he told her, "manufactured just outside of London. Very old firm, same outfit that makes the insides of grandfather clocks." He held out his hand in formal introduction. "Nate Vogel. Unfortunately, my name is a coincidence." And he added, in a voice she recognized as teacherly, "It means bird, you know."

Evangeline glanced down at her computer screen to check the date. September 26th. In three weeks it would be time for the Pact. She had already consulted her "Atlas of the Seven Continents" for Petrópolis (it was in Brazil), but what did she know of New Zealand? Nor would she come to George empty-handed, with nothing unusual of her own to tell.

On this ground she agreed to go bird-watching with Nate Vogel. After all, isn't the ludicrous also a kind of fanaticism, and must not the natural be made unnatural? And anyhow, she reflected, birds are the descendants of dinosaurs.

"You'd better put on your galoshes," he warned her. "Where we're going the soil can be moist. It's only a short drive." But galoshes were what Evangeline's grandmother had worn when it snowed, and in the stifling dry heat of late summer sandals were good enough.

Their destination turned out to be a swamp. He led her through a watery forest of waist-high yellow-haired cattails where mosquitoes hovered in swarms, and showed her how to keep her head down so as to be camouflaged by the wild tangle of vegetation all around. The air was too dense to breathe, and the mud was seeping upward between her naked toes. Small thin snakes—or were they large fat worms—came crawling out of the nowhere of this dizzying shiver of living things.

Evangeline said, "My feet are drowning."

"Quiet, don't speak, it makes vibrations they can feel. See over there?" He passed her the binoculars. His whisper was as thin as a hiss. "It's a saltmarsh sparrow, nothing special, they're common around here."

"What am I supposed to look for?" she whispered back.

"You have to do your homework first. You have to be prepared."

"Prepared for what?"

"The thrill of identification."

What Evangeline saw was a bird. It was a bird like any other bird. And, like any other bird, it instantly flew away.

"Now look what you've done," he said. "I told you not to speak. You've missed everything. Now we just have to wait."

Submissively, she handed back the binoculars. They sat side by side in silence, squatting in the wet. And then, disobeying his own rule, he explained exactly what she had missed: "The saltmarsh sparrow has a flat head with orange eyebrows and orange sidelocks and a speckled belly. The male is sexually promiscuous." Was this a direct quote from Audubon?

"I didn't know that birds are subject to moral standards," Evangeline said.

"Sh-h-h! There's another one. No, no, over there, to your left, quick, here, take the binoculars!"

This second bird was indistinguishable from the first. But now she knew what to look for: eyebrows and sidelocks, the thrill of identification. And she did feel a thrill, a horrible one. The bird was gazing at her with its single eye on the side of its flat head—a pterodactyl's cold indifferent Mesozoic eye.

They met again in the library on Monday afternoon. "I hope you enjoyed our little excursion yesterday," he said. "I hope you found it enlightening."

She decided to punish him. "I had to throw out my best sandals. They were soaked."

"What size are they? I'll be glad to get you a new pair."

But, instead, he brought her, on the following Monday, a small square box with a ribbon glued on its top. Inside was a necklace with a pendant: a shiny miniature monocular.

"It isn't real silver," he informed her. "It's chrome, so it won't ever tarnish. I thought you'd like it as a memento."

He had come without his seaman's cap, and also without his crayons. Evangeline thought he looked somewhat taller in the absence of the cap, as if it had been squashing the top of his head. And it was true that his hair stood up like a hedge. It irritated her that his eyelashes were almost invisibly pale. He was one of those self-flattered men who were still as blond as young children. The memento she slipped into her purse, intending to forget it.

He said, "So how about dinner Thursday next week?"

"Sorry," Evangeline said. "I have a meeting in Stamford."

"What kind of meeting?"

"I do have a private life," she retorted.

"Fine, then the week after," he said.

Evangeline was pleased to have outwitted him—the Pact was set for Wednesday. But ornithology had anyhow enlightened her: George was a bird in the bush, and the bush was on the nether side of the globe. He had abandoned his natural habitat and had migrated to unknown skies and foreign seasons. Had he evolved to new instincts? In the space of a year she had almost forgotten the color of his eyes. She longed for the thrill of identification.

On the Internet she read:

New Zealand is an island country in the southwestern Pacific Ocean. The country geographically comprises two main landmasses and numerous smaller islands. Because of its remoteness, it was one of the last lands to be inhabited by humans. During its long period of isolation, New Zealand developed a biodiversity of animal, fungal, and plant life. Some time between 1250 and 1300 CE, Polynesian settlers arrived and adapted a distinctive Maori culture. In 1642, a Dutch explorer became the first European to sight New Zealand. Bats and some marine animals are the sole native mammals. Indigenous flora are abundant, including rimu,

*tawa, matai, rata, and tussock. High waters skirt forests, parks,
and beaches.*

But the Internet couldn't tell her whether George's eyes
were brown or gray, or how and where he lived. Surely not
in commonplace university housing. Then in a little shack (he
would call it a cottage) on the rim of the fathomless Pacific,
together with a Maori lover? She knew what "marine animals"
meant. In the treacherous tides ringing the coast of New Zealand, the shadows of sharks, and also of dolphins. George would
seek out the sharks.

The train to Stamford had empty seats; it was the middle
of a weekday afternoon. And now the parking lot too was
gone. Still, hadn't George, spurred by the ingenuity of fore-
sight, promised that something, after all, would be there? And
something was: a swarming and a roaring of dump trucks and
cement mixers and steam shovels and muscular men in hard
hats and hired ragamuffins handing out anti-gentrification leaflets, all surrounding a mammoth billboard with a picture of a
very tall building and a newsworthy message in noisy purple
and green paint :

COMING SOON
STAMFORD'S FINEST LUXURY
APARTMENTS
WATCH US RISE

But it was George she was watching for. Was he late, or
was she too early? Or was it she who was late, and he'd given
up and gone back to his suite at the Waldorf? Impossible; he
wouldn't desert his most loyal adherent to the Pact. Or did he
suppose that she, like the others, had succumbed to the hollow
quotidian? A fine brown dust was beginning to thicken her
throat. Her lips were coated with grit. Then it came to her how
foolish she was: he knew better than to wait in a fog of dirt. He
was expecting her to show up at their old bench.

The bench was missing most of its slats. The bird droppings
had multiplied. And what species of bird might they be? There

were owls in Connecticut; in one of his most careful drawings Nate Vogel had crayoned a long-eared one. It almost resembled a rabbit. The subtlety of its colorings had required three separate shades of gray: dun, dove, and dusk.

But George was not there. After an hour and a half, and by now it was two and a half, he still was not there. She pondered why. Doubtless the university had promoted him, and he was no longer, like some freshly recruited underling, sent abroad on a superfluous errand—wasn't it clear that the world was already sufficiently cyberized? Or might it be that the ancient great-uncle had died in his absence, and he had no further reason to turn his back on New Zealand? The Pact was the fruit of his own, his central—his necessary—passion. Why would he abandon it? It was the seed of his Idea.

On the train back to Fordham—it was again rush hour, and so crowded that she had to stand holding on to an overhead strap—she all at once saw his Idea. Or she felt it, like a thunder coursing through the churn of the blood in her skull. George had allowed himself to disappear, it was his solitary will at work, it was fanaticism's ultimate flourish. He meant to shock her, he meant to undo her expectation, he meant to disappoint and to betray. The shock of his disappearance was not a negation of the Pact; it was its electrifying fulfillment.

The next week she consented to have dinner with Nate Vogel. His original notion of Thursday was a mistake. He preferred Saturday night, the traditional time, he said, for a real date. Date? This was galoshes again: the last traces of her grandmother's era. He had discovered a nice little bar right here in the neighborhood, four or five blocks from the library. On a mild autumn evening, when the library closed early for the weekend, they could walk there. She dreaded his intention: the dark, the booze, the thumping beat of the piped-in rock, the side-by-side intimacy of bodies in close quarters.

On the way, he asked whether she knew that vegetarians lived longer than meat eaters. "Somewhere between six and ten percent," he said. "And here we are. This is the place. I tried it out before I broached it."

The sign on the window read HEALTH BAR. There were rows and rows of salads to choose from, and little round tables with artificial flowers at the center of each. The lights were bright. The music was Mozart. He said, "The avocado with persimmon is excellent."

But Evangeline ordered eggplant.

"Did you know," he said, "that the persimmon means change? Because it's bitter when it's green and sweet when it turns orange."

He gave her his most importuning look. His breath was close, too close, to her own. For the first time she observed his eyes; they were the color of one of his most frequently used crayons. It was labelled taupe. Evangeline wondered whether there might also be an esoteric crayon that matched George's eyes. Aubergine, perhaps, like earth's most beautifully sculptured fruit.

And now he put out a forefinger to touch her lips; was this a presumptuous prelude to a kiss?

It was not. How chaste he was!

"I can't help noticing," he said, "that you have the archaic smile. Do you know what that is? Let's go to the Met and I'll show you. Is next Sunday okay?"

He took her to the Greek and Roman galleries. On plinth after plinth, a procession of ancient stone heads, each with its meaningful yet inscrutable smile.

"It could be a sign of revelry," he said, "or it could be derision. Nobody really knows."

"I choose derision," Evangeline said.

"Let's go look at the Buddha smiles. To compare."

He led her through the Asian halls, and then to Egypt, evading the sarcophagi to search for pharaonic mirth.

"We think we've got the cream of the crop in the Mona Lisa," he said, "but look at Nefertiti! Did you know that her left eye is missing? It was made of quartz, but they've never found it."

They sat on the topmost steps in front of the Met. The sun was abnormally hot for October, and the afternoon air had a dizzying haze. It seemed to Evangeline that they had walked endless miles, from one civilization to another. An ice cream cart was parked on the sidewalk below.

"Are you parched?" he asked, and came back with two orange popsicles. "Did you know how Indian summer got its name? From the Iroquois hunting season. Next time we could check out the local pinnipedia."

He was proposing an expedition to the Bronx Zoo. How wholesome he was!

They were leaning against the wrought-iron fence circling the sea lions' pool. The sea lions, sprawled on their boulders, too lethargic to dive, were all barking loudly in chorus. Against the din he said, "Do you know the difference between a seal and a sea lion? The sea lion has earflaps and can walk on its flippers. The seal has these apertures instead of ears and can only go on its belly. And did you know"—and here he grew excited—"that the hippopotamus evolved from the dolphin? In terms of aeons, it happened all of a sudden."

He bought her a balloon in the shape of a giraffe, and also two ice cream cones—her choice, one vanilla, one strawberry. But it was getting too cold for ice cream. Indian summer was over. They were both wearing sweaters. "And by the way," he said, "I hope you won't mind, but pretty soon I'll be moving out of the neighborhood."

"Why would you do that?" It came as a jolt to Evangeline that she was not indifferent to this announcement; somehow it embarrassed her. And why should she mind?

He had done his homework, he explained. Looked at all the want ads, asked around, got a tip about an opening in a well-funded private high school for girls, principal soon to retire, and so forth. All this was muddling: she had no inkling that Nate Vogel might be ambitious. How could a man so sure, so lacking in anxiety, so satisfied in his habits, so at home with equations, want to change his perfectly normal life? And no, he hadn't applied to the math department; he detested Euclid, he was sick of Pythagoras, he didn't care whether zero existed or not. Evangeline declined to believe him. For once he was making things up.

"It's in Connecticut," he told her. "The school. I got the job.

It means a big jump in pay. And they like it that I do math. It's all about budgets."

How uninspired to be gratified by something so banal as running a fancy school! As if Connecticut were kin to the dolphin-thronged coast of New Zealand.

And then she remembered that implausibility is the true authenticity. Otherwise how could the hippopotamus have once been a dolphin?

And then she thought, He always means what he says. And everything he says is so.

And then she thought, How wholesome he is, how chaste!

And then she thought, Chaste needn't mean celibate.

Six months later, she married him. And like Hygeia and Amphitrite before her, she decamped. Mouse One and Mouse Two were anyhow at war, vying for head librarian. Mouse Two had turned tiger and, by virtue of clearing out the cranks who commandeered whole tables for their hobbies, had won. He would have ousted Nate Vogel.

The girls' school was located in the suburbs of Stamford. Evangeline could hardly admit to surprise; everything that happens is inevitable, evolution is sudden. They were given a perk, a little house of their own, set in an acre of greenery; it was called the Principal's House. Still, she regretted that swamps and zoos were behind them.

"Posh," Evangeline said. "And those silly uniforms the girls have to wear." She was thirty-seven years old, the age of the beginning of nostalgia, when early discontent becomes regret. She regretted the long-ago loss of the green truck. She regretted that Mouse Two now reigned in place of the goddesses of water and well-being. She regretted that George had so far receded in her longings that she not only couldn't recall the color of his eyes; his voice too with all its clairvoyance, had faded. The words survived, but not the clarion call. George was nearly beyond retrieval, a tiny glint of a mote, like a wayward flea.

She did not regret marrying Nate Vogel. They named the baby Bella, after Evangeline's grandmother. Together, they worked to suspend a shiny miniature mobile over Bella's little bed, where it wafted and twisted and fitfully caught the light.

Bella gazed at it intelligently, though it was only a chrome monocular and not a real toy.

It was December. Evangeline liked to walk in the cold. Bella in her puffy swathings and Muscovite wool hat, under blankets in her carriage, was no more than an amorphous bundle. Evangeline wore furry Muscovite boots. A steamy cloud spilled out of her throat with every breath, but still she pushed the carriage everywhere, through unfamiliar streets and small icy plazas and rows of shops of every kind. She walked and walked: a private walk, a secret walk, secret even from Nate Vogel. And finally there it was, transfigured. Risen as pledged. It had renewed its surround, it had staunchly gentrified. Its fifteen luxury floors looked down on a lavish playground, where silky-cheeked children in thick winter regalia were bobbing on seesaws and shrieking down slides. Shivering nannies stood by. The ragamuffins were nowhere.

And next the bench. A different bench, stone sparkling with mica, impregnable to harm. Only the bird droppings were the same. Or were they? How do owls fare in December?

Bella was howling, and they were far from home, with miles to go. But Evangeline had seen what she wanted to see: that George was yet again not there.

April came, and Evangeline pushed Bella's stroller around the neighborhood, peering into the windows of stores. Trees grew all along the sidewalks. A bus snorted its way down the street. Bella pointed with her tiny finger and said "Buh." When a second bus followed in the fumy wake of the first, Bella pointed again and said "Buh-buh." She was already mastering arithmetic.

They passed a store with its door open; it was a bookshop going out of business, collateral damage of the new age of digital reading. Evangeline looked in. A man was on his knees, pulling books off their shelves and thrusting them into cardboard boxes. She could see only his elbows as he bent forward to the lowest shelf. He was wearing a nubbly tweed jacket; the elbow patches were of leather worn into creases, the color of ripened persimmon. When he stood and showed his face, it was again not George.

Nate Vogel was content. Every morning at breakfast the chatter of flocks of adolescent girls came to them through the open windows like undulating notes of nightingales. "What a pity," he said, "there aren't any nightingales around here. Not a single one. They winter in Africa and summer in Europe." He had looked up the history of the Principal's House. The school was founded just before the Battle of Appomattox. "Did you know," he said (and she was sometimes attentive), "that it was used by the Underground Railroad?" He no longer wore his seaman's cap; it was unsuitable for his office, it had no dignity. His hair stood up, an unplowed harvest, an improbable wheat field.

Bella too was content. Now she was mastering the art of two-leggedness.

One night in a dream Evangeline understood why she couldn't remember the color of George's eyes. They were colorless. A white light streamed out of them, turning everything translucent. When she awoke, she was uncertain of the meaning of her conscious life: was she no different from Ruby and Susan (formerly Olive), or was she, in truth, burning always with the hard, gemlike flame of her solitary will?

The Biographer's Hat

WHEN THE BIOGRAPHER of Emanuel Teller came to see me, he left behind his hat. It was the kind of hat a gaucho would wear, flat on top, wide-brimmed, but without the strings that tie under the chin. It was a very dark green, soft and fuzzy to the touch. It seemed familiar. I thought I knew that hat. As the biographer trotted down the stairs to the waiting taxi, I called out, "Hey! You forgot your hat!"

He didn't hear me; the driver was leaning on his horn.

I picked up the hat. It looked exactly like Emanuel Teller's hat in his photos.

Two weeks earlier, the biographer had informed me in an e-mail (it was easy to track me down online, he said) that he was coming from California to look up the remaining members of Emanuel Teller's old New York circle. He meant to settle in for some months to be near his quarry. They were much diminished by now, he supposed, and all of them elderly. They were dying off. Half of them were likely too sick to talk to him. He had already put down cash for a rented room on the Upper West Side and would soon be moving in. His idea was to be close to Emanuel Teller's old neighborhood, for the atmosphere. He gave the impression that he intended to keep on badgering these decrepit golden-agers.

"I'm a dead end, you're chasing air," I wrote back. "I once took a class he taught, that's all. Besides, that was long ago."

"No stone unturned. You're one of the very few who could fill me in on those elusive Early Years." The last two words were capitalized, as if they were already fixed in print, like a chapter heading.

So when the biographer turned up at my door I was more than skeptical, I was wary. If it was all right for him to pry into Emanuel Teller's life, he had no license to pry into mine. I didn't care to be depended on for posterity's sake.

His breath was a wintry cloud (February was still fierce), and there were fresh snowflakes on the fur collar of his coat. A coat with a fur collar! It made him look outmoded, like a Russian count. And then that gaucho's hat, and an ordinary briefcase. He told me he was on leave without pay from teaching at Berkeley—something to do with the farthest edge of the humanities, "where," he said, "free will meets Tao." By now Chinese philosophy had worn out its welcome. He intended to put all his energy into Emanuel Teller. He wasn't a tyro, he had already published a biography of Otto Blaustein, the man who invented the insight chamber. The book was a flop. It sold an embarrassing two hundred copies, and no wonder—who remembers Otto Blaustein? Even the insight chamber was ancient history. It was this device and its repute that had led him to Emanuel Teller. More than anything else, it was the insight chamber that had engendered Emanuel Teller's rise.

I took the biographer's wet coat and hung it over the shower rail in the bathroom. The fur collar squirted droplets, like a living animal shaking itself. When I reached for his hat, he backed away.

"You have to be careful with a hat like this," he said. "Especially if it got a bit soaked. Don't pat it dry, just leave it be." His voice, with its deep-bass vowels, signaled authority. I watched him search all around. His eyes were small and the lids were worn and sparsely lashed. His long earlobes drooped. Finally, he set the hat on a chair. "I'll just let it rest here. It's his, the real thing. His wife gave it to me."

"I thought his wife was dead," I said.

"She wasn't when I met her. You realize," he said, "that mine is the authorized biography. She trusted me right away, she was with me up to the hilt. That's why she let me have his hat. I didn't ask for it, she gave it to me."

"To wear," I said, "or to worship?"

"Don't mock it. Everything has hints. Nobody knows what a man who does himself in is thinking. Not even a wife. He had his secrets, and a life won't sell if it doesn't have secrets—I know that now. Blaustein was an open book. Say," he broke in, "would you have something hot to drink? I feel a cold coming on."

In the kitchen, the kettle was boiling, the teacups were ready, together with a plate of muffins. I had provided for a visit that seemed pointless. He was rushing me, distracting me. He wanted to know who I was and what I remembered. There are always these hints, he said, they come out of nowhere. He intended to pick my brain.

I protested that I was a proofreader for the *Village Sentinel*, a local newssheet, and could tell him nothing that touched on his subject. The *Sentinel* mostly had movie listings, and ads for restaurants and bars. It also had personal ads: fevered seekers of sex of every variety, sellers of used furniture, so-called researchers looking to hire an assistant for whatever purpose, families in need of a nanny. The wholesome and the raunchy—the *Sentinel* was far from fastidious. It was read all over New York and beyond. Tourists picked it up for the gossip.

"The *Sentinel*? You see, you see? Hints everywhere." The biographer gave out what could pass for a happy bleat. "I've hit the jackpot. They used to run pieces on the insight chamber, you didn't know that, did you? Before your time. In fact, it was the *Sentinel* that named Emanuel Teller a latter-day Mark Twain, did you know that? And he was the first to have one of those boxes. He used to sit in it for at least an hour a day. He believed in it. That's why I got one for myself, to feel how it worked. To see what it did for him. These things, you can't find them anymore, not even on eBay, so I built my own. In the end, I got nothing out of it and gave it away. You can always come up with another believer."

It was a long while since I had heard anyone speak of that forgotten old fad, three generations back. They were relics, sacral voodoo constructions. As far as I could tell, an insight chamber was nothing more than an oversized wooden box lined with alternating strips of goatskin and aluminum, and put together with brass screws. And where had he found the goatskin?

By now the plate of muffins was all crumbs. His eye scouted the pantry. He was hoping for more, even a full dinner. He was hungry, and I was dispirited. My own life, a relic in itself: a début role in a Surrealist play that featured a giant red radish front center stage. The venue was a thirty-seat theatre in a church basement; and nothing since. Flailing and failing, and, finally, waste. Why should I be made to dance to the song of Emanuel Teller's resurrection?

From his briefcase he fished out a fountain pen and a yellow legal pad. "Well, let's get going."

There was iron in his demand. He looked over to the hat on its chair as if it confirmed his will. As if the hat, and the fur-collared coat over the shower rail, and even the fountain pen, would keep him rooted until he had what he wanted. As if he meant to egg me on until I surrendered. The only way I might get rid of him was to acquiesce.

I was nineteen, I told him, when I enrolled in a helter-skelter seminar at the New School, on Twelfth Street, presided over by a middle-aged man dressed like a hobo wearing a hat. The class was listed as Victorian Prose and Verse. He explained that he was a pretender, a fake. At heart, he said, he was a bard, a minstrel, a reciter who had been selling himself for the money, mainly at high schools and women's lunch clubs, wherever they would have him. The New School was a lucky upgrade. He admitted that he had nothing like a fancy degree. The name of the course was a ruse. His Victorians were skewed toward make-believe, Edward Lear and Lewis Carroll and Beatrix Potter and Oscar Wilde, with plenty of doctored fairy tales thrown in. Even "The Arabian Nights," the unexpurgated edition. Right away, he was letting us know that he wasn't serious. And, except for theater, neither was I.

At the end, he promised to send a refund.

I could hear the reluctance in my prattle. Why must I yield to this invader? Why was I driven to go on—was it the force of the biographer's obstinacy, or of the hat? Its surface was sending out a faint autumnal fume, like faraway burning leaves.

The real lure was the Village, I said. I wasn't interested in Victorian anything. I was drawn to the lingering breaths of the old bohemia. Edna St. Vincent Millay had lived in the Village, and Hart Crane, and E. E. Cummings. And Eugene O'Neill!

If you looked out a certain window in Emanuel Teller's second-floor classroom you could sometimes spot, in a window opposite, Wystan Auden's ghost walking around in carpet slippers. Meanwhile, I imagined myself in the little playhouse on nearby Bleecker Street—some day, and soon, I was going to be Lavinia in "Mourning Becomes Electra." I was well prepared. What was I if not an ardent disciple of Stanislavski—emotion recollected in turmoil?

The fountain pen was tracking speedily across the yellow sheet. I followed the movement of the biographer's wide flat palm, the bulging knuckles, the knobby fingers.

"Is that his?" I asked. "The pen? Did his wife give you that, too?"

He ignored this. "Listen here," he said finally, and I saw him glancing yet again at the hat on the chair. "The man's dead, but he's alive in his things, what he held, what he wore. There's more tragedy in this pen than what you'd get out of a dozen operas, and God only knows what went on in that box—"

It was a brief but earnest speech, clearly rehearsed. It was plain that he was meaning to use it for all his interviews.

He urged me on. "Was he ever down in the dumps, did you ever see anything like that? There had to be inklings, you were on the spot, you could catch on to such things, suicides don't come out of the blue—"

"He wasn't *the* Emanuel Teller then," I said.

"He must've showed up with something of his own, one of his own riffs. With him, it was modernism be damned, and people still take him for nothing but a standup. My God, the man was an original, an *artist*—"

An artist? The biographer was deluded. A generation had grown old since the New School sacked Emanuel Teller. His one semester was denuded of its course credit. He had confessed outright that he was a fraud. He was no more than a showman and a scavenger; he fetched up, piecemeal, this and that shard from bawdy old legends and jokes. He had made his mark with the story of the two battling towns, Alef and Zed, one inhabited by sages, the other by dunces. He had filched it from the Norse. Out of rusting folklore he swiped tricksters and wedding jesters, and from these rags of foolery he made newer absurdities. He carried his insight chamber to late-night TV shows with their audience of millions, and popular plat-forms everywhere, revealing, he said, the visions and messages it delivered, all the while flaunting an amber flask of what he called his "elixir." He was, in fact, a run-of-the-mill ventril-oquist in a cowboy hat. The insight chamber was his Charlie McCarthy.

To the biographer I said, "I've told you everything I know."

"You've done me not an ounce of good, and I took two buses to get here. And, by the way, with the weather out there, can you help me out with a cab? I might not have enough cash."

He demanded his coat, shook out the fur (I was certain no animal had been sacrificed), and bounded down the stairs.

For the next few days I left the hat where he had placed it, on that chair, and stepped around it with a certain caution, as if it were important to stay out of its way. I saw no reason to remove it, and where would I keep it? He would miss it soon enough, though it was impossible to predict when he might retrieve it: better to have it ready to hand. It was an annoyance. I was learning not to be distracted by it, and I had no need of the chair it occupied; I rarely had visitors, and, besides, there were other chairs.

But after several weeks the biographer had not returned, and there was only the inescapable presence of the hat. Passing it one evening, I happened to notice a perceptible wilting—a shallow well was forming in the crown. It had sunk only slightly; after all this time, it was still not fully dry. Apparently, the moisture had begun to affect it. Dust lay along the brim like a gray salt. It had taken on the shape of a tongueless mouth, but when I sidled by some days afterward it seemed rather to resemble an eye: a dead eye lacking a pupil. This was alarming: it was the biographer's hat, but wasn't it also Emanuel Teller's hat, and hadn't I, entirely by chance, become its custodian? I was almost willing to believe that it had been deliberately abandoned. Still, why would the biographer not be eager to recover it? He had, after all, spoken of it as a kind of talisman. I was beginning to dislike the hat, even to resent it. A dead man's property, an intruder. I decided to banish it. Why must it draw my reluctant attention, day after day? Often, seeing how, little by little, it went on collapsing, the crown growing more and more sunken, the misshapen brim leering, I wanted to crush it. Yet I could not rid myself of it; it wasn't mine to dispose of.

And I knew what I must do. I wrapped the hat in a plastic bag from the grocery, and then in two or three more plastic bags, and found a place for it at the back of a closet, among old shoes I no longer wore but was unready to discard, and an ironing board that the rise of polyester had defeated, and also a discolored canvas cot the previous tenant had abandoned. The hat was well imprisoned.

The chair, though, was not as it had been. The hat had seeped a damp round stain into the fabric seat.

With spring closing in—it was coming on toward April—the *Sentinel*'s ads were increasing. I was at work in my office cubicle until late into the night, inserting commas and apostrophes in ten-point type for sadomasochistic trysts and lightly worn children's pajamas. My eyes were smarting. Longing for sleep, I climbed the stairs to my apartment.

The biographer was leaning against the door.

"Where were you? I've been waiting for the past two hours."

"You've come for the hat," I said.

"Well, not *for* it exactly. About it."

"You never got in touch."

"Why would I? I got all I could out of you."

"Well, come back another time if you want it. Right now it's packed away."

Though the night was warm, he was again wearing the coat with the fur collar. It hung open, revealing a grimy pink shirt.

"I don't want it. That's the whole point, you have to keep it. Someone's got to keep it. It's got to be kept. Preserved."

"If you don't want it, then why are you here?"

I put the key in the lock. He shouldered himself past me and stood on the other side of the door.

"The interviews were a bust. I ran into two cases of

Alzheimer's, and the rest on my list are kaput. You're the only one left. And I'm out of a job, got an e-mail from the provost, they're redirecting the department, I knew it was coming— look, can you put me up for a couple of nights?"

The provost? Out of a job? It came to me with a jab of conviction that his credentials, too, were likely sham. He had never taught Tao at Berkeley.

I said, "You're renting somewhere, aren't you, and I'm on my way to bed—"

"She threw me out. She was always complaining that I was late with the rent. As of now, I owe for the past two months, but she can't come after me. I gave her a made-up name and an address in California that doesn't exist."

This unnerved me. "I don't want you here," I told him. "You should leave now."

"I've got an idea. I've figured things out. Emanuel Teller's secret. Even his wife, especially his wife, didn't know it, so it should interest you. There's money in it. When I finish this bio, I'll give you a cut. You'll deserve it. It's all for the sake of the hat," he insisted. "A physical memento. And, listen, I don't mind sleeping on the floor. Unless you've got something better. How about this sofa?"

I saw that he was immovable. Something in his importuning made me unafraid. He was harmless. He was only a noisy blow- hard who had bilked his landlady. I went to the closet where the hat lay, suffocating in its plastic, and dragged out the cot. It had taken on the hat's odor of distant soot.

In the morning he slept late, helped himself from the refrig- erator, and explained that he was heading for the public library to do some deeper research. He had spent a night or two dozing in the waiting room of Grand Central, and some bastard had stolen his laptop. He wasn't taking his coat, he told me. It was too hot for spring and the fur collar was too much. I under- stood that the coat stood as a hostage and a warning: he had no intention of leaving.

But when I got home that evening it turned out that he had, after all, not gone out.

"Anyhow," he said, "the library's too crowded, you can't get near their computers. I've been moseying around to find where you keep yours, and I see that you've got a really good printer, the cheap ones always get jammed. How about if I stick around and get on with my idea? It's the chapter where you come in. A nice window in there, lots of light."

"Where I come in? You said you got nothing from me."

"But now that it's all worked out I'll get plenty, and you can fill in the gaps. By the way, I hope you've brought in some takeout. Your larder is too damn bare, and I could eat a horse."

I scrambled two eggs and made some toast, along with anything else I could find. He had already finished off two forgotten cans of sauerkraut.

"This coffee isn't so bad," he said. "You know how I got the idea? Believe it or not, it's from you. When you were going on about the Village, I mean in its heyday, all those old stories. Aline Bernstein and Eda Lou Walton, does anyone nowadays even recognize these names?"

I knew them. They were Village history: lovers and muses who protected, succored, rescued, housed, and fed the luminaries of the future. They were each a Pietà with a divinity in her lap.

"You could be the next one," he said. His reddened eyelids seemed on fire. His breath ran fast. "What Eda Lou Walton was to Henry Roth. She *made* him. What Aline Bernstein was to Thomas Wolfe. His desire was her desire until they broke up. You could be the one for Emanuel Teller. It isn't as if you don't have the proof of it. The actual proof—who else would be keeping his hat?"

I was suspicious of this excitement. I saw through it; I took it all in. It was a scenario, a deceit, a scheme he was determined to bring off—a whirlwind of lies, and he meant to sweep me into it.

"And those were older women," he pushed on. "The age difference is all to the good. Men like younger women, and young women are flattered to be loved by struggling gods-to-be. And then the young woman tires of her god, or feels betrayed, and breaks the god's heart. That's what you did to Emanuel Teller. You broke his heart and he did himself in."

I might have ridiculed him. I might have laughed. I might have been angered; I might have evicted him outright. He was a fool and a braggart and an interloper. But it was true: I had the hat. The hat was mine.

"It's just sensationalism. It isn't someone's real life, you're making it up—"

"That's just the point, it'll sell, there's drama in it. And scandal. It accounts for the suicide, nothing could be more plausible. And it's watertight. All his old cronies are dead or on the way out."

I said weakly, "You can't just change history."

"Why not? It's only a matter of perspective, of what's been overlooked. Even Shakespeare pulled that little trick. Is Ophelia for real? Who would deny her? All the world's a stage—"

He was shrewd; he knew how to thread an argument. He knew how to tempt. His power was in his why-not. Somehow he scented my shattered lust for the marquee. He was proposing a way out of the ignominy of the radish made of papier-mâché; he was offering me a stage and a role. A role! The hat immured in the closet was to be my theater, why not?

He was scrambling in his pockets, scratching and plucking, then he tossed a wrinkled envelope on the kitchen table. His plate was clean. He had eaten every scrap.

"Here," he said. His rasp smacked of victory. "Keep them, I have plenty more."

The envelope held a collection of fading newspaper clippings, all with photos of Emanuel Teller. Most were obituaries, but some showed him in the insight chamber, half in and half out, and wearing a hat. He was seriously graying, and well past how I recalled him. Publicity pictures, posed. In one or two, he was with a woman. The loyal widow who had given the biographer the cherished hat? Or an earlier lover, my rival? But no; the biographer assured me that I had no rival. I was Emanuel Teller's only infatuation. And it was I alone who had succored and rescued and housed and fed him in his darkening years. I was the young comforter of his old age.

And why not? All the men and women are merely players, they have their exits and their entrances, so why not?

*

He stayed on for more than a month. My grocery bill expanded mightily. He sat greedily at my computer every evening,
greedy for more and more invention, greedy for the notice to
come, and I at his side, making things up. The whirlwind had
consumed me—I succumbed, I felt, I saw, as if in the certainty
of memory, the shape of Emanuel Teller's eyes, the tragic turn
of his lips. My skin remembered the silk of his caresses, his
confidences, his kisses. He called me his pet, his nepenthe,
his anodyne. I was transfigured, I was Lavinia at last; the name
flew into my bloodstream as if born there. I knew how liaisons
decay into bitterness. How May and December are enemies by
nature. How love can kill. How impersonation can transmute
into reality.

I had become the biographer's collaborator.

"When you get to the breakup," he pressed, "make it
explosive. Volcanic. Tears, even." He wanted melodrama. He
coveted the wiles of Lady Macbeth. He wanted over-the-top.

Before he left, I gave the biographer five hundred dollars,
a good portion of my monthly earnings, and he handed me a
copy of his manuscript. "I printed out one extra. Hang on to
it, the original," he said. "It'll be worth something at auction."

He told me he had to get back to California. The New
York houses were too snooty, they had no imagination, they
were looking for footnotes, citations, verification. His previous
publisher hadn't been troubled by such nitpickings, and had
anyhow gone out of business. He was planning to submit to a
freewheeling press in Los Angeles, one that would surely seize
the opportunity to draw renewed attention to Emanuel Teller,
whose reputation, he conceded, the passage of years had begun
to erode.

"They'll grab a good story," he persisted. "And don't be
surprised when the journalists start coming at you like locusts.
Show them the hat, how you treasure it, how you grieve.
They'll run profiles in the magazines. People will want to get a
good look at the woman who seduced Emanuel Teller and got
him to kill himself."

He pointed a zealous finger at the manuscript. "You're right there in the Acknowledgments, and we'll split the royalties. I'll keep you posted, I'll be in touch. The title alone's a blockbuster."

I waited more than a year for him to make the sale, and another year or so for the reviews to come in, but "Emanuel Teller's Hidden Love" never turned up. The locusts failed to swarm. The biographer was silent. I tried once or twice to e-mail him; his account had been canceled.

On a night when the personals seeking hookups were especially explicit, and when I was again kept late at the *Sentinel*, I opened my door to an uncommon smell. I remembered it: the faint familiar wisps of a smoldering, a smokiness, a burning nearly smothered—but magnified, urgent. It was the hat in the closet. I took it out and unwound its wrappings and set it on the chair where it had left its mark and looked at it.

It was flattened, as if thrashed. The living leer had gone out of it. The hat was useless as witness and proof. Emanuel Teller's secret was never to be known; it was, as they say, safe. My last chance to tread the boards had fizzled, the footlights shut down, and why not? We players, after all, have our exits and entrances, don't we?

Sin

BY THE LAST week of April, the parking lot's long chain-link fence already bristles with its hundreds of attachments: coiled wire, duct tape, butterfly clips, boat hooks, coat hangers, pellets of industrial glue, nylon strips, braided strings, and whatever other contraptions stubborn ingenuity can dream up. Elsewhere, there are the uptown galleries, discreet and sleek as salons, with their Japanese pots on polished lion-pawed tables, and the walls behind them hung with small framed paintings ratified by catalogues signaling critical repute. And of course the grand museums with their marble stairs and broken-nosed Roman busts in halls mobbed by foreign tourists.—Well, so what and hoity-toity and never mind! With us fence daubers, it's catch-as-catch-can, whoever happens to pass by, and it's smelly too, because of the pretzel man's salty cart on one end of our sidewalk and the soda man's syrupy cart on the other, and always the sickening exhaust from the cars grumbling every half hour in and out of the parking lot. And the hard rain, coming on without so much as a warning cloud to shut down business for the day, and all of us scrambling to cover our merchandise with plastic sheeting, which anyhow the wind catches up and tangles and carries away, along with someone's still life.

I call it merchandise. I don't presume to call it art, though some of it might be, and our customers, or clients, or loitering gawkers, or whatever they are, mostly wouldn't know the difference. As for us, we're all sorts—do-it-yourself souvenir peddlers (you can pay a dollar to coat a six-inch plaster Statue of Liberty in silver glitter), or middle-aged Bennington graduates in jeans torn at the knee who speak of having a "flair," or homeless fakes, soused and stinking and grubbing for coins, who put up pages cut from magazines, or part-time coffee-shop servers self-described as art students. With the exception of the sidewalk chalkers who sprawl on their bellies, indisputably sovereign over their squares of pavement, we are warily territorial. We are all mindful of which piece of fence belongs to whom, and which rusted old folding chair, and who claims the fancier plastic kind swiped from outdoor tables set out by restaurants in the good weather. And there are thieves among us too: if you don't keep an eye out, half your supplies will disappear, and maybe even your wallet.

I am one of those art students, though it's been a long while since I stood before an easel staring at a bowl of overripe pears while trying to imagine them as pure color and innate form. This was happening in the Brooklyn studio of my mentor at the time—*mentor* was his word for it, at a fee of seventy-five dollars per session. He had a habit of repeating a single, faintly sadistic turn of phrase: what I needed was discipline, he told me, and as my mentor he was naturally obliged (the meanly intended clever laugh came here) to be my *tor*mentor. I had an unhealthy tendency toward literalism, he explained, which it was his responsibility to correct. He regarded himself as a disciple of the legendary Philip Guston, but only in his early period. After three months or so, I couldn't bring myself to believe in the platonic souls of pears, and besides, my uncle Joseph in Ohio, who was subsidizing those pears even while under the impression that I was learning fashion illustration, was coming to visit the Avenue A walkup I shared with a Cooper Union engineering student and his girlfriend. Joseph had taken me on as a good deed after my stepfather died. He wasn't exactly my uncle; he was my stepfather's brother, and he was proposing, along with some necessary business in New York, to look me up to see how I was doing. I saw then that the flow of money was about to dry up—the money for my tormentor and the money for my half of the rent: the engineering student was soon to graduate and marry and start a job upstate. Within two days Joseph flew back to Cincinnati, betrayed.

"Goddam it, Eva, you're a goddam *orphan*," he threw back at me, "and look at you, cohabiting with a pair of degenerates, and those imbecile oozings piled up in that dump, you've played me for a fool—"

He hadn't believed me when I told him that the study of swirls and random swipes was a prerequisite for fashion design.

Joseph's sloughing me off left me nervous: fences can't supply steady cash the way uncles do. Still, I knew I wasn't meant for the garment industry. Only a year ago I had been blissfully in love with the Pre-Raphaelites.

I began to wait tables from seven to midnight at La Bellamonte, an Italian restaurant down the street from the fence. And it was I who carried off two plastic sidewalk chairs, one for the portraitist (this was what we called ourselves), and one for the sitter. It was good to be literal—to work up a reasonable likeness—though not too much. For portraits, a bit of prettying was always preferable. Beginning about May, when the weather warmed up, straight through the middle of October, the money was reliable. I would charge according to how my sitter was dressed, though I was often wrong. I was amazed by the vanity of what I took to be, from the condition of their shoes, the poor: they were willing to pay as much as five dollars without giving me an argument, and sometimes I just tore the sheet off the pad and handed it over for free. Of course I sold what I could of the stuff I hung on the fence: these I splashed out quickly, between sitters—fanciful birds on branches, Greek-shaped vases overflowing with flowers (I had a botany book to copy from), invented landscapes, some with mountains, some with lakes. If there were lakes, I sketched in a boat with French lovers in old-fashioned headgear, huge feathered brims for the women and top hats for the men. From the local pharmacy, one of those acres-wide brilliantly lit warehouses where you could find anything from cheese crackers to lampshades, I bought cheap wood frames and painted them white. This gave the pictures on my three yards of fence almost a look of settled elegance.

Weekends, Sundays especially, are our busiest time, when people stroll by with their sodas or dripping popsicles (there's an ice cream vendor one block over) to watch the portraitists at work. For onlookers like ours, a portrait is an event requiring the courage to decide which of us to choose, and a certain daring even to submit to a twenty-minute sitting, surrounded by all the public kibbitzers who comment on the process, whether this person's nose is really wider than it's been shown, or taking note of a wattle that's been brushed away. Generally the crowd works itself up into a mood of untamed but not unfriendly hilarity. Yet sometimes it will be cruel.

It was cruel to the woman in the blue suit. She was not unfamiliar. I had spotted her yet again when, on the third Sunday in a row, she turned up, gaping with all the others circling round my easel. The weather was unusually hot for a late August afternoon coming on toward evening, and the baking pavement, with its crackle of pretzel crumbs, was still burning the feet of the pigeons; they were hopping more than pecking. Or else they were sated. As for me, I'd already counted one hundred and fifty-two dollars, more than enough for a single day's work, and was beginning to pack up the little it was my habit to take away for the night—brushes, paints, botany book, easel (the folding kind). The paintings I would leave where they were. I threw a worn tarp (pilfered from a car in the lot) over my part of the fence and with a piece of narrow rope knotted it through the gaps in the steel. What if rowdies came and ran off with my landscapes and flowers and boats? I would deem it a compliment, and anyhow I could readily splash out a few more.

By now many of the gawkers had dispersed, and the pretzel and soda men were long gone. But the diehards were still milling on the sidewalk, with bottles in paper bags bulging from hips and armpits. The woman in the blue suit was among them, cautious, attentive. Watchful.

As I was maneuvering the easel into its carrier, she called out, "Not yet, not yet!"

"Sorry," I said, "I'm just leaving, I can't be late."

"Why should I care, I'll take my turn now. I don't like it with that riffraff all around. So now."

"Sorry," I said again. "I've seen you before, haven't I? Then maybe next time? Or instead"—I lifted an edge of the tarp— "you could take home one of these, I'd let you have this one for half the price. A scene on the water." It was the feathered brim and the top hat.

"I don't want that kitsch. I want you at the easel. I want to see up close how you do it. I know what I want." This hint of disputation drew the diehards. Some of them already had the mouths of the bottles in their mouths. "All you people, get out of my way. Scum!"

Here was authority. And authority was money. The austere blue suit, of some summery fabric I couldn't name, the lapis necklace, the crucial absence of earrings, the gold loops on her wrists, and especially the tiny laced shoes, of that blue called midnight. Oddly small feet, a tidy head on a thin neck—she was small all over. Voice an uncontained ferocity. She looked to be—she could easily have been—a regular at the uptown galleries. And with her surliness she had mocked the surliest remnant of the crowd.

They mocked back. They called her cross-eyed (this she was, very slightly), they laughed at her skinny neck and her little feet, they laughed at me for surrendering to her whim. Once again I set up the easel. She took her place on one of the plastic chairs with an angry stubbornness that soon became a barrier. My own chair I had shoved aside; if I stood, I might dominate. Her face, I thought, had traces of insult, the eyelids tightened at the outer corners. How old was this woman? A portraitist, even my sort of sidewalk quick-job, relies on age; it animates character. But her fixed stare, guiding the brush and judging its pacings, gave out nothing. I bent closer to see the color of her irises. In the lessening light they had a yellow tint.

"Stop ogling," she spat out, "just get on with it, I'm not sitting here all night—"

The sun was dropping behind the parking lot. The last of the hecklers, finally bored, dwindled and scattered. I hurried to finish, forsaking detail, drizzling a mist of hair of indeterminate tone (was it brown, was it gray?), and privately calculated my price. The woman in the blue suit was rich; she had money. Rich people have good clothes, nice shoes, fine teeth. My uncle Joseph had paid thousands for his implants. On the other hand, this woman had sought out a street painter at a parking lot fence, so perhaps she was no different from the forlorn in their rotted sandals . . . yet how could this be? Her insistence had the brittle scrape of worldliness. She was a force. I lifted the sheet from the easel and held it out to her.

"Look at that thing, what would I want with that? It's the hand I'm after, I told you, seeing it up close, the grip, that little bit of hesitation just after—"

She snatched up her likeness—I'd caught her well enough, that angry lower lip, those inharmonious eyes—and tore it in two.

I said, "You have to pay anyway, I've done the work, you have to pay."

She drew from a flap of the blue suit a tiny blue purse. "Here, take this"—it was four one-hundred-dollar bills—"and there could be more. Does Sol Kerchek mean anything nowadays? I didn't think it would, you're too young."

I contemplated the name: nothing. I contemplated her money. It was still in her grasp.

"He's ancient history, people don't remember. I had some-one all picked out last month, a boy, I found him crouched in a corner so the guard wouldn't see. He was copying a Klimt. But in the end he was no good. He had the hand, but the whole thing was over his head. So," she said, "are you taking these or not?"

She wiggled the four bills under my chin. The engineer and his girlfriend, I knew, were already packing their belongings. In a few days they'd be gone, and my rent would instantly double.

"In the beginning," she pushed on, "you'd only have to clean brushes and so on, keep the place from getting overrun with rags. After that it's all up to him, whatever he wants."

"I've got a job, I don't have time for another—"

But already I saw that La Bellamonte would not soon claim me again.

She gave me that askew look; there was triumph in it.

"You don't have time for Sol Kerchek? You don't have time for a man whose work sits in Prague, in Berlin, in Cracow? In London? Those were the old days, but he's not dead yet, he's worth something. You should get on your knees for the privilege, you don't deserve what I'm offering—"

I shot back: "You ripped up my work, you called my stuff kitsch!"

"I say what I say and I see what I see." She stuffed the bills into the pocket of my shirt. "Come on, it's only a ten-minute walk from here."

I followed her then, threading through the gathering evening crowds on the sidewalks, past the red and green neon blinks of bars and suspect dance halls, past newsstands hung with key chains and caps and sunglasses, past check-cashing storefronts, bauble vendors, boys handing out flyers for fortune-tellers. The air was seeded with the fumes of lemony hookahs, and from the open doors of a row of ill-lit cafés, many with insolent old awnings, came the whine of guitars and a scattered pattern of clapping. We were coming now into darkened streets lined with tall silent after-hours glass-coated office buildings. A few windows were randomly lit.

"This is his place," the woman in the blue suit said. Between a pair of these giant vitrines stood a small clapboard house with a high stoop. Part of the siding was covered with stucco; the stucco showed meandering cracks, barely visible in the glow of the streetlamp. Crushed by the brutes on either flank, the little house seemed to quiver with its own insufficiency.

"We put in a skylight a few years ago, but with the way his eyes are now there's no point, all that construction debris and birdshit and whatnot, even the sun can't push through. And these monoliths they put up, there's no light anyhow. They tried to bribe us to sell, that's how they do it, but he wouldn't give in, it's like that with the old. Well look, here's something convenient."

I saw a concrete city trash bin.

She grabbed my easel—I had been carrying it tilted over my shoulder, like a rifle—and tossed it in. The plastic carrier tore with a screech.

"You won't need that anymore. There's a better one upstairs."

I trailed her up the eight steps of the stoop, denuded.

"It's these steps," she said. "He never goes out. And then the staircase going up, it's too much."

In the vestibule, an abrupt patter of foreign voices. The smell

of something frying. Sol, she told me, had the apartment at
the top. The whole place, from end to end, was his studio.
The people on the lower floor were a Filipino couple, the man
ailing; only the woman mattered, she brought Sol his dinner
every night, she cleaned his awful toilet, she changed his sheets.
I wouldn't have to do anything like that, she assured me. Maybe
now and then I could boil water for his tea, find him a crack-
er to go with it. My responsibility was solely to his art, did
I understand?

I asked about the hours and the money.

"The hours are whatever he says, whatever he wants. And let
me worry about the money."

She showed me what I took to be a business card and then
pinched it away. I had only a moment to see MARA KERCHEK,
CONSULTANT, and a row of digits below.

"He won't have a phone, he doesn't like to be bothered, he
says he can't hear. If you think you might want me, you can
text me."

"I can't," I admitted. "Someone swiped my phone. Nothing's safe at that fence—"

"Oh fine, incommunicado, the blind leading the blind. Go
get yourself a new one." It was a command. "Not that you'll
ever want me up there."

Mara Kerchek. So the old man must be her father. His door,
a heavy thing with carved scrolls, was half open. A relic purloined from some nobler house.

"Sol!" she called. "I've got someone."

I had expected him to be small, like Mara Kerchek. He was
stooped, with the bony spikes of massive shoulders leading
down to a pair of uncommonly large and dirty hands. Every
fingernail carried its load of dried paint, mostly blackened. A
wayward white thicket smothered his big head, and around it a
hint, even a halo, of hugeness, like a ghost of the mountain he
must once have been. The fuzz on his slippers was trembling.

"Mara, Mara!" With tentative balance he tipped forward to
embrace her, and I saw that his eyes, droop-lidded and milky-
pale and full of sleep, were emphatically unlike hers. She let
him hold out those monstrous hands long enough for a single

heave of his breath—ponderous, sluggish—and then patted
them away. Or was it a mild slap?

"My little Mara," he said. "All in blue, all in blue, look how
beautifully she dresses, she's always dressed that way, she knows
how to do it, she always knew, even at the start—"

But she cut him off. "He likes to talk a lot, don't you, Sol?
You don't have to listen," she told me. "And he won't use his
cane. The way he moves, make sure he uses his cane."

The little blue shoes quick-tapped down the stairs.

"She indulges me, you saw that." He was looking me over
with, I felt, a dubious fastidiousness. "Last time it was that boy,
couldn't tell his left from his right. But she means to please me,
she has a merciful heart."

"She was in a hurry to get away," I said.

"She has her work."

Under the muddy skylight (it was night now) I took in a
scene of stasis. Stillness and disuse. A tall thick-legged tripod,
naked and faceless as a skeleton, and near it a low table littered with dozens of dried-out paint pots and a jar of hideous
brushes, heavy and stiffened. A four-footed cane hooked over
a battered wooden chair. The dusky room itself as long and
narrow as some corridor in a gloomy hotel. At the far end
I made out a pair of dirty windows—dirty even in the dark.
And when I switched on the only lamps I could discover—all
three had torn silk shades—the cluttered walls on either side
of Kerchek's studio (it was Mara Kerchek who had named it
that) bluntly revealed what I had caught sight of but hadn't
accounted for. Those lumpy silhouettes were canvases, masses
of canvases stacked back to back, wild and unframed, flaming,
stricken with a crisis of color, the paint as dense as if sculpted.

And between the walls, a chaise longue, tattered only a
little, dangling crimson tassels over curly squat feet, islanded
in the void under the blinded skylight. All around, a public
smell—the smell of Kerchek's toilet. It drifted from space to
space, mingling, I imagined, with the fetid odors of worn and
crippling age. It was clear that the woman in the apartment
below was negligent; the care of the toilet, and the abhorrent
hollow of the grubby cubicle that was Kerchek's kitchen, and

the jungly bed I glimpsed in the dim hollow behind it, would fall to me, and what was I, why was I here? If sometimes the woman below failed to turn up with his meal, would I be obliged to forage in some nearby midnight diner for whatever might pass for Sol Kerchek's supper?

I got rid of the decaying brushes and filled the jar with my own. I made some small order in the sticky kitchen. I gathered up armfuls of paint-soaked oily rags furry with dust—the accumulation of years—and tossed them into the city's trash bin; my easel was gone. From under Kerchek's bed I pulled out a roll of canvas grayed by grime, and a torn cardboard box heaped with stale tubes of oils. I twisted one open; out sputtered a clot of brilliant turquoise.

And all the while the four-footed cane still hung disobediently from the wooden chair. Mara Kerchek had snapped out an order; Kerchek refused it. Then why shouldn't I defy Mara Kerchek, why must I satisfy Mara Kerchek? What would I do with a phone in this timeless feral place, where an old man's breathings were measured only by a faraway sun moving languidly across an opaque skylight? Here was freedom, and leisure, and unexpected ease. My wages, delivered by the woman below, sometimes came, and sometimes did not, and always in the shape of one-hundred-dollar bills sealed in an envelope coiled in masses of tape, its thickness impossible to predict. One envelope might be skimpy, the next one fat. I was content; ever since my uncle Joseph had given up on me, I had never felt so flush. Mara Kerchek herself kept away.

In the afternoons, it was Kerchek's habit to totter, caneless, toward that grotesquely ornamental object under the skylight, where he dropped into a doze. He lay there among its royal cushions like some misshapen odalisque, dozing and waking, dozing and waking, and soon enough he would shudder, hotly aware, into an excited cry, a remnant of some dream. His dreams, he told me, were omens and alarms—catastrophic, shaming. And more than once he explained how this misplaced Oriental curiosity came to flutter its fringes between the walls.

"My paradise, my sanctum," he said. "Look how my Mara indulges me. She found this marvel, who knows where she picked it up, she finds me everything, she found me that door, she found me that boy who didn't know his left hand from his right hand, she found me you, and do you know why? My foolish little Mara believes in instinct. She believes in resurrection. It's all mumbo jumbo. Superstition."

His voice puzzled me. Ingratiating, taunting, as if it concealed a fear.

In those early weeks, in the empty hours when Kerchek clung to his divan, and at other times too, I might easily have wandered off into the city streets on musings of my own, or walked the halls of the great museums uptown, where the world's imagination was stored. Instead, I searched out a pastry shop tucked among those glassed-in office buildings, and went every day to buy muffins and little cakes and canisters of foreign teas and blocks of oddly colored cheeses to fill Kerchek's blighted cupboard. And once, in a half-hidden alley, I blundered into a lively bodega, and returned with eggs and onions and potatoes and sometimes a bit of fish. In the evening, if the woman below brought up a soup that was too thin, or dry chicken parts more bone than flesh, I would cook up a stew or fry an egg. He was indifferent to my comings and goings. It was enough that I was there, to sit with him over teacups, mutely listening as he recited his sorrowful dreams, or spooled out what he called his misgivings, his guilts, his remorse.

"In those days," he always began, and then he would speak of the time before the war, and what war was that? All those wars, how was I to know, was it a war before I was born, or after? Why was I here, what was I meant to do?

The skylight was turning autumnal.

"Eva." He rasped this out with a lordliness that surprised me. After so many muffins and little pink cakes and cups of tea—after so many rueful mutterings—it was the first time he had spoken my name. Then he asked how old I was.

"I can't tell from your face. My eye can't see eyes. Faces gone, color no, my Mara in blue—" All this staccato, like gunshot.

I told him I was twenty-three. But I put my head down. To admit to this meagerness was a humiliation. Mara Kerchek had already parsed it: how could I deserve to be in this place with an old man's spiraling regrets, when I had none at all?

"Well, so much for that. My little Mara was twenty-six when we started, and how ambitious she was! And how cleverly she dressed even then, the way she carried herself, it gave her entry, you know, to the galleries, they saw her belief, they took on her belief—"

He stopped to attend to one of his slowly toiling breaths. I watched his torso, bent as it was, climb and recede, climb and recede.

"She hawked my work. After a while they came to her from everywhere. She made us rich. Never mind that she exaggerates, she lies a little, she indulges me, she makes you think Louvre, she makes you think Prado, it was nothing like that, but in those days," and he returned again to the time before the war, when his paintings were coveted, when his name was coveted, when there was everything all at once, everything new-born, a gluttony for the never before, schools and movements and trends and solemn revolutions, the orphists, the purists, the futurists, the vorticists, and soon the action painters, he was with it all, in the swim, in the maelstrom of all that delirium, and it was easy for Mara to make them rich. Especially during his divanist period (it was Mara who thought of calling it that), his conceptual nudes, his minimalist nudes, his spatter nudes, all of them parting their legs on sprawling velvet couches.

And sometimes, he told me, it was Mara who posed naked for him on that cheap chaise longue they'd bought, in those days, right out of the Sears, Roebuck catalogue.

I asked if Mara would come, if he expected her to come.

"She keeps away," I said.

"She has her work. It wears her out."

He stared me down with his milky eyes. Untamed wads of hair spilled over his collarbones. And again that stale aurora of things long eclipsed, those old grievances, if that's what they were, unfurling hour after hour, the same, the same. And then again the same. The spittle on his lip when he scraped out yet another weighty breath. He looked, I thought, like someone's abandoned messiah.

"My Mara is estranged," he said. "I've disappointed her, I haven't been good to her. She made us rich, I made her poor. After the war I made her poor."

Poor? The lapis pendant, the gold bracelets, the perfected blue shoes with their satin laces, the silken blue suit (was it silk, was it something else), the hundred-dollar bills?

I asked him if he would allow me to trim his hair.

His mind was all Mara. *Mara, Mara, my little Mara.* And wasn't I his echo? *Daughter, father,* banished words, useless here. Only Mara, Mara.

"She has a merciful heart," he said, "she indulges me, but still she casts me out, she doesn't relent. Year after year, after the war."

He told me where I might find a scissors—under the dirty windows, at the far end of his studio, beyond the skylight, in the deep drawers of a tall corner cabinet. The scissors were there, and a hammer and a vial of small black nails, and a roll of new canvas, and a sack of fresh tubes of oils. And a crisscross of stretcher bars. Mara, he explained, had ordered that boy to bring in all these useless things, that boy who didn't know his left hand from his right hand, and what good was any of it anyhow?

"The eye is the hand," he said. "And without the eye, the hand is as good as dead."

Shards of hair flew to the floor. I bent over him to do away with the tangled woolly forelock, and then his head was close against me, and I could feel in my ribs the heat of his history as he wove and unwove the knit of what was, how with all his generation of men (but he was older than most) he had been made to go to that faraway war, first in a massive ship, and then the landing on a blasphemous continent, its cities of slaughter, its trenches and shootings, planes like fleas in the sky, men who were wolves to men, women who covered their breasts with their hands, human flesh smoldering, and he saw and he saw and he saw, and he knew and he knew and he knew, and what he knew was that the body of the earth is cut in two by a ditch. A ditch between two walls.

But I had worked too close to the scalp. There was little left to cover the violated head. It was as if I had excavated a skull.

"In those days," he went on, "when the war was finished, when the war had evaporated, everything swept back to before, again the new, the new," and he told of the new office buildings, the new neighborhoods, the new hem lengths, the new markets, the galleries hungry for buyers, the collectors hungry for prestige, the contractors hungry to dazzle their suites, and oh how Mara believed! She assured him that he had only to resume. He was older than most, he was weary, he'd come out alive from the precincts of sin, and why, he asked, must he resume? She knew exactly, she was impatient to begin, she was inspired, the newest thing wasn't the newest thing, the newest thing was the oldest thing, she had been gazing, gazing, walking the Guggenheim, walking MoMA, in library reading rooms paging through catechisms of paintings, their periods, their masters, they fed her instincts, she had the clairvoyance of her instincts, and she hummed out the names of the old divanists, the old luxuriant gods, Modigliani, Matisse, Delacroix, Morisot, even Millet, even Boldini, divanists all, and more and more! She was in the thick of things, she was in the know, she could scent what the market craved, what it ought to crave, what she would teach it to crave, what the collectors devoured.

It was naked women lying down.

"She wanted me to go back to the divans. She wanted me to remake them in the shapes of all the new crazes, dance to the new tunes, old profits in new clothes, all her contacts were waiting, all her old clients, all those rich men looking for the latest thing. Retrofit, assemble, usurp, they could call it any fool name they liked, it was divans, divans, and what else was it but my Mara undressed and lying down? Still," he said, "look around, look around, and tell me if I haven't repented—"

He drilled a thick finger with its thickened fingernail through the darkening air, as if it could span the ditch between the walls, where, on either side, those heaps of canvases leaned moribund in the dust. The woman below came with his evening meal. The soup was again thin. He spooned it up and sent the rest away. Already, for many days, he had spurned the cheeses, the muffins, the little pink cakes; but he went on warming his hands on his teacup. I no longer sought out the pastry shop; it sickened him. The bodega, hidden in its alley, had anyhow failed. He took to using his cane.

In late November a peculiar brightness fell. Overhead, soundless cushions folding and unfolding: it had snowed in the night. The burdened skylight, soaked in sun, poured down rivers of white. The light, the light!

I asked if I might turn the canvases to the light.

"She couldn't move a single one," he said. "Not a one. The bleedings of three years, when I still had the eye, when I still had the hand. She begged for the divans. Instead I gave her these. Go turn them if you want, but I warn you, I warn you——"

I saw how heavily he lowered his big shoulder bones and the warp of his spine into the wooden chair where the cane had been shunned; but now he cherished it. And in an instant of shame I regretted cutting his hair. There was nothing to conceal his meaning. His meaning was transgression. He sat like a witness. It was, I felt, a vigil. Or a rite. A judgment. The vacant tripod stood nearby.

In that unnatural snowy light—or because of it, because it illumined the shadowy walls with unaccustomed clarity—I was at liberty to turn and turn each canvas, to see into this one, to inhabit that one, even to be repelled by all of them. To be warned and judged and sentenced. I saw how they were afflicted by a largeness. Even the smallest conveyed a looming. I saw what I imagined to be scenes, a ferryboat overturned, fires ingesting whole towns, drownings, earthquakes, scorching lava—but almost immediately I knew these to be illusions, the tricks of color and form and the impulsive licks of the brush. The tricks of largeness, of appetite for ruin. I thought of the scored palms of Kerchek's elephantine hands.

I crossed from wall to wall. Between these frenzies a ditch. Smoke, seared flesh, anguish, trains, engines, silent explosions. Yet hadn't he warned me? I was not to do what that ignorant boy had done, the boy who didn't know his left hand from his right hand. I was not to mistake a canvas on the left wall for

a canvas on the right wall. I was not to misplace, I was not to
compare. They were distinct, one wall from the other. And
mutually alien: each an enemy to its opposite. Each wall was an
archive. Each wall was a clamor. Each wall was a shriek. Right
wall was at war with left wall.

These, he told me, were his repudiations, his repentance. In
those days, when he still had his eye and his hand, they had the
power to redeem. And now they festered.

"Mara couldn't place any of them," he said. "They weren't
wanted. She didn't understand any of it, she didn't expect anyone
to understand, she wanted the divans, she wanted the profits,
they were there for the plucking, the postwar markets all on
fire, why was I scheming to make her poor, was it vengeance?"

The sun had passed over the skylight. Kerchek's studio—
how forlorn it was—returned to its daytime dusk. The canvases
were again what they had been: dead things decaying. In a
hidden corner of each of them, an obscure sign: *SK*, intertwined like an ampersand.

I confessed that I could see no breach between one wall and
the other. The wall on the right seemed no different from the
wall on the left.

"You don't see, you don't see? You with your eyes, you can't
see? It was Mara, my Mara, who made me see—"

I waited while he searched for his breath; I had learned to
wait. A little snake of a laugh crept out of his throat. It frightened me; it meant he was waning. His afternoon dozes had
grown longer and longer. I had cut his hair too close to the
scalp, his head was naked, and what if he died before Mara
came, what was I to do? And when would she come?

It was Mara herself, the joke of it, he told me, who drove
him on, who drove him into the work of the walls, if not for
Mara he might have succumbed to the divans, scores of divans,
hundreds of divans, seduced by the schools, the movements,
the profits, the old made new. If not for Mara, after the war.
She came to him, straight out, or how would he know to tell
it now? An inchling, she called it, she did away with it, what
else could she do, it was only an inchling, a pinch of fat in the
womb, so why did it matter?

His poor little ambitious Mara, hoping to lure her clients, her collectors, to please, to appease. Even then, even then.

And that discarded pinch of fat in the womb, was it the same as the poisonous brown seed of the apple, and if you crush the seed, you give the lie to the tree? Was it the same as the capsized ferry and its drownings? Was it the same as the bridge that collapses from age? Or the floods when the tide comes in, or the fires the winds ignite? Is the inferno in the belly of the earth the same as sin? Or the fever that kills? Is the river that dries no different from will? Who dares to fuse the two? Only a pinch of fat in the womb, so why must it matter?

"But I wept, you know," he said. "I wept. And then, because nothing mattered, not even a pinch of fat in the womb, I began to see again. I saw with all the strength of my body. Sin on one side, calamity on the other, with a ditch to keep them apart. Only men sin. Only women. It's an innocent God who wakens ruin."

I can't say that these were Kerchek's words. I can only say that this is what I heard. After all, he never spoke of God. He never mentioned sin, and hadn't he sneered at superstition? In fact, I remember that he said very little, only that once, long ago, while up to his knees in running blood on that blasphemous continent, Mara Kerchek conceived a child and did away with it.

And afterward—after letting out this small note—he went on dabbling his spoon in his soup.

The next day all that was forgotten. He warmed his hands on his morning tea and asked me plainly if I knew why Mara Kerchek had brought me to him.

"To be your assistant," I said. What else should I say?

"Did she do her hocus-pocus? Put you up for trial? My silly Mara with her sixth sense—"

"She called my work kitsch. She tore it up."

"Eva," he said, "come here. Give me your hand."

It startled me to hear him speak my name yet again; it seemed almost conspiratorial. I placed my left hand on his right hand. It lay there like a small salamander nestled among the mounds of his knuckles.

"Hocus-pocus," he said. "Abracadabra. She means to make it all come back to life. And do you know why?"

I had no answer. I feared his confidings, I feared his trust. If he was dying—the skin of his head was pitted and rusted and crumpled—if he was beginning to die, it wasn't for me to give him deliverance. He had a daughter for that!

"My Mara is sick of her work, it wears her out, I haven't been good to her. I've brought her down, I've made her poor—"

It was his usual chant. I thought I would tear through it outright.

I said, "Mara's work, what is it?"

"The same. Always the same. The clients, the consultations, the appraisals. These collectors, they want to possess but they don't know what they want to possess. She takes them around and shows them. Or else she goes up to their palaces, their penthouses, whatever they call them, to appraise what they already possess. The richer they are, the more they want to spell out the worth of things. The price. They're cautious, you know, so they pay in raw cash—"

Where was his breath? He was panting a little, a shallow gasp, and then another. A bit of a noise to go with it, and while I waited for the noise to subside, and for his breath to return, it came to me—how open it was—that Mara Kerchek in her silky blue suit, with her lapis necklace and satin shoeties, was a woman of the night.

In early December the day gave way to dark in seconds. The lamps were switched on before three, and Kerchek slept on, hour after hour, through the afternoon gloom. His feet, with their slippers fallen, overflowed the divan; the toenails tall and thick and jagged. The head on the ornate cushion a pallid dome. The soft ears uncovered. A remnant of biscuit left uneaten.

From the cabinet under the far windows I retrieved the scissors, the hammer, the vial of tacks. Out of the web of stretcher bars I chose four. I cut a length of fresh canvas, and hammered the bars into a precise fir square. I drew the canvas as taut as could be and tapped it down until it resisted the lightest dent of a fingertip. Then I snipped off the last wavering threads.

Through all this commotion I was vigilant. I kept watch

over Kerchek's breast: was it rising and descending, was this
wasted old man breathing? Was he deaf to the hammering? But
he slept on. The pale canvas in its frame, resting now on the
lip of the tripod, had the look of the white of an eye awaiting
its pupil.

And meanwhile in these short December days that rush into
night, the skylight turns biblical. Snow falls again, and then
again, the wintry wind arouses the sun: let there be light! But
the light is theatrical and brief, and must be made much of
while it lasts.

It was in just such a snowstruck radiant interval, when
Kerchek refused his dry biscuit and took up his cane and shed
his slippers and let himself warily down into those velvety
cushions to revisit his dreams (but the itch to reveal them had
lately weakened), that I began to paint the divan. The divan
overflowing with Kerchek.

I painted him slyly, slowly, thickly, hugely, with a raptness
new to my hand. I painted his collarbones, the bare ruined
pallor of his heels. I painted, with pity, his hands. I painted
his looted head, the flattened mouth, the wrinkled ovals of his
shuttered eyes. The ways of the fence, speed and slapdash, all for
the money, were wicked here.

And I painted the divan, the velvet, the crimson, the cushions, the curly squat legs, the kingly tassels. For ten days I
painted until it was too dark to see. I emptied the tubes of
their greens and reds and yellows and taupes, and thickened and
thinned them to grow into skin and weave and the gray of veins
and the delusions of sleep: a vessel for Kerchek's mind. I knew
what was in it. Dread and pity for such a daughter. Intoxicated
by such a daughter.

The woman below stopped coming. It was pointless, he
turned away. How I regretted cutting his hair, unclean, even
savage. I had meant it for his dignity. Instead it left the bones of
his face jutting. I painted them as if they were the crumbling
bones of a pharaoh. And it was with something like reverence
that I painted the divan: its sultan's cushions, its swaying tassels,
its regally curlicued feet. Soon he would die there, I thought,
on Mara Kerchek's divan.

The skylight's snow ebbed, the sun hid itself. The light was gone. A wind sent in the cold. The skin of Kerchek's hands, how like a membrane of thinnest isinglass, and under it the wormy dying veins. I covered his shoulders and arms with a blanket. He had no one to warm him. Mara kept away.

It was enough. Why was I here? The thing was finished.

"I'm going now, I have to go," I said, and looked down on him. "Mara will come," I told him. "Any day now she'll come."

He didn't wake. He didn't hear. I left him and went back to see what I had made. The figure on the divan, was it Kerchek? The resemblance was poor, who would know him? A heap of wornout passion. An unforgiven seer. The traitor father of a traitor daughter.

But the thing was done. Or almost. I picked up the brush with the slenderest tip and in a hidden fold of the canvas painted a tiny emblem: *SK*. It looked like an ampersand.

"Eva," he called. A voice hollowed by a stranded dream. "Eva, come here, I'm cold—"

His milky eyes were on guard. He took my hand, but this time he held me by the wrist and passed his heavy fingers over the palm. I felt how coarse they were.

"Do you have a mother? A father?"

"A stepfather, but he died."

"A child's hand. Small, like Mara's. She sees things in the fold of a thumb, in the turn of a crease." His fingers hardened on mine, one by one. "Mumbo jumbo, my Mara sees, she sees what she wants to see—"

It fell out like a plea.

"No," I said. "It's her father who sees."

"Mara? Mara's father is dead."

Was he a man condemning himself? Was it a sentence? A punishment? For the sin of making Mara poor.

"No, no, your daughter has a merciful heart, you say this yourself, she's bound to come soon—"

"My daughter? I have no daughter."

Was he grieving, was he lost? Or was it shame?

"You have Mara," I said.

I saw him let down his legs. I saw him pull himself up from

the divan. The crimson tassels swung. His old man's head shook.

"What are you saying? I have no child, I have no daughter."

I said again, "You have Mara."

"Mara, Mara." His throat thickened. His eyes blackened into char. He threw off his grip on my wrist. "Is that what you think? Is that what you believe? Who told you such blasphemy? That I am the man who would uncover his own daughter's naked-ness, that I am the father who would stretch out his daughter on a couch only to gaze on her lineaments? That I would oblige her to raise her hip for the curl of its arch, that I would beg her to part her thighs, and all for the sake of painter's gold? Ignorant girl, you don't know your left hand from your right hand, Mara is my wife, my little Mara, my wife, my wife—"

I can't say that these were Kerchek's words. I can only say that this was what I heard.

He sank back into the cushions. I saw his breast climb and recede, climb and recede.

"I have to go now," I said. "I can't stay," and left him there. Someone would find him. The woman below would find him. Or Mara would come.

Well, I'm back at La Bellamonte. Guido, the manager, gives me a second chance, he says, on condition that I never again walk out on the job. As penalty, he's taken five dollars off my old wages. What with the rent on my place, I can barely afford a new phone. Anyhow I've bought one. Who nowadays can live without such a thing? I've got a new shirt, too, with a zippered pocket to keep it safe. As for the rent, I was lucky enough to scout out a pair of art students from Cooper Union, to pay for half—Richard and Robert. They're focused and ambitious. Richard is heading for theater design, Robert for advertising. Like the engineer and his girlfriend, they sleep in one bed, mouth to mouth.

When the weather warms up, I'll go back to the fence. I won't do landscapes or seascapes or period lovers or flowers in vases or any of that sort of kitsch. I won't put anything up on the fence. I'll have a little table, the folding kind, and I'll filch a couple of chairs when Guido isn't looking, and what I'll do is miniatures. On fingernails, female and male. The women generally like ladies in long gowns. The men want snakes and daggers and girls' names circled in roses, the things you see tattooed on their biceps. All that, I'm told, is the newest craze down there at the fence, and brings in the money.

A Mercenary

Today we are all expressionists—men who
want to make the world outside themselves
take the form of their life within themselves.
—JOSEPH GOEBBELS

STANISLAV LUSHINSKI, A Pole and a diplomat, was not a Polish
diplomat. People joked that he was a mercenary, and would
sell his tongue to any nation that bargained for it. In certain
offices of the glass rectangle in New York he was known as "the
P.M."—which meant not so much that they considered him
easily as influential as the Prime Minister of his country (itself a
joke: his country was a speck, no more frightening than a small
wart on the western—or perhaps it was the eastern—flank of
Africa), but stood, rather, for Paid Mouthpiece.

His country. Altogether he had lived in it, not counting certain lengthy official and confidential visits, for something over
fourteen consecutive months, at the age of nineteen—that was
twenty-seven years ago—en route to America. But though it
was true that he was not a native, it was a lie that he was not a
patriot. Something in that place had entered him, he could not
shake out of his nostrils the musky dreamy fragrance of nights
in the capital—the capital was, as it happened, the third-largest
city, though it had the most sophisticated populace. There, his
colleagues claimed, the men wore trousers and the women
covered their teats.

The thick night-blossoms excited him. Born to a flagstoned
Warsaw garden, Lushinski did not know the names of flowers
beyond the most staid dooryard sprigs, daisies and roses, and
was hardly conscious that these heaps of petals, meat-white,
a red as dark and boiling as an animal's maw, fevered oranges
and mauves, the lobe-leafed mallows, all hanging downward
like dyed hairy hanged heads from tall bushes at dusk, were
less than animal. It was as if he disbelieved in botany, although

he believed gravely enough in jungle. He felt himself native to these mammalian perfumes, to the dense sweetness of so many roundnesses, those round burnt hills at the edge of the capital, the little round brown mounds of the girls he pressed down under the trees—he, fresh out of the roil of Europe; they, secret to the ground, grown out of the brown ground, on which he threw himself, with his tongue on their black-brown nipples, learning their language.

He spoke it not like a native—though he was master of that tangled clot of extraordinary inflections scraped on the palate, nasal whistles, beetle-clicks—but like a preacher. The language had no written literature. A century ago a band of missionaries had lent it the Roman alphabet and transcribed in it queer versions of the Psalms, so that

> thou satest in the throne judging right

came out in argot:

> god squat-on-earth-mound
> tells who owns
> accidentally-decapitated-by-fallen-tree-trunk
> deer,

and it was out of this Bible, curiously like a moralizing hunting manual, the young Lushinski received his lessons in syntax. Except for when he lay under a cave of foliage with a brown girl, he studied alone, and afterward (he was still only approaching twenty) translated much of Jonah, which the exhausted missionaries had left unfinished. But the story of the big fish seemed simple-minded in that rich deep tongue, which had fifty-four words describing the various parts and positions of a single rear fin. And for "prow" many more: "nose-of-boat-facing-brightest-star," or star of middle dimness, or dimmest of all; "nose-of-boat-fully-invisible-in-rain-fog"; half-visible; quarter-visible; and so on. It was an observant, measuring, meticulous language.

His English was less given to sermonizing. It was diplomat's

English: which does not mean that it was deceitful, but that it was innocent before passion, and minutely truthful about the order of paragraphs in all previous documentation.

He lived, in New York, with a mistress: a great rosy woman, buxom, tall and talkative. To him she was submissive.

In Geneva—no one could prove this—he lived on occasion with a strenuous young Italian, a coppersmith, a boy of twenty-four, red-haired and lean and not at all submissive.

His colleagues discovered with surprise that Lushinski was no bore. It astounded them. They resented him for it, because the comedy had been theirs, and he the object of it. A white man, he spoke for a black country: this made a place for him on television. At first he came as a sober financial attaché, droning economic complaints (the recently expelled colonial power had exploited the soil by excessive plantings; not an acre was left fallow; the chief crop—jute? cocoa? rye? Lushinski was too publicly fastidious ever to call it by its name—was thereby severely diminished, there was famine in the south). And then it was noticed that he was, if one listened with care, inclined to obliqueness—to, in fact, irony.

It became plain that he could make people laugh. Not that he told jokes, not even that he was a wit—but he began to recount incidents out of his own life. Sometimes he was believed; often not.

In his office he was ambitious but gregarious. His assistant, Morris Ngambe, held an Oxford degree in political science. He was a fat-cheeked, flirtatious young man with a glossy bronze forehead, perfectly rounded, like a goblet. He was exactly half Lushinski's age, and sometimes, awash in papers after midnight, their ties thrown off and their collars undone, they would send out for sandwiches and root beer (Lushinski lusted after everything American and sugared); in this atmosphere almost of equals they would compare boyhoods.

Ngambe's grandfather was the brother of a chief; his father had gone into trade, aided by the colonial governor himself. The history and politics of all this was murky; nevertheless Ngambe's father became rich. He owned a kind of assembly-line consisting of many huts. Painted gourds stood in the

doorways like monitory dwarfs; these were to assure prosperity. His house grew larger and larger; he built a wing for each
wife. Morris was the eldest son of the favorite wife, a woman
of intellect and religious attachment. She stuck, Morris said,
to the old faith. A friend of Morris's childhood—a boy raised
in the missionary school, who had grown up into a model
bookkeeper and dedicated Christian—accused her of scandal:
instead of the Trinity, he shouted to her husband (his employer), she worshipped plural gods; instead of caring for the Holy
Spirit, she adhered to animism. Society was progressing, and
she represented nothing but regression: a backslider into primi-
tivism. The village could not tolerate it, even in a female. Since
it was fundamental propriety to ignore wives, it was clear that
the fellow was crazy to raise a fuss over what one of a man's
females thought or did. But it was also fundamental propriety
to ignore an insane man (in argot the word for "insane" was, in
fact, "becoming-childbearer," or, alternatively, "bottom-hole-
mouth"), so everyone politely turned away, except Morris's
mother, who followed a precept of her religion: a female who
has a man (in elevated argot "lord") for her enemy must offer
him her loins in reconciliation. Morris's mother came naked
at night to her accuser's hut and parted her legs for him on the
floor. Earlier he had been sharpening pencils; he took the knife
from his pencil-pot (a gourd hollowed-out and painted, one of
Morris's father's most successful export items) and stabbed her
breasts. Since she had recently given birth (Morris was twenty
years older than his youngest brother), she bled both blood
and milk, and died howling, smeared pink. But because in her
religion the goddess Tanake declares before five hundred lords
that she herself became divine through having been cooked
in her own milk, Morris's mother, with her last cry, pleaded
for similar immortality; and so his father, who was less pious
but who had loved her profoundly, made a feast. While the
governor looked the other way, the murderer was murdered;
Morris was unwilling to describe the execution. It was, he said
in his resplendent Oxonian voice, "very clean." His mother
was ceremonially eaten; this accomplished her transfiguration.
Her husband and eldest son were obliged to share the principal

sacrament, the nose, "emanator-of-wind-of-birth." The six other wives—Morris called each of them Auntie—divided among them a leg steamed in goat's milk. And everyone who ate at that festival, despite the plague of gnats that attended the day, became lucky ever after. Morris was admitted to Oxford; his grandfather's brother died at a very great age and his father replaced him as chief; the factory acquired brick buildings and chimneys and began manufacturing vases both of ceramic and glass; the colonial power was thrown out; Morris's mother was turned into a goddess, and her picture sold in the villages. Her name had been Tuka. Now she was Tanake-Tuka, and could perform miracles for devout women, and sometimes for men.

Some of Ngambe's tales Lushinski passed off as his own observations of what he always referred to on television as "bush life." In the privacy of his office he chided Morris for having read too many Tarzan books. "I have only seen the movies," Ngambe protested. He recalled how in London on Sunday afternoons there was almost nothing else to do. But he believed his mother had been transformed into a divinity. He said he often prayed to her. The taste of her flesh had bestowed on him simplicity and geniality.

From those tedious interviews by political analysts Lushinski moved at length to false living rooms with false "hosts" contriving false conversation. He felt himself recognized, a foreign celebrity. He took up the habit of looking caressingly into the very camera with the red light alive on it, signaling it was sensitive to his nostrils, his eyebrows, his teeth and his ears. And under all that lucid theatrical blaze, joyful captive on an easy chair between an imbecile film reviewer and a cretinous actress, he began to weave out a life.

Sometimes he wished he could write out of imagination: he fancied a small memoir, as crowded with desires as with black leafy woods, or else sharp and deathly as a blizzard; and at the same time very brief and chaste, though full of horror. But he was too intelligent to be a writer. His intelligence was a version of cynicism. He rolled irony like an extra liquid in his mouth. He could taste it exactly the way Morris tasted his mother's nose. It gave him powers.

He pretended to educate. The "host" asked him why he, a white man, represented a black nation. He replied that Disraeli too had been of another race, though he led Britain. The "host" asked him whether his fondness for his adopted country induced him to patronize its inhabitants. This he did not answer; instead he hawked up into the actress's handkerchief—leaning right over to pluck it from her décolletage where she had tucked it— and gave the "host" a shocked stare. The audience laughed—he seemed one of those gruff angry comedians they relished.

Then he said: "You can only patronize if you are a customer. In my country we have no brothels."

Louisa—his mistress—did not appear on the programs with him. She worried about his stomach. "Stasek has such a very small stomach," she said. She herself had oversized eyes, rubbed blue over the lids, a large fine nose, a mouth both large and nervous. She mothered him and made him eat. If he ate corn she would slice the kernels off the cob and warn him about his stomach. "It is very hard for Stasek to eat, with his little stomach. It shrank when he was a boy. You know he was thrown into the forest when he was only six."

Then she would say: "Stasek is generous to Jews but he doesn't like the pious ones."

They spoke of her as a German countess—her last name was preceded by a "von"—but she seemed altogether American, though her accent had a fake melody either Irish or Swedish. She claimed she had once run a famous chemical corporation in California, and truly she seemed as worldly as that, an executive, with her sudden jagged gestures, her large hands all alertness, her curious attentiveness to her own voice, her lips painted orange as fire. But with Lushinski she could be very quiet. If they sat at some party on opposite sides of the room, and if he lifted one eyebrow, or less, if he twitched a corner of his mouth or a piece of eyelid, she understood and came to him at once. People gaped; but she was proud. "I gave up everything for Stanislav. Once I had three hundred and sixty people under me. I had two women who were my private secretaries, one for general work, one exclusively for dictation and correspondence. I wasn't always the way you see me now.

When Stasek tells me to come, I come. When he tells me to stay, I stay."

She confessed all this aloofly, and with the panache of royalty. On official business he went everywhere without her. It was true his stomach was very flat. He was like one of those playing-card soldiers in *Alice in Wonderland*: his shoulders a pair of neat thin corners, everything else cut along straight lines. The part in his hair (so sleekly black it looked painted on) was a clean line exactly above the terrifying pupil of his left eye. This pupil measured and divided, the lid was as cold and precise as the blade of a knife. Even his nose was a rod of machined steel there under the live skin—separated from his face, it could have sliced anything. Still, he was handsome, or almost so, and when he spoke it was necessary to attend. It was as if everything he said was like that magic pipe in the folktale, the sound of which casts a spell on its hearers' feet and makes the whole town dance madly, willy-nilly. His colleagues only remembered to be scornful when they were not face to face with him; otherwise, like everybody else, they were held by his mobile powerful eyes, as if controlled by silent secret wheels behind and his small smile that was not a smile, rather a contemptuous little mock-curtsy of those narrow cheeks, and for the moment they believed anything he told them, they believed that his country was larger than it seemed and was deserving of rapt respect.

In New York Morris Ngambe had certain urban difficulties typical of the times. He was snubbed and sent to the service entrance (despite the grandeur of his tie) by a Puerto Rican elevator man in an apartment house on Riverside Drive, he was knocked down and robbed not in Central Park but a block away by a gang of seven young men wearing windbreakers reading "Africa First, Harlem Nowhere"—a yellow-gold cap covering his right front incisor fell off, and was aesthetically replaced by a Dr. Korngelb of East Forty-ninth Street, who substituted a fine white up-to-date acrylic jacket. Also he was set upon by a big horrible dog, a rusty-furred female chow, who, rising from a squat, having defecated in the middle of the sidewalk, inexplicably flew up and bit deep into Morris's arm. Poor Morris had to go to Bellevue outclinic for rabies injections in his stomach.

For days afterward he groaned with the pain. "This city, this city!" he wailed to Lushinski. "London is boring but at least civilized. New York is just what they say of it—a wilderness, a jungle." He prayed to his mother's picture, and forgot that his own village at home was enveloped by a rubbery skein of gray forest with all its sucking, whistling, croaking, gnawing, perilously breathing beasts and their fearful eyes luminous with moonlight.

But at other times he did not forget, and he and Lushinski would compare the forests of their boyhoods. That sort of conversation always made Morris happy: he had been gifted with an ecstatic childhood, racing with other boys over fallen berries, feeling the squush of warm juice under his swift toes, stopping to try the bitter taste of one or two; and once they swallowed sour flies, for fun, and on a dare. But mostly there were games—so clever and elaborate he wondered at them even now, who had invented them, and in what inspired age long ago: concealing games, with complicated clue-songs attached, and quiet games with twigs of different sizes from different kinds of bark, requiring as much concentration as chess; and acrobatic games, boys suspended upside down from branches to stretch the muscles of the neck, around which, one day, the great width of the initiation-band would be fitted; and sneaking-up games, mimicking the silence of certain deer-faced little rodents with tender flanks who streaked by so quickly they could be perceived only as a silver blur. And best of all, strolling home after a whole dusty day in the bright swarm of the glade, insects jigging in the slotted sunbeams and underfoot the fleshlike fever-pad of the forest floor; and then, nearing the huts, the hazy smell of dusk beginning and all the aunties' indulgent giggles; then their hearts swelled: the aunties called them "lord"; they were nearly men. Morris—in those days he was Mdulgo-kt'dulgo ("prime-soul-born-of-prime-soul")—licked the last bit of luscious goat-fat from his banana leaf and knew he would one day weigh in the world.

Lushinski told little of his own forest. But for a moment its savagery wandered up and down the brutal bone of his nose.

"Wolves?" Morris asked; in his forest ran sleek red jackal

with black swaths down their backs, difficult to trap but not dangerous if handled intelligently, their heads as red as some of these female redheads one saw taking big immodest strides in the streets of London and New York. But wolves are northern terrors, Slavic emanations, spun out of snow and legends of the Baba Yaga.

"Human wolves," Lushinski answered, and said nothing after that. Sometimes he grew sullen all at once, or else a spurt of fury would boil up in him; and then Morris would think of the chow. It had never been determined whether the chow was rabid or not. Morris had endured all that wretchedness for nothing, probably. Lulu (this was Louisa: a name that privately disturbed Morris—he was ashamed to contemplate what these two horrid syllables denoted in argot, and prayed to his mother to help him blot out the pictures that came into his thoughts whenever Lushinski called her on the telephone and began with—O Tanake-Tuka!—"Lulu?")—Lulu also was sometimes bewildered by these storms which broke out in him: then he would reach out a long hard hand and chop at her with it, and she would remember that once he had killed a man. He had killed; she saw in him the power to kill.

On television he confessed to murder:

Once upon a time, long ago in a snowy region of the world called Poland, there lived a man and his wife in the city of Warsaw. The man ruled over a certain palace—it was a bank— and the woman ruled over another palace, very comfortable and rambling, with hundreds of delightful storybooks behind glass doors in mahogany cases and secret niches to hide toy soldiers in and caves under chairs and closets that mysteriously connected with one another through dark and enticing passageways—it was a rich fine mansion on one of the best streets in Warsaw. This noble and blessed couple had a little son, whom they loved more than their very lives, and whom they named Stanislav. He was unusually bright, and learned everything more rapidly than he could be taught, and was soon so accomplished that they rejoiced in his genius and could not get over their good luck in having given life to so splendid a little man. The cook used to bring him jigsaw puzzles consisting of one thousand pieces all seemingly of the same shape and color, just for the marvel of watching him make a picture out of them in no time at all. His father's chauffeur once came half an hour early, just to challenge the boy at chess; he was then not yet five, and the maneuvers he invented for his toy soliders were amusingly in imitation of the witty pursuits of the chessboard. He was already joyously reading about insects, stars, and trolley cars. His father had brought home for him one evening a little violin, and his mother had engaged a teacher of celebrated reputation. Almost immediately he began to play with finesse and ease.

In Stanislav there was only one defect—at least they thought it a defect—that grieved his parents. The father and mother were both fair, like a Polish prince and a Polish princess; the mother kept her golden hair plaited in a snail-like bun over each pink ear, the father wore a sober gray waistcoat under his satiny pink chin. The father was ruddy, the mother rosy, and when they looked into one another's eyes, the father's as gray as the buttery gray cloth of his vest, the mother's as clamorously blue as the blue chips of glass in her son's kaleidoscope, they felt themselves graced by God with such an extraordinary child, indeed a prodigy (he was obsessed by an interest in algebra)—but, pink and ruddy and golden and rosy as they were, the boy, it seemed, was a gypsy. His hair was black with a slippery will of its own, like a gypsy's, his eyes were brilliant but disappointingly black, like gypsy eyes, and even the skin of his clever small hands had a dusky glow, like gypsy skin. His mother grew angry when the servants called him by a degrading nickname—Ziggi, short for *Zigeuner*, the German word for gypsy. But when she forbade it, she did not let slip to them that it was the darkness she reviled, she pretended it was only the German word itself; she would not allow German to be uttered in that house— German, the language of the barbarian invaders, enemies of all good Polish people.

All the same, she heard them whisper under the stairs, or in the kitchen: *Zigeuner*; and the next day the Germans came, in helmets, in boots, tanks grinding up even the most fashionable streets, and the life of the Warsaw palaces, the fair father in his bank, the fair mother under her rose-trellis, came to an end.

The fair father and the fair mother sewed *zloty* in their under-clothes and took the dark child far off into a peasant village at the edge of the forest and left him, together with the money to pay for it, in the care of a rough but kind-hearted farmer until the world should right itself again. And the fair blessed couple fled east, hoping to escape to Russia: but on the way, despite fair hair and pale eyes and aristocratic manners and the cultivated Polish speech of city people with a literary bent, they were perceived to be non-Aryan and were roped to a silver birch at the other end of the woods and shot.

All this happened on the very day Stanislav had his sixth birthday. And what devisings, months and months ahead of time, there had been for that birthday! Pony rides, and a clown in a silken suit, and his father promising to start him on Euclid. . . . And here instead was this horrid dirty squat-necked man with a bald head and a fat nose and such terrible fingers with thick horny blackened nails like angle irons, and a dreadful witchlike woman standing there with her face on fire, and four children in filthy smocks peering out of a crack in a door tied shut with a rubber strap.

"He's too black," said the witch. "I didn't know he'd be a black one. You couldn't tell from the looks of *them*. He'll expose us, there's danger in it for us."

"They paid," the man said.

"Too black. Get rid of him."

"All right," said the man, and that night he put the boy out in the forest. . . .

But now the "host" interrupted, and the glass mouth of the television filled up with a song about grimy shirt collars and a soap that could clean them properly. "Ring around the collar," the television sang, and then the "host" asked, "Was that the man you killed?"

"No," Lushinski said. "It was somebody else."

"And you were only six?"

"No," Lushinski said, "by then I was older."

"And you lived on your own in the forest—a little child, imagine!—all that time?"

"In the forest. On my own."

"But how? How? You were only a child!"

"Cunning," Lushinski said. It was all mockery and parody. And somehow—because he mocked and parodied, sitting under the cameras absurdly smiling and replete with contradictions, the man telling about the boy, Pole putting himself out as African, candor offering cunning—an uneasy blossom of laughter opened in his listeners, the laughter convinced: he was making himself up. He had made himself over, and now he was making himself up, like one of those comedians who tell uproarious anecdotes about their preposterous relatives. "You see," Lushinski said, "by then the peasants wanted to catch me. They thought if they caught me and gave me to the Germans there would be advantage in it for them—the Germans might go easy on the village, not come in and cart away all the grain without paying and steal the milk—oh, I was proper prey. And then I heard the slaver of a dog: a big sick bulldog, I knew him, his name was Andor and he had chewed-up genitals and vomit on his lower jaw. He belonged to the sexton's helper who lived in a shed behind the parish house, a brute he was, old but a brute, so I took a stick when Andor came near and stuck it right in his eye, as deep as I could push it. And Andor comes rolling and yowling like a demon, and the sexton's helper lunges after him, and I grab Andor—heavy as a log, heavy as a boulder, believe me—I grab him and lift him and smash him right down against the sexton's helper, and he's knocked over on his back, by now Andor is crazy, Andor is screeching and sticky with a river of blood spilling out of his eye, and he digs his smelly teeth like spades, like spikes, like daggers, into the old brute's neck—"

All this was comedy: Marx Brothers, Keystone Kops, the audience is elated by its own disbelief. The bulldog is a dragon, the sexton's helper an ogre, Lushinski is only a storyteller, and the "host" asks, "Then that's the man you killed?"

"Oh no, Jan's Andor killed Jan."

"Is it true?" Morris wanted to know—he sat in the front row and laughed with the rest—and began at once to tell about the horrid chow on East Ninetieth Street; but Lulu never asked this. She saw how true. Often enough she shook him out of nightmares, tears falling from his nostrils, his tongue curling after air with hideous sucking noises. Then she brought him hot milk, and combed down his nape with a wet hand, and reminded him he was out of it all, Poland a figment, Europe a fancy, he now a great man, a figure the world took notice of.

He told no one who the man was—the man he killed: not even Lulu. And so she did not know whether he had killed in the Polish forest, or in the camp afterward when they caught him, or in Moscow where they took him, or perhaps long afterward, in Africa. And she did not know whether the man he killed was a gypsy, or a Pole, or a German, or a Russian, or a Jew, or one of those short brown warriors from his own country, from whom the political caste was drawn. And she did not know whether he had killed with his hands, or with a weapon, or through some device or ruse. Sometimes she was frightened to think she was the mistress of a murderer; and sometimes it gladdened her, and made her life seem different from all other lives, adventurous and poignant; she could pity and admire herself all at once.

He took Morris with him to Washington to visit the Secretary of State. The Secretary was worried about the threatened renewal of the northern tribal wars: certain corporate interests, he explained in that vapid dialect he used on purpose to hide the name of the one furious man whose fear he was making known, who had yielded his anxiety to the Secretary over a lunch of avocado salad, fish in some paradisal sauce, wine-and-mushroom-scented roast, a dessert of sweetened asparagus mixed with peppered apricot liqueur and surrounded by a peony-pattern of almond cakes—certain corporate interests, said the Secretary (he meant his friend), were concerned about the steadiness of shipments of the single raw material vital to the manufacture of their indispensable product; the last outbreak of tribal hostility had brought the cutting in the plantations to a dead halt; the shippers had nothing to send, and instead hauled some rotted stuff out of last year's discarded cuttings in the storehouses; it wouldn't do, an entire American industry depended on peace in that important region; but when he said "an entire American industry," he still meant the one furious man, his friend, whose young third wife had been at the luncheon too, a poor girl who carried herself now like a poor girl's idea of a queen, with hair expensively turned stiff as straw, but worth looking at all the same. And so again he said "that important region."

"You know last time with the famine up there," the Secretary continued, "I remember twenty years or so ago, before your time, I was out in the Cameroon, and they were at each other's throats over God knows what."

Morris said, "It was the linguistic issue. Don't think of 'tribes,' sir; think of nations, and you will comprehend better the question of linguistic pride."

"It's not a matter of comprehension, it's a matter of money. They wouldn't go to the plantations to cut, you see."

"They were at war. There was the famine."

"Mr. Ngambe, you weren't born then. If they had cut something, there wouldn't have been famine."

"Oh, that crop's not edible, sir," Morris protested: "it's like eating rope!"

The Secretary did not know what to do with such obtuseness; he was not at all worried about a hunger so far away which, full of lunch, he could not credit. His own stomach seemed a bit acid to him, he hid a modest belch. "God knows," he said, "what those fellows eat—"

But "Sir," said Lushinski, "you have received our documents on the famine in the south. The pressure on our northern stocks—believe me, sir, they are dwindling—can be alleviated by a simple release of Number Three grain deposits, for which you recall we made an appeal last week—"

"I haven't gotten to the Number Threes, Mr. Lushinski. I'll look them over this weekend, I give you my word. I'll put my staff right on it. But the fact is, if there's an outbreak—"

"Of cholera?" said Morris. "We've had word of some slight cholera in the south already."

"I'm talking about war. It's a pity about the cholera, but that's strictly internal. We can't do anything about it, unless the Red Cross . . . Now look here, we can't have that sort of interference again with cutting and with shipments. We can't have it. There has got to be a way—"

"Negotiations have begun between the Dt' and the Runda-bi," Morris said; he always understood when Lushinski wished him to speak, but he felt confused, because he could feel also that the Secretary did not wish him to speak and was in fact annoyed with him, and looked to Lushinski only. All at once bitterness ran in him, as when the Puerto Rican elevator man sent him to the service entrance: but then it ebbed, and he admonished himself that Lushinski was his superior in rank and in years, a man the Prime Minister said had a heart like a root of a tree in his own back yard. This was a saying derived from the Dt' proverb: the man whose heart is rooted in his own garden will betray your garden, but the man whose heart is rooted in your garden will take care of it as if it were his own. (In the beautiful compressed idiom of the Prime Minister's middle-region argot: *bl'kt pk'ralwa, bl'kt duwam pk'ralwi*.)

And so instead of allowing himself to cultivate the hard little knob of jealousy that lived inside his neck, in the very spot where he swallowed food and drink, Morris reminded himself of his patriotism—his dear little country, still more a concept than a real nation, a confederacy of vast and enviously competitive families, his own prestigious tribe the most prom-inent, its females renowned for having the sleekest skin, even grandmothers' flesh smooth and tight as the flesh of panthers. He considered how inventiveness and adaptability marked his father and all his father's brothers, how on the tribe-god's day all the other families had to bring his great-uncle baskets of bean-flour and garlic buds, how on that day his great-uncle took out the tall tribe-god from its locked hut, and wreathed a garland of mallows on its *lulu*, and the females were shut into the tribe-god's stockade, and how at the first star of night the songs from the females behind the wall heated the sky and every boy of fourteen had his new bronze collar hitched on, and then how, wearing his collar, Morris led out of the god's stockade and into the shuddering forest his first female of his own, one of the aunties' young cousins, a pliant little girl of eleven . . . .

In New York there were dangerous houses, it was necessary

to be married to be respectable, not to acquire a disease, in New York it was not possible for an important young man to have a female of his own who was not his wife; in London it was rather more possible, he had gone often to the bedsitter of Isabel Oxenham, a cheerful, bony, homely young woman who explained that being a Cockney meant you were born within the sound of Bow Bells and therefore she was a Cockney, but in New York there was prejudice, it was more difficult, in this Lushinski could not be his model. . . . Now he was almost listening to the Secretary, and oh, he had conquered jealousy, he was proud that his country, so tender, so wise, so full of feeling, could claim a mind like Lushinski's to represent it! It was not a foreign mind, it was a mind like his own, elevated and polished. He heard the Secretary say "universal," and it occurred to him that the conversation had turned philosophical. Instantly he made a contribution to it; he was certain that philosophy and poetry were his only real interests: his strengths.

"At bottom," Morris said, "there is no contradiction between the tribal and the universal. Remember William Blake, sir: 'To see a world in a grain of sand'—"

The Secretary had white hair and an old, creased face; Morris loathed the slender purple veins that made flower-patterns along the sides of his nose. The ugliness, the defectiveness, of some human beings! God must have had a plan for them if He created them, but since one did not understand the plan, one could not withhold one's loathing. It was not a moral loathing, it was only aesthetic. "Nationalism," Morris said, "in the West is so very recent: a nineteenth-century development. But in Africa we have never had that sort of thing. Our notion of nationhood is different, it has nothing political attached to it; it is for the dear land itself, the customs, the rites, the cousins, the sense of family. A sense of family gives one a more sublime concept: one is readier to think of the Human Family," but he thanked his mother that he was not related to this old, carmine-colored, creased and ugly man.

On the way back to New York in the shuttle plane Lushinski spoke to him like a teacher—avoiding English, so as not to be overheard. "That man is a peasant," he told Morris. "It is never necessary to make conversation with peasants. They are like their own dogs or pigs or donkeys. They only know if it rains. They look out only for their own corner. He will make us starve if we let him." And he said, using the middle-region argot of the Prime Minister, "Let him eat air," which was, in that place, a dark curse, but one that always brought laughter. In spite of this, and in spite of the funny way he pronounced *hl'tk*, "starve," aspirating it (*hlt'k*) instead of churning it in his throat, so that it came out a sort of half-pun for "take-away-the-virginity-of," Morris noticed again that whenever Lushinski said the word "peasant" he looked afraid. The war, of course, happened. For a week the cables flew. Lushinski flew too, to consult with the Prime Minister; he had letters from the Secretary, which he took with him to burn in the Prime Minister's ashtray. Morris remained in New York. One evening Lulu telephoned, to invite him to supper. He heard in her voice that she was obeying her lover, so he declined.

The war was more than fifty miles north of the capital. The Prime Minister's bungalow was beaten by rain; after the rain, blasts of hot wind shook the shutters. The leaves, which had been turned into cups and wells, dried instantly. Evaporation everywhere sent up steam and threads of rainbows. The air-conditioners rattled like tin pans. One by one Lushinski tore up the Secretary's letters, kindling them in the Prime Minister's ashtray with the Prime Minister's cigarette lighter—it was in the shape of the Leaning Tower of Pisa. Then he stoked them in the Prime Miniter's ashtray with the Prime Minister's Japanese-made fountain pen. Even indoors, even with the air-conditioners grinding away, the sunlight was dense with scents unknown in New York: rubber mingled with straw and tar and monkey-droppings and always the drifting smell of the mimosas. The Prime Minister's wife (he pretended to be monogamous, though he had left off using this one long ago)—rather, the female who had the status of the Prime Minister's wife—went on her knees to Lushinski and presented him with a sacerdotal bean-flour cake.

The war lasted a second week; when the Prime Minister signed the cease-fire, Lushinski stood at his side, wearing no expression at all. From the Secretary came a congratulatory cable; Lushinski read it under those perfumed trees, heavy as cabbage-heads, smoking and smoking—he was addicted to the local tobacco. His flesh drank the sun. The hills, rounder and greener than any other on the planet, made his chest blaze. From the airplane—now he was leaving Africa again—he imagined he saw the tarred roofs of the guerrilla camps in the shadows of the hills; or perhaps those were only the dark nests of vultures. They ascended, and through the window he fixed on the huge silver horn of the jet, and under it the white cloud-meadows.

In New York the Secretary praised him and called him a peacemaker. Privately Lushinski did not so much as twitch, but he watched Morris smile. They had given the Secretary air to eat! A month after the "war"—the quotation marks were visible in Lushinski's enunciation: what was it but a combination of village riots and semistrikes? only two hundred or so people killed, one of them unfortunately the Dt' poet L'duy—the price of the indispensable cuttings rose sixty percent, increasing gross national income by two thirds. The land was like a mother whose breasts overflow. This was Morris's image: but Lushinski said, "She has expensive nipples, our mother." And then Morris understood that Lushinski had made the war the way a man in his sleep makes a genital dream, and that the Prime Minister had transfigured the dream into wet blood.

The Prime Minister ordered a bronze monument to commemorate the dead poet. Along the base were the lines, both in argot and in English,

The deer intends	*Kt'ratalwo*
The lion fulfills.	*Mnep g'trpa*
Man the hunter	*Kt'bl ngaya wiba*
Only chooses sides.	*Gagl gagl mrpa.*

The translation into English was Lushinski's. Morris said worshipfully, "Ah, there is no one like you," and Lulu said, "How terrible to make a war just to raise prices," and Lushinski said, "For this there are many precedents."

To Morris he explained: "The war would have come in

any case. It was necessary to adjust the timing. The adjustment saved lives"—here he set forth the preemptive strategy of the Rundabi, and how it was foiled: his mouth looked sly, he loved tricks—"and simultaneously it accomplished our needs. Remember this for when you are Ambassador. Don't try to ram against the inevitable. Instead, tinker with the timing." Though it was after midnight and they were alone in Morris's office—Lushinski's was too grand for unofficial conversation—they spoke in argot. Lushinski was thirstily downing a can of Coca-Cola and Morris was eating salted crackers spread with apple butter. "Will I be Ambassador?" Morris asked. "One day," Lushinski said, "the mother will throw me out." Morris did not understand. "The motherland? Never!" "The mother," Lushinski corrected, "Tanake-Tuka." "Oh, never!" cried Morris, "you bring her luck." "I am not a totem," Lushinski said. But Morris pondered. "We civilized men," he said (using for "men" the formal term "lords," so that his thought ascended, he turned eloquent), "we do not comprehend what the more passionate primitive means when he says 'totem.'" "I am not afraid of words," Lushinski said. "You are," Morris said.

Lulu, like Morris, had also noticed a word which made Lushinski afraid. But she distinguished intelligently between bad memories and bad moods. He told her he was the century's one free man. She scoffed at such foolery. "Well, not the only one," he conceded. "But more free than most. Every survivor is free. Everything that can happen to a human being has already happened inside the survivor. The future can invent nothing worse. What he owns now is recklessness without fear."

This was his diplomat's English. Lulu hated it. "You didn't die," she said. "Don't be pompous about being alive. If you were dead like the others, you would have something to be pompous about. People call them martyrs, and they were only ordinary. If you were a martyr, you could preen about it."

"Do you think me ordinary?" he asked. He looked just then like a crazy man burning with a secret will; but this was nothing, he could make himself look any way he pleased. "If I were ordinary I would be dead."

She could not deny this. A child strung of sticks, he had

survived the peasants who baited and blistered and beat and hunted him. One of them had hanged him from the rafter of a shed, by the wrists. He was four sticks hanging. And his stomach shrank and shrank, and now it was inelastic, still the size of a boy's stomach, and he could not eat. She brought him a bowl of warm farina, and watched him push the spoon several times into the straight line of his mouth; then he put away the spoon; then she took his head down into her lap, as if it were the head of a doll, and needed her own thoughts to give it heat.

He offered her books.

"Why should I read all this? I'm not curious about history, only about you."

"One and the same," he said.

"Pompous," she told him again. He allowed her only this one subject. "Death," she said. "Death, death, death. What do you care? *You* came out alive." "I care about the record," he insisted. There were easy books and there were hard books. The easier ones were stories; these she brought home herself. But they made him angry. "No stories, no tales," he said. "Sources. Documents only. Politics. This is what led to my profession. Accretion of data. There are no holy men of stories," he said, "there are only holy men of data. Remember this before you fall at the feet of anyone who makes romances out of what really happened. If you want something liturgical, say to yourself, *what really happened*." He crashed down on the bed beside her an enormous volume: it was called *The Destruction*. She opened it and saw tables and figures and asterisks; she saw train-schedules. It was all dry, dry. "Do you know that writer?" she asked; she was accustomed to his being acquainted with everyone. "Yes," he said, "do you want to have dinner with him?" "No," she said.

She read the stories and wept. She wept over the camps. She read a book called *Night*; she wept. "But I can't separate all that," she pleaded, "the stories and the sources."

"Imagination is romance. Romance blurs. Instead count the numbers of freight trains."

She read a little in the enormous book. The title irritated her. It was a lie. "It isn't as if the whole *world* was wiped out.

It wasn't like the Flood. It wasn't *mankind*, after all, it was only one population. The Jews aren't the whole world, they aren't mankind, are they?"

She caught in his face a prolonged strangeness: he was new to her, like someone she had never looked at before. "What's the matter, Stasek?" But all at once she saw: she had said he was not mankind.

"Whenever people remember mankind," he said, "they don't fail to omit the Jews."

"An epigram!" she threw out. "What's the good of an epigram! Self-conscious! In public you make jokes, but at home—"

"At home I make water," and went into the bathroom.

"Stasek?" she said through the door.

"You'd better go read."

"Why do you want me to know all that?"

"To show you what you're living with."

"I know who I'm living with!"

"I didn't say *who*, I said *what*."

The shower water began.

She shouted, "You always want a bath whenever I say that word!"

"Baptism," he called. "Which word? Mankind?"

"Stasek!" She shook the knob; he had turned the lock. "Listen, Stasek, I want to tell you something. Stasek! I want to say something *important*."

He opened the door. He was naked. "Do you know what's important?" he asked her.

She fixed on his member; it was swollen. She announced, "I want to tell you what I hate."

"I hope it's not what you're staring at," he said.

"History," she said. "History's what I hate."

"Poor Lulu, some of it got stuck on you and it won't come off—"

"Stasek!"

"Come wash it away, we'll have a tandem baptism."

"I know what *you* hate," she accused. "You hate being part of the Jews. You hate that."

"I am not part of the Jews. I am part of mankind. You're not going to say they're the same thing?"

She stood and reflected. She was sick of his satire. She felt vacuous and ignorant. "Practically nobody knows you're a Jew," she said. "*I* never think of it. You always make me think of it. If I forget it for a while you give me a book, you make me read history, three wars ago, as remote as Attila the Hun. And then I say that word"—she breathed, she made an effort—"I say *Jew*, and you run the water, you get afraid. And then when you get afraid you *attack*, it all comes back on you, you attack like an animal—"

Out of the darkness came the illusion of his smile: oh, a sun! She saw him beautifully beaming. "If not for history," he said, "think! You'd still be in the *Schloss*, you wouldn't have become a little American girl, you wouldn't have grown up to the lipstick factory—"

"Did you leave the drain closed?" she said suddenly. "Stasek, with the shower going, how stupid, now look, the tub's almost ready to overflow—"

He smiled and smiled: "Practically nobody knows you're a princess."

"I'm *not*. It's my great-aunt—oh for God's sake, there it goes, over the side." She peeled off her shoes and went barefoot into the flood and reached to shut off the water. Her feet streamed, her two hands streamed. Then she faced him. "Princess! I know what it is with you! The more you mock, the more you mean it, but I know what it is! You want little stories, deep gossip, you want to pump me and pump me, you have a dream of royalty, and you know perfectly well, you've known it from the first *minute*, I've told and told how I spent the whole of the war in school in England! And then you say nonsense like 'little American girl' because you want that too, you want a princess and you want America and you want Europe and you want Africa—"

But he intervened. "I don't want Europe," he said.

"Pompous! Mockery! You want everything you're not, *that's* what it's about! Because of what you are!" She let herself laugh; she fell into laughter like one of his audiences. "An African! An African!"

"Louisa"—he had a different emphasis now: "I am an African," and in such a voice, all the sinister gaming out of it, the voice of a believer. Did he in truth believe in Africa? He did not take her there. Pictures swam in her of what it might be—herons, plumage, a red stalk of bird-leg in an unmoving pool, mahogany nakedness and golden collars, drums, black bodies, the women with their hooped lips, loin-strings, yellow fur stalking, dappled, striped . . . the fear, the fear.

He pushed his nakedness against her. Her hand was wet. Always he was cold to Jews. He never went among them. In the Assembly he turned his back on the ambassador from Israel; she was in the reserved seats, she saw it herself, she heard the gallery gasp. All New York Jews in the gallery. She knew the word he was afraid of. He pressed her, he made himself her master, she read what he gave her, she, once securely her own mistress, who now followed when he instructed and stayed when he ordered it, she knew when to make him afraid.

"You Jew," she said.

Without words he had told her when to say those words; she was obedient and restored him to fear.

Morris, despite his classical education, had no taste for Europe. No matter that he had studied "political science"—he turned it all into poetry, or, at the least, psychology; better yet, gossip. He might read a biography but he did not care about the consequences of any life. He remembered the names of Princess Margaret's dogs and it seemed to him that Hitler, though unluckily mad, was a genius, because he saw how to make a whole people search for ecstasy. Morris did not understand Europe. Nevertheless he knew he was superior to Europe, as people who are accustomed to a stable temperature are always superior to those who must live with the zaniness of the seasons. His reveries were attuned to a steady climate—summer, summer. In his marrow the crickets were always rioting, the mantises always flashing, sometimes a mantis stood on a leaf and put its two front legs one over the other, like a good child.

Lushinski seemed to him invincibly European: Africa was all light, all fine scent, sweet deep rain and again light, brilliance, the cleansing heat of shining. And Europe by contrast a coal, hellish and horrible, even the snows dark because humped and shadowy, caves, paw-prints of wolves, shoe-troughs of fleeing. In Africa you ran for joy, the joyous thighs begged for fleetness, you ran into veld and bush and green. In Europe you fled, it was flight, you ran like prey into shadows: Europe the Dark Continent.

Under klieg lights Lushinski grew more and more polished; he was becoming a comic artist, he learned when to stop for water, when to keep the tail of a phrase in abeyance. Because of television he was invited to talk everywhere. His stories were grotesque, but he told them so plausibly that he outraged everyone into nervous howls. People liked him to describe his student days in Moscow, after the Russian soldiers had liberated him; they liked him to tell about his suitcase, about his uniform.

He gave very little. He was always very brief. But they laughed. "In Moscow," he said, "we lived five in one room. It had once been the servant's room of a large elegant house. Twenty-seven persons, male and female, shared the toilet; but we in our room were lucky because we had a balcony. One day I went out on the balcony to build a bookcase for the room. I had some boards for shelves and a tin of nails and a hammer and a saw, and I began banging away. And suddenly one of the other students came flying out onto the balcony: 'People at the door! People at the door!' There were mobs of callers out there, ringing, knocking, yelling. That afternoon I received forty-six orders in three hours, for a table, a credenza, endless bookshelves, a bed, a desk, a portable commode. They thought I was an illegal carpenter working out in the open that way to advertise: you had to wait months for a State carpenter. One of the orders—it was for the commode—was from an informer. I explained that I was only a student and not in business, but they locked me up for hooliganism because I had drawn a crowd. Five days in a cell with drunkards. They said I had organized a demonstration against the regime.

"A little while afterward the plumbing of our communal toilet became defective—I will not say just how. The solid refuse had to be gathered in buckets. It was unbearable, worse than any stable. And again I saw my opportunity as a carpenter. I constructed a commode and delivered it to the informer—and oh, it was full, it was full. Twenty-seven Soviet citizens paid tribute."

Such a story made Morris uncomfortable. His underwear felt too tight, he perspired. He wondered why everyone laughed. The story seemed to him European, uncivilized. It was something that could have happened but probably did not happen. He did not know what he ought to believe.

The suitcase, on the other hand, he knew well. It was always reliably present, leaning against Lushinski's foot, or propped up against the bottom of his desk, or the door of his official car. Lushinski was willing enough to explain its contents: "Several complete sets of false papers," he said with satisfaction, looking the opposite of sly, and one day he displayed them. There were passports for various identities—English, French, Brazilian, Norwegian, Dutch, Australian—and a number of diplomas in different languages. "The two Russian ones," he boasted, "aren't forgeries," putting everything back among new shirts still in their wrappers.

"But why, why?" Morris said.

"A maxim. Always have your bags packed."

"But why?"

"To get away."

"Why?"

"Sometimes it's better where you aren't than where you are."

Morris wished the Prime Minister had heard this; surely he would have trusted Lushinski less. But Lushinski guessed his thought. "Only the traitors stay home," he said. "In times of trouble only the patriots have false papers."

"But now the whole world knows," Morris said reasonably. "You've told the whole world on television."

"That will make it easier to get away. They will recognize a patriot and defer."

He became a dervish of travel: he was mad about America and went to Detroit and to Tampa, to Cincinnati and to Biloxi. They asked him how he managed to keep up with his diplomatic duties; he referred them to Morris, whom he called his "conscientious blackamoor." Letters came to the consulate in New York accusing him of being a colonialist and a racist. Lushinski remarked that he was not so much that as a cyclist, and immediately—to prove his solidarity with cyclists of every color—bought Morris a gleaming ten-speed two-wheeler. Morris had learned to ride at Oxford, and was overjoyed once again to pedal into a rush of wind. He rode south on Second Avenue; he circled the whole Lower East Side. But in only two days his bike was stolen by a gang of what the police designated as "teen-age black male perpetrators." Morris liked America less and less.

Lushinski liked it more and more. He went to civic clubs, clubs with animal names, clubs with Indian names; societies internationalist and jingoist; veterans, pacifists, vegetarians, feminists, vivisectionists; he would agree to speak anywhere. No Jews invited him; he had turned his back on the Israeli ambassador. Meanwhile the Secretary of State withdrew a little, and omitted Lushinski from his dinner list; he was repelled by a man who would want to go to Cincinnati, a place the Secretary had left forever. But the Prime Minister was delighted and cabled Lushinski to "get to know the proletariat"—nowadays the Prime Minister often used such language; he said "dialectic," "collective," and "Third World." Occasionally he said "peoples," as in "peoples' republic." In a place called Oneonta, New York, Lushinski told about the uniform: in Paris he had gone to a tailor and asked him to make up the costume of an officer. "Of which nationality, sir?" "Oh, no particular one." "What rank, sir?" "High. As high as you can imagine." The coat was long, had epaulets, several golden bands on the sleeves, and metal buttons engraved with the head of a dead monarch. From a toy store Lushinski bought ribbons and medals to hang on its breast. The cap was tall and fearsomely military, with a strong bill ringed by a scarlet cord. Wearing this concoction, Lushinski journeyed to the Rhineland. In hotels they gave him the ducal suite and charged nothing, in restaurants he swept past everyone to the most devoted service, at airports he was served drinks in carpeted sitting rooms and ushered on board, with a guard, into a curtained parlor.

"Your own position commands all that," Morris said gravely. Again he was puzzled. All around him they rattled with hilarity. Lushinski's straight mouth remained straight; Morris brooded about impersonation. It was no joke (but this was years and years ago, in the company of Isabel Oxenham) that he sought out Tarzan movies: Africa in the Mind of the West. It could have been his thesis, but it was not. He was too inward for such a generality: it was his own mind he meant to observe. Was he no better than that lout Tarzan, investing himself with a chatter not his own? How long could the ingested, the invented, foreignness endure? He felt himself—himself, Mdulgo-kt'dulgo, called Morris, dressed in suit and tie, his academic gown thrown down on a chair twenty miles north of this cinema—he felt himself to be self-duped, an impersonator. The film passed (jungle, vines, apes, the famous leap and screech and fisted thump, natives each with his rubber spear and extra's face—janitors and barmen), it was a confusion, a mist. His thumb climbed Isabel's vertebrae: such a nice even row, up and down like a stair. The children's matinee was done, the evening film commenced. It was in Italian, and he never forgot it, a comedy about an unwilling imposter, a common criminal mistaken for a heroic soldier: General della Rovere.

The movie made Isabel's tears fall onto Morris's left wrist.

The criminal, an ordinary thug, is jailed; the General's political enemies want the General put away. The real General is a remarkable man, a saint, a hero. And, little by little, the criminal acquires the General's qualities, he becomes selfless, he becomes courageous, glorious. At the end of the movie he has a chance to reveal that he is not the real General della Rovere. Nobly, he chooses instead to be executed in the General's place, he atones for his past life, a voluntary sacrifice. Morris explained to Isabel that the ferocious natives encountered by Tarzan are in the same moral situation as the false General della Rovere: they accommodate, they adapt to what is expected. Asked to howl like men who inhabit no culture, they howl. "But they have souls, once they were advanced beings. If you jump into someone else's skin," he asked, "doesn't it begin to fit you?"

"Oi wouldn now, oi hev no ejucytion," Isabel said.

Morris himself did not know.

All the same, he did not believe that Lushinski was this sort of impersonator. A Tarzan perhaps, not a della Rovere. The problem of sincerity disturbed and engrossed him. He boldly asked Lushinski his views.

"People who deal in diplomacy attach too much importance to being believed," Lushinski declaimed. "Sincerity is only a maneuver, like any other. A quantity of lies is a much more sensible method—it gives the effect of greater choice. Sincerity offers only one course. But if you select among a great variety of insincerities, you're bound to strike a better course."

He said all this because it was exactly what Morris wanted to hear from him.

The Prime Minister had no interest in questions of identity. "He is not a false African," the Prime Minister said in a parliamentary speech defending his appointment, "he is a true advocate." Though vainglorious, this seemed plausible enough; but for Morris, Lushinski was not an African at all. "It isn't enough to be *politically* African," Morris argued one night; "politically you can assume the culture. No one can assume the cult." Then he remembered the little bones of Isabel Oxenham's back. "Morris, Morris," Lushinski said, "you're not beginning to preach Negritude?" "No," said Morris; he wanted to speak of religion, of his mother; but just then he could not—the telephone broke in, though it was one in the morning and not the official number, rather his own private one, used by Louisa. She spoke of returning to her profession; she was too often alone. "Where are you going tomorrow?" she asked Lushinski. Morris could hear the little electric voice in the receiver. "You say you do it for public relations," she said, "but why really? What do they need to know about Africa in Shaker Heights that they don't know already?" The little electric voice forked and fragmented, tiny lightnings in her lover's ear.

The next day a terrorist from one of the hidden guerrilla camps in the hills shot the Prime Minister's wife at a government ceremony with many Westerners present; he had intended to shoot the Prime Minister. The Prime Minister, it was noted, appeared to grieve, and ordered a bubble-top for his car and a bulletproof vest to wear under his shirt. In a cable he instructed Lushinski to cease his circulation among the American proletariat. Lulu was pleased. Lushinski began to refuse invitations; his American career was over. In the Assembly he spoke— "with supernal," Morris acknowledged, "eloquence"—against terrorism; though their countries had no diplomatic relations, and in spite of Lushinski's public snub, the Israeli ambassador applauded, with liquid eyes. But Lushinski missed something. To address an international body representing every nation on the planet seemed less than before; seemed limiting; he missed the laughter of Oneonta, New York. The American provinces moved him—how gullible they were, how little they knew, or would ever know, of cruelty's breadth! A country of babies. His half-year among all those cities had elated him, a visit to an innocent star: no sarcasm, cynicism, innuendo grew there; such nice church ladies; a benevolent passiveness which his tales, with their wily spikes, could rouse to nervous pleasure.

Behind Lushinski's ears threads of white hairs sprang; he worried about the Prime Minister's stability in the aftermath of the attack. While the representative from Uganda "exercised," Lushinski sneered, "his right of reply"—"The distinguished representative from our sister-country to the north fabricates dangerous adventures for make-believe pirates who exist only in his fantasies, and we all know how colorfully, how excessively, he is given to whimsy"—Lushinski drew on his pad the head of a cormorant, with a sack under its beak. Though there was no overt resemblance, it could pass nevertheless for a self-portrait.

In October he returned to his capital. The Prime Minister had a new public wife. He had replenished his ebullience, and no longer wore the bulletproof vest. The new wife kneeled before Lushinski with a bean-flour cake. The Prime Minister was sanguine: the captured terrorist had informed on his colleagues, entire nests of them had been cleaned out of four nearby villages. The Prime Minister begged Lushinski to allow him to lend him one of his younger females. Lushinski examined her and accepted. He took also one of Morris's sisters and with these two went to live for a month alone in a white villa on the blue coast.

Every day the Prime Minister sent a courier with documents and newspapers; also the consular pouch from New York.

Morris in New York: Morris in a city of Jews. He walked. He crossed a bridge. He walked. He was attentive to their houses, their neighborhoods. Their religious schools. Their synagogues. Their multitudinous societies. Announcements of debates, ice cream, speeches, rallies, delicatessens, violins, felafel, books. Ah, the avalanche of their books!

Where their streets ended, the streets of the blacks began. Mdulgo-kt'dulgo in exile among the kidnapped—cargo-Africans, victims with African faces, lost to language and faith; impostors sunk in barbarism, primitives, impersonators. Emptied-out creatures, with their hidden knives, their swift silver guns, their poisoned red eyes, christianized, made not new but neuter, fabricated: oh, only restore them to their inmost selves, to the serenity of orthodoxy, redemption of the true gods who speak in them without voice!

Morris Ngambe in New York. Alone, treading among traps, in jeopardy of ambush, with no female.

And in Africa, in a white villa on the blue coast: the Prime Minister's gaudy pet, on a blue sofa before an open window, smoking and smoking, under the breath of the scented trees, under the sleek palms of a pair of young females, smoking and caressing—snug in Africa, Lushinski.

In Lushinski's last week in the villa, the pouch from New York held a letter from Morris.

The letter:

A curious note concerning the terrorist personality. I have just read of an incident which took place in a Jerusalem prison. A captive terrorist, a Japanese who had murdered twenty-nine pilgrims at the Tel Aviv airport, was permitted to keep in his cell, besides reading matter, a comb, a hairbrush, a nailbrush, and a fingernail clippers. A dapper chap, apparently. One morning he was found to have partially circumcised himself. His instrument was the clippers. He lost consciousness and the job was completed in the prison hospital. The doctor questioned him. It turned out he had begun to read intensively in the Jewish religion. He had a Bible and a text for learning the Hebrew language. He had begun to grow a beard and earlocks. Perhaps you will understand better than I the spiritual side of this matter.

You recall my remarks on culture and cult. Here is a man who wishes to annihilate a society and its culture, but he is captivated by its cult. For its cult he will bleed himself.

Captivity leading to captivation: an interesting notion.

It may be that every man at length becomes what he wishes to victimize.

It may be that every man needs to impersonate what he first must kill.

Lushinski recognized in Morris's musings a lumpy parroting of *Reading Gaol* mixed with—what? Fanon? Genet? No; only Oscar Wilde, sentimentally epigrammatic. Oscar Wilde in Jerusalem! As unlikely as the remorse of Gomorrah. Like everyone the British had once blessed with Empire, Morris was a Victorian. He was a gentleman. He believed in civilizing influences; even more in civility. He was besotted by style. If he thought of knives, it was for buttering scones.

But Lushinski, a man with the nose and mouth of a knife, and the body of a knife, understood this letter as a blade between them. It meant a severing. Morris saw him as an impersonator. Morris uncovered him; then stabbed. Morris had called him a transmuted, a transfigured, African. A man in love with his cell. A traitor. Perfidious. A fake.

Morris had called him Jew.

—Morris in New York, alone, treading among traps, in jeopardy of ambush, with no female. He knew his ascendancy. Victory of that bird-bright forest, glistening with the bodies of boys, over the old terror in the Polish woods.

Morris prayed. He prayed to his mother: down, take him down, bring him something evil. The divine mother answers sincere believers: O Tanake-Tuka!

And in Africa, in a white villa on the blue coast, the Prime Minister's gaudy pet, on a blue sofa before an open window, smoking and smoking, under the breath of the scented trees, under the shadow of the bluish snow, under the blue-black pillars of the Polish woods, under the breath of Andor, under the merciless palms of peasants and fists of peasants, under the rafters, under the stone-white hanging stars of Poland—Lushinski.

Against the stones and under the snow.

Virility

YOU ARE TOO young to remember Edmund Gate, but I knew him when he was Elia Gatoff in knickers, just off the boat from Liverpool. Now to remember Edmund Gate at all, one must be a compatriot of mine, which is to say a centagenerian. A man of one hundred and six is always sequestered on a metaphysical Elba, but on an Elba without even the metaphor of a Napoleon—where, in fact, it has been so long forgotten that Napoleon ever lived that it is impossible to credit his influence, let alone his fame. It is harsh and lonely in this country of exile—the inhabitants (or, as we in our eleventh decade ought more accurately to be called, the survivors) are so sparse, and so maimed, and so unreliable as to recent chronology, and so at odds with your ideas of greatness, that we do indeed veer toward a separate mentality, and ought in logic to have a flag of our own. It is not that we seclude ourselves from you, but rather that you have seceded from us—you with your moon pilots, and mohole fishermen, and algae cookies, and anti-etymological reformed spelling—in the face of all of which I can scarcely expect you to believe in a time when a plain and rather ignorant man could attain the sort of celebrity you people accord only to vile geniuses who export baby-germs in plastic envelopes. That, I suppose, is the worst of it for me and my countrymen in the land of the very old—your isolation from our great. Our great and especially our merely famous have slipped from your encyclopaedias, and will vanish finally and absolutely when we are at length powdered into reconstituted genetic ore—mixed with fish flour, and to be taken as an antidote immediately after radiation-saturation: a detail and a tangent, but I am subject to these broodings at my heavy age, and occasionally catch myself in egotistical yearning for an ordinary headstone engraved with my name. As if, in a population of a billion and a quarter, there could be space for that entirely obsolete indulgence!—and yet, only last week, in the old Preserved Cemetery, I visited Edmund Gate's grave, and viewed his monument, and came away persuaded of the beauty of that ancient, though wasteful, decorum. We have no room for physical memorials nowadays; and nobody pays any attention to the pitiful poets.

Just *here* is my huge difficulty. How am I to convince you that, during an interval in my own vast lifetime, there was a moment when a poet—a plain, as I have said, and rather ignorant man—was noticed, and noticed abundantly, and noticed magnificently and even stupendously? You will of course not have heard of Byron, and no one is more eclipsed than dear Dylan; nor will I claim that Edmund Gate ever rose to *that* standard. But he was recited, admired, worshiped, translated, pursued, even paid; and the press would not let him go for an instant. I have spoken of influence and of fame; Edmund Gate, it is true, had little influence, even on his own generation—I mean by this that he was not much imitated—but as for fame! Fame was what we gave him plenty of. We could give him fame—in those days fame was ours to give. Whereas you measure meanly by the cosmos. The first man to the moon is now a shriveling little statistician in a Bureau somewhere, superseded by the first to Venus, who, we are told, lies all day in a sour room drinking vodka and spitting envy on the first to try for Pluto. Now it is the stars which dictate fame, but with us it was *we* who made fame, and we who dictated our stars.

He died (like Keats, of whom you will also not have heard) at twenty-six. I have this note not from Microwafer Tabulation, but from the invincible headstone itself. I had forgotten it and was touched. I almost thought he lived to be middle-aged: I base this on my last sight of him, or perhaps my last memory, in which I observe him in his underwear, with a big hairy paunch, cracked and browning teeth, and a scabby scalp laid over with a bunch of thin light-colored weeds. He looked something like a failed pugilist. I see him standing in the middle of a floor without a carpet, puzzled, drunk, a newspaper in one hand and the other tenderly reaching through the slot in his shorts to enclose his testicles. The last words he spoke to me were the words I chose (it fell to me) for his monument: "I am a man."

He was, however, a boy in corduroys when he first came to me. He smelled of salami and his knickers were raveled at the pockets and gave off a saltiness. He explained that he had walked all the way from England, back and forth on the deck. I later gathered that he was a stowaway. He had been sent ahead to Liverpool on a forged passport (these were Czarist times), from a place full of wooden shacks and no sidewalks called Glusk, with instructions to search out an old aunt of his mother's on Mersey Street and stay with her until his parents and sisters could scrape up the papers for their own border-crossing. He miraculously found the Liverpudlian aunt, was received with joy, fed bread and butter, and shown a letter from Glusk in which his father stated that the precious sheets were finally all in order and properly stamped with seals almost identical to real government seals: they would all soon be reunited in the beckoning poverty of Golden Liverpool. He settled in with the aunt who lived tidily in a gray slum and worked all day in the back of a millinery shop sewing on veils. She had all the habits of a cool and intellectual spinster. She had come to England six years before—she was herself an emigrant from Glusk, and had left it legally and respectably under a pile of straw in the last of three carts in a gypsy caravan headed westward for Poland. Once inside Poland (humanely governed by Franz Josef), she took a train to Warsaw, and liked the book stores there so much she nearly stayed forever, but instead thoughtfully lifted her skirts onto another train—how she hated the soot!—to Hamburg, where she boarded a neat little boat pointed right at Liverpool. It never occurred to her to go a little further, to America: she had fixed on English as the best tongue for a foreigner to adopt, and she was suspicious of the kind of English Americans imagined they spoke. With superior diligence she began to teach her great-nephew the beautiful and clever new language; she even wanted him to go to school, but he was too much absorbed in the notion of waiting, and instead ran errands for the greengrocer at three shillings a week. He put pennies into a little tin box to buy a red scarf for his mother when she came. He waited and waited, and looked dull when his aunt talked to him in English at night, and waited immensely, with his whole body. But his mother and father and his sister Feige and his sister Gittel never arrived. On a rainy day in the very month he burst into manhood (in the course of which black rods of hairs appeared in the trench of his upper lip), his aunt told him, not in English, that it was no use waiting any longer: a pogrom had murdered them all. She put the letter, from a cousin in Glusk, on exhibit before him—his mother, raped and slaughtered; Feige, raped and slaughtered; Gittel, escaped but caught in the forest and raped twelve times before a passing friendly soldier saved her from the thirteenth by shooting her through the left eye; his father, tied to the tail of a Cossack horse and sent to have his head broken on cobblestones.

All this he gave me quickly, briefly, without excitement, and with a shocking economy. What he had come to America for, he said, was a job. I asked him what his experience was. He reiterated the fact of the greengrocer in Liverpool. He had the queerest accent; a regular salad of an accent.

"That's hardly the type of preparation we can use on a newspaper," I said.

"Well, it's the only kind I've got."

"What does your aunt think of your leaving her all alone like that?"

"She's an independent sort. She'll be all right. She says she'll send me money when she can."

"Look here, don't you think the money ought to be going in the opposite direction?"

"Oh, I'll never have any money," he said.

I was irritated by his pronunciation—"mawney"—and I had theories about would-be Americans, none of them complimentary, one of which he was unwittingly confirming. "There's ambition for you!"

But he startled me with a contradictory smile both iron and earnest. "I'm very ambitious. You wait and see," as though we were already colleagues, confidants, and deep comrades. "Only what *I* want to be," he said, "they don't ever make much money."

"What's that?"

"A poet. I've always wanted to be a poet."

I could not help laughing at him. "In English? You want to do English poetry?"

"English, righto. I don't *have* any other language. Not any more."

"Are you positive you have English?" I asked him. "You've only been taught by your aunt, and no one ever taught *her*."

But he was listening to only half, and would not bother with any talk about his relative. "That's why I want to work on a paper. For contact with written material."

I said strictly, "You could read books, you know."

"I've read *some*." He looked down in shame. "I'm too lazy. My mind is lazy but my legs are good. If I could get to be a reporter or something like that I could use my legs a lot. I'm a good runner."

"And when," I put it to him in the voice of a sardonic archangel, "will you compose your poems?"

"While I'm running," he said.

I took him on as office boy and teased him considerably. Whenever I handed him a bit of copy to carry from one cubbyhole to another I reminded him that he was at last in contact with written material, and hoped he was finding it useful for his verse. He had no humor but his legs were as fleet as he had promised. He was always ready, always at attention, always on the alert to run. He was always *there*, waiting. He stood like a hare at rest watching the typewriters beat, his hands and his feet nervous for the snatch of the sheet from the platen, as impatient as though the production of a column of feature items were a wholly automatic act governed by the width of the paper and the speed of the machine. He would rip the page from the grasp of its author and streak for the copy desk, where he would lean belligerently over the poor editor in question to study the strokes of this cringing chap's blue pencil. "Is that what cutting is?" he asked. "Is that what you call proofreading? Doesn't 'judgment' have an 'e' in it? Why not? There's an 'e' in 'judge,' isn't there? How come you don't take the 'e' out of 'knowledgeable' too? How do you count the type for a headline?" He was insufferably efficient and a killing nuisance.

In less than a month he switched from those ribbed and reeky knickers to a pair of grimy trousers out of a pawnshop, and from the ample back pocket of these there protruded an equally ample dictionary with its boards missing, purchased from the identical source: but this was an affectation, since I never saw him consult it. All the same we promoted him to proofreader. This buried him. We set him down at a dark desk in a dungeon and entombed him under mile-long strips of galleys and left him there to dig himself out. The printshop helped by providing innumerable shrdlus and inventing further typographical curiosities of such a nature that a psychologist would have been severely interested. The city editor was abetted by the whole reporting staff in the revelation of news stories rivaling the Bible in luridness, sexuality, and imaginative abomination. Meanwhile he never blinked, but went on devotedly taking the "e" out of "judgment" and putting it back for "knowledge-able," and making little loops for "omit" wherever someone's syntactical fancy had gone too rapturously far.

When I looked up and spotted him apparently about to mount my typewriter I was certain he had risen from his cellar to beg to be fired. Instead he offered me a double information: he was going to call himself Gate, and what did I think of that?—and in the second place he had just written his first poem.

"First?" I said. "I thought you've been at it all the while."

"Oh no," he assured me. "I wasn't ready. I didn't have a name."

"Gatoff's a name, isn't it?"

He ignored my tone, almost like a gentleman. "I mean a name suitable for the language. It has to match somehow, doesn't it? Or people would get the idea I'm an impostor." I recognized this word from a recent fabrication he had encountered on a proof—my own, in fact: a two-paragraph item about a man who had successfully posed as a firewarden through pretending to have a sound acquaintance with the problems of water-pressure systems, but who let the firehouse burn down because he could not get the tap open. It was admittedly a very inferior story, but the best I could do; the others had soared

beyond my meager gleam, though I made up for my barrenness by a generosity of double negatives. Still, I marveled at
his quickness at self-enrichment—the aunt in Liverpool, I was
certain, had never talked to him, in English, of impostors.

"Listen," he said thickly, "I really feel you're the one who
started me off. I'm very grateful to you. You understood
my weakness in the language and you allowed me every
opportunity."

"Then you like your job down there?"

"I just wish I could have a light on my desk. A small bulb
maybe, that's all. Otherwise it's great down there, sure, it gives
me a chance to think about poems."

"Don't you pay any attention to what you're reading?" I
asked admiringly.

"Sure I do. I always do. That's where I get my ideas. Poems
deal with Truth, right? One thing I've learned lately from
contact with written material is that Truth is Stranger than Fiction." He uttered this as if fresh from the mouths of the gods.
It gave him a particular advantage over the rest of us: admonish
him that some phrase was as old as the hills, and he would
pull up his head like a delighted turtle and exclaim, "Now
that's perfect. What a perfect way to express antiquity. That's
true, the hills have been there since the earth was just new.
Very good! I congratulate you"—showing extensive emotional
reverberation, which I acknowledged after a time as his most
serious literary symptom.

The terrible symptom was just now vividly tremulous.
"What I want to ask you," he said, "is what you would think
of Edmund for a poet's name. In front of Gate, for instance."

"*My* name is Edmund," I said.

"I know, I know. Where would I get the idea if not from
you? A marvelous name. Could I borrow it? Just for use on
poems. Otherwise it's all right, don't be embarrassed, call me
Elia like always."

He reached for his behind, produced the dictionary, and
cautiously shook it open to the Fs. Then he tore out a single
page with meticulous orderliness and passed it to me. It covered Fenugreek to Fylfot, and the margins were foxed with an

astonishing calligraphy, very tiny and very ornate, like miniature crystal cubes containing little bells.

"You want me to read this?" I said.

"Please," he commanded.

"Why don't you use regular paper?"

"I like words," he said. "Fenugreek, an herb of the pea
family. Felo-de-se, a suicide. I wouldn't get that just from
a blank sheet. If I see a good word in the vicinity I put it
right in."

"You're a great borrower," I observed.

"Be brutal," he begged. "Tell me if I have talent."

It was a poem about dawn. It had four rhymed stanzas and
coupled "lingered" with "rosy-fingered." The word Fuzee was
strangely prominent.

"In concept it's a little on the hackneyed side," I told him.

"I'll work on it," he said fervently. "You think I have a
chance? Be brutal."

"I don't suppose you'll ever be an original, you know,"
I said.

"You wait and see," he threatened me. "I can be brutal too."

He headed back for his cellar and I happened to notice his
walk. His thick round calves described forceful rings in his
trousers, but he had a curiously modest gait, like a preoccupied
steer. His dictionary jogged on his buttock, and his shoulders
suggested the spectral flutes of a spectral cloak, with a spectral
retinue following murmurously after.

"Elia," I called to him.

He kept going.

I was willing to experiment. "Edmund!" I yelled.

He turned, very elegantly.

"Edmund," I said. "Now listen. I mean this. Don't show me
any more of your stuff. The whole thing is hopeless. Waste your
own time but don't waste mine."

He took this in with a pleasant lift of his large thumbs. "I
never waste anything. I'm very provident."

"Provident, are you?" I made myself a fool for him: "Aha,
evidently you've been inditing something in and around the
Ps—"

"Puce, red. Prothorax, the front part of an insect. Plectrum, an ivory pick."

"You're an opportunist," I said. "A hoarder. A rag-dealer. Don't fancy yourself anything better than that. Keep out of my way, Edmund," I told him.

After that I got rid of him. I exerted—if that is not too gross a word for the politic and the canny—a quiet urgency here and there, until finally we tendered him the title of reporter and sent him out to the police station to call in burglaries off the blotter. His hours were midnight to morning. In two weeks he turned up at my desk at ten o'clock, squinting through an early sunbeam.

"Don't you go home to sleep now?" I asked.

"Criticism before slumber. I've got more work to show you. Beautiful new work."

I swallowed a groan. "How do you like it down at headquarters?"

"It's fine. A lovely place. The cops are fine people. It's a wonderful atmosphere to think up poems in. I've been extremely fecund. I've been pullulating down there. This is the best of the lot."

He ripped out Mimir to Minion. Along the white perimeter of the page his incredible handwriting peregrinated: it was a poem about a rose. The poet's beloved was compared to the flower. They blushed alike. The rose minced in the breeze; so did the lady.

"I've given up rhyme," he announced, and hooked his eyes in mine. "I've improved. You admit I've improved, don't you?"

"No," I said. "You've retrogressed. You're nothing but hash. You haven't advanced an inch. You'll never advance. You haven't got the equipment."

"I have all these new words," he protested. "Menhir. Eximious. Suffruticose. Congee. Anastrophe. Dandiprat. Trichiasis. Nidificate."

"Words aren't the only equipment. You're hopeless. You haven't got the brain for it."

"All my lines scan perfectly."

"You're not a poet."

He refused to be disappointed; he could not be undermined. "You don't see any difference?"

"Not in the least.—Hold on. A difference indeed. You've bought yourself a suit," I said.

"Matching coat and pants. Thanks to you. You raised me up from an errand boy."

"That's America for you," I said. "And what about Liverpool? I suppose you send your aunt something out of your salary?"

"Not particularly."

"Poor old lady."

"She's all right as she is."

"Aren't you all she's got? Only joy, apple of the eye and so forth?"

"She gets along. She writes me now and then."

"I suppose you don't answer much."

"I've got my own life to live," he objected, with all the ardor of a man in the press of inventing not just a maxim but a principle. "I've got a career to make. Pretty soon I have to start getting my things into print. I bet you know some magazine editors who publish poems."

It struck me that he had somehow discovered a means to check my acquaintance. "That's just the point. They publish *poems*. You wouldn't do for them."

"You could start me off in print if you wanted to."

"I don't want to. You're no good."

"I'll get better. I'm still on my way. Wait and see," he said.

"All right," I agreed, "I'm willing to wait but I don't want to see. Don't show me any more. Keep your stuff to yourself. Please don't come back."

"Sure," he said: this was his chief American acquisition. "You come to me instead."

During the next month there was a run of robberies and other nonmatutinal felonies, and pleasurably and with relief I imagined him bunched up in a telephone booth in the basement of the station house, reciting clot after clot of criminal boredoms into the talking-piece. I hoped he would be hoarse enough and weary enough to seek his bed instead of his fortune, especially if he conceived of his fortune as conspicuously involving me. The mornings passed, and, after a time, so did my dread—he never appeared. I speculated that he had given me up. I even ventured a little remorse at the relentlessness of my dealings with him, and then a courier from the mail room loped in and left me an enormous envelope from an eminent literary journal. It was filled with dozens and dozens of fastidiously torn-out dictionary pages, accompanied by a letter to me from the editor-in-chief, whom—after a fashion—I knew (he had been a friend of my late and distinguished father): "Dear Edmund, I put it to you that your tastes in gall are not mine. I will not say that you presumed on my indulgence when you sent this fellow up here with his sheaf of horrors, but I will ask you in the future to restrict your recommendations to *simple* fools—who, presumably, turn to ordinary foolscap in their hour of folly. P.S. In any case I never have, and never hope to, print anything containing the word 'ogdoad.'"

One of the sheets was headed Ogam to Oliphant.

It seemed too savage a hardship to rage all day without release: nevertheless I thought I would wait it out until midnight and pursue him where I could find him, at his duties with the underworld, and then, for direct gratification, knock him down. But it occurred to me that a police station is an inconvenient situation for an assault upon a citizen (though it did not escape me that he was still unnaturalized), so I looked up his address and went to his room.

He opened the door in his underwear. "Edmund!" he cried. "Excuse me, after all I'm a night worker—but it's all right, come in, come in! I don't need a lot of sleep anyhow. If I slept I'd never get any poems written, so don't feel bad."

Conscientiously I elevated my fists and conscientiously I knocked him down.

"What's the idea?" he asked from the floor.

"What's the idea is right," I said. "Who told you you could go around visiting important people and saying I sicked you on them?"

He rubbed his sore chin in a rapture. "You heard! I bet you heard straight from the editor-in-chief himself. You would.

You've got the connections, I knew it. I told him to report right to you. I knew you'd be anxious."

"I'm anxious and embarrassed and ashamed," I said. "You've made me look like an idiot. My father's oldest friend. He thinks I'm a sap."

He got up, poking at himself for bruises. "Don't feel bad for me. He didn't accept any at all? Is that a fact? Not a single one?" I threw the envelope at him and he caught it with a surprisingly expert arc of the wrist. Then he spilled out the contents and read the letter. "Well, that's too bad," he said. "It's amazing how certain persons can be so unsympathetic. It's in their nature, they can't help it. But I don't mind. I mean it's all compensated for. Here *you* are. I thought it would be too nervy to invite you—it's a very cheap place I live in, you can see that—but I knew you'd come on your own. An aristocrat like yourself."

"Elia," I said, "I came to knock you down. I *have* knocked you down."

"Don't feel bad about it," he repeated, consoling me. He reached for my ear and gave it a friendly pull. "It's only natural. You had a shock. In your place I would have done exactly the same thing. I'm very strong. I'm probably much stronger than you are. You're pretty strong too, if you could knock me down. But to tell the truth, I sort of *let* you. I like to show manners when I'm a host."

He scraped forward an old wooden chair, the only one in the room, for me to sit down on. I refused, so he sat down himself, with his thighs apart and his arms laced, ready for a civilized conversation. "You've read my new work yourself, I presume."

"No," I said. "When are you going to stop this? Why don't you concentrate on something sensible? You want to be a petty police reporter for the rest of your life?"

"I hope not," he said, and rasped his voice to show his sincerity. "I'd like to be able to leave this place. I'd like to have enough money to live in a nice American atmosphere. Like you, the way you live all alone in that whole big house."

He almost made me think I had to apologize. "My father left

it to me. Anyway, didn't you tell me you never expected to get rich on poetry?"

"I've looked around since then, I've noticed things. Of America expect everything. America has room for anything, even poets. Edmund," he said warmly, "I know how you feel. R.I.P. I don't have a father either. You would have admired my father—a strapping man. It's amazing that they could kill him. Strong. Big. No offense, but he restrained himself, he never knocked anyone down. Here," he pleaded, "you just take my new things and look them over and see if that editor-in-chief was right. You tell me if in his shoes you wouldn't publish me, that's all I want."

He handed me Gharri to Gila Monster: another vapid excrescence in the margins. Schuit to Scolecite: the same. But it was plain that he was appealing to me out of the pathos of his orphaned condition, and from pity and guilt (I had the sense that he would regard it as a pogrom if I did not comply). I examined the rest, and discovered, among his daisies and sunsets, a fresh theme. He had begun to write about girls: not the abstract Beloved, but real girls, with names like Shirley, Ethel, and Bella.

"Love poems," he said conceitedly. "I find them very moving."

"About as moving as the lovelorn column," I said, "if less gripping. When do you get the time for girls?"

"Leonardo da Vinci also had only twenty-four hours in his day. Ditto Michelangelo. Besides, I don't go looking for them. I attract them."

This drew my stare. "You attract them?"

"Sure. I attract them right here. I hardly ever have to go out. Of course that sort of arrangement's not too good with some of the better types. They don't go for a poet's room."

"There's not a book in the place," I said in disgust.

"Books don't make a poet's room," he contradicted. "It depends on the poet—the build of man he is." And, with the full power of his odious resiliency, he winked at me.

The effect on me of this conversation was unprecedented: I suddenly began to see him as he saw himself, through the lens of his own self-esteem. He almost looked handsome. He had changed; he seemed larger and bolder. The truth was merely that he was not yet twenty and that he had very recently grown physically. He remained unkempt, and his belly had a habit of swelling under his shirt; but there was something huge starting in him.

About that time I was asked to cover a minor war in the Caribbean—it was no more than a series of swamp skirmishes —and when I returned after eight weeks I found him living in my house. I had, as usual, left the key with my married sister (it had been one of my father's crotchets—he had several—to anticipate all possible contingencies, and I carried on the custom of the house), and he had magically wheedled it from her: it turned out he had somehow persuaded her that she would earn the gratitude of his posterity by allowing him to attain the kind of shelter commensurate with his qualities.

"Commensurate with your qualities," I sing-songed at him. "When I heard that, I knew she had it verbatim. All right, Elia, you've sucked the place dry. That's all. Out." Every teacup was dirty and he had emptied the whiskey. "You've had parties," I concluded.

"I couldn't help it, Edmund. I've developed so many friend-ships recently."

"Get out."

"Ah, don't be harsh. You know the little rooms upstairs? The ones that have the skylight? I bet those were maids' rooms once. You wouldn't know I was there, I promise you. Where can I go where there's so much good light? Over at the precinct house it's even worse than the cellar was, they use only forty-watt bulbs. The municipality is prodigiously parsimonious. What have I got if I haven't got my eyesight?

> *Take my pen and still*
> *I sing. But deny*
> *My eye*
> *And Will*
> *Departs the quill."*

"My reply remains Nil," I said. "Just go."

He obliged me with a patronizing laugh. "That's very good. Deny, Reply. Quill, Nil."

"No, I mean it. You can't stay. Besides," I said sourly, "I thought you gave up rhymes long ago."

"You think I'm making it up about my eyes," he said. "Well, look." He darted a thick fist into a pocket and whipped out a pair of glasses and put them on. "While you were gone I had to get these. They're pretty strong for a person of my age. I'm not supposed to abuse my irises. These peepers cost me equal to nearly a month's rent at my old place."

The gesture forced me to study him. He had spoken of his qualities, but they were all quantities: he had grown some more, not upward exactly, and not particularly outward, but in some textural way, as though his bigness required one to assure oneself of it by testing it with the nerve in the fingertip. He was walking around in his underwear. For the first time I took it in how extraordinarily hairy a man he was. His shoulders and his chest were a forest, and the muscles in his arms were globes darkened by brush. I observed that he was thoroughly aware of himself; he held his torso like a bit of classical rubble, but he captured the warrior lines of it with a certain prideful agility.

"Go ahead, put on your clothes," I yelled at him.

"It's not cold in the house, Edmund."

"It is in the street. Go on, get out. With or without your clothes. Go."

He lowered his head, and I noted in surprise the gross stems of his ears. "It would be mean."

"I can take it. Stop worrying about my feelings."

"I'm not referring just to you. I left Sylvia alone upstairs when you came in."

"Are you telling me you've got a *girl* in this house right now?"

"Sure," he said meekly. "But you don't mind, Edmund. I know you don't. It's only what you do yourself, isn't it?"

I went to the foot of the staircase and shouted: "That's enough! Come down! Get out!"

Nothing stirred.

"You've scared her," he said.

"Get rid of her, Elia, or I'll call the police."

"That would be nice," he said wistfully. "*They* like my poems. I always read them aloud down at the station house. Look, if you really want me to go I'll go, and you can get rid of Sylvia yourself. You certainly have a beautiful spacious house here. Nice furniture. I certainly did enjoy it. Your sister told me a few things about it—it was very interesting. Your sister's a rather religious person, isn't she? Moral, like your father. What a funny man your father was, to put a thing like that in his will. Fornication on premises."

"What's this all about?" But I knew, and felt the heat of my wariness.

"What your sister mentioned. She just mentioned that your father left you this house only on condition you'd never do anything to defame or defile it, and if you did do anything like that the house would go straight to her. Not that she really needs it for herself, but it would be convenient, with all those children of hers—naturally I'm only quoting. I guess you wouldn't want me to let on to her about Regina last Easter, would you?— You see, Edmund, you're even sweating a little bit yourself, look at your collar, so why be unfair and ask me to put on my clothes?"

I said hoarsely, "How do you know about Regina?"

"Well, I don't really, do I? It's just that I found this bunch of notes from somebody by that name—Regina—and in one or two of them she says how she stayed here with you over Easter and all about the two of you. Actually, your sister might be a little strait-laced, but she's pretty nice, I mean she wouldn't think the family mansion was being desecrated and so on if *I* stayed here, would she? So in view of all that don't you want to give your consent to my moving in for a little while, Edmund?"

Bitterly I gave it, though consent was academic: he had already installed all his belongings—his dictionary (what was left of it: a poor skeleton, gluey spine and a few of the more infrequent vocabularies, such as K, X, and Z), his suit, and a cigar box filled with thin letters from Liverpool, mostly unopened. I wormed from him a promise that he would keep to the upper part of the house; in return I let him take my typewriter up with him.

What amazed me was that he kept it tapping almost every evening. I had really believed him to be indolent; instead it emerged that he was glib. But I was astonished when I occasionally saw him turn away visitors—it was more usual for him to grab, squeeze, tease and kiss them. They came often, girls with hats brimmed and plumed, and fur muffs, and brave quick little boots; they followed him up the stairs with crowds of poems stuffed into their muffs—their own, or his, or both—throwing past me jagged hillocks and troughs of laughter, their chins hidden in stanzas. Then, though the space of a floor was between us, I heard him declaim: then received a zephyr of shrieks; then further laughter, ebbing; then a scuffle like a herd of zoo antelope, until, in the pure zeal of fury, I floundered into the drawing room and violently clapped the doors to. I sat with my book of maps in my father's heavy creaking chair near a stagnant grate and wondered how I could get him out. I thought of carrying the whole rude tale of his licentiousness to my sister—but anything I might say against a person who was plainly my own guest would undoubtedly tell doubly against myself (so wholesome was my father's whim, and so completely had he disliked me), and since all the money had gone to my sister, and only this gigantic curio of a house to me, I had the warmest desire to hold onto it. Room for room I hated the place; it smelled of the wizened scrupulousness of my burdensome childhood, and my dream was to put it on the market at precisely the right time and make off with a fortune. Luckily I had cozy advice from real-estate friends: the right hour was certainly not yet. But for this house and these hopes I owned nothing, not counting my salary, which was, as my sister liked to affirm, beggar's pay in the light of what she called our "background." Her appearances were now unhappily common. She arrived with five or six of her children, and always without her husband, so that she puffed out the effect of having plucked her offspring out of a cloud. She was a small, exact woman, with large, exact views, made in the exact image of a pious bird, with a cautious jewel of an eye, an excessively arched and fussy breast, and two very tiny and exact nostril-points. She admired Elia and used to ascend to his rooms, trailing progeny, at his bedtime, which is to say at nine o'clock in the morning, when I would be just departing the house for my office; whereas the poetesses, to their credit, did not become visible until romantic dusk. Sometimes she would telephone me and recommend that I move such-and-such a desk—or this ottoman or that highboy —into his attic to supply him with the comforts due his gifts.

"Margaret," I answered her, "have you seen his stuff? It's all pointless. It's all trash."

"He's very young," she declared—"you wait and see," which she reproduced in his idiom so mimetically that she nearly sounded like a Glusker herself. "At your age he'll be a man of the world, not a house-hugging eunuch."

I could not protest at this abusive epithet, vibrantly meant for me; to disclaim my celibacy would have been to disclaim my house. Elia, it appeared, was teaching her subtlety as well as ornamental scurrility—"eunuch" had never before alighted on Margaret's austere tongue. But it was true that since I no longer dared to see poor Regina under our old terms—I was too perilously subject to my guest's surveillance—she had dropped me in pique, and though I was not yet in love, I had been fonder of Regina than of almost anyone. "All right," I cried, "then let him be what he can."

"Why that's *everything*," said Margaret; "you don't realize what a find you've got in that young man."

"He's told you his designs on fame."

"Dear, he doesn't have to tell me. I can *see* it. He's unbelievable. He's an artist."

"A cheap little immigrant," I said. "Uncultivated. He never reads anything."

"Well, that's perfectly true, he's *not* effete. And about being a foreigner, do you know that terrible story, what they did to his whole family over there? When you survive a thing like that it turns you into a man. A fighter. Heroic," she ended. Then, with the solemnity of a codicil: "Don't call him little. He's big. He's enormous. His blood hasn't been thinned."

"He didn't *survive* it," I said wearily. "He wasn't even there when it happened. He was safe in England, he was in Liverpool, for God's sake, living with his aunt."

"Dear, please don't exaggerate and *please* don't swear. I see in him what I'm afraid I'll never see in you: because it isn't there. Genuine manliness. You have no tenderness for the children, Edmund, you walk right by them. Your own nieces and nephews. Elia is remarkable with them. That's just a single example."

I recited, "Gentleness Is the True Soul of Virility."

"That's in very bad taste, Edmund, that's a very journalistic way to express it," she said sadly, as though I had shamed her with an indelicacy: so I assumed Elia had not yet educated her to the enunciation of this potent word.

"You don't like it? Neither do I. It's just that it happens to be the title of the manly artist's latest ode," which was a fact. He had imposed it on me only the night before, whereupon I ritually informed him that it was his worst banality yet.

But Margaret was unvanquishable; she had her own point to bring up. "Look here, Edmund, can't you do something about getting him a better job? What he's doing now doesn't come near to being worthy of him. After all, a police station. And the hours!—"

"I take it you don't think the police force an influence suitable to genuine manliness," I said, and reflected that he had, after all, managed to prove his virility at the cost of my demonstrating mine. I had lost Regina; but he still had all his poetesses.

Yet he did, as I have already noted, now and then send them away, and these times, when he was alone in his rooms, I would listen most particularly for the unrelenting clack of the typewriter. He was keeping at it; he was engrossed; he was serious. It seemed to me the most paralyzing sign of all that this hollow chattering of his machine was so consistent, so reliable, so intelligible, so without stutter or modest hesitation—it made me sigh. He was deeply deadly purposeful. The tapping went on and on, and since he never stopped, it was clear that he never thought. He never daydreamed, meandered, imagined, meditated, sucked, picked, smoked, scratched or loafed. He simply tapped, forefinger over forefinger, as though these sole active digits of his were the legs of a conscientious and dogged errand boy. His investment in self-belief was absolute in its ambition, and I nearly pitied him for it. What he struck off the page was spew and offal, and he called it his career. He mailed three dozen poems a week to this and that magazine, and when the known periodicals turned him down he dredged up the unknown ones, shadowy quarterlies and gazettes printed on hand-presses in dubious basements and devoted to matters anatomic, astronomic, gastronomic, political, or atheist. To the publication of the Vegetarian Party he offered a pastoral verse in earthy trochees, and he tried the organ of a ladies' tonic manufacturing firm with fragile dactyls on the subject of corsets. He submitted everywhere, and I suppose there was finally no editor alive who did not clutch his head at the sight of his name. He clattered out barrage after barrage; he was a scourge to every idealist who had ever hoped to promote the dim cause of numbers. And leaf by leaf, travel journals shoulder to shoulder with Marxist tracts, paramilitarists alongside Seventh-Day Adventists, suffragettes hand in hand with nudists—to a man and to a woman they turned him down, they denied him print, they begged him at last to cease and desist, they folded their pamphlets like Arab tents and fled when they saw him brandishing so much as an iamb.

Meanwhile the feet of his fingers ran; he never gave up. My fright for him began almost to match my contempt. I was pitying him now in earnest, though his confidence remained as unmoved and oafish as ever. "Wait and see," he said, sounding like a copy of my sister copying him. The two of them put their heads together over me, but I had done all I could for him. He had no prospects. It even horribly developed that I was looked upon by my colleagues as his special protector, because when I left for the trenches my absence was immediately seized on and he was fired. This, of course, did not reach me until I returned after a year, missing an earlobe and with a dark and ugly declivity slashed across the back of my neck. My house guest had been excused from the draft by virtue of his bad eyesight, or perhaps more accurately by virtue of the ponderous thickness of his lenses; eight or ten of his poetesses tendered him a party in celebration of both his exemption and his myopia, at which he unflinchingly threw a dart into the bull's-eye of a target-shaped cake. But I was myself no soldier, and went only as a correspondent to that ancient and so primitive war, naïvely pretending to encompass the world, but Neanderthal according to our later and more expansive appetites for annihilation. Someone had merely shot a prince (a nobody—I myself cannot recall his name), and then, in illogical consequence, various patches of territory had sprung up to occupy and individualize a former empire. In the same way, I discovered, had Elia sprung up—or, as I must now consistently call him (lest I seem to stand apart from the miraculous change in his history), Edmund Gate. What I mean by this is that he stepped out of his attic and with democratic hugeness took over the house. His great form had by now entirely flattened my father's august chair, and, like a vast male Goldilocks, he was sleeping in my mother's bed—that shrine which my father had long ago consecrated to disuse and awe: a piety my sister and I had soberly perpetuated. I came home and found him in the drawing room, barefoot and in his underwear, his dirty socks strewn over the floor, and my sister in attendance mending the holes he had worn through the heels, invigilated by a knot of her children. It presently emerged that she had all along been providing him with an allowance to suit his tastes, but in that first unwitting moment when he leaped up to embrace me, at the same time dragging on his shirt (because he knew how I disliked to see him undressed), I was stunned to catch the flash of his initials—"E.G."—embroidered in scarlet silk on a pair of magnificent cuffs.

"Edmund!" he howled. "Not one, not two—two *dozen!* Two dozen in the past two months alone!"

"Two dozen what?" I said, blinking at what had become of him. He was now twenty-one, and taller, larger, and hairier than ever. He wore new glasses (far less formidable than the awful weights his little nose had carried to the draft board), and these, predictably, had matured his expression, especially in the area of the cheekbones: their elderly silver frames very cleverly contradicted that inevitable boyishness which a big face is wont to radiate when it is committed to surrounding the nose of a cherub. I saw plainly, and saw it for myself, without the mesmerizing influence of his preening (for he was standing before me very simply, diligently buttoning up his shirt), that he had been increased and transformed: his fantastic body had made a simile out of him. The element in him that partook of the heathen colossus had swelled to drive out everything callow—with his blunt and balding skull he looked (I am willing to dare the vulgar godliness inherent in the term) like a giant lingam: one of those curious phallic monuments one may suddenly encounter, wreathed with bright chains of leaves, on a dusty wayside in India. His broad hands wheeled, his shirttail flicked; it was clear that his scalp was not going to be friends for long with his follicles—stars of dandruff fluttered from him. He had apparently taken up smoking, because his teeth were already a brown ruin. And with all that, he was somehow a ceremonial and touching spectacle. He was massive and dramatic; he had turned majestic.

"Poems, man, poems!" he roared. "Two dozen poems sold, and to all the best magazines!" He would have pulled my ear like a comrade had I had a lobe to pull by, but instead he struck me down into a chair (all the while my sister went on peacefully darning), and heaped into my arms a jumble of the most important periodicals of the hour.

"Ah, there's more to it than just that," my sister said.

"How did you manage all this?" I said. "My God, here's one in *The Centennial*! You mean Fielding accepted? Fielding actually?"

"The sheaf of horrors man, that's right. He's really a very nice old fellow, you know that, Edmund? I've lunched with him three times now. He can't stop apologizing for the way he embarrassed himself—remember, the time he wrote you that terrible letter about me? He's always saying how ashamed he is over it."

"Fielding?" I said. "I can't imagine Fielding—"

"Tell the rest," Margaret said complacently.

"Well, tomorrow we're having lunch again—Fielding and Margaret and me, and he's going to introduce me to this book publisher who's very interested in my things and wants to put them between, how did he say it, Margaret?—between something."

"Boards. A collection, all the poems of Edmund Gate. You see?" said Margaret.

"I *don't* see," I burst out.

"You never did. You haven't the vigor. I doubt whether you've ever really *penetrated* Edmund." This confused me, until I understood that she now habitually addressed him by the name he had pinched from me. "Edmund," she challenged—which of us was this? from her scowl I took it as a finger at myself—"you don't realize his level. It's his *level* you don't realize."

"I realize it," I said darkly, and let go a landslide of magazines: but *The Centennial* I retained. "I suppose poor Fielding's gone senile by now. Wasn't he at least ten years older than Father even? I suppose he's off his head and they just don't have the heart to ship him out."

"That won't do," Margaret said. "This boy is getting his recognition at last, that's all there is to it."

"I know what he means, though," Edmund said. "I tell them the same thing, I tell them exactly that—all those editors, I tell them they're crazy to carry on the way they do. You ought to hear—"

"Praise," Margaret intervened with a snap: "praise and more praise," as if this would spite me.

"I never thought myself those poems were *that* good," he said. "It's funny, they were just an experiment at first, but then I got the hang of it."

"An experiment?" I asked him. His diffidence was novel, it was even radical; he seemed almost abashed. I had to marvel: he was as bemused over his good luck as I was.

Not so Margaret, who let it appear that she had read the cosmic will. "Edmund is working in a new vein," she explained.

"Hasn't he always worked in vain?" I said, and dived into *The Centennial* to see.

Edmund slapped his shins at this, but "He who laughs last," said Margaret, and beat her thimble on the head of the nearest child: "What a callous man your uncle is. Read!" she commanded me.

"He has a hole in the back of his neck and only a little piece of ear left," said the child in a voice of astute assent.

"Ssh," said Margaret. "We don't speak of deformities."

"Unless they turn up as poems," I corrected; and read; and was startled by a dilation of the lungs, like a horse lashed out of the blue and made to race beyond its impulse. Was it his, this clean stupendous stuff? But there was his name, manifest in print: it was his, according to *The Centennial*, and Fielding had not gone senile.

"Well?"

"I don't know," I said, feeling muddled.

"He doesn't know! Edmund"—this was to Edmund—"he doesn't know!"

"I can't believe it."

"He can't believe it, Edmund!"

"Well, neither could I at first," he admitted.

But my sister jumped up and pointed her needle in my face. "Say it's good."

"Oh, it's good. I can see it's good," I said. "He's hit it for once."

"They're *all* like that," she expanded. "Look for yourself."

I looked, I looked insatiably, I looked fanatically, I looked frenetically, I looked incredulously—I went from magazine to magazine, riffling and rifling, looking and looting and shuffling, until I had plundered them all of his work. My booty dumbfounded me: there was nothing to discard. I was transfixed; I was exhausted; in the end it was an exorcism of my stupefaction. I was converted, I believed; he had hit it every time. And not with ease—I could trace the wonderful risks he took. It *was* a new vein; more, it was an artery, it had a pump and a kick; it was a robust ineluctable fountain. And when his book came out half a year later, my proselytization was sealed. Here were all the poems of the periodicals, already as familiar as solid old columns, uniquely graven; and layered over them like dazzling slabs of dappled marble, immovable because of the perfection of their weight and the inexorability of their balance, was the aftermath of that early work, those more recent productions to which I soon became a reverential witness. Or, if not witness, then auditor: for out of habit he still liked to compose in the attic, and I would hear him type a poem straight out, without so much as stopping to breathe. And right afterward he came down and presented it to me. It seemed, then, that nothing had changed: only his gift and a single feature of his manner. Unerringly it was a work of—yet who or what was I to declare him genius?—accept instead the modest judgment of merit. It was a work of merit he gave me unerringly, but he gave it to me—this was strangest of all—with a quiescence, a passivity. All his old arrogance had vanished. So had his vanity. A kind of tranquillity kept him taut and still, like a man leashed; and he went up the stairs, on those days when he was seized by the need for a poem, with a languidness unlike anything I had ever noticed in him before; he typed, from start to finish, with no falterings or emendations; then he thumped on the stairs again, loomed like a thug, and handed the glorious sheet over to my exulting grasp. I supposed it was a sort of trance he had to endure—in those dim times we were only just beginning to know Freud, but even then it was clear that, with the bursting forth of the latent thing, he had fallen into a relief as deep and curative as the sleep of ether. If he lacked—or skipped—what enthusiastic people call the creative exaltation, it was because he had compressed it all, without the exhibitionism of prelude, into that singular moment of power—six minutes, or eight minutes, however long it took him, forefinger over forefinger, to turn vision into alphabet.

He had become, by the way, a notably fast typist.

I asked him once—this was after he had surrendered a new-hatched sheet not a quarter of an hour from the typewriter—how he could account for what had happened in him.

"You used to be awful," I reminded him. "You used to be unspeakable. My God, you were vile."

"Oh, I don't know," he said in that ennui, or blandness, that he always displayed after one of his remarkable trips to the attic, "I don't know if I was *that* bad."

"Well, even if you weren't," I said—in view of what I had

in my hand I could no longer rely on my idea of what he had been—"this! This!" and fanned the wondrous page like a triumphant flag. "How do you explain *this*, coming after what you were?"

He grinned a row of brown incisors at me and gave me a hearty smack on the ankle. "Plagiarism."

"No, tell me really."

"The plangent plagiarism," he said accommodatingly, "of the plantigrade persona.—Admit it, Edmund, you don't like the Ps, you never did and you never will."

"For instance," I said, "you don't do *that* any more."

"Do what?" He rubbed the end of a cigarette across his teeth and yawned. "I still do persiflage, don't I? I do it out of my pate, without periwig, pugree, or peril."

"That. Cram grotesque words in every line."

"No, I don't do that any more. A pity, my dictionary's practically all gone."

"Why?" I persisted.

"I used it up, that's why. I *finished* it."

"Be serious. What I'm getting at is why you're different. Your stuff *is* different. I've never seen such a difference."

He sat up suddenly and with inspiration, and it came to me that I was observing the revival of passion. "Margaret's given that a lot of thought, Edmund. *She* attributes it to maturity."

"That's not very perspicacious," I said—for the sake of the Ps, and to show him I no longer minded anything.

But he said shortly, "She means virility."

This made me scoff. "She can't even get herself to say the word."

"Well, maybe there's a difference in Margaret too," he said.

"She's the same silly woman she ever was, and her husband's the same silly stockbroker, the two of them a pair of fertile prudes—she wouldn't recognize so-called virility if she tripped over it. She hates the whole concept—"

"She likes it," he said.

"What she likes is euphemisms for it. She can't face it, so she covers it up. Tenderness! Manliness! Maturity! Heroics! She hasn't got a brain in her head," I said, "and she's never gotten anything done in the world but those silly babies, I've lost count of how many she's done of *those*—"

"The next one's mine," he said.

"That's an imbecile joke."

"Not a joke."

"Look here, joke about plagiarism all you want but don't waste your breath on fairy tales."

"Nursery tales," he amended. "I never waste anything, I told you. That's just it, I've gone and plagiarized Margaret. I've purloined her, if you want to stick to the Ps."—Here he enumerated several other Ps impossible to print, which I am obliged to leave to my reader's experience, though not of the parlor. "And you're plenty wrong about your sister's brains, Edmund. She's a very capable businesswoman—she's simply never had the opportunity. You know since my book's out I have to admit I'm a bit in demand, and what she's done is she's booked me solid for six months' worth of recitations. And the fees! She's getting me more than Edna St. Vincent Millay, if you want the whole truth," he said proudly. "And why not? The only time that dame ever writes a good poem is when she signs her name."

All at once, and against his laughter and its storm of smoke, I understood who was behind the title of his collected poems. I was confounded. It was Margaret. His book was called *Virility*.

A week after this conversation he left with my sister for Chicago, for the inauguration of his reading series.

I went up to his attic and searched it. I was in a boil of distrust; I was outraged. I had lost Regina to Margaret's principles, and now Margaret had lost her principles, and in both cases Edmund Gate had stood to profit. He gained from her morality and he gained from her immorality. I began to hate him again. It would have rejoiced me to believe his quip: nothing could have made me merrier than to think him a thief of words, if only for the revenge of catching him at it—but he could not even be relied on for something so plausible as plagiarism. The place revealed nothing. There was not so much as an anthology of poetry, say, which might account for his extraordinary burgeoning; there was not a single book of any kind—that sparse and pitiful wreck of his dictionary, thrown into a corner together with a cigar box, hardly signified. For the rest, there were only an old desk with his—no, my—typewriter on it, an ottoman, a chair or two, an empty chest, a hot bare floor (the heat pounded upward), and his primordial suit slowly revolving in the sluggish airs on a hanger suspended from the skylight, moths nesting openly on the lapels. It brought to mind Mohammed and the Koran; Joseph Smith and the golden plates. Some mysterious dictation recurred in these rooms: his gift came to him out of the light and out of the dark. I sat myself down at his desk and piecemeal typed out an agonized letter to Regina. I offered to change the terms of our relationship. I said I hoped we could take up again, not as before (my house was in use). I said I would marry her.

She answered immediately, enclosing a wedding announcement six months old.

On that same day Margaret returned. "I left him, of *course* I left him. I had to, not that he can take care of himself under the circumstances, but I sent him on to Detroit anyhow. If I'm going to be his manager, after all, I have to *manage* things. I can't do all that from the provinces, you know—I have to *be* here, I have to see people . . . ah, you can't imagine it, Edmund, they want him everywhere! I have to set up a regular office, just a *little* switchboard to start with—"

"It's going well?"

"Going well! What a way to put it! Edmund, he's a phenomenon. It's supernatural. He has *charisma*, in Chicago they had to arrest three girls, they made a human chain and lowered themselves from a chandelier right over the lectern, and the lowest-hanging one reached down for a hair of his head and nearly tore the poor boy's scalp off—"

"What a pity," I said.

"What do you *mean* what a pity, you don't follow, Edmund, he's a celebrity!"

"But he has so few hairs and he thinks so much of them," I said, and wondered bitterly whether Regina had married a bald man.

"You have no right to take that tone," Margaret said. "You

have no idea how modest he is. I suppose that's part of his appeal—he simply has no ego at all. He takes it as innocently as a baby. In Chicago he practically looked over his shoulder to see if they really meant *him*. And they *do* mean him, you can't imagine the screaming, and the shoving for autographs, and people calling bravo and fainting if they happen to meet his eyes—"

"Fainting?" I said doubtfully.

"Fainting! My goodness, Edmund, don't you read the headlines in your own paper? His audiences are three times as big as Caruso's. Oh, you're hard, Edmund, you admit he's good but I say there's a terrible wall in you if you don't see the power in this boy—"

"I see it over you," I said.

"Over me! Over the world, Edmund, it's the world he's got now—I've already booked him for London and Manchester, and here's this cable from Johannesburg pleading for him—oh, he's through with the backwoods, believe you me. And look here, I've just settled up this fine generous contract for his next book, with the reviews still piling in from the first one!" She crackled open her briefcase, and flung out a mass of files, lists, letterheads, schedules, torn envelopes with exotic stamps on them, fat legal-looking portfolios, documents in tiny type— she danced them all noisily upon her pouting lap.

"His second book?" I asked. "Is it ready?"

"Of course it's ready. He's remarkably productive, you know. Fecund."

"He pullulates," I suggested.

"His own word exactly, how did you hit it? He can come up with a poem practically at will. Sometimes right after a reading, when he's exhausted—you know it's his shyness that exhausts him that way—anyhow, there he is all fussed and worried about whether the next performance will be as good, and he'll suddenly get this—well, *fit,* and hide out in the remotest part of the hotel and fumble in his wallet for bits of paper—he's always carrying bits of folded paper, with notes or ideas in them I suppose, and shoo everyone away, even me, and *type* (he's awfully fond of his new typewriter, by the way)—he just types the glory right out of his soul!" she crowed. "It's the energy of genius. He's *authentic*, Edmund, a profoundly energetic man is profoundly energetic in all directions at once. I hope at least you've been following the reviews?"

It was an assault, and I shut myself against it. "What will he call the new book?"

"Oh, he leaves little things like the titles to me, and I'm all for simplicity.—*Virility II*," she announced in her shocking business-magnate voice. "And the one after that will be *Virility III*. And the one after that—"

"Ah, fecund," I said.

"Fecund," she gleamed.

"A bottomless well?"

She marveled at this. "How is it you always hit on Edmund's words exactly?"

"I know how he talks," I said.

"A bottomless well, he said it himself. Wait and see!" she warned me.

She was not mistaken. After *Virility* came *Virility II*, and after that *Virility III*, and after that an infant boy. Margaret named him Edmund—she said it was after me—and her husband the stockbroker, though somewhat puzzled at this human production in the midst of so much literary fertility, was all the same a little cheered. Of late it had seemed to him, now that Margaret's first simple switchboard had expanded to accommodate three secretaries, that he saw her less than ever, or at least that she was noticing him less than ever. This youngest Edmund struck him as proof (though it embarrassed him to think about it even for a minute) that perhaps she had noticed him more than he happened to remember. Margaret, meanwhile, was gay and busy—she slipped the new little Edmund ("Let's call *him* III," she laughed) into her packed nursery and went on about her business, which had grown formidable. Besides the three secretaries, she had two assistants: poets, poetasters, tenors, altos, mystics, rationalists, rightists, leftists, memoirists, fortune-tellers, peddlers, everyone with an *idée fixe* and therefore suitable to the lecture circuit clamored to be bundled into her clientele. Edmund she ran ragged. She ran him to Paris, to Lisbon, to Stockholm, to Moscow; nobody understood him in any of these places, but the title of his books translated impressively into all languages. He developed a sort of growl—it was from always being hoarse; he smoked day and night—and she made him cultivate it. Together with his accent it caused an international shudder among the best of women. She got rid of his initialed cuffs and dressed him like a prize fighter, in high laced black brogans and tight shining T-shirts, out of which his hairiness coiled. A long bladder of smoke was always trailing out of his mouth. In Paris they pursued him into the Place de la Concorde yelling "*Virilité! Virilité!*" "*Die Manneskraft!*" they howled in Munich. The reviews were an avalanche, a cataclysm. In the rotogravure sections his picture vied with the beribboned bosoms of duchesses. In New Delhi glossy versions of his torso were hawked like an avatar in the streets. He had long since been catapulted out of the hands of the serious literary critics—but it was the serious critics who had begun it. "The Masculine Principle personified, verified, and illuminated." "The bite of Pope, the sensuality of Keats." "The quality, in little, of the very greatest novels. Tolstoyan." "Seminal and hard." "Robust, lusty, male." "Erotic."

Margaret was ecstatic, and slipped a new infant into her bursting nursery. This time the stockbroker helped her choose its name: they decided on Gate, and hired another nanny to take care of the overflow.

After *Virility IV* came *Virility V*. The quality of his work had not diminished, yet it was extraordinary that he could continue to produce at all. Occasionally he came to see me between trips, and then he always went upstairs and took a turn around the sighing floors of his old rooms. He descended haggard and slouching; his pockets looked puffy, but it seemed to be only his huge fists he kept there. Somehow his fame had intensified that curious self-effacement. He had divined that I was privately soured by his success, and he tried bashfully to remind me of the days when he had written badly.

"That only makes it worse," I told him. "It shows what a poor prophet I was."

"No," he said, "you weren't such a bad prophet, Edmund."

"I said you'd never get anywhere with your stuff."

"I haven't."

I hated him for that—Margaret had not long before shown me his bank statement. He was one of the richest men in the country; my paper was always printing human-interest stories about him—"Prosperous Poet Visits Fabulous Patagonia." I said, "What do you mean you haven't gotten anywhere? What more do you want from the world? What else do you think it can give you?"

"Oh, I don't know," he said. He was gloomy and sullen. "I just feel I'm running short on things."

"On triumphs? They're all the time comparing you to Keats. Your pal Fielding wrote in *The Centennial* just the other day that you're practically as great as the Early Milton."

"Fielding's senile. They should have put him away a long time ago."

"And in sales you're next to the Bible."

"I was brought up on the Bible," he said suddenly.

"Aha. It's a fit of conscience? Then look, Elia, why don't you take Margaret and get her divorced and get those babies of yours legitimized, if that's what's worrying you."

"They're legitimate enough. The old man's not a bad father. Besides, they're all mixed up in there, I can't tell one from the other."

"Yours are the ones named after you. You were right about Margaret, she's an efficient woman."

"I don't worry about that," he insisted.

"*Some*thing's worrying you." This satisfied me considerably.

"As a matter of fact—" He trundled himself down into my father's decaying chair. He had just returned from a tour of Italy; he had gone with a wardrobe of thirty-seven satin T-shirts and not one of them had survived intact. His torn-off sleeves sold for twenty lira each. They had stolen his glasses right off his celebrated nose. "I like it here, Edmund," he said. "I like your house. I like the way you've never bothered about my old things up there. A man likes to hang on to his past."

It always bewildered me that the style of his talk had not changed. He was still devoted to the insufferably hackneyed.

He still came upon his clichés like Columbus. Yet his poems
. . . but how odd, how remiss! I observe that I have not even
attempted to describe them. That is because they ought certainly to be *presented*—read aloud, as Edmund was doing all
over the world. Short of that, I might of course reproduce
them here; but I must not let my narrative falter in order to
make room for any of them, even though, it is true, they would
not require a great deal of space. They were notably small and
spare, in conventional stanza-form. They rhymed consistently
and scanned regularly. They were, besides, amazingly simple.
Unlike the productions of Edmund's early phase, their language was pristine. There were no unusual words. His poems
had the ordinary vocabulary of ordinary men. At the same
time they were immensely vigorous. It was astonishingly easy
to memorize them—they literally could not be forgotten. Some
told stories, like ballads, and they were exhilarating yet shocking stories. Others were strangely explicit love lyrics, of a kind
that no Western poet had ever yet dared—but the effect was
one of health and purity rather than scandal. It was remarked
by everyone who read or heard Edmund Gate's work that only
a person who had had great and large experience of the world
could have written it. People speculated about his life. If the
Borgias, privy to all forms of foulness, had been poets, someone said, they would have written poems like that. If Teddy
Roosevelt's Rough Riders had been poets, they would have
written poems like that. If Genghis Khan and Napoleon had
been poets, they would have written poems like that. They
were masculine poems. They were political and personal,
public and private. They were full of both passion and ennui,
they were youthful and elderly, they were green and wise.
But they were not beautiful and they were not dull, the way
a well-used, faintly gnarled, but superbly controlled muscle is
neither beautiful nor dull.

They were, in fact, very much like Margaret's vision
of Edmund Gate himself. The poet and the poems were
indistinguishable.

She sent her vision to Yugoslavia, she sent it to Egypt, she
sent it to Japan. In Warsaw girls ran after him in the street

to pick his pockets for souvenirs—they came near to picking his teeth. In Copenhagen they formed an orgiastic club named "The Forbidden Gate" and gathered around a gatepost to read him. In Hong Kong they tore off his underwear and stared giggling at his nakedness. He was now twenty-five; it began to wear him out.

When he returned from Brazil he came to see me. He seemed more morose than ever. He slammed up the stairs, kicked heavily over the floors, and slammed down again. He had brought down with him his old cigar box.

"My aunt's dead," he said.

As usual he took my father's chair. His burly baby's-head lolled.

"The one in Liverpool?"

"Yeah."

"I'm sorry to hear that. Though she must have gotten to be a pretty old lady by now."

"She was seventy-four."

He appeared to be taking it hard. An unmistakable misery creased his giant neck.

"Still," I said, "you must have been providing for her nicely these last few years. At least before she went she had her little comforts."

"No. I never did a thing. I never sent her a penny."

I looked at him. He seemed to be nearly sick. His lips were black. "You always meant to, I suppose. You just never got around to it," I ventured; I thought it was remorse that had darkened him.

"No," he said. "I couldn't. I didn't have it then. I couldn't afford to. Besides, she was always very self-reliant."

He was a worse scoundrel than I had imagined. "Damn you, Elia," I said. "She took you in, if not for her you'd be murdered with your whole family back there—"

"Well, I never had as much as you used to think. That police station job wasn't much."

"Police station!" I yelled.

He gave me an eye full of hurt. "You don't follow, Edmund. My aunt died before all this fuss. She died three years ago."

"Three years ago?"

"Three and a half maybe."

I tried to adjust. "You just got the news, you mean? You just heard?"

"Oh, no. I found out about it right after it happened."

Confusion roiled in me. "You never mentioned it."

"There wasn't any point. It's not as though you *knew* her. Nobody knew her. I hardly knew her myself. She wasn't anybody. She was just this old woman."

"Ah," I said meanly, "so the grief is only just catching up with you, is that it? You've been too busy to find the time to mourn?"

"I never liked her," he admitted. "She was an old nuisance. She talked and talked at me. Then when I got away from her and came here she wrote me and wrote me. After a while I just stopped opening her letters. I figured she must have written me two hundred letters. I saved them. I save everything, even junk. When you start out poor, you always save everything. You never know when you might need it. I never waste anything." He said portentously, "Waste Not, Want Not."

"If you never answered her how is it she kept on writing?"

"She didn't have anybody else to write to. I guess she had to write and she didn't have anybody. All I've got left are the ones in here. This is the last bunch of letters of hers I've got." He showed me his big scratched cigar box.

"But you say you saved them—"

"Sure, but I used them up. Listen," he said. "I've got to go now, Edmund, I've got to meet Margaret. It's going to be one hell of a fight, I tell you."

"What?" I said.

"I'm not going anywhere else, I don't care how much she squawks. I've had my last trip. I've got to stay home from now on and do poems. I'm going to get a room somewhere, maybe my old room across town, *you* remember—where you came to see me that time?"

"Where I knocked you down. You can stay here," I said.

"Nah," he said. "Nowhere your sister can get at me. I've got to work."

"But you've *been* working," I said. "You've been turning out new poems all along! That's been the amazing thing."

He hefted all his flesh and stood up, clutching the cigar box to his dinosaurish ribs.

"I haven't," he said.

"You've done those five collections—"

"All I've done are those two babies. Edmund and Gate. And they're not even my real names. That's all I've done. The reviews did the rest. Margaret did the rest."

He was suddenly weeping.

"I can't tell it to Margaret—"

"Tell what?"

"There's only one bundle left. No more. After this no more. It's finished."

"Elia, what in God's name is this?"

"I'm afraid to tell. I don't know what else to do. I've *tried* to write new stuff. I've tried. It's terrible. It's not the same. It's not the same, Edmund. I can't do it. I've told Margaret that. I've told her I can't write any more. She says it's a block, it happens to all writers. She says don't worry, it'll come back. It always comes back to genius."

He was sobbing wildly; I could scarcely seize his words. He had thrown himself back into my father's chair, and the tears were making brooks of its old leather cracks.

"I'm afraid to tell," he said.

"Elia, for God's sake. Straighten up like a man. Afraid of what?"

"Well, I told you once. I told you because I knew you wouldn't believe me, but I *did* tell you, you can't deny it. You could've stopped me. It's your fault too." He kept his face hidden.

He had made me impatient. "What's my fault?"

"I'm a plagiarist."

"If you mean Margaret again—"

He answered with a whimper: "No, no, don't be a fool, I'm through with Margaret."

"Aren't those collections yours? They're not yours?"

"They're mine," he said. "They came in the mail, so if you mean are they mine *that* way—"

I caught his agitation. "Elia, you're out of your mind—"

"She wrote every last one," he said. "In Liverpool. Every last line of every last one. Tante Rivka. There's only enough left for one more book. Margaret's going to call it *Virility VI*," he bawled.

"Your aunt?" I said. "She wrote them all?"

He moaned.

"Even the one—not the one about the—"

"All," he broke in; his voice was nearly gone.

He stayed with me for three weeks. To fend her off I telephoned Margaret and said that Edmund had come down with the mumps. "But I've just had a cable from Southern Rhodesia!" she wailed. "They need him like mad down there!"

"You'd better keep away, Margaret," I warned. "You don't want to carry the fever back to the nursery. All those babies in there—"

"Why should he get an infant's disease?" she wondered; I heard her fidget.

"It's just the sort of disease that corresponds to his mentality."

"Now stop that. You know that's a terrible sickness for a grown man to get. You know what it does. It's awful."

I had no idea what she could be thinking of; I had chosen this fabrication for its innocence. "Why?" I said. "Children recover beautifully—"

"Don't be an imbecile, Edmund," she rebuked me in my father's familiar tone—my father had often called me a scientific idiot. "He might come out of it as sterile as a stone. Stop it, Edmund, it's nothing to laugh at, you're a brute."

"Then you'll have to call his next book *Sterility*," I said.

He hid out with me, as I have already noted, for nearly a month, and much of the time he cried.

"It's all up with me."

I said coldly, "You knew it was coming."

"I've dreaded it and dreaded it. After this last batch I'm finished. I don't know what to do. I don't know what's going to happen."

"You ought to confess," I advised finally.

"To Margaret?"

"To everyone. To the world."

He gave me a teary smirk. "Sure. The Collected Works of Edmund Gate, by Tante Rivka."

"Vice versa's the case," I said, struck again by a shadow of my first shock. "And since it's true, you ought to make it up to her."

"You can't make anything up to the dead." He was wiping the river that fell from his nose. "My reputation. My poor about-to-be-mutilated reputation. No, I'll just go ahead and get myself a little place to live in and produce new things. What comes now will be *really* mine. Integrity," he whined. "I'll save myself that way."

"You'll ruin yourself. You'll be the man of the century who fizzled before he made it to thirty. There's nothing more foolish-looking than a poet who loses his gift. Pitiful. They'll laugh at you. Look how people laugh at the Later Wordsworth. The Later Gate will be a fiasco at twenty-six. You'd better confess, Elia."

Moodily he considered it. "What would it get me?"

"Wonder and awe. Admiration. You'll be a great sacrificial figure. You can say your aunt was reticent but a tyrant, she made you stand in her place. Gate the Lamb. You can say anything."

This seemed to attract him. "It *was* a sacrifice," he said. "Believe me it was hell going through all of that. I kept getting diarrhea from the water in all those different places. I never could stand the screaming anywhere. Half the time my life was in danger. In Hong Kong when they stole my shorts I practically got pneumonia." He popped his cigarette out of his mouth and began to cough. "You really think I ought to do that, Edmund? Margaret wouldn't like it. She's always hated sterile men. It'll be an admission of my own poetic sterility, that's how she'll look at it."

"I thought you're through with her anyhow."

Courage suddenly puffed him out. "You bet I am. I don't think much of people who exploit other people. She built that business up right out of my flesh and blood. Right out of my marrow."

He sat at the typewriter in the attic, at which I had hammered out my futile proposal to Regina, and wrote a letter to his publisher. It was a complete confession. I went with him to the drugstore to get it notarized. I felt the ease of the perfect confidant, the perfect counsel, the perfect avenger. He had spilled me the cup of humiliation, he had lost me Regina; I would lose him the world.

Meanwhile I assured him he would regain it. "You'll go down," I said, "as the impresario of the nearly-lost. You'll go down as the man who bestowed a hidden genius. You'll go down as the savior who restored to perpetual light what might have wandered a mute inglorious ghost in the eternal dark."

On my paper they had fired better men than I for that sort of prose.

"I'd rather have been the real thing myself," he said. The remark seemed to leap from his heart; it almost touched me.

"Caesar is born, not made," I said. "But who notices Caesar's nephew? Unless he performs a vast deep act. To be Edmund Gate was nothing. But to shed the power of Edmund Gate before the whole watching world, to become little in oneself in order to give away one's potency to another—*that* is an act of profound reverberation."

He said wistfully, "I guess you've got a point there," and emerged to tell Margaret.

She was wrathful. She was furious. She was vicious. "A lady wrote 'em?" she cried. "An old Jewish immigrant lady who never even made it to America?"

"My Tante Rivka," he said bravely.

"Now Margaret," I said. "Don't be obtuse. The next book will be every bit as good as the ones that preceded it. The quality is exactly the same. He picked those poems at random out of a box and one's as good as another. They're all good. They're brilliant, you know that. The book won't be different so its reception won't be different. The profits will be the same."

She screwed up a doubtful scowl. "It'll be the last one. He says *he* can't write. There won't be any more after this."

"The canon closes," I agreed, "when the poet dies."

"This poet's dead all right," she said, and threw him a spiteful laugh. Edmund Gate rubbed his glasses, sucked his cigarette, rented a room, and disappeared.

Margaret grappled in vain with the publisher. "Why not *Virility* again? It was good enough for the other five. It's a selling title."

"This one's by a woman," he said. "Call it *Muliebrity*, no one'll understand you." The publisher was a wit who was proud of his Latin, but he had an abstract and wholesome belief in the stupidity of his readers.

The book appeared under the name *Flowers from Liverpool*. It had a pretty cover, the color of a daisy's petal, with a picture of Tante Rivka on it. The picture was a daguerrotype that Edmund had kept flat at the bottom of the cigar box. It showed his aunt as a young woman in Russia, not very handsome, with large lips, a circular nose, and minuscule light eyes—the handle of what looked strangely like a pistol stuck out of her undistinguished bosom.

The collection itself was sublime. By some accident of the unplanned gesture the last poems left in Edmund Gate's cracked cigar box had turned out to be the crest of the poet's vitality. They were as clear and hard as all the others, but somehow rougher and thicker, perhaps more intellectual. I read and marveled myself into shame—if I had believed I would dash his career by inducing him to drop his connection with it, I had been worse than misled. I had been criminal. Nothing could damage the career of these poems. They would soar and soar beyond petty revenges. If Shakespeare was really Bacon, what difference? If Edmund Gate was really Tante Rivka of Liverpool, what difference? Since nothing can betray a good poem, it is pointless to betray a bad poet.

With a prepublication copy in my hand I knocked at his door. He opened it in his underwear: a stink came out of him. One lens was gone from his glasses.

"Well, here it is," I said. "The last one."

He hiccuped with a mournful drunken spasm.

"The last shall be first," I said with a grin of disgust; the smell of his room made me want to run.

"The first shall be last," he contradicted, flagging me down with an old newspaper. "You want to come in here, Edmund? Come in, sure."

But there was no chair. I sat on the bed. The floor was splintered and his toenails scraped on it. They were long filthy crescents. I put the book down. "I brought this for you to have first thing."

He looked at the cover. "What a mug on her."

"What a mind," I said. "You were lucky to have known her."

"An old nuisance. If not for her I'd still be what I was. If she didn't run out on me."

"Elia," I began; I had come to tell him a horror. "The publisher did a little biographical investigation. They found where your aunt was living when she died. It seems," I said, "she was just what you've always described. Self-sufficient."

"Always blah blah at me. Old nuisance. I ran out on her, couldn't stand it."

"She got too feeble to work and never let on to a soul. They found her body, all washed clean for burial, in her bed. She'd put on clean linens herself and she'd washed herself. Then she climbed into the bed and starved to death. She just waited it out that way. There wasn't a crumb in the place."

"She never asked me for anything," he said.

"How about the one called 'Hunger'? The one everybody thought was a battle poem?"

"It was only a poem. Besides, she was already dead when I got to it."

"If you'd sent her something," I said, "you might have kept Edmund Gate going a few years more. A hardy old bird like that could live to be a hundred. All she needed was bread."

"Who cares? The stuff would've petered out sooner or later anyhow, wouldn't it? The death of Edmund Gate was unavoidable. I wish you'd go away, Edmund. I'm not used to feeling this drunk. I'm trying to get proficient at it. It's killing my stomach. My bladder's giving out. Go away."

"All right."

"Take that damn book with you."

"It's yours."

"Take it away. It's your fault they've turned me into a

woman. I'm a man," he said; he gripped himself between the legs; he was really very drunk.

All the same I left it there, tangled in his dirty quilt.

Margaret was in Mexico with a young client of hers, a baritone. She was arranging bookings for him in hotels. She sent back a photograph of him in a swimming pool. I sat in the clamorous nursery with the stockbroker and together we rattled through the journals, looking for reviews.

"Here's one. 'Thin feminine art,' it says."

"Here's another. 'A lovely girlish voice reflecting a fragile girlish soul: a lace valentine.'"

"'Limited, as all domestic verse must be. A spinster's one-dimensional vision.'"

"'Choked with female inwardness. Flat. The typical unimaginativeness of her sex.'"

"'Distaff talent, secondary by nature. Lacks masculine energy.'"

"'The fine womanly intuition of a competent poetess.'"

The two youngest children began to yowl. "Now, now Gatey boy," said the stockbroker, "now, now, Edmund. Why can't you be good? Your brothers and sisters are good, *they* don't cry." He turned to me with a shy beam. "Do you know we're having another?"

"No," I said. "I didn't know that. Congratulations."

"She's the New Woman," the stockbroker said. "Runs a business all by herself, just like a man."

"Has babies like a woman."

He laughed proudly. "Well, she doesn't do that one by herself, I'll tell you that."

"Read some more."

"Not much use to it. They all say the same thing, don't they? By the way, Edmund, did you happen to notice they've already got a new man in *The Centennial*? Poor Fielding, but the funeral was worthy of him. Your father would have wept if he'd been there."

"Read the one in *The Centennial*," I said.

"'There is something in the feminine mind which resists largeness and depth. Perhaps it is that a woman does not get the chance to sleep under bridges. Even if she got the chance, she would start polishing the piles. Experience is the stuff of art, but experience is not something God made woman for . . .' It's just the same as the others," he said.

"So is the book."

"The title's different," he said wisely. "This one's by a woman, they all point that out. All the rest of 'em were called *Virility*. What happened to that fellow, by the way? He doesn't come around."

The babies howled down the ghost of my reply.

I explained at the outset that only last week I visited the grave of Edmund Gate, but I neglected to describe a curious incident that occurred on that spot.

I also explained the kind of cameraderie elderly people in our modern society feel for one another. We know we are declining together, but we also recognize that our memories are a kind of national treasury, being living repositories for such long-extinct customs as burial and intra-uterine embryo-development.

At Edmund Gate's grave stood an extraordinary person—a frazzled old woman, I thought at first. Then I saw it was a very aged man. His teeth had not been trans-rooted and his vision seemed faint. I was amazed that he did not salute me—like myself, he certainly appeared to be a centagenerian—but I attributed this to the incompetence of his eyes, which wore their lids like hunched capes.

"Not many folks around here nowadays," I said. "People keep away from the old Preserved Cemeteries. My view is these youngsters are morbid. Afraid of the waste. They have to use everything. We weren't morbid in our time, hah?"

He did not answer. I suspected it was deliberate.

"Take this one," I said, in my most cordial manner, inviting his friendship. "This thing right here." I gave the little stone a good knock, taking the risk of arrest by the Outdoor Museum Force. Apparently no one saw. I knocked it again with the side of my knuckle. "I actually knew this fellow. He was famous in his day. A big celebrity. That young Chinese fellow, the one who just came back from flying around the edge of the Milky

Way, well, the fuss they made over *him*, that's how it was with this fellow. This one was literary, though."

He did not answer; he spat on the part of the stone I had touched, as if to wash it.

"You knew him too?" I said.

He gave me his back—it was shaking horribly—and minced away. He looked shriveled but of a good size still; he was uncommonly ragged. His clothing dragged behind him as though the covering over the legs hobbled him; yet there was a hint of threadbare flare at his ankle. It almost gave me the sense that he was wearing an ancient woman's garment, of the kind in fashion seventy years ago. He had on queer old-fashioned woman's shoes with long thin heels like poles. I took off after him—I am not slow, considering my years—and slid my gaze all over his face. It was a kettle of decay. He was carrying a red stick—it seemed to be a denuded lady's umbrella (an apparatus no longer known among us)—and he held it up to strike.

"Listen here," I said hotly, "what's the matter with you? Can't you pass a companionable word? I'll just yell for the Museum Force, you and that stick, if you don't watch it—"

"I watch it," he said. His voice burst up and broke like boiling water—it sounded vaguely foreign. "I watch it all the time. That's my monument, and believe you me I watch it. I won't have anyone else watch it either. See what it says there? 'I am a man.' You keep away from it."

"I'll watch what I please. You're no more qualified than I am," I said.

"To be a man? I'll show you," he retorted, full of malice, his stick still high. "Name's Gate, same as on that stone. That's my stone. They don't make 'em any more. *You'll* do without."

Now this was a sight: madness has not appeared in our society for over two generations. All forms of such illness have vanished these days, and if any pops up through some genetic mishap it is soon eliminated by Electromed Procedure. I had not met a madman since I was sixty years old.

"Who do you say you are?" I asked him.

"Gate, born Gatoff. Edmund, born Elia."

This startled me: it was a refinement of information not on the monument.

"Edmund Gate's dead," I said. "You must be a literary historian to know a point like that. I knew him personally myself. Nobody's heard of him now, but he was a celebrated man in my day. A poet."

"Don't tell *me*," the madman said.

"He jumped off a bridge dead drunk."

"That's what you think. That so, where's the body? I ask you."

"Under that stone. Pile of bones by now."

"I thought it was in the river. Did anybody ever pull it out of the river, hah? You've got a rotten memory, and you look roughly my age, boy. My memory is perfect: I can remember perfectly and I can forget perfectly. That's my stone, boy. I survived to see it. That stone's all there's left of Edmund Gate." He peered at me as though it pained him. "He's dead, y'know."

"Then you can't be him," I told the madman; genuine madmen always contradict themselves.

"Oh yes I can! I'm no dead poet, believe you me. I'm what survived him. He was succeeded by a woman, y'know. Crazy old woman. Don't tell *me*."

He raised his bright stick and cracked it down on my shoulder. Then he slipped off, trembling and wobbling in his funny shoes, among the other monuments of the Preserved Cemetery.

He had never once recognized me. If it had really been Elia, he would certainly have known my face. That is why I am sure I have actually met a genuine madman for the first time in over forty years. The Museum Force at my request has made an indefatigable search of the Cemetery area, but up to this writing not so much as his pointed heel-print has been discovered. They do not doubt my word, however, despite my heavy age; senility has been eliminated from our modern society.

Bloodshed

BLEILIP TOOK A Greyhound bus out of New York and rode through icy scenes half-urban and half-countrified until he arrived at the town of the hasidim. He had intended to walk, but his coat pockets were heavy, so he entered a loitering taxi. Though it was early on a Sunday afternoon he saw no children at all. Then he remembered that they would be in the yeshivas until the darker slant of the day. Yeshivas not yeshiva: small as the community was, it had three or four schools, and still others, separate, for the little girls. Toby and Yussel were waiting for him and waved his taxi down the lumpy road above their half-built house—it was a new town, and everything in it was new or promised: pavements, trash cans, septic tanks, newspaper stores. But just because everything was unfinished, you could sniff rawness, the opened earth meaty and scratched up as if by big animal claws, the frozen puddles in the basins of ditches fresh-smelling, mossy.

Toby he regarded as a convert. She was just barely a relative, a third or fourth cousin, depending on how you counted, whether from his mother or from his father, who were also cousins to each other. She came from an ordinary family, not especially known for its venturesomeness, but now she looked to him altogether uncommon, freakish: her bun was a hairpiece pinned on, over it she wore a bandanna (a *tcheptichke*, she called it), her sleeves stopped below her wrists, her dress was outlandishly long. With her large red face over this costume she almost passed for some sort of peasant. Though still self-reliant, she had become like all their women.

She served him orange juice. Bleilip, feeling his bare bald head, wondered whether he was expected to say the blessing, whether they would thrust a headcovering on him: he was baffled, confused, but Yussel said, "You live your life and I'll live mine, do what you like," so he drank it all down quickly. Relief made him thirsty, and he drank more and more from a big can with pictures of sweating oranges on it—some things they bought at a supermarket like all mortals.

"So," he said to Toby, "how do you like your *shtetl*?"

She laughed and circled a finger around at the new refrigerator, vast-shouldered, gleaming, a presence. "What a village we are! A backwater!"

"State of mind," he said, "that's what I meant."

"Oh, state of mind. What's that?"

"Everything here feels different," was all he could say.

"We're in pieces, that's why. When the back rooms are put together we'll seem more like a regular house."

"The carpenter," Yussel said, "works only six months a year—we got started with him a month before he stopped. So we have to wait."

"What does he do the rest of the year?"

"He teaches."

"He teaches?"

"He trades with Shmulka Gershons. The other half of the year Shmulka Gershons lays pipes. Six months *Gemara* with the boys, six months on the job. Mr. Horowitz the carpenter also."

Bleilip said uncertainly, meaning to flatter, "It sounds like a wonderful system."

"It's not a *system*," Yussel said.

"Yussel goes everywhere, a commuter," Toby said: Yussel was a salesman for a paper-box manufacturer. He wore a small trimmed beard, very black, black-rimmed eyeglasses, and a vest over a rounding belly. Bleilip saw that Yussel liked him—he led him away from Toby and showed him the new hot air furnace in the cellar, the gas-fired hot water tank, the cinder blocks piled in the yard, the deep cuts above the road where the sewer pipes would go. He pointed over a little wooded crest—they could just see a bit of unpainted roof. "That's our yeshiva, the one our boys go to. It's not the toughest, they're not up to it. They weren't good enough. In the other yeshiva in the city they didn't give them enough work. Here," he said proudly, "they go from seven till half-past six."

They went back into the house by the rear door. Bleilip believed in instant rapport and yearned for closeness—he wanted to be close, close. But Yussel was impersonal, a guide, he froze Bleilip's vision. They passed through the bedrooms and again it seemed to Bleilip that Yussel was a real estate agent, a bureaucrat, a tourist office. There were a few shelves of books—holy books, nothing frivolous—but no pictures on the walls, no radio anywhere, no television set. Bleilip had brought with him, half-furtively, a snapshot of Toby taken eight or nine years before: Toby squatting on the grass at Brooklyn College, short curly hair with a barrette glinting in it, high socks and loafers, glimpse of panties, wispy blouse blurred by wind, a book with its title clear to the camera: Political Science. He offered this to Yussel: "A classmate." Yussel looked at the wall. "Why do I need an image? I have my wife right in front of me every morning." Toby held the wallet, saw, smiled, gave it back. "Another life," she said.

Bleilip reminded her, "The joke was which would be the bigger breakthrough, the woman or the Jew—" To Yussel he explained, "She used to say she would be the first lady Jewish President."

"Another life, other jokes," Toby said.

"And this life? Do you like it so much?"

"Why do you keep asking? Don't you like your own life?"

Bleilip liked his life, he liked it excessively. He felt he was part of society-at-large. He told her, without understanding why he was saying such a thing, "Here there's nothing to mock at, no jokes."

"You said we're a village," she contradicted.

"That wasn't mockery."

"It wasn't, you meant it. You think we're fanatics, primitives."

"Leave the man be," Yussel said. He had a cashier's tone, guide counting up the day's take, and Bleilip was grieved, because Yussel was a survivor, everyone in the new town, except one or two oddities like Toby, was a survivor of the deathcamps or the child of a survivor. "He's looking for something. He wants to find. He's not the first and he won't be the last." The rigid truth of this—Bleilip had thought his purposes darkly hidden—shocked him. He hated accuracy in a survivor. It was an affront. He wanted some kind of haze, a nostalgia for suffering perhaps. He resented the orange juice can, the appliances, the furnace, the sewer pipes. "He's been led to expect saints," Yussel said. "Listen, Jules," he said, "I'm not a saint and Toby's not a saint and we don't have miracles and we don't have a rebbe who works miracles."

"You have a rebbe," Bleilip said; instantly a wash of blood filled his head.

"He can't fly. What we came here for was to live a life of study. Our own way, and not to be interrupted in it."

"For the man, not the woman. You, not Toby. Toby used to be smart. Achievement goals and so forth."

"Give the mother of four sons a little credit too, it's not only college girls who build the world," Yussel said in a voice so fair-minded and humorous and obtuse that Bleilip wanted to knock him down—the first lady Jewish President of the United States had succumbed in her junior year to the zealot's private pieties, rites, idiosyncrasies. Toby was less than lucid, she was crazy to follow deviants, not in the mainstream even of their own tradition. Bleilip, who had read a little, considered these hasidim actually christologized: everything had to go through a mediator. Of their popular romantic literature he knew the usual bits and pieces, legends, occult passions, quirks, histories—he had heard, for instance, about the holiday the Lubavitcher hasidim celebrate on the anniversary of their master's release from prison: pretty stories in the telling, even more touching in the reading—poetry. Bleilip, a lawyer though not in practice, an ex-labor consultant, a fund-raiser by profession, a rationalist, a *mitnagid* (he scarcely knew the word), purist, skeptic, enemy of fresh revelation, enemy of the hasidim!—repelled by the sects themselves, he was nevertheless lured by their constituents. Refugees, survivors. He supposed they had a certain knowledge the unscathed could not guess at.

He said: "Toby makes her bed, she lies in it. I didn't come expecting women's rights and God knows I didn't come expecting saints."

"If not saints then martyrs," Yussel said.

Bleilip said nothing. This was not the sort of closeness he coveted—he shunned being seen into. His intention was to be a benefactor of the feelings. He glimpsed Yussel's tattoo-number (it almost seemed as if Yussel just then lifted his wrist to display it) without the compassion he had schemed for it. He had come to see a town of dead men. It spoiled Bleilip's mood that Yussel understood this.

At dusk the three of them went up to the road to watch the boys slide down the hill from the yeshiva. There was no danger: not a single car, except Bleilip's taxi, had passed through all day. The snow was a week old, it was coming on to March, the air struck like a bell-clapper, but Bleilip could smell through the cold something different from the smell of winter. Smoke of woodfire seeped into his throat from somewhere with a deep pineyness that moved him: he had a sense of farness, clarity, other lands, displaced seasons, the brooks of a village, a foreign bird piercing. The yeshiva boys came down on their shoe-soles, one foot in front of the other, lurching, falling, rolling. A pair of them tobogganed past on a garbage-can lid. The rest jostled, tumbled, squawked, their yarmulkas dropping from their heads into the snow like gumdrops, coins, black inkwells. Bleilip saw hoops of halos wheeling everywhere, and he saw their ear-curls leaping over their cheeks, and all at once he penetrated into what he took to be the truth of this place—the children whirling on the hillside were false children, made of no flesh, it was a crowd of ghosts coming down, a clamor of white smoke beat on the road. Yussel said, "I'm on my way to *mincha*, want to come?" Bleilip's grandfather, still a child but with an old man's pitted nose, appeared to be flying toward him on the lid. The last light of day split into blue rays all around them; the idea of going for evening prayer seemed natural to him now, but Bleilip, privately elated, self-proud, asked, "Why, do you need someone?"—because he was remembering what he had forgotten he knew. Ten men. He congratulated his memory, also of his grandfather's nose, thin as an arrow—the nose, the face, the body, all gone into the earth—and he went on piecing together his grandfather's face, tan teeth that gave out small clicks and radiated stale farina, shapely gray half-moon eyes with fleshy lids, eyebrows sparse as a woman's, a prickly whiskbroom of a mustache whiter than cream. Yussel took him by the arm: "Pessimist, joker, here we never run short, a *minyan* always without fail, but come, anyhow you'll hear the rebbe, it's our turn for him." Briefly behind them Bleilip saw Toby moving into the dark of the door, trailed by two pairs of boys with golden earlocks: he felt the shock of that sight, as if a beam of divinity had fixed on her head, her house. But in an instant he was again humiliated by the sting of Yussel's eye—"She'll give them supper," he said merely, "then they have homework." "You people make them work." "Honey on the page is only for the beginning," Yussel said, "afterward comes hard learning."

Bleilip accepted a cap for his cold-needled skull and they toiled on the ice upward toward the schoolhouse: the rebbe gave himself each week to a different *minyan*. When Bleilip reached for a prayer-shawl inside a cardboard box Yussel thumbed a No at him, so he dropped it in again. No one else paid him any attention. Through the window the sky deepened; the shouts were gone from the hill. Yussel handed him a *sidur*, but the alphabet was jumpy and strange to him: it needed piecing together, like his grandfather's visage. He stood up when the others did. Then he sat down again, fitting his haunches into a boy's chair. It did not seem to him that they sang out with any special fervor, as he had read the hasidim did, but the sounds were loud, cadenced, earnest. The leader, unlike the others a mutterer, was the single one wearing the fringed shawl—it made a cave for him, he looked out of it without mobility of heart. Bleilip turned his stare here and there into the tedium—which was the rebbe? He went after a politician's face: his analogy was to the mayor of a town. Or a patriarch's face—the father of a large family. They finished *mincha* and herded themselves into a corner of the room—a long table (three planks nailed together, two sawhorses) covered by a cloth. The cloth was grimy: print lay on it, the backs of old *sidurim*, rubbing, shredding, the backs of the open hands of the men. Bleilip drew himself in; he found a wooden folding chair and wound his legs into the rungs, away from the men. It stunned him that they were not old, but instead mainly in the forties, plump and in their prime. Their cheeks were blooming hillocks above their beards; some wore yarmulkas, some tall black hats, some black hats edged with fur, some ordinary fedoras pushed back, one a workman's cap. Their mouths especially struck him as extraordinary—vigorous, tender, blessed. He marveled at their mouths until it came to him that they were speaking another language and that he could follow only a little of it: now and then it was almost as if their words were visibly springing out of their mouths, like flags or streamers. Whenever he understood the words the flags whipped at him, otherwise they collapsed and vanished with a sort of hum. Bleilip himself was a month short of forty-two, but next to these pious men he felt like a boy; even his shoulder-blades weakened and thinned. He made himself concentrate: he heard *azazel*, and he heard *kohen gadol*, they were knitting something up, mixing strands of holy tongue with Yiddish. The noise of Yiddish in his ear enfeebled him still more, like Titus's fly—it was not an everyday language with him, except to make cracks with, jokes, gags. . . . His dead grandfather hung from the ceiling on a rope. Wrong, mistaken, impossible, uncharacteristic of his grandfather!—who died old and safe in a Bronx bed, mischief-maker, eager aged imp. The imp came to life and swung over Bleilip's black corner. Here ghosts sat as if already in the World-to-Come, explicating Scripture. Or whatever. Who knew? In his grandfather's garble the hasidim (refugees, dead men) were crying out Temple, were crying out High Priest, and the more Bleilip squeezed his brain toward them, the more he comprehended. Five times on the tenth day of the seventh month, the Day of Atonement, the High Priest changes his vestments, five times he lowers his body into the ritual bath. After the first immersion garments of gold, after the second immersion white linen, and wearing the white linen he confesses his sins and the sins of his household while holding on to the horns of a bullock. Walking eastward, he goes from the west of the altar to the north of the altar, where two goats stand, and he casts lots for the goats: one for the Lord, one for Azazel, and the one for the Lord is given a necklace of red wool and will be slaughtered and its blood caught in a bowl, but first the bullock will be slaughtered and its blood caught in a bowl; and once more he confesses his sins and the sins of his household, and now also the sins of the children of Aaron, this holy people. The blood of the bullock is sprinkled eight times, both upward and downward, the blood of the goat is sprinkled eight times, then the High Priest comes to the goat who was not slaughtered, the one for Azazel, and now he touches it and confesses the sins of the whole house of Israel, and utters the name of God, and pronounces the people cleansed of sin. And Bleilip, hearing all this through the web of a language gone stale in his marrow, was scraped to the edge of pity and belief, he pitied the hapless goats, the unlucky bullock, but more than this he pitied the God of Israel, whom he saw as an imp with a pitted nose dangling on a cord from the high beams of the Temple in Jerusalem, winking down at His tiny High Priest—now he leaps in and out of a box of water, now he hurries in and out of new clothes like a quick-change vaudevillian, now he sprinkles red drops up and red drops down, and all the while Bleilip, together with the God of the Jews, pities these toy children of Israel in the Temple long ago. Pity upon pity. What God could take the Temple rites seriously? What use does the King of the Universe have for goats? What, leaning on their dirty tablecloth—no vestments, altars, sacrifices—what do these survivors, exemptions, expect of God now?

All at once Bleilip knew which was the rebbe. The man in the work-cap, with a funny flat nose, black-haired and red-bearded, fist on mouth, elbows sunk into his lap—a self-stabber: in all that recitation, those calls and streamers of discourse, this blunt-nosed man had no word: but now he stood up, scratched his chair backward, and fell into an ordinary voice. Bleilip examined him: he looked fifty, his hands were brutish, two fingers missing, the nails on the others absent. A pair of muscles bunched in his neck like chains. The company did not breathe and gave him something more than attentiveness. Bleilip reversed his view and saw that the rebbe was their child, they gazed at him with the possessiveness of faces seized by a crib, and he too spoke in that mode, as if he were addressing parents, old fathers, deferential, awed, guilty. And still he was their child, and still he owed them his guilt. He said: "And what comes next? Next we read that the *kohen gadol* gives the goat fated for Azazel to one of the *kohanim*, and the *kohen* takes it out into a place all bare and wild, with a big cliff in the middle of it all, and he cuts off a bit of the red wool they had put on it, and ties it onto a piece of rock to mark the place, and then he drives the goat over the edge and it spins down, down, down, and is destroyed. But in the Temple the worship may not continue, not until it is known that the goat is already given over to the wilderness. How can they know this miles away in the far city? All along the way from the wilderness to Jerusalem, poles stand up out of the ground, and on top of every pole a man, and in the hand of every man a great shawl to shake out, so that pole flies out a wing to pole, wing after wing, until it comes to the notice of the *kohen gadol* in the Temple that the goat has been dashed into the ravine. And only then can the *kohen gadol* finish his readings, his invocations, his blessings, his beseechings. In the neighborhood of Sharon often there are earthquakes: the *kohen gadol* says: let their homes not become their graves. And after all this a procession, no, a parade, a celebration, all the people follow the *kohen gadol* to his own house, he is safe out of the Holy of Holies, their sins are atoned for, they are cleansed and healed, and they sing how like a flower he is, a lily, like the moon, the sun, the morning star among clouds, a dish of gold, an olive tree. . . . That, gentlemen, is how it was in the Temple, and how it will be again after the coming of Messiah. We learn it"—he tapped his book—"in *Mishna Yoma, Yoma*—Targum for Day, *yom hakipurim*, but whose is the atonement, whose is the cleansing? Does the goat for Azazel atone, does the *kohen gadol* cleanse and hallow us? No, only the Most High can cleanse, only we ourselves can atone. Rabbi Akiva reminds us: 'Who is it that makes you clean? Our Father in Heaven.' So why, gentlemen, do you suppose the Temple was even then necessary, why the goats, the bullock, the blood? Why is it necessary for all of this to be restored by Messiah? These are questions we must torment ourselves with. Which of us would slaughter an animal, not for sustenance, but for an idea? Which of us would dash an animal to its death? Which of us would not feel himself to be a sinner in doing so? Or feel the shame of Esau? You may say that those were other days, the rituals are obsolete, we are purer now, better, we do not sprinkle blood so readily. But in truth you would not say so, you would not lie. For animals we in our day substitute men. What the word Azazel means exactly is not known—we call it wilderness, some say it is hell itself, demons live there. But whatever we mean by 'wilderness,' whatever we mean by 'hell,' surely the plainest meaning is *instead of.* Wilderness instead of easeful places, hell and devils instead of plenitude, life, peace. Goat instead of man. Was there no one present in the Temple who, seeing the animals in all their majesty of health, shining hair, glinting hooves, timid nostrils, muscled like ourselves, gifted with tender eyes no different from our own, the whole line creature trembling—was there no one there when the knife slit the fur and skin and the blood fled upward who did not feel the splendor of the living beast? Who was not in awe of the miracle of life turned to carcass? Who did not think: *how like that goat I am! The goat goes, I stay, the goat instead of me.* Who did not see in the goat led to Azazel his own destiny? Death takes us too at random, some at the altar, some over the cliff. . . . Gentlemen, we are this moment so to speak in the Temple, the Temple devoid of the Holy of Holies—when the Temple was destroyed it forsook the world, so the world itself had no recourse but to pretend to be the Temple by mockery. In the absence of Messiah there can be no *kohen gadol,* we have no authority to bless multitudes, we are not empowered, we cannot appeal except for ourselves, ourselves alone, in isolation, in futility, instead we are like the little goats, we are assigned our lot, we are designated for the altar or for Azazel, in either case we are meant to be cut down. . . . O little fathers, we cannot choose, we are driven, we are not free, we are only *instead of*: we stand *instead of,* instead of choice we have the yoke, instead of looseness we are pointed the way to go, instead of freedom we have the red cord around our throats, we were in villages, they drove us into camps, we were in trains, they drove us into showers of poison, in the absence of Messiah the secular ones made a nation, enemies bite at it. All that we do without Messiah is in vain. When the Temple forsook the world, and the world presumed to mock the Temple, everyone on earth became a goat or a bullock, he-animal or she-animal, all our prayers are bleats and neighs on the way to a forsaken altar, a teeming Azazel. Little fathers! How is it possible to live? When will Messiah come? You! You! Visitor! You're looking somewhere else, who are you not to look?"

He was addressing Bleilip—he pointed a finger without a nail.

"Who are you? Talk and look! Who!"

Bleilip spoke his own name and shook: a schoolboy in a schoolroom. "I'm here with the deepest respect, Rabbi. I came out of interest for your community."

"We are not South Sea islanders, sir, our practices are well known since Sinai. You don't have to turn your glance. We are not something new in the world."

"Excuse me, Rabbi, not new—unfamiliar."

"To you."

"To me," Bleilip admitted.

"Exactly my question! Who are you, what do you represent, what are you to us?"

"A Jew. Like yourselves. One of you."

"Presumption! Atheist, devourer! For us there is the Most High, joy, life. For us trust! But you! A moment ago I spoke your own heart for you, *emes?*"

Bleilip knew this word: truth, true, but he was only a visitor and did not want so much: he wanted only what he needed, a certain piece of truth, not too big to swallow. He was afraid of choking on more. The rebbe said, "You believe the world is in vain, *emes?*"

"I don't follow any of that, I'm not looking for theology—"

"Little fathers," said the rebbe, "everything you heard me say, everything you heard me say in a voice of despair, emanates from the liver of this man. My mouth made itself his parrot. My teeth became his beak. He fills the study-house with a black light, as if he keeps a lump of radium inside his belly. He would eat us up. Man he equates with the goats. The Temple, in memory and anticipation, he considers an abattoir. The world he regards as a graveyard. You are shocked, Mister Bleilip, that I know your kidneys, your heart? Canker! Onset of cholera! You say you don't come for 'theology,' Mister Bleilip, and yet you have a particular conception of us, *emes?* A certain idea."

Bleilip wished himself mute. He looked at Yussel, but Yussel had his eyes on his sleeve-button.

"Speak in your own language, please"—Bleilip was unable to do anything else—"and I will understand you very well. Your idea about us, please. Stand up!"

Bleilip obeyed. That he obeyed bewildered him. The crescents of faces in profile on either side of him seemed sharp as scythes. His yarmulka fell off his head but, rising, he failed to notice it—one of the men quickly clapped it back on. The stranger's palm came like a blow.

"Your idea," the rebbe insisted.

"Things I've heard," Bleilip croaked. "That in the Zohar it's written how Moses coupled with the Shekhina on Mount Sinai. That there are books to cast lots by, to tell fortunes, futures. That some Rabbis achieved levitation, hung in air without end, made babies come in barren women, healed miraculously. That there was once a Rabbi who snuffed out the Sabbath light. Things," Bleilip said, "I suppose legends."

"Did you hope to witness any of these things?"

Bleilip was silent.

"Then let me again ask. Do you credit any of these things?"

"Do you?" asked Bleilip.

Yussel intervened: "Forbidden to mock the rebbe!"

But the rebbe replied, "I do not believe in magic. That there are influences I do believe."

Bleilip felt braver. "Influences?"

"Turnings. That a man can be turned from folly, error, wrong choices. From misery, evil, private rage. From a mistaken life."

Now Bleilip viewed the rebbe; he was suspicious of such hands. The hands a horror: deformity, mutilation: caught in what machine?—and above them the worker's cap. But otherwise the man seemed simple, reasoned, balanced, after certain harmonies, sanities, the ordinary article, no mystic, a bit bossy, pedagogue, noisy preacher. Bleilip, himself a man with a profession and no schoolboy after all, again took heart. A commonplace figure. People did what he asked, nothing more complicated than this—but he had to ask. Or tell, or direct. A monarch perhaps. A community needs to be governed. A human relationship: of all words Bleilip, whose vocabulary was habitually sociological, best of all liked "relationship."

He said, "I don't have a mistaken life."

"Empty your pockets."

Bleilip stood without moving.

"Empty your pockets!"

"Rabbi, I'm not an exercise, I'm not a demonstration—"

"Despair must be earned."

"I'm not in despair," Bleilip objected.

"To be an atheist is to be in despair."

"I'm not an atheist, I'm a secularist," but even Bleilip did not know what he meant by this.

"Esau! For the third time: empty your pockets!"

Bleilip pulled the black plastic thing out and threw it on the table. Instantly all the men bent away from it.

"A certain rebbe," said the rebbe very quietly, "believed every man should carry two slips of paper in his pockets. In one pocket should be written: 'I am but dust and ashes.' In the other: 'For my sake was the world created.' This canker fills only one pocket, and with ashes." He picked up Bleilip's five-and-ten gun and said "Esau! Beast! Lion! To whom did you intend to do harm?"

"Nobody," said Bleilip out of his shame. "It isn't real. I keep it to get used to. The feel of the thing. Listen," he said, "do you think it's easy for me to carry that thing around and keep on thinking about it?"

The rebbe tried the trigger. It gave out a tin click. Then he wrapped it in his handkerchief and put it in his pocket. "We will now proceed with *ma'ariv*," he said. "The study hour is finished. Let us not learn more of this matter. This is Jacob's tent."

The men left the study table and took up their old places, reciting. Bleilip, humiliated (the analogy to a teacher confiscating a forbidden toy was too exact), still excited, the tremor in his groin worse, was in awe before this incident. Was it amazing chance that the rebbe had challenged the contents of his pockets, or was he a seer? At the conclusion of *ma'ariv* the men dispersed quickly; Bleilip recognized from Yussel's white stare that this was not the usual way. He felt like an animal they were running from. He intended to run himself—all the way to the Greyhound station—but the rebbe came to him. "You," he said (*du*, as if to an animal, or to a child, or to God), "the other pocket. The second one. The other side of your coat."

"What?"

"Disgorge."

So Bleilip took it out. And just as the toy gun could instantly be seen to be a toy, all tin glint, so could this one be seen for what it was: monstrous, clumsy and hard, heavy, with a scarred trigger and a barrel that smelled. Dark, no gleam. An actuality, a thing for use. Yussel moaned, dipping his head up and down. "In my house! Stood in front of my wife with it! With two!"

"With one," said the rebbe. "One is a toy and one not, so only one need be feared. It is the toy we have to fear: the incapable—"

Yussel broke in, "We should call the police, rebbe."

"Because of a toy? How they will laugh."

"But the other! This!"

"Is it capable?" the rebbe asked Bleilip.

"Loaded, you mean? Sure it's loaded."

"Loaded, you hear him?" Yussel said. "He came as a curiosity-seeker, rebbe, my wife's cousin, I had no suspicion of this—"

The rebbe said, "Go home, Yussel. Go home, little father."

"Rebbe, he can shoot—"

"How can he shoot? The instrument is in my hand."

It was. The rebbe held the gun—the real one. Again Bleilip was drawn to those hands. This time the rebbe saw. "Buchenwald," he said. "Blocks of ice, a freezing experiment. In my case only to the elbow, but others were immersed wholly and perished. The fingers left are toy fingers. That is why you have been afraid of them and have looked away."

He said all this very clearly, in a voice without an opinion.

"Don't talk to him, rebbe!"

"Little father, go home."

"And if he shoots?"

"He will not shoot."

Alone in the schoolhouse with the rebbe—how dim the bulbs, dangling on cords—Bleilip regretted that because of the dishonor of the guns. He was pleased that the rebbe had dismissed Yussel. The day (but now it was night) felt full of miracles and lucky chances. Thanks to Yussel he had gotten to the rebbe. He never supposed he would get to the rebbe himself—all his hope was only for a glimpse of the effect of the rebbe. Of influences. With these he was satisfied. He said again, "I don't have a mistaken life."

The rebbe enclosed the second gun in his handkerchief. "This one has a bad odor."

"Once I killed a pigeon with it."

"A live bird?"

"You believers," Bleilip threw out, "you'd cut up those goats all over again if you got the Temple back!"

"Sometimes," the rebbe said, "even the rebbe does not believe. My father when he was the rebbe also sometimes did not believe. It is characteristic of believers sometimes not to believe. And it is characteristic of unbelievers sometimes to believe. Even you, Mister Bleilip—even you now and then believe in the Holy One, Blessed Be He? Even you now and then apprehend the Most High?"

"No," Bleilip said; and then: "Yes."

"Then you are as bloody as anyone," the rebbe said (it was his first real opinion), and with his terrible hands put the bulging white handkerchief on the table for Bleilip to take home with him, for whatever purpose he thought he needed it.

Shots

I CAME TO photography as I came to infatuation—with no special talent for it, and with no point of view. Taking pictures —when *I* take them, I mean—has nothing to do with art and less to do with reality. I'm blind to what intelligent people call "composition," I revile every emanation of "grain," and any drag through a gallery makes me want to die. As for the camera as *machine*—well, I know the hole I have to look through, and I know how to press down with my finger. The rest is thingama- jig. What brought me to my ingenious profession was no idea of the Photograph as successor to the Painting, and no pleasure in darkrooms, or in any accumulation of clanking detritus.

Call it necrophilia. I have fallen in love with corpses. Dead faces draw me. I'm uninformed about the history of pho- tography—1832, the daguerreotype, mercury vapor; what an annoyance that so blatant a thing as picture-taking is consid- ered worth applying a history to!—except to understand how long a past the camera has, measured by a century-old length of a woman's skirt. People talk of inventing a time machine, as if it hadn't already been invented in the box and shutter. I have been ravished by the last century's faces, now motes in their graves—such lost eyes, and noses, and mouths, and earlobes, and dress-collars: my own eyes soak these up; I can never leave off looking at anything brown and brittle and old and decaying at the edges.

The autumn I was eleven I found the Brown Girl. She was under a mound of chestnut-littered leaves near five tall trash barrels in a corner of the yard behind the Home for the Elderly Female Ill. Though the old-lady inmates were kept confined to a high balcony above the browning grass of their bleak over- grown yard, occasionally I would see some witless half-bald refugee shuffling through a weed-sea with stockings rolled midway down a sinewy blue calf engraved by a knotted garter. They scared me to death, these sticks and twigs of brainless ancients, rattling their china teeth and howling at me in foreign tongues, rolling the bright gems of their mad old eyes inside their nearly visible crania. I used to imagine that if one of these fearful witches could just somehow get beyond the gate, she would spill off garters and fake teeth and rheumy eye-whites and bad smells and stupid matted old flesh, and begin to bloom all plump and glowing and ripe again: Shangri-La in reverse.

What gave me this imagining was the Brown Girl. Any one of these pitiful decaying sacks might once have been the Brown Girl. If only someone had shot a kind of halt-arrow through the young nipples of the Brown Girl at the crest of her years, if only she had been halted, arrested, stayed in her ripeness and savor!

The Brown Girl lived. She lay in a pile of albums dumped into the leaves. It seemed there were hundreds of her: a girl in a dress that dropped to the buttons of her shoes, with an arched bosom and a hint of bustle, and a face mysteriously shut: you never once saw her teeth, you never once saw the lips in anything like the hope of a smile; laughter was out of the question. A grave girl; a sepia girl; a girl as brown as the ground. She must have had her sorrows.

Gradually (to my eyes suddenly) I saw her age. It wasn't that the plain sad big-nosed face altered: no crinkles at the lids, no grooves digging out a distinct little parallelogram from nostril-sides to mouth-ends—or, if these were in sight, they weren't what I noticed. The face faded out—became not there. The woman turned to ghost. The ghost wore different clothes now, too familiar to gape at. The fingers were ringless. The eyes whitened off. Somehow for this melancholy spinster's sake the first rule of the box camera was always being violated: not to put the sun behind your subject. A vast blurred drowning orb of sun flooded massively, habitually down from the upper right corner of her picture. Whoever photographed her, over years and years and years, meant to obliterate her. But I knew it was no sun-bleach that conspired to efface her. What I was seeing— what I *had* seen—was time. And not time on the move, either, the illusion of stories and movies. What I had seen was time as stasis, time at the standstill, time at the fix; the time (though I hadn't yet reached it in school) of Keats's Grecian urn. The face faded out because death was coming: death the changer, the collapser, the witherer; death the bleacher, blancher, whitener.

The truth is, I'm looked on as a close-mouthed professional, serious about my trade, who intends to shut up and keep secrets when necessary. I repel all "technical" questions—if someone wants to discuss the make of my camera (it's Japanese), or my favorite lens, or some trick I might have in developing, or what grade of paper I like, I'll stare her down. Moonings on Minor White's theories I regard as absolutely demeaning. I have a grasp on what I am about, and it isn't any of that.

What it is, is the Brown Girl. I kept her. I kept her, I mean, in a pocket of my mind (and one of her pictures in the pocket of my blouse); I kept her because she was dead. What I expect you to take from this is that I *could* keep her *even though* she was dead. I wasn't infatuated by her (not that she was the wrong sex: infatuation, like any passion of recognition, neglects gender); she was too oppressed and brown and quiet for that. But it was she who gave me the miraculous hint: a hint derived from no science of mechanics or physics, a rapturous hint on the other side of art, beyond metaphor, deep in the wonderfully literal. What she made me see was that if she wasn't a girl any more, if she wasn't a woman any more, if she was very likely not even a member of the elderly female ill any more (by the time her photos fell among the leaves, how long had she been lying under them?), still I *had* her, actually and physically and with the certainty of simple truth. I could keep her, just as she used to be, because someone had once looked through the bunghole of a box and clicked off a lever. Whoever had desultorily drowned her in too much sun had anyhow given her a monument two inches wide and three inches long. What happened then was here now. I had it in the pocket of my blouse.

Knowing this—that now will become then, that huge will turn little—doesn't cure. I walk around the wet streets with a historian now, a tenured professor of South American history: he doesn't like to go home to his wife. Somehow it always rains when we meet, and it's Sam's big blue umbrella, with a wooden horse's head for a handle, that preoccupies me this instant. Which is strange: he hasn't owned it for a whole year. It was left in a yellow garish coffee shop on the night side of a street you couldn't trust, and when Sam went back, only ten minutes later, to retrieve it, of course it wasn't there.

At that time I didn't care about one thing in Sam's mind. I had to follow him, on assignment, all through a course of some public symposia he was chairing. We had—temporarily—the same employer. His college was setting up a glossy little booklet for the State Department to win South American friends with: I had to shoot Sam on the podium with Uruguayans, Sam on the podium with Brazilians, Sam on the podium with Peruvians, and so forth. It was a lackluster job—I had just come, not so long ago, from photographing an intergalactic physicist whose bravest hope was the invention of an alphabet to shoot into the kindergartens of the cosmos—so it was no trouble at all not to listen to the speeches while I shot the principals. Half the speeches were in Portuguese or Spanish, and if you wanted to you could put on earphones anywhere in the hall and hear a simultaneous translation. The translator sat at the squat end of the long symposium table up on the stage with Sam and the others, but kept his microphone oddly close to his lips, like a kiss, sweat sliding and gleaming along his neck—it seemed he was tormented by that bifurcated concentration. His suffering attracted me. He didn't count as one of the principals—the celebrity of the day (now it was night, the last of the dark raining afternoon) was the vice-consul of Chile—but I shot him anyhow, for my own reasons: I liked the look of that shining sweat on his bulging Adam's apple. I calculated my aim (I'm very fast at this), shot once, shot again, and was amazed to see blood spring out of a hole in his neck. The audience fell apart— it was like watching an anthill after you've kicked into it; there was a spaghetti of wires and police; the simultaneous translator was dead: It made you listen for the simultaneous silence of the principal speaker, but the Chilean vice-consul only swerved his syllables into shrieks, with his coat over his head; he was walked away in a tremor between two colleagues suddenly sprouting guns. A mob of detectives took away my film; it was all I could do to keep them from arresting my camera: I went straight to Sam—it was his show—to complain. "That's *film* in there, not bullets." "It's evidence now," Sam said. "Who wanted to do that?" I said. "God knows," Sam said; "they didn't do what they wanted anyhow," and offered six political possibilities, each of which made it seem worthwhile for someone to do away with the Chilean vice-consul. He found his umbrella under the table and steered me out. The rain had a merciless wind in it, and every glassy sweep of it sent fountains spitting upward from the pavement. We stood for a while under his umbrella (he gripping the horse's head hard enough to whiten his knuckles) and watched them carry the simultaneous translator out. He was alone on a stretcher; his duality was done, his job as surrogate consummated. I reflected how quickly vertical becomes horizontal. "You knew him," I said.

"Only in a public way. He's been part of all these meetings."

"So have I," I said.

"I've watched you watching me."

I resisted this. "That's professional watching. It's more like stalking. I always stalk a bit before I shoot."

"You talk like a terrorist," Sam said, and began a history of South American conspiracy, which group was aligned with whom, who gave asylum, who withheld it, who the Chilean vice-consul's intimates across several borders were, at this instant plotting vengeance. He had exactly the kind of mentality—cumulative, analytical—I least admired, but since he also had the only umbrella in sight, I stuck with him. He was more interested in political factionalism—he had to get everything sorted out, and his fascination seemed to be with the victims—than in his having just sat two feet from a murder. "My God," I said finally, "doesn't the power of inaccuracy impress you? It could've been you on that stretcher."

"I don't suppose *you* ever miss your target," he said.

"No," I said, "but I don't shoot to kill."

"Then you're not one of those who want to change the

world," he said, and I could smell in this the odor of his melancholy. He was a melancholic and an egotist; this made me a bit more attentive. His umbrella, it appeared, was going to pilot him around for miles and miles; I went along as passenger. We turned at last into a coffee shop—this wasn't the place he lost the horse's head in—and then turned out again, heated up, ready for more weather. "Don't you ever go home?" I asked him.

"Don't you?"

"I live alone."

"I don't. I hate my life," he said.

"I don't blame you. You've stuffed it up with South American facts."

"Would you like North American facts better?"

"I can't take life in whole continents," I protested.

"The thing about taking it in continents is that you don't have to take it face by face."

"The faces are the best part."

"Some are the worst," Sam said.

I looked into his; he seemed a victim of factionalism himself, as if you become what you study. He had rather ferocious eyes, much too shiny, like something boiling in a pot—the ferocity made you think them black, but really they were pale—and black ripe rippled hair and unblemished orderly teeth, not white but near-white. "Which faces are the worst?"

"Now I'll go home," he said.

The murder had cut short the series of symposia; the South Americans scattered, which was too bad—they were Sam's source of vitality. But it never occurred to either of us that we might not meet again officially, and often enough we did—he on a platform, myself with camera. Whether this meant that all the magazine people I knew—the ones who were commissioning my pictures—were all at once developing a fevered concern for South American affairs (more likely it was for terrorism) is a boring question. I know I wasn't. I never wanted to listen to Sam on the subjects he was expert in, and I never did. I only caught what I thought of as their "moans"—impure and simmering and winnowing and sad. The sounds that came through his microphone were always intensely public: he was, his audience maintained—loyalists, they trotted after him from speech to speech—a marvelous generalist. He could go from predicting the demand for bauxite to tracing migrations of Indian populations, all in a single stanza. He could connect disparate packets of contemporary information with a linking historic insight that took your breath away. He was a very, very good public lecturer; all his claque said so. He could manage to make anyone (or everyone but me) care about South America. Still, I had a little trick in my head as he declaimed and as I popped my flashbulbs, not always at him—more often at the distinguished sponsors of the event. I could tell they were distinguished from the way they dragged me up to the dais to photograph them—it showed how important they were. Sometimes they wanted to be photographed just before Sam began, and sometimes, with their arms around him, when he was just finished, themselves grinning into Sam's applause. All the while I kept the little trick going.

The little trick was this: whatever he said that was vast and public and South American, I would simultaneously translate (I hoped I wouldn't be gunned down for it) into everything private and personal and secret. This required me to listen shrewdly to the moan behind the words—I had to blot out the words for the sake of the tune. Sometimes the tune would be civil or sweet or almost jolly—especially if he happened to get a look at me before he ascended to his lectern—but mainly it would be narrow and drab and resigned. I knew he had a wife, but I was already thirty-six, and who didn't have a wife by then? I wasn't likely to run into them if they didn't. Bachelors wouldn't be where I had to go, particularly not in public halls gaping at the per capita income of the interior villages of the Andes, or the future of Venezuelan oil, or the fortunes of the last Paraguayan bean crop, or the differences between the centrist parties in Bolivia and Colombia, or whatever it was that kept Sam ladling away at his tedious stew. I drilled through all these sober-shelled facts into their echoing gloomy melodies: and the sorrowful sounds I unlocked from their casings—it was like breaking open a stone and finding the music of the earth's wild core boiling inside—came down to the wife, the wife, the wife. That was the tune Sam was moaning all the while: wife wife wife. He didn't like her. He wasn't happy with her. His whole life was wrong. He was a dead man. If I thought I'd seen a dead man when they took that poor fellow out on that stretcher, I was stupidly mistaken; *he* was ten times deader than that. If the terrorist who couldn't shoot straight had shot *him* instead, he couldn't be more riddled with gunshot than he was this minute—he was smoking with his own death.

In the yellow garish coffee shop he went on about his wife— he shouldn't be telling me all this, my God, what the hell did he think he was doing; he was a fool; he was a cliché; he was out of a cartoon or an awful play; he was an embarrassment to himself and to me. It was either a trance or a seizure. And then he forgot his umbrella, and ran back after it, and it was gone. It wouldn't have had, necessarily, to be a desperate thief who stole his horse's head that night; it might easily have been a nice middle-class person like ourselves. A nice middle-class person especially would have hated to be out in such a drenching without a shred of defense overhead—Sam charged on into gales of cold rain, and made me charge onward too: for the first time he had me by the hand. I wouldn't let him keep it, though—I had to bundle my camera under my coat.

"How long are we going to walk in this?" I said.

"We'll walk and walk."

"I've got to go home or I'll soak my equipment," I complained.

"I'm not going home."

"Don't you ever go home?"

"My whole life is wrong," he said.

We spilled ourselves into another coffee place and sat there till closing. My shoes were seeping and seeping. He explained Verity: "I admire her," he said. "I esteem her, you wouldn't believe how I esteem that woman. She's a beautiful mother. She's strong and she's bright and she's independent and there's nothing she can't do."

"Now tell her good points," I said.

"She can fix a car. She always fixes the car. Puts her head into the hood and fixes it. She builds furniture. We live in a madhouse of excess property—she built every stick of it. She saws like a madwoman. She *sews* like a madwoman—I don't mean just *clothes*. She sews her own clothes and the girls' clothes too. What I mean is she *sews*—bedspreads and curtains and upholstery, even *car* upholstery. And she's got a whole budding career of her own. I've made her sound like a bull, but she's really very delicate at whatever she does—she does plates, you know."

"License plates?"

"She's done *some* metalwork—her minor was metallurgy—but what I'm talking about is ceramics. Porcelain. She does painted platters and pots and pitchers and sells them to Bloomingdale's."

"She's terrific," I said.

"She's terrific," he agreed. "There's nothing she can't do."

"Cook?"

"My God, *cook*," he said. "French, Italian, Indian, whatever you want. And bakes. Pastries, the difficult stuff, crusts made of cloud. She's a domestic genius. We have this big harp—hell, it was busted, a skeleton in a junk shop, so she bought it cheap and repaired it—she plays it like an angel. You think you're in heaven inside that hell. She plays the piano, too—classics, ragtime, rock. She's got a pretty nice singing voice. She's good at basketball—she practically never misses a shot. Don't ask me again if I admire her."

I asked him again if he admired her.

"I'm on my knees," he groaned. "She's a goddamn goddess. She's powerful and autonomous and a goddamn genius. Christ," he said, "I hate my life."

"If I had someone like that at home," I said, "I'd never be out in the rain."

"She could abolish the weather if she wanted to, only she doesn't want to. She has a terrific will."

I thought this over and was surprised by my sincerity: "You ought to go home," I told him.

"Let's walk."

After that we met more or less on purpose. The South American fad wore off—there was a let-up in guerrilla activity down there—and it got harder to find him in public halls, so I went up to his college now and then and sat in on his classes, and afterward, rain or shine, but mostly rain, we walked. He told me about his daughters—one of them was nearly as terrific as Verity herself—and we walked with our arms hooked. "Is something happening here?" I inquired. "Nothing will ever happen here," he said. We had a friend in common, the editor who'd assigned me to photographing that intergalactic physicist I've mentioned; it turned out we were asked, Sam with Verity, myself as usual, to the editor's party, in honor of the editor's ascension. There were some things the editor hadn't done which added immensely to his glory; and because of all the things he hadn't done they were making him vice-chancellor of Sam's college. I did justice to those illustrious gaps and omissions: I took the host, now majestic, and his wife, their children, their gerbil, their maid. I shot them embedded in their guests. I dropped all those pictures behind me like autumn leaves. I hadn't brought my usual Japanese spy, you see; I'd carried along a tacky Polaroid instead—instant development, a detective story without a detective, ah, I disliked that idea, but the evening needed its jester. I aimed and shot, aimed and shot, handing out portraits deciduously. Verity had her eye on all this promiscuity; she was blond and capacious and maybe capricious; she seemed without harm and without mercy.

"You're the one who shot the simultaneous translator," she said.

"Judicial evidence," I replied.

"Now let me," she said, "ask you something about your trade. In photography, do you consistently get what you expect?"

I said: "It's the same as life."

Verity expressed herself: "The viewfinder, the viewfinder!"

"I always look through that first," I admitted.

"And then do you get what you see? I mean can you predict exactly, or are you always surprised by what comes out?"

"I can never predict," I told her, "but I'm never surprised."

"That's fatalism," Verity said. Her voice was an iron arrow;

she put her forefinger into my cheek as humbly as a bride. "Talk about shots, here's a parting one. You take a shot at Sam, no expectations. He's not like life. He's safe. He's *good*."

He was safe and he was good: Sam the man of virtue. She knew everything exactly, even when everything was nothing she knew it exactly, she was without any fear at all; jealousy wasn't in her picture; she was more virtuous than he was, she was big, she had her great engine, she was her own cargo. And you see what it is with infatuation: it comes on you as quick as a knife. It's a bullet in the neck. It gets you from the outside. One moment you're in your prime of health, the next you're in anguish. Until then—until I had the chance to see for myself how clear and proud his wife was—Sam was an entertainment, not so entertaining after all. Verity was the Cupid of the thing, Verity's confidence the iron arrow that dragged me down. She had her big foot on her sour catch. I saw in her glow, in her sureness, in her pride, in her tall ship's prow of certitude, the plausibility of everything she knew: he'd have to go home in the end.

But the end's always at the end; in the meantime there's the meantime.

How to give over these middle parts? I couldn't see what I looked like, from then on, to Sam: all the same I had my automatic intelligence—light acting on a treated film. I was treated enough; Verity had daubed me. Since I was soaked in her solution, infatuation took, with me, a mechanical form— if you didn't know how mechanical it was, you would have imagined it was sly. I could listen now to everything Sam said. Without warning, I could *follow* him; I discovered myself in the act of wanting more. I woke up one morning in a fit of curiosity about the quantity of anthracite exports on the Brazilian littoral. I rooted in hard-to-find volumes of Bolívar's addresses. I penetrated the duskier hells of the public library and boned up on every banana republic within reach. It was astounding: all at once, and for no reason—I mean for *the* reason—Sam interested me. It was like walking on the lining of his brain.

On the South American issue he was dense as a statue. He had never noticed that I hadn't paid attention to his subject before; he didn't notice that I was attentive now. His premise was that everyone alive without exception was all the time infatuated with the former Spanish Empire. On *my* subject, though, Sam was trying; it was because of Verity; she had made him ambitious to improve himself with me.

"Verity saw at that party," he said, "that you had the kind of camera that gets you the picture right away."

"Not exactly right away. You have to wait a minute," I corrected.

"Why don't you use a camera like that all the time? It's magic. It's like a miracle."

"Practical reasons of the trade. The farther you are from having what you think you want, the more likely you are to get it. It's just that you have to wait. You really have to *wait*. What's important is the waiting."

Sam didn't get it. "But it's *chemistry*. The image is already on the film. It's the same image one minute later or two months later."

"You're too miracle-minded even for a historian," I admonished him. "It's not like that at all. If you have a change of heart between shooting your picture and taking it out of the developer, the picture changes too." I wanted to explain to him how, between the exposure and the solution, history comes into being, but telling that would make me bleed, like a bullet in the neck, so I said instead, "Photography is *literal*. It gets what's *there*."

Meanwhile the rain is raining on Sam and me. We meet in daylight now, and invent our own occasions. We hold hands, we hook arms, we walk through the park. There is a mole on his knuckle which has attached itself to my breathing; my lungs grasp all the air they can. I want to lay my tears on the hairs of his fingers. Because of the rain, the daylight is more like twilight; in this perpetual half of dusk, the sidewalks a kind of blackened purple, like fallen plums, we talk about the past and the future of the South American continent. Verity is in her house. I leave my camera behind too. Our faces are rivers, we walk without an umbrella, the leaves splash. When

I can't find Sam on my own, I telephone Verity; she stops the motor of her sewing machine and promises to give him the message when he returns. He comes flying out to meet me, straight from his Committee on Inter-American Conditions; I'm practically a colleague now, and a pleasure to talk to about Ecuadorian peonage. He tells me he's never had a mistress and never will; his wife is too remarkable. I ask him whether he's ever walked in a summer rain this way with anyone else. He admits he has; he admits it hasn't lasted. "The rain hasn't lasted? Or the feeling?" He forgets to answer. I remember that *he* is only interested; it's I who feel. We talk some more about the native religions still hiding out in the pampas; we talk about the Jewish gauchos in nineteenth-century Argentina. He takes it all for granted. He doesn't realize how hard I've had to study. A big leaf like a pitcher overturns itself all over our heads, and we make a joke about Ponce de León and the Fountain of Youth. I ask him then if he'll let me take his picture in the park, under a dripping linden tree, in a dangerous path, so that I can keep him forever, in case it doesn't last.

I see that he doesn't understand. He doesn't understand: unlike me, he's not under any special spell, he's not in thrall to any cult. That's the rub always—infatuation's unilateral or it doesn't count as real. I think he loves me—he may even be "in love"—but he's not caught like me. He'd never trace my life over as I've traced over his brain waves. He asks me why I want to shoot him under the linden tree. I tell him the truth I took from his wife: virtue ravishes me. I want to keep its portrait. I am silent about the orphaned moment we're living in now, how it will leave us. I feel, I feel our pathos. We are virtue's orphans. The tree's green shoots are fleeting; all green corrupts to brown. Sam denies that he's a man of virtue. It's only his guilt about Verity: she's too terrific to betray.

He consents to having his picture taken in the sopping park if I agree to go home with him afterward.

I say in my amazement, "I can't go home with you. She's *there*."

"She's always there."

"Then how can I go home with you?"

"You have to *see*. It's all been too obscure. I want you to know what I know."

"I know it, you've told me. You've told and told."

"You have to get the smell of it. Where I am and how I live. Otherwise you won't believe in it. You won't know it," he insists. "Such cozy endurances."

"You endure them," I said.

"Yesterday," he said, "she brought home a box of old clothes from the Salvation Army. From a thrift shop. From an old people's home, who knows where she got it from. Pile of rags. She's going to sew them into God's bright ribbons. A patchwork quilt. She'll spin straw into gold, you'll see."

"She's terrific."

"She's a terrific wife," he says.

We walk to my place, pick up my camera—I stop to grab my light meter for the rain's sake—and walk crosstown to the park again. I shoot Sam, the man of virtue, under the dripping linden tree. Although I am using my regular equipment, it seems to me the picture's finished on the spot. It's as if I roll it out and fix it then and there. Sam has got his back against the bark, and all the little wet leaves lick down over his bumpy hair. He resembles a Greek runner resting. His face is dappled by all those heart-shaped leaves, and I know that all the rest of my life I'll regret not having shot him in the open, in a field. But my wish for now is to speckle him and see him darkle under the rainy shade of a tree. It comes to me that my desire—oh, my desire! it stings me in the neck—is just now not even for Sam's face: it's for the transitoriness of these thin vulnerable leaves, with their piteous veins turned upward toward a faintness of liverish light.

We walk the thirty-one blocks, in the quickening rain, to his place. It's only a four-room apartment, but Verity's made a palace of it. Everything plain is converted into a sweetness, a furriness, a thickness of excess. She weaves, she knits. She's an immense spider building out of her craw. The floors are piled with rugs she's woven, the chairs with throws she's knit. She's cemented up a handy little fireplace without a flue; it really works, and on a principle she invented herself. She's carpentered all the bookcases—I catch the titles of the four books Sam's written; he's a dignitary and a scholar, after all—and overhead there wafts and dazzles the royal chandelier she found in the gutter and refurbished. Each prism slid through her polishing and perfecting fingers. Verity resurrects, Verity's terrific—you can't avoid thinking it. She's got her big shoulders mounted over her sewing machine in the corner of the living room, hemming brown squares. "It's weird, you wouldn't believe it," she says, "*all* the stuff in this box they gave me is brown. It's good rich fabric, though—a whole load of clothes from dead nuns. You know what happened? A convent dissolved, the young nuns broke their vows and ran to get married."

"That's *your* story," Sam says.

Verity calls her daughter—only one of the girls is at home, the other is away at college. Clearly this one isn't the daughter that's so much like Verity. She has a solemn hard flank of cheek and no conversation. She carries out a plate of sliced honey cake and three cups of tea; then she hides herself in her bedroom. A radio is in there; gilded waves of Bach tremble out of it. I look around for Verity's harp.

"Hey, let's dress you up," Verity says out of her teacup; she's already downed a quantity of cake. "There's stuff in that box that would just fit you. You've got a waist like our girls. I wish *I* had a waist like that." I protest; I tell her it's too silly. Sam smolders with his sour satisfaction, and she churns her palms inside the box like a pair of oars. She pulls out a long skirt, and a blouse called a bodice, and another blouse to wear under that, with long sleeves. Sam pokes my spine and nudges me into the girl's bedroom, where there's a tall mirror screwed into the back of the door. I look at myself.

"Period piece!" says Verity.

I'm all in brown, as brown as leaves. The huge high harp, not gold as I imagined it but ivory, is along the wall behind me. I believe everything Sam has told about the conquistadores. I believe everything he's told about Verity. He's a camera who never lies. His wet hair is black as olives. He belongs to his wife, who's terrific. She's put a nun's bonnet on herself. She has an old-fashioned sense of fun—the words come to me out of, I think, Louisa May Alcott: she likes costume and dress-up. Soon she will have us guessing riddles and playing charades. They are a virtuous and wholesome family. The daughter, though her look is bone, is fond of Bach; no junk music in such a household. They are sweeter than the whole world outside. When Sam is absent the mother and her daughter climb like kittens into a knitted muff.

I shoot Verity wearing the nun's bonnet.

"Look at *you!*" she cries.

I return to the mirror to see. I am grave; I have no smile. My face is mysteriously shut. I'm suffering. Lovesick and dreamsick, I'm dreaming of my desire. I am already thirty-six years old, tomorrow I will be forty-eight years old, and a crafty parallelogram begins to frame the space between my nose and mouth. My features are very distinct—I will live for years and years before they slide out of the mirror. I'm the Brown Girl in the pocket of my blouse. I reek of history. If, this minute, I could glide into a chemical solution, as if in a gondola, splashed all over and streaming with wet silver, would the mirror seize and fix me, like a photographic plate? I watch Sam's eyes, poached and pale and mottled with furious old civilizations, steaming hatred for his wife. I trip over the long drapery of my nun's hem. All the same I catch up my camera without dropping it—my ambassador of desire, my secret house with its single shutter, my chaste aperture, my dead infant, husband of my bosom. Their two heads, hers light, his black, negatives of each other, are caught side by side in their daughter's mirror. I shoot into their heads, the white harp behind. Now they are exposed. Now they will stick forever.

Usurpation (Other People's Stories)

OCCASIONALLY A WRITER will encounter a story that is his, yet is not his. I mean, by the way, a writer of *stories*, not one of these intelligences that analyze society and culture, but the sort of ignorant and acquisitive being who moons after magical tales. Such a creature knows very little: how to tie a shoelace, when to go to the store for bread, and the exact stab of a story that belongs to him, and to him only. But sometimes it happens that somebody else has written the story first. It is like being robbed of clothes you do not yet own. There you sit, in the rapt hall, seeing the usurper on the stage caressing the manuscript that, in its deepest turning, was meant to be yours. He is a transvestite, he is wearing your own hat and underwear. It seems unjust. There is no way to prevent him.

You may wonder that I speak of a hall rather than a book. The story I refer to has not yet been published in a book, and the fact is I heard it read aloud. It was read by the author himself. I had a seat in the back of the hall, with a much younger person pressing the chair-arms on either side of me, but by the third paragraph I was blind and saw nothing. By the fifth paragraph I recognized my story—knew it to be mine, that is, with the same indispensable familiarity I have for this round-flanked left-side molar my tongue admires. I think of it, in all that waste and rubble amid gold dental crowns, as my pearl.

The story was about a crown—a mythical one, made of silver. I do not remember its title. Perhaps it was simply called "The Magic Crown." In any event, you will soon read it in its famous author's new collection. He is, you may be sure, very famous, so famous that it was startling to see he was a real man. He wore a conventional suit and tie, a conventional haircut and conventional eyeglasses. His whitening mustache made him look conventionally distinguished. He was not at all as I had expected him to be—small and astonished, like his heroes.

This time the hero was a teacher. In the story he was always called "the teacher," as if how one lives is what one is.

The teacher's father is in the hospital, a terminal case. There is no hope. In an advertisement the teacher reads about a wonder-curer, a rabbi who can work miracles. Though a rational fellow and a devout skeptic, in desperation he visits the rabbi and learns that a cure can be effected by the construction of a magical silver crown, which costs nearly five hundred dollars. After it is made the rabbi will give it a special blessing and the sick man will recover. The teacher pays and in a vision sees a glowing replica of the marvelous crown. But afterward he realizes that he has been mesmerized.

Furiously he returns to the rabbi's worn-out flat to demand his money. Now the rabbi is dressed like a rich dandy. "I telephoned the hospital and my father is still sick." The rabbi chides him—he must give the crown time to work. The teacher insists that the crown he paid for be produced. "It cannot be seen," says the rabbi, "it must be believed in, or the blessing will not work."

The teacher and the rabbi argue bitterly. The rabbi calls for faith, the teacher for his stolen money. In the heart of the struggle the teacher confesses with a terrible cry that he has really always hated his father anyway. The next day the father dies.

With a single half-archaic word the famous writer pressed out the last of the sick man's breath: he "expired."

Forgive me for boring you with plot-summary. I know there is nothing more tedious, and despise it myself. A rabbi whose face I have not made you see, a teacher whose voice remains a shadowy moan: how can I burn the inside of your eyes with these? But it is not my story, and therefore not my responsibility. I did not invent any of it.

From the platform the famous writer explained that the story was a gift, he too had not invented it. He took it from an account in a newspaper—which one he would not tell: he sweated over fear of libel. Cheats and fakes always hunt themselves up in stories, sniffing out twists, insults, distortions, transfigurations, all the drek of the imagination. Whatever's made up they grab, thick as lawyers against the silky figurative. Still, he swore it really happened, just like that—a crook with his crooked wife, calling himself rabbi, preying on gullible people, among them educated men, graduate students even; finally they arrested the fraud and put him in jail.

Instantly, the famous writer said, at the smell of the word "jail," he knew the story to be his.

This news came to me with a pang. The silver crown given away free, and where was I?—I who am pocked with newspaper-sickness, and hunch night after night (it pleases me to read the morning papers after midnight) catatonically fixed on shipping lists, death columns, lost wallets, maimings, muggings, explosions, hijackings, bombs, while the unwashed dishes sough thinly all around.

It has never occurred to me to write about a teacher; and as for rabbis, I can make up my own craftily enough. You may ask, then, what precisely in this story attracted me. And not simply attracted: seized me by the lung and declared itself my offspring—a changeling in search of its natural mother. Do not mistake me: had I only had access to a newspaper that crucial night (the *Post*, the *News*, the *Manchester Guardian*, *St. Louis Post-Dispatch*, *Boston Herald-Traveler*, ah, which, which? and where was I? in a bar? never; buying birth control pills in the drugstore? I am a believer in fertility; reading, God forbid, a *book?*), my own story would have been less logically decisive. Perhaps the sick father would have recovered. Perhaps the teacher would not have confessed to hating his father. I might have caused the silver crown to astonish even the rabbi himself. Who knows what I might have sucked out of those swindlers! The point is I would have fingered out the magical parts.

Magic—I admit it—is what I lust after. And not ordinary magic, which is what one expects of pagan peoples; their religions declare it. After all, half the world asserts that once upon a time God became a man, and moreover that whenever a priest in sacral ceremony wills it, that same God-man can climb into a little flat piece of unleavened bread. For most people nowadays it is only the *idea* of a piece of bread turning into God—but is that any better? As for me, I am drawn not to the symbol, but to the absolute magic act. I am drawn to what is forbidden.

Forbidden. The terrible Hebrew word for it freezes the tongue—*asur*; Jewish magic. Trembling, we have heard in Deuteronomy the No that applies to any slightest sniff of occult disclosure: how mighty is Moses, peering down the centuries into the endlessness of this allure! Astrologists, wizards and witches: *asur*. The Jews have no magic. For us bread may not tumble into body. Wine is wine, death is death.

And yet with what prowess we have crept down the centuries after amulets, and hidden countings of letters, and the silver crown that heals: so it is after all nothing to marvel at that my own, my beloved, subject should be the preternatural—everything anti-Moses, all things blazing with their own wonder. I long to be one of the ordinary peoples, to give up our agnostic God whom even the word "faith" insults, who cannot be imagined in any form, whom the very hope of imagining offends, who is without body and cannot enter body . . . oh, why can we not have a magic God like other peoples?

Some day I will take courage and throw over being a Jew, and then I will make a little god, a silver godlet, in the shape of a crown, which will stop death, resurrect fathers and uncles; out of its royal points gardens will burst.—That story! Mine! Stolen! I considered: was it possible to leap up on the stage with a living match and burn the manuscript on the spot, freeing the crown out of the finished tale, restoring it once more to a public account in the press? But no. Fire, even the little humble wobble of a match, is too powerful a magic in such a place, among such gleaming herds. A conflagration of souls out of lust for a story! I feared so terrible a spell. All the same, he would own a carbon copy, or a photographic copy: such a man is meticulous about the storage-matter of his brain. A typewriter is a volcano. Who can stop print?

If I owned a silver godlet right now I would say: Almighty

small Crown, annihilate that story; return, return the stuff of it to me.

A peculiar incident. Just as the famous writer came to the last word—"expired"—I saw the face of a goat. It was thin, white, blurry-eyed; a scraggly fur beard hung from its chin. Attached to the beard was a transparent voice, a voice like a whiteness—but I ought to explain how I came just then to be exposed to it. I was leaning against the wall of that place. The fading hiss of "expired" had all at once fevered me; I jumped from my seat between the two young people. Their perspiration had dampened the chair-arms, and the chill of their sweat, combined with the hotness of my greed for this magic story which could not be mine, turned my flesh to a sort of vapor. I rose like a heated gas, feeling insubstantial, and went to press my head against the cold side wall along the aisle. My brain was all gas, it shuddered with envy. Expired! How I wished to write a story containing that unholy sound! How I wished it was I who had come upon the silver crown. . . . I must have looked like an usher, or in some fashion a factotum of the theater, with my skull drilled into the wall that way.

In any case I was taken for an official: as someone in authority who lolls on the job.

The goat-face blew a breath deep into my throat.

"I have stories. I want to give him stories."

"*What* do you want?"

"Him. Arrange it, can't you? In the intermission, what d'you say?"

I pulled away; the goat hopped after me.

"How? When?" said the goat. "Where?" His little beard had a tremor. "If he isn't available here and now, tell me his mailing address. I need criticism, advice, I need help—"

We become what we are thought to be; I became a factotum.

I said pompously, "You should be ashamed to pursue the famous. Does he know you?"

"Not exactly. I'm a cousin—"

"*His* cousin?"

"No. That rabbi's wife. She's an old lady, my mother's uncle was her father. We live in the same neighborhood."

"What rabbi?"

"The one in the papers. The one he swiped the story from."

"That doesn't oblige him to read you. You expect too much," I said. "The public has no right to a writer's private mind. Help from high places doesn't come like manna. His time is precious, he has better things to do." All this, by the way, was quotation. A famous writer—not this one—to whom I myself sent a story had once stung me with these words; so I knew how to use them.

"Did he say you could speak for him?" sneered the goat. "Fame doesn't cow me. Even the famous bleed."

"Only when pricked by the likes of you," I retorted. "Have you been published?"

"I'm still young."

"Poets before you died first and published afterward. Keats was twenty-six, Shelley twenty-nine, Rimbaud—"

"I'm like these, I'll live forever."

"Arrogant!"

"Let the famous call me that, not you."

"At least I'm published," I protested; so my disguise fell. He saw I was nothing so important as an usher, only another unknown writer in the audience.

"Do *you* know him?" he asked.

"He spoke to me once at a cocktail party."

"Would he remember your name?"

"Certainly," I lied. The goat had speared my dignity.

"Then take only one story."

"Leave the poor man alone."

"*You* take it. Read it. If you like it—look, only if you like it!—give it to him for me."

"He won't help you."

"Why do you think everyone is like you?" he accused—but he seemed all at once submerged, as if I had hurt him. He shook out a vast envelope, pulled out his manuscript, and spitefully began erasing something. Opaque little tears clustered on his eyelashes. Either he was weeping or he was afflicted with pus. "Why do you think I don't deserve some attention?"

"Not of the great."

"Then let me at least have yours," he said.

The real usher just then came like a broom. Back! Back! Quiet! Don't disturb the reading! Before I knew it I had been swept into my seat. The goat was gone, and I was clutching the manuscript.

The fool had erased his name.

That night I read the thing. You will ask why. The newspaper was thin, the manuscript fat. It smelled of stable: a sort of fecal stink. But I soon discovered it was only the glue he had used to piece together parts of corrected pages. An amateur job.

If you are looking for magic now, do not. This was no work to marvel at. The prose was not bad, but not good either. There are young men who write as if the language were an endless bolt of yard goods—you snip off as much as you need for the length of fiction you require: one turn of the loom after another, everything of the same smoothness, the texture catches you up nowhere.

I have said "fiction." It was not clear to me whether this was fiction or not. The title suggested it was: "A Story of Youth and Homage." But the narrative was purposefully inconclusive. Moreover, the episodes could be interpreted on several "levels." Plainly it was not just a story, but meant something much more, and even that "much more" itself meant much more. This alone soured me; such techniques are learned in those hollowed-out tombstones called Classes in Writing. In my notion of these things, if you want to tell a story you tell it. I am against all these masks and tricks of metaphor and fable. That is why I am attracted to magical tales: they mean what they say; in them miracles are not symbols, they are conditional probabilities.

The goat's story was realistic enough, though self-conscious. In perfectly ordinary, mainly trite, English it pretended to be incoherent. That, as you know, is the fashion.

I see you are about to put these pages down, in fear of another plot-summary. I beg you to wait. Trust me a little. I will get through it as painlessly as possible—I promise to abbreviate everything. Or, if I turn out to be long-winded, at least to be interesting. Besides, you can see what risks I am taking. I am unfamiliar with the laws governing plagiarism, and here I am, brazenly giving away stories that are not rightfully mine. Perhaps one day the goat's story will be published and acclaimed. Or perhaps not: in either case he will recognize his plot as I am about to tell it to you, and what furies will beat in him! What if, by the time *this* story is published, at this very moment while you are reading it, I am on my back in some filthy municipal dungeon? Surely so deep a sacrifice should engage your forgiveness.

Then let us proceed to the goat's plot:

An American student at a yeshiva in Jerusalem is unable to concentrate. He is haunted by worldly desires; in reality he has come to Jerusalem not for Torah but out of ambition. Though young and unpublished, he already fancies himself to be a writer worthy of attention. Then why not the attention of the very greatest?

It happens that there lives in Jerusalem a writer who one day will win the most immense literary prize on the planet. At the time of the story he is already an old man heavy with fame, though of a rather parochial nature; he has not yet been to Stockholm—it is perhaps two years before the Nobel Prize turns him into a mythical figure. ["Turns him into a mythical figure" is an excellent example of the goat's prose, by the way.] But the student is prescient, and fame is fame. He composes a postcard:

> There are only two
> religious writers in the world.
> You are one and I am
> the other. I will come to visit you.

It is true that the old man is religious. He wears a skullcap, he threads his tales with strands of the holy phrases. And he cannot send anyone away from his door. So when the student appears, the old writer invites him in for a glass of tea, though homage fatigues him; he would rather nap.

The student confesses that his own ambitiousness has brought him to the writer's feet: he too would wish one day to be revered as the writer himself is revered.

—I wish, says the old writer, I had been like you in my youth. I never had the courage to look into the face of anyone I admired, and I admired so many! But they were all too remote; I was very shy. I wish now I had gone to see them, as you have come to see me.

—Whom did you admire most? asks the student. In reality he has no curiosity about this or anything else of the kind, but he recognizes that such a question is vital to the machinery of praise. And though he has never read a word the old man has written, he can smell all around him, even in the old man's trousers, the smell of fame.

—The Rambam, answers the old man. —Him I admired more than anyone.

—Maimonides? exclaims the student. —But how could you visit Maimonides?

—Even in my youth, the old man assents, the Rambam had already been dead for several hundred years. But even if he had not been dead, I would have been too shy to go and see him. For a shy young man it is relieving to admire someone who is dead.

—Then to become like you, the student says meditatively, it is necessary to be shy?

—Oh yes, says the old man. —It is necessary to be shy. The truest ambition is hidden in shyness. All ambitiousness is hidden. If you want to usurp my place you must not show it, or I will only hang to it all the more tightly. You must always walk with your head down. You must be a true *ba'al ga'avah*.

—A *ba'al ga'avah?* cries the student. —But you contradict yourself! Aren't we told that the *ba'al ga'avah* is the man whom God most despises? The self-righteous self-idolator? It's written that him alone God will cause to perish. Sooner than a murderer!

It is plain that the young man is in good command of the sources; not for nothing is he a student at the yeshiva. But he is perplexed, rattled. —How can I be like you if you tell me to be a *ba'al ga'avah?* And why would you tell me to be such a thing?

—The *ba'al ga'avah*, explains the writer, is a supplanter: the man whose arrogance is godlike, whose pride is like a tower. He is the one who most subtly turns his gaze downward to the ground, never looking at what he covets. I myself was never cunning enough to be a genuine *ba'al ga'avah*; I was always too timid for it. It was never necessary for me to feign shyness, I was naturally like that. But you are not. So you must invent a way to become a genuine *ba'al ga'avah*, so audacious and yet so ingenious that you will fool God and will live.

The student is impatient. —How does God come into this? We're talking only of ambition.

—Of course. Of *serious* ambition, however. You recall: "All that is not Torah is levity." This is the truth to be found at the end of every incident, even this one. —You see, the old man continues, my place can easily be taken. A blink, and it's yours. I will not watch over it if I forget that someone is after it. But you must make me forget.

—How? asks the student, growing cold with greed.

—By never coming here again.

—It's a joke!

—And then I will forget you. I will forget to watch over my place. And then, when I least look for it to happen, you will come and steal it. You will be so quiet, so shy, so ingenious, so audacious, I will never suspect you.

—A nasty joke! You want to get rid of me! It's mockery, you forget what it is to be young. In old age everything is easier, nothing burns inside you.

But meanwhile, inside the student's lungs, and within the veins of his wrists, a cold fog shivers.

—Nothing burns? Yes; true. At the moment, for instance, I covet nothing more lusty than my little twilight nap. I always have it right now.

—They say (the student is as cold now as a frozen path, all his veins are paths of ice), they say you're going to win the Nobel Prize! For literature!

—When I nap I sleep dreamlessly. I don't dream of such things. Come, let me help you cease to covet.

—It's hard for me to keep my head down! I'm young, I want what you have, I want to be like you!

Here I will interrupt the goat's story to apologize. I would not be candid if I did not confess that I am rewriting it; I am almost making it my own, and that will never do for an act of plagiarism. I don't mean only that I have set it more or less in order, and taken out the murk. That is only by the way. But, by sticking to what one said and what the other answered, I have broken my promise; already I have begun to bore you. Boring! Oh, the goat's story was boring! Philosophic stories make excellent lullabies.

So, going on with my own version (I hate stories with ideas hidden in them), I will spring out of paraphrase and invent what the old man does.

Right after saying "Let me help you cease to covet," he gets up and, with fuzzy sleepy steps, half-limps to a table covered by a cloth that falls to the floor. He separates the parts of the cloth, and now the darkness underneath the table takes him like a tent. In he crawls, the flaps cling, his rump makes a bulge.

He calls out two words in Hebrew: *ohel shalom!* and backs out, carrying with him a large black box. It looks like a lady's hat box.

"An admirer gave me this. Only not an admirer of our own time. A predecessor. I had it from Tchernikhovsky. The poet. I presume you know his work?"

"A little," says the student. He begins to wish he had boned up before coming.

"Tchernikhovsky was already dead when he brought me this," the old man explains. "One night I was alone, sitting right there—where you are now. I was reading Tchernikhovsky's most famous poem, the one to the god Apollo. And quite suddenly there was Tchernikhovsky. He disappointed me. He was a completely traditional ghost, you could see right through him to the wall behind. This of course made it difficult to study his features. The wall behind—you can observe for yourself—held a bookcase, so where his nose appeared to be I could read only the title of a Tractate of the Mishnah. A ghost can be seen mainly in outline, unfortunately, something like an artist's charcoal sketch, only instead of the blackness of charcoal, it is the narrow brilliance of a very fine white light. But what he carried was palpable, even heavy—this box. I was not at all terror-stricken, I can't tell you why. Instead I was bemused by the kind of picture he made against the wall—'modern,' I would have called it then, but probably there are new words for that sort of thing now. It reminded me a little of a collage: one kind of material superimposed on another kind which is utterly different. One order of creation laid upon another. Metal on tissue. Wood on hide. In this case it was a three-dimensional weight superimposed on a line—the line, or luminous congeries of lines, being Tchernikhovsky's hands, ghost hands holding a real box."

The student stares at the box. He waits like a coat eager to be shrunk.

"The fact is," continues the old writer, "I have never opened it. Not that I'm not as inquisitive as the next mortal. Perhaps more so. But it wasn't necessary. There is something about the presence of an apparition which satisfies all curiosity forever—the deeper as well as the more superficial sort. For one thing, a ghost will tell you everything, and all at once. A ghost may *look* artistic, but there is no finesse to it, nothing indirect or calculated, nothing suggesting *raffinement*. It is as if everything gossamer had gone simply into the stuff of it. The rest is all grossness. Or else Tchernikhovsky himself, even when alive and writing, had a certain clumsiness. This is what I myself believe. All that pantheism and earth-worship! That pursuit of the old gods of Canaan! He thickened his tongue with clay. All pantheists are fools. Likewise trinitarians and gnostics of every kind. How can a piece of creation be its own Creator?

"Still, his voice had rather a pretty sound. To describe it is to be obliged to ask you to recall the sound of prattle: a baby's purr, only shaped into nearly normal cognitive speech. A most pleasing combination. He told me that he was reading me closely in Eden and approved of my stories. He had, he assured me, a number of favorites, but best of all he liked a quite short tale—no more than a notebook sketch, really—about why the Messiah will not come.

"In this story the Messiah is ready to come. He enters a synagogue and prepares to appear at the very moment he hears the congregation recite the 'I believe.' He stands there and listens, waiting to make himself visible on the last syllable of the verse 'I believe in the coming of the Messiah, and even if he tarry I will await his coming every day.' He leans against the Ark and listens, listens and leans—all the time he is straining his ears. The fact is he can hear nothing: the congregation buzzes with its own talk—hats, mufflers, business, wives, appointments, rain, lessons, the past, next week . . . the prayer is obscured, all its syllables are drowned in dailiness, and the Messiah retreats; he has not heard himself summoned.

"This, Tchernikhovsky's ghost told me, was my best story. I was at once suspicious. His baby-voice hinted at ironies, I caught a tendril of sarcasm. It was clear to me that what he liked about this story was mainly its climactic stroke: that the Messiah is prevented from coming. I had written to lament the tarrying of the Messiah; Tchernikhovsky, it seemed, took satisfaction exactly in what I mourned. 'Look here,' he tinkled at me—imagine a crow linked to a delicious little gurgle, and the whole sense of it belligerent as a prizefighter and coarse as an old waiter—'now that I'm dead, a good quarter-century of deadness under my dust, I've concluded that I'm entirely willing to have you assume my eminence. For one thing, I've been to Sweden, pulled strings with some deceased but still influential Academicians, and arranged for you to get the Nobel Prize in a year or two. Which is beyond what I ever got for myself. But I'm aware this won't interest you as much as a piece of eternity right here in Jerusalem, so I'm here to tell you you can have it. You can'—he had a babyish way of repeating things—'assume my eminence.'

"You see what I mean about grossness. I admit I was equally coarse. I answered speedily and to the point. I refused.

"'I understand you,' he said. 'You don't suppose I'm pious enough, or not pious in the right way. I don't meet your yeshiva standards. Naturally not. You know I used to be a doctor, I was attracted to biology, which is to say to dust. Not spiritual enough for you! My Zionism wasn't of the soul, it was made of real dirt. What I'm offering you is something tangible. Have some common sense and take it. It will do for you what the Nobel Prize can't. Open the box and put on whatever's inside. Wear it for one full minute and the thing will be accomplished.' "

"For God's sake, what *was* it?" shrieks the student, shriveling into his blue city-boy shirt. With a tie: and in Jerusalem! (The student is an absurdity, a crudity. But of course I've got to have him; he's left over from the goat's story, what else am I to do?)

"Inside the box," replies the old writer, "was the most literal-minded thing in the world. From a ghost I expected as much. The whole idea of a ghost is a literal-minded conception. I've used ghosts in my own stories, naturally, but they've always had a real possibility, by which I mean an ideal possibility: Elijah, the True Messiah. . . ."

"For God's sake, the box!"

"The box. Take it. I give it to you."

"What's in it?"

"See for yourself."

"Tell me first. Tchernikhovsky told *you*."

"That's a fair remark. It contains a crown."

"What kind of crown?"

"Made of silver, I believe."

"*Real* silver?"

"I've never looked on it, I've explained this. I *refused* it."

"Then why give it to me?"

"Because it's meant for that. When a writer wishes to usurp the place and power of another writer, he simply puts it on. I've explained this already."

"But if I wear it I'll become like Tchernikhovsky—"

"No, no, like me. Like me. It confers the place and power of the giver. And it's what you want, true? To be like me?"

"But this isn't what you advised a moment ago. *Then* you said to become arrogant, a *ba'al ga'avah*, and to conceal it with shyness—"

(Quite so. A muddle in the plot. That was the goat's story, and it had no silver crown in it. I am still stuck with these leftovers that cause seams and cracks in my own version. I will have to mend all this somehow. Be patient. I will manage it. Pray that I don't bungle it.)

"Exactly," says the old writer. "That's the usual way. But if you aren't able to feign shyness, what is necessary is a short cut. I warned you it would demand audacity and ingenuity. What I did not dare to do, you must have the courage for. What I turned down you can raise up. I offer you the crown. You will see what a short cut it is. Wear it and immediately you become a *ba'al ga'avah*. Still, I haven't yet told you how I managed to get rid of Tchernikhovsky's ghost. Open the box, put on the crown, and I'll tell you."

The student obeys. He lifts the box onto the table. It seems light enough, then he opens it, and at the first thrust of his hand into its interior it disintegrates, flakes off into dust, is blown off at a breath, consumed by the first alien molecule of air, like something very ancient removed from the deepest clay tomb and unable to withstand the corrosive stroke of light.

But there, in the revealed belly of the vanished box, is the crown.

It appears to be made of silver, but it is heavier than any

earthly silver—it is heavy, heavy, heavy, dense as a meteorite. Puffing and struggling, the student tries to raise it up to his head. He cannot. He cannot lift even a corner of it. It is weighty as a pyramid.

"It won't budge."

"It will after you pay for it."

"You didn't say anything about payment!"

"You're right. I forgot. But you don't pay in money. You pay in a promise. You have to promise that if you decide you don't want the crown you'll take it off immediately. Otherwise it's yours forever."

"I promise."

"Good. Then put it on."

And now lightly, lightly, oh so easily as if he lifted a straw hat, the student elevates the crown and sets it on his head.

"There. You are like me. Now go away."

And oh so lightly, lightly, as easily as if the crown were a cargo of helium, the student skips through Jerusalem. He runs! He runs into a bus, a joggling mob crushed together, everyone recognizes him, even the driver: he is praised, honored, young women put out their hands to touch his collar, they pluck at his pants, his fly unzips and he zips it up again, oh fame! He gets off the bus and runs to his yeshiva. Crowds on the sidewalk, clapping. So this is what it feels like! He flies into the yeshiva like a king. Formerly no one blinked at him, the born Jerusalemites scarcely spoke to him, but now! It is plain they have all read him. He hears a babble of titles, plots, characters, remote yet familiar—look, he thinks, the crown has supplied me with a ready-made bibliography. He reaches up to his head to touch it: a flash of cold. Cold, cold, it is the coldest silver on the planet, a coldness that stabs through into his brain. Frost encases his brain, inside his steaming skull he hears more titles, more plots, names of characters, scholars, wives, lovers, ghosts, children, beggars, villages, candlesticks—what a load he carries, what inventions, what a teeming and a boiling, stories, stories, stories! His own; yet not his own. The Rosh Yeshiva comes down the stairs from his study: the Rosh Yeshiva, the Head, a bony miniaturized man grown almost entirely inward and upward into a spectacular dome, a brow shaped like the front of an academy, hollowed-out temples for porticoes, a resplendent head with round dead-end eye-glasses as denying as bottle-bottoms and curl-scribbled beard and small attachments of arms and little antlike legs thin as hairs; and the Rosh Yeshiva, who has never before let fall a syllable to this obscure tourist-pupil from America, suddenly cries out the glorious blessing reserved for finding oneself in the presence of a sage: Blessed are You, O God, Imparter of wisdom to those who fear Him! And the student in his crown understands that there now cleave to his name sublime parables interpreting the divine purpose, and he despairs, he is afraid, because suppose he were obliged to write one this minute? Suppose these titles clamoring all around him are only empty pots, and he must fill them up with stories? He runs from the yeshiva, elbows out, scattering admirers and celebrants, and makes for the alley behind the kitchen—no one ever goes there, only the old cats who scavenge in the trash barrels. But behind him—crudely sepulchral footsteps, like thumps inside a bucket, he runs, he looks back, he runs, he stops—Tchernikhovsky's ghost! From the old writer's description he can identify it easily. "A mistake," chimes the ghost, a pack of bells, "it wasn't for you."

"What!" screams the student.

"Give it back."

"What!"

"The crown," pursues the baby-purr voice of Tchernikhovsky's ghost. "I never meant for that old fellow to give it away."

"He said it was all right."

"He tricked you."

"No he didn't."

"He's sly sly sly."

"He said it would make me just like him. And I am."

"No."

"Yes!"

"Then predict the future."

"In two years, the Nobel Prize for Literature!"

"For him, not for you."

"But I'm *like* him."

" 'Like' is not the same as the same. You want to be the same? Look in the window."

The student looks into the kitchen window. Inside, among cauldrons, he can see the roil of the students in their caps, spinning here and there, in the pantry, in the Passover dish closet even, past a pair of smoky vats, in search of the fled visitor who now stares and stares until his concentration alters seeing; and instead of looking behind the pane, he follows the light on its surface and beholds a reflection. An old man is also looking into the window; the student is struck by such a torn rag of a face. Strange, it cannot be Tchernikhovsky: he is all web and wraith; and anyhow a ghost has no reflection. The old man in the looking-glass window is wearing a crown. A silver crown!

"You see?" tinkles the ghost. "A trick!"

"I'm old!" howls the student.

"Feel in your pocket."

The student feels. A vial.

"See? Nitroglycerin."

"What is this, are you trying to blow me up?"

Again the small happy soaring of the infant's grunt. "I remind you that I am a physician. When you are seized by a pulling, a knocking, a burning in the chest, a throb in the elbow-crook, swallow one of these tablets. In coronary insufficiency it relaxes the artery."

"Heart failure! Will I die? Stop! I'm young!"

"With those teeth? All gums gone? That wattle? Dotard! Bag!"

The student runs; he remembers his perilous heart; he slows. The ghost thumps and chimes behind. So they walk, a procession of two, a very old man wearing a silver crown infinitely cold, in his shadow a ghost made all of lit spider-thread, giving out now and then with baby's laughter and odd coarse curses patched together from Bible phrases; together they scrape out of the alley onto the boulevard—an oblivious population there.

"My God! No one knows me. Why don't they know me here?"

"Who should know you?" says Tchernikhovsky.

"In the bus they yelled out dozens of book titles. In the streets! The Rosh Yeshiva said the blessing for seeing a sage!"

But now in the bus the passengers are indifferent; they leap for seats; they snore in cozy spots standing up, near poles; and not a word. Not a gasp, not a squeal. Not even a pull on the collar. It's all over! A crown but no king.

"It's stopped working," says the student, mournful.

"The crown? Not on your life."

"Then you're interfering with it. You're jamming it up."

"That's more like the truth."

"Why are you following me?"

"I don't like misrepresentation."

"You mean you don't like magic."

"They're the same thing."

"Go away!"

"I never do that."

"*He* got rid of you."

"Sly sly sly. He did it with a ruse. You know how? He refused the crown. He took it but he hid it away. No one ever refused it before. Usurper! Coveter! *Ba'al ga'avah!* That's what he is."

The student protests, "But he *gave* me the crown. 'Let me help you cease to covet,' that's exactly what he said, why do you call him *ba'al ga'avah?*"

"And himself? *He's* ceased to covet, is that it? That's what you think? You think he doesn't churn saliva over the Nobel Prize? Ever since I told him they were speculating about the possibility over at the Swedish Academicians' graveyard? Day and night that's all he dreams of. He loves his little naps, you know why? To sleep, perchance to dream. He imagines himself in a brand-new splendiferous bow-tie, rear end trailing tails, wearing his skullcap out of public arrogance, his old wife up there with him dressed to the hobbledorfs—in Stockholm, with the King of Sweden! That's what he sees, that's what he dreams, he can't work, he's in a fever of coveting. You think it's different when you're old?"

"I'm not old!" the student shouts. A willful splinter, he peels himself from the bus. Oh, frail, his legs are straw, the dry knees wrap close like sheaves, he feels himself pouring out, sand from a sack. Old!

Now they are in front of the writer's house. "Age makes no matter," says the ghost, "the same, the same. Ambition levels, lust is unitary. Lust you can always count on. I'm not speaking of the carnal sort. Carnality's a brevity—don't compare wind with mountains! But lust! Teetering on the edge of the coffin there's lust. After mortality there's lust, I guarantee you. In Eden there's nothing but lust." The ghost raps on the door—with all his strength, and his strength is equal to a snowflake. Silence, softness. "Bang on the thing!" he commands, self-disgusted; sometimes he forgets he is incorporeal.

The student obeys, shivering; he is so cold now his three or six teeth clatter like chinaware against a waggling plastic bridge anchored in nothing, his ribs shake in his chest, his spine vibrates without surcease. And what of his heart? Inside his pocket he clutches the vial.

The old writer opens up. His fists are in his eyes.

"We woke you, did we?" gurgles Tchernikhovsky's ghost.

"You!"

"Me," says the ghost, satisfied. "*Ba'al ga'avah!* Spiteful! You foisted the crown on a kid."

The old writer peers. "Where?"

The ghost sweeps the student forward. "I did him the service of giving him long life. Instantly. Why wait for a good thing?"

"I don't want it! Take it back!" the student cries, snatching at the crown on his head; but it stays on. "You said I could give it back if I don't want it any more!"

Again the old writer peers. "Ah. You keep your promise. So does the crown."

"What do you mean?"

"It promised you acclaim. But it generates this pest. Everything has its price."

"Get rid of it!"

"To get rid of the ghost you have to get rid of the crown."

"All right! Here it is! Take it back! It's yours!"

The ghost laughs like a baby at the sight of a teat. "Try and take it off then."

The student tries. He tears at the crown, he flings his head upward, backward, sideways, pulls and pulls. His fingertips flame with the ferocious cold.

"How did *you* get rid of it?" he shrieks.

"I never put it on," replies the old writer.

"No, no, I mean the ghost, how did you get rid of the ghost!"

"I was going to tell you that, remember? But you ran off."

"You sent me away. It was a trick, you never meant to tell."

The ghost scolds: "No disputes!" And orders, "Tell now."

The student writhes; twists his neck; pulls and pulls. The crown stays on.

"The crown loosens," the old writer begins, "when the ghost goes. Everything dissolves together—"

"But *how?*"

"You find someone to give the crown to. That's all. You simply pass it on. All you do is agree to give away its powers to someone who wants it. Consider it a test of your own generosity."

"Who'll want it? Nobody wants such a thing!" the student shrieks. "It's stuck! Get it off! Off!"

"*You* wanted it."

"Prig! Moralist! *Ba'al ga'avah!* Didn't I come to you for advice? Literary advice, and instead you gave me this! I wanted help! You gave me metal junk! Sneak!"

"Interesting," observes the ghost, "that I myself acquired the crown in exactly the same way. I received it from Ibn Gabirol. Via ouija board. I was skeptical about the method but discovered it to be legitimate. I consulted him about some of his verse-forms. To be specific, the problem of enjambment, which is more difficult in Hebrew than in some other languages. By way of reply he gave me the crown. Out of the blue it appeared on the board—naked, so to speak, and shining oddly, like a fish without scales. Of course there wasn't any ghost attached to the crown then. I'm the first, and you don't think I *like* having to materialize thirty minutes after someone's put it on? What I need is to be left in peace in Paradise, not this business of being on call the moment someone—"

"Ibn Gabirol?" the old writer breaks in, panting, all attention. Ibn Gabirol! Sublime poet, envied beyond envy, sublimeness without heir, who would not covet the crown of Ibn Gabirol?

"He said *he* got it from Isaiah. The quality of ownership keeps declining apparently. That's why they have me on patrol. If someone unworthy acquires it—well, that's where I put on my emanations and dig in. Come on," says the ghost, all at once sounding American, "let's go." He gives the student one of his snowflake shoves. "Where you go, I go. Where I go, you go. Now that you know the ropes, let's get out of here and find somebody who deserves it. Give it to some goy for a change. 'The righteous among the Gentiles are as judges in Israel.' My own suggestion is Oxford, Mississippi, Faulkner, William."

"Faulkner's dead."

"He is? I ought to look him up. All right then. Someone not so fancy. Norman Mailer."

"A Jew," sneers the student.

"Can you beat that. Never mind, we'll find someone. Keep away from the rot of Europe—Kafka had it once. Maybe a black. An Indian. Spic maybe. We'll go to America and look."

Moistly the old writer plucks at the ghost. "Listen, this doesn't cancel the Prize? I still get it?"

"In two years you're in Stockholm."

"And me?" cries the student. "What about me? What happens to me?"

"You wear the crown until you get someone to take it from you. Blockhead! Dotard! Don't you *listen?*" says the ghost: his accent wobbles, he elides like a Calcuttan educated in Paris.

"No one wants it! I told you! Anyone who really needs it you'll say doesn't deserve it. If he's already famous he doesn't need it, and if he's unknown you'll think he degrades it. Like me. Not fair! There's no *way* to pass it on."

"You've got a point." The ghost considers this. "That makes sense. Logic."

"So get it off me!"

"However, again you forget lust. Lust overcomes logic."

"Stop! Off!"

"The King of Sweden," muses the old writer, "speaks no

Hebrew. That will be a difficulty. I suppose I ought to begin to
study Swedish."

"Off! Off!" yells the student. And tugs at his head, yanks at
the crown, pulling, pulling, seizing it by the cold points. He
throws himself down, wedges his legs against the writer's desk,
tumbling after leverage; nothing works. Then methodically he
kneels, lays his head on the floor, and methodically begins to
beat the crown against the wooden floor. He jerks, tosses, taps,
his white head in the brilliant crown is a wild flashing hammer;
then he catches at his chest; his knuckles explode; then again he
beats, beats, beats the crown down. But it stays stuck, no blow
can knock it free. He beats. He heaves his head. Sparks spring
from the crown, small lightnings leap. Oh, his chest, his ribs,
his heart! The vial, where is the vial? His hands squirm toward
his throat, his chest, his pocket. And his head beats the crown
down against the floor. The old head halts, the head falls, the
crown stays stuck, the heart is dead.

"Expired," says the ghost of Tchernikhovsky.

Well, that should be enough. No use making up any more of it.
Why should I? It is not my story. It is not the goat's story. It is
no one's story. It is a story nobody wrote, nobody wants, it has
no existence. What does the notion of a *ba'al ga'avah* have to do
with a silver crown? One belongs to morals, the other to magic.
Stealing from two disparate tales I smashed their elements one
into the other. Things must be brought together. In magic
all divergences are linked and locked. The fact is I forced the
crown onto the ambitious student in order to punish.

To punish? Yes. In life I am, though obscure, as generous
and reasonable as those whom wide glory has sweetened; earlier
you saw how generously and reasonably I dealt with the goat.
So I am used to being taken for everyone's support, confidante,
and consolation—it did not surprise me, propped there against
that wall in the dark, when the goat begged me to read his
story. Why should he not? My triumph is that, in my unre-
nown, everyone trusts me not to lie. But I always lie. Only on
paper I do not lie. On paper I punish, I am malignant.

For instance: I killed off the student to punish him for

arrogance. But it is really the goat I am punishing. It is an excellent thing to punish him. Did he not make his hero a student
at the yeshiva, did he not make him call himself "religious"?
But what is that? What is it to be "religious"? Is religion any
different from magic? Whoever intends to separate them ends
in proving them to be the same.

The goat was a *ba'al ga'avah!* I understood that only a *ba'al
ga'avah* would dare to write about "religion."

So I punished him for it. How? By transmuting piety into
magic.

Then—and I require you to accept this with the suddenness
I myself experienced it: *as if by magic*—again I was drawn to
look into the goat's story; and found, on the next-to-last page,
an address. He had rubbed out (I have already mentioned this)
his name; but here was a street and a number:

**18 Herzl Street
Brooklyn, N.Y.**

A street fashioned—so to speak—after the Messiah. Here
I will halt you once more to ask you to take no notice of the
implications of the goat's address. It is an aside worthy of
the goat himself. It is he, not I, who would grab you by the
sleeve here and now in order to explain exactly who Theodor
Herzl was—oh, how I despise writers who will stop a story
dead for the sake of showing off! Do you care whether or not
Maimonides (supposing you had ever heard of that lofty saint)
tells us that the messianic age will be recognizable simply by the
resumption of Jewish political independence? Does it count if,
by that definition, the Messiah turns out to be none other than
a Viennese journalist of the last century? Doubtless Herzl was
regarded by his contemporaries as a *ba'al ga'avah* for brazening
out, in a modern moment, a Hebrew principality. And who is
more of a *ba'al ga'avah* than the one who usurps the Messiah's
own job? Take Isaiah—was not Isaiah a *ba'al ga'avah* when he
declared against observance—"I hate your feasts and your new
moons"—and in the voice, no less, of the Creator Himself?

But thank God I have no taste for these notions. Already

you have seen how earnestly my mind is turned toward hatred of metaphysical speculation. Practical action is my whole concern, and I have nothing but contempt for significant allusions, nuances, buried effects.

Therefore you will not be astonished at what I next undertook to do. I went—ha!—to the street of the Messiah to find the goat.

It was a place where there had been conflagrations. Rubble tentatively stood: brick on brick, about to fall. One remaining configuration of wall, complete with windows but no panes. The sidewalk underfoot stirred with crumbs, as of sugar grinding: mortar reduced to sand. A desert flushed over tumbled yards. Lintels and doors burned out, foundations squared like pebbles on a beach: in this spot once there had been cellars, stoops, houses. The smell of burned wood wandered. A civilization of mounds—who had lived here? Jews. There were no buildings left. A rectangular stucco fragment—of what? synagogue maybe—squatted in a space. There was no Number 18—only bad air, light flying in the gape and gash where the fires had driven down brick, mortar, wood, mothers, fathers, children pressing library cards inside their pockets—gone, finished.

And immediately—as if by magic—the goat!

"You!" I hooted, exactly as, in the story that never was, the old writer had cried it to Tchernikhovsky's shade.

"You've read my stuff," he said, gratified. "I knew you could find me easy if you wanted to. All you had to do was want to."

"Where do you live?"

"Number 18. I knew you'd want to."

"There isn't any 18."

He pointed. "It's what's left of the shul. No plumbing, but it still has a good kitchen in the back. I'm what you call a squatter, you don't mind?"

"Why should I mind?"

"Because I stole the idea from a book. It's this story about a writer who lives in an old tenement with his typewriter and the tenement's about to be torn down—"

The famous author who had written about the magic crown

had written that story too; I reflected how some filch their fiction from life, others filch their lives from fiction. What people call inspiration is only pilferage. "You're not living in a tenement," I corrected, "you're living in a synagogue."

"What used to be. It's a hole now, a sort of cave. The Ark is left though, you want to see the Ark?"

I followed him through shards. There was no front door.

"What happened to this neighborhood?" I said.

"The Jews went away."

"Who came instead?"

"Fire."

The curtain of the Ark dangled in charred shreds. I peered inside the orifice which had once closeted the Scrolls: all blackness there, and the clear sacrificial smell of things that have been burned.

"See?" he said. "The stove works. It's the old wood-burning kind. For years they didn't use it here, it just sat. And now—resurrection." Ah: the clear sacrificial smell was potatoes baking.

"Don't you have a job?"

"I write, I'm a writer. And no rent to pay anyhow."

"How do you drink?"

"You mean *what*." He held up a full bottle of Schapiro's kosher wine. "They left a whole case intact."

"But you can't wash, you can't even use the toilet."

"I pee and do my duty in the yard. Nobody cares. This is freedom, lady."

"Dirt," I said.

"What's dirt to Peter is freedom to Paul. Did you like my story? Sit."

There was actually a chair, but it had a typewriter on it. The goat did not remove it.

"How do you take a bath?" I persisted.

"Sometimes I go to my cousin's. I told you. The rabbi's wife."

"The rabbi from this synagogue?"

"No, he's moved to Woodhaven Boulevard. That's Queens. All the Jews from here went to Queens, did you know that?"

"*What* rabbi's wife?" I blew out, exasperated.

"I *told* you. The one with the crown. The one they wrote about in the papers. The one *he* lifted the idea of that story from. A rip-off that was, my cousin ought to sue."

Then I remembered. "All stories are rip-offs," I said. "Shakespeare stole his plots. Dostoyevski dug them out of the newspaper. Everybody steals. *The Decameron*'s stolen. Whatever looks like invention is theft."

"Great," he said, "that's what I need. Literary talk."

"What did you mean, you knew I would want to come?— Believe me, I didn't come for literary talk."

"You bet. You came because of my cousin. You came because of the crown."

I was amazed: instantly it coursed in on me that this was true. I had come because of the crown; I was in pursuit of the crown.

I said: "I don't care about the crown. I'm interested in the rabbi himself. The crown-blesser. What I care about is the psychology of the thing."

This word—"psychology"—made him cackle. "He's in jail, I thought you knew that. They got him for fraud."

"Does his wife still have any crowns around?"

"One."

"Here's your story," I said, handing it over. "Next time leave your name in. You don't have to obliterate it, rely on the world for that."

The pus on his eyelids glittered. "Alex will obliterate the world, not vice versa."

"How? By bombing it with stories? The first anonymous obliteration. The Flood without a by-line," I said. "At least everything God wrote was publishable. Alex what?"

"Goldflusser."

"You're a liar."

"Silbertsig."

"Cut it out."

"Kupferman. Bleifischer. Bettler. Kenigman."

"All that's mockery. If your name's a secret—"

"I'm lying low, hiding out, they're after me because I helped with the crowns."

I speculated, "You're the one who made them."

"No. She did that."

"Who?"

"My cousin. The rabbi's wife. She crocheted them. What he did was go buy the form—you get it from a costume loft, stainless steel. She used to make these little pointed sort of *gloves* for it, to protect it, see, and the shine would glimmer through, and then the customer would get to keep the crown-cover, as a sort of guarantee—"

"My God," I said, "what's all that about, why didn't *she* go to jail?"

"Crocheting isn't a crime."

"And you?" I said. "What did you do in all that?"

"Get customers. Fraudulent solicitation, that's a crime."

He took the typewriter off the chair and sat down. The wisp of beard wavered. "Didn't you like my story?" he accused. The pages were pressed with an urgency between his legs.

"No. It's all fake. It doesn't matter if you've been to Jerusalem. You've got the slant of the place all wrong. It doesn't matter about the yeshiva either. It doesn't matter if you really went to see some old geezer over there, you didn't get anything right. It's a terrible story."

"Where do you come off with that stuff?" he burst out. "Have *you* been to Jerusalem? Have *you* seen the inside of a yeshiva?"

"No."

"So!"

"I can tell when everything's fake," I said. "What I mean by fake is raw. When no one's ever used it before, it's something new under the sun, a whole new combination, that's bad. A real story is whatever you can predict, it has to be familiar, anyhow you have to know how it's going to come out, no exotic new material, no unexpected flights—"

He rushed out at me: "What you want is to bore people!"

"I'm a very boring writer," I admitted; out of politeness I kept from him how much his story, and even my own paraphrase of it, had already bored me. "But in *principle* I'm right. The only good part in the whole thing was explaining about the *ba'al ga'avah*. People hate to read foreign words, but at least it's ancient wisdom. Old, old stuff."

Then I told him how I had redesigned his story to include a ghost.

He opened the door of the stove and threw his manuscript in among the black-skinned potatoes.

"Why did you do that?"

"To show you I'm no *ba'al ga'avah*. I'm humble enough to burn up what somebody doesn't like."

I said suspiciously, "You've got other copies."

"Sure. Other potatoes too."

"Look," I said, riding malice, "it took me two hours to find this place, I have to go to the yard."

"You want to take a leak? Come over to my cousin's. It's not far. My cousin's lived in this neighborhood sixty years."

Furiously I went after him. He was a crook leading me to the house of crooks. We walked through barrenness and canker, a ruined city, store-windows painted black, one or two curtained by gypsies, some boarded, barred, barbed, old newspapers rolling in the gutter, the sidewalks speckled with viscous blotch. Overhead a smell like kerosene, the breath of tenements. The cousin's toilet stank as if no one had flushed it in half a century; it had one of those tanks high up, attached to the ceiling, a perpetual drip running down the pull chain. The sink was in the kitchen. There was no soap; I washed my hands with Ajax powder while the goat explained me to his cousin.

"She's interested in the crown," he said.

"Out of business," said the cousin.

"Maybe for her."

"Not doing business, that's all. For nobody whatsoever."

"I'm not interested in buying one," I said, "just in finding out."

"Crowns is against the law."

"For healing," the goat argued, "not for showing. She knows the man who wrote that story. You remember about that guy, I told you, this famous writer who took—"

"Who took! Too much fame," said the cousin, "is why Saul sits in jail. Before newspapers and stories we were left in peace, we helped people peacefully." She condemned me with an oil-surfaced eye, the colorless slick of the ripening cataract. "My husband, a holy man, him they put in jail. Him! A whole year, twelve months! A man like that! Brains, a saint—"

"But he fooled people," I said.

"In helping is no fooling. Out, lady. You had to pee, you peed. You needed a public facility, very good, now out. I don't look for extra customers for my toilet bowl."

"Goodbye," I said to the goat.

"You think there's hope for me?"

"Quit writing about ideas. Stay out of the yeshiva, watch out for religion. Don't make up stories about famous writers."

"Listen," he said—his nose was speckled with pustules of lust, his nostrils gaped—"you didn't like that one, I'll give you another. I've got plenty more, I've got a crateful."

"What are you talking," said the cousin.

"She knows writers," he said, "in person. She knows how to get things published."

I protested, "I can hardly get published myself—"

"You published something?" said the cousin.

"A few things, not much."

"Alex, bring Saul's box."

"That's not the kind of stuff," the goat said.

"Definitely. About expression I'm not so concerned like you. What isn't so regular, anyone with a desire and a pencil can fix it."

The goat remonstrated, "What Saul has is something else, it's not *writing*—"

"With connections," said the cousin, "nothing is something else, everything is writing. Lady, in one box I got my husband's entire holy life work. The entire theory of healing and making the dead ones come back for a personal appearance. We sent maybe to twenty printing houses, nothing doing. You got connections, I'll show you something."

"Print," I reminded her, "is what you said got the rabbi in trouble."

"Newspapers. Lies. False fame. Everything with a twist. You

call him rabbi, who made from him a rabbi? The entire world says rabbi, so let it be rabbi. There he sits in jail, a holy man what did nothing his whole life to harm. Whatever a person asked for, this was what he gave. Whatever you wanted to call him, this was what he became. Alex! Take out Saul's box, it's in the bottom of the dresser with the crown."

"The crown?" I said.

"The crown is nothing. What's something is Saul's brain. Alex!"

The goat shut his nostrils. He gave a snicker and disappeared. Through the kitchen doorway I glimpsed a sagging bed and heard a drawer grind open.

He came back lugging a carton with a picture of tomato cans on it. On top of it lay the crown. It was gloved in a green pattern of peephole diamonds.

"Here," said the cousin, "is Saul's ideas. Listen, that famous writer what went to steal from the papers—a fool. If he could steal what's in Saul's brain, what would he need a newspaper? Read!" She dipped a fist into a hiss of sheets and foamed up a sheaf of them. "You'll see, the world will rush to put in print. The judge at the trial—I said to him, look in Saul's box, you'll see the truth, no fraud. If they would read Saul's papers, not only would he not sit in jail, the judge with hair growing from his ears they would throw out!"

I looked at the goat; he was not laughing. He reached out and put the crown on my head.

It felt lighter than I imagined. It was easy to forget you were wearing it.

I read:

Why does menkind not get what they wish for? This is an easy solution. He is used to No. Always No. So it comes he is afraid to ask.

"The power of positive thinking," I said. "A philosopher."

"No, no," the cousin intervened, "not a philosopher, what do philosophers know to heal, to make real shadows from the dead?"

Through thinning threads of beard the goat said, "Not a philosopher."

I read:

Everything depends what you ask. Even you're not afraid to ask, plain asking is not sufficient. If you ask in a voice, there got to be an ear to listen in. The ear of Ha-shem, King of the Universe. (His Name we don't use it every minute like a shoelace.) A Jew don't go asking Ha-shem for inside information, for what reason He did this, what ideas He got on that, how come He let happen such-and-such a pogrom, why a good person loved by one and all dies with cancer, and a lousy bastard he's rotten to his partner and cheats and plays the numbers, this fellow lives to 120. With questions like this don't expect no replies, Ha-shem don't waste breath on trash from fleas. Ha-shem says, My secrets are My secrets, I command you what you got to do, the rest you leave to Me. This is no news that He don't reveal His deepest business. From that territory you get what you deserve, silence.

"What are you up to?" said the goat.

"Silence."

"Ssh!" said the cousin. "Alex, so let her read in peace!"

For us, not one word. He shuts up, His mouth is locked. So how come G-d conversed in history with Adam, with Abraham, with Moses? All right, you can argue that Moses and Abraham was worth it to G-d to listen to, what they said Ha-shem wanted to hear. After all they fed Him back His own ideas. An examination, and already they knew the answers. Smart guys, in the whole history of menkind no one else like these couple of guys. But with Adam, new and naked with no clothes on, just when the whole world was born, was Adam different from me and you? What did Adam know? Even right from wrong he didn't know yet. And still G-d thought, to Adam it's worthwhile to say a few words, I'm not wasting my breath. So what was so particular about Adam that he got Ha-shem's attention, and as regards me and you He don't blink an eye? Adam is better than me and you? We don't go around like a nudist colony, between good and lousy we already know what's what, with or without apples. To me and you G-d should also talk!

"You're following?" the cousin urged. "You see what's in Saul's brain? A whole box full like this, and sits in jail!"

But when it comes wishes, when it comes dreams, who says No? Who says Ha-shem stops talking? Wishes, dreams, imaginations —like fishes in the head. Ha-shem put in Joseph's head two good dreams, were they lies? The truth and nothing but the truth! Q.E.D. To Adam Ha-shem spoke one way, and when He finishes with Moses he talks another way. In a dream, in a wish. That *epikoros* Sigmund Freud, he also figured this out. Whomever says Sigmund Freud stinks from sex, they're mistaken. A wish is the voice, a dream is the voice, an imagination is the voice, all is the voice of Ha-shem the Creator. Naturally a voice is a biological thing, who says No? Whatsoever happens inside the human is a biological thing.

"What are you up to?" the goat asked again.
"Biology."
"Don't laugh: A man walked in here shaking all over, he walked out okay, I saw it myself."
The cousin said mournfully, "A healer."
"I wrote a terrific story about that guy, I figured what he had was cystic fibrosis, I can show you—"
"There isn't any market for medical stories," I said.
"This was a miracle story."
"There are no miracles."
"That's right!" said the cousin. She dug down again into the box. "One time only, instead of plain writing down, Saul made up a story on this subject exactly. On a yellow piece paper. Aha, here. Alex, read aloud."
The goat read:

One night in the middle of dim stars Ha-shem said, No more miracles! An end with miracles, I already did enough, from now on nothing.

So a king makes an altar and bows down. "O Ha-shem, King

of the Universe, I got a bad war on my hands and I'm taking a beating. Make a miracle and save the whole country." Nothing doing, no miracle.

Good, says Ha-shem, this is how it's going to be from now on.

So along comes the Germans, in the camp they got a father and a little son maybe twelve years old. And the son is on the list to be gassed tomorrow. So the father runs around to find a German to bribe, G-d knows what he's got to bribe him with, maybe his wife's diamond ring that he hid somewhere and they didn't take it away yet. And he fixes up the whole thing, tomorrow he'll bring the diamond to the German and they'll take the boy off the list and they won't kill him. They'll slip in some other boy instead and who will know the difference?

Well, so that could be the end, but it isn't. All day after everything's fixed up, the father is thinking and thinking, and in the middle of the night he goes to an old rabbi that's in the camp also, and he tells the rabbi he's going to save his little son.

And the rabbi says, "So why come to me? You made your decision already." The father says, "Yes, but they'll put another boy in his place." The rabbi says, "Instead of Isaac, Abraham put a ram. And that was for G-d. You put another child, and for what? To feed Moloch." The father asks, "What is the law on this?" "The law is, Don't kill."

The next day the father don't bring the bribe. And his eyes don't never see his beloved little child again. Well, so that could be the end, but it isn't. Ha-shem looks at what's happening, here is a man what didn't save his own boy so he wouldn't be responsible with killing someone else. Ha-shem says to Himself, I made a miracle anyhow. I blew in one man so much power of My commandments that his own flesh and blood he lets go to Moloch, so long he shouldn't kill. That I created even one such person like this is a very great miracle, and I didn't even notice I was doing it. So now positively no more.

And after this the destruction continues, no interruptions. Not only the son is gassed, but also the father, and also the boy what they would have put in his place. And also and also and also, until millions of bones of alsos goes up in smoke. About miracles Ha-shem don't change his mind except by accident. So the question menkind has to ask their conscience is this: If the father wasn't such a good commandment-keeper that it's actually a miracle to find a man like this left in the world, what could happen instead? And if only one single miracle could slip through before G-d notices it, which one? Suppose this father didn't use up the one miracle, suppose the miracle is that G-d will stop the murderers altogether, suppose! Instead: nothing doing, the father on account of one kid eats up the one miracle that's lying around loose. For the sake of one life, the whole world is lost.

But on this subject, what's written in our holy books? What the sages got to say? The sages say different: If you save one life only, it's like the whole world is saved. So which is true? Naturally, whatever's written is what's true. What does this prove? It proves that if you talk miracle, that's when everything becomes false. Men and women! Remember! No stories from miracles! No stories and no belief!

"You see?" said the cousin. "Here you have Saul's theories exactly. Whoever says miracles, whoever says magic, tells a lie. On account of a lie a holy man sits in a cage."

"And the crown?" I asked.

She ignored this. "You'll help to publish. You'll give to the right people, you'll give to connections—"

"But why? Why do you need this?"

"What's valuable you give away, you don't keep it for yourself. Listen, is the Bible a secret? The whole world takes from it. Is Talmud a secret? Whatever's a lie should be a secret, not what's holy and true!"

I appealed to the goat. He was licking his fingertips. "I can't digest any of this—"

"You haven't had a look at Saul," he said, "that's why."

The cousin said meanly, "I saw you put on her the crown."

"She wants it."

"The crown is nothing."

"She wants it."

"Then show her Saul."

"You mean in prison?" I said.

"In the bedroom on the night table."

The goat fled. This time he returned carrying a small gilded tin frame. In it was a snapshot of another bearded man.

"Look closely."

But instead of examining the photograph, I all at once wanted to study the goat's cousin. She was one of those tiny twig-thin old women who seem to enlarge the more you get used to their voices. It was as if her whine and her whirr were a pump, and pumped her up; she was now easily as tall as I (though I am myself not very tall) and expanding curiously. She was wearing a checked nylon housedress and white socks in slippers, above which bulged purplish varicose nodules. Her eyes were terribly magnified by metal-rimmed lenses, and looked out at me with the vengefulness of a pair of greased platters. I was astonished to see that a chromium crown had buried itself among the strings of her wandering hairs: having been too often dyed ebony, they were slipping out of their follicles and onto her collarbone. She had an exaggerated widow's peak and was elsewhere a little bit bald.

The goat too wore a crown.

"I thought there was only one left," I objected.

"Look at Saul, you'll see the only one."

The man in the picture wore a silver crown. I recognized him, though the light was shut off in him and the space of his flesh was clearly filled.

"Who is this?" I said.

"Saul."

"But I've seen him!"

"That's right," the cousin said.

"Because you wanted to," said the goat.

"The ghost I put in your story," I reminded him, "this is what it looked like."

The cousin breathed. "You published that story?"

"It's not even written down."

"Whose ghost was it?" asked the goat.

"Tchernikhovsky's. The Hebrew poet. A *ba'al ga'avah*. He wrote a poem called 'Before the Statue of Apollo.' In the last line God is bound with leather thongs."

"Who binds him?"

"The Jews. With their phylacteries. I want to read more," I said.

The two of them gave me the box. The little picture they set on the kitchen table, and they stood over me in their twinkling crowns while I splashed my hands through the false rabbi's stories. Some were already browning at the margins, in ink turned violet, some were on lined school paper, written with a ball-point pen. About a third were in Yiddish; there was even a thin notebook all in Russian; but most were pressed out in pencil in an immigrant's English on all kinds of odd loose sheets, the insides of old New Year greeting cards, the backs of cashiers' tapes from the supermarket, in one instance the ripped-out leather womb of an old wallet.

Saul's ideas were:

sorcery, which he denied.
levitation, which he doubted.
magic, which he sneered at.
miracles, which he denounced.
healing, which he said belonged in hospitals.
instant cures, which he said were fancies and delusions.
the return of deceased loved ones, which he said were wishful.
    hallucinations.
the return of dead enemies, which ditto.
plural gods, which he disputed.
demons, which he derided.
amulets, which he disparaged and repudiated.
Satan, from which hypothesis he scathingly dissented.

He ridiculed everything. He was a rationalist.

"It's amazing," I said, "that he looks just like Tchernik-hovsky."

"What does Tchernikhovsky look like?" one of the two crowned ones asked me; I was no longer sure which.

"I don't know, how should I know? Once I saw his picture in an anthology of translations, but I don't remember it. Why are there so many crowns in this room? What's the point of these crowns?"

Then I found the paper on crowns:

You take a real piece mineral, what kings wear. You put it on, you become like a king. What you wish, you get. But what you get you shouldn't believe in unless it's real. How do you know when something's real? If it lasts. How long? This depends. If you wish for a Pyramid, it should last as long like a regular Pyramid lasts. If you wish for long life, it should last as long like your own grandfather. If you wish for a Magic Crown, it should last as long like the brain what it rests on.

I interrupted myself: "Why doesn't he wish himself out of prison? Why didn't he wish himself out of getting sentenced?"

"He lets things take their course."

Then I found the paper on things taking their course:

From my own knowledge I knew a fellow what loved a woman, Beylinke, and she died. So he looked and looked for a twin to this Beylinke, and it's no use, such a woman don't exist. Instead he married a different type altogether, and he made her change her name to Beylinke and make love on the left side, like the real Beylinke. And if he called Beylinke! and she forgot to answer (her name was Ethel) he gave her a good knock on the back, and one day he knocked hard into the kidney and she got a growth and she died. And all he got from his forcing was a lonesome life.

Everything is according to destiny, you can't change nothing. Not that anybody can know what happens before it happens, not even Ha-shem knows which dog will bite which cat next week in Persia.

"Enough," said one of the two in the crowns. "You read and

you took enough. You ate enough and you drank enough from
this juice. Now you got to pay."

"To pay?"

"The payment is, to say thank you what we showed you
everything, you take and you publish."

"Publishing isn't the same as Paradise."

"For some of us it is," said one.

"She knows from Paradise!" scoffed the other.

They thrust the false rabbi's face into my face.

"It isn't English, it isn't even coherent, it's inconsistent,
it's crazy, nothing hangs together, nobody in his right mind
would—"

"Connections you got."

"No."

"That famous writer."

"A stranger."

"Then somebody else."

"There's no one. I can't make magic—"

"*Ba'al ga'avah!* You're better than Saul? Smarter? Cleverer?
You got better ideas? You, a nothing, they print, and he sits in
a box?"

"I looked up one of your stories. It stank, lady. The one
called 'Usurpation.' Half of it's swiped, you ought to get sued.
You don't know when to stop. You swipe other people's stories
and you go on and on, on and on, I fell asleep over it. Boring!
Long-winded!"

The mass of sheets pitched into my lap. My fingers flashed
upward: there was the crown, with its crocheted cover, its
blunted points. Little threads had gotten tangled in my hair. If
I tugged, the roots would shriek. Tchernikhovsky's paper eyes
looked frightened. Crevices opened on either side of his nose
and from the left nostril the gray bone of his skull poked out, a
cheekbone like a pointer.

"I don't have better ideas," I said. "I'm not interested in
ideas, I don't care about ideas. I hate ideas. I only care about
stories."

"Then take Saul's stories!"

"Trash. Justice and mercy. He tells you how to live, what

to do, the way to think. Righteousness fables, morality tales. Didactic stuff. Rabbinical trash," I said. "What I mean is *stories*. Even you," I said to the goat, "wanting to write about writers! Morality, mortality! You people eat yourself up with morality and mortality!"

"What else should a person eat?"

Just then I began to feel the weight of the crown. It pressed unerringly into the secret tunnels of my brain. A pain like a grief leaped up behind my eyes, up through the temples, up, up, into the marrow of the crown. Every point of it was a spear, a nail. The crown was no different from the bone of my head. The false rabbi Tchernikhovsky tore himself from the tin prison of his frame and sped to the ceiling as if gassed. He had bluish teeth and goblin's wings made of brown leather. Except for the collar and cravat that showed in the photograph, below his beard he was naked. His testicles were leathery. His eyeballs were glass, like a doll's. He was solid as a doll; I was not so light-headed as to mistake him for an apparition. His voice was as spindly as a harpsichord: "Choose!"

"Between what and what?"

"The Creator or the creature. God or god. The Name of Names or Apollo."

"Apollo," I said on the instant.

"Good," he tinkled, "blessings," he praised me, "flowings and flowings, streams, brooks, lakes, waters out of waters."

Stories came from me then, births and births of tellings, narratives and suspenses, turning-points and palaces, foam of the sea, mermen sewing, dragons pullulating out of quicksilver, my mouth was a box, my ears flowed, they gushed legends and tales, none of them of my own making, all of them acquired, borrowed, given, taken, inherited, stolen, plagiarized, usurped, chronicles and sagas invented at the beginning of the world by the offspring of giants copulating with the daughters of men. A king broke out of the shell of my left eye and a queen from the right one, the box of my belly lifted its scarred lid to let out frogs and swans, my womb was cleft and stories burst free of their balls of blood. Stories choked the kitchen, crept up the toilet tank, replenished the bedroom, knocked off the goat's crown, knocked off the cousin's crown, my own crown in its coat contended with the vines and tangles of my hair, the false rabbi's beard had turned into strips of leather, into whips, the whips struck at my crown, it slid to my forehead, the whips curled round my arm, the crown sliced the flesh of my forehead.

At last it fell off.

The cousin cried out her husband's name.

"Alex," I called to the goat: the name of a conqueror, Aristotle's pupil, the arrogant god-man.

In the hollow streets which the Jews had left behind there were scorched absences, apparitions, usurpers. Someone had broken the glass of the kosher butcher's abandoned window and thrown in a pig's head, with anatomical tubes still dripping from the neck.

When we enter Paradise there will be a cage for storywriters, who will be taught as follows:

All that is not Law is levity.

But we have not yet ascended. The famous writer has not. The goat has not. The false rabbi has not; he sits out his year. A vanity press is going to bring out his papers. The bill for editing, printing, and binding will be $1,847.45. The goat's cousin will pay for it from a purse in the bottom bowel of the night table.

The goat inhabits the deserted synagogue, drinking wine, littering the yard with his turds. Occasionally he attends a public reading. Many lusts live in his chin-hairs, like lice.

Only Tchernikhovsky and the shy old writer of Jerusalem have ascended. The old writer of Jerusalem is a fiction; murmuring psalms, he snacks on leviathan and polishes his Prize with the cuff of his sleeve. Tchernikhovsky eats nude at the table of the nude gods, clean-shaven now, his limbs radiant, his youth restored, his sex splendidly erect, the discs of his white ears sparkling, a convivial fellow; he eats without self-restraint from the celestial menu, and when the Sabbath comes (the

Sabbath of Sabbaths, which flowers every seven centuries in the perpetual Sabbath of Eden), as usual he avoids the congregation of the faithful before the Footstool and the Throne. Then the taciturn little Canaanite idols call him, in the language of the spheres, kike.

Levitation

A PAIR OF novelists, husband and wife, gave a party. The husband was also an editor; he made his living at it. But really he was a novelist. His manner was powerless; he did not seem like an editor at all. He had a nice plain pale face, likable. His name was Feingold.

For love, and also because he had always known he did not want a Jewish wife, he married a minister's daughter. Lucy too had hoped to marry out of her tradition. (These words were hers. "Out of my tradition," she said. The idea fevered him.) At the age of twelve she felt herself to belong to the people of the Bible. ("A Hebrew," she said. His heart lurched, joy rocked him.) One night from the pulpit her father read a Psalm; all at once she saw how the Psalmist meant *her*; then and there she became an Ancient Hebrew.

She had huge, intent, sliding eyes, disconcertingly luminous, and copper hair, and a grave and timid way of saying honest things.

They were shy people, and rarely gave parties.

Each had published one novel. Hers was about domestic life; he wrote about Jews.

All the roil about the State of the Novel had passed them by. In the evening after the children had been put to bed, while the portable dishwasher rattled out its smell of burning motor oil, they sat down, she at her desk, he at his, and began to write. They wrote not without puzzlements and travail; nevertheless as naturally as birds. They were devoted to accuracy, psychological realism, and earnest truthfulness; also to virtue, and even to wit. Neither one was troubled by what had happened to the novel: all those declarations about the end of Character and Story. They were serene. Sometimes, closing up their notebooks for the night, it seemed to them that they were literary friends and lovers, like George Eliot and George Henry Lewes.

In bed they would revel in quantity and murmur distrustingly of theory. "Seven pages so far this week." "Nine-and-a-half, but I had to throw out four. A wrong tack." "Because you're doing first person. First person strangles. You can't get out of their skin." And so on. The one principle they agreed on was the importance of never writing about writers. Your protagonist always has to be someone *real*, with real work-in-the-world—a bureaucrat, a banker, an architect (ah, they envied Conrad his shipmasters!)—otherwise you fall into solipsism, narcissism, tedium, lack of appeal-to-the-common-reader; who knew what other perils.

This difficulty—seizing on a concrete subject—was mainly Lucy's. Feingold's novel—the one he was writing now—was about Menachem ben Zerach, survivor of a massacre of Jews in the town of Estella in Spain in 1328. From morning to midnight he hid under a pile of corpses, until a "compassionate knight" (this was the language of the history Feingold relied on) plucked him out and took him home to tend his wounds. Menachem was then twenty; his father and mother and four younger brothers had been cut down in the terror. Six thousand Jews died in a single day in March. Feingold wrote well about how the mild winds carried the salty fragrance of fresh blood, together with the ashes of Jewish houses, into the faces of the marauders. It was nevertheless a triumphant story: at the end Menachem ben Zerach becomes a renowned scholar.

"If you're going to tell about how after he gets to be a scholar he just sits there and *writes*," Lucy protested, "then you're doing the Forbidden Thing." But Feingold said he meant to concentrate on the massacre, and especially on the life of the "compassionate knight." What had brought him to this compassion? What sort of education? What did he read? Feingold would invent a journal for the compassionate knight, and quote from it. Into this journal the compassionate knight would direct all his gifts, passions, and private opinions.

"Solipsism," Lucy said. "Your compassionate knight is only another writer. Narcissism. Tedium."

They talked often about the Forbidden Thing. After a while

they began to call it the Forbidden City, because not only
were they (but Lucy especially) tempted to write—solipsistically,
narcissistically, tediously, and without common appeal—about
writers, but, more narrowly yet, about writers in New York.

"The compassionate knight," Lucy said, "lived on the Upper
West Side of Estella. He lived on the Riverside Drive, the West
End Avenue, of Estella. He lived in Estella on Central Park
West."

The Feingolds lived on Central Park West.

In her novel—the published one, not the one she was writing
now—Lucy had described, in the first person, where they lived:

> By now I have seen quite a few of those West Side apart-
> ments. They have mysterious layouts. Rooms with doors
> that go nowhere—turn the knob, open: a wall. Someone
> is snoring behind it, in another apartment. They have
> made two and three or even four and five flats out of
> these palaces. The toilet bowls have antique cracks that
> shimmer with moisture like old green rivers. Fluted
> columns and fireplaces. Artur Rubinstein once paid rent
> here. On a gilt piano he raced a sonata by Beethoven.
> The sounds went spinning like mercury. Breathings all
> lettered now. Editors. Critics. Books, old, old books,
> heavy as centuries. Shelves built into the cold fireplace;
> Freud on the grate, Marx on the hearth, Melville, Haw-
> thorne, Emerson. Oh God, the weight, the weight.

Lucy felt herself to be a stylist; Feingold did not. He believed
in putting one sentence after another. In his publishing house
he had no influence. He was nervous about his decisions. He
rejected most manuscripts because he was afraid of mistakes;
every mistake lost money. It was a small house panting after
profits; Feingold told Lucy that the only books his firm respected belonged to the accountants. Now and then he tried to
smuggle in a novel after his own taste, and then he would be
brutal to the writer. He knocked the paragraphs about until
they were as sparse as his own. "God knows what you would
do to mine," Lucy said; "bald man, bald prose." The horizon

of Feingold's head shone. She never showed him her work. But they understood they were lucky in each other. They pitied every writer who was not married to a writer. Lucy said: "At least we have the same premises."

Volumes of Jewish history ran up and down their walls; they belonged to Feingold. Lucy read only one book—it was *Emma*—over and over again. Feingold did not have a "philosophical" mind. What he liked was event. Lucy liked to speculate and ruminate. She was slightly more intelligent than Feingold. To strangers he seemed very mild. Lucy, when silent, was a tall copper statue.

They were both devoted to omniscience, but they were not acute enough to see what they meant by it. They thought of themselves as children with a puppet theater: they could make anything at all happen, speak all the lines, with gloved hands bring all the characters to shudders or leaps. They fancied themselves in love with what they called "imagination." It was not true. What they were addicted to was counterfeit pity, and this was because they were absorbed by power, and were powerless.

They lived on pity, and therefore on gossip: who had been childless for ten years, who had lost three successive jobs, who was in danger of being fired, which agent's prestige had fallen, who could not get his second novel published, who was *persona non grata* at this or that magazine, who was drinking seriously, who was a likely suicide, who was dreaming of divorce, who was secretly or flamboyantly sleeping with whom, who was being snubbed, who counted or did not count; and toward everyone in the least way victimized they appeared to feel the most immoderate tenderness. They were, besides, extremely "psychological": kind listeners, helpful, lifting hot palms they would gladly put to anyone's anguished temples. They were attracted to bitter lives.

About their own lives they had a joke: they were "secondary-level" people. Feingold had a secondary-level job with a secondary-level house. Lucy's own publisher was secondary-level; even the address was Second Avenue. The reviews of their books had been written by secondary-level reviewers. All their friends were secondary-level: not the presidents or partners of the respected firms, but copy editors and production assistants; not the glittering eagles of the intellectual organs, but the wearisome hacks of small Jewish journals; not the fiercely cold-hearted literary critics, but those wan and chattering daily reviewers of film. If they knew a playwright, he was off-off-Broadway in ambition and had not yet been produced. If they knew a painter, he lived in a loft and had exhibited only once, against the wire fence in the outdoor show at Washington Square in the spring. And this struck them as mean and unfair; they liked their friends, but other people—why not they?— were drawn into the deeper caverns of New York, among the lions.

New York! They risked their necks if they ventured out to Broadway for a loaf of bread after dark; muggers hid behind the seesaws in the playgrounds, junkies with knives hung upside down in the jungle gym. Every apartment a lit fortress; you admired the lamps and the locks, the triple locks on the caged-in windows, the double locks and the police rods on the doors, the lamps with timers set to make burglars think you were always at home. Footsteps in the corridor, the elevator's midnight grind; caution's muffled gasps. Their parents lived in Cleveland and St. Paul, and hardly ever dared to visit. All of this: grit and unsuitability (they might have owned a snowy lawn somewhere else); and no one said their names, no one had any curiosity about them, no one ever asked whether they were working on anything new. After half a year their books were remaindered for eighty-nine cents each. Anonymous mediocrities. They could not call themselves forgotten because they had never been noticed.

Lucy had a diagnosis: they were, both of them, sunk in a ghetto. Feingold persisted in his morbid investigations into Inquisitional autos-da-fé in this and that Iberian market-place. She herself had supposed the inner life of a housebound woman—she cited *Emma*—to contain as much comedy as the cosmos. Jews and women! They were both beside the point. It was necessary to put aside pity; to look to the center; to abandon selflessness; to study power.

They drew up a list of luminaries. They invited Irving Howe,

Susan Sontag, Alfred Kazin, and Leslie Fiedler. They invited
Norman Podhoretz and Elizabeth Hardwick. They invited Philip
Roth and Joyce Carol Oates and Norman Mailer and William
Styron and Donald Barthelme and Jerzy Kosinski and Truman
Capote. None of these came; all of them had unlisted numbers,
or else machines that answered the telephone, or else were in
Prague or Paris or out of town. Nevertheless the apartment
filled up. It was a Saturday night in a chill November. Taxis
whirled on patches of sleet. On the inside of the apartment
door a mound of rainboots grew taller and taller. Two closets
were packed tight with raincoats and fur coats; a heap of coats
smelling of skunk and lamb fell tangled off a bed.

The party washed and turned like a sluggish tub; it lapped
at all the walls of all the rooms. Lucy wore a long skirt, violet-
colored, Feingold a lemon shirt and no tie. He looked paler than
ever. The apartment had a wide center hall, itself the breadth
of a room; the dining room opened off it to the left, the living
room to the right. The three party-rooms shone like a triptych:
it was as if you could fold them up and enclose everyone into
darkness. The guests were free-standing figures in the niches
of a cathedral; or else dressed-up cardboard dolls, with their
drinks, and their costumes all meticulously hung with sashes
and draped collars and little capes, the women's hair variously
bound, the men's sprouting and spilling: fashion stalked, Feingold moped. He took in how it all flashed, manhattans and
martinis, earrings and shoe-tips—he marveled, but knew it was
a falsehood, even a figment. The great world was somewhere
else. The conversation could fool you: how these people talked!
From the conversation itself—grains of it, carried off, swallowed by new eddyings, swirl devouring swirl, every moment
a permutation in the tableau of those free-standing figures or
dolls, all of them afloat in a tub—from this or that hint or
syllable you could imagine the whole universe in the process
of ultimate comprehension. Human nature, the stars, history—
the voices drummed and strummed. Lucy swam by blank-eyed,
pushing a platter of mottled cheeses. Feingold seized her: "It's a
waste!" She gazed back. He said, "No one's here!" Mournfully
she rocked a stump of cheese; then he lost her.

He went into the living room: it was mainly empty, a few lumps on the sofa. The lumps wore business suits. The dining room was better. Something in formation: something around the big table: coffee cups shimmering to the brim, cake cut onto plates (the mock-Victorian rosebud plates from Boots's drug store in London: the year before their first boy was born Lucy and Feingold saw the Brontës' moors; Coleridge's house in Highgate; Lamb House, Rye, where Edith Wharton had tea with Henry James; Bloomsbury; the Cambridge stairs Forster had lived at the top of)—it seemed about to become a regular visit, with points of view, opinions; a discussion. The voices began to stumble; Feingold liked that, it was nearly human. But then, serving round the forks and paper napkins, he noticed the awful vivacity of their falsetto phrases: actors, theater chatter, who was directing whom, what was opening where; he hated actors. Shrill puppets. Brainless. A double row of faces around the table; gurgles of fools.

The center hall—swept clean. No one there but Lucy, lingering.

"Theater in the dining room," he said. "Junk."

"Film. I heard film."

"Film too," he conceded. "Junk. It's mobbed in there."

"Because they've got the cake. They've got all the food. The living room's got nothing."

"My God," he said, like a man choking, "do you realize *no one came*?"

The living room had—had once had—potato chips. The chips were gone, the carrot sticks eaten, of the celery sticks nothing left but threads. One olive in a dish; Feingold chopped it in two with vicious teeth. The business suits had disappeared. "It's awfully early," Lucy said; "a lot of people had to leave." "It's a cocktail party, that's what happens," Feingold said. "It isn't *exactly* a cocktail party," Lucy said. They sat down on the carpet in front of the fireless grate. "Is that a real fireplace?" someone inquired. "We never light it," Lucy said. "Do you light those candlesticks ever?" "They belonged to Jimmy's grandmother," Lucy said, "we never light them."

She crossed no-man's-land to the dining room. They were serious in there now. The subject was Chaplin's gestures.

In the living room Feingold despaired; no one asked him, he began to tell about the compassionate knight. A problem of ego, he said: compassion being superconsciousness of one's own pride. Not that he believed this; he only thought it provocative to say something original, even if a little muddled. But no one responded. Feingold looked up. "Can't you light that fire?" said a man. "All right," Feingold said. He rolled a paper log made of last Sunday's *Times* and laid a match on it. A flame as clear as a streetlight whitened the faces of the sofa-sitters. He recognized a friend of his from the Seminary—he had what Lucy called "theological" friends—and then and there, really very suddenly, Feingold wanted to talk about God. Or, if not God, then certain historical atrocities, abominations: to wit, the crime of the French nobleman Draconet, a proud Crusader, who in the spring of the year 1247 arrested all the Jews of the province of Vienne, castrated the men, and tore off the breasts of the women; some he did not mutilate, and only cut in two. It interested Feingold that Magna Carta and the Jewish badge of shame were issued in the same year, and that less than a century afterward all the Jews were driven out of England, even families who had been settled there seven or eight generations. He had a soft spot for Pope Clement IV, who absolved the Jews from responsibility for the Black Death. "The plague takes the Jews themselves," the Pope said. Feingold knew innumerable stories about forced conversions, he felt at home with these thoughts, comfortable, the chairs seemed dense with family. He wondered whether it would be appropriate—at a cocktail party, after all!—to inquire after the status of the Seminary friend's agnosticism: was it merely that God had stepped out of history, left the room for a moment, so to speak, without a pass, or was there no Creator to begin with, nothing had been created, the world was a chimera, a solipsist's delusion?

Lucy was uneasy with the friend from the Seminary; he was the one who had administered her conversion, and every encounter was like a new stage in a perpetual examination. She was glad there was no Jewish catechism. Was she a backslider?

Anyhow she felt tested. Sometimes she spoke of Jesus to the children. She looked around—her great eyes wheeled—and saw that everyone in the living room was a Jew.

There were Jews in the dining room too, but the unruffled, devil-may-care kind: the humorists, the painters, film reviewers who went off to studio showings of *Screw on Screen* on the eve of the Day of Atonement. Mostly there were Gentiles in the dining room. Nearly the whole cake was gone. She took the last piece, cubed it on a paper plate, and carried it back to the living room. She blamed Feingold, he was having one of his spasms of fanaticism. Everyone normal, everyone with sense—the humanists and humorists, for instance—would want to keep away. What was he now, after all, but one of those boring autodidacts who spew out everything they read? He was doing it for spite, because no one had come. There he was, telling about the blood-libel. Little Hugh of Lincoln. How in London, in 1279, Jews were torn to pieces by horses, on a charge of having crucified a Christian child. How in 1285, in Munich, a mob burned down a synagogue on the same pretext. At Eastertime in Mainz two years earlier. Three centuries of beatified child martyrs, some of them figments, all called "Little Saints." The Holy Niño of LaGuardia. Feingold was crazed by these tales, he drank them like a vampire. Lucy stuck a square of chocolate cake in his mouth to shut him up. Feingold was waiting for a voice. The friend from the Seminary, pragmatic, licked off his bit of cake hungrily. It was a cake sent from home, packed by his wife in a plastic bag, to make sure there was something to eat. It was a guaranteed no-lard cake. They were all ravenous. The fire crumpled out in big paper cinders.

The friend from the Seminary had brought a friend. Lucy examined him: she knew how to give catechisms of her own, she was not a novelist for nothing. She catechized and catalogued: a refugee. Fingers like long wax candles, snuffed at the nails. Black sockets: was he blind? It was hard to tell where the eyes were under that ledge of skull. Skull for a head, but such a cushioned mouth, such lips, such orderly expressive teeth. Such a bone in such a dry wrist. A nose like a saint's. The face of Jesus. He whispered. Everyone leaned over to hear.

He was Feingold's voice: the voice Feingold was waiting for.

"Come to modern times," the voice urged. "Come to yesterday." Lucy was right: she could tell a refugee in an instant, even before she heard any accent. They all reminded her of her father. She put away this insight (the resemblance of Presbyterian ministers to Hitler refugees) to talk over with Feingold later: it was nicely analytical, it had enough mystery to satisfy. "Yesterday," the refugee said, "the eyes of God were shut." And Lucy saw him shut his hidden eyes in their tunnels. "Shut," he said, "like iron doors"—a voice of such nobility that Lucy thought immediately of that eerie passage in Genesis where the voice of the Lord God walks in the Garden in the cool of the day and calls to Adam, "Where are you?"

They all listened with a terrible intensity. Again Lucy looked around. It pained her how intense Jews could be, though she too was intense. But she was intense because her brain was roiling with ardor, she wooed mind-pictures, she was a novelist. *They* were intense all the time; she supposed the grocers among them were as intense as any novelist; was it because they had been Chosen, was it because they pitied themselves every breathing moment?

Pity and shock stood in all their faces.

The refugee was telling a story. "I witnessed it," he said, "I am the witness." Horror; sadism; corpses. As if—Lucy took the image from the elusive wind that was his voice in its whisper— as if hundreds and hundreds of Crucifixions were all happening at once. She visualized a hillside with multitudes of crosses, and bodies dropping down from big bloody nails. Every Jew was Jesus. That was the only way Lucy could get hold of it: otherwise it was only a movie. She had seen all the movies, the truth was she could feel nothing. That same bulldozer shoveling those same sticks of skeletons, that same little boy in a cap with twisted mouth and his hands in the air—if there had been a camera at the Crucifixion Christianity would collapse, no one would ever feel anything about it. Cruelty came out of the imagination, and had to be witnessed by the imagination.

All the same, she listened. What he told was exactly like the movies. A gray scene, a scrubby hill, a ravine. Germans in helmets, with shining tar-black belts, wearing gloves. A ragged bundle of Jews at the lip of the ravine—an old grandmother, a child or two, a couple in their forties. All the faces stained with grayness, the stubble on the ground stained gray, the clothes on them limp as shrouds but immobile, as if they were already under the dirt, shut off from breezes, as if they were already stone. The refugee's whisper carved them like sculptures—there they stood, a shadowy stone asterisk of Jews, you could see their nostrils, open as skulls, the stony round ears of the children, the grandmother's awful twig of a neck, the father and mother grasping the children but strangers to each other, not a touch between them, the grandmother cast out, claiming no one and not claimed, all prayerless stone gums. There they stood. For a long while the refugee's voice pinched them and held them, so that you had to look. His voice made Lucy look and look. He pierced the figures through with his whisper. Then he let the shots come. The figures never tee-tered, never shook: the stoniness broke all at once and they fell cleanly, like sacks, into the ravine. Immediately they were in a heap, with random limbs all tangled together. The refugee's voice like a camera brought a German boot to the edge of the ravine. The boot kicked sand. It kicked and kicked, the sand poured over the family of sacks.

Then Lucy saw the fingers of the listeners—all their fingers were stretched out.

The room began to lift. It ascended. It rose like an ark on waters. Lucy said inside her mind, "This chamber of Jews." It seemed to her that the room was levitating on the little grains of the refugee's whisper. She felt herself alone at the bottom, below the floorboards, while the room floated upward, carrying Jews. Why did it not take her too? Only Jesus could take her. They were being kidnapped, these Jews, by a messenger from the land of the dead. The man had a power. Already he was in the shadow of another tale: she promised herself she would not listen, only Jesus could make her listen. The room was ascending. Above her head it grew smaller and smaller, more and more remote, it fled deeper and deeper into upwardness.

She craned after it. Wouldn't it bump into the apartment

upstairs? It was like watching the underside of an elevator, all dirty and hairy, with dust-roots wagging. The black floor moved higher and higher. It was getting free of her, into loftiness, lifting Jews.

The glory of their martyrdom.

Under the rising eave Lucy had an illumination: she saw herself with the children in a little city park. A Sunday afternoon early in May. Feingold has stayed home to nap, and Lucy and the children find seats on a bench and wait for the unusual music to begin. The room is still levitating, but inside Lucy's illumination the boys are chasing birds. They run away from Lucy, they return, they leave. They surround a pigeon. They do not touch the pigeon; Lucy has forbidden it. She has read that city pigeons carry meningitis. A little boy in Red Bank, New Jersey, contracted sleeping sickness from touching a pigeon; after six years, he is still alseep. In his sleep he has grown from a child to an adolescent; puberty has come on him in his sleep, his testicles have dropped down, a benign blond beard glints mildly on his cheeks. His parents weep and weep. He is still asleep. No instruments or players are visible. A woman steps out onto a platform. She is an anthropologist from the Smithsonian Institution in Washington, D.C. She explains that there will be no "entertainment" in the usual sense; there will be no "entertainers." The players will not be artists; they will be "real peasants." They have been brought over from Messina, from Calabria. They are shepherds, goatherds. They will sing and dance and play just as they do when they come down from the hills to while away the evenings in the taverns. They will play the instruments that scare away the wolves from the flock. They will sing the songs that celebrate the Madonna of Love. A dozen men file onto the platform. They have heavy faces that do not smile. They have heavy dark skins, cratered and leathery. They have ears and noses that look like dried twisted clay. They have gold teeth. They have no teeth. Some are young; most are in their middle years. One is very old; he wears bells on his fingers. One has an instrument like a butter churn: he shoves a stick in and out of a hole in a wooden tub held under his arm, and a rattling screech spurts out of it. One blows on two slender pipes simultaneously. One has a long strap, which he rubs. One has a frame of bicycle bells; a descendant of the bells the priests used to beat in the temple of Minerva.

The anthropologist is still explaining everything. She explains the "male" instrument: three wooden knockers; the innermost one lunges up and down between the other two. The songs, she explains, are mainly erotic. The dances are suggestive.

The unusual music commences. The park has filled with Italians—greenhorns from Sicily, settled New Yorkers from Naples. An ancient people. They clap. The old man with the bells on his fingers points his dusty shoe-toes and slowly follows a circle of his own. His eyes are in trance, he squats, he ascends. The anthropologist explains that up-and-down dancing can also be found in parts of Africa. The singers wail like Arabs; the anthropologist notes that the Arab conquest covered the southernmost portion of the Italian boot for two hundred years. The whole chorus of peasants sings in a dialect of archaic Greek; the language has survived in the old songs, the anthropologist explains. The crowd is laughing and stamping. They click their fingers and sway. Lucy's boys are bored. They watch the man with the finger-bells; they watch the wooden male pump up and down. Everyone is clapping, stamping, clicking, swaying, thumping. The wailing goes on and on, faster and faster. The singers are dancers, the dancers are singers, they turn and turn, they are smiling the drugged smiles of dervishes. At home they grow flowers. They follow the sheep into the deep grass. They drink wine in the taverns at night. Calabria and Sicily in New York, sans wives, in sweat-blotched shirts and wrinkled dusty pants, gasping before strangers who have never smelled the sweetness of their village grasses!

Now the anthropologist from the Smithsonian has vanished out of Lucy's illumination. A pair of dancers seize each other. Leg winds over leg, belly into belly, each man hopping on a single free leg. Intertwined, they squat and rise, squat and rise. Old Hellenic syllables fly from them. They send out high elastic cries. They celebrate the Madonna, giver of fertility and fecundity. Lucy is glorified. She is exalted. She comprehends.

Not that the musicians are peasants, not that their faces and feet and necks and wrists are blown grass and red earth. An enlightenment comes on her: she sees what is eternal: before the Madonna there was Venus; before Venus, Aphrodite; before Aphrodite, Astarte. The womb of the goddess is garden, lamb, and babe. She is the river and the waterfall. She causes grave men of business—goatherds are men of business—to cavort and to flash their gold teeth. She induces them to blow, beat, rub, shake and scrape objects so that music will drop out of them.

Inside Lucy's illumination the dancers are seething. They are writhing. For the sake of the goddess, for the sake of the womb of the goddess, they are turning into serpents. When they grow still they are earth. They are from always to always. Nature is their pulse. Lucy sees: she understands: the gods are God. How terrible to have given up Jesus, a man like these, made of earth like these, with a pulse like these, God entering nature to become god! Jesus, no more miraculous than an ordinary goatherd; is a goatherd miracle? Is a leaf? A nut, a pit, a core, a seed, a stone? Everything is miracle! Lucy sees how she has abandoned nature, how she has lost true religion on account of the God of the Jews. The boys are on their bellies on the ground, digging it up with sticks. They dig and dig: little holes with mounds beside them. They fill them with peach pits, cherry pits, cantaloupe rinds. The Sicilians and Neapolitans pick up their baskets and purses and shopping bags and leave. The benches smell of eaten fruit, running juices, insect-mobbed. The stage is clean.

The living room has escaped altogether. It is very high and extremely small, no wider than the moon on Lucy's thumbnail. It is still sailing upward, and the voices of those on board are so faint that Lucy almost loses them. But she knows which word it is they mainly use. How long can they go on about it? How long? A morbid cud-chewing. Death and death and death. The word is less a human word than an animal's cry; a crow's. Caw caw. It belongs to storms, floods, avalanches. Acts of God. "Holocaust," someone caws dimly from above; she knows it must be Feingold. He always says this word over and over and over. History is bad for him: how little it makes him seem! Lucy decides it is possible to become jaded by atrocity. She is bored by the shootings and the gas and the camps, she is not ashamed to admit this. They are as tiresome as prayer. Repetition diminishes conviction; she is thinking of her father leading the same hymns week after week. If you said the same prayer over and over again, wouldn't your brain turn out to be no better than a prayer wheel?

In the dining room all the springs were running down. It was stale in there, a failed party. They were drinking beer or Coke or whiskey-and-water and playing with the cake crumbs on the tablecloth. There was still some cheese left on a plate, and half a bowl of salted peanuts. "The impact of Romantic Individualism," one of the humanists objected. "At the Frick?" "I never saw that." "They certainly are deliberate, you have to say that for them." Lucy, leaning abandoned against the door, tried to tune in. The relief of hearing atheists. A jacket designer who worked in Feingold's art department came in carrying a coat. Feingold had invited her because she was newly divorced; she was afraid to live alone. She was afraid of being ambushed in her basement while doing laundry. "Where's Jimmy?" the jacket designer asked. "In the other room." "Say goodbye for me, will you?" "Goodbye," Lucy said. The humanists—Lucy saw how they were all compassionate knights—stood up. A puddle from an overturned saucer was leaking onto the floor. "Oh, I'll get that," Lucy told the knights, "don't think another thought about it."

Overhead Feingold and the refugee are riding the living room. Their words are specks. All the Jews are in the air.

The Bloodline of the Alkanas

CYRUS ALKANA WAS my father, and if you can recognize this name, you belong to an inconspicuous substratum of humanity—a coterie, if such things can still be said to exist. He had his little following, cranks and fanatics like himself, including an out-of-favor critic who once dubbed him "the American Keats." If this was launched as a compliment, it landed as a disparagement. Keats was exactly the trouble, the reason for my father's obscurity—and not only Keats, but Shelley and Wordsworth and Coleridge and Tennyson and Swinburne, all those denizens of a fading antiquity. It wasn't that my father worshiped these old poets who had crowded the back pages of his grade-school spelling book—he regarded himself as one of their company, a colleague and companion.

It was presumed by his enemies (he had many more of these than readers) that his formal literary education had stopped with those spellers—at sixteen he left Thrace High School in upstate New York for a job as a copyboy at the *Beacon-Herald*, the local newspaper, snatching stories fresh from the typewriter to speed them to the big clattering linotype machines. He wasn't so much running away from school as he was running away from home—there was something at home he didn't like, some influence or threat that repelled him. It couldn't have been his parents, because my father always behaved like a man who had been lavishly nurtured, and in marrying my mother he had lucked into the same cushioned indulgence. Still, some element of family there was that he wanted never again to be close to—a raving sister in an attic, or a herd of brutish cousins who habitually beat him up? He never hinted at anything of the kind; I never heard him speak of family at all. The little that came drifting down to me was only that he lived by himself in a rooming house until he could stiffen his spine for the move to New York. If I had an aunt, even a mad one, I was never to know it.

It was this cramped beginning that led him to the harvesting of enemies. The American Keats, they mocked, was no more than a small-town autodidact. Modernism had left him behind, or else he had never been aware of its arrival, dizzied as he was by groves and rivulets and dawns and goddesses and nymphs. His mind was afloat with cosmic visions—infinity, and transcendence, and the sublime. Which was the least of it: born into the wrong century, he sometimes spattered his lines with 'tis and o'er and e'en. These, my mother said in my father's defense, were conscious grace notes, not, as his accusers claimed, outlandish bad habits.

My mother regularly defended my father: it was he alone who was taking a stand for Beauty, lately driven from the world by the conspiracy of a self-styled avant-garde who despised not merely the cradlings of iambic pentameter, but the very skein and pith of magic and mystery.—All this, in fact, was how my mother spoke. She had long ago learned to be a copy of my father. She even copied his distaste for me.

At nine I had begun to dismantle all the clocks in our apartment, and soon discovered how to reassemble their parts. Out of waxed paper, school paste, and bits of wood pried from the backs of picture frames I built fragile model airplanes, with the thinnest of wing struts. At twelve, on purpose to provoke, I announced that I had seen God, and that His name was Geometry. (My father dismissed God; he cared only for the gods.) I was absorbed by shapes and their measurements, the height and width of tables and bureaus and doors, everything hard to the touch and substantially *there*. I determined early on that I would shun the vapor of words my parents exhaled, as from some mist-producing internal fungus—my mother's, being imitative, somehow more egregious than my father's. These enveloping clouds of words, and the rapture they induced, my father called "the Bestowal." It was a term I heard often, especially in relation to its absence in me.

"The child lacks it," he would say.

"She is wanting in it," my mother would agree.

They had named me Sidney (mistakenly, my father pointed out) after a pair of antiquated poets born centuries apart: Sir Philip Sidney and Sidney Lanier, both of whom, my mother frequently reminded me, "were known to work in your father's vein." She spoke as if they had long ago publicly acknowledged their debt to Cyrus Alkana. I had never cared enough to look up either one.

The Bestowal had come, according to my father, through an ancestral line leading back as far as the poet-prophets Micah and Isaiah, but more immediately through a rumor of one Rafael Alkana, who was said to have set down torrents of God-praises, in rhyming Ladino couplets, in the margins of his prayerbook. In the Inquisitional trauma of that distant fifteenth-century departure from a myth-clad Iberia to an equally shrouded Anatolia, the sacred volume was lost—in shipwreck or conflagration, whichever version one preferred.

"Lost yet not lost," my father said, "whence, even in the latter-day idiom of the New World, the power of language suffuses the bloodline of the Alkanas." And recited:

> Frigate or trireme,
> Oarsmen or steam,
> Onward they ploughed,
> Spirits unbowed,
> Unto the invincible dream.

Though *whence* and *unto* were recognizably also among his grace notes, it was unclear whether these lines were his own, or a fragment of some admired minor lyrical Victorian.

I did not understand my father's talk. I sensed only that there was some undeniable connection between these enigmatic outbursts and the mundane truth that we were always worrying about money. I was by then a demanding fifteen, shamed by the way we lived in a three-room flat on the fifth floor of a Bronx walkup. The kitchen window looked out on a narrow shaft that plummeted down into a bleak courtyard mobbed by rows of metal barrels. I slept on a pull-out bed abutting a steam radiator, on top of which the current crop of my father's books was heaped, so that in winter I was assaulted by the peculiar odor of heated binding glue.

These books, it was my habit to notice, were never the same for long. They changed their colors and thicknesses—some were squat, some tall and lean, and most had slips of paper, my father's scribbles, stuck between the leaves. They all came from the public library at the end of our street, a red-brick Carnegie whose coal furnace shook the building with its winter roar. This was as far into the outer world as my father was willing to go. "He lives in his head," my mother insisted, and by this she meant me to grasp that my father's cerebrations were the equivalent of what other fathers had: a regular job. And more: in that labyrinthine space, she implied, were museums and galleries and opera houses and lecture halls and cathedrals and landscapes and monuments: the whole of civilization. If his mind was a kind of Parthenon, then what need had he of the common street?

For herself, though, it was different, and for a certain brief period during my childhood (it didn't long outlast my father's contempt), she ran off to the trolley stop on weekend evenings to begin a rattling journey to the city's buzz and hum. There were free excitements everywhere, in cafés and parks and lofts and barrooms so dark you could scarcely see the faces around you, where readers stood at ill-lit lecterns and shot out ugly staccato syllables, the women in shawls and sandals, the half-bald men dangling mournful gray hanks of hair from behind their ears. Sometimes, to rid my father of what he scorned as my prattle, she took me with her. I disliked these forced excursions and their puffed-up dronings. Once, as a bribe, she bought for me from a street vendor a mechanical toy with many moving parts—by shifting them cleverly, you could construct a tunnel or a tower or a bridge. But mostly she went alone, returning breathless and exhilarated, and smelling foully of cigarette. "Barbarians!" she called out to my father. "Nothing down there but ranting pygmies, rotten as rat's hair, no *music* in it, no *sense*, no *vision*, there's not one in the bunch worth Cyrus Alkana's fingernail clippings—"

Still, whatever supernal faculty the Bestowal may have conferred on my father, it was she who paid the rent.

"He hadn't planned on it, not in the least," she told me when, embarrassed, I went on pressing her: why, unlike other men, was my father content to remain unemployed? "Upstate was a desert for a mind like that, so when he came down to New York he thought he'd find work in a publishing house, even if he hadn't a shred of ordinary credentials—they all wanted a college degree. It didn't impress those fools that he'd read absolutely everything. In fact," she reminded me—it was an anecdote I knew by heart—"when I first set eyes on your father, it was in the cellar of a used-book store on Fourth Avenue, and he had his nose in Pindar, of all things!"

I never troubled to discover who or what this Pindar was; it was enough to know that if not for my mother's enchantment in that damp Fourth Avenue cellar twenty years before, I might have been spared the Alkana bloodline. Instead, three months short of what was to have been her graduation from Vassar, my mother took a job as a receptionist in a small law firm not far from the Bronx Zoo, where she could occasionally hear the barks of the sea lions in their outdoor pool; and then began her life as Cyrus Alkana's shield and support. It was a blessing, she said, that he had been forcibly exempted from the tedious workaday world of offices. Her credo—on behalf of my father—was, she informed me, Solitude and Time, those faithful begetters of the muses. Cyrus Alkana's exaltations were not to be distracted by the shabby incursions of the everyday. Most evenings, when she was too tired or impatient to cook, she would bring us dinner in paper cartons from a local eatery, and would soon sit down to the secondhand Remington that occupied the farther end of the kitchen table, a kind of shrine dedicated to my father's papers, many of them accumulated in overflowing folders. Here she would transcribe Solitude and Time's daily yield, emitting joyful little chirps while tapping away until past midnight.

But my father's exertions were not always the melodious lines of those squarish sonnets and spreading odes that so excited my mother. Often—too often—they were raging letters flung out to his enemies and detractors, and though my mother might plead and remonstrate, she trusted finally in the sacral might of his every outcry, and in the respectful eye of a just posterity. It fell to me to witness the composition of these diatribes, how he splashed them out ferociously with every dip into the ink bottle (my father despised fountain pens), and how he exulted in wickedly ingenious imprecations, oblivious to my watchfulness. Until she came to type them at night, my mother regularly missed these afternoon thunderings—she would depart early in the morning for the sea lions' chorus, while my school day ended at three; I had all the advantage of seeing Cyrus Alkana actually at work. I had been given my own key, with instructions not to disturb my father's labors.

And sometimes there were no labors. I would find my father in my parents' bedroom, lying down, shoeless, with his pale naked feet dangling like animal parts, and his dusty socks curled at one elbow. This pleased me. It meant I would have the kitchen to myself, and could slam the icebox door if I liked, or crackle cookie wrappers without being reprimanded. I was tempted to slip back into the bedroom to stare down at him—it was my only chance to look at my father without having him look back at me. He had a way of twisting his lower lip to show his disappointment. I felt he always saw in me the work of some jealous spirit (he pretended to believe in such things), his bad luck in having spawned an Alkana perversely passed over by the whims of the Bestowal. He had small close-set very black eyes rimmed by short sparse reddish lashes, placed not quite horizontally (the left one seemed to list toward an ear) in a big head made bigger by a bulky bush of red hair. His eyebrows too were red. Adam, he liked to say, was made of red clay, but his own ruddiness was inherited from King David; I think he was burdened by the inescapable notice it commanded. A tiny tic or tremor went on pulsing through the shut lids. He was sleeping deeply, snoring with drumlike monotony. It was somehow understood between us that I was not to disclose these instances of idleness to my mother. She was confident that his ambition, like her belief in him, was indefatigable.

And it was because of her relentless advocacy that my

father began at last to see his things in print. "His things"—
this was how my mother, who rarely spoke simply, spoke of
Cyrus Alkana's elevated verse. It was the simplicity of humbled
gratitude: she knew herself to be the privileged guardian of
a fabled cache of royal jewels about to be put out for public
display. Each a peerless emerald or pearl, they had all, one by
one, been denied publication by this or that obtuse periodical.
But my mother had been too shy. Her newest idea was that
a volume of these resplendent strophes, strung together like
some priceless Oriental necklace, must irresistibly dazzle even
the dullest editorial eye—in pursuit of which she typed, she
admired, she inspired, she burnished, and you could almost say
she influenced. And certainly she wrapped the finished product in carefully smoothed-out brown paper cut from grocery
bags, and wrote down the publisher's address in her best Palmer
script, and carried the precious package to the post office to be
weighed and stamped and sent off to its fate. In our family, it
was my mother who was in charge of outgoing mail.

But because one's fate is what one must create (her favorite
homily), she had already set in motion something else. On a
rainy Saturday afternoon, when my father had gone out, hatless
as always, his hair jutting floridly over his ears, on one of his
impulsive rambles to the public library, I heard my mother at
the Remington, typing more slowly than usual, stopping and
then starting again, with long silences in between. It was not
her ordinary pace, that rapid and even cadence of a practiced
amanuensis.

She looked up when she felt me watching from the doorway.

"Don't dare ask me what I'm doing," she ordered. "I have to
think—can't you see I'm thinking?"

"About what?"

"Getting them to pay attention. Publishers. Editors. You
have to have a hook—"

It wasn't, I knew, that she thought me worthy of being her
confidante; but since a conspirator must have an accomplice,
even if an inferior one, she earnestly pumped out the rest: "A
celebratory imprimatur. An introduction, a kind of preamble.
Or call it a preface. That's what I'm doing."

Whatever she was finally willing to name it, it described the poet's circumstances from his birth in backward Thrace to the present flowering of his genius, citing his resemblance to the grandest bards of Albion—and it went off together with each brown-paper packet. Whether or not the tone of these glorifications was persuasive, I could not judge; it was out of my ken and over my head. And my father, it seemed, was kept out of it from the start. Yet what came of it all was three startlingly immediate offers of publication, one from a respected old press (this she quickly dismissed), and the others from two large commercial houses known for their popular successes.

My mother was elated. "We'll go with the biggest fish," she told me. "A reward for swallowing the bait."

The biggest fish, she admitted, had proposed a minnow of an advance while stipulating a single indispensable condition: that the bait be included in the body of the book itself as an enticing illumination of Cyrus Alkana's lines. I saw her hesitate; she had to think it over, she said. She had schemed it only as a worm on a hook, she hadn't expected to go public with it. In the end she had to agree—why lose the big fish for the sake of withholding the inconsequential worm? And the bait, she privately confessed—but only to me, her reluctant confederate—was this: the sole signatory to the gushing endorsement she had quietly fabricated was Alexander Alcott.

It was a name even I could recognize. You couldn't speak, in those years, of an Eliot or a Pound, without, for fairness, adding an Alcott. Alexander Alcott, I knew, was chief among my father's enemies, routinely reviled together with those graven grand luminaries, the acknowledged titans of modernism. That such rarefied figures could be so readily familiar to me, I owed to my father's raucous and tireless hatreds.

"But does he know you've done that?" I asked.

My mother let out an impatiently innocent grunt. "Does who know what?"

"Alexander Alcott. That you used his name that way."

"Oh, I don't need that fool's permission for anything. Besides, I told them over there that I had it—publishers make such fusses over nonsense."

"But what if he finds out and sues?"

"Lawyer talk at your age? Sidney dear, you're a bit of a fool yourself, aren't you? He's bound to find out—think of the publicity that's coming! It won't make a bit of difference to him, he's got fame enough to spare, and he's worthless anyhow. The fellow's nothing but a pestilence, and these days it's pestilence that wins the prizes and the prestige. He's *listened* to, more's the pity, his rubbish gets taught in the schools, he's in all the anthologies, and Lord knows your father isn't, not yet—"

She went on in this way, and though I resented being called a fool, I was more frightened than hurt. I thought her horribly reckless.

A good-sized volume of Cyrus Alkana's verses, under the unwieldy title *Thou Shouldst Be Living at This Hour*, was brought out the following spring. It was reviewed here and there, and could be glimpsed, spottily, in the bookstores, but soon disappeared. My mother blamed this short shelf life on the miscalculation of a long-winded title; she took the trouble to inform me, with an uneasy sigh, that my father, who relied on her for much else, had insisted on it. When I dared to ask him what it meant, he rolled his eyes and puckered his bottom lip and said only that it was something out of Wordsworth anyone with a brain in her head ought to know. I had intended this mostly innocuous question as a preliminary breach into more dangerous territory: what I really hoped to hear was what my father thought of Alexander Alcott's incursion into Cyrus Alkana's inviolate precincts. I opened my mouth and nothing came out: I hadn't the courage to put it to him.

Instead I turned to my mother.

"He still doesn't know it was you," I accused. "Shouldn't he *know* who wrote that stuff?"

"If you tell him, my dear Sidney, I'll poison your cocoa," she said mildly. "And don't call it stuff, it's an appreciation. He understands it was the publisher who wanted it—the salespeople over there, for the noise it would make. Well, we've been *having* a bit of noise, haven't we? People are noticing—"

"But how can he *like* it? He can't like it, can he?"

"The idea of your father liking the likes of an Alexander

Alcott, what a joke—he despises him, you've heard it yourself, those blistering letters, look how he keeps me up every night typing whatever's got stuck in his craw. Not that the ones to Alcott ever get into the mailbox."

"They don't?"

"And why should they? It wouldn't be politic, not when he's been so gracious and helped us out and done us a service. Listen, dearie," she said, "this Alcott's a rascal like the rest of them, and it gives your father no end of pleasure to see some fool of a charlatan come crawling on his knees, flattering and fawning away in that nice little preface of his."

"*Your* nice little preface—"

"That's only a quibble. Your father, wonderful man, takes it as a vindication and a surrender, and so do I—imagine, here's the venerated Alexander Alcott practically admitting that in the war between the Pure and the Sham, it's the Pure that carries the day."

She had flown into the Alkana sublime once again, and I could almost see the capital letters in the shine of her eyes.

There was no reviewer, meanwhile, who did not remark on the seeming anomaly of Alexander Alcott's exuberant praise for a sensibility so radically different from his own. The disparity was so glaring, the *Nation* admonished, that it could hardly have been inspired by collegial generosity—Alkana and Alcott were no more colleagues than they were brothers-in-arms, and it was an exceedingly strange pod that could contain two such unlike peas. This, it turned out, was to become the general theme: that a sophisticated artist imbued with the subtlest vibrations of the Zeitgeist had, inconceivably, lent his influence to the grotesque delusions of an archaist. The wonderment was so intense, and so confounding, that it brought on a second edition. The impetus for this miracle bubbled up, to start with, at those notorious dinner parties run by the literary set, a pack of up-to-date gossips (this was my mother's view) who followed the critics solely in order to tear into their arguments. From this narrowest of sanctums a wildfire of curiosity began to spread into the larger arena of the magazines: why had Alcott done it? And then: but *had* he done it? It was impossible, it made no sense, so vast a reputation stooping to crown with such extravagant laurels a negligible versifier—a mere mimic of the outmoded.

Outmoded? Cyrus Alkana spat out his grievance in phalanxes of rancor rushed off to the journals that spurned him. Did his assailants suppose they owned the language from the root up, and could do with it, by seigneurial right, whatever they wished? And what they wished to do with it, my father declaimed, was to pull off their shallow showy tricks—they said it themselves, straight out! These jabbering fakers mooing away at their slogans—make it new, break it down, chop it up, thin it out! And all of it morose, and ugly, and desolating, a wasteland! It wasn't only the language they were after, it was the tongue and the teeth and the eyeballs and the optic nerve itself, until they got all the way back into the human brain, to modernize even that.

Yet Cyrus Alkana was acquiring a faction of his own: he had his little coterie, his loyal little junta, the hot-blooded coven of his fans. The critic who had named him the American Keats now compared him to the school of Rembrandt, those ingenious disciples whose paintings, far from being imitations, "quaffed," he crowed, "from the selfsame celestial spring." How these accolades animated my mother! Praise for my father might be too sparse, or too bizarre, or too strenuously infatuated, but it satisfied her that after so many years in exile he had attained the recognition he had always deserved. It appeared not to trouble her that we still lived as thinly as we had before. My father may have arrived at a kind of fame, but even I could see that it came not so much from his devotees as from his detractors. The ongoing flood of those assaults on his enemies (you couldn't class it as correspondence, since there were never any answers) brought him, it developed, more notice from the reigning literati than whatever fading rumble was left of the shock of publication. There was no third edition. No one turned up to interview him. Occasionally the odd essay or two, like shards churned out of the dry soil of an abandoned dig, would crop up in this or that marginal journal. It might be a zealous study of the titular *Thou*—did it address the poet's soul, or the solitary reader, or the spirit of Wordsworth himself? Or else it would happen that Cyrus Alkana was cited in some university panel on forgotten minor figures.

In the two quiet years following what my mother happily went on calling my father's "apotheosis"—the flurry was long over—the deepest and most perplexing silence was the terrible muteness of Alexander Alcott. I had been wildly apprehensive all along. He had been the object of the minutest inquisitiveness; his repute had been usurped, even molested; some hinted at blackmail. And still he held his tongue. He made no mention of the abuse of his name. He wrote and spoke nothing in public or, as far as anyone could tell, in private. He raised no accusation or threat of anything remotely punitive. Week after week, month after month, I had been fearing a thunderclap: a dangerous letter, or the door bursting open, with police in pursuit. Again and again I badgered my mother—why was she so indifferent, how could she be so certain that there wouldn't be some sudden repercussion, a disgrace that might fall on us at any moment, and what would she do then?

"Oh, we're just fleas as far as he's concerned," she said, waving me off. "He doesn't take any notice, we're nothing to him, it would only be a comedown for the high-and-mighty Alexander Alcott to be bothered with us—"

"Is that why you took the risk? When you really don't know anything about him, the way he thinks, how he might take it—"

"How he might take it? You can see how he's taken it. He doesn't care. There never *was* a risk."

But another time she had a more deliberate argument.

"Did it ever occur to you," she began, "that the fellow might actually *admire* your father?"

"How could he? You're always saying they have nothing in common, they're opposites—"

"And out of opposition affinity grows. Suppose he's finally allowed himself a good look at what he said about your father—"

"What *you* said—"

"—and recognized the truth of it."

"The truth of what?"

"The truth of falling in love. A sort of conversion," she said, and here her voice, which was ordinarily excitedly soprano, darkened into a clairvoyant hush. "That's why he has nothing to complain of, he doesn't make a fuss, he leaves us alone. Because he's satisfied, because he *sees*. Because he *knows*."

I could only stare; there was nothing more to say. I was by now in my last year of high school, and had absorbed enough of her willfulness to recognize that this newest theory was as capricious as it was preposterous—the modernist Alcott suddenly smitten by the antiquarian Alkana! And all of it resting on (what else could it be called?) a forgery. She had robbed him of his name; she stood ready to concoct his inmost sentiments. There was more at stake than my childhood notions had been able to swallow, when I was repeatedly told that my father was genuine and noble, and that his enemies weren't. And if proof was wanted, only see: my father's lines rhymed, and theirs didn't.

The next afternoon, when my father was again napping—his naps were becoming longer and more frequent—I put on my galoshes and walked through rapidly thickening snow to the public library. My arms were heavy with pretext: my mother, frugal as always, frowning on overdue fines, had instructed me that morning to return my father's latest batch of borrowed books, still piled on the radiator next to my bed. I was familiar with their hot smell, but had scarcely noticed their titles—the same hoary bards, the same sunsets and rivers and dryads, the same blurry infinities of a gods-infested cosmos. Except for the preoccupied librarian at the desk, who appeared to be sorting through files of index cards, the reading room was deserted and nearly silent; there was only the distant subterranean growl of the ancient furnace under our feet. The storm had done its work—I had the place to myself, and uninterrupted hours before me. And in this fortuitously secret space, below high windows palely lit and snow-muffled, I found the man I had come to look for: my father's enemy, my mother's dupe.

Or almost found him. The more I followed his tracings—he seemed to be everywhere—the more elusive he grew. Even so, you couldn't escape him. He took up whole chapters in one academic study after another, he proliferated in the bibliographies, and in the dictionaries he turned up between *alcohol* and *alcove.* Two or three essays in the serious journals attempted to uncover a venerable literary connection: was he a descendant of those estimable New England idealists, the Brook Farm Alcotts? Could he claim a cousinship, however distant, with the admirable Louisa May? There was no conclusive proof favoring a yes or a no; the genealogical paths were murky. None of this mattered to me; none of it counted. It was the living man I was after, so I burrowed into the glossy weeklies, into those "human interest" articles that confirm renown by adding to it. His name and his fame were titillating enough to land him there, among the politicians and movie stars—hadn't Eliot himself once filled a football stadium, declaiming before thousands of fans who'd never read a line? But Alexander Alcott disdained the public. He declined to be photographed. Yet as I leafed through mounds of mostly stale magazines I came on plenty of photos: in lieu of the poet, they were all, disappointingly, of the poet's house, taken from different angles. A modest stucco, set back from a countrified road. Rosebushes on either side of a door painted red.

Here and there, speculations seeped through—a marriage to an older widow who died; a speech hindrance, slight, intermittent, the cause of a raw self-consciousness. But these were only stories sprinkled among other stories. He lived alone. He was "reclusive," "reserved," "secretive." He "disliked leaving his house," though some could remember how, long ago, when he was still in his twenties, he had gone roaming together with other would-be young poets, scions of the new movement, to recite in parks and cafés. He was the only one to have lasted. The rest ended mainly as stockbrokers or insurance men; and two drank themselves to death. All these stories were sparse and uncertain. Was there a broken heart, a failed love? Of his childhood, I could discover nothing at all. It was as if he had been born out of a crater in the moon, and it gave me a chill to read that he was known to be irascible, a man with a heavy temper and a hidden grudge.—Or was it that the librarian, closing for the day, had already shut down the heat? It struck me as odd (I thought of my mother's cryptic affinity of opposites) that Alexander Alcott, exactly like my father, was unwilling to step past his own threshold; and that he too was easily roused to rage. A hollow equation: despite these echoing traits, Alcott was everywhere revered—he was in all the magazines!—while my father was more and more falling into eclipse.

By the time I got home, the snow had crept up to my ankles, and my mother was standing at the stove, stirring a pot. It was an unfamiliar scene. Her office had been dismissed earlier than usual. Even the neighboring sea lions had been herded indoors to avoid the rough weather.

She was quick to confront me. "Sidney!" The name itself was accusation; peevishly, she tugged at my wet sleeve. "Look at you, your hair all soaked through. What in the world have you been up to, what kept you so long?"

I had prepared a covering lie. When I told it, it sounded true. What need had my mother of the actual Alcott, when she so relished her moist inventions? And I hated the hobbling weight of my hair; she had forced me to let it grow to below my waist ("Pre-Raphaelite tresses," she said) to please my father.

"I got to looking through a bunch of college catalogues," I threw out, "and I think I've found just the place I want."

"And what place is that?"

On the spot I invented a name. "Kansas Polytech. For engineering."

"Girls can't be engineers," my mother said. "They won't let you, it's not any sort of normal occupation for a girl. Besides, who's going to pay for your room and board way off in some godforsaken nowhere? Not to mention the tuition, when right here you've got a perfectly fine city college that won't cost a penny—"

"You know my grades are good. I'll get a scholarship."

From his customary chair, his elbows lost in a surf of papers, my father growled, "Ah, let her go. The Bestowal's skipped her anyhow."

The Bestowal? I was past seventeen, sick of all such illusions, and more than ready to flee our moonbeam lives. It was math, it was physics, it was logic and dirt I was after, and brick and steel and cement—solid everyday things—and how a bridge can curve in the air like an arrow in flight, with seemingly nothing to keep it there. Some months afterward, I did in fact win a scholarship, not to some mythically faraway Kansas, but to an even more distant yet beckoning Texas: a full scholarship, together with a gratifyingly ample stipend. My mother in her melancholy letters never stopped insisting that I had been invited to study structural engineering at Texas A&M solely because of someone's mistaken impression that Sidney was a boy.

Until my father died nearly four years later, at the start of my last semester, I never went home again; I was glad to put half a continent between us. And then, as it happened, I was compelled to miss the funeral. A freak autumn blizzard followed by massive flooding had drowned Texan highways and railroad tracks, thwarting travel. My mother sadly reported that there were only three at the graveside: herself, the librarian from down the street, and the man who had named my father the American Keats; it was he who recited—*by heart*, my mother wrote—Cyrus Alkana's fourteen-stanza "Ode to the Aegean Cybele." She had been lamenting my father's decline all along, week after week, year after year: how the afternoon naps were now beginning in the mornings (he was always tired), and how, little by little, he had given up castigating his enemies—because finally there were no more enemies. No one took any notice, good or bad, of Cyrus Alkana: it had come to that. There were no new verses. The Remington was silent. The books languishing on the radiator, browning at their margins, had become shockingly overdue, until the librarian herself came to collect them. The heap of folders on the farther end of the kitchen table remained stagnant. "From a peak in Darien," my mother summed up, "to the Slough of Despond." She had retired to care for my father; she had a small pension.

There was no mention of Alexander Alcott. The name and the incident had receded into worse than oblivion—into a kind of caricature, an ephemeral embarrassment in the long march of my mother's besotted loyalty to Cyrus Alkana. Even the troubled shame her deceit had once caused me, and my own childish terror of retribution, had faded away. I was preoccupied now with weight-bearing walls, I had begun designing simple beams and columns, I was learning to calculate the load

capacity of steel. In thrall to my slide rule and gravity's recal-
citrance, I was—finally—freed from the lying romance of my
father's house. To celebrate, I cut my hair very short, close to
the scalp. In the mirror I saw the head of a boy. It pleased me
to have acquired the look of a proper engineer. I tossed away
my dresses and skirts, and took to wearing pants and rough
shirts that buttoned the wrong way. In the campus cafeteria,
crammed into a fifty-cent automatic photo booth, I sat for my
portrait. With a mechanical click, a long row of boys' heads
emerged from a slot. The most cheerful of the bunch I mailed
to my mother. She never acknowledged it.

But when the floods had dried up and the rails were cleared,
and my father had been in his grave for nearly a month, my
mother wrote urgently again, begging me to come: what was to
be done with his precious papers, his treasure trove, his golden
egg, his soul's lantern, was it all to be condemned to perpetual
night? Whom could she turn to for advice? She was helpless:
the lone votary who had likened my father to Keats was useless
for practical matters, not a thread or shred of any other literary
connection remained, and only she and I were witnesses to the
glory that lay in the scores of bulging folders she was daily
uncovering in neglected corners and closets.

I dreaded those papers, and suspected her intent. Surely she
didn't suppose that I would gaze, admire, and at last be swept
away—what was the Aegean Cybele to me? She knew my
detachment. Or did she imagine (and what might my mother
not imagine?) that I could somehow lead her to certain grandly
monumental Texan libraries eager to enshrine Cyrus Alkana's
hallowed archive? I was, despite all, an authentic Alkana—of
the bloodline if not of the Bestowal. She meant to lure me back,
to draw me in—to keep me imprisoned in that dank emptiness
that was just now invading my lungs as I climbed the stairs to
my parents' old flat. It was no more than a ruse, this implausible
commotion over my father's papers: I was to be his surrogate,
her stay against Cyrus Alkana's extinction.

The grimy fake marble steps and the iron balustrade with
its rusting scrolls were the same as they had always been. The
shrunken hallways and dusky stairwells groaned out their old

echoes. Even the smell of the place was everything I remembered—a sour fume of changelessness, defeat, aging. Silence
and loneliness. Two flights above (I had by now arrived at
the third-floor landing) a muddy wash of voices swelled and
ebbed—and then I heard the shutting of a door, and downward
footsteps.

I looked up, and looked again; I stood where I was. Through
the gaps in the railings I saw a man descending. One hand slid
lightly along the banister, the other gripped a fedora. He was
moving easily, firmly, confident of his tread. He wore a long
tweed coat with a velvet collar. His shoes were impeccable,
the leather unscuffed, the laces orderly. On the fourth landing,
glancing below, he hesitated, startled; clearly he had expected
the way to be unobstructed. But I stood where I was, taking
him in. I recognized the ruddy mass of his hair, the color now
much subdued, the wilderness of it tamed and civilized. He had
grown a pinkish mustache, overrun by white, that oddly hid
his upper lip. As he came nearer, I caught the tilt of his left eye
listing toward an ear, like a skiff about to capsize—but his gait
was strong, he was robust all over, and he passed me by with a
stranger's nod. My tongue felt frozen in my mouth. How could
he know me, with my boy's head, and my pants and borrowed
lumberjacket?

It was my father. I had never before seen him so well-
dressed.

Ruse! Deceit! Lie! The pretext of his papers? No, the
unthinkable, the heinous: my mother the trickster! Had she
concocted his decline and his dying, and all of it to snatch me
back?

I took the last two flights at a gallop, and faced the door that
would open into the life I had repudiated—that enervated life
of mist and chimera. Into the scarred lock I thrust the old key
my mother had pressed on me long ago. It had taught me to be
surreptitious.

She was standing at a window, looking into the street
below—watching, I thought, my father go. But where? And
in a coat with a velvet collar! When she turned, alerted by the
cat's squeal of the doorknob, I saw how the skin of her jaw hung

loose, and how sparse, nearly naked, her eyebrows had become: it gave her a worn abandoned stare.

But her voice was lively. "Oh, what a pity, such a pity," she sang out. "Here you are, and you've just missed him." And then: "Sidney! Your hair, what have you done to yourself? Just look at you, what a getup, I couldn't believe that photo, how your father would be appalled—"

She spoke as if the years of my absence had all at once dissolved, as if my having just then materialized was no more than a daily commonplace.

But I would not allow her to distract me. "You made me come back," I said: bitterly, coldly. "And all for nothing."

"For nothing? If only you'd got here on time! He sent a note ahead—it went to the publisher, so it was delayed almost a week, it turned up only day before yesterday, and by then you'd left, you were on the train for sure, there was no way I could let you know. How I wish you had seen him!"

"Let me know?" I could catch hold only of the tail of this whirlwind. "I did see him," I said. "On the stairs, coming down, he didn't recognize me—"

"Condolences, he called it. But Sidney, it was so much more, and imagine, Alexander Alcott right in this very *spot*! In this very room!"

A rush of shame; the fury drained out of my throat. She was pulling at my sleeve—her old proprietary habit—and I followed where she led. Was she the captive of a delusion? She was ill, her senses were deteriorating, she believed my father was dead, and not five minutes ago I had seen him alive! And hale! And in a coat with a velvet collar! And worse, horrifyingly worse: she had mistaken him for his most hated antagonist.

The kitchen table was littered with remnants of a repast: empty teacups and lavish little colored cakes of a kind that had never before appeared in our household. A sugar bowl where once stood a perpetual bottle of ink. The Remington too gone from its place, as if a cavity had been carved out of the air.

"You see," she said, "he even brought me these pretty petit fours, that's how gentlemanly he was! And he told me things I never knew, things your father kept to himself—"

It was brutal to listen to. I could think of nothing to say to these muddles, and while she went to find another cup for me (she filled it with weak tea grown cold), I looked all around, searching for evidences of my father: some vagrant sheet with his obsessive scratchings, an ink-stained pamphlet with a note stuck in it, his coddled old dipping pen. There were only the bare plates and their pink-and-yellow crumbs.

"I always understood it was Cain and Abel between those two," she went on, "but I never dreamed they'd been so young, boys no more than fifteen or so, hotheads, a falling-out like that, and even now it isn't clear who was Cain and who was Abel, except that he had that lip all covered up—"

It was unendurable. I broke in headlong: "*What* boys, for God's sake what *is* it! And where was he going just now, he never used to bother about a hat—"

"Oh Sidney, don't be so dense"—her old tone. "Can't you see how remarkable it is? That he *came*? That he was here? He saw the obituary, a tiny little thin thing, no more than six lines, it didn't at all add up to your father's proper stature, but still, the blood between them—"

"Blood? What are you saying?"

"The blood of the Alkanas. That's what brought him."

She told me then what she admitted she had always known: it was my father's great secret, she said, he had never once spoken of it, and she had never violated what she perceived to be a sacred ban—a ban rooted in an insatiable rage; or in guilt; or in shame. Or perhaps even in fossilized indifference. But she had known his secret for years, and had, in truth, known more of it than he knew himself.

All this I submitted to with a skepticism mixed with fear: what fraud was she brewing now? The purposeful drama of it, her small pale eyes theatrically effulgent, where was she intending to take me?

"I saw him just that one time," she said, "on Bleecker Street, down a staircase into a smoky cellar, candles set in saucers, a dozen chairs in a circle, that sort of place. A reading along with two others, vile simpleminded stuff, red wheelbarrows and chickens, he didn't read well at all, and he had that little notch over his mouth. He was already calling himself by that pretentious name he took on, not that it had any shine to it then. But I knew right away."

It was as if she was drawing me on with tightening straps, and where was she taking me?

I asked, "What did you know?"

"The hidden thing. That my husband had a brother."

And again, cautiously: "How could you know that? If you never saw him before?"

"Because of the resemblance. Except for that notch. And when I got home that night I never told your father any of it."

The illogic, the waywardness! The fantasy, the delusion!

I surrendered docility and tore into her wildly. "You ran into someone years ago who looked a little like my father and you decided he was my father's brother—"

"What a fool you are, you have no imagination, you don't understand, you can't *see*! There wasn't an iota of difference, every cell of him, every grain and pore of him, every hair on his head! Identical! And that's the one the world adores, not your father, they throw garlands around his neck . . . how your father despised that man, and he had no inkling . . ."

Her face collapsed into its grooves, and it came to me—heavily, grievously, ruinously—that my mother's trick was not of this moment. It was lifelong. My father and his dithyrambs were dead, obliterated, and the man in the coat with the velvet collar was his enemy, whom the world had wreathed in garlands.

But still she was dogged, and it spiraled out, the maelstrom of it, Cain and Abel, Jacob and Esau . . . Cyrus and Alexander, all of them twinned in the womb, contending even there. And then the falling-out, the horrid divide, that delta of flesh cut out of a lip, the outcry, the blood . . . "You can't really get a good look at it," she said, "a bit of a slash, like a sewed-up harelip, it was only one of those little pocketknives, an argument between boys, that's what he was telling me—"

An argument between boys? Prodigious boys, extraordinary boys, boys who were already preserving their verses in packets tied with knotted string, wondrous and singular boys, though doubled by the bloodline of the Alkanas; and it was over the

bloodline of the Alkanas that they fought: whether it was destined to course through the cosmos or through a grain of sand,
whether it was to be venerable and honored or new-made and
radical, whether it was sunk in overgrown ancient scum or alive
in the pulse of the modern . . . even then, even then, in their
teens! Not over a skate or a pair of purloined socks, or whatever trivial spats ordinary boys turn into wars. The knife that
sliced the lip might easily, by a finger's length, have pierced eye
or throat—his brother's knife, captured and wielded by your
father. One boy owned the knife, the other used it. The intent
to maim, mutual. The rage, mutual. How alike they were,
striving for supremacy! And then he ran away, your father, the
almost-murderer, the runaway criminal who might so easily
have blinded his brother, or killed him . . .

My mother recited these passionate claims with a strained
breathlessness, while I, disbelieving, shocked into ridicule,
went on numbly stirring my tepid tea. "Are you telling me—
did *he* tell you—that it was a fight over—what a piece of
nonsense—*style*?"

"You stupid engineer!" she cried out. "All you have any feeling for is dust—bricks, concrete, who knows what you're after,
looking like that, and you a born Alkana! It was the Bestowal,
it was your father fighting against the tide to have his life! Even
then he would never go with the tide, don't you see? And in
spite of it, when it comes to the marrow of things, there's not a
droplet's difference between them . . . Do you know why that
man came today? Do you understand why?"

"No," I said.

"And just think how worried you once were, how afraid you
were that he'd punish us—"

"It was long ago," I said.

"I knew he'd never harm us. I always knew it."

"You stole his name, you abused him."

"Oh, his name! He gave up his name, didn't he? He got rid
of it—not to be tainted by his brother, his derided brother, his
brother the . . . *archaist*." The word was ruthless: she trickled
out a covetous little laugh, half pain, half victory. "It was his
fame I stole. For your father's sake, to catch the world's eye,

to get him into print. But I knew," she breathed out grandly, "he'd never harm us."

"My father was harmed. You made him a butt."

"You're hard on me, aren't you—when all my life I've been a person of forbearance. I never let on to your father that the man he most detested carried his own blood in his veins."

"His blood, his veins! How could you *not* expect some retaliation—at least a protest? How could you not? You gave out a hundred different reasons—"

"There was only one reason."

Again the tightening straps; the reins were now wholly in her hands.

I asked, "And what was that?"

"He didn't mind. It's exactly the thing he came to tell me. That he didn't mind, he'd never minded. And I always trusted that he wouldn't. Because," she persisted, "they were breast to breast even before they were born."

She stopped and looked me over; her nostrils danced in wary distaste. I saw that she was judging me less by what she took to be my indecency of feeling than by my shorn boy's head.

When I left her—she didn't try to keep me, after all—I understood that my guileless mother would go on believing forever in the binding force of the bloodline of the Alkanas. And I made no further move to dispute it.

It was the librarian from down the street who salvaged my father's papers. They were stored in the library's cavernous underground—one hundred and twenty-three cardboard boxes of unsorted manuscripts, some typed, many more handwritten in the blue-black ink he favored—*awaiting*, my mother wrote in the last letter I ever had from her, *the unborn critic who will restore him to his rightful peers*. But when some years later a nearby water main burst and inundated the old building's outmoded electrical and heating systems, the library had to be demolished (no engineer would touch it), washing away what a very few still revere as Cyrus Alkana's lordly if unsung art.

The Story of My Family

Nowhere in the west was the chasm between
the old world and the new so wide as in the
lands of the pope-king.
—DAVID KERTZER,
The Kidnapping of Edgardo Mortara

IF YOU ARE unfortunate enough to bear a name trailing a history, as I am, you will understand why I have decided to change
mine—though not quite yet. I must live with the original until
I have squeezed out of it the last syllable of iniquity. A great
sin was committed against this name, the name of an honest
and peaceful family, and whether the choice of an American
commonplace will serve as anodyne, I can hardly predict. It
was in 1940 that my own fraction of these relations arrived here
from Bologna to escape the racial laws. My widowed father,
Isacco Giacobbe Mortara, had already been expelled from the
university, where he taught philosophy. And it was in this same
year, 1940, that my great-uncle, Pio Edgardo Mortara, died at
age 88, after living out his last years in a monastery in Belgium.
The incident that had made a small boy notorious was by then
mainly forgotten, except by a handful of scholars, and was
regularly attributed to mediaeval ignominy, as if modernity—
railway, telegraph, photography—hadn't at the time already
permeated everywhere.

Photography! How often I have studied that face—the face
of Father Pio in a posed photo. Those round black eyes seem
both to protrude and to lie peculiarly flat, like a screen laid over
a marble egg, as if declining to see, or else as if able to see only
what they already know. It is a look that refutes, and denies, and
abhors curiosity. In the same photo a woman is seated before
him. She is soberly dressed, a mother in mourning, all black
satin and black ribbons. Her downcast head speaks agony, agony.

When I ultimately came face-to-face with Father Pio—the very one, the legend, the scandal—I was myself a child of eight. He had returned to Bologna to visit my father, his nephew; in his mature years it was his habit to seek out this and that remnant of kin, sometimes to proselytize, sometimes not. I was at the time alone in our apartment, darkened by too many draperies and densely adorned lampshades and antimacassars on velvet armchairs, all the heavy assurances of our Bolognese comforts. I let him in, as I had been told to do, prepared to explain that my father was delayed and would soon arrive. In the dining room a bottle of wine had been set out. He declined to sit, and simply stood there, in his long black gown and short black cape. It was as if he had no legs, no arms, only a neck with its Adam's apple rimmed by a white cloth. His hat, round and black and broad, lay on the table.

He said, "Tua madre è a casa?"

His voice was dark and thick, and his speech was no longer like ours.

I told him that my mother was not at home. She was dead.

His answer frightened me. He spoke it not as a man to a child, but as a child to another child. As if daring to tell a secret.

"Anche mia madre è morta," he said.

And to my relief soon afterward my father hurried in, bustling and breathless and apologetic: "My students, they linger, they chatter, they jabber away, I can't get rid of them!" My father was always apologetic, and always outwardly cheery, though now and then, in quieter periods, I would see him tighten his mouth into a saddened twist.

The two men sat down together. The wine stood uncorked. I was sent away, but listening from a distance was useless—the talk was too quick, and on matters too long-ago for me to understand. Something, a kind of skip in the rise and fall in their grownups' voices, made them sound alike.

When the visitor left—an arm in its black sleeve crept out from the cape to lift his hat—my father said, "What a pity, what a pity."

To my mind, there was more to be afraid of than to feel sorry for. Father Pio for me was a black crow that had flown into our lives and was never seen again. A crow that spoke like a small boy.

When my father and I landed at last in New York on a Portuguese ship—he to begin again at the New School, which had arranged for our visas and his employment—our circumstances had become severely stripped. We settled into a small apartment in the borough of Queens, where everything, even the table and chairs, seemed deprived of ornament. My father, who was adept at several languages, tutored me in English, and I went every morning to the public school, where there was a scattering of other foreign children, but none from Bologna, and not one who had a father like mine.

My father's scholarly preoccupations were with Stoics and Essenes; he intended to pry out their affinities by seeing Job in Stoics and Zeno in Essenes. This was so lively and new and disconcerting that it made him popular as a teacher. And still these quixotic notions were far from his inmost broodings. I sometimes imagined that I had two fathers, the ebullient professor with his checkered accent surrounded by delighted students, and the grief-besotted descendant of a tragic history who propelled me into his private convulsions. It was as if our tiny windowless kitchen were a kind of clandestine theater where that distant tableau of outrage and violation could be called up out of the air. Yet we ourselves had been hounded by tyranny, by Mussolini and his fascist polizia, so why was my father inflamed by a vanquished pope, an obsolete and silenced inquisitor?

Even as a young child I argued with him.

He said, always with the same words, "When you're older you'll understand. You think it distant, but nothing is distant, it's as close as you are to me," and he would fetch me up against his scratchy shirt, and kiss me; but how could I believe him, when I knew that I was alive and breathing his breath, and that the boy he was possessed by had even less reality than the unlikely uncle who dressed like a crow?

It was at moments like these that I felt infiltrated by the fearsome incorporeality of my father's phantoms. As we sat in the little kitchen, he with the newspaper at his elbow, eating the supper he had affably and efficiently cooked, some evocative word or phrase might all at once erupt under his eye, and he would speak of the boy as if he, like me, were alive and near and breathing his breath. Or as though there might at any instant come the knock on the door, and the boy—or was it I?—would be snatched away. Whether these visions were my father's or my own, I cannot say. Nor can I call them hallucinations, or drift-ings of displaced dreams, or willed delusions, or dramatizations torn out of my father's fevers—but whatever they were, it was in such untethered intervals that I saw what he saw and knew what he knew.

Allow me to add: only in part. My father was embedded, as I could not be, in those faded chronicles of the Resorgimento, the decline and defeat of the papal states, the rise of the king-dom of Italy, and all the rest. And though I have since absorbed (I mean conscientiously pursued) this same history, I apprehend all the more now what I took in only by instinct then: that none of it touched him, that he was indifferent to the boy as the spore of all these upheavals, that it was the boy, solely the boy, the living boy in the darkened room, the boy standing there, sobbing, bewildered, the boy, the boy, the boy. The boy whose life called to ours: my father's life, and mine.

In Bologna the pith of summer's heat is set to boiling chiefly in July and August, but on the 23rd of the blazing June of 1858 the rooftops were sizzling as they never had before. In the household of Solomone and Marianna Mortara, the shutters were closed and the draperies drawn, to keep out the assault of the furnace that pressed all around. Even so, the small rooms were stifling, and children of various ages, five boys and the twins Ernesta and Erminia, lay sprawled and enervated on beds and sofas. Imelda, the baby, was at her mother's breast. Both mother and infant were streaming with sweat. It was the afternoon hour of *riposo*, when Solomone—the family called him Momolo—had as usual shut up his shop, and he and Riccardo, his oldest son, went looking for respite, strolling through the shadowy cool of the neighborhood's ancient colonnades, and then stopping for iced vino in a nearby café. Riccardo had a knack for numbers, and Momolo thought he might soon be useful in the shop.

As they approached home—the Mortara apartment occupied the lower half of the house—Riccardo noticed that the
door was wedged open by the boot of a man in uniform.

"Papa," he said, "there's a soldier, and look, another one
inside—"

What they saw was the pope's military police, a uniformed
marshal and his deputy, a brigadier in ordinary dress; and Marianna holding up two paralyzed naked fists, howling, imploring.

The marshal thrust a hand into a crevice alongside his epaulets and drew out a paper. He chose a boy who stared back at
him with petrified eyes.

"What is your name?" he said.

"Arnoldo."

"And you?"

"Augusto."

"You?"

"Aristide."

"You, and your brother hiding behind you—"

"Ercole. Edgardo."

"Come here, little one. Don't be afraid. Tell me your full
name."

"Edgardo Levi."

"How old are you, Edgardo?"

"Six."

The marshal consulted his paper.

"This is the one," he said, and placed his hand, the one not
gripping the paper, on Edgardo's head. His fingers explored
among the black curls—what was he searching for there?—and
then on to the small thin neck, where a pendant of some kind
dangled from a jeweler's chain.

"What's this?"

"Whatever it is," the other man said, "we'll soon get him a
better one."

The marshal was inwardly disappointed; he hadn't found
the soft baby horns that all Jews are born with. Turning to
Momolo, he asked, "Are you the head of this family and the
father of this boy?"

Marianna shrieked, "It's a mistake, a horrible mistake—Momolo, tell him he's come to the wrong house, tell him to go away—"

"I am here as a representative of Father Pier Gaetano Feletti, the Inquisitor in service to the pope. Your son is a Christian, and according to law may not be reared under a Jewish roof. I am instructed to remove him to Rome, to the House of the Catechumens."

Momolo said, "You have no right, my son is a Jewish child circumcised into the Covenant, and you have no right to override the natural claim of his parents."

"Baptism overrides your superstitions," the other man said.

"Baptism! Rome!" Marianna wailed. "Oh my God, my God, what are you blathering, never on this earth—"

"Madam," the marshal said, "your son will be treated kindly, you need not be anxious, and now, Edgardo, give me your hand, the horses are ready, and in Rome you'll have a new father."

Momolo thundered: "I am his father, and you will not take him!"

The marshal's fingers crept to the silver buttons on his blue coat. "These," he said, "are my authority and my right."

The thunder collapses. Pleading, Momolo begs to keep the boy another night, but the day's reprieve will mean nothing, the boy will be led to the carriage weeping, gasping, his backward look straining toward his mama, why doesn't she come after him, why does she crouch there with her mouth open, why is his papa immobile, silent, and here is the carriage with four huge horses snorting, and never before has he been in a carriage, and why must he go to Rome when all he wants is mama, mama, they tell him Rome is where his new father the pope lives, and where he too will live in a fine big house, what are they saying, what are they saying, what is happening . . . . . but no no no, make an end of it, this clumsiness cannot stand, and what have I done, such oafish play-acting and cardboard speeches, a scene no one can animate, no one has witnessed. A scene? Call it a blasphemy. An Inquisitor in service to the Pope, and in burgeoning, fermenting modernity? Railways, telegraph, photography, international journalism, public gas lamps in every municipal thoroughfare! What consumes my father is a sensation, a ravaging tide, a moment rent out of time, an instance of immateriality knit out of pure will. Phantasmagoria betrayed into words, words, words, oh make an end of this farce, this melodrama, this treacle!

I will not attempt it again. I am not a playwright. History is not a theater. As for the House of Catechumens, my father inhabits it, he inhales it, the fetid odor of the strange repugnant food, the unholy mixing of meat and milk, and how the boy in his new clothes eats nothing, he can chew and swallow none of it, they have taken away his mezuzah, his little locket and its bit of parchment inscribed with the Sh'ma, he had already begun to learn his Hebrew letters, but now he is told he must learn his catechism, and from the slim gold chain on his neck hangs a medallion engraved with a woman sheltering an infant, and he cries because it makes him think of his mama nursing Imelda, he cries and he cries until the well of his tears is emptied, he is parched and famished, he chews their strange and repugnant meat, he swallows their forbidden wine, he is afraid of the Rector, afraid not to obey him because of his scowl, but when he studies his catechism the Rector smiles and pets him, no wonder they say the Jews are clever, the baptized boy is a prodigy, a prodigy!

My father in our kitchen in Queens, transfixed, ensorcelled, and I with him: the stuff of tale and myth, Circe and Juliet, the powerful potion secretly introduced, sometimes with an incantation, sometimes not. And in Bologna, in modernity, the servant girl, simple, devout, illiterate, unseen, clandestinely performing a baptism on the fevered Edgardo, and all for the sake of saving his soul if he should die. How, with what water, from where? Well, bucket, pitcher, cup? The brevity of the formula, the sacral eternity of the mutation. The fever is transient and the boy does not die. Yet in a fleeting particle of a second my father's uncle, Edgardo Levi Mortara, is transfigured from Jewish child to Christian neophyte, and never mind Momolo's repeated importunings, the futile interventions of the Rothschilds, of Sir Moses Montefiore, knighted by Victoria, of

Napoleon the Third of France, of the Jews of Rome, of the foreign press, never mind the zealots of civic equality, the armed
proponents of Italian nationhood who mean to wrest the papal
lands from the Church's grasp, never mind the weight of the
future—never mind all of it. The baptized boy Edgardo is now
a man, and the man is my great-uncle, Father Pio Mortara.

I was fully independent when my father died, and long before.
This I owe to him. He had always urged me not to lose the little
native Italian I still retained from childhood, and to master not
only the breadth of the language and its literature, but also its
annals and politics—wasn't it politics that had turned us into
panicked refugees? At twenty, I was already employed as a
research assistant for an eminent historian of Italian fascism, but
I was soon earning my living—*our* living, in fact, my father's
and mine—as a translator of commercial documents. As my
father declined, his professorial ruminations on Essenes and
Stoics waned, and he was encouraged to retire from teaching.
From then on, his obsession with our heritage of crisis and
catastrophe became mine alone.

   Since the trappings of my work often made it opportune for
me to travel to Italy, and to Rome in particular, it became my
habit to search out the oldest congregants in one synagogue
after another: did they remember hearing of Edgardo Mortara,
the stolen Jewish child? Or had they seen the priest himself in
the flesh? Fruitless excursions—what do I suppose I may find?
The name of the child, blotted out. The name of the Inquisitor,
vanished. But only at first. If I persist and return again and
again, then wisps of incidents, rumors, fables, figments, fantasies, might somehow rise like a vagrant mist to coalesce into
what claims to be memory. What must I call these legendary
strands that lodge in the unaware spirits of generations? And
what am I to make of these wavering semblances? *The rabbis of
Rome, summoned by law from the ghetto to utter in embroidered speech
their gratitude to the pope for his charitable solicitude, and standing at
the side of the papal throne, a small solemn boy in clerical robes. A visit
to the grownup Edgardo by his mother, fearful, grieving, her back to
him, unable to look him in the eye. Edgardo, shedding his friar's dress,*

*and in ordinary street clothes fleeing his father. His brother Riccardo in
the uniform of the antipapal forces, and Edgardo leaping at him, hissing
"Satan! Satan!"*

Myths and mirages. Or do such streaks of lamentation—the
story of my family—hang trapped in Italy's ancient winds to
be swept among strangers? And if you who do not carry the
bitter name of Mortara are riddled and dizzied by such lurking
images, what of my father's leanings, and of his legacy to me?

It was not until many months after his death that I felt driven to
open a certain drawer in my father's desk. There was no obstacle, no lock and no key, no prohibition of any kind. I expected
nothing to surprise. In fact, I was already familiar with much
of the contents of this private space: his curious map (he called
it our geography lesson) of our flight south from the carabinieri
in Bologna, moving perilously in farmers' carts by night and
hidden for the price of a few lire in villages along the way, until
we came to Livorno, where we cowered under the bombings,
and where the remainder of my mother's jewels bought us a
corner of the engine room of a freighter to Lisbon—and from
there, after weeks of travail, and always in fear of errant torpe-
does, to our American deliverance.

Here too were my father's folders of ingeniously webbed
notes on his Greek thinkers and Hebrew ascetics (they had
earned him deference but no glory), and the envelope that preserved the handful of salvaged photos of my mother. Her face
was not young. As the deadly child born of late middle age, I
had long been careful to keep away from evidences of the life
I had expunged.

It was among these worn and meager snapshots that I discovered my father's correspondence with Father Pio Mortara.
There are no letters from my father to his uncle (he had apparently made no copies), and Edgardo's replies, on the letterhead
of the abbey of the Canons Regular, are all dated in the years
of my very early childhood. If I had ever been aware of these
papers before, I have no memory of it. Nor do I see any mark
of intimacy—every letter from the priest falls into a missionary
fervor—until the one dated last, confined to the margins of a

page torn from a missal. The baptized prodigy, renowned for his fluency in Latin, French, Spanish, Flemish, German, Basque, preaching to Jews as far away as Mainz, Munich, Paris, Breslau . . . but in this furtive plaint to my father, it is as if—as if, as if!—the small boy, the terrified captive child Edgardo, speaks. He comes to me now as a voice tangled in the prickle of our old Bolognese consonants, evading, prevaricating, entreating. I see him looking back, I hear him beseeching. A smothered appeal, a wilderness that eludes my telling. And what was the force, what was the pledge, that my father uttered to bring such whispers, such whimpers, such naked bleats, into helpless being?

Ricordo mea madre.	I remember my mother.
Ricordo mio padre.	I remember my father.
Ricordo quasi i miei fratelli e mie sorelle.	I almost remember my brothers and sisters.
Mea madre mi ha abbandonato.	My mother gave me up.
Mio padre ha cercato di portarmivia.	My father tried to steal me.
Cosa sono?	What am I?
Chi sono?	Who am I?
Cosa posso fare?	What can I do?

Below these lines I recognize, in my father's hand, three sparse words:

pity pity pity

Actors

MATT SORLEY, BORN Mose Sadacca, was an actor. He was a
character actor and (when they let him) a comedian. He had
broad, swarthy, pliant cheeks, a reddish widow's peak that was
both curly and balding, and very bright teeth as big and orderly
as piano keys. His stage name had a vaguely Irish sound, but
his origins were Sephardic. One grandfather was from Constantinople, the other from Alexandria. His parents could still
manage a few words of the old Spanish spoken by the Jews who
had fled the Inquisition, but Matt himself, brought up in Ben-
sonhurst, Brooklyn, was purely a New Yorker. The Brooklyn
that swarmed in his speech was useful. It got him parts.

Sometimes he was recognized in the street a day or so
following his appearance on a television lawyer series he was
occasionally on call for. These were serious, mostly one-shot
parts requiring mature looks. The pressure was high. Clowning
was out, even in rehearsals. Matt usually played the judge (three
minutes on camera) or else the father of the murder victim
(seven minutes). The good central roles went to much younger
men with rich black hair and smooth flat bellies. When they
stood up to speak in court, they carefully buttoned up their
jackets. Matt could no longer easily button his. He was close to
sixty and secretly melancholy. He lived on the Upper West Side
in a rent-controlled apartment with a chronic leak under the
bathroom sink. He had a reputation for arguing with directors;
one director was in the habit of addressing him, rather nastily,
as Mr. Surly.

His apartment was littered with dictionaries, phrase books,
compendiums of scientific terms, collections of slang, encyclopedias of botany, mythology, history. Frances was the one
with the steady income. She worked for a weekly crossword
puzzle magazine, and by every Friday had to have composed

three new puzzles in ascending order of complexity. The job
kept her confined and furious. She was unfit for deadlines and
tension; she was myopic and suffered from eyestrain. Her neck
was long, thin, and imperious, with a jumpy pulse at the side.
Matt had met her, right out of Tulsa, almost twenty years ago
on the tiny stage of one of those downstairs cellar theaters in
the Village—the stage was only a clearing in a circle of chairs.
It was a cabaret piece, with ballads and comic songs, and neither
Matt nor Frances had much of a voice. This common deficiency
passed for romance. They analyzed their mutual flaws endlessly
over coffee in the grimy little café next door to the theater.
Because of sparse audiences, the run petered out after only two
weeks, and the morning after the last show Matt and Frances
walked downtown to City Hall and were married.

Frances never sang onstage again. Matt sometimes did, to
get laughs. As long as Frances could stick to those Village cellars
she was calm enough, but in any theater north of Astor Place
she faltered and felt a needlelike chill in her breasts and forgot
her lines. And yet her brain was all storage. She knew words
like "fenugreek," "kermis," "sponson," "gibberellin." She was
angry at being imprisoned by such words. She lived, she said,
behind bars; she was the captive of a grid. All day long she
sat fitting letters into squares, scrambling the alphabet, inventing definitions made to resemble conundrums, shading in the
unused squares. "Grid and bear it," she said bitterly, while Matt
went out to take care of ordinary household things—buying
milk, picking up his shirts from the laundry, taking his shoes
to be resoled. Frances had given up acting for good. She
didn't like being exposed like that, feeling nervous like that,
shaking like that, the needles in her nipples, the numbness in
her throat, the cramp in her bowel. Besides, she was embarrassed about being nearsighted and hated having to put in
contact lenses to get through a performance. In the end she
threw them in the trash. Offstage, away from audiences,
she could wear her big round glasses in peace.

Frances resented being, most of the time, the only bread-
winner. After four miscarriages she said she was glad they
had no children, she couldn't imagine Matt as a father—he

lacked gumption, he had no get-up-and-go. He thought it was demeaning to scout for work. He thought work ought to come to him because he was an artist. He defined himself as master of a Chaplinesque craft; he had been born into the line of an elite tradition. He scorned props and despised the way some actors relied on cigarettes to move them through a difficult scene, stopping in the middle of a speech to light up. It was false suspense, it was pedestrian. Matt was a purist. He was contemptuous of elaborately literal sets, rooms that looked like real rooms. He believed that a voice, the heel of a hand, a hesitation, the widening of a nostril, could furnish a stage. Frances wanted Matt to hustle for jobs, she wanted him to network, bug his agent, follow up on casting calls. Matt could do none of these things. He was an actor, he said, not a goddamn peddler.

It wasn't clear whether he was actually acting all the time (Frances liked to accuse him of this), yet even on those commonplace daytime errands, there was something exaggerated and perversely open about him: an unpredictability leaped out and announced itself. He kidded with all the store help. At the Korean-owned vegetable stand, the young Mexican who was unpacking peppers and grapefruits hollered across to him, "Hey, Mott, you in a movie now?" For all its good will, the question hurt. It was four years since his last film offer, a bit part with Marlon Brando, whom Matt admired madly, though without envy. The role bought Matt and Frances a pair of down coats for winter, and a refrigerator equipped with an ice-cube dispenser. But what Matt really hoped for was getting back onstage. He wanted to be in a play.

At the shoe-repair place his new soles were waiting for him. The proprietor, an elderly Neapolitan, had chalked *Attore* across the bottom of Matt's well-worn slip-ons. Then he began his usual harangue: Matt should go into opera. "I wouldn't be any good at it," Matt said, as he always did, and flashed his big even teeth. Against the whine of the rotary brush he launched into "La donna è mobile." The shoemaker shut off his machine and bent his knees and clapped his hands and leaked tears down the accordion creases that fanned out from the corners of his eyes. It struck Matt just then that his friend Salvatore had the fairy-tale crouch of Geppetto, the father of Pinocchio; the thought encouraged him to roll up the legs of his pants and jig, still loudly singing. Salvatore hiccupped and roared and sobbed with laughter.

Sometimes Matt came into the shop just for a shine. The shoemaker never let him pay. It was Matt's trick to tell Frances (his awful deception, which made him ashamed) that he was headed downtown for an audition, and wouldn't it be a good idea to stop first to have his shoes buffed? The point was to leave a decent impression for next time, even if they didn't hire you this time. "Oh, for heaven's sake, buy some shoe polish and do it yourself," Frances advised, but not harshly; she was pleased about the audition.

Of course there wasn't any audition—or if there was, Matt wasn't going to it. After Salvatore gave the last slap of his flannel cloth, Matt hung around, teasing and fooling, for half an hour or so, and then he walked over to the public library to catch up on the current magazines. He wasn't much of a reader, though in principle he revered literature and worshiped Shakespeare and Oscar Wilde. He looked through the *Atlantic* and *Harper's* and *The New Yorker*, all of which he liked; *Partisan Review, Commentary*, magazines like that, were over his head.

Sitting in the library, desultorily turning pages, he felt himself a failure and an idler as well as a deceiver. He stared at his wristwatch. If he left this minute, if he hurried, he might still be on time to read for Lionel: he knew this director, he knew he was old-fashioned and meanly slow—one reading was never enough. Matt guessed that Lionel was probably a bit of a dyslexic. He made you stand there and do your half of the dialogue again and again, sometimes three or four times, while he himself read the other half flatly, stumblingly. He did this whether he was seriously considering you or had already mentally dismissed you: his credo was fairness, a breather, another try. Or else he had a touch of sadism. Directors want to dominate you, shape you, turn you into whatever narrow idea they have in their skulls. To a director an actor is a puppet—Geppetto with Pinocchio. Matt loathed the ritual of the audition; it was humiliating. He was too much of a pro to be put through these things, his track record ought to speak for itself, and why didn't it? Especially with Lionel; they had both been in the business for years. Lionel, like everyone else, called it "the business." Matt never did.

He took off his watch and put it on the table. In another twenty minutes he could go home to Frances and fake it about the audition: it was the lead Lionel was after, the place was full of young guys, the whole thing was a misunderstanding. Lionel, believe it or not, had apologized for wasting Matt's time.

"Lionel apologized?" Frances said. Without her glasses on, she gave him one of her naked looks. It was a way she had of avoiding seeing him while drilling straight through him. It made him feel damaged.

"You never went," she said. "You never went near that audition."

"Yes I did. I did go. That shit Lionel. Blew my whole day."

"Don't kid me. You didn't go. And Lionel's not a shit, he's been good to you. He gave you the uncle part in *Navy Blues* only three years ago. I don't know why you insist on forgetting that."

"It was junk. Garbage. I'm sick of being the geezer in the last act."

"Be realistic. You're not twenty-five."

"What's realistic is if they give me access to my range."

And so on. This was how they quarreled, and Matt was pained by it: it wasn't as if Frances didn't understand how much he hated sucking up to directors, waiting for the verdict on his thickening fleshy arms, his round stomach, his falsely grinning face, his posture, his walk, even his voice. His voice he knew passed muster: it was like a yo-yo, he could command it to tighten or stretch, to torque or lift. And still he had to submit to scrutiny, to judgment, to prejudice, to whim. He hated having to be obsequious, even when it took the form of jolliness, of ersatz collegiality. He hated lying. His nose was growing from all the lies he told Frances.

On the other hand, what was acting if not lying? A good actor is a good impostor. A consummate actor is a consummate deceiver. Or put it otherwise: an actor is someone who falls into the deeps of self-forgetfulness. Or still otherwise: an actor is a puppeteer, with himself as puppet.

Matt frequently held forth in these trite ways—mostly to himself. When it came to philosophy, he didn't fool anybody, he wasn't an original.

"You got a call," Frances said.

"Who?" Matt said.

"You won't like who. You won't want to do it, it doesn't fit your range."

"For crying out loud," Matt said. "Who was it?"

"Somebody from Ted Silkowitz's. It's something Ted Silkowitz is doing. You won't like it," she said again.

"Silkowitz," Matt groaned. "The guy's still in diapers. He's sucking his thumb. What's he want with me?"

"That's it. He wants you and nobody else."

"Cut it out, Frances."

"See what I mean? I know you, I knew you'd react like that. You won't want to do it. You'll find some reason."

She pulled a tissue from inside the sleeve of her sweater and began to breathe warm fog on her lenses. Then she rubbed them with the tissue. Matt was interested in bad eyesight—how it made people stand, the pitch of their shoulders and necks. It was the kind of problem he liked to get absorbed in. The stillness and also the movement. If acting was lying, it was at the same time mercilessly and mechanically truth-telling. Watching Frances push the earpieces of her glasses back into the thicket of her hair, Matt thought how pleasing that was, how quickly and artfully she did it. He could copy this motion exactly; he drew it with his tongue on the back of his teeth. If he looked hard enough, he could duplicate anything at all. Even his nostrils, even his genitals, had that power. His mind was mostly a secret kept from him—he couldn't run it, it ran him, but he was intimate with its nagging pushy heat.

"It's got something to do with Lear. Something about King Lear," Frances said. "But never mind, it's not for you. You wouldn't want to play a geezer."

"Lear? What d'you mean, Lear?"

"Something like that, I don't know. You're supposed to show up tomorrow morning. If you're interested," she added; he understood how sly she could be. "Eleven o'clock."

"Well, well," Matt said, "good thing I got my shoes shined." Not that he believed in miracles, but with Silkowitz anything was possible: the new breed, all sorts of surprises up their baby sleeves.

Silkowitz's building was off Eighth Avenue, up past the theater district. The neighborhood was all bars, interspersed with dark little slots of Greek luncheonettes; there was a sex shop on the corner. Matt, in suit and tie, waited for the elevator to take him to Silkowitz's office, on the fifth floor. It turned out to be a cramped two-room suite: a front cubicle for the receptionist, a boy who couldn't have been more than nineteen, and a rear cubicle for the director. The door to Silkowitz's office was shut.

"Give him a minute. He's on the phone," the boy said. "We've run into a little problem with the writer."

"The writer?" Matt said stupidly.

"She died last night. After we called you about the Lear thing."

"I thought the writer died a long time ago."

"Well, it's not *that* Lear."

"Matt Sorley," Silkowitz yelled. "Come on in, let's have a look. You're the incarnation of my dream—I'm a big fan, I love your work. Hey, all you need is a Panama hat."

The hat crack was annoying; it meant that Silkowitz was familiar mainly with one of Matt's roles on that television show—it was his signature idiosyncrasy to wear a hat in court until the judge reprimanded him and made him take it off.

Matt said, "The writer's *dead?*"

"We've got ourselves a tragedy. Heart attack. Two A.M., passed away in intensive care. Not that she's any sort of spring chicken. Marlene Miller-Weinstock, you know her?"

"So there's no play," Matt said; he was out of a job.

"Let me put it this way. There's no playwright, which is an entirely different thing."

"Never heard of her," Matt said.

"Right. Neither did I, until I got hold of this script. As far as I know she's written half a dozen novels. The kind that get published and then disappear. Never wrote a play before. Face it, novelists can't do plays anyhow."

"Oh, I don't know," Matt said. "Gorky, Sartre, Steinbeck. Galsworthy. Wilde." It came to him that Silkowitz had probably never read any of these old fellows from around the world. Not that Matt had either, but he was married to someone who had read them all.

"Right," Silkowitz conceded. "But you won't find Miller-Weinstock on that list. The point is what I got from this woman is raw. Raw but full of bounce. A big look at things."

Silkowitz was cocky in a style that was new to Matt. Lionel, for all his arrogance, had an exaggerated courtly patience that ended by stretching out your misery; Lionel's shtick was to keep you in suspense. And Lionel had a comfortingly aging face, with a firm deep wadi slashed across his forehead, and a wen hidden in one eyebrow. Matt was used to Lionel—they were two old war horses, they knew what to expect from each other. But here was Silkowitz with his baby face—he didn't look a lot older than that boy out there—and his low-hung childishly small teeth under a bumpy tract of exposed fat gums: here was Silkowitz mysteriously dancing around a questionable script by someone freshly deceased. The new breed, they didn't wait out an apprenticeship, it was drama school at Yale and then the abrupt ascent into authority, reputation, buzz. The sureness of this man, sweatshirt and jeans, pendant dangling from the neck, a silver ring on his thumb, hair as sleek and flowing as a girl's—the whole thick torso glowing with power. Still a kid, Silkowitz was already on his way into Lionel's league: he could make things happen. Ten years from now the scruffy office would be just as scruffy, just as out of the way, though presumably more spacious; the boy out front would end up a Hollywood agent, or else head out for the stock exchange in a navy blazer with brass buttons. Lionel left you feeling heavy, superfluous, a bit of an impediment. This Silkowitz, an enthusiast, charged you up: Matt had the sensation of an electric wire going up his spine, probing and poking his vertebrae.

"Look, it's a shock," Silkowitz said. "I don't feel good about it, but the fact is I never met the woman. Today was supposed to be the day. Right this instant, actually. I figured first organize the geriatric ward, get the writer and the lead face to face. Well, no sweat, we've still got our lead."

"Lead," Matt said; but "geriatric," quip or not, left him sour.

"Right. The minute I set eyes on the script I knew you were the one. As a matter of fact," Silkowitz said, flashing a pair of clean pink palms, "I ran into Lionel the other night and he put me on to you."

These two statements struck Matt as contradictory, but he kept his mouth shut. He had his own scenario, Silkowitz scouting for an old actor and Lionel coming up with Matt: "Call Sorley. Touchy guy, takes offense at the drop of a hat, but one hundred percent reliable. Learns his lines and shows up." Showing up being nine-tenths of talent.

Matt was businesslike. "So you intend to do the play without the writer."

"We don't need the writer. It's enough we've got the blueprint. As far as I'm concerned, theater's a director's medium."

Oh, portentous: Silkowitz as infant lecturer. And full of himself. If he could do without the writer, maybe he could do without the actor?

Silkowitz handed Matt an envelope. "Photocopy of the script," he said. "Take it home. Read it. I'll call you, you'll come in again, we'll talk."

Matt hefted the envelope. Thick, not encouraging. In a way Silkowitz was right about novelists doing plays. They overwrite, they put in a character's entire psychology, from birth on: a straitjacket for an actor. The actor's job is to figure out the part, to feel it out. Feather on feather, tentative, groping. The first thing Matt did was take a black marking pen and cross out all the stage directions. That left just the dialogue, and the dialogue made him moan: monologues, soliloquies, speeches. Oratory!

"Never mind," Frances said. "Why should *you* care? It's work, you wanted to work."

"It's not that the idea's so bad. Takes off from the real thing."

"So what's the problem?"

"I can't do it, that's the problem."

Naturally he couldn't do it. And he resented Silkowitz's demand that he trek all the way down to that sex-shop corner again—wasn't the telephone good enough? Silkowitz threw out the news that he couldn't proceed, he couldn't think, except in person: he was big on face to face. As if all that counted was his own temperament. With a touch of spite Matt was pleased to be ten minutes late.

A young woman was in the outer cubicle.

"He's waiting for you," she said. "He's finishing up his lunch."

Matt asked where the boy was.

Silkowitz licked a plastic spoon and heaved an empty yogurt cup into a wastebasket across the room. "Quit. Got a job as assistant stage manager in some Off Off. So, what d'you say?"

"The part's not for me. I could've told you this straight off on the phone. The character's ten years older than I am. Maybe fifteen."

"You've got plenty of time to grow a beard. It'll come in white."

"I don't know anything about the background here, it's not my milieu."

"The chance of a lifetime," Silkowitz argued. "Who gets to play Lear, for God's sake?"

Matt said heavily, bitterly, "Yeah. The Lear of Ellis Island. Just off the boat."

"That's the ticket," Silkowitz said. "Think of it as a history play."

Matt sat there while Silkowitz, with lit-up eyes, lectured. A history riff for sure. Fourth, fifth generation, steerage troubles long ago strained out of his blood—it was all a romance to little Teddy Silkowitz. Second Avenue down at Twelfth, the old Yiddish theater, the old feverish plays. Weeping on the stage, weeping in all the rows. Miller-Weinstock ("May she rest in peace," Silkowitz put in) was the daughter of one of those pioneer performers of greenhorn drama; the old man, believe it or not, was still alive at ninety-six, a living fossil, an actual breathing known-to-be-extinct duck-billed dodo. That's where she got it from—from being his daughter. Those novels she turned out, maybe they were second rate, who knows? Silkowitz didn't know—he'd scarcely looked at the handful of reviews she'd sent—and it didn't matter. What mattered was the heat that shot straight out of her script, like the heat smell of rusted radiators knocking in worn-out five-story tenements along Southern Boulevard in the thirties Bronx, or the whiff of summer ozone at the trolley-stop snarl at West Farms. It wasn't those Depression times that fired Silkowitz—it wasn't that sort of recapturing he was after. Matt was amazed—Matt who worshiped nuance, tendril, shadow, intimation, instinct, Matt who might jig for a shoemaker but delivered hints and shadings to the proscenium, Matt who despised exaggeration, caricature, going over the top, Matt for whom the stage was holy ground . . . And what did little Teddy Silkowitz want?

"Reversal," Silkowitz said. "Time to change gears. The changing of the guard. Change, that's what! Where's the overtness, the overture, the passion, the emotion? For fifty, sixty years all we've had is mutters, muteness, tight lips, and, goddamn it, you can't hear their voices, all that Actors Studio blather, the old religion, so-called inwardness, a bunch of Quakers waiting for Inner Light—obsolete! Dying, dead, finished! Listen, Matt, I'm talking heat, muscle, human anguish. Where's the theatrical *noise?* The big speeches and declamations? All these anemic monosyllabic washed-out two-handers with their impotent little climaxes. Matt, let me tell you my idea, and I tell it with respect, because I'm in the presence of an old-timer, and I want you to know I know my place. But we're in a new era now, and someone's got to make that clear—" Silkowitz's kindling look moved all around, from desk to floor to ceiling; those hot eyes, it seemed to Matt, could scald the paint off the walls. "This is what I'm for. Take it seriously. My idea is to restore the old lost art of melodrama. People call it melodrama to put it down, but what it is is open feeling, you see what I mean? And the chance came out of the blue! From the daughter of the genuine article!"

Matt said roughly (his roughness surprised him), "You've got the wrong customer."

"Look before you leap, pal. Don't try to pin that nostalgia stuff on me. The youthful heart throbbing for grandpa's world. That's what you figure, right?"

"Not exactly," Matt fibbed.

"That's not it, honest to God. It's the largeness—big feelings, big cries. Outcries! The old Yiddish theater kept it up while it was dying out everywhere else. Killed by understatement. Killed by abbreviation, downplaying. Killed by sophistication, modernism, psychologizing, Stanislavsky, all those highbrow murderers of the Greek chorus, you see what I mean? The Yiddish Medea. The Yiddish Macbeth! Matt, it was *big!*"

"As far as I'm concerned," Matt said, "the key word here is old-timer."

"There aren't many of your type around," Silkowitz admitted. "Look, I'm saying I really want you to do this thing. The part's yours."

"A replay of the old country, that's my type? I was doing Eugene O'Neill before you were born."

"You've read the script, it's in regular English. American as apple pie. Lear on the Lower East Side! We can make that the Upper West Side. And those daughters—I've got some great women in mind. We can update everything, we can do what we want."

"Yeah, we don't have the writer to kick around." Matt looked down at his trouser cuffs. They were beginning to fray at the crease; he needed a new suit. "I'm not connected to any of that. My mother's father came from Turkey and spoke Ladino."

"A Spanish grandee, no kidding. I didn't realize. You look—"

"I know how I look," Matt broke in. "A retired pants presser." He wanted to play Ibsen, he wanted to play Shaw! Henry Higgins with Eliza. Something grand, aloof, cynical; he could do Brit talk beautifully.

Silkowitz pushed on. "Lionel says he's pretty sure you're free."

Free. The last time Matt was on a stage (televison didn't count) was in Lionel's own junk play, a London import, where

Matt, as the beloved missing uncle, turned up just before the final curtain. That was more than three years ago; by now four.

"I'll give it some thought," Matt said.

"It's a deal. Start growing the beard. There's only one thing. A bit of homework you need to do."

"Don't worry," Matt said, "I know how the plot goes. Regan and Goneril and Cordelia. I read it in high school."

But it wasn't Shakespeare Silkowitz had in mind: it was Eli Miller the nonagenarian. Silkowitz had the old fellow's address at a "senior residence." Probably the daughter had mentioned its name, and Silkowitz had ordered his underling—the boy, or maybe the girl—to look it up. It was called the Home for the Elderly Children of Israel, and it was up near the Cloisters.

"Those places give me the creeps," Matt complained to Frances. "The smell of pee and the zombie stare."

"It doesn't have to be like that. They have activities and things. They have social directors. At that age maybe they go for blue material, you never know."

"Sure," Matt said. "The borscht belt up from the dead and unbuckled. You better come with me."

"What's the point of that? Silkowitz wants you to get the feel of the old days. In Tulsa we didn't *have* the old days."

"Suppose the guy doesn't speak English? I mean just in case. Then I'm helpless."

So Frances went along; Tulsa notwithstanding, she knew some attenuated strands of household Yiddish. She was a demon at languages anyhow; she liked to speckle her tougher crosswords with *cri de coeur*, *Mitleid*, *situación difícil*. She had once studied ancient Greek and Sanskrit.

A mild January had turned venomous. The air slammed their foreheads like a frozen truncheon. Bundled in their down coats, they waited for a bus. Icicles hung from its undercarriage, dripping black sludge. The long trip through afternoon dark took them to what seemed like a promontory; standing in the driveway of the Home for the Elderly Children of Israel, they felt like a pair of hawks surveying rivers and roads and inch-tall buildings. "*The Magic Mountain*," Frances muttered as they left

the reception desk and headed down the corridor to room 1-A:
Eli Miller's digs.

No one was there.

"Let's trespass," Frances said. Matt followed her in. The
place was overheated; in two minutes he had gone from chill
to sweat. He was glad Frances had come. At times she was capable of an unexpected aggressiveness. He saw it now and then
as she worked at her grids, her lists of synonyms, her trickster
definitions. Her hidden life inside those little squares gave off
an electric ferocity. She was prowling all around 1-A as if it was
one of her boxes waiting to be solved. The room was cryptic enough: what was it like to be so circumscribed—a single
dresser crowded with tubes and medications, a sagging armchair
upholstered in balding plush, a bed for dry bones—knowing it
to be your last stop before the grave? The bed looked more like
a banquet table, very high, with fat carved legs; it was covered
all over with a sort of wrinkly cloak, heavy maroon velvet
tasseled at the corners—a royal drapery that might have been
snatched from the boudoir of a noblewoman of the Tsar's court.
A child's footstool stood at the bedside.

"He must be a little guy," Frances said. "When you get old
you start to shrink."

"Old-timer," Matt spat out. "Can you imagine? That's what
he called me actually."

"Who did?"

"That twerp Silkowitz."

Frances ignored this. "Get a look at that bedspread or whatever it is. I'd swear a piece of theater curtain. And the bed!
Stage furniture. Good God, has he read all this stuff?"

Every space not occupied by the dresser, the chair, and the
bed was tumbled with books. There were no shelves. The books
rose up from the floorboards in wobbly stacks, with narrow
aisles between. Some had fallen and lay open like wings, their
pages pulled from their spines.

"German, Russian, Hebrew, Yiddish. A complete set of
Dickens. Look," Frances said, "*Moby-Dick!*"

"In the atrium they told me visitors," said a voice in the
doorway. It was the brassy monotone of the almost-deaf, a horn

bereft of music. Frances hiked up her glasses and wiped her right hand on her coat: *Moby-Dick* was veiled in grime.

"Mr. Miller?" Matt said.

"Bereaved, sir. Eli Miller is bereaved."

"I heard about your daughter. I'm so sorry," Matt said; but if this was going to be a conversation, he hardly knew how to get hold of it.

The old man was short, with thick shoulders and the head of a monk. Or else it was Ben Gurion's head: a circle of naked scalp, shiny as glass, and all around it a billowing ring of pearl-white hair, charged with static electricity. His cheeks were a waterfall of rubbery creases. One little eye peeped out from the flow, dangerously blue. The other was sealed into its socket. You might call him ancient, but you couldn't call him frail. He looked like a man who even now could take an ax to a bull.

He went straight to the stepstool, picked it up, and tossed it into the corridor; it made a brutal clatter.

"When I go out they put in trash. I tell them, Eli Miller requires no ladders!" With the yell of the deaf he turned to Frances. "She was a woman your age. What, you're fifty? Your father, he's living?"

"He died years ago," Frances said. Her age was private; a sore point.

"Naturally. This is natural, the father should not survive the child. A very unhappy individual, my daughter. Divorced. The husband flies away to Alaska and she's got her rotten heart. A shame, against nature—Eli Miller, the heart and lungs of an elephant! Better a world filled with widows than divorced." He curled his thick butcher's arm around Frances's coat collar. "Madam, my wife if you could see her you would be dumb-struck. She had unusually large eyes and with a little darkening of the eyelids they became larger. Big and black like olives. Thirty-two years she's gone. She had a voice they could hear it from the second balcony, rear row."

Matt caught Frances's look: it was plain she was writing the old fellow off. *Not plugged in,* Frances was signaling, *nobody home upstairs, lost his marbles.* Matt decided to trust the better possibility: a bereaved father has a right to some indulgence.

"There's real interest in your daughter's play," he began; he spoke evenly, reasonably.

"An ambitious woman. Talent not so strong. Whoever has Eli Miller for a father will be ambitious. Eli Miller's talent, this is another dimension. What you see here"—he waved all around 1-A—"are remnants. Fragments and vestiges! *The Bewildered Bridegroom*, 1924!" He pinched a bit of the maroon velvet bedspread and fingered its golden tassel. "From the hem of Esther Borodovsky's dress hung twenty-five like this! And four hundred books on the walls of Dr. Borodovsky! That's how we used to do it, no stinginess! And who do you think played the Bridegroom? Eli Miller! The McKinley Square Theater, Boston Road and 169th, they don't forget such nights, whoever was there they remember!"

Matt asked, "You know your daughter wrote a play? She told you?"

"And not only the Bridegroom! Othello, Macbeth, Polonius. Polonius the great philosopher, very serious, very wise. Jacob Adler's Shylock, an emperor! Tomashefsky, Schwartz, Carnovsky!"

"Matt," Frances whispered, "I want to leave *now*."

Matt said slowly, "Your daughter's play is getting produced. I'm *in* it. I'm an actor."

The old man ejected a laugh. His dentures struck like a pair of cymbals; the corona of his magnetic hair danced. "Actor, actor, call yourself what you want, only watch what you say in front of Eli Miller! My daughter, first it's *romanen*, now it's a play! Not only is the daughter taken before the father but also the daughter is mediocre. Always mediocre. She cannot ascend to the father! Eli Miller the pinnacle! The daughter climbs and falls. Mediocre!"

"Matt, let's go," Frances growled.

"And this one?" Again the old man embraced her; Frances recoiled. "This one is also in it?"

"Here," Matt said, and handed Eli Miller one of Teddy Silkowitz's cards. "If you want to know more, here's the director." He stopped; he thought better of what he was about to say. But he said it anyway: "He admires your daughter's work."

"Eli Miller's Polonius, in the highest literary Yiddish, sir! Standing ovations and bravo every night. Every matinee. Three matinees a week, that's how it was. Bravo bravo. By the time she's born, it's after the war, it's 1948, it's finishing up, it's practically gone. Gone—the whole thing! After Hitler, who has a heart for tragedy on a stage? Anyhow no more actors, only movie stars. Please, sir, do me a favor and name me no names, what is it, who is it, who remembers? But Eli Miller and Esther Borodovsky, also Dr. Borodovsky, whoever was there they remember!"

"With or without you," Frances warned, "I'm going."

Matt hung on. "Your daughter's play," he said, "is out of respect for all that. For everything you feel."

"What are you saying? I know what she is! My daughter, all her life she figures one thing, to take away Eli Miller's soul. This is why God makes her mediocre, this is why God buries the daughter before the father!"

They left him with tears running out of the one blue eye.

"I think you incited him," Frances said. "You just went ahead and provoked him." They were huddled in the bus shelter, out of the wind. It was five o'clock and already night.

Matt said, "An old actor, maybe he was acting."

"Are you kidding?" Frances said; hunched inside the bulk of her coat, she was shivering.

"You're always telling me *I* do that."

"Do what?"

"Act all the time."

"Oh, for Pete's sake," Frances said. "Why did you make me come anyhow? My toes are numb."

Late in February, a day of falling snow, rehearsals began. Silkowitz had rented a cellar in a renovated old building in the West Forties, in sight of the highway and the river. The space had a stage at one end and at the other a sort of stockade surrounding a toilet that occasionally backed up. The ceiling groaned and shuddered. A far-off piano thumped out distracting rhythms: there was a dance studio overhead. The cast was smaller than Matt had expected—the three female roles had been reduced to two. Silkowitz had spent the past month reviewing the script, and was still not satisfied. No sooner did Matt learn the moves of a scene than the director had second thoughts and rearranged the blocking. To Matt's surprise, the boy who had been in Silkowitz's office was there, presiding over a notebook; Silkowitz had brought him back to be stage manager. Matt calculated that the kid had six weeks' experience.

Silkowitz had put himself in charge of secrets. Each rehearsal session felt like a cabal from which the actors were excluded. Strangers came and went, carrying portfolios. Silkowitz never introduced any of them. "This is going to be a tight job, nothing extraneous. I believe in collaboration with all my heart, but just remember that collaboration runs through me," he announced. And another time: "My intention is to clot the curds." It was a tyranny that outstripped even Lionel's. The veneer was on the shabby side, but there was a stubborn complacency beneath. Matt, who had his own ideas and liked to cavil, was disinclined to argue with Silkowitz. The director would stop him mid-sentence to murmur against a wall with one of those coming and going unknowns: it was a discussion of the set, or some question about the lighting; or there would be the incidental music to consider. The house was already booked, Silkowitz reported—a two-hundred-and-ninety-nine-seater west of Union Square—and he had nailed down a pair of invisible backers, whom he did not name. Silkowitz had a reputation for working fast: what seemed important yesterday no longer mattered today. He scarcely listened when Matt began to tell about the visit to Eli Miller. "Good, good," he replied, "right," and turned away to look over someone's swatch of cloth. It was as if he had never insisted on the journey to the Home for the Elderly Children of Israel.

At the end of each day's rehearsal, the director sat on the edge of the stage and drew the actors around him in a half-circle and gave them his notes. And then came the daily exhortation: what he wanted from them all, he said, was more passion, more susceptibility. He wanted them to be drinking metaphorical poison; he wanted them to pour out blood and bile and bitter gall.

"Especially you, Matt. You're underplaying again. Forget that less-is-more business, it's crap! More energy! We've got to hear the thunderclap."

Matt's throat hurt. He was teaching himself to howl. He had abandoned all his customary techniques: his vocal cords seemed perplexed by these new uses. He felt his chest fill with a curious darkness. In the morning, before taking the subway down to rehearsal, he tramped through the blackening snow to the public library and found a warm spot near a radiator and fell into *King Lear*, the original. He saw how those selfish women were stripping the old guy to the bone—no wonder he howls!

He was heading back to the subway when it occurred to him that it was weeks since he had stepped into the shoe-repair shop.

Salvatore did not know him.

"Hey, Salvatore!" Matt called in that stagy roar Silkowitz liked, and attempted an abbreviated version of his little comic jig. But in his clumsy buckled-up snow boots he could only stamp.

Salvatore said over the noise of his machines, "You got shoes to fix, mister?"

"What's the matter with *you?*" Matt said.

"*Il attore!*"

The trouble was the beard, the shoemaker said. Who could see it was his friend Matteo? What was the beard *for?* Had he gone into opera after all? With the beard he looked one hundred years old. This frightened Matt. Just as Silkowitz had predicted, Matt's whiskers had grown in stark white: he was passing for an old-timer in earnest.

And it was true: in a way he *had* gone into opera. Marlene Miller-Weinstock's primal voice still reverberated, even with Silkowitz's changes. His changes were logistical: he had moved the locale, updated the era, and accommodated the names of the characters to contemporary ears. Marlene Miller-Weinstock's play was a kind of thirties costume drama, and Silkowitz had modernized it. That was all. The speeches were largely unaltered. Grandiloquence! There were no insinuations or intimations, none of those shrewd hesitations Matt loved to linger over. His gods were ellipsis and inference. Hers were bombast and excitation. Matt's particular skill was in filling in the silent spaces: he did it with his whole elastic face, and in the stance of his legs—a skeptical tilt of knee, an ironical angle of heel. But Marlene Miller-Weinstock's arias left no room for any play of suggestion or uncertainty. Fury ruled; fury and conviction and a relentless and fiery truth. It came to Matt that fury *was* truth; it amazed him that this could be so. His actor's credo had always been the opposite: glimmer and inkling are truth, hint and intuition are truth; nuance is essence. What Marlene Miller-Weinstock was after was malevolence, rage, even madness: vehemence straight out; shrieks blasted from the whirlwind's bowel. She was all storm. In the gale's wild din—inside all that howling—Matt was learning how to hear the steady blows of some interior cannon. The booms were loud and regular: it was his own heartbeat.

Those two women with him on that dusty ill-lit stage—he felt apart from them, he saw them as moving shadows of himself. He felt apart from the men, one of whom he had worked with before, under Lionel's direction. And in the darkened margins of the place, on folding chairs along the wall, here was the boy with his notebook, and Silkowitz next to him, faintly panting, kicking his foot up and down as if marching to an unheard band. But Matt had pushed through a vestibule of embarrassment (it was shame over being made to howl) into some solitary chamber, carpeted and tapestried; it was as if he had broken through a membrane, a lung, behind which a sudden altar crouched, covered with Eli Miller's heavy tasseled bedspread. In this chamber Matt listened to his heart-beat. He understood that it wasn't Silkowitz who had led him here. Silkowitz was a literalist, a sentimentalist, a theorist—one of these, or all. Mainly he was flashy. Silkowitz's bets were on the future. He had nothing to do with this voluptuous clamor, Matt inside the gonging of his own rib cage, alone and very large; terrifyingly huge there on that dusty ill-lit stage. Marlene Miller-Weinstock had drawn him in. Or her father had. Inside his howl, Matt was beginning to believe the father's accusation:

the daughter had taken hold of the father in order to copy his soul.

Silkowitz was pleased. "You've got it together," he told Matt. "Stick with Matt," he said to the others. He praised Matt for being everywhere at once, like a rushing ghost; for looking into the women's eyes with a powerful intimacy beyond naturalism; for what he called "symbolic stature" and "integration into the scene." All this puzzled Matt. He hated the lingo. It wasn't what he was feeling, it wasn't what he was doing. He had no consciousness of being part of a company. He wasn't serving the company, whatever Silkowitz might think. He was in pursuit of his grand howl. He wanted to go on living inside it. When rehearsals were over he kept to himself and hurried to the subway.

Ten days before the opening, Silkowitz moved the cast to the theater. It was a converted movie house; the stage was undersized but workable. To get to the men's dressing room you had to go through a narrow airless tunnel with great rusted pipes sweating overhead. The place was active, swarming. The boy with the notebook kept on checking his lists and schedules; he seemed professional enough. Wires crisscrossed the floor. Taped music traveled on phantom waves between scenes. Big wooden shapes materialized, pushed back and forth along the apron. Silkowitz had a hand in everything, running from corner to corner, his long girlish hair rippling, the silver thumb ring reddening in the light of the Exit sign whenever he glided past it.

Frances had decided to attend these final days of rehearsal. Silkowitz made no objection. She came hauling a tote bag, and settled into the next-to-last row, laying out her dictionaries and references and pencils on the seats around her. She worked quietly, but Matt knew she was attentive and worried. He was indifferent to her inspections and judgments; he was concentrating on his howl. She mocked it as rant, but it didn't trouble her that Matt had departed from his usual style—he was doing his job, he was giving the director what he wanted. What it meant was a paycheck. And by now Matt couldn't claim, either, that Silkowitz was egging him on. The director was taking in

whatever Matt was emitting. He was emitting a sea of lamentation. Frances dumped her papers back into the tote and listened.
Matt was standing downstage, alone, in profile, leaning forward like a sail in the wind, or like the last leaf of a wintry
tree. He looked wintry himself. It was the day's concluding
run-through; the rest of the cast had left. Matt was doing his
solo scene near the end of the second act. His big belly had
mostly sunk. Lately he had no appetite. He was never hungry.
His beard had lengthened raggedly; a brownish-yellowish tinge
showed at the tips. He seemed mesmerized, suffering. He was
staring ahead, into the dark of the wings.

He turned to Silkowitz. "Someone's out there," he said.

"There shouldn't be," Silkowitz said. "Sally's kid's sick, she
went home. And anyhow her cue brings her in the other way.
Is that electrician still working back there?" he called to the boy
with the notebook.

"Everyone's gone," the boy called back.

Matt said hoarsely, "I thought I saw someone." He had let
his hair grow down to meet the beard. His eyes were birdlike,
ringed with creases.

"O.K., call it a day. You're not the only one who's dead
tired," Silkowitz said. "Go get some sleep."

On the way to the subway, Frances beside him, Matt brooded. "There was a guy out there. He was coming from the men's
toilet, I saw him."

"It's the neighborhood. Some creep wandered in."

"He was there yesterday too. In the middle of that same
speech. I think someone's hiding out."

"Where? In the men's toilet?"

"Ever since we got to the theater. I saw him the first day."

"You never said anything."

"I wasn't sure he was there."

He was sorry he had spoken at all. It wasn't something he
wanted to discuss with Frances. She had ridiculed his howl; now
she was telling him it was worse than rant, he was hamming
it up. The ignorance, the obtuseness! He was seized, dissolved,
metamorphosed. His howl had altered him: the throat widens
and becomes a highway for specters, the lungs an echo chamber

for apparitions. His howl had floated him far above Frances, far above Silkowitz. Silkowitz and Lionel, what did it matter? They were the same, interchangeable, tummlers and barkers, different styles, what did it matter? Silkowitz was attracted to boldness and color, voices as noisy as an old music hall; he was as helpless as Frances to uncover what lay in the cave of the howl. As for the actors, Matt saw them as automatons; he was alone, alone. Except for the man who was hiding out, lurking, gazing.

"My God, Matt," Frances exploded, "you're hallucinating all over the place. It's enough you've started to *look* the part, you don't have to go crazy on top of it. Don't expect me to go there again, I'm keeping away, I've got my deadlines anyhow."

That night her grids sprouted "urus," "muleta," "athanor," "stammel," "nystagmic," "mugient." She worked into the dawn and kept her head down. Occasionally she stopped to polish her lenses. Matt knew her to be inexorably logical.

The day before dress rehearsal, Matt brought his shoes in for a shine. Salvatore seemed wary. Matteo, he said, no longer looked one hundred years old; he looked two hundred.

"You know," Matt said carefully—he had to whisper now to preserve his howl—"there's something better than opera."

Salvatore said there was nothing better than opera. What could be better than opera? For the first time he let Matt pay for his shine.

Dress rehearsal went well, though a little too speedily. The man in the wings had not returned. Silkowitz sat with the cast and gave his last notes. He did not address Matt. Odors of coffee and pastries wafted, and with unexpected lust Matt devoured a bagel spread with cream cheese. He understood himself to be in possession of a deep tranquility. All around him there was nervous buffoonery, witticisms, unaccountable silliness; it was fruition, it was anticipation. The director joined in, told jokes, teased, traded anecdotes and rumors. A journalist, a red-haired woman from the *Times*, arrived to interview Silkowitz. He had hired an industrious publicist; there had been many such journalists. This one had just come from speaking to Lionel, she said, to cover the story from another angle: how, for instance, a more traditional director might view the goings-on down near Union Square. Lionel had responded coolly: he was a minimalist; he repudiated what he took to be Teddy Silkowitz's gaudy postmodern experimentalism. Would he show up at the opening? No, he thought not.

"He'll be here," Silkowitz told the interviewer. The little party was breaking up. "And don't I know what's bugging him. He used to do this sort of thing himself. He was a child actor at the old Grand Theater downtown."

"Oh, come on. Lionel's an Anglophile."

"I read up on it," Silkowitz assured her. "In 1933 he played the boy Shloymele in *Mirele Efros*. God forbid anybody should find out."

The cast, packing up to go home, laughed; wasn't this one of Silkowitz's show-biz gags? But Matt was still contemplating the man in the wings. He had worked himself up to unhealthy visions. It was likely that Frances was right; at least she was sensible. Someone had sneaked in from the street. A homeless fellow sniffing out a warm corner to spend the night. A drunk in need of a toilet. Or else a stagehand pilfering cigarettes on the sly. A banner, a rope, an anything, swaying in the narrow wind that blew through a crack in the rafters. Backstage—deserted at the end of the day, inhabited by the crawling dark.

On the other hand, he knew who it was; he knew. It was the old guy. It was Eli Miller, come down on the M-4 bus from his velvet-curtained bed in the Home for the Elderly Children of Israel.

Lionel would keep his word. He would stay away. Matt had his own thoughts about this, on a different track from Silkowitz's. Matt as Lear! Or a kind of Lear. Lionel had never given Matt the lead in anything; he was eating crow. Naturally he wouldn't put in an appearance. Thanks to Marlene Miller-Weinstock—swallowing her father's life, vomiting out a semblance of Lear—it was a case of Matt's having the last laugh.

In the clouded dressing-room mirror, preparing during intermission for the second act, he thickened his eyebrows with paint and white gum and spilled too much powder all over his beard—the excesses and accidents of opening night. He stepped out of his newly polished shoes to stand on bare feet and then pulled on his costume: a tattered monkish robe. Sackcloth. A tremor shook his lip. He examined the figure in the mirror. It was himself, his own horrifying head. He resembled what he remembered of Job—diseased, cut down, humiliated. The shoemaker if he could see him would add another hundred years.

The first act had survived the risks. Silkowitz had all along worried that the audience, rocked by the unfamiliar theatricality—the loudness, the broadness, the brazenness, the bigness—would presume something farcical. He was in fear of the first lone laugh. A shock in the serpent's tail pulses through to its tongue. An audience is a single beast, a great vibrating integer, a shifting amoeba without a nucleus. One snicker anywhere in its body can set off convulsions everywhere, from the orchestra to the balcony. Such were the director's sermons, recounting the perils ahead; Matt habitually shut out these platitudes. And more from that cornucopia—think of yourselves, Silkowitz lectured them all, as ancient Greek players on stilts, heavily, boldly masked; the old plays of Athens and the old plays of Second Avenue are blood cousins, kin to kin. Power and passion! Passion and power!

Were they pulling it off? During the whole first act, a breathing silence.

Sweating, panting his minor pant, Silkowitz came into the dressing room. Matt turned his back. A transgression. An invasion. Where now was that sacred stricture about the inviolability of an actor's concentration in the middle of a performance, didn't that fool Silkowitz know better? A rip in the brain. Matt was getting ready to lock it up—his brain; he was goading it into isolation, into that secret chamber, all tapestried and tasseled. He was getting ready to enter his howl, and here was Silkowitz, sweating, panting, superfluous, what was he doing here, the fool?

"Your wife said to give you this." Silkowitz handed Matt a folded paper. He recognized it as a sheet from the little spiral pad Frances always carried in her pocketbook. It was her word-collector.

"Not now. I don't want this now." The fool!

"She insisted," Silkowitz said, and slid away. He looked afraid; for the first time he looked respectful. Matt felt his own force; his howl was already in his throat. What was Frances up to? Transgression, invasion!

He read: "metamerism," "oribi," "glyptic," "enatic"—all in Frances's compact, orderly fountain-pen print. But an inch below, in rapid pencil: "*Be advised. I saw him. He's here.*"

She had chosen her seat herself: front row balcony, an aerie from which to spot the reviewers and eavesdrop on the murmurs, the sighs, the whispers. She meant to spy, to search out who was and wasn't there. Aha: then Lionel was there. He was in the audience. He had turned up after all—out of rivalry. Out of jealousy. Because of the buzz. To get the lay of Silkowitz's land. An old director looking in on a young one: age, fear, displacement. They were saying Lionel was past it; they were saying little Teddy Silkowitz, working on a shoestring out of a dinky cell over a sex shop, was cutting edge. So Lionel was out there, Lionel who made Matt audition, who humiliated him, who stuck him with the geezer role, a bit part in the last scene of a half-baked London import.

> As flies to wanton boys are we to the gods; they kill
> us for their sport.
> Unaccommodated man is no more but such a poor,
> bare, fork'd animal as thou art.

Lear on the heath—now let Lionel learn what a geezer role could be, and Matt in it!

Lionel wasn't out there. He would not come for Silkowitz, he would not come for Matt. Matt understood this. It was someone else Frances had seen.

He made his second-act entrance. The set was abstract, filled with those cloth-wrapped wooden free forms that signified the city. Silkowitz had brought the heath to upper Broadway. But no one laughed, no one coughed. It was Lear all the same, daughter-betrayed, in a storm, half mad, sported with by the gods, a poor, bare, forked animal, homeless, shoeless, crying in the gutters of a city street on a snowy night. The fake snow drifted down. Matt's throat let out its unholy howl; it spewed out old forgotten exiles, old lost cities, Constantinople, Alexandria, kingdoms abandoned, refugees ragged and driven, distant ash heaps, daughters unborn, Frances's wasted eggs and empty uterus, the wild roaring cannon of a human heartbeat.

A noise in the audience. Confusion; another noise. Matt moved downstage, blinded, and tried to peer through the lights. A black silhouette was thudding up the middle aisle, shrieking. Three stairs led upward to the apron; up thudded the silhouette. It was Eli Miller in a threadbare cape, waving a walking stick.

"This is not the way! This is not the way!" Eli Miller yelled, and slammed his stick down again and again on the floor of the stage. "Liars, thieves, corruption! In the mother tongue, with sincerity, not from such a charlatan like this!" He thudded toward Matt; his breath was close. It smelled of farina. Matt saw the one blue eye, the one dead eye.

"Jacob Adler, *he* could show you! Not like this! Take Eli Miller's word for it, this is not the way! You weren't there, you didn't see, you didn't hear!" With his old butcher's arm he raised his stick. "People," he called, "listen to Eli Miller, they're leading you by the nose here, it's charlatanism! Pollution! Nobody remembers! Ladies and gentlemen, my daughter, she wasn't born yet, mediocre! Eli Miller is telling you, this is not the way!"

Back he came to Matt. "You, you call yourself an actor? You with the rotten voice? Jacob Adler, this was a thunder, a rotten voice is not a thunder! Maurice Schwartz, the Yiddish Art Theater, right around the corner it used to be, there they did everything beautiful, Gordin, even Herzl once, Hirschbein, Leivick, Ibsen, Molière. Lear! And whoever was there, whoever saw Jacob Adler's Lear, what they saw was not of this earth!"

In a tide of laughter the audience stood up and clapped—a volcano of applause. The laughter surged. Silkowitz ran up on the stage and hauled the old man off, his cape dithering behind

him, his stick in the air, crying Lear, Lear. Matt was still loitering there in his bare feet, watching the wavering cape and the
bobbing stick, when the curtain fell and hid him in the dark.
Many in the audience, Frances informed him later, laughed
until they wept.

At Fumicaro

FRANK CASTLE KNEW everything. He was an art critic; he was a book critic; he wrote on politics and morals; he wrote on everything. He was a journalist, both in print and weekly on the radio; he had "sensibility," but he was proud of being "focused." He was a Catholic; he read Cardinal Newman and François Mauriac and Étienne Gilson and Simone Weil and Jacques Maritain and Graham Greene. He reread *The Heart of the Matter* a hundred times, weeping (Frank Castle could weep) for poor Scobie. He was a parochial man who kept himself inside a frame. He had few Protestant and no Jewish friends. He said he was interested in happiness, and that was why he liked being Catholic. Catholics made him happy.

Fumicaro made him happy. To get there he left New York on an Italian liner, the *Benito Mussolini*. Everything about it was talkative but excessively casual. The schedule itself was casual, and the ship's engines growled in the slip through a whole day before embarkation. Aboard, the passageways were packed with noisy promenaders—munchers of stuffed buns with their entrails dripping out (in all that chaos the dock peddlers had somehow pushed through), quaffers of colored fizzy waters.

At the train station in Milan he found a car, at an exorbitant rate, to take him to Fumicaro. He was already hours late. He was on his way to the Villa Garibaldi, established by a Chicago philanthropist who had set the place up for conferences of a virtuous nature. The Fascists interfered, but not much, out of a lazy sense of duty; so far, only a convention of lepidopterists had been sent away. One of the lepidopterists had been charged with supplying information, not about butterflies, to gangs of anti-Fascists in their hideouts in the hills around Fumicaro.

There were wonders all along the road: dun brick houses Frank Castle had thought peculiar only to certain neighborhoods in the Bronx, each with its distinctive four-sided roof and, in the dooryard of each, a fig tree tightly mummified in canvas. It was still November, but not cold, and the banks along the spiraling mountain route were rich with purple flowers. As they ascended, the driver began to hum a little, especially where the curves were most hair-raising, and when a second car came hurtling into sight from the opposite direction in a space that seemed too narrow even for one, Frank Castle believed death was near; and yet they passed safely and climbed higher. The mountain grew more and more decorous, sprouting antique topiary and far flecks of white villas.

In the Villa Garibaldi the three dozen men who were to be his colleagues were already at dinner, under silver chandeliers; there was no time for him to be taken to his room. The rumbling voices put him off a bit, but he was not altogether among strangers. He recognized some magazine acquaintances and three or four priests, one of them a public charmer whom he had interviewed on the radio. After the conference—it was called "The Church and How It Is Known," and would run four days—almost everyone was planning to go on to Rome. Frank Castle intended to travel to Florence first (he hoped for a glimpse of the portrait of Thomas Aquinas in the San Marco), and then to Rome, but on the fourth day, entirely unexpectedly, he got married instead.

After dinner there was a sluggish session around the huge conference board in the hall next to the dining room—Frank Castle, who had arrived hungry, now felt overfed—and then Mr. Wellborn, the American director, instructed one of the staff (a quick hollow-faced fellow who had waited on Frank Castle's table) to lead him down to the Little Annex, the cottage where he was to sleep. It was full night now; there was a stone terrace to cross, an iron staircase down, a pebbled path weaving between lofty rows of hedges. Like the driver, the waiter hummed, and Frank Castle looked to his footing. But again there was no danger—only a strangeness, and a fragrance so alluring that his nostrils strained after it with appetite. The entrance to the Little Annex was an engaging low archway. The waiter set down Frank Castle's suitcase on the gravel under the arch, handed him a big cold key, and pointed upward to a circular flight of steps. Then he went humming away.

At the top of the stairs Frank Castle saw a green door, but there was no need for the key—the door was open; the lamp was on. Disorder; the bed unmade, though clean sheets were piled on a chair. An empty wardrobe; a desk without a telephone; a bedside cabinet, holding the lit gooseneck; a loud clock and a flashlight; the crash of water in crisis. It was the sound of a toilet flushing again and again. The door to the toilet gaped. He went in and found the chambermaid on her knees before it, retching; in four days she would be his wife.

He was still rather a young man, yet not so young that he was unequal to suddenness. He was thirty-five, and much of his life had flowered out of suddenness. He did not know exactly what to do, but he seized a washcloth, moistened it with cold water at the sink, and pressed it against the forehead of the kneeling woman. She shook it off with an animal sound.

He sat on the rim of the bathtub and watched her. He did not feel especially sympathetic, but he did not feel disgust either. It was as if he were watching a waterfall—a thing belonging to nature. Only the odor was unnatural. Now and then she turned her head and threw him a wild look. *Condemn what thou art, that thou mayest deserve to be what thou art not*, he said to himself; it was Saint Augustine. It seemed right to him to think of that just then. The woman went on vomiting. A spurt of colorless acrid liquid rushed from her mouth. Watching serenely, he thought of some grand fountain where dolphins, or else infant cherubim, spew foamy white water from their bottomless throats. He saw her shamelessly: she was a solid little nymph. She was the coarse muse of Italia. He recited to himself, *If to any man the tumult of the flesh were silenced, silenced the phantasies of earth, waters, and air, silenced, too, the poles.*

She reached back with one hand and grasped the braid that lay along her neck. Her nape, bared, was running with sweat, and also with tears that trailed from the side of her mouth and around. It was a short robust neck, like the stem of a mushroom.

"Are you over it?" he said.

She lifted her knees from the floor and sat back on her heels.

Now that she had backed away from it, he could see the shape of the toilet bowl. It was, to his eyes, foreign-looking: high, much taller than the American variety, narrow. The porcelain lid, propped upright, was bright as a mirror. The rag she had been scrubbing it with was lost in her skirt.

Now she began to hiccup.

"Is it over?"

She leaned her forehead along the base of the washstand. The light was not good—it had to travel all the way from the lamp on the table in the bedchamber and through the door, dimming as it came; nevertheless her color seemed high. Surely her lips were swollen; they could not have been intended to bulge like that. He believed he understood just how such a face ought to have been composed. With her head at rest on the white pillar of the sink, she appeared to him (he said these words to himself slowly and meticulously, so clarified and prolonged was the moment for him) like an angel seen against the alabaster column that upholds the firmament. Her hiccups were loud, frequent; her shoulders jerked, and still the angel did not fall.

She said, "*Le dispiace se mi siedo qui? Sono molto stanca.*"

The pointless syllables—it was his first day in Italy—made him conscious of his stony stare. His own head felt stone: was she a Medusa?—those long serpents of her spew. It occurred to him that, having commenced peacefully enough, he was far less peaceful now. He was, in fact, staring with all his might, like a statue, a stare without definition or attachment, and that was foolish. There was a glass on the shelf over the sink. He stood up and stepped over her feet (the sensation of himself as great arch-of-triumph darkening her body) and filled the glass with water from the tap and gave it to her.

She drank as quickly as a child, absorbed. He could hear her throat race and shut on its hinge, and race again. When the glass was empty she said, "*Molto gentile da parte sua. Mi sento così da ieri. É solo un piccolo problema.*" All at once she saw how it was for him: he was a foreigner and could not understand. Recognition put a smoke of anxiety over her eyes. She said loudly, "*Scusi,*" and lapsed into a brevity of English as peculiar as any he had ever heard, surprising in that it was there at all:

"No belief!" She jumped up on her thick legs and let her braid hang. "*Ho vomitato!*" she called—a war cry roughened by victorious good humor. The rag separated itself from the folds of her big skirt and slid to the floor, and just then, while he was contemplating the density of her calves and the wonder of their roundness and heaviness, she seemed as he watched to grow lighter and lighter, to escape from the rough aspiring weight that had pulled her up, and she fell like a rag, without a noise.

Her lids had slapped down. He lifted her and carried her—heaved her—onto the bed and felt for her pulse. She was alive. He had never before been close to a fainted person. If he had not seen for himself how in an instant she had shut herself off, like a faucet turned, he would have been certain that the woman he had set down on the naked gray mattress was asleep.

The night window was no better than a blind drawn to: no sight, no breath, no help. Only the sweet grassy smells of the dark mountainside. He ran halfway down the spiral stone staircase and then thought, Suppose, while I am gone, the woman dies. She was only the chambermaid; she was a sound girl, her cheeks vigorous and plump; he knew she would not die. He locked the door and lay down beside her in the lamplight, riding his little finger up and down her temple. It was a marvel and a luxury to be stretched out there with her, unafraid. He assured himself she would wake and not die.

He was in a spiritual condition. He had been chaste for almost six months—demandingly pure, even when alone, even inside his secret mind. His mind was a secret cave, immaculately swept and spare. It was an initiation. He was preparing himself for the first stages of a kind of monasticism. He did not mean that he would go off and become a monk in a monastery: he knew how he was of the world. But he intended to be set apart in his own privacy: to be strong and transcendent, above the body. He did not hope to grow into a saint, yet he wanted to be more than ordinary, even while being counted as "normal." He wanted to possess himself first, so that he could yield himself, of his own accord, to the forces of the spirit.

Now here was his temptation. It seemed right—foreordained—that he would come to Italy to be lured and tempted.

The small rapture versus the greater rapture—the rapture in the body and the rapture in God, and he was for the immensity. Who would not choose an ocean, with its heaven-tugged tides, over a single drop? He looked down at the woman's face and saw two wet black drops, each one an opened eye.

"Do you feel sick again? Are you all right?" he said, and took away his little finger.

"No belief! No belief!"

The terrible words, in her exhausted croak, stirred him to the beginning of a fury. What he had done, what he had endured, to be able to come at last to belief! And a chamber-maid, a cleaner of toilets, could cry so freely against it!

He knew her meaning: she was abashed, shame punched out her tears, she was sunk in absurdity and riddle. But still it shook him—he turned against her—because every day of his life he had to make this same pilgrimage to belief all over again, starting out each dawn with the hard crow's call of no belief.

"No belief! No belief!" she croaked at him.

"Stop that."

She raised herself on her wrist, her arm a bent pole. "Signore, *mi scusi*, I make the room—"

"Stay where you are."

She gestured at the pile of sheets on the chair, and fell back again.

"Do they know you're sick? Does Mr. Wellborn know?"

She said laboriously, "I am two day sick." She touched her stomach and hiccupped. "I am no sick two day like now."

He could not tell from this whether she meant she was better or worse. "Do you want more water?"

"Signore, *grazie*, no water."

"Where do you stay?" He did not ask where she lived; he could not imagine that she lived anywhere.

Her look, still wet, trailed to the window. "In the town."

"That's all the way down that long road I drove up."

"*Sì.*"

He reflected. "Do you always work so late?"

"Signore, in this morning when I am sick I no make the room, I come back to make finish the room. I make finish all the room"—her eyes jumped in the direction of the Villa—"only the signore's room I no make."

He let out his breath: a wind so much from the well of his ribs that it astonished him. "They don't know where you are." He was in awe of his own lung. "You can stay here," he said.

"Oh, Signore, *grazie*, no—"

"Stay," he said, and elevated his little finger. Slowly, slowly, he dragged it across her forehead. A late breeze, heavy with the lazy fragrance of some alien night bloomer, had cooled her. He tasted no heat in the tiny salted cavern between her nose and her mouth. The open window brought him the smell of water; during the taxi's climb to the Villa Garibaldi he had scarcely permitted himself a glimpse of old shining Como, but now his nostrils were free and full: he took in the breath of the lake while again letting out his own. He unbuttoned his shirt and wiped every cranny of her face with it, even inside her ears; he wiped her mushroom neck. He had worn this shirt all the way from Leghorn, where the *Benito Mussolini* had docked, to Milan, and from the train station in Milan to Fumicaro. He had worn it for twenty hours. By now it was dense with the exhalations of Italy, the sweat of Milan.

When he spoke of Milan she pushed away his shirt. Her mother, she told him, lived in Milan. She was a maid at the Hotel Duomo, across from the cathedral. Everyone called her Caterina, though it wasn't her name. It was the name of the previous maid, the one who got married and went away. They were like that in Milan. They treated the maids like that. The Duomo was a tourist hotel; there were many Americans and English; her mother was quick with foreign noises. Her mother's English was very good, very quick; she claimed to have learned it out of a book. An American had given her a bilingual dictionary to keep, as a sort of tip.

In Milan they were not kind. They were so far north they were almost like Germans or Swiss. They cooked like the Swiss, and they had cold hearts like the Germans. Even the priests were cold. They said ordinary words so strangely; they accused Caterina of a mischief called "dialect," but the mischief was theirs, not hers. Caterina had a daughter, whom she had left behind in Calabria. The daughter lived with Caterina's old mother, but when the daughter was thirteen Caterina had summoned her north to Milan, to work in the hotel. The daughter's name was Viviana Teresa Accenno, and it was she who now lay disbelieving in Frank Castle's bed in the Little Annex of the Villa Garibaldi. Viviana at thirteen was very small, and looked no more than nine or ten. The manager of the Duomo did not wish to employ her at all, but Caterina importuned, so he put the girl into the kitchen to help with the under-chefs. She washed celery and broccoli; she washed the grit out of the spinach and lettuce. She reached with the scrub brush under the stove and behind it, crevices where no one else could fit. Her arm then was a little stick for poking. Unlike Caterina, she hardly ever saw any Americans or English. Despite the bilingual dictionary, Viviana did not think that her mother could read anything at all—it was only that Caterina's tongue was so quick. Caterina kept the dictionary at the bottom of her wardrobe; sometimes she picked it up and cradled it, but she never looked into it. Still, her English was very fine, and she tried to teach it to Viviana. Viviana could make herself understood, she could say what she had to, but she could never speak English like Caterina.

Because of her good English Caterina became friends with the tourists. They gave her presents—silk scarves, and boxes made of olivewood, with celluloid crucifixes resting on velveteen inside, all the useless things tourists are attracted to—and in return she took parties out in the evenings; often they gave her money. She led them to out-of-the-way restaurants in neighborhoods they would never have found on their own, and to a clever young cobbler she was acquainted with, who worked in a shoe factory by day but measured privately for shoes at night. He would cut the leather on a Monday and have new shoes ready on a Wednesday—the most up-to-date fashions for the ladies, and for the gentlemen oxfords as sober and sturdy as anyone could wish. His prices were as low as his workmanship was splendid. The tourists all supposed he stole the leather from the factory, but Caterina guaranteed his probity and assured them this could not be. His jacket pockets were heavy with bits of leather of many shapes, and also straps and buckles, and tiny corked flacons of dye.

Caterina had all these ways of pleasing tourists, but she would not allow Viviana to learn any of them. Every Easter she made Viviana go back to spend a whole week with the grandmother in Calabria, and when Viviana returned, Caterina had a new Easter husband. She had always had a separate Milan husband, even when her Calabria husband, Viviana's father, was alive. It was not bigamy, not only because Caterina's Calabria husband had died long ago but also because Caterina had never, strictly speaking, been married in the regular way to the Milan husband. It wasn't that Caterina did not respect the priests; each day she went across the street and over the plaza to the cathedral to kneel in the nave, as broad as a sunless grassless meadow. The floor was made holy by the bones of a saint shut up in a box in front of the altar. All the priests knew her, and tried to persuade her to marry the Easter husband, and she always promised that very soon she would. And they in turn promised her a shortcut: if only she showed good will and an honest faith, she could become a decent wife overnight.

But she did not, and Viviana at length understood why: the Easter husband kept changing heads. Sometimes he had one head, sometimes another, sometimes again the first. You could not marry a husband who wore a different head all the time. Except for the heads, the Easter husband was uniformly very thin, from his Adam's apple all the way down to his fancy boots. One Easter he wore the cobbler's head, but Caterina threw him out. She said he was a thief. A silver crucifix she had received as a present from a Scottish minister was missing from the bottom of the wardrobe, though the bilingual dictionary was still there. But the cobbler came back with the news that he had a cousin in Fumicaro, where they were looking for maids for the American villa there; so Caterina decided to send her daughter, who was by now sixteen and putting flesh on her buttocks. For an innocent, Caterina said, the money was safer than in Milan.

And just then the grandmother died; so Caterina and Viviana and the cobbler all traveled down to Calabria for the funeral. That night, in the grandmother's tiny house, Viviana had a peculiar adventure, though as natural as rain; it only felt peculiar because it had never happened before—she had always trusted that someday it would. The cobbler and Caterina were crumpled up together in the grandmother's shabby bed; Caterina was awake, sobbing: she explained how she was a dog loose in the gutters, she belonged nowhere, she was a woman without a place, first a widow, now an orphan and the mother of an orphan. The highfaluting priests in the cathedral could not understand how it was for a widow of long standing. If a widow of long standing, a woman used to making her own way, becomes a wife, they will not allow her to make her own way anymore, she will be poorer as a poor man's wife than as a widow. What can priests, those empty pots, those eunuchs, know of the true life of a poor woman? Lamenting, Caterina fell asleep, without intending to, and then the cobbler with his bony shadow slipped out from the grandmother's bed and circled to the corner where Viviana slept, though now she was as wide awake as could be, in her cot near the stove, a cot dressed up during the day with a rosy fringed spread and crocheted cushions patterned with butterflies. The grandmother had let Viviana hug the pretty cushions at night, as if they were stuffed dolls. Viviana's lids were tight. She imagined that the saint's bones had risen from their northern altar and were sliding toward her in the dark. Caterina kept on clamorously breathing through the tunnel of her throat, and Viviana squeezed her shut eyes down on the butterflies. If she pressed them for minutes at a time, their wings would appear to flutter. She could make their wings stir just by pressing down on them. It seemed she was making the cobbler shudder now as he moved, in just that same way; her will was surely against it, and yet he was shuddering close to the cot. He had his undershirt on, and his bony-faced smile, and he shivered, though it was only September and the cabbage-headed trees in her grandmother's yard were luxuriant in the Calabrian warmth.

After this she came to Fumicaro to work as a chambermaid at the Villa Garibaldi; she hadn't told her mother a thing about where the cobbler had put his legs and his arms, and not only

because he had shown her the heavy metal of his belt. The
cobbler was not to blame; it was her mother's mourning that
was at fault, because if Caterina had not worn herself out with
mourning the cobbler would have done his husband business in
the regular way, with Caterina; and instead he had to do it with
Viviana. All men have to do husband business, even if they
are not regular husbands; it is how men are. How you are also,
Signore, an American, a tourist.

It was true. In less than two hours Frank Castle had become the
lover of a child. He had carried her into his bed and coaxed her
story from her, beginning with his little finger's trip across her
forehead. Then he had let his little finger go riding elsewhere,
riding and riding, until her sweat returned, and he began to
sweat himself; the black night window was not feeding them
enough air. Air! It was like trying to breathe through a straw.
He drew the key from the door and steered her, both of them
barefoot, down the curling stairs, and walked with her out
onto the gravel, through the arch. There was no moon, only
a sort of gliding whitish mist low to the ground, and transi-
tory; sometimes it was there, sometimes not. At the foot of
the invisible hill, below the long hairy slope of mountainside,
Como stretched like a bit of black silk nailed down. A galaxy
prickled overhead, though maybe not: lights of villas high up,
chips of stars—in such a blackness it was impossible to know
the difference. She pointed far out, to the other side of the lake:
nothingness. Yet there, she said, stood the pinkish palace of Il
Duce, filled with seventy-five Fascist servants, and a hundred
soldiers who never slept.

After breakfast, at the first meeting of the morning, a young
priest read a paper. It seemed he had forgotten the point of
the conference—public relations—and was speaking devoutly,
illogically. His subject was purity. The flesh, he said, is holy
bread, like the shewbread of the Israelites, meant to be consecrated for God. To put it to use for human pleasure alone
is defilement. The words inflamed Frank Castle: he had told
Viviana to save his room for last and to wait for him there in the

afternoon. At four o'clock, after the day's third session, while the others went down the mountain—the members had been promised a ride across Como in a motor launch—he climbed to the green door of the Little Annex and once again took the child into his bed.

He knew he was inflamed. He felt his reason had been undermined, like a crazy man's. He could not get enough of this woman, this baby. She came to him again after dinner; then he had to attend the night session, until ten; then she was in his bed again. She was perfectly well. He asked her about the nausea. She said it was gone, except very lightly, earlier that day; she was restored. He could not understand why she was yielding to him this way. She did whatever he told her to. She was only afraid of meeting Guido, Mr. Wellborn's assistant, on her way to the Little Annex: Guido was the one who kept track of which rooms were finished, and which remained, and in what order. Her job was to make the beds and change the towels and clean the floors and the tub. Guido said the Little Annex must be done first. It was easy for her to leave the Little Annex for last—it had only two rooms in it, and the other was empty. The person who was to occupy the empty room had not yet arrived. He had sent no letter or telegram. Guido had instructed Viviana to tend to the empty room all the same, in case he should suddenly make his appearance. Mr. Wellborn was still expecting him, whoever it was.

On the third day, directly after lunch, it was Frank Castle's turn to speak. He was, after all, he said, only a journalist. His paper would be primarily neither theological nor philosophical—on the contrary, it was no more than a summary of a series of radio interviews he had conducted with new converts. He would attempt, he said, to give a collective portrait of these. If there was one feature they all had in common, it was what Jacques Maritain named as "the impression that evil was truly and substantially someone." To put it otherwise, these were men and women who had caught sight of demons. Let us not suppose, Frank Castle said, that—at the start—it is the love of Christ that brings souls into the embrace of Christ. It is fear; sin; evil; true cognizance of the Opposer. The corridor to

Christ is at bottom the Devil, just as Judas was the necessary corridor to redemption.

He read for thirty minutes, finished to a mainly barren room, and thought he had been too metaphorical; he should have tried more for the psychological—these were modern men. They all lived, even the priests, along the skin of the world. They had cleared out, he guessed, in order to walk down the mountain into the town in the brightness of midday. There was a hot chocolate shop, with pastry and picture postcards of Fumicaro: clusters of red tiled roofs, and behind them, like distant ice cream cones, the Alps—you could have your feet in Italy and your gaze far into Switzerland. Around the corner from the hot chocolate place, he heard them say, there was a little box of a shop, with a tinkling bell, easily overlooked if you didn't know about it. It was down an alley as narrow as a thread. You could buy leather wallets, and ladies' pocketbooks, also of leather, and shawls and neckties labeled *seta pura*. But the true reason his colleagues were drawn down to the town was to stand at the edge of Como. Glorious disc of lake! It had beckoned them yesterday. It beckoned today. It summoned eternally. The bliss of its flat sun-shot surface; as dazzling as some huge coin. The room had emptied out toward it; he was not offended, not even discontent. He had not come to Fumicaro to show how clever he could be (nearly all these fellows were clever), or how devout; he knew he was not devout enough. And not to discover new renunciations, and not to catch the hooks the others let fly. And not even to be tested. He was beyond these trials. He had fallen not into temptation but into happiness. Happy, happy Fumicaro! He had, he saw, been led to Fumicaro not for the Church—or not directly for the Church, as the conference brochure promised—but for the explicit salvation of one needful soul.

She was again waiting for him. He was drilled through by twin powers: the power of joy, the power of power. She was obedient, she was his own small nun. The roundness of her calves made him think of loaves of round bread, bread like domes. She asked him—it was in a way remarkable—whether his talk had been a success. His "talk." A "success." She was alert, shrewd. It was clear she had a good brain. Already she was catching on. Her mind skipped, it was not static; it was a sort of burr that attached itself to whatever passed. He told her that his paper had not been found interesting. His listeners had drifted off to look at Como. Instantly she wanted to take him there—not through the town, with its lures for tourists, but down an old stone road, mostly overgrown, back behind the Villa Garibaldi, to the lake's unfrequented rim. She had learned about it from some of the kitchen staff. He was willing, but not yet. He considered who he was; where he was. A man on fire. He asked her once more if she was well. Only a little in the morning not, she said. He was not surprised; he was prepared for it. She had missed, she said, three bleedings. She believed she might be carrying the cobbler's seed, though she had washed herself and washed herself. She had cleaned out her insides until she was as dry as a saint.

She lay with her head against his neck. Her profile was very sharp. He had seen her head a hundred times before, in museums: the painted walls of Roman villas. The oversized eyes with their black oval shine, the nose broad but so splendidly symmetrical, the top lip with its two delectably lifted points. Nevertheless she was mysteriously not handsome. It was because of her caste. She was a peasant's child. Her skin was tawny—as if a perpetual brown shadow had dropped close against it, partly translucent. A dark lens stretched over her cheeks, through which he saw, minutely, the clarity of her youth. He thought she was too obedient; she had no pride. Meekness separated her from beauty. She urged her mouth on his neck and counted: *Settembre, Ottobre, Novembre*, all without the bleeding.

He began to explain the beginning of his plan: in a week or two she would see New York.

"New York! No belief!" She laughed—and there was her gold tooth!—and he laughed too, because of his idiocy, his recklessness; he laughed because he had really lost his reason now and was giving himself over to holy belief. She had been disclosed to him, and on her knees; it followed that he had been sent. Her laughter was all youth and clarity and relief— what she had escaped! Deliverance. His was clownishness: he

was a shaman. And recognition: he was a madman, driven like
a madman, or an idiot.

"You're all right," he said. "You'll be all right."

She went on laughing. "No belief! No belief! *Dio, Dio!*"
She laughed out the comedy of her entanglements: a girl like
herself, who had no husband, and goes three bleedings without
bleeding, will be, she said, "finish"—she had seized the idiom
out of the air. There was no place for her but the ditch. There
would never be a regular husband for her—not in Fumicaro,
not in Milano, not at home in Calabria, not anywhere on any
piece of God's earth inhabited by the human family. No one
would touch her. They would throw her in the ditch. She was
in hell. Finish. God had commanded the American signore to
pull her out from the furnace of hell.

He explained again, slowly (he was explaining it to himself),
in a slow voice, with the plainest words he could muster, that
he would marry her and take her home with him to America.
To New York.

"New York!" She *did* believe him; she believed him on the
instant. Her trust was electric. The beating of her belief entered
his rib cage, thrashing and plunging its beak into his spine. He
could not help himself: he was his own prisoner, he was inside
his own ribs, pecking there. "New York!" she said. For this she
had prayed to the Holy Bambino. Oh, not for New York, she
had never prayed for America, who could dream it!

No belief: he would chain himself to a rock and be flung
into the sea, in order to drown unbelief.

Therefore he would marry Viviana Teresa Accenno. It was
his obeisance. It was what had brought him to Italy; it was what
had brought him to the Little Annex of the Villa Garibaldi.
There were scores of poor young women all over Italy—perhaps in Fumicaro itself—in her position. He could not marry
them all. Her tragedy was a commonplace. She was a noisy aria
in an eternal opera. It did not matter. This girl was the one
he had been led to. Now the power traveled from him to her;
he felt the pounding of her gratitude, how it fed her, how it
punished him, how she widened herself for him, how stalwart
she was, how nervy! He was in her grip, she was his slave; she

had the vitality of surrender. For a few moments it made her his master.

He did not return to the salons and chandeliers of the Villa Garibaldi that day—not for the pre-dinner session or for the after-dinner session; and not for dinner either. From then on everything went like quicksilver. Viviana ran to find Guido, to report that she was short of floor wax; he gave her the key to the supply closet, which was also the wine cellar. Easeful Fumicaro! where such juxtapositions reigned. She plucked a flask of each: wax and wine. Mr. Wellborn blinked at such pilfering; it kept the staff content. It was only Guido who was harsh. Still, it was nothing at all for her to slip into the kitchen and spirit away a fat fresh bread and a round brick of cheese. They trod on ivy that covered the path under the windows of the grand high room that held the meadow-long conference board. Frank Castle could hear the cadenced soughing of the afternoon speaker. The sun was low but steady. She took him past enormous bricked-up arches, as tall as city apartment buildings. In the kitchen, where they were so gullible, they called it the Roman aqueduct, but nobody sensible supposed that Romans had once lived here. It was *stupido*, a tale for children. They say about the Romans that they did not have God; the priests would not let them linger in holy Italy if they did not know Jesus, so they must have lived elsewhere. She did not doubt that they had once existed, the Romans, but elsewhere. In Germany, maybe in Switzerland. Only never in Italy. The Pope of those days would never have allowed infidels to stay in such a place as Fumicaro. Maybe in Naples! Far down, under their feet, they could descry a tiny needle: it was the bell tower of the ancient church in Fumicaro. Frank Castle had already inquired about this needle. It had been put there in the twelfth century. Wild irises obscured the stone road; it wound down and down, and was so spare and uneven that they had to go single file. They met no one. It was all theirs. He had a sense of wingedness: how quickly they came to the lip of Como. The lake was all gold. A sun-ball was submerged in it as still as the yolk of an egg, and the red egg on the horizon also did not move. They encamped in a wilderness—thorny bushes and a jumble of long-necked, thick-speared grasses.

The wine was the color of light, immaculately clear, and warm, and wonderfully sour. He had never before rejoiced in such a depth of sourness—after you swallowed some and contemplated it, you entered the second chamber of the sourness, and here it was suddenly applelike. Their mouths burst into orchards. They were not hungry; they never broke off even a crumb of the bread and cheese; of these they would make a midnight supper, and in the early morning they would pay something to the milk driver, who would carry them as far as he could. The rest of the trip they would go by bus, like ordinary people. Oh, they were not ordinary! And in Milan Viviana would tell Caterina everything—everything except where the cobbler had put his legs and his arms; she would not mention the cobbler at all—and Caterina would lead them across the plaza into the cathedral, and the priests would marry them in the shortcut way they had always promised to Caterina and her Easter husband.

It was nearly night. Como had eaten the red egg; it was gone. Streaks of white and pink trailed over water and sky. There was still enough light for each to see the other's face. They passed the bottle of wine between them, back and forth, from hand to hand, stumbling upward, now and then wandering wide of the path—the stones were sometimes buried. A small abandoned shrine blocked the way. The head was eroded, the nose chipped. "This must be a Roman road," he told her. "The Romans built it."

"No belief!" It was becoming their life's motto.

The air felt miraculously dense, odorous with lake and bush. It could almost be sucked in, it was so liquidly thick. They spiraled higher, driving back the whiplike growth that snapped at their eyes. She could not stop laughing, and that made him start again. He knew he was besotted.

Directly in front of them the grasses appeared to part. Noises; rustle and flutter and an odd abrasive sound—there was no mistake, the bushes were moving. The noises ran ahead with every step they took; the disturbance in the bushes and the growling scrape were always just ahead. He thought of the malcontents who were said to have their hiding places in the mountains—thugs; he thought of the small mountain beasts that might scramble about in such a place—a fox? He was perfectly ignorant of the usual habitat of foxes. Then—in what was left of the dusk—he caught sight of a silhouette considerably bigger and less animate than a fox. It was a squarish thing kicking against the vegetation and scudding on the stones. It looked to be attached to a pallid human shape, broad but without glimmer, also in silhouette.

"Hello?" said an elderly American voice. "Anybody back there speak English?"

"Hello," Frank Castle called.

The square thing was a suitcase.

"Damn cab let me off at the bottom. Said he wouldn't go up the hill in the dark. Didn't trust his brakes. Damn lazy thieving excuse—I paid him door to door. This can't be the regular way up anyhow."

"Are you headed for the Villa Garibaldi?"

"Three days late to boot. You mixed up in it? Oh, it just stirs my blood when they name a bed to sleep in after a national hero."

"I'm mixed up in it. I came on the *Benito Mussolini*," Frank Castle said.

"Speaking of never getting a night's sleep. So did I. Didn't see you aboard. Didn't see anyone. Stuck to the bar. Not that I can see you now, getting pitch black. Don't know where the hell I am. Dragging this damn thing. Is that a kid with you? I'll pay him to lug my bag."

Frank Castle introduced himself, there on the angle of the mountainside, on the Roman road, in the tunneling night. He did not introduce Viviana. All his life it would be just like that. She crept back off the bit of path into the thornbushes.

"Percy Nightingale," the man said. "Thank you kindly but never mind, if the kid won't take it, I'll carry it myself. Damn lazy types. How come you're on the loose, they haven't corralled you for the speeches?"

"You've missed mine."

"Well, I don't like to get to these things too early. I can sum up all the better if I don't sit through too many speeches—I do a summing-up column for the *All-Parish Taper*. Kindles Brooklyn and Staten Island. What've I missed besides you?"

"Three days of inspiration."

"Got my inspiration in Milan, if you want the truth. Found a cheapo hotel with a bar and had myself a bender. Listen, if you get up to Milan again take a gander at the *Last Supper*—it's just about over. Peeling. I give it no more'n fifty years. And for God's sake don't skip that messed-up *Pietà*—half done, arms and legs in such a tangle you wouldn't believe. Extra legs stuck in. My God, what now?" They had come flat out against a wall.

Viviana jumped into the middle of the stone road and zigzagged leftward. An apparition of battlements: high box hedges. Without any warning they had emerged right under the iron staircase abutting the kitchen of the Villa Garibaldi.

Climbing, the man with the suitcase said, "The name's familiar. Haven't I heard you on the radio, WJZ, those interviews with convicts?"

"Converts."

"I know what I said."

Viviana had evaporated.

"Are you the one Mr. Wellborn's expecting?"

"Mister who?"

"Wellborn," Frank Castle said. "The director. You'd better go to his office first. I think we're going to be neighbors."

"Love thy neighbor as thyself. He doesn't sound like a Wop."

"He's a Presbyterian from New Jersey."

"Myself, I'm a specialist. Not that I ever got my degree. I specialize in Wops and Presbyterians. Ad hoc and à la carte. We all have to make a living."

In his cups, Frank Castle thought. Then he remembered that he was drunk himself. He dug into his pocket and said with patient annoyance, "You know you can still catch the night session if you want. Here, take my program. It lists the whole conference. They were handing these out after Mass on the first day."

Percy Nightingale said, "After Mass? Liturgy giving birth to jargon. The sublime giving birth to what you'd damn well better be late arriving at."

But it was too dark to read.

In the Little Annex, behind the green door, Frank Castle began to pack. The wine had worn off. He wondered whether his stupefying idea—his idiocy—would wear off. He tested his will: was it still firm? He had no will. He had no purpose. He did not know what he was thinking. He was not thinking of a wedding. He felt infinitely bewildered. He stood staring at his shirts. Had Viviana run down the mountain again, into Fumicaro, to fetch her things from her room? They had not planned that part. Somehow he took it for granted that she had no possessions, or that her possessions did not matter, or were invisible. He saw that he had committed the sin of heroism, which always presumes that everyone else is unreal, especially the object of rescue. She was the instrument of his carnality, the occasion of his fall; no more than that, though that was too much. He had pushed too far. A stranger, a peasant's child. He was no more capable of her salvation than of his own.

The doorknob turned. He hardly understood what he would say to her. After all, she was a sort of prostitute, the daughter of a sort of prostitute. He did not know exactly what these women were—the epiphenomena, he supposed, of the gradual movement, all over the globe, of the agricultural classes to the city. He was getting his reason back again. She, on her side, was entirely reasonable. An entrapment. Such women are always looking for free tickets to the New World. She had planted herself in his room—just his luck—to pretend sickness. All right, she hadn't pretended; he could see it wasn't pretense. All the more blatant. A scheme; a pit; a noose. With her bit of English she had examined the conference lists and found her eligible prey: an unmarried man. The whole roster were married men—it was only the priests and himself. So she had done her little research. A sensible girl who goes after what she wants. He was willing to give her some money, though God was his witness he didn't have so much that he could take on an extended program of philanthropy—his magazine, the *Sacral Review*, was making good his expenses. All the same he had to pinch. It was plain to him that she had never expected him to redeem the impulse of his dementia. It was his relief—the relief he felt in coming to his senses—that she had all along meant to exploit. Relief and the return of sanity were what he had to pay for. Mild enough blackmail. He wrenched his head round.

There stood Nightingale, anxiously jubilating and terrifically white. He had, so far, been no more than an old man's voice in the night, and to the extent that a voice represents a soul, he had falsified, he had misrepresented utterly. He was no older than Frank Castle, and it was not only that he was alarmingly indistinct—his ears were blanched; his mouth was a pinkish line; his eyes, blue overrinsed to a transparency, were humps in a face as flat as zinc. He was almost blotted out. His look was a surprise: white down to his shoes, and immensely diffident. His shirt was white, his thighs were white, his shoes the same, and even shyer; he was self-effacing. He had already taken off his pants—he was without dazzle or glare. Washed out to a Celtic pallor. Frank Castle was unsure, with all this contradiction between words and appearance, where to put his confidence.

"You're right. Neighbors," Nightingale said. "You can have your program back. I've got the glory of my own now. It's a wonder *any*one shows up for these things. It puts the priests to sleep, not that you can tell the difference when they're awake. I don't mind myself forgoing the pleasure"—he shook open the little pamphlet—"of, get this, 'Approaches to Bigotry.' 'The Church and the Community, North, East, South, West.' 'The Dioceses of Savannah, Georgia, and Denver, Colorado, Compared.' 'Parish or Perish . . .' My God, I wish I could go to bed."

"No one's forcing you to attend," Frank Castle said.

"You bet they're not. If I sum up better by turning up late, I sum up best if I don't turn up at all. Listen, I like a weight on me when I sleep. No matter what the climate or the weather, put me in the tropics, I've got to have plenty of blankets. I told them so in the office—they're sending the chambermaid. Not that she isn't taking her own sweet time. No wonder,

godforsaken place they've stuck us in, way down here. The rest
get to sleep like princes in the palace. I know about me, I always
get the short straw, but what's your crime, you're not up at the
big house? . . . Hey, you packing?"

Was he really packing? There were his shirts in a mound,
folded and waiting to be folded, and his camera; there was his
open suitcase.

"Not that I blame you, running off. Three days of it should
do anyone." Nightingale tossed the pamphlet on the bed.
"You've paid your dues. Especially if you got to stick in your
two cents with the speechifying—what on?"

Footsteps on the circling stairs. Heavy goat steps. Viviana,
obscured by blankets. She did not so much as glance in.

"Interviews with convicts," Frank Castle said.

Nightingale guffawed—the pouncing syllables of a hawk,
the thread of the lips drawn covertly in. A hider. Recklessness
at war with panic. Mistrusting the one, Frank Castle believed
in the other. Panic. "What's your fix on these fellows? Cradle
Catholics in my family since Adam, if not before, but I got my
catechism from Father Leopold Robin."

"Never heard of him."

"Wouldn't expect you to. *Né* Rabinowitz."

Frank Castle felt himself heat up. The faintest rise of verti-
go. It was stupid to give in to peculiar sensations just because
Viviana hadn't looked in the door. He said, "Would you mind
asking the chambermaid"—the word tugged at his tongue, as if
it had fallen into something glutinous—"to stop by when she's
finished at your place? They haven't changed my towels—"

"A whole speech on seeing the light? That's what you did?
Too pious for me."

"Scientific. I put in the statistics. Enough to please even a
specialist. How many converts per parish, what kinds of converts, from what kinds of backgrounds."

But he was listening to the small sounds in the next room.

Nightingale said, "Clare Boothe Luce. There's your trophy."

"We get all sorts these days. Because of the ascent of the
Devil. Everyone's scared of the Devil. The rich and the poor.
The soft and the arrogant—"

"And who's the Devil? You one of these fellows think Adolf's the new Satan? At least he holds off against the Commies."

"I'm willing to think you're the Devil," Frank Castle said.

"You're the touchy one."

"Well, a bit of the Devil's in all of us."

"Touchy and pious—I told you pious. Now you wouldn't think it would take a year to drop two blankets on a bed! All right, I'll send you that girl." He took two steps into the corridor and turned back. "This Father Robin wore the biggest crucifix you ever saw. Maybe it only looked big—I was just a kid. But that's how it is with these convicts—they're self-condemned, so they take their punishment more seriously than anybody. It gives me the willies when they come in hotter'n Hades. They act like a bunch of Holy Rollers with lights in their sockets. Show me a convert, I'll show you a fellow out to get even with someone. They're killers."

"Killers?"

"They kill the old self for the sake of the new self. Conversion," Nightingale said, "is revenge."

"You're forgetting Christ."

"Oh Jesus God. I never forget Christ. Why else would I end up in this goddamn shack in this godforsaken country? Maybe the Fascists'll make something out of these Wops yet. Put some spine in 'em. You want that girl? I'll get you that girl."

Left to himself, Frank Castle dropped his head into his hands. With his eyes shut, staring into the flesh of the lids, he could see a whirligig of gold flecks. He had met a man and instantly despised him. It seemed to him that everyone here, not counting the handful of priests, was a sham—mountebanks all. And, for that matter, the priests as well. Public-relations types. Journalists, editors. In an older time these people would have swarmed around the marketplace selling indulgences and hawking pigs' hair.

The chambermaid came in. She was a fleshless uncomprehending spindly woman of about forty, perspiring at the neck, with ankles like balloons. There was a purple mark in the middle of her left cheek. "Signore?" she said.

He went into the toilet and brought out a pair of fresh bath towels. "I won't need these. I'm leaving. You might as well do whatever you want with them."

She shook her head and backed away. He had already taken it in that she would not be able to follow a word. And anyhow his charade made no sense. Still, she accepted the towels with a maddening docility; she was no different from Viviana. Any explanation, no explanation, was all the same to these creatures.

He said, "Where's the other maid who always comes?"

The woman stared.

"Viviana," he said.

"Ah! *L'altra cameriera.*"

"Where is she?"

With the towels stuck firmly under one armpit, she lifted her shoulders and held out her palms; then shut the door smartly behind her. A desolation entered him. He decided to attend the night session.

The meadow-long conference board had grown slovenly. Notebooks, squashed paper balls, pencils without points, empty pitchers and dirty cups, an exhausted coffee urn, languid eye-glasses lying with their earpieces askew; here and there a leg thrown up on the table. Formality had vanished, decay was crawling through. The meeting was well under way; the speaker was citing Pascal. It was very like a chant—he had sharp tidy hand gestures, a grocer slicing cheese. " 'Not only do we understand God only through Jesus Christ, but we understand ourselves only through Jesus Christ. We understand life and death only through Jesus Christ. Outside Jesus Christ we do not know what life is, nor death, nor God, nor ourselves.' These words do not compromise; they do not try to get along with those who are indifferent to them, or with those who would laugh at them. They are neither polite nor gentle. They take their stand, and their stand is eternal and absolute. Today the obligation of Catholic public relations is not simply to defend the Church, though there is plenty of that to be done as well. In America especially we live with certain shadows, yet here in the mountains and valleys of Fumicaro, in glorious Italy, the Church is a serene mother, and it is of course easy to forget that she is troubled elsewhere. Elsewhere she is defamed as the refuge of superstition. She is accused of unseemly political advantages. She is assaulted as a vessel of archaism and as an enemy of the scientific intelligence. She is pointed to as an institution whose whole raison d'être is the advance of clerical power. Alas, the Church in her true soul, wearing her heavenly garments, is not sufficiently understood or known.

"All this public distortion is real enough, but our obligation is even more fundamental than finding the right lens of clarification to set over the falsifying portrait. The need to defend the Church against the debasement of the ignorant or the bigoted is, how shall we call it, a mere ripple in the sacred river. Our task as opinion makers—and we should feel no shame over this phrase, with all its American candor, for are we not Americans at an American colloquy, though we sit here charmed by the antiquity of our surroundings?—our task, then, is to show the timelessness of our condition, the applicability of our objectifying vision even to flux, even to the immediate instant. We are to come with our banner inscribed Eternity, and demonstrate its pertinence in the short run; indeed, in the shortest run of all, the single life, the single moment. We must let flower the absolute in the concrete, in the actual rise and fall of existence. Our aim is transmutation, the sanctification of the profane."

It was impossible to listen; Nightingale was right. Frank Castle sank down into some interior chamber of mind. He was secretive; he knew this about himself. It was not that he had habits of concealment, or that, as people say, he kept his own counsel. It was instead something akin to sensation, an ache or a bump. Self-recognition. Every now and then he felt the jolt of who he was and what he had done. He was a man who had invented his own designations. He was undetermined. He was who he said he was. No one, nothing, least of all chance, had placed him. Like Augustine, he interpreted himself, and hotly. Oh, hotly. Whereas this glacial propagandist, reciting his noble text, bleating out "absolute" and "concrete" and "transmutation," had fallen into his given slot like a messenger from fate. Once fallen, fixed. Rooted. A stalactite.

Far behind the speaker, just past the lofty brass-framed

doorway—a distance of several pastures, a whole country-side—a plump little figure glimmered. Viviana! There she was; there she stood. You would need a telescope to bring her close. Even with his unaccoutered eye, Frank Castle noticed how nicely she was dressed. If he had forgotten that she might have possessions, here was something pleasant—though it was only a blouse and skirt. She was clutching an object, he could not make out what. The blouse had a bright blue ribbon at the neck, and long sleeves. It might have been the ribbon, or the downward flow of the sleeves, or even the skirt, red as paint, which hung lower than he was used to—there was a sudden propriety in her. The wonderful calves were hidden: those hot globes he had only that afternoon drawn wide apart. Her thighs, too, were as hot and heavy as corn bread. Across such a space her head, remote and even precarious, was weighted down, like the laden head of a sunflower. She was absorbed by the marble floor tiles of the Villa Garibaldi. She would not come near. She eclipsed herself. She was a bit of shifting reflection.

He wondered if he should wait the speaker out. Instead he got up—every step a crash—and circled the table's disheveled infinitude. No one else moved. He was a scandal. Under the chandelier the speaker stuck to his paper. Frank Castle had done the same the day before, when they had all walked out on him for a ride across Como. Now here he was deserting, the only one to decamp. It was almost ten o'clock at night; the whole crew of them had been up since eight. One had made a nest of his rounded arms and was carefully, sweetly, cradling his face down into it. Another was propped back with his mouth open, brazenly asleep, something between a wheeze and a snuffle puffing intermittently out.

In the hall outside he said, "You've changed your clothes."

"We go Milano!"

She was in earnest then. Her steady look, diverted down-ward, was patient, docile. He did not know what to make of her; but her voice was too high. He set an admonitory finger over his own mouth. "Where did you disappear to?"

"I go, I put"—he watched her labor after the words; excitement throttled her—"*fiore. Il santo!* To make *un buon viaggio.*"

He was clear enough about what a *santo* was. "A saint? Is there a saint here?"

"You see before, in the road. You see," she insisted. She held up a metal cylinder. It was the flashlight from his bedside cabinet in the Little Annex. "Signore, come."

"Do you have things? You're taking things?"

"*La mia borsa, una piccolo valigia.* I put in the signore's room."

They could not stand there whispering. He followed where she led. She took him down the mountainside again, along the same half-buried road, to a weedy stone stump. It was the smothered little shrine he had noticed earlier. It grew right up out of the middle of the path. The head, with its rotted nose, was no more than a smudge. Over it, as tall as his hipbone, a kind of stone umbrella, a shelter like an upside-down U, or a fragment of vertical bathtub, seemed to be turning into a mound of wild ivy. Spiking out of this dense net was the iris Viviana had stuck there.

"San Francesco!" she said; the kitchen staff had told her. Such hidden old saints were all over the hills of Fumicaro.

"No," Frank Castle said.

"*Molti santi.* You no belief? Signore, see! San Francesco."

She gave him the flashlight. In its white pool everything had a vivid glaze, like a puppet stage. He peered at the smudge. Goddess or god? Emperor's head, mounted like a milestone to mark out sovereignty? The chin was rubbed away. The torso had crumbled. It hardly looked holy. Depending on the weather, it might have been as old as a hundred years, or a thousand; two thousand. Only an archeologist could say. But he did not miss how the flashlight conjured up effulgence. A halo blazed. Viviana was on her knees in the scrub; she tugged him down. With his face in leaves he saw the eroded fragment of the base, and, half sunken, an obscure tracing, a single intact word: DELEGI. I chose; I singled out. Who chose, what or who was singled out? Antiquity alone did not enchant him: the disintegrating image of some local Roman politico or evanescent godlet. The mighty descend to powder and leave chalk on the fingertips.

Her eyes were shut; she was now as she had been in her small faint, perfectly ordered; but her voice was crowded with fierce little mutterings. She was at prayer.

"Viviana. This isn't a saint."

She stretched forward and kissed the worn-away mouth.

"You don't know *what* it is. It's some old pagan thing."

"San Francesco," she said.

"No."

She turned on him a smile almost wild. The thing in the road was hallowed. It had a power; she was in thrall to sticks and stones. "*Il santo*, he pray for us." In the halo of the flashlight her cheeks looked oiled and sleek and ripe for biting. She crushed her face down into the leaves beside his own—it was as if she read him and would consent to be bitten—and said again, "Francesco."

He had always presumed that sooner or later he would marry. He had spiritual ambition; yet he wanted to join himself to the great protoplasmic heave of human continuity. He meant to be fruitful: to couple, to procreate. He could not be continent; he could not sustain purity; he was not chaste. He had a terrible inquisitiveness; his fall with Viviana was proof enough. He loved the priests, with their parched lip-corners and glossy eyes, their enigmatic loins burning for God. But he could not become like them; he was too fitful. He had no humility. Sometimes he thought he loved Augustine more than God. *Imitatio Dei:* he had come to Christ because he was secretive, because Jesus lived, though hiddenly. Hence the glory of the thousand statues that sought to make manifest the reticent Christ. Sculptors, like priests, are least of all secretive.

Often it had seemed to Frank Castle that, marriage being so open a cell, there was no one for him to marry. Wives were famous for needing explanations. He could not imagine being married to a bookish sort—an "intellectual"—but also he feared this more than anything. He feared a wife who could talk and ask questions and analyze and inquire after his history. Sometimes he fancied himself married to a rubber doll about his own size. She would serve him. They would have a rubber child.

A coldness breathed from the ground. Already hoarfrost was beginning to gather—a blurry veil over the broken head in the upended tub.

He said, "Get up."

"Francesco."

"Viviana, let's go." But he hung back himself. She was a child of simple intuitions, a kind of primitive. He saw how primitive she was. She was not a rubber doll, but she would keep clear of the precincts of his mind. This gladdened him. He wondered how such a deficiency could make him so glad.

She said for the third time, "Francesco." He understood finally that she was speaking his name.

They spent the night in his room in the Little Annex. At six the milk driver would be grinding down from the kitchen lot past the arch of the Little Annex. They waited under a brightening sunrise. The mist was fuming free of the mountainside; they could see all the way down to Como. Quietly loitering side by side with the peasant's child, again Frank Castle knew himself slowly churning into chaos: half an hour ago she had stretched to kiss his mouth exactly as she had stretched to kiss the mouth of the pagan thing fallen into the ground. He was mesmerized by the strangeness he had chosen for himself: a whole life of it. She was clinging to his hand like an innocent; her fingers were plaited into his. And then, out of the blue, as if struck by a whirlwind, they were not. She tore herself from him; his fingers were ripped raw; it seemed like a seizure of his own skin; he lost her. She had hurled herself out of sight. Frank Castle watched her run—she looked flung. She ran into the road and down the road and across, behind the high hedges, away from the bricked-up vaults of the Roman aqueduct.

Percy Nightingale was descending from those vaults. Under his open overcoat a pair of bare bluish-white knees paraded.

"Greetings," he called, "from a practiced insomniac. I've been examining the local dawn. They do their dawns very nicely in these parts, I'll give 'em that. What detritus we travelers gather as we move among the realms—here you are with two bags, and last night I'm sure I saw you with only one. You don't happen to have any extra booze in one of those?" He stamped vaguely round in an uneven try at a circle. "Who was that rabbit who fled into the bushes?"

"I think you scared it off," Frank Castle said.

"The very sight of me? It's true I'm not dressed for the day. I intend to pull on my pants in time for breakfast. You seem to be waiting for a train."

"For the milk driver."

"Aha. A slow getaway. You'd go quicker with the booze driver. I'd come along for kicks with the booze driver."

"The fact of the matter," Frank Castle said in his flattest voice, "is that you've caught me eloping with the chambermaid."

"What a nice idea. Satan, get thee behind me and give me a push. Long and happy years to you both. The scrawny thing with the pachyderm feet and the birthmark? She made up my bed very snugly—I'd say she's one of the Roman evidences they've got around here." He pointed his long chin upward toward the aqueduct. "Since you didn't invite me to the exhumation, I won't be expected to be invited to the wedding. Believe it or not, here's your truck."

Frank Castle picked up Viviana's bag and his own and walked out into the middle of the road, fluttering his green American bills; the driver halted.

"See you in the funny papers," Nightingale yelled.

He sat in the seat next to the driver's and turned his face to the road. It snaked left and then left again: any moment now a red-skirted girl would scuttle out from behind a dip in the foliage. He tried to tell this to the driver, but the man only chirped narrowly through his country teeth. The empty steel milk cans on the platform in the back of the truck jiggled and rattled; sometimes their flanks collided—a robust clang like cymbals. It struck him then that the abyss in his entrails was his in particular: it wasn't fright at being discovered and judged that had made her bolt, but practical inhibition—she was canny enough, she wasn't about to run off with a crazed person. Lust! He had come to his senses yesterday, though only temporarily; she had come to hers today, and in the nick of time. After which it occurred to him that he had better look in his wallet. Duped.

She had robbed him and escaped. He dived into his pocket.

Instantly the driver's open palm was under his nose.

"I paid you. *Basta*, I gave you *basta*."

The truck wobbled perilously around a curve, but the hand stayed.

"Good God! Keep hold of the wheel, can't you? We'll go off the road!"

He shook out a flood of green bills onto the seat. Now he could not know how much she had robbed him of. He did not doubt she was a thief. She had stolen cheese from the kitchen and wine from a locked closet. He thought of his camera. It would not surprise him if she had bundled it off in a towel or in a pillowcase in the night. Thievery had been her motive from the beginning. Everything else was ruse, snare, distraction, flimflam; she was a sort of gypsy, with a hundred tricks. He would never see her again. He was relieved. The freakishness of the past three days stung him; he grieved. Never again this surrender to the inchoate; never again the abyss. A joke! He had almost eloped with the chambermaid. Damn that Nightingale!

They rattled—sounding now like a squad of carillons—into Fumicaro. Here was the promenade; here was the hot chocolate shop; here was the church with its bell tower; here was morning-dazzled Como—high and pure the light that rose from it. "Autobus," he commanded the driver. He had spilled enough green gold to command. The country teeth showed the bliss of the newly rich. He was let out at an odd little turn of gossipy street, which looked as if it had never in all its existence heard tell of an autobus; and here—"No belief!"—was Viviana, panting hard. She could not catch her breath, because of the spy. A spy had never figured in their fears, God knows! A confusion and a danger. The spy would be sure to inform Guido, and Guido would be sure to inform Mr. Wellborn, or, worse yet, the cobbler's cousin, who, as it happened, was Guido's cousin too, only from the other side of the family. And then they would not let her go. No, they would not! They would keep her until her trouble became visible and ruinous, and then they would throw her into the ditch. The spy was an untrustworthy man. He was the man they had met on the hill,

who took her for a boy. He was the man in the empty room of
the Little Annex. The other *cameriera* had told her that on top
of all the extra blankets she had brought him he had put all the
towels there were, and then, oh! he pulled down the curtains
and piled them on top of the towels. And he stood before the
other *cameriera* shamelessly, without his *pantaloni!* And so what
could she do? She flew down the secret stone path, she flew
right past San Francesco without stopping, to get to the autobus
piazza before the milk driver.

Droplets of sweat erupted in a phalanx on her upper lip.
She gave him the sour blink of an old woman; he glimpsed the
Calabrian grandmother, weathered by the world's suspicions.
"You think I no come?"

He would not tell her that he thought she had stolen.

"No belief!" Out tumbled her hot laugh, redolent of his bed
in the Little Annex. "When *questo bambino* finish"—she pressed
the cushion of her belly—"you make new *bambino*, O.K.?"

In Milan in the evening (his fourth in Italy), in a cramped cold
chapel in the cathedral, within sight of the relic, they were
married by a priest who was one of Caterina's special friends.

Caterina herself surprised him: she was dressed like a businesswoman. She wore a black felt hat with a substantial brim;
she was substantial everywhere. Her head was set alertly on a
neck that kept turning, as if wired to a generator; there was
nothing she did not take in with her big powerful eyes. He
perceived that she took *him* in, all in a gulp. Her arm shot out
to smack Viviana, because Viviana, though she had intended
never to tell about the cobbler, on her wedding day could not
dissemble. The arm drew back. Caterina would not smack
Viviana in front of a tourist, an American, on her wedding day.
She was respectful. Still, it was a slander—the cobbler did not
go putting seeds into the wombs of innocent girls. Twisting her
neck, Caterina considered the American.

"Three days? You are friend of my Viviana three days,
Signore?" She tapped her temple, and then made circles in
the air with her forefinger. "For what you want to marry my
Viviana if you no put the seed?"

He knew what a scoundrel he seemed. The question was terrifying; but it was not meant for him. They went at it, the mother and the daughter, weeping and shrieking, in incomprehensible cascades: it was an opera, extravagant with drama, in a language he could not fathom. All this took place in Caterina's room in the Hotel Duomo, around the corner from a linen closet as capaciously filled with shelves as a library; he sat in a chair face to face with the wardrobe in which the bilingual dictionary was secreted. The door was at his right hand—easy enough to grab the knob and walk away. For nearly an hour he sat. The two barking mouths went on barking. The hands clenched, grasped, pushed. He was detached, distant; then, to his amazement, at a moment of crescendo, when the clamor was at its angriest, the two women fell into a fevered embrace. Implausible as it was, preposterous as it was, Caterina was sending Viviana to America. *Un colpo di fulmine! Un fulmine a ciel sereno!*

Just before the little ceremony, the priest asked Frank Castle how he would feel about a child that was—as he claimed—not his. Frank Castle could not think what to say. The priest was old and exhausted. He spoke of sin as an elderly dog who is too sick to be companionable—yet you are used to him, you can't do without him, you can't bring yourself to get rid of him. The wedding ring was Caterina's.

Frank Castle exchanged his return ticket for two others on the *Stella Italiana*, sailing for New York in ten days. It was all accident and good luck: someone had canceled. There were two available places. That left time for the marriage to be accorded a civil status: the priest explained to Caterina that though in the eyes of God Viviana was now safe, they had to fetch a paper from the government and get it stamped. This was the law.

There was time for Milan. It was a curiosity: Viviana had been brought to this northern treasure-city as a girl of thirteen and still did not know where the *Last Supper* was. Caterina knew; she even knew who had made it. "Leonardo da Vinci," she recited proudly. But she had never seen it. She took Viviana away to shop for a trousseau; they bought everything new but shoes, because Viviana was stubborn. She refused to go to the cobbler. "*Ostinata!*" Caterina said, but a certain awe had begun to creep into her fury. Viviana had found an American husband who talked on the radio in New York! Il Duce talked on the radio, too, and they could hear him as far away as America. Viviana a bride! Married, and to a tourist! These were miracles. Someone, Caterina said, had kissed a saint.

The *Last Supper* was deteriorating. It had to be looked at from behind a velvet rope. Viviana said it was a pity the camera hadn't yet been invented when Our Lord walked the earth—a camera would get a *much* better picture of Our Lord than the one in the flaking scene on the wall. Frank Castle taught her how to use his camera, and she snapped him everywhere; they snapped each other. They had settled into Caterina's room, but they had to come and go with caution, so that the manager would not know. It cost them nothing to stay in Caterina's room. Caterina did not say where she went to sleep; she said she had many friends who would share. When Viviana asked her who they were, Caterina laughed. "The priests!" she said. All over the Duomo, Frank Castle was treated with homage, as a person of commercial value. He was an American with an Italian wife. In the morning they had coffee in the dining room. The waiter gave his little bow. Viviana was embarrassed. At the Villa Garibaldi she had deferred to the waiters; no one was so low as the *cameriera*. It made her uncomfortable to be served. Frank Castle told her she was no longer a *cameriera*; soon she would be an American. Unforgiving, she confided that Caterina had gone to stay with the cobbler.

He took her—it was still Nightingale's itinerary—to see the unfinished *Pietà* in a castle with bartizans and old worn bricks; schoolchildren ran in and out of the broad grassy trench that had once been the moat, but Viviana was unmoved. It was true that she admired the luster of Our Lady's lifelike foot, as polished as the marble flagging of the Villa Garibaldi; the rest was mainly rough rock. She thought it ridiculous to keep a thing like that on display. Our Lord didn't have a face. The Virgin didn't have a face. They looked like two ghouls. And this they called religion! What sense was it that the *muratore* who made it was famous—his sprawling Jesus was no more beautiful or *sacro* than a whitewashed wall falling down. And without a face! She let Frank Castle take her picture in her new bird-speckled dress in front of all that rubble, and meanwhile she described the statue of Our Lady that had stood on a shelf in her own plain room at Fumicaro. The Madonna's features were perfect in every detail—there were wonderful tiny eyelashes glued on, made of actual human hair. And all in the nicest brightest colors, the eyes a sweet blue, the cheeks rosy. The Holy Bambino was just as exact. He had a tiny bellybutton with a blue rhinestone in it, to match Our Lady's blue robe, and under his gauzy diaper he even had a lacquered penis that showed through, the color of a human finger, though much tinier. He had tiny celluloid fingernails! A statue like that, Viviana said, is *molto sacro*—she had kneeled before it a thousand times. She had cried penitential floods because of the bleeding that did not come. She had pleaded with Our Lady for intercession with the Holy Bambino, and the Holy Bambino had heard her prayer. She had begged the Holy Bambino, if He could not make the bleeding come, to send a husband, and He had sent a husband.

They walked through rooms of paintings: voluptuous Titians; but Frank Castle was startled only by the solidity of Viviana. Ardor glowed in her. He had arrived in Italy with two little guidebooks, one for Florence and one for Rome, but he had nothing for Milan. Viviana herself was unmapped. Everything was a surprise. He could not tell what lay around the corner. He marveled at what he had done. On Monday, at Fumicaro, Augustine and philosophy; on Thursday, the chattering of a brown-eyed bird-speckled simple-minded girl. His little peasant wife, a waif with a baby inside her! All his life he would feel shame over her. To whom could he show her without humiliation?

Her ignorance moved and elevated him. He thought of Saint Francis rejoicing in the blows and ridicule of a surly innkeeper: *Willingly and for the love of Christ let me endure pains and insults and shame and want, inasmuch as in all other gifts of God we may not glory, since they are not ours but God's.* Frank Castle understood that he would always be mocked because of this girl; he went on snapping his camera at her. How robust she was, how gleaming, how happy! She was more hospitable to God than anyone who hoped to find God in books. She gave God a home everywhere—in old Roman tubs, in painted wooden dolls: sticks and stones. He saw that no one had taught her to clean her fingernails. He puzzled over it: she was a daughter of a trader in conveniences, she was herself a kind of commodity; she believed herself fated, a vessel for anyone's use. He had married shame. Married! It was what he had done. But he felt no remorse; none. He was exhilarated—to have had the courage for such a humbling!

In front of them, hanging from a crossbar, was a corpse made of oak. It was the size of a real man, and had the head of a real man. It wore a wreath made of real brambles, and there were real holes in its body, with real nails beaten into them.

Viviana dropped to the floor and clasped her hands.

"Viviana, people don't pray here."

Her mouth went on murmuring.

"You don't *do* that in a place like this."

"*Una chiesa*," she said.

"People don't pray in museums." Then it came to him that she did not know what a museum was. He explained that the pictures and the statues were works of art. And he was married to her! "There aren't any priests here," he said.

She shot him a look partly comical and partly shocked. Even priests have to eat, she protested. The priests were away, having their dinner. Here it was almost exactly like the *chiesa* at Fumicaro, only more crowded. At the other *chiesa*, where they kept the picture of the *Last Supper*, there were also no priests to be seen, and did that prove that it wasn't a *chiesa?* Caterina had always told her how ignorant tourists were. Now she would have to put in an extra prayer for him, so that he could feel more sympathy for the human hunger of priests.

She dipped her head. Frank Castle circled all around the medieval man of wood. Red paint, dry for centuries, spilled from the nail holes. Even the back of the figure had its precision: the draw of the muscles elongated in fatigue. The carver had not stinted anywhere. Yet the face was without a grain of devout inspiration. It was as if the carver had cared only for the

carving itself, and not for its symbol. The man on the crossbar
was having his live body imitated, and that was all. He was a
copy of the carver's neighbor perhaps, or else a cousin. When
the carving was finished, the neighbor or cousin stepped down,
and together he and the carver hammered in the nails.

The nails. Were they for pity? They made him feel cruel.
He reflected on their cruelty—piety with a human corpse at
its center, what could that mean? The carver and his model,
beating and beating on the nails.

In the streets there were all at once flags, and everywhere big
cloth posters of Il Duce flapping on the sides of buildings. Il
Duce had a frog's mouth and enormous round Roman eyes. Was
it a celebration? He could learn nothing from Viviana. When
he asked Caterina, she spat. Some of the streets were miraculously enclosed under a glass dome. People walked and shopped
in a greenish undersea twilight. Masses of little tables freckled
the indoor sidewalks. Mobs went strolling, all afternoon and
all night, with an exuberance that stunned him. All of Milan
was calling out under glass. They passed windows packed with
umbrellas, gloves, shoes, pastries, silk ties, marzipan. There
was the cathedral itself, on a giant platter, made all of white
marzipan. He bought a marzipan goose for Viviana, and from
a peddler a little Pinocchio on a string. Next to a bookstore,
weaving in and out of the sidewalk coffee-drinkers—"*Turista?
Turista?*"—boys were handing out leaflets in French and English. Frank Castle took one and read: "Only one of my ancestors
interests me: there was a Mussolini in Venice who killed his
wife who had betrayed him. Before fleeing he put two Venetian
scudi on her chest to pay for her funeral. This is how the people
of Romagna are, from whom I descend."

They rode the elevator to the top of the cathedral and
walked over the roofs, among hundreds of statues. Behind each
figure stood a dozen others. There were saints and martyrs and
angels and gryphons and gargoyles and Romans; there were
Roman soldiers whose decorated sword handles and buskins
sprouted the heads of more Roman soldiers. Viviana peered out
through the crenelations at the margins of the different roofs,

and again there were hundreds of sculptures; thousands. The statues pullulated. An army of carvers had swarmed through these high stones, century after century, striking shape after amazing shape. Some were reticent, some ecstatic. Some were motionless, some winged. It was a dream of proliferation, of infinity: of figures set austerely inside octagonal cupolas, and each generative flank of every cupola itself lavishly friezed and fructified; of limbs erupting from limbs; of archways efflorescing; of statues spawning statuary. What looked, from the plaza below, like the frothiest lacework or egg-white spume here burst into solidity, weight, shadow and dazzlement: a derangement of plenitude tumbling from a bloated cornucopia.

A huge laughter burst out of Frank Castle's lung. On the hot copper roof he squatted down and laughed.

"What? What?" Viviana said.

"You could be here years and years," he said. "You would never finish! You would have to stay up in the air your whole life!"

"What?" she said. "What I no finish?"

He had pulled out his handkerchief and was pummeling his wet eyes. "If—if—" But he could not get it out.

"What? What? Francesco—"

"If—suppose—" The laughter felt like a strangulation; he coughed out a long constricted breath. "Look," he said, "I can see you falling on your goddamn knees before every *one* of these! Viviana," he said, "it's a *chiesa!* The priests aren't eating dinner! The priests are down below! Under our feet! You could be up here," he said—now he understood exactly what had happened at Fumicaro; he had fixed his penance for life—"a thousand years!"

A Hebrew Sibyl

MY MOTHER WAS a native of this place, though my father, a trader in pots, was not. Each year, usually in the spring, he came from his home country to buy the wares of our region. He would remain with us, if the weather and the sea's temper held, into the last days of summer. He spoke our language well, and could read and write in our alphabet. Still, the kiln masters, who could not, called him *barbaros*, and laughed at his clumsiness with our easy "th." The lekythoi flasks, for instance, he pronounced "lekydoi"; it made him sound childish. Behind his back he was resented and disliked, even as he brought us prosperity.

It was my father's practice to choose the pots he intended to purchase at the very moment they were taken from the kilns and set out on wooden slats to cool. He did this with a certain harsh and almost contemptuous speed; he knew instantly what wouldn't do, never mind that to any ordinary eye the skyphos or krater he spurned as imperfect might be altogether indistinguishable from those he deemed flawless. And then, after the favored pots were wrapped in linen strips and cushioned in straw and sent on to the port town in a procession of donkey carts, they would be filled (so my father explained to me) with oils and syrups and perfumes of a kind not to be found in his own land. Yet not all: only those vessels designed for freight. The others, prized solely for their beauty, were destined, he said, for the tables of scholars and aristocrats.

There was still another reason my father was derided, this one far more grave than his foreigner's tongue. He was a confessed atheist. It was on this account that my mother had no communal standing as his wife, and was subjected to unkind whisperings: she was called concubine, bondmaid, helot; and sometimes, to my shame, harlot. My father had refused the customary marriage rites under the aegis of Hestia, to whose favor my mother had been dedicated at birth, and whose chapel was one of the grandest. When I was old enough to go about by myself, I often wandered there, to stand between the gilded pilasters and stare upward at her image. I went alone; I was always alone. Like my mother, I was not wholly shunned—our polis was too orderly for something so noticeably offensive. Instead, we were discreetly, almost politely, avoided. But here, in the goddess's dim cool shrine, Hestia's arms, outstretched as if ready to embrace, seemed welcoming, even as they overawed with their stony weight. A fire was kept burning in a brazier in her vast lap, tended by a very young acolyte, a boy my own age, dressed like the priests in a pleated white tunic fringed at the ankles. With each shudder of the tossing flames, the goddess's breasts flashed like bucklers; shadows wavered over her massive round toes. And then, as I looked on steadily, her eyes with their carved pupils shifted her gaze to me. I saw that she knew me for what I was: the outcome of my mother's humiliation and my father's subversion.

But my father was insouciant, scorning whatever reached us of these disparagements. And in the months he was with us, we were happy. He had built for us a fine large house, rather more plain than ostentatious; somehow, not because of its size but because of my father's presence, it signified wealth. Indoors, the walls were stippled with brilliant frescoes, landscapes thickened by fruit-bearing orchards, and skies rife with colorful birds. He had forbidden the usual scenes from the lives of the gods; there were to be no gods in our house. My mother protested, but vaguely. She was uncommonly compliant, especially when he teased and kissed her. He called her his camelopard: she had a long neck, on which her small head turned silkily, eyeing him as if to fix him in place. Her tentative smile darkened when the sun's slant began to hint at autumn and his nearing departure. She had been no more than seventeen, one of many earthquake orphans under the care of the polis, when he found her. Though by then seven years had passed, she was still in mourning for her parents. She had seen them devoured by a black crevice widening and widening, out of which a wild fang of blaze leaped up to snatch them, two living torches, into the ravenous abyss. My reticent mother rarely spoke of this, and when she did, it was with a shiver of obeisance, I hardly knew to whom. The gods, the priests, our sibyl? The *barbaros* who had inexplicably succored her, and given her shelter and the child who was to become his delight?

That I was my father's delight I was fully confident. I was his delight, and his darling, and his joy; and also his little sparrow, and his pearl, and his pomegranate, and his garden of love. These were his fanciful names for me, and many more. He made me believe (and for a long time I did believe it) that he came every year not to see to his business at the kilns, but solely to marvel at how much I had grown, and to bring me presents of woven bracelets and pendants of polished stone and necklaces strung with beads that were really the shells of tiny sea creatures. He told me of the great fishes that swam singing and sighing alongside his ship, huge monstrous things with hairy fins and glistening eyes, and of how when it stormed in the night the waves turned into thrashing tongues frothing at the lips of prow and stern; and that he bore these queer perils all for the sake of once again taking into his arms his little sparrow, his darling, his garden of love, his only delight.

And then would begin my father's anxious questioning: what did I like best to eat? And why did I refuse wine? Where were my playmates, why was I so often alone? Why did I leave my mother, only to loiter among the chapels? What did I do there?

I answered dutifully but aslant. How could I admit, as I stood ringed by the sweetness of his embrace, that my father was the cause of our isolation? Though he periodically engaged a number of household servants, as soon as he departed they would instantly vanish. During the long months of his absence, my mother wrapped herself in loneliness. No one came to us. In a corner, on a little lion-footed tripod table covered with a woolen cloth, she kept an image of Hestia, her protectress. It was carved out of cedar and no taller than her forearm. In the spring, as my father's return approached, she hid it away. Even I, who lived within the sound of her thin breathing, hardly knew

where. All this because my father was *atheos*, and we carried his
stain—my mother less than I. It was I who carried his blood.

What I dared not tell was how I came to fear the taste of wine.
My mother and I drank clear water with our meals, but often
enough our cups held wine mixed with water, a faintly half-
sweet, half-bitter flavor that, chiefly in the depth of summer, I
swallowed greedily. My father, oddly, always avoided our wine,
even when it was much diluted. And he had another strange
refusal: with a quick thrust of his hand he declined all bread,
whether wheat or barley—but only for a certain set of eight
days; and after that he would eat normally. My mother did not
question these incomprehensible omissions. It was how they
lived in his home country, she told me, where even the bread
and the wine were unlike our own.

But now I could no longer endure the taste or look or smell
of wine. I would not touch any cup that had once held so much
as a drop of it. The faintest vinous aroma, even at a distance,
struck me as ominous, redolent of the terror that had inflamed
me one melancholy afternoon, after my mother and I had said
our farewells to my father. The air, with its memory of last
year's abandonment, had already begun to grow sick with its
presentiments of loneliness. My father clasped each of us close,
confiding, to my mother especially, assurances of future comforts, and nestling my face in the familiar bristle of his beard; yet
I could see in his eyes that his thoughts were more of departure
than of far-off arrival. All that morning he had been supervis-
ing the noisy loading of the caravan, while the donkeys yawped
amid their droppings, and the drivers abused one another with
friendly curses. The moment the last cart was out of sight, my
mother's waning smiles flattened into the cheerless silence that
would, I knew, afflict her for many weeks.

And so I fled into the late-summer heat, and went to walk
again among the chapels. My mother was glad to have me go;
I understood that she meant to take out from its hiding place,
unobserved, the diminutive image of her protectress, and
would set beside it the ritual dishes of figs and sacred seeds. It
puzzled me how so shrunken a figure could claim to hold equal
power with the towering Hestia in the grandeur of her proper

shrine, but my mother's belief was steadfast. As water will flow into any vessel prepared to receive it, she instructed me, so must the presence of the goddess flow into her material incarnation, no matter if it is no bigger than a hand's breadth . . . *ouai*, she murmured, if only your father would not deny it!

Secretly I was tempted to deny it too, and as I stole into the dusk of Hestia's chapel (always it was my single-minded destination), and saw at the far end of its shrouded nave the goddess's mighty lineaments, my mother's tiny replica seemed no more than a childish toy. I had come out of desire, and also out of fear; I feared my father's denial, and my own. Yet by now my father was irretrievably gone, my mother was sick at heart, and in the hallowed twilight of that place I felt sheltered by the force and majesty of the goddess's brooding head and broad thighs, those marble hills in whose valley rested the sacred fire. All things were small beside her, my unhappy mother smaller still.

The acolyte was not alone. A woman stood before the altar at Hestia's feet. She was neither young nor old, her waist was thick and round as a pumpkin, and she was pouring a dark syrup from a narrow flask into the swirling well of the libation bowl. The dense liquid fell in waves and folds, and when the flask was emptied, she placed next to the bowl a barley cake that smelled of honey. The acolyte held out a rattling cup. The woman dropped in a drachma and hurried away.

I distrusted this boy. He was dressed like the priests, but he was not a priest; he was only a boy.

"You always come," he said. I had never before heard his voice; it was the voice of a female child. Was it because he was not permitted to speak, and could not remember how? I watched him as he sidled to the altar to tend to his duty there— was he not the goddess's servant? But instead he broke off a bit of the cake and licked the beads of honey seeping out.

"Want some?" he said in his strange squeal. "It's for the priests, though."

"Are you allowed?"

He gave me a sly look. "They won't know, will they?"

He picked up a ladle and dipped it into the libation bowl.

I saw him sip, and sip again. The wine shimmered and shook in its krater, and then it glinted and shuddered at the rim of the ladle. I was all at once ravished by an invincible thirst; on this parched day of my father's leavetaking, I had forgotten food and drink. I took in the smell, a wild and sour stench, as of some small animal's dung. It was the spoor of the wine, and the wine was in the ladle, trembling there, moving closer, until a droplet touched my lip and wet my tongue, when the stench turned all at once deliriously sweet, like butterflies liquefied, or bird-beaks pounded into flowery powder, and I drank, deeply, thirstily, drivenly, a violator, a betrayer of the priests and the goddess herself, but I was indifferent, my throat was a vine on fire, my fingers crawled like twisted vines, vines charred white coiled round all my parts, I was alone, alone, swept up by a burning whirlwind and thrown into an airless void, I belonged nowhere, and I was afraid, afraid of the flame between the goddess's thighs, afraid of my lips and my tongue and the smoldering coals that were my eyes; and I was afraid of what I suddenly and terribly *knew*.

It was a long time before I could return to that place. When I did, the acolyte kept his distance. He never again spoke to me.

And when my father had been gone for several weeks, and we were in our customary seclusion, my mother one day confided to me, all unexpectedly, what she had long understood to be my father's secret. It was only because of the earthquake that he had taken her, she told me, an orphan tainted by the wrath of Hades, and it was because of the earthquake that she was not the proper wife of a proper husband, and was made to suffer now like some grieving widow, though she was not a widow, and what was she then, if she was not a proper wife? My mother's recurrent malaise too often plagued our solitude, and I saw that she was again falling into forlornness. It was her habit to skirt any talk of the cataclysm that had despoiled her earlier years, particularly when I was nearby to hear it; she wished to shield me from these old scenes, even if in their remoteness from our ordinary landscape they seemed to me no different from fables. Yet now, in the fever of her telling (it came upon her like a seizure), she spoke over and over of the wrath of Hades whose punishment it was, the ruination of houses and orchards and animals and crops, the ruination of everything civilized, and how in the bleak aftermath of the last of the tremors she had lingered for many hours half-naked in her torn tunic at the brink of the steaming trench; and she told of the looting that followed, and the riots when there was little to eat, and the knives and the fury and the bloodshed. The wrath of Hades? All this impressed me as a passing figment of her disordered temper: how did such long-ago wounds accord with our sedate and harmonious polis, governed by the priests under the inspiration of our sibyl? And had not those wounds been transfigured by the newcomer to our restrained and measured realm, my mother's savior, the redeemer of her misfortunes—my father?

"And did I not know it," she wailed, "did I not know it even then? He comes and he comes, but one time he will not come, the sea will break his vessel, he will stop his breath among the fishes, or else, or else," in a voice almost too thin to grasp, "one day he will not come because he no longer wishes to come."

I asked why my father, who loved me so, would not ever wish to come.

And then my mother confessed what she believed to be my father's great deceit. In his home country, she told me, he had a proper wife, how could it be otherwise? And a proper family, and yes, a foreign daughter, how could it be otherwise?

I believed her belief. I believed it even more intently than I believed her belief in the dark god's spite: how should my guileless mother merit the lash of his underworld? But the other daughter, how my envious imaginings stung! Did she love my father as yearningly as I? It rankled me that a foreign girl could bask under his fond eye nearly all the year, while me he held close only for a summer's blink. And did she not speak his home-country tongue, as I could not, and was she not intimate with his home-country ways? How often and often had I wished that my father were one of us!—though sometimes, as I contemplated my mother pleading before her protectress's small shrine, it came to me that the other daughter might be no more than a phantom, the lurking creature of my mother's frights.

But when my father returned, all these darknesses fled. His ship had skimmed a stormless sea, he was hale and ruddy-cheeked from the prickly northern winds, and oh! the presents he brought, brooches inlaid with turquoise, and baskets woven in many colors heaped with gleaming olives different in shape and taste from ours, and scarves and bracelets and a glossy bronze looking-glass, and even sandals hung with silver beads, unlike any we had ever seen. My mother brightened; her toy Hestia had already been rushed into its hiding place. Immediately fresh troops of servants were bustling everywhere, sweeping out neglected corners, crisscrossing the courtyard, fetching water and grinding meal, all the while showing uncommon deference. It was easy then to put away jealousy: how plain it was that my father could *not* love a foreign child more than he loved his pearl, his pomegranate, his little sparrow!

And now we were happy once more. In the mornings my father went to the kilns, and again in the late afternoon, but the hours in between belonged to my mother and me. Together we set out for the fields, carrying pouches of cakes and fruit. We walked until the footpaths ended and everything before us was brush and tangles of green, and then my father would be sure to tell us that the fields of his own land were no different; it was only the families of wildflowers that were not the same. Or else, to flavor our lavish dinners of fish or lamb, we would visit the market stalls in the agora, in search of herbs and spices he was familiar with and we were not. My father would sometimes allow me to go with him to the kilns before sunset, to tally and mark with his mark the pots he had purchased that day. The tedium and the dust and the heat and the incessant shouting of the kiln masters, he warned, would tire me. But despite the lingering smoke and the biting smells of glaze and moist clay, I was never wearied there, where the armies of finished pots marched in brilliant rows—how I loved to see their shapes and colors! Some had handles like ears, and others were thin-necked and fat-bellied, and on their flanks so many patterns, scrolls or stripes or leaves curled like snails.

Even so, what enchanted me more than all the rest were the pots that told stories: figures in motion, bearing kraters or kneeling or with uplifted arms gripping weapons, all devotedly and meticulously painted, as if they could come alive if only they willed it. Like any child of our polis, I knew their stories well: here was Gaia, here was Poseidon with his trident, and Demeter and Zeus, and poor frightened Persephone, dragged by deathly Hades into the chasm's cruel gullet. And still my father coveted them all!

For the very first time I dared to question him. Hadn't he banned from the fresh walls of our new-built house any fresco depicting the gods, no matter how it would have pleased my mother, whose every solace he unfailingly sought to indulge? And now look—all these sanctified chronicles on pots, and as always he intended to take them away with him!

My father caressed my cheeks, a tender habit meant to calm me, though now it could not. "Oh my little bird," he said, "only see how beautiful, the tunics of the women, how the cloth folds and unfolds, like shadow and light, and the limbs of the men, their force—"

"But they are *gods*!" I cried. Could he not see, did he not know?

"In my home country they will not be gods, they will be what they are, beautiful mortal men and beautiful mortal women."

And I thought: how barren, how deprived, was my father's far-off land, where beauty was denied to the gods.

It was after this troubled colloquy (and wasn't it almost a quarrel?) that my father began to ply me with strange tales. They were, he said, the history of his home country. We would rest in the courtyard in the thick of the afternoon, when the air quivered from heat, and the pavement sizzled, and the servants dozed over their tasks, and my mother napped in the shuttered cool of an inner room. Then my father told of an infant saved from drowning by a king's daughter, who reared him to grandeur in the royal palace, only to see him lead a fearsome rebellion. He told of a youth who knew the meaning of dreams, whose envious brothers sold him into a foreign kingdom, where he rose out of a dungeon to become a powerful vizier. He told of a great flood that swallowed the earth, except for one old drunkard with his one small boat, who salvaged all future life. He told of an ill-starred voyager, who, thrown overboard by terrified sailors, fell into the belly of a mammoth fish. He told of a boy who brought down a giant with nothing more formidable than a simple slingshot.

My father told all these stories, and many more. Some I shrank from and some I wondered at; but privately I judged them inferior—what were they, after all, but the earthbound dry happenings of the ordinary world, haplessly cut off from the dazzlements of Olympus? Men, not gods, struggled in these tales, while *our* histories, how glorious they were!—the rages and lusts and jealousies of goddesses and gods, how they caused the skies to rumble and the seas to churn, how the lot of humankind hung from their passions, and how, if they were drawn to the love of a mortal, what heroes, Heracles and Achilles, erupted from their loins!

I said nothing of this to my father.

Instead, I asked whether in his home country they kept a sibyl, as we did.

No, my father said. And I began to pity him a little: it seemed to me then that my father, *barbaros* and *atheos*, must live in an uncivilized land. This dim inkling of a divide, finer than a spider's line, made me cling to him all the more, and to the everyday pleasures of our little family. We went on wandering the fields, the three of us, often lying contented and laughing in the long grasses with our heads flattening the wildflowers, and our noses yellowed by pollen, and our mouths purpled from the juice of the grapes we had eaten. And still—though he was not, he did not wish to be, one of us—I was my father's darling, his sparrow, his pomegranate, his garden of love.

But I determined that I would no longer go walking among the chapels, and that the great gleaming Hestia in her cathedral shrine would never again lure me.

Year after year, unwaveringly, I kept this private vow, both when my father was happily with us and in the dreary months of my mother's melancholia when he was not. There were seasons that brought him to us in the earliest days of spring, and other times when summer had already reached its midpoint. All this fickleness rested, he teased, on the temperament of the sailors: an indolent crew dallies and dawdles. Or if the big fishes knock their heavy tails against the starboard, like cats begging for a morsel. But we knew he meant the whims of the hungering sea.

One year, when the summer was beginning to drift toward exhaustion, my father had still not come.

"It must be the winds," I said, "flying hard against him."

Or I said, to lighten my mother's thoughts, "How lazy those sailors are."

Or I said, "The sea cats are crowding his path."

And then I said, "Surely he will come, he always comes, soon he will come, he has never not come—"

But my mother said, "He will not come."

And he did not.

From then on, my mother descended into grieving. We were invariably alone. Our suppers were meager. Morning and evening I heard my mother's murmured pleas and lamentations before her small protectress, now always out of its hiding place; but the propitiatory dishes were bare.

"*Ouai*," she soughed, "he is drowned, he is drowned," and covered the twist of her mouth with her pale hands, on which I could see the gray ridges of veins like the ridges made by cart tracks in earth after rain.

Or else she said in her flat strained voice, "He has chosen his proper family, it is his proper place."

And was this not, I thought, the very reason for the fierceness of our love? Because he was not, and did not wish to be, one of us—and yet had he not come to succor and rejoice us?

But my mother said bitterly, "It was only for the kilns that he came, and never for us. Never did he come for us."

And I saw that grief was coarsening and muddling my mother's heart. She was willing now, more and more, to speak of the earthquake, and of the wild time afterward, those fearful years of chaos and violence, as dire as the upheaval itself. She told and retold (how tedious it was!) the old familiar tales of how the priests in despair had summoned our sibyl from the far north, and how they kept her secluded, no one knew where—grove, or cave, or forest—and how through the sway of her divinations and prophecies our polis was at length pacified and cleansed. These storied events had neither impressed nor dismayed my father; the sibyl, he would chide my mother, was mere woman, and many women were wise who never governed . . . and then my mother would clasp her breast as if a tiny beast were strangling there, and cry out, "*Ouai, atheos!*"

In those sorrowful days of mourning, my father's erasure from our lives returned to her awry: it was the earthquake that had devoured him, and never the sea; or she would fall into a dreamy lassitude and promise that my father was certain to come again when the sun burned hot on the lintel and flocks of foreign birds filled the skies. And sometimes, because I gave no obeisance to her little Hestia, and passed it by without so much as a glance, she charged me with denying the gods, and turned her plaintive look on me to ask, "Who will there be to marry one such as you?"

In this way, half-bewildered and maundering, my mother sickened. She vomited the gruel I pressed on her and spat out the water in her cup, and the skin of her neck frayed like a wrinkled rope, and in the spring, when my father once more did not come, she died. Season after season, month upon month, time relentlessly dividing itself, I sat solitary in my father's house (so I regarded it), and saw the pavement in the courtyard crack, and a wilderness of scrub creep up through a mazy map of fissures, and watched as the frescoes faded and flaked into a drizzle of powder at a finger's touch.

But I had not forgotten the hoard of my treasures—my father's countless gifts of brooches and necklaces and pendants and bracelets, each with its precious stones, and the sandals with their silver beads, too beautiful to have ever been worn, and the bronze looking-glass. I had long ago given up adorning myself; these things were useless to me now. One by one, I took them to the agora to sell, lest I become impoverished. It was only the bronze looking-glass that I thought to keep.

I disliked these periodic excursions to the market stalls, infrequent though they were. The sharp smell of spices pierced and saddened me: here our little family had once loitered, while my father sorted through ruffled leaves and roots and tubers and tubs of ground bark with the same determined delicacy he brought to choosing lekythoi at the kilns, as if a sprig of fenugreek was as lovely to his eye as a painted jar. But now, caught among the roiling streams of tattle that agitated the agora, I knew myself to be a rumor, a byword, a warning; yet I hardly understood why. Was I not as native to our polis as any passerby? The stares of the merchants unsettled me—they retreated into the dark of their stalls as I approached. Was it because I was a woman alone, an abandoned relic in a hollow ruin, childless, unwanted? Was it because I rarely cared to speak? To whom should I speak, and to what end? Who would love me as I had once been loved by my father?

In the bronze looking-glass I saw what I was. My father's eyes gazed back at me with unfamiliar ferocity; swollen blue-black pockets bulged beneath them. My hair, white as a cloud, unbound and untamed, was as vagrant as some massive shrub torn up by an unforgiving wind. My mouth frightened me: a hive of terrible silences.

In my fifty-seventh year, long after even the looking-glass had been sold, our sibyl died. Very few could remember a time when she was not the unseen guardian of our decorum and our laws; for us, she was ageless and faceless. Her lineage was unknown. No one had ever heard her voice. It was said that the goddess to whom she was pledged had decreed at her birth that she was not to live beyond two hundred years.

And soon a savage tumult seized our polis. Bins of ripened fruits overturned and trampled in the marketplace, stalls barricaded, old women wailing in the confusion. Menacing packs of youths heaving boulders downhill, to crash into whatever stood in their path. Thieves running free, hauling their prey. Trembling curs prowling in the night, sniffing for scraps, the tattered fur hanging loose from their bellies. Everywhere fear—fear of brokenness, fear of hunger, fear of bloodletting and malice.

Only I was left unharmed, I with my snarled coils of hair, my speech idled and shattered, sitting day after day under the lintel of my father's decaying house, listening to the groans and maledictions of a dying polis. Fires on the hills, fires in the fields, the chapels on fire, the agora smoldering, always the fires: the sun veiled in smoke.

It was on just such an afternoon of burning air that the priests came. I saw them at first at a distance, a procession of seven shrouded figures, and supposed it to be yet another rite of expiation to stem the crawling flames. I had often witnessed these futile parades as they passed, chanting and swinging their censers, as if those small vessels of heated coals had the power to extinguish the greater conflagration. As they moved nearer, they were more easily defined: all wore long pleated white garments fringed at the anklebone and flecked with soot. Six were bare-headed and clean-shaven; two of these were clearly acolytes in their teens, and one was a withered patriarch with a palsied chin. The seventh, whom I took to be their chief, wore a gilded circlet round his head, and plaited through his abundant beard were sooty ribbons of colored silk.

But this time there were no censers, and no chanting, and the silent cortege drifted unfathomably toward me, until it stopped directly before my feet.

One of the acolytes knelt and removed my sandals. At a word from the priest with the palsied chin—who appeared to be their spokesman, though not their leader—the other invaded the dirty gloom of my father's house and quickly brought out my mother's toy Hestia. Her little shrine had remained in its old corner, untouched and untended; but the lion-footed table that held it I had long ago sold.

I was instructed to follow where I was led, past the blighted agora into fields of grasses like blackened straw, and onward through soot-blasted fields farther yet, where my father had never taken us, and over a rise and beyond it, and finally into a place of stones. Here the fires had never reached. I was made to walk on my naked feet, so that they might toughen and grow hard and invulnerable, no matter that the thistles were piercing my heels, or that my soles were torn and bloodied. The stones rose tall and taller as we proceeded, until they seemed to form a kind of grotto, a cavern of earth and stone through which ran a trickle of icy water. I was shown the nearby spring that was its source: I was permitted to drink of this spring, and to relieve myself there, but it was forbidden to bathe in its water, except for when the moon was shrunk to the shape of a fingernail. It was forbidden to forage for leaves or berries: I must be satisfied with what, morning and evening, the acolytes would bring. If it turned cold, I was not to plead for a fire; again I must be content with whatever habit or vesture the acolytes might offer. It was forbidden to speak to the acolytes. It was forbidden to cover my feet; it was an offense to the gods. It was forbidden to depart from this place; it was a profanation. It was forbidden to eat or drink on the days designated for the coming of the priests: my body must be purified in preparation.

These were the precepts imparted to me by the priest with the palsied chin.

The chief priest, who until then had been mute, now spoke; out of his throat came a crooked falsetto. It was his duty, he said, to recite the evidences and conditions, the signs and confirmations, that had brought me to this hour of initiation. It was known that my mother had, despite all, been a woman of piety, dedicated to Hestia, before whose domestic shrine she had faithfully submitted her reverence; and that after her death, having denuded my house of all manner of precious things, as affirmed by the merchants of the agora, I retained and continued my mother's allegiance: the proof being the shrine itself, carried away by an acolyte enjoined to seek corroboration. Secondly, it was known that even from earliest childhood it was my passion to frequent the holy chapels in order to search out the veracity and power of their deities. Thirdly, it was attested by the kiln masters that as a young girl I was heard disputing with my father on behalf of the gods. And fourthly—

As if overcome by a chill, the chief priest halted. Already there were intimations of the night to come, deepened by the long cold shadows of the stones. I looked into his face, that part of it visible above the great beard with its ornaments, and in the dwindling light saw an elderly man my own age, whose voice was strangely broken and stunted and shrill, akin to an infant's cry; and I knew him.

Fourthly, he resumed in that childlike pitch, your father's blood has become as water, and now you are freed and made holy. Dangerous and despised, an interloper and a blasphemer, he came among us only to usurp our native treasure. Him the gods have justly destroyed. Behold! I, Grand Priest and First Servant to the Oracle, hereby annul the stain!

The acolytes, meanwhile, had brought me to a flat stone close to the spring, where, encircled by a tall ring of concealing stones, I was made to prostrate myself. Over me stood the chief priest. He himself, he piped, was witness to the child I once was, and how in the cathedral shrine of Hestia, guardian of the civic hearth, and in the glimmer of the sacral flame between her thighs, he saw me overtaken by those signs of election given only to whom the goddess anoints: the sacerdotal frenzy, its telltale howls and whirlings, the shrieks of terror and elation at the instant of possession. It was by the will of the goddess that I should be as I now was: old and foretold, and virgin, and a woman apart.

As I lay there, smelling the damp earth, my face a brief space above the ground, I was aware of something alive and moist licking its way across the naked soles of my feet. It humped and curled as it slid into view: here was the habitation of snakes.

And so began what I was to become. To all these things—the admonitions and the testimonies, the rites and the annunci- ations—I had easily acquiesced. It was as well to live among stones as to linger emptily under the rotted lintel of my father's house. And if I wished, might I not readily escape this place— to go where? Too quickly I learned that my naked feet were my prison. When one bloody wound healed, another would open—either I blundered into a nest of thorns, or unwitting- ly cut my heel on a half-buried stone, sharp as an arrow. By cushioning leaves and grasses on a scrap of bark, and twining them round with the vines that crawled among the stones, I contrived to be roughly shod. The acolytes, I discovered, were indifferent to this and every other transgression. When I spoke to them, they answered freely; in the absence of the priests, they were no more than careless boys. I would hear them laughing and cavorting as they approached, and too often it happened that the meal they were carrying was spilled; and then I was left to go hungry.

It was from the acolytes that I came to know how our sibyl had met her death—not by divine command, as proclaimed by the priests, but by the bite of a snake in the heel. A commonplace: such a calamity might befall anyone, even in so mundane and frequented a spot as the agora itself. I had no fear of the snakes; they lived as I now lived, earthbound among the stones. I saw them as neighbors and companions, and at times amused myself by trailing them to their lairs; in this way I stumbled on a trove of sweet berries to gladden my hunger. Now and again, when one of these beasts lay motionless in a coil, in a fit of rapture I would be moved to study the colors and patterns of its skin, as I had once been stirred by the colors and patterns of my father's pots at the kilns. And all around, the stones in the changing light showed their changing tempers: the configurations of their small shadowed juttings and hollows came to resemble human features. More than once it seemed that my father's face looked out at me.

I had no desire to leave this place. It was sufficient. My feet, latterly growing callused and tough, were at last freeing me to wander away—yet why should I? If a piercing wind invaded, or if the sun blazed too harshly, the tall stones shielded me. I bathed when I pleased, I slept and woke when I pleased. The acolytes, like the days and the nights in their passing, came and went. The polis and its disorders were distant.

But I was in dread of the moon. I watched as it swelled, evening by evening; soon the priests would return. And at the time fixed for divination, when the moon was white and round and seamed with bluish veins, they arrived as they had before, in a procession, wordlessly. Behind them came the acolytes, carrying great waxed tablets—so many petitions and devotions, undertakings and devisings, ordinances and decrees, how they frightened me! All were to pass through me when the goddess entered my body.

I was made to wear a gown of pure linen—it girdled my neck and fell to my knees; my breasts it left bare. I was ashamed of my old woman's dried-up nipples and wrinkled dugs, but for these too I had been chosen: the proud gods disdain rivals to their beauty. No one envies a crone.

And my feet were again naked, but ugly and yellowed and hard as shells.

The chief priest drew me to the spring, where I was made to mount the flat stone of my initiation. Here I was to remain sequestered by the surrounding upright stones, and here I was to summon the goddess. Had I eaten or drunk that day? I said I had not. Though the acolytes had been instructed to withhold my meals, all afternoon I had glutted on berries and cupped my hands at the spring.

Then now you must drink.

He set down at my feet a silver kalyx and left me. I saw through the gaps in the stones how the priests with their tablets had gathered in a knot, silent and waiting; but I saw only their backs. It was forbidden to come near. It was forbidden to witness the act of possession.

I picked up the kalyx and looked into its mouth. Swaying from side to side, as if agitated by some double tide, was a viscous purple sea. Its odor was foul. Its fumes were bitter.

And what must I do now?

I lifted my arms to the white moon and called to the goddess. Come. Come, I called, again and again. Come. Only come.

She did not come, and what must I do now?

The moonlight had carved small pits and grooves in the stones that hemmed me round like sentinels, and I saw my father's eyes, black and lidless, gaping out of the nearest stele; and I knew what I must not do.

I must not succumb. I must not surrender.

I stood erect on the sacral mound and from the lip of the kalyx slowly, slowly, spilled stain upon stain into the waters of the spring, observing how purple bled into red, and how red paled to clear transparency, until the spring flowed as innocently as before.

And then I gave out a great hideous shriek, and another, and another, my throat grappling more and more violently in its box, and I beat the stone at my feet, pounding and pounding with the silver kalyx, until a savage ringing raged all around, as if a phalanx of gongs were tumbling out of the night, and I spewed out unearthly words that were no words, only crippled syllables and feral growls and squeals, and I barked like a hound and hissed like a cat, and humped and crawled on my belly in the way of the snakes, and I clawed at my hair to twist it into worms, and thrashed and flailed on my slab, and writhed and cackled and yowled, and all the while I held on and held on, I would not succumb, I dared not surrender; and the goddess did not come.

She did not come, and I fell to the ground emptied, breathless; spent. No shaft of exaltation had penetrated the hollows of my body, I was what I was born to be, no more than mortal woman, and below all my clamor a brutal silence, the silence of the oracle that never was and never will be, the merciless silence of the goddess who never was and never will be, and now the voices of the priests, chanting, importuning, praising and blessing the goddess's terrifying power, her pity and absolution, crying out their tremulous petitions and grievances, their perplexities and yearnings, their ordinances and vainglorious decrees, all in submission to the sublime will—and what was I to do now, I who am deceiver and dissembler, false in ecstasy, false in frenzy, I who carry the blood of him who was not, and did not wish to be, one of us?

I have since outlived them all, the chief priest with his castrato mewlings, and the priest with the palsied chin, and I have outlived even the heedless acolytes, all of them given way to new priests and new careless boys. Always there will be the priests, and always there will be my companions the snakes with their unfeeling eyes and radiant skins, and always and always the tall stones that shelter my shrine. Nowadays I cover my feet with thick leather clogs (I have already been bitten twice, but mildly, and the fever soon passed), and when it is very cold, I make a fire if it pleases me (the acolytes bring the wood), and all in all I live as I like, and am content.

In the roundings of time, the acolytes seem always the same, the older reticent, the younger garrulous, and both uncommonly beautiful—the chief priests, I believe, choose them for their lovely mouths and soft napes. The younger is eager to give me news of the polis, how once in an unhappy autumn the remnants of my father's house were razed to rubble by a whirling storm, brief and already half-forgotten, which was said to cause scores of ships to be shattered, so that the traders no longer arrive, and the kiln masters are gone elsewhere to establish their craft anew. And in the fields beyond the agora, there are now wine presses and oil presses, bringing much prosperity. The charred grasses are again green, and the wildflowers dense, and throughout the polis order and serenity.

The priests go on, as of old, appealing to the goddess for holy guidance; but it is I who sanction and govern and make the laws, though the priests cannot know this. I no longer fear the growing moon and the wine with its treacheries, and the coming of the priests in procession cannot shake me. I am their mistress, and if I howl and convulse on the sacred mound, I do it not to indulge their belief, but to scorn it: the gods are a lie. Yet how accuse these solemn elders of delusion? As much accuse the snakes of their venom; it is their truth.

And I have learned, in time, to reveal the goddess's answer in the form of a puzzle, or a riddle, or an enigma with as many sides as a polygon: when diligently parsed, they cannot fail of reason or usefulness. As for the wine, always I am careful to paint the waters of the spring with its ebbing colors; but sometimes I leave a little at the bottom of the kalyx to give to the acolytes when they bring the morning meal. The older is reluctant and afraid, but the younger drinks lustily.

My father's image has faded from the nubs and crevices of the stones, and I scarcely ever look for it there. But on still summer nights, when ships are safe at sea, and the snakes hide in their thickets, and the spring runs soundlessly, and even the stones are tranquil, I think of that primitive and barbarous land, my father's home country, where their tongue is not our tongue, and their bread is not our bread, and their tales are not our tales, and they keep no sibyl and know no gods . . . then who is it that gives them their laws, lacking, as they do, one such as I?

What Happened to the Baby?

WHEN I WAS a child, I was often taken to meetings of my Uncle Simon's society, the League for a Unified Humanity. These meetings, my mother admitted, were not suitable for a ten-year-old, but what was she to do with me? I could not be left alone at night, and my father, who was a detail man for a pharmaceutical company, was often away from home. He had recently been assigned to the Southwest: we would not see him for weeks at a time. To our ears, places like Arizona and New Mexico might as well have been far-off planets. Yet Uncle Simon, my mother told me proudly, had been to even stranger regions. Sometimes a neighbor would be called in to look after me while my mother went off alone to one of Uncle Simon's meetings. It was important to go, she explained, if only to supply another body. The hall was likely to be half empty. Like all geniuses, Uncle Simon was—"so far," she emphasized—unappreciated.

Uncle Simon was not really my uncle. He was my mother's first cousin, but out of respect, and because he belonged to an older generation, I was made to call him uncle. My mother revered him. "Uncle Simon," she said, "is the smartest man you'll ever know." He was an inventor, though not of mundane things like machines, and it was he who had founded the League for a Unified Humanity. What Uncle Simon had invented, and was apparently still inventing, since it was by nature an infinite task, was a wholly new language, one that could be spoken and understood by everyone alive. He had named it GNU, after the African antelope that sports two curved horns, each one turned toward the other, as if striving to close a circle. He had traveled all over the world, picking up roots and discarding the less common vowels. He had gone to Turkey and China and many countries in South America, where he interviewed

Indians and wrote down, in his cryptic homemade notation, the sounds they spoke. In Africa, in a tiny Xhosa village hidden in the wild, he was inspired by observing an actual yellow-horned gnu. And still, with all this elevated foreign experience, he lived, just as we did, in a six-story walkup in the East Bronx, in a neighborhood of small stores, many of them vacant. In the autumn the windows of one of these stores would all at once be shrouded in dense curtains. Gypsies had come to settle in for the winter. My mother said it was the times that had emptied the stores. My father said it was the Depression. I understood it was the Depression that made him work for a firm cruel enough to send him away from my mother and me.

Unlike my mother, my father did not admire Uncle Simon. "That panhandler," he said. "God only knows where he finds these suckers to put the touch on."

"They're cultured Park Avenue people," my mother protested. "They've always felt it a privilege to fund Simon's expeditions."

"Simon's expeditions! If you ask me, in the last fifteen years he's never gotten any farther than down the street to the public library to poke his nose in the *National Geographic*."

"Nobody's asking, and since when are you so interested? Anyhow," my mother said, "it's not Simon who runs after the money, it's *her*."

"Her," I knew, was Uncle Simon's wife, Essie. I was not required to call her aunt.

"She dresses up to beat the band and flatters their heads off," my mother went on. "Well, someone's got to beg, and Simon's not the one for that sort of thing. Who's going to pay for the hall? Not to mention his research."

"Research," my father mocked. "What're you calling research? Collecting old noises in order to scramble them into new noises. Why doesn't he go out and get a regular job? A piece of work, those two—zealots! No, I've got that wrong, he's the zealot, and she's the fawning ignoramus. Those idiot jingles! Not another penny, Ruby, I'm warning you, you're not one of those Park Avenue suckers with money to burn."

"It's only for the annual dues—"

"The League for Scrambling Noises. Ten bucks down the sewer." He put on his brown felt fedora, patted his vest pocket to check for his train ticket, and left us.

"Look how he goes away angry," my mother said, "and all in front of a child. Phyllis dear, you have to understand. Uncle Simon is ahead of his time, and not everyone can recognize that. Daddy doesn't now, but someday he surely will. In the meantime, if we don't want him to come home angry, let's not tell that we've been to a meeting."

Uncle Simon's meetings always began the same way, with Uncle Simon proposing a newly minted syllable, explaining its derivation from two or three alien roots, and the membership calling out their opinions. Mostly these were contentious, and there were loud arguments over whether it was possible for the syllable in question to serve as a verb without a different syllable attached to its tail. Even my mother looked bored during these sessions. She took off her wool gloves and then pulled them on again. The hall was unheated, and my feet in their galoshes were growing numb. All around us a storm of furious fingers holding lit cigarettes stirred up halos of pale smoke, and it seemed to me that these irritable shouting men (they were mostly men) detested Uncle Simon almost as much as my father did. How could Uncle Simon be ahead of his time if even his own League people quarreled with him?

My mother whispered, "You don't have to be upset, dear, it's really all right. It's just their enthusiasm. It's what they have to do to decide, the way scientists do experiments, try and try again. We're sitting right in the middle of Uncle Simon's laboratory. You'll see, in the end they'll all agree."

It struck me that they would never all agree, but after a while the yelling ebbed to a kind of low communal grumbling, the smoke darkened, and the next part of the meeting, the part I liked best (or disliked least) commenced. At the front of the hall, at the side, was a little platform, broad enough to accommodate one person. Two steps led up to it, and Uncle Simon's wife mounted them and positioned herself. "The opera star," my mother said into my ear. Essie was all in yellow silk, with a yellow silk rose at her collarbone, and a yellow silk rose in her graying hair. She had sewn this dress herself, from a tissue-paper pattern bought at Kresge's. She was a short plump flat-nosed woman who sighed often; her blackly gleaming pumps with their thin pedestals made her look, I thought, like Minnie Mouse. Her speaking voice too was mouselike, too soft to carry well, and there was no microphone.

" 'Sunshine Beams,'" she announced. "I will first deliver my poem in English, and then I will render it in the lovely idiom of GNU, the future language of all mankind, as translated by Mr. Simon Greenfeld."

It was immediately plain that Essie had designed her gown to reflect her recitation:

Sunshine Beams

If in your most radiant dreams
You see the yellow of sunshine beams,
Then know, O Human Race all,
That you have heard the call
Of Humanity Unified.
So see me wear yellow with pride!
For it means that the horns of the gnu are
    meeting at last,
And the Realm of Unity has come to pass!

"Yellow horn, yellow horn, each one toward his fellow horn" was the refrain, repeated twice.

"The opera star and the poetess," my mother muttered. But then something eerie happened: Essie began to sing, and the words, which even I could tell were silly, were transmuted into reedlike streams of unearthly sounds. I felt shivery all over, and not from the cold. I was not unused to the hubbub of foreign languages: a Greek-speaking family lived across the street, the greengrocer on the corner was Lebanese, and our own building vibrated with Neapolitan and Yiddish exuberances. Yet what we were hearing now was something altogether alien. It had no affinity with anything recognizable. It might just as well have issued from the mouths of mermaids at the bottom of the sea.

"Well?" my mother said. "How beautiful, didn't I tell you? Even when it comes out of *her*."

The song ended in a pastel sheen, like the slow decline of a sunset.

Uncle Simon held up his hand against the applause. His voice was hoarse and high-pitched and ready for battle. "For our next meeting," he said, "the program will feature a GNU rendition, by yours truly, of Shelley's 'To a Skylark,' to be set to music by our own songbird, Esther Rhoda Greenfeld, so please everyone be sure to mark the date . . ."

But the hall was in commotion. A rocking boom was all at once erupting from the mostly empty rear rows, drowning Uncle Simon out. Three men and two women were standing on their chairs and stamping their feet, drumming faster and faster. This was, I knew, no more unexpected than Essie's singing and Uncle Simon's proclamations. It burst out at the close of nearly every meeting, and Uncle Simon reveled in the clamor. These were his enemies and rivals; but no, he had no rivals, my mother informed me afterward, and he took it as a compliment that those invaders, those savages, turned up at all, and that they waited until after Essie had finished. They waited in order to ridicule her, but what was their ridicule if not envy? They were shrieking out some foolish babble, speaking in tongues, pretending a parody of GNU, and when they went off into their customary chanting, wasn't that the truest sign of their defeat, of their envy?

"ZA-men-hof! ZA-men-hof!" Uncle Simon's enemies were howling. They jumped off their seats and ran down the aisle toward the podium, bawling right into Uncle Simon's reddening face.

"Esper-ANto! Esper-ANto! ZA-men-hof!"

"We'd better leave," my mother said, "before things get rough." She hurried me out of the hall without stopping to say goodnight to Uncle Simon. I saw that this would have been impossible anyhow. He had his fists up, and I wondered if his enemies were going to knock him down. He was a small man, and his nearsighted eyes were small and frail behind their fat lenses. Only his ridged black hair looked robust, scalloped like the sand when the tide has run out.

Though I had witnessed this scene many times in my child-hood, it was years before I truly fathomed its meaning. By then my father had, according to my mother, "gone native": he had fallen in love with the Southwest and was bringing back hand-woven baskets from New Mexico for my mother's rubber plants, and toy donkeys made of layers of colored crepe paper for me. I was in my late teens when he persuaded my mother to move to Arizona. "Ludicrous," she complained. "I'll be a fish out of water out there. I'll be cut off from everything." She worried especially about what would happen to Uncle Simon, who was now living alone downtown, in a room with an icebox and a two-burner stove hidden behind a curtain. That Essie! A divorce! It was a scandal, and all of it Essie's doing: no one in our family had ever before succumbed to such shame. She had accused Uncle Simon of philandering.

"What a viper that woman is," my mother said. "And all on top of what she did to the baby." She was filling a big steamer trunk with linens and quilts. The pair of creases between her eyebrows tightened. "Who knows how those people out there think—out there I might just as well be a greenhorn straight off the boat. I'd rather die than live in such a place, but Daddy says he's up for a raise if he sticks to the territory."

I had heard about the baby nearly all my life. Uncle Simon and Essie had not always been childless. Their little girl, eleven months old and already walking, had died before I was born. Her name was Henrietta. They had gone to South America on one of Uncle Simon's expeditions—in those days Essie went everywhere with him. "She never used to let him out of her sight," my mother recounted. "She was always jealous. Suspicious. She expected Simon to be no better than she was, that's the truth. You know she was already pregnant at the wed-ding, so she was grateful to him for marrying her. As well she should be, considering that who could tell whose baby it was anyway, maybe Simon's, maybe not. If you ask me, not. She'd had a boyfriend who had hair just like Simon's, black and wiry.

The baby had a headful of black curls. The poor little thing caught one of those diseases they have down there, in Peru or Bolivia, one of those places. Leave it to Essie, would any normal mother drag a baby through a tropical swamp?"

"A swamp?" I asked. "The last time you told about the baby it was a desert."

"Desert or swamp, what's the difference? It was something you don't come down with in the Bronx. The point is Essie killed that child."

I was happy that the move to the Southwest did not include me. I had agitated to attend college locally, chiefly to escape Arizona. My father had paid for a year's tuition at NYU, and also for half the rent of a walkup on Avenue A that I shared with another freshman, Annette Sorenson. The toilet was primitive—it had an old-fashioned pull chain and a crack in the overhead tank that leaked brown sludge. The bathtub was scored with reddish stains that couldn't be scrubbed away, though Annette went at it with steel wool and bleach. She cried nearly every night, not from homesickness but from exasperation. She had come from Briar Basin to NYU, she confided, because it was located in Greenwich Village. ("Briar Basin, Minnesota," she said; she didn't expect me to know that.) She was on the lookout for bohemia, and had most of Edna St. Vincent Millay's verse by heart. She claimed she had discovered exactly which classroom Thomas Wolfe had once taught in. She explored the nearby bars, but legend eluded her. Her yearnings were commonplace in that neighborhood: she wanted to act someday, and in the meantime she intended to inhale the atmosphere. She was blond and large all over. Her shoulder blades were a foot and a half apart and her wrist bones jutted like crab apples. I thought of her as a kind of Valkyrie. She boasted, operatically, that she wasn't a virgin.

I took Annette with me to visit Simon. I had long ago dropped the "Uncle"; I was too old for that. My mother's letters were reminding me not to neglect him. A twenty-dollar bill was sometimes enclosed, meant for delivery to Simon. I knew my father believed the money was for me; now and then he would add an admonitory line. Essie was still living in the old apartment in the Bronx, supporting herself well enough. She had a job in a men's clothing store and sat all day in a back room doing alterations, letting out seams and shortening sleeves. I suspected that Simon was on the dole. It seemed unlikely, after all this time, that he was still being shored up by his Park Avenue idealists.

"Is your uncle some sort of writer?" Annette asked as we climbed the stairs. The wooden steps creaked tunefully; the ancient layers of paint on the banisters were thickly wrinkled. I had told her that Simon was crazy about words. "I mean really crazy," I said.

Simon was sitting at a bridge table lit by a gooseneck lamp. A tower of dictionaries was at his left. A piece of questionable-looking cheese lay in a saucer on his right. In between was a bottle of ink. He was filling his fountain pen.

"My mother sends her love," I said, and handed Simon an envelope with the twenty-dollar bill folded into a page torn from my Modern History text. Except for a photograph of a zeppelin, it was blank. My father's warning about how not to be robbed in broad daylight was always to keep your cash well swaddled. "Otherwise those Village freaks down there will sure as shooting nab it," he wrote at the bottom of my mother's letter. But I had wrapped the money mostly to postpone Simon's humiliation: maybe, if only for a moment, he would think I was once again bringing him one of my mother's snapshots of cactus and dunes. She had lately acquired a box camera; in order not to be taken for a greenhorn, she was behaving like a tourist. At that time I had not yet recognized that an occasional donation might not humiliate Simon.

He screwed the cap back on the ink bottle and looked Annette over.

"Who's this?"

"My roommate. Annette Sorenson."

"A great big girl, how about that. Viking stock. You may be interested to know that I've included a certain uncommon Scandinavian diphthong in my work. Zamenhof didn't dare. He looked the other way. He didn't have the nerve." Behind his glasses Simon was grinning. "Any friend of my niece Phyllis

I intend to like. But never an Esperantist. You're not an Esperantist, are you?"

This, or something like it, was his usual opening. I had by now determined that Essie was right: Simon was a flirt, and something more. He went for the girls. Once he even went for me: he put out a hand and cupped my breast. Then he thought better of it. He had, after all, known me from childhood; he desisted. Or else, since it was January, and anyhow I was wearing a heavy wool overcoat, there wasn't much of interest worth cupping. For my part, I ignored it. I was eighteen, with eyes in my head, beginning to know a thing or two. I had what you might call an insight. Simon coveted more than the advancement of GNU.

On my mother's instructions I opened his icebox. A rancid smell rushed out. There was a shapeless object green at the edges—the other half of the cheese in his saucer. The milk was sour, so I poured it down the toilet. Simon was all the while busy with his spiel, lecturing Annette on the evil history of Esperanto and its ignominious creator and champion, Dr. Ludwik Lazar Zamenhof, of Bialystok, Poland.

"There they spoke four languages, imagine that! Four lousy languages! And this is what inspires him? Four languages? Did he ever go beyond European roots? Never! The man lived inside a puddle and never stepped out of it. Circumscribed! Small! Narrow!"

"I'll be right back," I called out from the doorway, and went down to the grocery on the corner to replenish Simon's meager larder. I had heard this grandiose history too many times: how Simon alone had ventured into the genuinely universal, how he had roamed far beyond Zamenhof's paltry horizons into the vast tides of human speech, drawing from these a true synthesis, a compact common language unsurpassed in harmony and strength. Yet tragically eclipsed—eclipsed by Zamenhof's disciples, those deluded believers, those adorers of a false messiah! An eye doctor, that charlatan, and look how he blinds all his followers: Germanic roots, Romance roots, Slavic, and then he stops, as if there's no India, no China, no Arabia! No Aleutian Islanders! Why didn't the fellow just stick to the polyglot

Yiddish he was born into and let it go at that? Did he ever set foot twenty miles into the Orient, into the Levant? No! Then why didn't he stick to Polish? An eye doctor who couldn't see past his own nose. *Hamlet* in Esperanto, did you ever hear of such chutzpah?

And so on: Esperanto, a fake, a sham, an injustice!

As I was coming up the stairs, carrying bread and milk and eggs in the straw-handled Navajo bag my mother had sent as a present for Simon, I heard Annette say, "But I never knew Esperanto even *existed*," and I saw that Simon had Annette's hand in his. He was circling her little finger with a coarse thumb that curved backward like a twisted spoon. She didn't seem to mind.

"You shouldn't call him crazy," she protested. "He's only disappointed." By then we were already in the street. She looked up at Simon's fourth-floor window. It flashed back at her like a signal: it had caught the late sun. I noticed that she was holding a white square of paper with writing on it.

"What's that?"

"A word he gave me. A brand-new word that no one's ever used before. He wants me to learn it."

"Oh my God," I said.

"It means 'enchanting maiden,' isn't that something?"

"Not if maiden's supposed to be the same as virgin."

"Cut it out, Phyllis, just stop it. He thinks I can help."

"You? How?"

"I could recruit. He says I could get young people interested."

"I'm young people," I said. "I've never been interested, and I've had to listen to Simon's stuff all my life. He bores me silly."

"Well, he told me you take after your father, whatever that means. A prophet is without honor in his own family, that's what he said."

"Simon isn't a prophet, he's a crank."

"I don't care what he is. You don't get to meet someone like that in Minnesota. And he even wears sandals!"

It seemed she had found her bohemian at last. The sandals were another of my mother's presents. Like the photos of the cactus and the dunes, they were intended as souvenirs of distant Arizona.

After that, though Annette and I ate and slept within inches of each other, an abyss opened between us. There had never been the chance of a friendship. I was serious and diligent, she was not. I attended every class. Annette skipped most of hers. She could spurt instant tears. I was resolutely dry-hearted. Besides, I had my suspicions of people who liked to show off and imagined they could turn into Katharine Cornell, the famous actress. Annette spoke of "thespians" and "theater folk," and began parading in green lipstick and black stockings. But even this wore off after a time. She was starting to take her meals away from our flat. She kept a secret notebook with a mottled cover, bound by a strap connected to a purple sash tied around her waist. I had nothing to say to her, and when in a month or so she told me she had decided to move out ("I need to be with my own crowd," she explained), I was altogether relieved.

I was also troubled. I was afraid to risk another roommate: would my father agree to shouldering the full rent? I put this anxiety in a letter to Arizona; the answer came, unexpectedly, from my father, and not, as usual, in a jagged postscript below my mother's big round slanted Palmer-method penmanship. The extra money, he said, wouldn't be a problem. "Believe it or not," he wrote, "your mother thinks she's a rich woman, she's gone into business! There she was, collecting beaded belts and leather dolls, and God only knows what other cheap junk people like to pick up out here, and before I can look around, she's opened up this dinky little gift shop, and she's got these gullible out-of-staters paying good dollars for what costs your mother less than a dime. Trinkets! To tell the truth, I never knew she had this nonsense in her, and neither did she."

This time it was my mother who supplied the postscript— but I observed it had a later date, and I guessed she had mailed the letter without my father's having seen her addendum. It was a kind of judicial rider: she had put him in the dock. "I don't know why your dad is so surprised," she complained in a tone so familiar that I could almost hear her voice in the sprawl of her handwriting. "I've always had an artistic flair, whether or not it showed, and I don't much appreciate it when your dad puts me down like that, just because he's disillusioned with being stuck out here. He says he's sick and tired of it and misses home, but I don't, and my gallery is already beginning to look like a success, it's all authentic Hopi work! But that's the way your dad is—anywhere there's culture and ambition, he just has to put it down. For years he did it to Simon, and now he's doing it to me. And Phyllis dear, speaking of Simon, he ought to be eating his greens. I hope you're remembering to bring him a salad now and then." A fifty-dollar bill dropped out of the envelope.

That my mother was writing to me without my father's knowledge did not disturb me. It was of a piece with her long-ago attempts to conceal our attendance at Simon's old meetings. But I felt the heat of my guilt: I had neglected Simon, I hadn't looked in on him for . . . I hardly knew how many weeks it might have been. Weeks, surely; two months, three? I resented those visits; I resented the responsibility my mother had cursed me with. Simon was worse than a crank and a bore. He was remote from my youth and my life. I thought of him as a bad smell, like his icebox.

But I obediently chopped up lettuce and cucumber and green peppers, and poured a garlic-and-oil dressing over all of it. Then, with the fifty-dollar bill well wrapped in waxed paper and inserted into a folded piece of cardboard with a rubber band around it, I went to see Simon. Two flights below the landing that led to his place I could already hear the commotion vibrating out of it: an incomprehensible clamor, shreds of laughter, and a strangely broken wail that only vaguely passed for a chant. The door was open; I looked in. A mob of acolytes was swarming there—no, not swarming after all: in the tiny square of Simon's parlor, with its sofa-bed in one corner and its makeshift pantry, a pair of wooden crates, in the other, there was hardly a clear foot of space to accommodate a swarming. Yet what I saw through a swaying tangle of elbows and legs had all the buzz and teeming of a hive: a squatting, a slouching, a splaying, a leaning, a curling up, a lying down. And in the center of this fleshy oscillation, gargling forth the syllables of GNU, stood Annette. She stood like a risen tower, solid as bricks. She seemed to be cawing—croaking, crackling, chirring—though in the absence of anything intelligible, how was it possible to tell? Were these the sounds and cadences of the universal tongue? I could not admit surprise: from the start Annette had been so much my unwanted destiny. What else could she be now, having materialized here, in the very bosom of GNU? Or, if she wasn't to be *my* destiny, she intended to be Simon's. She was resurrecting his old meetings—it was plain from the spirit of the thing that this wasn't the first or the last. Anyhow it was flawed. No enemies lurked among these new zealots, if they were zealots at all.

At that time there were faddists of various persuasions proliferating up and down the Village, anarchists who dutifully went home every night to their mothers' kitchens, a Hungarian monarchist with his own following, free-verse poets who eschewed capital letters, cultists who sat rapturously for hours in orgone boxes, cloudy Swedenborgians, and all the rest. These crazes never tempted me; my early exposure to Simon's fanatics had been vaccination enough. As for where Annette had fetched this current crew, I supposed they were picked up from the looser margins of her theater crowd. There were corroboratory instances, here and there, of black stockings and green lipstick. And no Esperantists. Zamenhof was as alien to these recruits as—well, as GNU had been two months ago. Not one of them would have been willing to knock Simon down.

Annette lifted her face from her mottled notebook. All around her the wriggling knots of torsos turned inert and watchful.

"Oh my God, it's Phyllis," she said. "What're you doing here? Can't you see we're in the middle of things, we're *work*ing?"

"I'm just bringing a green salad for my uncle—"

"Little Green Riding Hood, how sweet. She's not his actual *niece*," Annette explained to the mob. "She doesn't give a hoot about him. Hey, Phyl, you don't think we'd let a man like that starve? And if you want to know what a real green salad looks like, here's a green salad." She swooped to the floor and swept up a large straw basket (yet another of my mother's souvenirs) heaped with verdant dollars. "This week's dues," she told me.

I surveyed the bodies at my feet, sorting among them. "Where is he?"

"Simon? Not here. Thursday's his day away, but he gave us the new words last time, so we carry on. We do little dialogues, we're getting the hang of it. We're his pioneers," she declaimed: Katharine Cornell to the hilt.

"And then it'll spread all over," a voice called out.

"There, you see?" Annette said. "Some people understand. Poor Phyl's never figured it out. Simon's going against the Bible, he's an atheist."

"Is that what he tells you?"

"You are *such* a dope," she spat out. "The Tower of Babel's why he got to thinking about GNU in the first place, wasn't it? So that things would go back to the way they were. The way it was before."

"Before what? Before they invented lunatic asylums? Look," I said, "as far as I'm concerned Simon's not exactly right in the head, so I'm supposed to—" But I broke off shamefacedly. "I have to watch out for him, he's sort of my responsibility."

"As far as you're concerned? How far is that? How long's it been since you showed up anyhow?"

Annette, I saw, was shrewder than I could ever hope to be. She was stupid and she was earnest. The stupidity would last; the earnestness might be fleeting, but the combination ignited a volcanic purposefulness: she had succeeded in injecting a bit of living tissue into Simon's desiccated old fossil. She was a first-rate organizer. I wondered how much of that weekly green salad she took away with her. And why not? It was a commission on dues. It was business.

"Where *is* he?" I insisted. I was still holding the bowl of cut vegetables, and all at once discovered a tremor in my hands: from fury, from humiliation.

"He went to visit a family member. That's what he said."

"A family member? There aren't any around here, there's only me."

"He goes every Thursday, I guess to see his wife."

"His ex-wife. He's been divorced for years."

"Well, *he* didn't want that divorce, did he? He's a man who *likes* being affectionate—maybe not to you. He gives back what he's given, that's why, and believe me he doesn't need you to turn up with your smelly old veggies once in a blue moon." Behind her the mob was breaking up. It was distracted, it was annoyed, it was impatient, it was uprooted, it was stretching its limbs. It was growling, and not in the universal tongue. "Just look what you've done," Annette accused, "barging in like that. We were doing so beautifully, and now you've broken the spell."

Circumspectly, I wrote the news to my mother. I had been to Simon's flat, I said, and things were fine. They were boiling away. His old life had nicely recommenced: he had a whole new set of enthusiasts. His work was reaching the next generation; he even had an agent to help him out. I did not tell her that I hadn't in fact *seen* Simon, and I didn't dare hint that he might be courting Essie again: wasn't that what Annette had implied? Nor did I confess that I had unwrapped the fifty-dollar bill and kept it for myself. I had no right to it; it couldn't count as a commission. I had done nothing for Simon. I had failed my mother's charge.

My mother's reply was long in coming. In itself this was odd enough: I had expected an instant happy outcry. With lavish deception I had depicted Simon's triumphant renewal, the future of GNU assured, crowds of mesmerized and scholarly young people streaming to his lectures—several of which, I lied, were held in the Great Hall of Cooper Union, at the very lectern Lincoln himself had once sanctified.

And it was only Annette, it was only the Village revolving on its fickle wheel: soon the mob would be spinning away to the next curiosity.

But my mother was on a wheel of her own. She was whirling on its axle, and Simon was lately at the distant perimeter. Her languorously sweeping Palmer arches were giving way to crabbed speed. She was out of time, she informed me, she had no time, no time at all, it was good to hear that Simon was doing well, after all these years he was finally recovered from that fool Essie, that witch who had always kept him down, but so much was happening, happening so fast, the gallery was flooded with all these tourists crazy for crafts, the place was wild, she was exhausted, she'd had to hire help, and meanwhile, she said, your father decided to retire, it was all to the good, she needed him in the gallery, and yes, he had his little pension, that was all right, never mind that it was beside the point, there was so much stock and it sold so fast that she'd had to buy the building next door to store whatever came in, and what came in went out in a day, and your father, can you imagine, was keeping the books and calling himself Comptroller, she didn't care what he called himself, they were importing like mad, all these kachina dolls from Japan, they certainly *look* like the real thing, the customers don't know the difference anyhow . . .

It seemed she was detaching herself from Simon. The kachinas had freed her. I was not sorry that I had deceived her; hadn't she taught me how to deceive? For my part, I had no desire to look after Simon. He was hokum. He was snake oil. What may have begun as a passion had descended into a con. Simon's utopia was now no more than a Village whim, and Annette its volatile priestess. But what had Essie, sewing her old eyes out in the lint-infested back room of a neighborhood haberdashery, to do with any of it—on Thursdays or any other day? She had thrown him out, and for reason. I surmised that along with Simon's infidelities she had thrown out her fidelity to GNU. How many strapping young Annettes had he cosseted over the decades?

I did not go back to Simon's place. I did what I could to chuck him out of my thoughts—but there were reminders and impediments. My mother in her galloping prosperity had taken to sending large checks. The money was no longer for Simon, she assured me; I had satisfied her that he was launched on what, in my telling, was a belated yet flowering career. The money was for me: for tuition and rent and textbooks, of course, but also for new dresses and shoes, for the movies, for treats. With each check—they were coming now in scrappy but frequent maternal rushes—Simon poked a finger in my eye. He invaded, he abraded, he gnawed. I began to see that I would never be rid of him. Annette and her mob would drop him. He would fall from her eagle's claws directly into my unwilling hands. And still I would not go back.

Instead I went down into the subway at Astor Place (where, across a broad stretch of intersection, loomed my lie: the venerable red brick of Cooper Union), and headed for the Bronx and Essie. I found her where time had left her, in apartment 2-C on the second floor of the old walkup. It was not surprising that she did not recognize me. We had last met when I was twelve and a half; emulating my mother, I had been reliably rude.

"You're who?" She peered warily through the peephole. On my side I saw a sad brown eye startled under its drooping hood.

"It's Phyllis," I said. "Ruby and Dan's daughter. From down the block."

"They left the neighborhood years ago. I don't know where they went. Ask somebody else."

"Essie, it's *Phyllis*," I repeated. "My mother used to take me to hear Uncle Simon."

She let me in then, and at the same time let out the heavy quick familiar sigh I instantly recognized: as if some internal calipers had pinched her lung. She kept her look on me fixedly yet passively, like someone sitting in a movie house, waiting for the horses on the screen to rear up.

"How about that, Simon's cousin's kid," she said. "Your mother never liked me."

"Oh no, I remember how she admired your singing—"

"She admired Simon. She thought he was the cat's pajamas. Like every other female he ever got near, the younger the better. I wouldn't put it past him if he had some girlie in his bed right now, wherever he is."

"But he comes to see you, and he wouldn't if he didn't want to be"—I struggled for the plainest word—"together. Reconciled, I mean. At his age. Now that he's . . . older."

"He comes to see me? Simon?" The horses reared up in her eyes. "Why would he want to do that after all this time?"

I had no answer for this. It was what I had endured an hour or more in the subway to find out. If Simon could be restored to Essie, then—as Annette had pronounced—things would go back to the way they once were. The Tower of Babel had nothing to do with it; it was rather a case of Damocles' sword, Simon's future dangling threateningly over mine. I wanted him back in the Bronx. I wanted him reinstalled in 2-C. I wanted Essie to claim him.

Her rooms had the airless smell of the elderly. They were hugely overfurnished—massive, darkly oiled pieces, china figurines on every surface. A credenza was littered with empty bobbins and crumpled-up tissue paper. An ancient sewing machine with a wrought-iron treadle filled half a wall; the peeling bust of a mannequin was propped against it. In the bedroom a radio was playing; through spasms of static I heard fragments of opera. Though it was a mild Sunday afternoon in early May, all the windows were shut—despite which, squads of flies were licking their feet along the flanks of the sugar bowl. The kitchen table (Essie had led me there) was covered with blue-flowered oilcloth, cracked in places, so that the canvas lining showed through. I waved the flies away. They circled just below the ceiling for an idling minute, then hurled themselves against the panes like black raindrops. The smell was the smell of stale changelessness.

Essie persisted, "Simon hasn't been here since never mind how long it is. Since the divorce. He never comes."

"Not on Thursdays?" The question hung in all its foolishness. "I heard he goes to visit family, so I thought—"

"I'm not Simon's family, not anymore. I told you, I haven't seen him in years. Where would you get an idea like that?"

"From . . . his assistant. He has an assistant now. A kind of manager. She sets up his meetings."

"His manager, his assistant, that's what he calls them. Then he goes out and diddles them. And how come he's still having those so-called meetings? Who's paying the bills?" She coughed out a disordered laugh that was half a viscous sigh. "Those famous Park Avenue moneybags?"

The laugh was too big for her body. Her bones had contracted, leaving useless folds of puckered fallen skin. Her hands were horribly veined.

"Listen, girlie," she said, "Simon doesn't come, nobody comes. I do a fitting for a neighbor, I sew up a hem, I put in a pocket, that's who comes. A bunch of the old Esperantists used to show up, this was when Simon left, but then it stopped. By now they're probably dead. The whole thing is dead. It's a wonder Simon isn't dead."

The flies had settled back on the sugar bowl. I stood up to leave. Nothing could be clearer: there would be no reconciliation. 2-C would not see Simon again.

But Essie was pulling at my sleeve. "Don't think I don't know where he goes anyhow. Maybe not Thursdays, who could figure Thursdays, but every week he goes there. He always goes there, it never stops."

"Where?"

I asked it reluctantly. Was she about to plummet me into a recitation of Simon's history of diddlings? Did she think me an opportune receptacle for an elderly divorcée's sour old grievances?

"Why should I tell you where? What have you got to do with any of it? Simon never told your mother, he never told anyone, so why should I tell *you*? Sit down," she commanded. "You want something to drink? I've got Coca-Cola."

The bottle had been opened long ago. The glass was smudged. I felt myself ensnared by a desolate hospitality. Having got what I came for—or not having got it—I wanted to hear nothing more.

But she had my arm in her grip. "At my time of life I'm not still squatting down there in the back room of somebody's pants store, you understand? I've got my own little business, I do my fittings right here in my own dining room. The point is I'm someone who can make a living. I could always make a living. My God, your mother was gullible! What wouldn't she believe, she swallowed it all."

My mother gullible? She who was at that very hour gulling her tourists into buying Pueblo artifacts factory-made in Japan?

"If you mean she believed in Simon—"

"She believed everything." She released me then, and sank

into a deflecting whisper. "She believed what happened to the baby."

So it was not simple grievance that I took from Essie that afternoon. It was broader and deeper and wilder and stranger. And what she was deflecting—what she was repudiating as trivia and trifle, as pettiness and quibble—was Simon and his diddlings. He had his girlies—his assistants, his managers—and for all she cared, staring me down, wasn't I one of them? No, he wouldn't go so far as his cousin's kid, and even if he did, so what? It hardly interested her anyhow that I was his cousin's kid, the offspring of a simple-minded woman, an imbecile who would believe anything, who swallowed it all, a chump for any hocus-pocus . . .

"Ruby had her kid," she said—torpidly, as though reciting an algebraic equation—"she had *you*, and by then what did I have? An empty crib, and then nothing, nothing, empty—"

When I left Essie four hours later, I knew what had happened to the baby. At Astor Place I ascended, parched and hungry, from the subway's dark into the dark of nine o'clock: she had offered me nothing but that stale inch of Coke. Instead she had talked and talked, loud and low, in her mouselike whisper, too often broken into by her big coarse bitter croak of a laugh. It *was* a joke, she assured me, it was a joke and a trick, and now I would know what a gullible woman my mother was, how easy it was to deceive her; how easy it was to trick the whole world. She clutched at me, she made me her muse, she gave me her life. She made me *see*, and why? Because her child was dead and I was not, or because my mother was a gullible woman, or because there were flies in the room? Who could really tell why? I had fallen in on her out of the blue, out of the ether, out of the past (it wasn't *my* past, I hadn't come to be anyone's muse, I had only come to dispose of Simon): I was as good, for giving out her life, as a fly on the wall. And did I want her to sing? She could still sing some stanzas in GNU, she hadn't forgotten how.

I did not ask her to sing. She had hold of me with her finger-nails in my flesh, as if I might escape. She drew me back, back, into her young womanhood, when she was newly married to Simon, with Retta already two months in the womb and Simon in his third year at City College, far uptown, dreaming of philology, that funny-sounding snobby stuff (as if a boy from the Bronx could aspire to such goings-on!), unready for marriage and fatherhood, and seriously unwilling. And that was the first of all the jokes, because finally the other boy, the one from Cincinnati who was visiting his aunt (the aunt lived around the corner), and who met Essie in the park every night for a week, went home to Ohio . . . She didn't tell Simon about that other boy, the curly-haired boy who pronounced all his *r*'s the midwestern way; even under the wedding canopy Simon had no inkling of the Ohio boy. He believed only that he was behaving as a man should behave who has fathered a child without meaning to. It was the first of all the jokes, the first of all the tricks, but the joke was on herself too, since she was just as much in the dark as anyone: was Retta's papa the Ohio boy, or Simon? Simon had to leave school then, and went to work as a salesman in a men's store on East Tremont Avenue. Essie had introduced him to her boss; she was adept with a needle, and had already been shortening trousers and putting in pleats and letting out waists for half a year.

Their first summer they did what in those days all young couples with new babies did. They fled the burning Bronx sidewalks, they rented a *kochaleyn* in the mountains, in one of those Catskill bungalow colonies populated by musty one-room cottages set side by side, no more than the width of a clothes line between them. Every cottage had its own little stove and icebox and tiny front porch. The mothers and babies spent July and August in the shade of green leaves, among wild tiger lilies as orange as the mountain sunsets, and the fathers came up from the city on weekends, carrying bundles of bread and rolls and oily packets of pastries and smoked whitefish. It was on one of these weekends that Essie decided to tell Simon the joke about the baby, it was so much on her mind, and she thought it would be all right to tell him now because he liked the baby so much, he was mad about Retta, and the truth is the truth, so why not? She had been brought up to tell the truth, even if sometimes the truth is exactly like a joke.

But he did not take it as a joke. He took it as a trick, and for the next two weekends he kept away. Essie, alone with her child and humiliated, went wandering through the countryside, discovering who her neighbors were, and what sort of colony they'd happened into. All the roads were plagued by congregations of wasps, and once the baby, pointing and panting, spied a turtle creeping in the dust. They followed the turtle across the road, and found a community of Trotskyites, beyond which, up the hill, were the Henry George people, and down toward the village a nest of Tolstoyans. Whoever they were, they all had rips in their clothes, they all required mending, they all wanted handmade baby dresses, they all had an eye on styles for the fall, and Essie's summertime business was under way.

When Simon returned, out of sorts, Essie informed him that in the interim she had taken in fifty-four dollars and twenty-five cents, she could get plenty more if only she had a sewing machine, and besides all that, there was a peculiar surprise that might interest him: next door on one side, next door on the other, and all around, behind them and in front of them—why hadn't she noticed it sooner? but she was preoccupied with the baby, and now with the sewing—their neighbors were chattering in a kind of garble. Sometimes it sounded like German, sometimes like Spanish (it never sounded like Yiddish), and sometimes like she didn't know what. Groups of them were gathering on the little porches, which were no more than leaky wooden lean-tos; they seemed to be studying; they were constantly exchanging comments in their weird garble. They even spoke the weird garble to their older children, who rolled their eyes and answered in plain English.

Which was how Simon fell in among the Esperantists. Bella was one of them. She lived four cottages down, and had a little boy a month or two older than Retta. Julius, her husband, turned up only rarely; his job, whatever it was, kept him at work right through the weekend. Bella ordered a dimity blouse and a flowered skirt (dirndl was the fashion) and came often to sit with Essie while she diligently sewed. The two babies, with their pull toys and plush bears, prattled and crowed at their feet. It was a pleasant time altogether, and Simon, when he arrived from the city, seeing the young women sweetly side by side with their children crawling all around them, seemed no longer out of sorts. He was silent now about Essie's deception, if it *was* a deception, because, after all, Essie herself wasn't certain, and the boy from Ohio was by now only a moment's vanished vapor. Besides, Retta's pretty curls were as black and billowy as Simon's own, and Essie was earning money, impressively more than Simon would ever make selling men's underwear in the Bronx. One August afternoon he arranged to have a second-hand sewing machine delivered to the cottage. Essie jumped up and kissed him, she was so pleased; it was as if the sleek metal neck of the sewing machine had restored them to each other.

After that Essie's orders increased, and on Saturday and Sunday mornings, while she worked her treadle, Simon went round to one porch or another, happy in the camaraderie of the Esperantists. They were eager for converts, of course, and he wanted nothing so much as to be converted. Of all of them, Bella was the most advanced. She was not exactly their leader, but she was an expert teacher, and actually had in her possession a letter of praise from Lidia Zamenhof, Zamenhof's own daughter and successor. Bella had sent her a sonnet in fluent Esperanto; Lidia replied that Bella's ingenuity in creating rhyming couplets in the new language remarkably exceeded that of Ludwik Zamenhof himself. There was nothing concerning Esperanto that Bella did not know; she knew, for instance, that the Oomoto religion in Japan held Esperanto to be a sacred language and Zamenhof a god. Zamenhof a god! Simon was entranced; Essie thought he envied Bella even more than he was inspired by her. Also, she felt a little ashamed. It was all those outlandish words Simon loved, he was possessed by them, words had always been his *ambition*, and on account of his wife and the child whose hair was as black and thick as his own he had been compelled to surrender words for a life of shirts and ties, boxer shorts and suspenders.

So when Bella asked Essie to take charge of her little boy for just two hours that evening—perhaps he could be put to bed together with Retta, and Bella would come to fetch him afterward—Essie gladly took the child in her arms, and stroked his warm silky nape, and did the same with Retta, whose nape was every bit as silky, and sang both babies to sleep, while Simon walked with Bella through the grassy dusk to be tutored in the quiet of her porch. An electric cord led indoors; there was a lamp and a table and a bottle of citronella to ward off the mosquitoes and (the point of it all) Bella's weighty collection of Esperanto journals.

It was more than the two hours Bella had promised (it was closer to five, and the crickets had retired into their depth-of-night silence) when she and Simon returned. Simon had under his arm a fat packet of Bella's journals, borrowed to occupy his empty weekday evenings in the city; but it was Bella, not Simon, who explained this. Essie had fallen into a doze in the old stained armchair next to the big bed—Simon and Essie's marital bed—where she had set the babies down, nestled together under one blanket. Retta's crib was too narrow for the two of them; they lay head to head, their round foreheads nearly touching, breathing like a single organism. Bella looked down at her sleeping boy, and murmured that it was a pity to take him out into the cold night air, he was so snug, why wake him, and could she leave him there until morning? She would arrive early to carry him off, and in the meantime wasn't Essie comfortable enough right where she was, in that nice chair, and Simon wouldn't mind a cushion on the floor, would he, it would only be for a few more hours . . .

Bella went away, and it was as if she had plotted to keep Simon from Essie that night. But surely this was a worthless imagining: settling into his cushion at Essie's feet, Simon was fixed with all the power and thirst of his will on Bella's journals; he intended to study them until he could rival Bella, he meant to pursue and conquer the language that was to be humanity's salvation, the structure of it, its strange logic and beauty, and already tonight, he said, he had made a good beginning—and then, without a sign, in the middle of it all, he sent out a soft snore, a velvety vibrating hum. Haplessly alert now, Essie tried not to follow her thoughts. But the night was long, there was so much left of it, and the mountain chill crept round her shoulders, and except for the private voice inside her, a voice that nagged with all its secret confusions, there was nothing to listen to—only one of the babies turning, and Simon's persistent dim hum. She went on listening, she wasn't the least bit drowsy, she forced her eyelids shut and they clicked wide again, of their own accord, like a mechanical doll's. Simon's hum—was it roughening into a wheeze, or something more brutish than a wheeze? A spiraling unnatural noise; an animal being strangled. But the animal noise wasn't coming from Simon, it was hurtling out of one of the babies—a groaning, and then a yowling—good God, was it Retta? No, no, not Retta, it was Bella's boy! She leaped up to see what was the matter: the child's face was mottled, purple and red, his mouth leaked vomit, he was struggling to breathe . . . She touched his head. It was wildly hot: a tropical touch.

"Simon!"

She pummeled him awake.

"There's something wrong, you have to get down to the village right away, you have to get to the doctor's, the boy's sick—"

"It's the middle of the night, Essie, for God's sake! Bella's coming for the kid first thing, and maybe by then it'll pass—"

"Simon, I'm telling you, he's *sick*—"

In those uncomplicated years none of the *kochaleyns* had a telephone, and few of the families owned cars. On Friday evenings the husbands, Simon among them, made their way up the mountainside from the train station by means of the one ancient village taxi, or else they trudged with their suitcases and their city bundles along the mile of dusty stone-strewn road, between high weedy growths, uphill to the colonies of cottages. The village itself was only a cluster of stores on either side of the train station, and a scattering of old houses inhabited by the year-round people. The doctor was one of these. His office was in his front parlor.

"Go!" Essie cried. Then she thought of the danger to Retta, so close to the feverish child, and seized her and nearly threw her, sobbing, and awakened now by the excitement, into her crib; but the thin little neck under the moistly knotted curls was cool.

"I ought to stop at Bella's, don't you think, and let her know—"

"No, no, don't waste a minute, what's the point, what can she do? Oh listen to him, you've got to hurry, the poor thing can't catch his breath—"

"It's Bella's kid, she'll know what to do," he urged. "It's happened before."

"What makes you think that?"

"Bella told me. She said it in Esperanto actually, when we were working on it last week—"

"Never mind that gibberish, just go and get the doctor!"

Gibberish. She had called the universal language, the language of human salvation, gibberish.

He started down the road to the village: it meant he had to pass Bella's cottage. Her windows were unlit, and he went on. But a few yards beyond her door, he stopped and turned back—how perverse it seemed, how unreasonable, it wasn't right not to tell the mother, and probably the kid would get better anyhow, it was a long walk down the mountain in the dark and cold of the country night, Essie had hurried him out without so much as a sweater, and why wake the poor doctor, a doctor needs his sleep even more than ordinary people, why not hold off till morning, a decent hour, wasn't the main thing to let Bella know?

And here, waiting and waiting, was Essie, with the boy folded in her lap; she kept him there, in the big armchair, lifting him at times (how heavy he was!) to pace from one wall of the narrow room to the other. Now and then she wiped the soles of his feet with a dampened cloth, until he let out a little shudder—almost, it seemed, of satisfaction. But mainly she stood at the window, her wrists aching from the child's weight, watching the sky alter from an opaque square of black to a ghostly pinkish stripe. Retta had long since grown quiet: she lay in the tranquil ruddiness of waxworks sleep, each baby fist resting beside an ear. And finally the white glint of morning struck the windowsill and lit the walls; and at half past eight the doctor came, together with Simon and Bella. He had driven them both up from the village in his Ford. The child was by now perfectly safe, he said, there was nothing the matter that he wouldn't get over, and wasn't the mother told repeatedly not to feed him milk? Her son was clearly allergic to milk, and still she had forgotten, and put some in his pudding.

"You know your boy's had these episodes before," the doctor said, peevishly, "and he may have them again. Because, dear lady, you don't *listen*."

And Bella, apologizing, said, "It's a good thing anyhow we didn't drag you out of your bed at three o'clock in the morning, the way some people would have—"

Essie knew what "some people" meant, but who was "we"?

"While I'm here," the doctor said, "I suppose I ought to have a look at the other one."

"She's fine," Essie said. "She slept through the rest of the night like an angel. Just look, she's still asleep—"

The doctor looked. He shook Retta. He picked up her two fists; they fell back.

"Good God," the doctor said. "This child is dead."

They buried her on the outskirts of a town fifteen miles to the west, in a small nonsectarian cemetery run by an indifferent undertaker who sold them a dog-sized coffin. There was no ceremony; no one came, no one was asked to come. A private burial, a secret burial. In the late afternoon a workman dug out a cavity in the dry soil; down went the box. Simon and Essie stood alone at the graveside and watched as the shovelfuls of earth flew, until the ground was level again. Then they left the *kochaleyn* and for the rest of the summer rented a room not far from the cemetery. Simon went every day to sit beside the grave. At first Essie went with him; but after a while she stayed away. How he wailed, how he hammered and yammered! She could not endure it: too late, that spew, too late, his shame, his remorse, his disgrace: if only he'd gone earlier for the doctor . . . if only he hadn't stopped to see Bella . . . if only he hadn't told her the kid's all right, there's no emergency, my wife exaggerates, morning's time enough to bring the doctor . . . if only he hadn't knocked on Bella's door, if only she hadn't let him in!

In her flat whisper Essie said, "What happened to the baby, maybe it wouldn't have happened—"

She understood that Simon had become Bella's lover that night. She was silent when she saw him carry out Bella's journals and set them afire. The smell of Esperanto burning remained in his clothes for days afterward.

She did not know what the doctor could have done; she knew only that he hadn't been there to do it.

Summer after summer they returned to the town near the cemetery, far from all the *kochaleyns* that were scattered along the pebbly dirt roads in those parts, and settled into the top floor of a frame house owned by a deaf old widower. Simon never went back to his job in the men's store, but Essie kept busy at her sewing machine. She placed a two-line advertisement in the Classified column of the local paper—"Seamstress, Outfits Custom-Made"—and had more orders than ever. Simon no longer sat by the little grave every day; instead, he turned his vigil into a driven penance, consecrating one night each week to mourning. Their first year it was Saturday—it was on a Saturday night that Retta had died. The following year it was Tuesday: Simon had burned Bella's journals on a Tuesday evening. Always, whatever the day and whatever the year and whatever the weather, he walked out into the midnight dark, and lingered there, among the dim headstones, until daybreak. Essie had no use for this self-imposed ritual. It was made up, it was another kind of gibberish out there in the night. She scorned it: what did it mean, this maundering in the cemetery's rime to talk to the wind? He had deceived her with Bella, he had allowed Retta to die. Essie never spoke of Retta; only Simon spoke of her. He remembered her first steps, he remembered her first words, he remembered how she had pointed with her tiny forefinger at this and that beast at the zoo. "Tiger," she said. "Monkey," she said. And when they came to the yellow-horned gnu, and Simon said "Gnu," Retta, mistaking it for a cow, blew out an elongated "Moo." And how Simon and Essie had laughed at that! Retta was dead; Simon was to blame, he had deceived her with Bella, and what difference now if he despised Bella, if he had made a bonfire of Bella's journals, if he despised everything that smacked of Bella, if he despised Esperanto, and condemned it, and called it delusion and fakery—what difference all of that, if Retta was dead?

It was not their first summer, but the next, when Simon was setting aside Tuesdays to visit his shrine ("His shrine," Essie said bitterly to herself), that he began writing letters to Esperanto clubs all over the city, all over the world—nasty letters, furious letters. "Zamenhof, your false idol! Your god!" he wrote. "Why don't you join the Oomoto, you fools!"

This was the start of Simon's grand scheme—the letters, the outcries, the feverish heaps of philological papers and books with queer foreign alphabets on their spines. Yet in practice it was not grand after all; it was extraordinarily simple to execute. Obscure lives inspire no inquisitiveness. If your neighbor tells you he was born in Pittsburgh when he was really born in Kalamazoo, who will trouble to search out his birth certificate? As for solicitous—or prying—relations, Essie had been motherless since childhood, and her father had remarried a year after her own marriage to Simon. Together with his new wife he ran a hardware store in Florida; he and Essie rarely corresponded. Simon himself had been reared in the Home for Jewish Orphans: his only living connection was his cousin Ruby—gullible Ruby, booby Ruby! The two of them, Simon and Essie, were as rootless as dandelion spores. They had to account to no one, and though Simon continued jobless, there was money enough, as long as Essie's treadle purred. She kept it purring: her little summertime business spread to half a dozen towns nearby, and her arrival in May was regularly greeted by a blizzard of orders for the following autumn. She changed her ad to read "Get Set for Winter Warmth in Summer Heat," and had an eye out for the new styles in woolen jackets and coats. She bought, at a discount, discarded pieces of chinchilla and learned to sew fur collars and linings. And all the while Simon was concocting GNU. He named it, he said, in memory of Retta at the zoo; and besides, it announced itself to the ear as New—only see how it superseded and outshone Esperanto, that fake old carcass!

In the fall of each year they moved back to the Bronx. By now Essie owned two sewing machines. "My city Singer and my country Singer," she liked to say, and in the winter worked her treadle as tirelessly as in the summer, while Simon went out proselytizing. He printed up fliers on yellow paper, with long rows of sponsors—lists that were anonymous but for their golden Park Avenue addresses—and tacked them on telephone poles.

It was not surprising, Essie thought, that GNU could attract its earliest adherents—all the *kochaleyns* come home for the winter, and more: the Trotskyites, the Henry George people, the Tolstoyans, the classical music lovers who went to the free concerts at Lewisohn Stadium, the Norman Thomas loyalists, the Yiddish Bundists, the wilder Hebraists, the evolving Thomas Merton mystics, the budding young Taoists and Zen Buddhists, the aging humanists and atheists, the Ayn Rand enthusiasts . . . and, most dangerously, the angry Esperantists. But after the first few meetings, too many of Simon's would-be converts fell away, the merely inquisitive to begin with, the rest out of boredom, or resentment over dues, or because the rental hall was unheated (the stinginess of those Park Avenue donors!), or because the accustomed messianisms they had arrived with were more beguiling than Simon's ingrown incantations.

"What these people need to keep them interested," Simon argued, "is entertainment. If it's a show they want, Essie, let's give them a show, how about it?"

So Essie was recruited to sing. She had not immediately agreed; the idea of it repelled her, but only until she perceived the use of it; the ruse of it. She was already complicit in Simon's scheme—give your little finger to the devil, and he'll take your whole arm. And even the little finger was not so spare: no matter what Simon's yellow fliers boasted, it was Essie's industry at her two sewing machines that paid for the rental hall. Well then, all right, she'd sing! It turned out, besides, that she had a way with a rhyme. Her rhymes were inconsequential ditties, private mockeries—the latest of her mockeries: the Park Avenue philanthropists were the first of her inventions. As for her singing voice, it had no range, and she was nearly breathless at the close of a long verse, but she poured into it the fury and force of her ridicule, and her ridicule had the sound of conviction. She put herself in the service of Simon's gibberish—why not, why not? Retta was dead, Simon was to blame! Her performances in the cold hall—the costume, the patter, the ditties—were her own contraption, her secret derision, her revenge for what happened to the baby.

And still Simon's meetings shrank and shrank, until only the quarrelsome diehards remained, and Simon's enemies, the Esperantists.

"Jealousy!" he said. "Because I've outdone them, I've finished them off. And it's Bella who's sending them, it's got to be Bella, who else?"

But it was Essie. She knew where they were, she knew how to find them: she had helped Simon with all those letters calling them fools, she had written their names on the envelopes. Slyly, clandestinely, she summoned them, and they were glad to come, and stand on chairs, and stomp and chant and shriek and pound and threaten. Simon, that usurper, with his shabby homemade mimicry of the real thing, had called them fools! They were pleased to shout him down, and some were even pleased to put up their fists in defense of the sole genuine original universal language, Zamenhof's! Essie herself gave the signal: when she ended those nonsensical couplets, when she hopped off the little podium, the assault began.

She let it go on, winter after winter, with the summer's expeditions to look forward to. From a secondhand bookshop she bought herself a world atlas, and instructed Simon in latitudes and longitudes, all those remote wadis and glaciers and canyons and jungles and steppes he was to explore from May through August (she always with him on every trek, never mind how hazardous), all for the purpose of uncovering fresh syllables to feed and fatten his GNU—while here they sat, the two of them, from May through August, lapping up their suppers of bananas and sour cream at the kitchen counter, half of which held Essie's faithful Singer, on the top floor of the deaf old widower's decaying house.

She let it go on, the meetings winter after winter in the

city, in the summers hidden away in their mountain townlet close to Retta's grave. She let it go on until it was enough, until her mockery was slaked, until the warring Esperantists had left him sufficiently bruised to satisfy her. There was more to it than spite, the almost carnal relishing of spite, the gloating pleasure of punishing Simon with his own stick. It was the fantastical stick itself: Essie's trickster apparatus, the hoax of those exotic wanderings, when all the world—simple-minded, credulous world!—believed them to be . . . where? Wherever Dravido-Munda, Bugi, Veps, Brahui, Khowar, Oriya, Ilokano, Mordvinian, Shilha, Jagatai, Tipura, Yurak, and all other teeming tongues, were spoken. From May through August, Essie's atlas marked out these shrewdly distant regions; and on a Tuesday, or a Sunday, or any chosen day of the week, Simon moaned out his gibberish beside Retta's grave in the misty night air.

It did not take long for Annette and her crowd to tire of GNU. They cleared out, I learned afterward, on one of those Thursdays that took Simon conveniently away: there were no goodbyes. When I went to see him again, he was alone. This time, and all the times that followed, I was not prodded by my mother. Her mind was on business; she trusted that Simon was still, as she put it, *blooming*, and I did not disabuse her. She too, she reported, was blooming like mad—it was no longer economical to import the kachinas, so she had gone into producing them on her own. She'd bought up a bit more property, and had a little factory buzzing away, which made not only replicas of the dolls, but all manner of other presumably local artifacts, shawls no Indian had ever worn, moccasins no Indian had ever trod in. Many of these she had designed herself ("I do have this flair," she reminded me), and to tell the truth, they were an improvement on the raw-looking native stuff. My father wrote often, asking when I was coming out for a visit, since from my mother's point of view a trip to New York was out of the question: they had their hands full, the business was so demanding. I answered with commonplace undergraduate complaints—I had too many papers overdue, catching up would consume the

winter break, and as for vacation later in the year, I was intending to take courses all summer long.

I was becoming an easy liar. My papers were not overdue. I
was reluctant to witness my mother's pride in turning out fakes.

The checks she continued to send (with my father's signature
over "Comptroller" in print) grew bigger and bigger. I cashed
them and gave the money to Simon. He took it sadly, idly,
without protest. He was unshaven and wore his sandals on bare
feet. His toenails were overgrown and as thick as oyster shells.
His breath was bad; he had an abscess on a molar that sometimes
tormented him and sometimes receded. I begged him to see a
dentist. Little by little I had begun to look after him. I tipped
the grocery boy and hired the janitor to take a brush to the
toilet bowl. He had given up those fruitless hours among alien
lexicons; but every Thursday he put on his frayed city hat, with
its faded grosgrain ribbon, and locked the door of his flat and
did not return until late the next afternoon. I imagined him in
a rattling train headed upstate, toward a forgotten town in the
Catskills; I imagined him kneeling in the dark in damp grass
alongside a small stone marker. I went so far as to conjecture
what Thursday might commemorate to a mind as deluded as
Simon's: suppose it was on a Thursday that Essie had confessed
her doubts about the baby; suppose it was on a Thursday that
Simon first heard about the curly-haired boy from Cincinnati—then the grieving guilty mourner at the graveside might
not be a father at all, but only the man Essie had gulled into
marriage long ago. If he did not know which one he was, the
father or the dupe, why should he not be half mad?

And what if everything Essie had confided was a fickle fable,
myself (like those flies to her sugar bowl) lured into it, a partner
to Simon's delusions?

The sophomore term began. One morning on my way to
class I saw, across the street, Annette and two young men. The
men were dressed in gray business suits and striped ties and
had conventional short haircuts. All three were carrying leather
briefcases. Annette herself looked less theatrical than I remembered her, though I could not think why. She wore a silk scarf
and sober shoes with sharp little heels.

"Hey, Phyl," she called. "How's your uncle nowadays?"

Unwillingly, I crossed the street.

"Tim. John. My old roommate," she introduced me. Close up, I noticed the absence of lipstick. "Is Simon O.K.? I have to tell you, he changed my life."

"You wrecked his."

"Well, you were right, maybe I took him too seriously. But I got something out of it. I'm in the School of Commerce now. I've switched to accounting, I'm a finance major."

"Just like Katharine Cornell."

"No, really, I have this entrepreneurial streak. I figured it out just from running Simon's meetings."

"Sure, all that green salad," I said, and walked off.

I did not honestly believe that Annette had wrecked Simon's life. It was true that her defection had left him depleted, but some inner deterioration, from a source unknown to me, was gnawing at him. Perhaps it was age: he was turning into a sick old man. The tooth abscess, long neglected, had affected his heart. He suffered from repeated fits of angina and for relief swallowed handfuls of nitroglycerin. He implored me to visit more often; there were no more Thursdays away. I had come to suspect these anyhow—was it conceivable after so many decades that he would still be looking to set his thin haunches on the damp ground of a graveyard, and in snowy winter to boot? Had there been, instead, a once-a-week lover? One of those girlies he diddled? Or Bella, secretly restored? He had no lover now. When he put out a hand to me, it was no longer an attempt to feel for my breast. He hoped for comfort, he wanted to hold on to warmth. The old man's hand that took mine was bloodlessly cold.

I loitered with him through tedious afternoons. I brought him petit fours and tins of fancy tea. While he dozed over his cup, I emptied the leaves out of their gilt canister and filled it with hundred-dollar bills: froth and foam of my mother's fraudulent prosperity. I tried to wake him into alertness: I asked why he had stopped working on GNU.

"I haven't stopped."

"I don't see you *do*ing it—"

"I think about it. It's in my head. But lately . . . well, what good does it do, you can't beat the Esperantists. Zamenhof, that swindler, he had it all sewed up long ago, he cornered the market." He blinked repeatedly; he had acquired a distracting twitch. "Is Ruby getting on all right out there? I remember how she hated to go. You know," he said, "your mother was always steadfast. The only one who was steadfast was my cousin Ruby."

Some weeks after this conversation I went to see Essie; it would be for the last time.

"Simon's dead," I told her.

"Simon? How about that." She took it in with one of her shallow breathy sighs, and all at once blazed up into rage. "Who made the arrangements? Who! Was it you? If he's buried *there*, next to Retta, I swear I'll have him dug up and thrown out!"

"It's all right, my mother took care of it. On the telephone, long distance, from Arizona. He's over in Staten Island, my parents own some plots."

"Ruby took care of it? Well, at least that, *she* doesn't know where Retta is. She thinks it was Timbuktu, what happened to the baby. I've told you and told you, your silly mother never knew a thing—"

The apartment had its familiar smell. I had done what I came for, and was ready to leave. But I noticed, though the mannequin still kept its place against the wall, that the sewing machine was gone.

"I got rid of it. I sold it," she said. "I saved up, I've got plenty. There never was a time when I couldn't make a living, no matter what. Even after the divorce. But people came in those days, it was like a condolence call. I don't suppose anyone's coming now."

I said lamely, "I'm here."

"Ruby's kid, why should I care? I mean the Esperanto people, they're the ones who came. Because they saw I was against Simon. Some of them brought flowers, can you believe it?"

"If you were against him," I said, "why did you go along with everything?"

"I told you why. To get even."

"A funny way of getting even, if you did just what he wanted."

"My God, the apple doesn't fall far from the tree, just like your mother, blind as a bat. You don't think I'd let anybody know my own husband managed to kill off my own child right in my own bed, do you?"

She was all zigzag and contradiction: she had taken revenge on Simon; she had protected him. She was both sword and shield. Was this what an improvisational temperament added up to? I was certain now that no word Essie uttered could be trusted.

She had little more to say about Simon, and there was little more she cared to hear. But before I left she pushed her brownish face, wrinkled as a walnut, into mine, and told me something I have never forgotten.

"Listen," she said, "that goddamn universal language, you want to know what it is? Not Esperanto, and not Simon's gibberish either. I'll tell you, but only if you want to know."

I said I did.

"Everyone uses it," she said. "Everyone, all over the world."

And was that it really, what Essie gave out just then in her mercurial frenzied whisper? Lie, illusion, deception, she said—was that it truly, the universal language we all speak?

The Conversion of the Jews

> They lived in narrow streets and lanes obscure,
>   Ghetto and Judenstrass, in murk and mire;
> Taught in the school of patience to endure
>   The life of anguish and the death of fire. . . .
>
> Pride and humiliation hand in hand
>   Walked with them through the world
>   where'er they went;
> Trampled and beaten were they as the sand,
>   And yet unshaken as the continent.
> —HENRY WADSWORTH LONGFELLOW,
> "The Jewish Cemetery at Newport"

IN THE SUMMER of 1933, while traveling in a tour bus through the Judean desert, Solomon Adelberg, twenty-four years old, disembarked, hauled up his backpack, and ascended a hill where, halfway up, a medieval monastery was perched. Like many other resourceful Americans, he had arranged beforehand (the reply was in his pocket) for permission to visit. But he was not a sightseer on the hunt for souvenirs. He was an earnest student of philology. Also, he was very thin, as if he had devoured himself all the way down to the bone. Often his throat and his chest burned like ice. He knew his own character; he had decided, at least for the time being, to become a permanent celibate. It was more than enough that King Solomon, his namesake, was said to have had seven hundred wives.

By origin, the monastery was Dominican, a connection that had frayed more than two centuries ago. Only the library had survived the friars' long sleep, though barely; even its soporific dust, felled by time, failed to fly up. The monks were modern men, and entrepreneurs, and regarded themselves more as custodians of a tourist attraction than spiritual zealots. Many were widowers. To gratify the sightseers, their robes were black. The

library itself was an unfathomable sanctum they were barred
from, not by rule but by indifference.

The business of the monastery was the crafting of icons.
On china plates and mugs and bowls and teapots the monks
painted haloed images of saints, many genuine, others inspired
by invention. They worked from templates, filling in the lines,
like children with their coloring books. The buses stopped at
the foot of the hill, waited for their passengers to come down
with their purchases, and went on to Jerusalem, where still
more of the icons could be found in the Old City *shuks*. But
who would venture there? That year, all through Jerusalem, all
through the Holy Land, there was rioting.

Solomon Adelberg waved the bus on without him. He
had arrived as a researcher, and meant to stay (the monastery
charged hotel rates for a bed and no bath), though the likeli-
hood of discovery was almost nil. He was looking for the work
of a certain convert. It was intuition, guesswork, probability—
hope, in fact—that had brought him here. What he knew, what
every linguistic adept knew, was that an unrecorded portion of
Pablo Christiani's writings had been sent here for safekeeping
in the year 1265 by Pope Clement IV. Most were copies of
official declarations, but some were purported to be clandestine
and dangerous confessions.—Or were these hoary certainties
no better than mere wishfulness?

Pablo's history was fully preserved. Born into a pious Jewish
family, he was a Dominican friar dedicated to the conversion
of the Jews. He journeyed to all the synagogues of Aragon
to harangue, and if that fell short, to coerce, and if that too
appeared useless, to punish. He appealed to Clement to compel
the wearing of the Jew-badge. He ordered the confiscation of
Jewish books, most particularly the Talmud, to be burned to
ash in great smoldering heaps. Confident of his own mastery
of Jewish sources, he prevailed on King James of Aragon to
sponsor a public disputation in the royal palace in the great city
of Barcelona, under the scrutiny of the world: he alone would
confound Moshe ben Nachman, the most eminent Talmudist
of the age, second only to Maimonides, with proofs of the Gospels taken from the Talmud itself. But James judged the Jew

the winner, and the next day Moshe ben Nachman, accused of blasphemy, fled for his life to Acre in the Holy Land. The pope was more powerful than the king, and Pablo had the ear of the pope.

Solomon dismissed all this. He scorned the stale stuff of encyclopedias. It was to the mazy byways of the unspoken mind of Pablo Christiani that he was drawn. He was after impulses, inducements, animating subterranean drives. A philologist must be an excavator. So he had learned from his teacher, his mentor, the sovereign of his thought: tread where no one else has trod. The library was no more than a filthy niche in an old stone wall, crusted with the dung of rodents and bats. The monastery itself was defunct. Its archives were choked by the smell and the spew of heedless decay—no roster or index hinted at what it might hold. Shells of ancient generations of dead insects crackled under Solomon's soles. And his teacher too was dead.

After three days he gave up. As he was preparing to leave and was paying his bill, the abbot—and wasn't he also the sales manager?—asked whether he had found what he was looking for. Solomon said he had not. To ease his disappointment, the abbot offered him a discount if he would buy one of the icons displayed on a nearby table. The images were mostly all authentic portraits of saints, he said, copied from the paintings in museum catalogues. The monastery had a substantial collection of these.

Solomon was irritated. A philologist ought not to be mistaken for a primitive believer.

"Not interested," he said.

"Pick out a nice one and pray to it, and you'll get whatever you wish."

And there they were: rows of painted saints, male and female, on polished pottery, each beatific head ringed by light.

"Not interested," he said again.

"Then let me help you," the abbot urged. "We're overstocked just now, so how about I let you have one for free? It might do you some good."

Solomon picked up, not entirely at random, the image of

a woman. Despite the halo, it was a human face. It had a long
narrow column of a nose and a small pink mouth and gazed
up at him from a medium-size oval platter. He set it down—it
meant nothing to him—and made his way in the gathering
heat through the stones of the hillside. At the bottom the bus
snorted out a cloud of impatient exhaust. The passengers sat like
wilted stalks; they had come from the rioting in Jaffa, where
Jonah had fled, and were besieged while buying toy whales in
the market.

But Solomon was anyhow in possession of the portrait of the
saint on the oval platter. The abbot had slipped it into his backpack; he was intent on salvaging the soul of a philologist. And
Solomon did believe in the notion of souls, and all else that was
mystical and cryptic. After all, his teacher at the university, his
mentor, the sovereign of his thought, had been Merton Ames,
a champion of the efficacy of magic, Kabbalah, all things tinged
by the gnostic and the hysteric. He was a heretic, a wild card
who argued that there were Gospels and Testaments yet to be
revealed. And Solomon was Merton Ames's disciple: this was
the reason he shunned saints. They sought everything material,
tangible, mortal, carnal. They were morbidly preoccupied by
willed starvation, rags, straw beds, self-flagellation. St. Catherine of Siena claimed her marriage to the Savior could be
attested to by her wedding ring, the circlet of flesh that had
been cut from his circumcision. St. Joan insisted that the voices
she heard were actual, not hallucinatory. And both were skilled
worldly politicians. It was Catherine who brought the papacy
from Avignon to Rome. It was Joan who threw the English out
of France.

A full six months had elapsed when Solomon was surprised
by the alien touch of an unfamiliar object. He had put his
unwitting hand on the icon. At home on Henry Street in New
York, aware of the growing paucity of his socks (he had been
wearing his shoes without them), he was finally emptying his
backpack. The saint had sunk to the bottom, lost among his
unwashed things. Miraculously, she had sustained no chip or
crack. Yet what was he to do with her? She was unwelcome.

She was illicit, clearly she had been smuggled, she was a whim, she had trespassed, she was nameless. And when and where had she lived, which year in all the centuries of saints? Philologists had long been studying the telltale disparities in the utterances of holy women. In the north, Solomon knew, young oblates, the cherished daughters of gentlewomen, were given to the Lord out of the ranks of the nobility. In the rougher south they were divinely seized peasants. In Aragon, a full quarter of the canonized were female; unlike in some orders, it was not uncommon for the friars to venerate and confide in these, who, like persuasive mothers, coddled and counseled them, and in death supplied body parts to be worshipped as relics.

When Solomon uncovered the sacral platter there in the grimy pit of his backpack, what came to him—what flooded him—was an untamed surmise, though not without precedent: Mary Magdalene and St. Catherine had from the beginning been patronesses and intercessors for the friars. Might Pablo himself have been bound by just such a hallowed yoke, a sainted confidante?

Then suppose, thought Solomon, Pablo's buried disclosures, if they existed, were not in an obscure manuscript in some esoteric hiding place? The science of philology—how words can alter the meaning and motives of history—cried out for exposure of the unknown. What had stirred the Jew Sha'ul ben Kish to become Pablo Christiani? Did the secret of this avowal loiter in the breast of a consecrated virgin?

Solomon was electrified: *Tread where no one else has trod.* If Pablo had come under the benevolence of such a confessor, might this very portrait now under his hand carry her face? Daring was the philologist's calling, experiment his means of conviction. Hypothesis could lead, if not to truth (what is truth?), then to fresh possibility. Why not grasp beyond the hackneyed hope of detecting fragments of parchments in ancient monasteries and caves? Manuscripts, manuscripts! Monasteries and caves and parchments! That road had been well trod.

Suppose, Solomon thought further, he were to release himself from the constrictions of the expected, the accepted? Merton Ames, his teacher, had started out as a traditional

Episcopal priest. Notoriously, he had veered toward sorcery and spells and magical revelations. Why should Merton Ames's votary not do the same?

Early the next morning, he hurried to seek out, in an aging redbrick tenement on Eldridge Street criss-crossed by a web of rusting fire escapes, that mecca of audacious thinkers—the Medieval Library of Gnostic Teachings, founded by Merton Ames. It housed the historic accounts of the Registry of Female Penitents, many of them self-mortifiers renowned for miracles of healing. Christina Mirabilis, a shepherd girl who suffered a seizure, died, rose from the dead, and threw herself into flames and icy waters, neither burning nor freezing; Lutgardis, blinded by a vision of the Heart of Jesus, benefactress of the blind and the maimed; Margaret of Ypres, who stuffed her bosom with nettles and thorns for the sake of imitatio Dei. Was it vainglorious to dream that among these enshrined women he would find one whom Pablo might in his lifetime have known? But Christina and Lutgardis and Margaret were all from the Low Lands, and besides, their dispositions hardly promised spiritual welcome or intimacy. Also, their lives were geographically far from Pablo in Spain. If Pablo were to have had a confidante and confessor, she must be a living neighbor in Aragon.

As Solomon was leafing dispiritedly through the record of localized thirteenth-century female saints—too many were present only in relics of skulls or jawbones—Jacob Sadacca, a former fellow student of Merton Ames, a rival, a close-at-hand antagonist in comradely dress, whom Solomon had long envied, came to sit down beside him. Sadacca was already a subject of newspaper features. He had twice been interviewed on the radio. And like Solomon, he too was twenty-four: a prodigy. He claimed that his scholarly instincts had been sharpened by a converso ancestor, yet another Jacob Sadacca, who was one of the last to be burned at the stake. As late as the middle of the nineteenth century! This history had drawn him, he said, to the study of Inquisitional documents, where—in the unlikely cellars of a Coptic convent—he had unearthed a philological treasure, inscribed in an amalgam of Portuguese, Aramaic, and

an early dialect of Coptic. The lives of generations would be
devoured by the labors of its decipherment.

"So," Jacob asked, "did your exertions in that clerical factory in the desert yield anything?"

"There were riots all over," Solomon said. "And arson and
bombs. The British could do nothing. The tourists were scared
out of their wits."

"Meaning you got nothing."

"I'm looking in a different direction."

"Meaning?"

Solomon hid his defeat under a grunt.

"Away from the hackneyed," he said. But he knew what he
meant, and where he intended to go.

"Well, good luck," Jacob said meanly, and meandered back
to his own carrel, with its towers of what appeared to be lexical
etymologies. Solomon was satisfied that he had struck back with
a wounding insult, whether Jacob recognized it or not. What
could be more familiar than still another decaying esoteric
parchment, still another subterranean find? Stale, hackneyed,
trite! There were untrustworthy rumors that thousand-year-old
scrolls in clay canisters were concealed in underground caves
somewhere in the vicinity of the Dead Sea, but even if such
an improbable cache were true, then yet again manuscripts,
manuscripts, philology's outworn standby!

In that single transporting moment of . . . what must he call
it? emancipation, liberation from the established, the customary—Solomon knew that he had glimpsed something untried,
original, even revolutionary. Pablo's own voice echoed alive on
the tongue of a woman who was a willing conduit, an oracle!
One whose sanctity was conveyed not through the anguish of
flesh, but as a repository of the icy fumes of mortal confession.
A living sepulchre of secrets. He had only to unveil her.

The Registry of Female Penitents was catalogued alphabeti-
cally, though this was of no use to Solomon; he had no inkling
of the name of the sanctified figure he was searching for. In his
impatience he came upon two St. Catherines, one St. Magdalene, three St. Marys . . . and one born Anne of Alquaréz, a
village in Aragon that Pablo had surely frequented, since in its

humbled synagogue he had preached to the stubborn Jews the example of Anne, the Mother of the Mother of the Savior.

But Anne of Alquaréz was never called by her birth name. As an initiate at the age of ten she had ingeniously named herself Azed. St. Azed! A to Zed, Alpha to Omega, the First and the Last, Divine Infinity itself! Plainly this must be the insignia of the chosen confessor—known, inevitably known, to friar Pablo in Aragon. She was *found*, rescued, fetched out into the dizzying light: St. Azed of Alquaréz! He could spy in her history no record of willed penury or humiliation, of fleshly replication of the Lord's travail; her mode and her mark, he concluded, was pure spirit, her soul flew up to join the Absolute, she was all Ear, attentive to voices, the voices of angels, the voices of men. To the voice, he was ready to believe, of Pablo Christiani.

There was in the Registry, besides, her portrait, painted by an artist of the time in the conventional style of the time: haloed, illumined, awestruck eyes fixed upward to the heavens. Whether tonsured male or hooded female, they were all alike, the Catherines, the Marys, the singular Azed. Then how was he truly to know whether the face on the oval platter was the orphic, the oracular, the confidential Azed who was privy to the admissions of Pablo Christiani?

Philology taught him how. Encountering some arcane glyph, how often does the philologist stare hopelessly into the void of the indecipherable, when, all unexpectedly, lightning intuition dispels blindness, and meaning penetrates enigma? In this way, Solomon *saw*; he saw and he knew. The St. Azed of Alquaréz who had languished in his knapsack was Pablo's secret confessor.

It was Solomon Adelberg's habit to breakfast on Thursday mornings with his rival Jacob Sadacca in a local coffee shop. This had continued for some months, and though some of the talk was not-so-benign banter (Jacob, who had several girl-friends, one at a time in sequence, was pleased to recite and compare their traits), some of it was distinctly not. There were intervals when the conversation was significant; not for nothing had each of them been a student of Merton Ames. The coffee shop was foul with cigarette smells—neither one of them smoked—and the early din was unsustainable, so they turned instead to Solomon's rooms on Henry Street. By agreement, Jacob came bearing two large cinnamon rolls, while Solomon supplied the butter and the jam and the tea kettle.

On this Thursday in July, at an already sweltering eight o'clock, the discussion was itself seriously heated, even if recurrent and far from new. Ten years before, while the rivals were still in their teens, Merton Ames had been charged with forgery. He had presented the thesis that had earned him his repute as innovator—the Son of the Father as a magician, a practitioner of ritual healings and cures rooted in the believer's susceptibility. It came with all the proper substantiating tenets and trappings: the remote monastery, the lost-and-found forgotten parchment, cautiously photographed and then dutifully replaced in its niche, the attendant public excitement over the discovery. All this followed by Merton Ames's acclaimed return to the monks to retrieve the authentic chronicle for display. And then its unaccountable disappearance!

Jacob said, "But when they say it looks a lot like Merton pulled off a forgery, it's out-and-out professional jealousy, what else could it be?" Their mentor had urged, at least on his favorites, the use of his first name. It was, he said, a sign of his trust; they would never join the camp of the doubters.

But Solomon felt targeted by this remark. "They!" he spat out. "Who cares what they say? It doesn't have to be jealousy. There could be dozens of reasons for why the original went missing."

"Name one," Jacob said.

"It could have been stolen."

"And the thief, after all these years, never caught? Nobody even suspected? Look, if it's tea we're having," Jacob complained, "why isn't there any sugar? Or at least a slice of lemon? And by the way, whatever became of your fancy new direction? The one that's meant to turn philology upside-down."

"I never said anything like that."

"But you meant it."

This was unanswerable, so it was the quibbles—the missing

condiments—that took a new direction that morning. Why couldn't they sometimes have ginger tea? Or a bit of interesting cheese?

And meanwhile the portrait of St. Azed of Alquaréz stood propped up among Solomon's everyday cups and saucers on a kitchen shelf nearby, unnoticed by the prodigy.

They had been speaking of false representation, of deliberate fakery, of pulling the wool over honest scholarly eyes. Of guilt! Neither Solomon nor Jacob believed that their teacher had committed any such crime: it was calumny, what an outrage even to imagine it! But for the rest of that day Solomon was moved to question himself. A tendril of mistrust crept back. In invoking Azed, was he devising a kind of forgery of his own? And again, what form was it to take? A séance? A trance? Wisps and waverings of antiquated sounds in transit from the faraway past? And how was he to record it, if not as yet another scorned manuscript, but with no thousand-year-old parchment to validate it? Of course he would be thought guilty of fabrication, as his teacher had been before him. But Merton Ames had belonged to that inspired party of originators, scholars valorous enough to catch hold of new meanings in traditional formulas, resolute enough to withstand the skeptics. And what evidence did Solomon Adelberg have for his own excitements? No more than his oval platter, traced from a museum catalogue.

Still, he must undertake a ceremony of evidence, and yes, a ceremony it must be. The mood, the space, the time, must call forth the saint's temperament. At midnight, in the glimmering light of her nimbus, in the holiness of candle and wine. But ought not a ceremony to have a witness, or will it hover forever as a mist, unheard, disbelieved? And who was to be the witness?

The next Thursday morning brought a disappointment. The bakery was out of cinnamon rolls, and Jacob arrived with ordinary kaisers, which neither of them liked. A hard rain had soaked through the bag; the rolls were soggy and inedible.

"Don't you have anything else? Always an empty larder?"

They had their tea with stale crackers, and Solomon

understood that Jacob was slyly mocking him for having no new ideas.

"I've got some news," Jacob said. "I'm getting an award from the Philology Society. I just found out."

"Another one? What for?" Solomon asked. But his throat burned as if coated with frost.

"It's brand-new, they call it the Fresh Paths in Inquisitional Studies Prize. It comes with two hundred and fifty dollars. I'm thinking of buying a secondhand Ford if I save up."

And wasn't Azed of Alquaréz exactly such a Fresh Path? And wasn't she also the different direction he had recklessly boasted of, even when he hadn't so much as known her name? Philology is a science; seclusion is imperative until its premise can be proven, demonstrated, enacted. Witnessed. And for this he must recruit a sympathetic bystander. Jacob was not sympathetic.

"Well, well, so congratulations," Solomon said.

"Your turn will come," his rival assured him. His tone was not kind.

The voice was dim, far, quick, strange, often incomprehensible. But it was, undeniably, a species of Spanish—an offshoot of Old Spanish, half-Portuguese and half-Catalan, the medieval idiom of Aragon. The more syllables it emitted, the more Solomon's strivings could pierce its undulations. It was as if they had risen out of the void fully prepared, brooking no probings, no questions. As if they had caught any call, any summons that circled the air, like a moth to be pinched out of the ether. Solomon's fever alone had invoked it.

Pablo Christiani, the voice affirmed, had come to her as a Jew. However much he may have skirted it, it was as a Jew that he came, and it was as a Jew that she received him. But he seemed too much a rationalist, and wasn't this what marked him as a Jew? For herself, she had touched the garment of the Lord, and knew it, and felt its silken threads, and felt her soul dissolved in it. This was why Pablo Christiani had sought her out—to fall into the embrace of her purity, of her easy and natural faith.

He had come to confess, the voice said, but he was perplexed as to what he had to confess.

Jacob said, "I don't hear a thing."

"Try harder," Solomon insisted. "You're not attuned."

"All I can catch is a kind of static. Like a bad radio."

"You're not ready. You're resisting. Look at her eyes."

These had earlier been compliant in their devout upward stare. Yet now they were alive, in motion, swimming with rebellious light.

And then Solomon too heard the static, and the white glare of her eyes blinded his own, and the voice was drowned in silence. But still, still, his confidence was restored; he understood. Wasn't it because Pablo was a believer that he must bring the Jews to follow him in his newborn conviction? To peel away the scales that darkened Jewish perception?—But what flimsy speculation, the ardent goodwill of the evangelizer, any skeptic could puncture it with a feather! It must be something more robust, more of the worldly, the cynical. Then why not ambition, raw ambition? Greed for domination? The lure of punishing authority, of the ritual robes, of the menacing sermons, of the burning books, of the expulsions, the humiliations of the Jew-badge, the forced disputations that incited rioting against the arrogant Jews—who would not yearn for such command, who would not relish such zeal? What recalcitrant Jew, with his finger on the pages of the cursèd Talmud, could attain it, could live it? Which was the stronger—bona fide devotion, or the fruits and rewards of an archbishop? Why remain a pawn among the persecuted when a clever scholar and able administrator might flourish in the company of the powerful?

But was this what Azed of Alquaréz was telling him, or was it Solomon's own suspicions, his own judgment, obscuring her, muffling her bleats? He was losing her, the granules of her breath were by now no more than a hiss, or were they his own gasps of bereavement? He searched her face for some sign: the roving, distracted, and faltering eyes, the quiescent indifferently breathing narrow nostrils, the mouth . . . There was something amiss with the mouth. Was it a creak, a crack, what was he hearing, what was he seeing? The halo darkened, snuffed, the deceiving tremor of the fitful candle flame, and from brow to chin a split, a splintering, a slash—the icon severed in a shower of fragments, all at once capsized by a deadly smash.

"I was just reaching for the wine," Jacob said, laughing—his rival, the prodigy, the destroyer, laughing, mocking!—"while you were sunk in all that mumbo jumbo. What a farce, you're just too lazy for the kind of digging that I do. You're always looking for shortcuts. You see what good it does you, and we wouldn't even have had the wine if I hadn't brought it—"

On the floor at their feet lay a scattering of shards, islands in a bloodred sea. On the kitchen table three thick volumes had toppled—Merton Ames's heretical yet lauded trilogy on the Savior's conjury, the supportive spine that had held the oval platter upright.

Was it Jacob's blow that had undone her, or was this diminishing, this fading, the prompt of conscience of the saint herself? No matter. She was gone. The mind of the Jew Pablo Christiani, scourge of the Jews of Aragon, could not be retrieved.

It was not long after the loss of the icon that Solomon Adelberg reneged on his vow of celibacy. On his twenty-fifth birthday he gave it up. His girlfriend's name was Celeste. He declined to look her up in the Registry of Female Penitents: he was done with holy women. Then how could he know that Sister Maria Celeste was the convent-bred daughter of Galileo, the astronomer who deduced that the earth circled the sun, a blasphemy that offended doctrine? Celibacy, Solomon finally perceived, gave birth to veneration, and veneration to the saint Azed, who, like all other purifying icons and penitents, could hardly rise to the enlightened science of philology. He blamed Jacob for his misstep, and it was true: Jacob had confessed to being complicit. It was he, after all, who had brought the wine.

As for the conversion of the Jews. Whoever today remembers Pablo Christiani remembers him solely as the Jew he was. But who remembers the philologist Solomon Adelberg, Pablo's pursuer, who leaves no trace as scholar and finder?

Dictation

IN THE EARLY summer of 1901, Lamb House, Henry James's exurban domicile in Rye, was crowded with flowers. At the close of the morning's dictation, Mary Weld, his young amanuensis, had gone out to the back garden with scissors in hand, to cut the thorny vines that clung to the heat of a surrounding brick wall. On the entrance hall table, on the parlor mantelpiece, on the dining room sideboard—everywhere in the house where the eyes of the expected visitors might fall—she scattered rose-filled vases. Then she mounted her bicycle and rode off.

The visitors did not arrive until late afternoon. Tea was already laid, as usual with safe and respectable toast and jam, but also with the perilously sweet and oily pastries James was so fond of, though they made his teeth hurt horribly. Even before the knocker was lifted, he knew they had come: here were the wheels of the trap scraping on gravel, and the pony's skipping gait, and a child's angry howl when he was taken from his mother and set down before an alien door. James stood waiting, nervously braiding his fingers—Lamb House was unaccustomed to the presence of a noisy, unpredictable, and certainly precarious three-year-old boy, and one with so un-English a name.

Four years before, James had summoned Joseph Conrad to lunch at 34 DeVere Gardens, his London flat. The two of them sat in the unsteady yellow light of newly installed electric bulbs and talked of the nature of fiction—yet not quite as writer to writer. Conrad was a stringy, leathery, youthful-looking man of nearly forty, a literary cipher, virtually unknown. As an act of homage, he had sent James a copy of *Almayer's Folly*, his first—at that time his only—novel. James saw something extraordinary in it, even beyond the robustness of style and subject: he saw shrewdness, he saw fervency, he saw intuition, he saw authority; he saw, in rougher circumstance, humanity. In a way, he saw a psychological simulacrum of himself—and in a Polish seaman!

Awed and self-conscious, Conrad could scarcely lick away the grains of crumpet lingering on his lower lip. He understood himself to be a novice still, perpetually distraught and uncertain: was his stuff any good at all? And he worried, in these rooms of high privilege, and under the false yellow light with its unholy flicker, whether his pronunciation was passable. Sometimes he used words, marvelous English words, that he had only *read*, and when he spoke the marvelous words, no matter how intimately he felt them, their syllables, striking the surprised eyes of his hearers, seemed all in the wrong tones: he could not bring out, except in ink, that sublimely organized Anglo-Saxon speech. Polish was otherwise constructed; now and then he borrowed the counterpoint of its ornate melodies, but he would never again write in his native language. He would not—he could not—speak to his wife in any foreign voice; she knew no language other than her own. Despite what was called a "natural" intelligence, she had little education. She was sensible and good-hearted and straightforward and comfortably dependable. He harbored some small shame over her, and was ashamed of his shame. He hid it, as much as he could, even from himself. He had learned, early on, the difference between common sense and infatuation; marriage meant the former. In this initial colloquy with the Master (he hoped others would follow), he was reluctant to disclose that he was, in fact, a new husband, and that he had only recently, and willingly, thrown himself into the coils of domesticity. There was nothing in his wife's character to attract James's always inquisitive ear—was this why he was blotting out his Jessie? Or was it because James, in all the nobility of his supreme dedication, led an unencumbered bachelor life, altogether freed to his calling? While a man with a wife, and perhaps soon with a child . . .

DeVere Gardens had saluted the coming century—the nascent twentieth—with artificial illumination, and also with an innovation growing more and more commonplace. It was said that the Queen had requested the new thing for her secretary, who had refused it in terror. On a broad surface reserved for it in a far corner of the room where the older writer sat discoursing, and the younger went on nodding his chin with an affirmative and freshly inaugurated little pointed beard, stood the Machine. It stood headless and armless and legless—brute shoulders merely: it might as well have been the torso of a broken god. Even at a distance it struck Conrad as strange and repulsive, the totem of a foreign civilization to which, it now appeared, James had uncannily acclimated. The thing was large and black and glossy, and in height it ascended in tiers, like a stadium. Each round key was shielded by glass and rimmed by a ring of metal. James had been compelled to introduce the Machine into his labors after years of sweeping a wrist across paper; gripping a pen had become too painful. To relieve the recurring cramp, he hired William MacAlpine, a stenographer, who recorded in shorthand James's dictation and then transcribed it on the Machine; but it soon turned out to be more efficient to speak directly to the thing itself, with MacAlpine at the keys.

Their glassy surfaces were catching the overhead light. Shifting his head, Conrad saw blinking semaphores.

"I note, sir," James remarked, "that you observe with some curiosity the recent advent of a monstrously clacking but oh so monumentally modern Remington. The difficulty of the matter is that my diligent typewriter, a plausible Scot conveniently reticent, is at bottom too damnably expensive, and I believe I can get a highly competent little woman for half, *n'est-ce pas*? May I presume, Mr. Conrad, that you, in the vigor of youth, as it were, are not of a mind to succumb to a mechanical intercessor, as I, heavier with years, perforce have succumbed?"

Dictation? Dependence? Inconceivable separation of hand from paper, inner voice leaching into outer, immemorial sacred solitude shattered by a breathing creature always in sight, a tenacious go-between, a constantly vibrating interloper, the human operator! The awful surrender of the fructuous mind that lives on paper, lives *for* paper, paper and ink and nothing else! Squinting upward at the electrical sorcery suspended from the ceiling, a thread of burning wire that mimicked and captured in its tininess the power of fire, it occurred to Conrad that Jessie at her sewing might covet this futuristic advantage. As for himself and the Machine . . . never. He had his seaman's good right hand, and the firm mast of his pen, and the blessèd ocean of paper, as white as a sail and as relentless as the wind.

"An amanuensis?" he replied. "No, Mr. James, I am not so progressive. Indeed I loathe revolution. I have run steam in my day, but I was trained to the age of sail. I fear I am wedded to my bad old habits."

Not long after Conrad's introduction to DeVere Gardens, James gave up the implacable press and rush of London and went to live in the country, in his cherished Lamb House—an established householder at last. He took MacAlpine and the Machine with him. But on this warm June afternoon in 1901, when Conrad and Jessie and their son Borys came to visit, changes were evident on both sides. For one, MacAlpine had been replaced by the highly competent (and cheaper) little woman James had hoped for: Miss Weld. And for another, James now knew to a certainty that Conrad had a wife—a plump wife made all the plumper by a plethora of bulging and writhing bundles, among them the screeching child forcibly lifted over the threshold, a multiform traveling nursery to serve his exigencies, and a dangling basket of ripe plums. Her tread was nevertheless light, though with a bit of a limp from a knee injured in girlhood. The plums, she explained, were for their host, not that the little boy wouldn't like two or three, if Mr. James wouldn't mind, and would Mr. James please excuse the child, he'd been dozing the whole eighteen miles from Kent, it was the waking so abruptly when they arrived set him off . . . She had the unschooled accent of the streets; her father had toiled in a warehouse.

Conrad, James saw, kept apart from wife and son, as if they had been strangers who were for some unfathomable reason attaching themselves to his affairs. He was much altered from the grateful young acolyte of DeVere Gardens. He carried himself with a look that hinted at a scarred and haughty nature. He had since brought out half a dozen majestic works of fiction; two of them, *The Nigger of the "Narcissus"* and *Lord Jim*, had already placed him as a literary force. He and James regularly exchanged fresh volumes as soon as they were out; each acknowledged the other as an artist possessed—though in private each man harbored his reservation and his doubt. James thought Conrad a thicket of unrestrained profusion. Conrad saw James as heartless alabaster. Writing, Conrad had confided, meant dipping his pen in his own blood and pulling out pieces of flesh. He was always despairing, and as a family man he was always in need of money. Very often he was ill. His nerves were panicked and untrustworthy. Those long-ago voyages in the tropics, Malaysia and Africa, had left him debilitated—the effects of malaria contracted in the Congo, and a persistent gout that frequently landed him in bed. The gout assaulted his joints; his writing hand was no good. There were times when it was agony to hold on to a pen. He had set Jessie to making fair copies of his big hurling hurting scrawl; she was eager and diligent, but when he looked over her neatly lettered sheets, he found foolish misreadings, preposterous omissions. She was not suited for the work. She was bright enough, she could compose an acceptable sentence on her own in decent everyday practical prose; she understood much of the ordinary world; she understood *him*; it was only that she lacked an eye for his lightning storms, his wild rushes and terrifying breathlessness. It grieved him that she was capable of converting a metaphor into a literalism (but this too was a metaphor), and she in her good plain way grieved that she could not satisfy his ferociously driven greed for the word, the marvelous English word. His handwriting was so difficult! But she had a cousin, she reminded him, a cousin who had gone to secretarial school; the cousin was properly trained, surely she would do better? The cousin was hired. She did not do better.

James was contemplating the child. That red elastic mouth with its tiny teeth, those merciless unstinting rising howls, was there to be no end to it? Was there a devil in this small being? And was this hellish clamor, and these unwanted plums with their sour skins, the common fruit of all marriage? Ah, the lesson in it!

"My dear Mrs. Conrad," he began in his most companionably embracing manner (the graciousness of mere twaddle, he liked privately to call it), "is it not possible that a simple bribe might induce calm in the breast of this vociferous infant? Here you are, my little man, a tart truly sublime upon the palate—"

Borys reached for the truly sublime stickiness and threw it in the air and resumed the rhythm of his protests: he wailed and he flailed, and Jessie said cheerily, with a glance at her stoically indifferent husband, "Oh do forgive us, Mr. James, but all these lovely bunches of roses . . . then would there be a garden? Borys would love a romp in a garden, and this, you see, will permit you and Mr. Conrad to enjoy each other's company, would it not? I assure you that Borys and I will be very happy in the outdoors."

James did not hesitate. "Mrs. Smith," he called, "would you kindly oblige us—"

A servant materialized from a hidden corridor, bearing a large steaming iron kettle. A smell of spirits came with her.

"Sir, will you be wanting the hot water for the teapot now?"

"Not quite yet, Mrs. Smith. Mrs. Conrad and this very delightful young man will be pleased to be escorted to the floral precincts beyond the premises, and I beg you, Mrs. Smith, do take away that perilous object before we are all scalded to embers—"

Mrs. Smith looked confused, but Jessie picked up Borys and followed her. The woman walked unsteadily, spilling boiling droplets. Mr. James, Jessie thought, was undoubtedly an unearthly intelligence—had he actually uttered "floral precincts"? Still, she pitied him. He had no wife to run his house. A wife would have a notion or two about what to do with a drunken servant!

She did not know what the two men talked about that long afternoon. As usual, she was shut out, though she thirsted to hear. There was a cat in the garden, and Borys was sufficiently amused through the hours of exile. If only Mr. James would come out to see how charming her little boy really was! But Mrs. Smith had been directed to carry half the tea things into the garden, where she set a table for Jessie and the child. Plainly, it was Conrad who had maneuvered this arrangement—or so Jessie believed. Her nostrils tightened: the woman did smell awfully of whiskey, and her faltering steps over the uneven ground made the tray of pastries wobble. One of them dropped to the grass nearby, luring the cat, who gave it a lick and left it alone. Soon a party of ants massed underfoot. But except for the ants, and after a time a squad of circling bees, it was pleasant in these secluded floral precincts (oh, that remarkable man's way of speaking!); she had taken along her sewing, and Borys was content to stalk the cat along the wall, or to draw its silky tail through his fingers. Mrs. Smith, in a second appearance, had inexplicably brought out the basket of plums. Jessie was alarmed, and felt it an insult to their host, when, looking up from her needle, she noticed that Borys had eaten every last one. He had also consumed four of the sticky tarts, and finally fell asleep in the late sun, with his head on the cat.

When they had thanked Mr. James, and Jessie had apologized for the disappeared plums, and they had said their goodbyes, and were halfway home in the trap, Jessie asked Conrad what had been the chief points of the conversation indoors.

"Books," said Conrad. And then: "That damnable racket, what on earth was ailing the boy?"

"It was only he was hungry," Jessie said. "But what was Mr. James telling you?"

"You oughtn't to have brought the fruit. He doesn't like them raw."

"Is *that* what the two of you talked about?"

"Only in passing. Books mostly."

"His own? Yours?"

"Everybody's, so make an end of it, Jess. And we won't be taking the boy again, that's clear."

The plums had been mentioned, yes, but only because of the tarts—Mrs. Smith, tipsy as she regrettably too often was in her kitchen, had despite this impediment a knack, James said, for the manufacture of fruit pastries, which doubtless accounted for the size of his butter bill. From the cost of dairy, they passed on to writerly gossip—H. G. Wells was in the general neighborhood, at Sandgate on the coast, and Stephen Crane, the brilliant

young American, at Brede, a mere eight-mile bicycle run to
Rye; and also Ford Madox Hueffer, at Winchelsea. In fact, Hueffer had turned up only yesterday, bringing Edmund Gosse. So
many intimate connections! In this very season, with an eye to
the market, Conrad and Hueffer were collaborating on a novel,
hoping to win the popular libraries—a thing that bemused
James, since their separate styles had little in common. This
observation led naturally to a discussion of style, and whether it
remains distinct from the writer's intrinsic personality. Conrad
thought not. The novelist, he argued (while out of the blue a
shooting pain was assaulting his knuckles), surely the novelist stands confessed in his works? On the other hand, James
countered (but the hurt just then was in both the poor visitor's
hands: that cursèd gout flaring up when least desired!), the artist
multiplies his confessions, thereby concealing his inmost self.
The talk went back and forth in this way, the two labyrinthine
minds locking and unlocking, and how, after all, was Conrad
reasonably to recount it all to Jessie when she pressed him on
it, as she was certain to do? James was free; there was no one
to press him; yet Conrad was determined to press him now. As
for style, he persisted, was there not an intervening influence,
a contamination or a crippling, however you may tell it, when
the roiling abyss, in whose bottommost bowel the secrets of
language lie coiled, is thrown open to mundane elements? *Cher
maître*, what of your Machine, your MacAlpines and Welds!
Your sharers and intercessors!

It was past sundown when Conrad and Jessie reached their
cramped old farmhouse—a property rented from Hueffer, and
not far from Winchelsea, to facilitate the collaboration. After
Borys had been put to bed, and Jessie had resumed her sewing,
Conrad fell into his old complaint.

"It came on so, Jess, the pain in my hands, that I could hardly
keep my wits. And worse in the right, as always."

"Oh my dear, and you haven't held a pen all day—"

"I had it from Mr. James that he has done well enough with
his Remington these last years. I had rather thought it a vise,
but he assures me that the whole of *The Ambassadors* was spoken
aloud, and he believes it has enriched his tone—he feels his very

breathing has gone into it. That glorious lavishness, dictated! And he finds Miss Weld decidedly a jewel. Jess, I have been too faint-hearted. Likely one can get one of these Remingtons at a fair price—Mr. James calculated for me the cost of his own. I'm confident we'll soon be able to afford it, especially if all goes right with Hueffer and the work."

Jessie let out a small snort. "The work," she said. "It appears to me it's you does most of it. It's not him that'll make your fortune. A man who won't keep his own name, and goes about calling himself Ford Ford, like a stutterer!"

"But you see," he held firm, "it's not to be just the cost of the Remington—"

"Of course I see. There's to be a Miss Weld. You want a jewel of your own." Her warming good humor came tumbling out in all its easy laughter. "Well, Mr. Conrad, this *will* be a revolution! And here you let me think the two of you were talking all afternoon about plums."

Winter in Lamb House, when few visitors came, was lonely for Henry James; too often an insidious depression set in. At times he felt defined by it. It was, he admitted—especially to himself—deeper than anything else in his character, deeper even than the subterranean windings of his art. An extraordinary avowal: in the country he kept it hidden under great gusts of hospitality. But London, whatever its flaws, had never been openly lonely, and the Reform Club, where he took up seasonal residence in spacious upper rooms, and could entertain guests at luncheon in the pillared splendors below, was the metropolis at its finest. His windows oversaw the rooftops and chimney pots of handsome embassies and lofty mansions. It was here that he shaved off his whitening beard, itself a reason for melancholy: he thought it made him look old. And it was here, on a rainy afternoon in January of 1910, that Miss Lilian Hallowes and Miss Theodora Bosanquet almost did not meet.

Conrad and his wife had come to London to consult a surgeon. Jessie was suffering from the effects of her last knee operation (there had already been several), and would need yet another—some years earlier, she had fallen on the pavement during a shopping excursion, further damaging the trouble-some injury of her teens. She had begun to take on the life of a serious cripple. Availing himself of an interval in the day's plans—Jessie was resting in their hotel—Conrad had arranged for Miss Hallowes to deliver some newly transcribed pages of his current work to the Reform Club, where James, learning his friend was in town, had invited him for one of their old talks. Conrad's instructions were plain: he had some neces-sary revisions in mind, and meant to apply them immediately; Miss Hallowes was to make herself known to the concierge, and was then simply to ascend to Mr. James's quarters, hand over the typewritten sheets to her employer, and rapidly and unobtrusively depart. Any chance of an encounter with Miss Bosanquet, however fleeting, must be urgently avoided. It was an hour when James would likely be dismissing Miss Bosanquet at the close of the morning's dictation. He was intermittently engaged at this time in composing the prefaces for his crowning New York Edition; his ambition was to gather up, and at last to perfect, all the novels and tales, the labors of a lifetime. He intended to vet each one, line by line, imposing his maturer style on his earlier manner, and he was looking forward to hear-ing Conrad's view of this obsessive revisiting—after so many years, did Conrad still hold to his theory that style confesses the inner man? And what if style were finally to be altered? Might it not signify that one's essential self, one's ostensibly immutable character, was, in fine, mutable?

When Conrad, considerably rain-dampened, penetrated the Grecian luxuriances of the Reform Club's lower halls, he had no inkling that this was to be the quizzical, possibly the fraught, theme of the visit. But he knew anyhow that the simultaneous appearance of the two ladies, in the presence of himself and James, would be damnably awkward. Miss Hallowes had seen (was constantly seeing) into the blackest recesses of his mind. She was privy to his hesitations, his doubts, his reversals, and certainly his excitements; she was in the most crucial sense his double, since everything that came out of him she instantly duplicated on the Machine. His thoughts ran straight through her, unchanged, unmitigated, unloosed. Without doubt the

same was true with respect to James and the spirited Miss
Bosanquet: every vibration of James's sensibility ran through
the woman who served and observed—how could it be otherwise? These two, Miss Hallowes and Miss Bosanquet, brought
together even momentarily, could only mean exposure. In Miss
Hallowes's face, in her posture, in the very shape and condition
of her shoes, James would detect, with the divining rod that was
his powerful instinct, the secret thing Conrad harbored against
him: that the Master's cosmopolitanism, his civilized restraint,
his perfection of method, his figures so finished, chiseled, and
carved, were, when you came down to it, stone. Under the
glow lay heartlessness and cold. And in Miss Bosanquet's face
and posture and perhaps even in the shape and condition of
her shoes, Conrad himself might recognize, frighteningly, the
arrow of James's hidden dislike.

These vulnerable premonitions did not come to pass. Luckily, Miss Bosanquet had already left when Conrad knocked and
James opened, and patted Conrad on the back, and led him in
and stood him before the fire with many a "delighted to see
you" and exclamations of "my dear, good fellow" and worried
inquiries about poor Mrs. Conrad's health, and exhortations to
a libation of sherry, and urgings to take the chair that allowed
a view of the grand edifice opposite, which housed the Turkish legation: a green crescent and a green star were painted on
its roof. And then another knock, and it was Miss Hallowes,
precisely as directed, bringing the latest portion of the sea tale
Conrad was thinking of calling "The Second Self," or "The
Secret Stranger," though he might yet settle on something
else . . .

"I'm much obliged to you, Miss Hallowes," he said, accept-
ing the moist folder; she had struggled to shelter it under her
coat. "Mr. James, may I present the very person your example
inspired? My amanuensis, Miss Hallowes, who flies off to enjoy
her day in London, despite this wretched weather—"

Under her wet clumsy hat with its wet little feather, Miss
Hallowes's somewhat obvious nose reddened. She had a long
neck—she was long all over—at the base of which sat a bun.
The bun confined brown hair, the sort of brown that is so

common as to be always overlooked, except in a very pretty woman. Miss Hallowes was not a very pretty woman. She was thirty-seven, just starting a jowl. It was mostly inconspicuous, but formed a soft round bulge whenever she lowered her head. Her head, bending over the Machine, was usually lowered. Sometimes the quick agitation of her fingers and shoulders shook out her bun and uncaged it from its pins, and then her hair would cascade down over her long back; she wondered if Mr. Conrad noticed. She had been employed by him for the past six years, and was and was not a member of the household—rather like a governess in a book. She often took Borys to school. Yet after all this time Mr. Conrad still misspelled her Christian name, and wrote it as "Lillian," with two *l*'s, when it had only one, and referred to her as his "girl." She was gratified that he had not said "my girl" to Mr. James, who was right now looking at her, or *into* her, with those lantern eyes he had. He was much fatter than she had expected, and showed a paunch and a developed jowl that reminded her humiliatingly of the probable future of her own. She was dripping on his nice carpet; outdoors it was raining like mad; she wished she could go stand in front of his fire. Her feet were soaked through, and cold. But she was not to stay—she understood she was merely a necessary intrusion. If only Mr. James would not judge her by the ruin of her shoes!

She said, "How do you do, Mr. James," and moved to the door. Her hand was on the knob, but it was already vigorously turning, as if of itself, and a hand on the other side of the door slid through, and brushed against her own, and in leaped Miss Bosanquet.

"I do apologize, I was nearly on my way out—I seem to have forgotten my umbrella—"

The forgotten umbrella! Worn device, venerable ruse! Yet perhaps not—it was a fact, after all, that Miss Bosanquet, with James's permission, habitually kept an umbrella in his rooms. It hadn't been raining so heavily when she arrived at ten o'clock, and she was insouciant about such nonsense as getting a little wet—unlike some ladies, who behaved as if they were made of sugar and were bound to melt. But even Miss Bosanquet might acknowledge the need of an umbrella when the rain bounced upward from the pavement and a cutting wind pelted icy rivers into one's face: hence the contingency article in the Master's cupboard. The morning's drizzle had by now blown into a brutish January storm, which might very well explain why Miss Bosanquet burst in to fetch her umbrella just as Miss Hallowes was leaving, all inadvertently touching Miss Hallowes's large interesting hand.

Possibly there was another explanation. As Miss Bosanquet, having been discharged for the day, was passing through the monumental lower hall on her way out to the street, she heard a voice speaking the Master's name. A tall woman with a disheveled bun and wearing a charmingly silly hat stood at the concierge's desk, announced that she was expected, and asked where she might find Mr. James's apartment. She walked on through the hall's massive columns, halting to remove from under her coat a folder of the kind used to enclose manuscript. This was unquestionably odd: Miss Bosanquet was scrupulously cognizant of every sacred sheet of paper that entered or left the Master's sanctum; every hallowed word he breathed aloud danced through her agile fingertips and registered indelibly in her brain. Was this woman, apparently summoned by the Master, some hidden competitor? Under the excessive burden of preparing his strenuous New York Edition, did he feel that he required *two* amanuenses, one for the earlier part of the day, the other for the later? Miss Bosanquet was aware that she had had predecessors—and that she outshone them all: was there now to be a rival? For the too-costly MacAlpine the Master had found other employment, and Miss Weld had gone off in the bloom of her youth to be married. The last, a Miss Lois Baker, was sometimes called on, Miss Bosanquet knew, when she herself was compelled to be absent: could this be the same Miss Baker harried and hurried, who was just then stopping to prop the suspicious folder against the base of a pillar while she rearranged the pins in her bun? She had loosened her hair; it swept free before she could scoop it up again, and in this one disclosing moment, when the length of it swung innocently by its own dark weight, Miss Bosanquet reflected that Miss Baker,

if Miss Baker it was, resembled a mermaid all at once released
from a spell—she was certainly wet enough! Were shining
scales and a forked tail concealed, together with some errant
manuscript, under her coat? Her long lurking body, like a mermaid cast up on solid earth, was spilling puddles on the marble
floor. She had a broad shy mouth in a broad shy face, the sort of
face you might see in an old painting of the Madonna, where
the model had clearly been a plain peasant girl, coarse-skinned,
yet with a transcendentally devoted mien. Miss Baker's eyes, if
Miss Baker it was, were too small, and the lobes of her nostrils
too fleshy, but standing there, with her hands lifted to the back
of her neck, and looking all around, as if under the ceiling of
some great cathedral, she seemed dutiful and unguarded and
glowingly virginal. She picked up the folder and went on.

For ten minutes Miss Bosanquet lingered and pondered,
lingered and pondered—and there *was* the question of the
umbrella, was there not? So when she returned to the Master's
rooms and dared to rush in, unexpectedly caressing the hand of
the departing Miss Baker on the other side of the door . . . but
no! It could not be Miss Baker, despite all. Miss Bosanquet was
astonished to see that the Master, in the interim following her
own departure, had received a guest, and the guest (impossible
not to recognize him) was the renowned Mr. Joseph Conrad;
and *therefore*, she instantly calculated, the manuscript the putative Miss Baker had been carrying pertained not to the Master,
but to Mr. Conrad. Here was the proof: the folder was already
in the grip of Mr. Conrad's nervously pinching fingers, and
why was he pinching it in that strange way, and glaring at the
two ladies as if they might do him some obscure harm?

It was done. It was inescapable. These women were not
supposed to have met, and by the grace of God had eluded
meeting—yet here they were, side by side: he almost thought
he had seen them fugitively clasping hands. A baleful destiny
works through confluences of the commonplace—that damnable umbrella! He pinched the folder Miss Hallowes had freshly
delivered (she was punctual as usual), and pinched it again,
pressing it hotly against his ribs—a shield to ward off that avidly
staring Miss Bosanquet, who had the bright shrewd look of

a keeper of secrets. What disadvantageous word, product of a supernal critical mind, had the Master confided in her? What fatal flaw—he was doomed to flaw, to sweat and despair—was she privately rehearsing, fixed as she was on this newest burden of his toil? That his tales were all Chinese boxes and nested matrioshkas, narrators within narrators, that he was all endlessly dangling strings, that he suffered from a straggle of ungoverned verbiage? In Miss Bosanquet's confident ease in the presence of the Master, he divined James's sequestered judgment—sequestered for the nonce, but might he not one day thrust it into print? *Mr. Conrad is to be greatly admired, but so flawed as not to be excessively revered.* Miss Bosanquet, who understood reverence, gave it all away in her long sharp look. And poor Miss Hallowes, with her little worshipful eyes (he sometimes suspected that he was worshiped by Miss Hallowes), what dour elements of his own sequestered view of the Master was *she* giving away? He wished they would vanish, the two of them!

But the Master came forward, and in his most expansively seigneurial manner introduced Miss Bosanquet to Miss Hallowes. "An unprecedented hour," he pronounced, "unforeseen in the higher mathematics, when parallel handmaidens collide. Can you hear, my dear Conrad, as thunder on Olympus, the clash of the Remingtons?" And when they were gone, Miss Bosanquet brandishing her retrieved umbrella, and Miss Hallowes in her dreadful shoes following as if led by an orchestral baton, he asked, "And do you find your Miss Hallowes satisfactory then?"

"Quite satisfactory," Conrad said.

"She discerns your meaning?"

"Entirely."

"Miss Bosanquet—you see how lively and rather boyish she is—yet she is worth all the other females I have had put together. Among the faults of my previous amanuenses—not by any means the *only* fault—was their apparent lack of comprehension of what I was driving at. And Miss Bosanquet is admirably discreet."

"One must expect no less."

"Miss Hallowes, I take it, you deem a *bijou*."

"Indeed," said Conrad, though he remarked to himself that Jessie more and more believed otherwise.

"Do give me your arm, or I shall never fit you under," Miss Bosanquet urged. "It's a wonder you haven't brought your own. Miss Hallowes, you're waterlogged!"

"I surely did set out with one, but the wind turned it inside out and swept it halfway into the square, and I couldn't go after it because Mr. Conrad so dislikes unpunctuality—"

"What a felicitous misfortune! The stars have favored us, Miss Hallowes—had you been delayed by a single minute, it's not likely that you and I should be splashing along arm in arm . . . I should so value half an hour with you—may I ask whether you have some immediate obligation—"

"I must look in on my mother, who hasn't been well."

"I plead only for half an hour. Shall we duck into the nearest Lyons and get out of the wet? I believe I am acquainted with every tearoom in the vicinity. I frequently bring Mr. James his morning crullers."

Miss Hallowes thought guiltily of her mother; but she was not so punctual with her mother as she was with Mr. Conrad. "It *would* be a pleasure to dry off my feet."

"Oh, your poor swimming feet!" cried Miss Bosanquet— which struck Miss Hallowes as perhaps too familiar from someone she had met not twenty minutes ago; and yet Miss Bosanquet's body was warm against her, holding her close under the narrow shelter of the umbrella.

When they were seated and had a pair of brown china teapots and a sticky sugar bowl between them, Miss Bosanquet asked, as if they were old intimates, "And how *is* your mother?"

"She suffers from an ailment of the heart. My mother is a widow, and very much alone. It is not only illness that troubles her. She is very often sad."

"Then how providential," Miss Bosanquet said, "to have a daughter to lighten her spirits—"

"They cannot be so easily lightened. My mother is in mourning."

"Her loss is so recent?"

"Not at all. It is more than five years since my brother died. For my mother the hurt remains fresh."

"Your mother must be a woman of uncommon feeling. And perhaps you are the same, Miss Hallowes?"

So suddenly private an exchange, and in so public a place! Though the few windows were gray and streaming, the tea-room's big well-lit space with its rows of little white tables was almost too bright to bear. She felt uncomfortably surrounded and pressured, and Miss Bosanquet was looking at her so penetratingly that it made her ashamed. Through some unworldly distillation of reciprocal sympathy, Miss Bosanquet was somehow divining her humiliation, and more: she was granting it license, she was inviting secrets.

"Your brother," she said, "could not have been in good health?"

"He was entirely well."

"I take it that he was cut down in some unfortunate accident—"

"He was a suicide."

"Oh my poor Miss Hallowes. But how—"

"He shot himself. In privacy, in the first-class compartment of a moving train."

All around them there was the chink of cutlery, and a shaking out of mackintoshes, and the collective noise of mixed chatter, pierced now and then by a high note of laughter, and the pungent smell of wet wool. Miss Hallowes marveled: to have told *that* about Warren, how unlike herself it was! But Miss Bosanquet was taking it in without condemnation, and with all the naturalness and practiced composure of a nurse, or a curate; or even some idolatrous healer.

"I understand perfectly," Miss Bosanquet said. "Your mother can hardly have recovered from such a tragedy. She leans on you? She depends on you?"

"All that is true."

"And she has become your life?"

"Mr. Conrad is my life."

Miss Bosanquet bent forward; the hollows in her thin cheeks darkened; her thin shoulders hovered over her teacup. "We are

two of a kind, Miss Hallowes. You with Mr. Conrad, I with
Mr. James. In the whole history of the world there have been
very few as privileged as you and I. We must talk more of this.
I presume you are living with your mother?"

"I have a flat in the Blessington Road, but I often stop with
her for days at a time."

"And how did you come to Mr. Conrad?"

"I was employed by a secretarial office, and he found me
there. He seemed pleased with my work and took me on."

"My own beginning in a similar office was, I fear, a trifle
more devious. I deliberately trained myself for Mr. James.
Certain chapters of *The Ambassadors* were being dictated from
a stenographer's transcription. I heard that Mr. James was dissatisfied and in need of a steady amanuensis, and I set myself to
learn to type. It was a plot—I schemed it all. You will judge me
a dangerous woman!"

"You are very direct."

"Yes, I am very direct. I think you must begin to call me
Theodora. For a very few friends I am Teddie, but you may start
with Theodora. And what am I to call *you*, Miss Hallowes?"

Miss Hallowes gave out a small worried cough. She hoped it
did not mean she was catching cold. She said, "I'm sure it's time
I ought to be off to my mother—"

"Please don't evade me. We have too much in common.
We are each in an extraordinary position. Mr. James and Mr.
Conrad are men of genius, and posterity will honor us for being
the conduits of genius."

"I never think of posterity. I think only of Mr. Conrad, and
how to serve him. The truth is—I am certain he is aware of it—
he said it outright in a letter to Mr. Pinker, a letter that I myself
typed—he is so often unconscious of me, he never realized—he
told Mr. Pinker that were he to allow it I should work for him
for nothing. And I should. Besides, Miss Bosanquet—"

"Theodora."

"—Mr. Pinker is also a conduit, as you put it. All Mr. Conrad's work passes through him."

"And Mr. James's as well. But Mr. Pinker is merely a literary
agent. Mr. Pinker is secondary. He is in fact tertiary. No one

in future will know his name, I assure you. It isn't Mr. Pinker who is blessed to listen to the breathings, and the silences, and the sighs, and the pacings . . . sometimes, when Mr. James and I have been at work for hours, he will quietly place a piece of chocolate near my hand, and will even unwrap the silver foil for me—"

"There are occasions when Mr. Conrad is worn out at the end of the day and he and I sit in opposite chairs in his study and smoke. Mrs. Conrad doesn't like it at all."

"Smoke? Then you are an advanced woman!"

"Not so advanced as you, Miss Bosanquet—but you are very young and more accustomed than I to the new manners."

"*Theodora*. And I am past thirty. If by 'the new manners' you mean the use of our Christian names . . . but look, our lives are so alike, we are almost sisters! It's unnatural for sisters to be so formal—have you no sisters?"

Miss Hallowes said gravely, "Only the two brothers, and one is dead."

"Then you will have a sister in me, and you may confide anything you wish. It's you who seem so young—have you never been in love?"

Miss Hallowes tried out her new little cough once more. It was not a cold coming on; it was recognition. Miss Bosanquet—*Theodora*—was entering a wilderness of strangling vines. In love? She believed, indeed she knew (and had declared it in Mrs. Conrad's hearing!), that Mr. Conrad's works were imprinted on her heart, and would remain so even after her death. The truth was she had loved him, mutely, for six whole years. Mr. Conrad never guessed it; he saw her, she supposed, as an enigmatically living limb of the Machine, and the operation of the Machine was itself enigmatic to him. But Mrs. Conrad, though simple and prosaic, had strong intuitions and watchful eyes, and ears still more vigilant. It had happened more than once that when Miss Hallowes and the family—it now included baby John—were at dinner, and if Miss Hallowes asked for the butter, Mrs. Conrad would turn away her head.

But she confessed none of this to, to . . . Theodora.

She said instead, "You may call me Lilian, but please never

Lily. And if you should ever write my name, you must write it with one *l*, not two."

"Then let me have your hand, Lilian."

Theodora reached over the sugar bowl and fondled the hand she had first touched on the other side of the Master's door. The palm was wide and soft and unprepared for womanly affection.

"Let us meet again very soon," she said.

When Lilian parted from her mother that evening, it was later than she had expected. She had stopped at a butcher's for lamb chops, a treat Mrs. Hallowes relished, and cooked them, and tried to turn the conversation from Warren. Her mother's plaints inevitably led to Warren, and then, predictably, to Lilian and the usual quarrel. Warren had been thirty-seven when he shot himself ("when he was taken," her mother said), exactly the age Lilian was now. To her mother this number was ominous. It signified the end of possibility, the closing down of a life. The dark fate of the unmarried.

"Thirty-seven! It's no good to be alone, dear, just look at your own poor mum, without another soul in the house. I'd be stone solitary if you didn't come by. And there you are, shut up all day long with that old man, and what future are you to get from it?"

"Mr. Conrad isn't old. He's fifty-three, and has young children."

"Yes, and don't I always get an earful, Borys and John, Borys and John. You talk as if they're yours, getting them presents and such. That'd be well and good if you had one or two of your own. Every year you've spent with Mr. Conrad is a year thrown to the winds. I truly think he's wicked, keeping you confined, using you up like that—"

"Mother, please—"

"It's not that I haven't looked into that book of stories you gave me this last Christmas, when what I really needed was a nice warm woolen muffler—"

"Mother, I gave you the muffler too, and a pair of gloves, don't you remember? And you've got your new tea cosy right there on the pot."

"—that wicked wicked *Heart of Darkness*, such a horrifying tale I never in my life could imagine. What must be in that man's mind!"

"It's a very great mind. Mr. Conrad is a very great writer. Posterity will treasure him."

Posterity. How improbable: that formidable word, how it sprang out in all its peculiar awkwardness, not at all the kind of thing that fit her mother's kitchen—the very word Miss Bos . . . *Theodora* . . . had uttered only hours before.

"Well, there you're right," her mother said. "The man has sons, that's the only posterity, if you want to say it like that, any normal person ought to care about. And when you lose one of your own, like our Warren—"

Her mother broke into weeping, and Lilian felt relieved; she was not callous, but she was used to her mother's tears, and preferred them to the subject of a marriage that would never be.

In her bed in the tiny flat in the Blessington Road, Lilian lay listening. She had hung a tall looking-glass on one wall to give the cell-like room an illusion of breadth, and from her pillow she could contemplate her reflection. She saw the white pillow behind her; she saw her head on the pillow. She saw her white face, dim in the half-dark, and (she fancied) ghostly. But she was not a ghost—she was ordinary flesh, as kneadable as dough, a woman's body alone in a bed, with her hand on her breast. A woman's hand, which no one had ever stroked—only that evanescent grazing at Mr. James's door, and that oddly enthralling caress across the tearoom table. Theodora had taken her hand and turned it over and over, and then comically pretended to read her palm, like a gypsy seer; and then she plaited her own hand through Lilian's, and looked at her . . . how to say it?—cannily, almost tantalizingly, as no one had ever looked at her before; as if some unfathomable purpose were pulsing between them. Out of her pillow voices were rising, known and perilous voices: all week she had labored beside Mr. Conrad, capturing the slow windings of the voices as they came twisting out of his viscera, or else hurtled out in violent tornado coilings, so that her fingers had to fly after them, rattling the

Machine, rattling the lamps, rattling Mrs. Conrad's porcelain figurines. They were the very voices she had carried that day to the Reform Club—the heart of a tale still uncompleted, not yet named. The voices were in her ears, in her throat, in the whorls of her fingers. *My double. My second self. My feeling of identity. Our secret partnership. My secret sharer.* The voices shook her, they frightened her, and when Mr. Conrad broke off at last, she saw how spent he was. She too was spent. He took out his flint lighter and put it back in his pocket. He wasn't getting it right, he told her, not even the title, and who knew when the thing might be ready for print? He would not smoke now—he was flushed and sickly and untidy, as though he had been vomiting all afternoon.

She lifted her hand from her breast, and with her other hand delicately, tentatively tapped it, patted it, smoothed it, ran her fingers along the knuckles and under the yielding arch of the palm—just so had Theodora played with her hand in the tea-shop, making a toy of it, and then, *then*—raising it, smiling and smiling, as if about to put the curious plaything to her lips. That knowing smile, and the surprising small shudder that crept along her spine—a woman seeming almost to wish to kiss a woman's hand! It stirred and troubled her—the sensation was so much like . . . that moment once, or moments, when, turning too hastily from the Machine to pass the day's sheaf of typed sheets to Mr. Conrad, a flurry of papers slipped from her, loosed and strewn, landing on the carpet, the two of them plucking and stooping and kneeling ("a pair of coolies in a rice paddy," he growled), their heads close and their hands entangled . . . The ends of his fingers were hard, and the veins in his wrists were thin blue ropes under her eyes: a sailor's worn claw, and the unforeseen movement of it, its gritty touch, rocked her and affected her with a kind of thirst. And there was Mrs. Conrad in the doorway, looking in angrily, and it was only Mr. Conrad holding out his hand to help Miss Hallowes up from her knees.

From the alley below her bedroom window—the filtering panes that sheathed her in a dusky mist of almost-light—Lilian heard a sharp clatter: a metal trash barrel overturned. The fox

again, scavenging. A sly fox out of a fable, a fox that belonged
in a wood—but there are sightings of foxes in the outlying
streets of London, and once, coming home in the winter night
from her mother's, she had glimpsed a brown streak under the
lamppost; and then it was gone. And another time, in the early
morning—the woman and the animal, both of them solitary,
two stragglers separated from the pack, transfixed, staring,
panicked into immobility. The fox's eyes were oddly lit, as if
glittering pennies had got into its sockets; its ears stood straight
up; its white tail hung low, like a shamed flag; its flanks trembled. A nervous wild thing. It twitched the upper muscle of its
long snout—she saw the zigzag glint of teeth, the dangerous
grin of ambush. How beautiful it was!

And the voices in the pillow persisted, growing louder with
every repeated cry: *my double, my secret self, our secret partnership*
. . . In her dry-hearted bed Lilian held up her two hands and
matched them one against the other, thumb to thumb, and
observed how persuasively, how miraculously, they made an
almost identical pair.

What was most remarkable was that there was never a contest
between them. They were not destined to be rivals or champions of rivals. In her very first note Theodora had insisted
on this. The note was also an invitation: was Lilian fond of
theater, and would she be willing to accompany Theodora to
the Lyceum Tuesday next, to see Mrs. Patrick Campbell as Lady
Macbeth? Lilian had promised to have dinner with her mother
that evening, and how could she disappoint her? But she did,
and her mother wept. Similar disappointments followed, until
her mother's mood hardened still more, and her tears increased:
it was nearly like losing another child, she said, since she was
left to be abandoned and alone, with that unfeeling Mr. Conrad
claiming Lilian's nights as well, and what a cruel waste of a
young woman's life!

It was so jolly to be with Theodora—she truly was like a
sister. In the theater, at the most shivery instant, when Lady
Macbeth was gazing at her bloody hand and muttering "Out,
damned spot," Theodora drew Lilian into her arms to shelter

her from the fright of it, and this time really did kiss her, on her left temple, on her cheek, on her chin, and almost, almost on her lips. And Theodora had so many ideas for outings, some of them (or so it struck Lilian) just on the edge of risk or even threat. It became a teasing commonplace between them that Theodora was bold and Lilian was faint-hearted—though it was only Theodora who did the teasing, as if Lilian's reticence were merely a sham, since of course Lilian was the daring one: hadn't she agreed to come ice-skating, when she had never skated in all her life before? Teetering on the ice, Lilian's unaccustomed feet seemed to belong to someone else—the blades skittered uncontrollably, and her heart in its unfamiliar cavern vibrated madly—but Theodora's strong saving embrace was firm at her waist, and the warmth of her breath was feathery under her ear, laughing: "Oh my brave Lily, you're so red in the face you look positively painted!" It was the first time Theodora had called her Lily; she did not protest. After this, an excursion to the New Forest, where freshly falling snow obliterated the paths, and ownerless horses roamed free and untrammeled, sidling toward the human intruders and sniffing after crumbs with their dark vast smoldering nostrils and yolk-colored eye-whites and rolling imbecile eyeballs and gigantic mindless heads, as menacing as the massive mechanisms of train wheels seen too close.

There were parts of London Theodora knew, shadowy corners Lilian had never ventured into, and incense-stung cellars where motley strangers squabbled in raucous remote accents, like hotheaded revelers at an incomprehensible carnival. And sometimes the carnival turned up in Theodora's rooms at the top of an old row house, with a skylight, and on the black-papered walls murky blurry paintings that looked as if they had been dropped in a tub of water and got smeared all over. Women in rippling shawls, gripping the strawlike stems of wine glasses, moved stubbornly from painting to painting: each fiercely stained rectangle seemed an argument to be won. But at length these fearsome women went away, and Theodora said, "All this nice chardonnay left, and you haven't had a drop. I hope you haven't been brought up Temperance, Lil!"

"Mother and I used to take a beer or so with Warren, but never since. And Mr. Conrad, when he's not in company with ladies, prefers . . . well, the other sort."

"I won't ply you with whiskey, my dear, we'll leave that to the men, but wine you must have. One glass to gladden your heart, two to gladden mine."

Lilian obeyed and drank, with small hesitant sips. The moon was in the skylight, and the inky walls with their perplexing daubs pressed against her spine. She felt she had been lured to a far lighthouse built on a rock in the middle of a treacherous estuary. It was plain that Theodora had concocted all these unusual scenes and adventures to amuse and thrill her; she understood this—but why?

"Say Teddie and I'll tell you," Theodora commanded.

Lilian looked into her glass—the wine made a kind of mirror, a gathering of morning dews, and her eye lay dreaming there, pale as a lily and unexpectedly lovely, a tiny round calm pond lazily twirling, and unnaturally lit, like the fox's eye.

"Teddie," she said faintly, and let Theodora kiss her again, in her strange new way. She did not really like this—she did not like it at all—but she had a secret trick, a hidden lever at the back of her brain that she could raise or lower, nearly at will, whenever Theodora kissed her with that wary slow incautious kiss, as though unlatching a forbidden room. The trick was dangerous (everything that derived from Theodora was dangerous): Lilian touched the secret lever in her mind, and immediately Theodora became Mr. Conrad. Now and then a glowering unwelcome apparition wearing the face of Mrs. Conrad erupted on the underside of her tongue, and then Theodora was again Theodora; but most often Theodora's insistent mouth was wickedly transformed into Mr. Conrad's—she could almost decipher his puzzling primordial Polish whisperings, and sense the wiry brush of his mustache.

The wine was drained; the moon too was drained from its surrounding glass. Under the blackened skylight Theodora was smiling her heralding smile. "You will remember," she said, "my admission the afternoon we met—"

"When you ambushed me," Lilian said.

"Yes, yes, you brazen thing, call it what you will. I've explained all that, and aren't you glad? We are friends, and sisters, and very soon we shall be sharers in a glorious act. It has only been a question of courage, of aspiring to courage, and there can be no aspiration without training. You recall," Theodora pressed on, "how I trained myself to become worthy of Mr. James. I wished to be the companion—yes, the companion!—of the greatest writer of the age."

Lilian said flatly, "Mr. Conrad is the greatest writer of the age."

"This will not be our quarrel. We shall have no quarrel at all. I believe I can boast that I have made you braver than you were—as one guides a lily afloat on a leaf into unknown waters. You have grown accustomed to the unaccustomed—even to a modicum of shock. You have been enrolled, you have been tutored, you have been apprenticed. I am happy that I have sometimes astonished you. But you must be braver now than you have ever been, if we are to have our success."

"To sit beside Mr. Conrad, and hear his voice each day of my life, is the only success I have ever desired."

"Lily, there is more. Much, much more."

"I want no more than I have."

"You do, Lily, you do. And you deserve more."

"I am merely an amanuensis. Why must I deserve more?"

"Because," Theodora said, "more is already in the power of your grasp. There is more to be had, if only we dare to take it. Please note that I say 'we.' It cannot be achieved save in partnership. We are warp and weft, you and I. You are the lily, and I am the leaf that carries you."

Lilian took a breath; she was famished for air. Theodora was proposing . . . what? That she become an accomplice of sorts, but toward what impenetrable end? Her pulse was quivering as it had quivered on the ice, but she hadn't really been frightened then, or in the theater (it was only Mrs. Patrick Campbell and some red stuff), or when the wells of the horses' nostrils blasted their steamy fumes, or among the Wiltshire steles in twilight, or in those cellars . . . Everything Theodora had led her to was untried and unnerving and curiously beautiful, even when it was repellent (she thought of the fox and its creamy dark gums glimpsed above the spiky teeth); she had never been afraid of any of it. She was afraid now, when Theodora, taking her hand, went on turning it this way and that, turning it as she had done in the teashop long ago, as if she could turn away her fear.

"Think, Lily," Theodora urged, "you deem yourself 'merely' an amanuensis. Merely! I dislike this 'merely,' yet let us examine it. In all the past, has there ever been an amanuensis who has earned immortality? Who leaves a distinguishing mark on the unsuspecting future? One who stands as an indelible presence?"

Lilian withdrew her hand as if Theodora had set it on fire; she jumped up. "Is this a game?" she cried. "I am Mr. Conrad's secretary! Merely his secretary! It's Mr. Conrad who is immortal! His force, his vision! Why do you try to equate us, why do you trivialize?"

"Sit down, my silly Lily. You are too impatient—I am attempting to engage you in a profundity. I do not trivialize. We are speaking of the generations. If your Mr. Conrad should be venerated as far into the time to come as, let us say, the twenty-first century, then I concede he may be counted among the immortals. And Mr. James unquestionably. But are they interchangeable, these likely immortals? You must know Mr. James's belief—I hope I don't offend—so he once put it to me—that Mr. Conrad's novels on occasion take on the aspect of huge fluid puddings—"

"And for my part," Lilian retorted, "I have heard Mr. Conrad tell Mr. Wells that Mr. James's tales simply evade, that they leave behind no more than a phosphorescent trail—"

"Enough! And never mind. There will be no competition—I insist on it."

Lilian softened. Theodora was genuinely not looking to provoke. In her most teasing affectionate sisterly way, hadn't she called Lilian "my silly"?—the tenderest sort of chaffing. Besides, Mr. James and Mr. Conrad were indeed not interchangeable, Mr. Conrad being so much the superior. What Mr. Conrad knew of the sea, and of the ambivalence of men's souls! Whereas Mr. James was . . . *American*. Theodora was threatening nothing—it was one of her larks, an innocuous game after all, a frolic, no different from that eccentric play of the kisses, or those confounding moments in the Stonehenge dusk once, when Theodora masked her face with her gloved hands and spread the fingers and peered through them as though each one were a small upright stone pillar, and ground out a mocking phantom Druid liturgy made up of coarse guttural lunatic syllables—so that Lilian, taken aback, had a little scare, until Theodora's laughter burbled out and left her feeling stupid. "It's your mother," Theodora chided, "your lugubrious mother— she's stunted you with all that gloom. She leaves you no space for mischief. Oh my poor Lily, when will you learn to play?"

So it was only play. A diversion. Fear? What was there to fear? But the skylight was as dense as the walls, oppressively so: the whole weight of stony astronomies seemed about to crash in on their heads. And here was Theodora, larking about with talk of eternal life for those forgettable wisps of ephemera who are faithful at their Machines day after day, typing, typing, typing, until they disintegrate into the dust of the earth . . .

"Think!" said Theodora. "Everlastingness for such as us! Who!"

Conciliating, Lilian overreached. "Boswell," she said finally.

"Boswell immortal? As an amanuensis? Never! An annoying sycophant. His only occupation was to follow in Dr. Johnson's wake, whether he was wanted or not."

"Still, he set down whatever Johnson spoke—"

"He wasn't wanted. Johnson didn't *choose* him. An amanuensis must be chosen. You and I, Lily, have been chosen. Try again."

Lilian released a dreary sigh. This diversion—this digression (but from what goal?)—was not to her taste. Perhaps it was true that like her mother—like Mr. Conrad himself!—she had been born to an uneasy lingering gloom. "Then Moses," she said, "who took dictation directly from the author. And was certainly chosen. Now there it is, done, your riddle is solved."

"Not satisfactorily. Truly," Theodora scoffed, "what have you and I to do with Moses? All those tedious Jewish rules! I ask you, my dearest Lily, why must we be confined by rules, when all the world's joy runs past them? I promised you a profundity.

The chance lies before us—we shall be the first. If only you have courage enough, we two, separately and entwined, will live forever. Forever, Lily! The generations will *feel* what we do."

Under the skylight, opaque and invisible, and between the cryptic blotches on the walls, darkened now to a row of indistinct smudges (a single lamp stood in a distant corner), Theodora's look sent out a feral copper gleam. It came to Lilian then, sadly, horribly—oh, horribly—that it was not a game at all: she was being drawn instead into some dire scheme of an unbalanced spirit.

"No one," she said (and to her surprise, she heard her mother's bleak reproachful wisdom creeping up from her own throat), "no one can live forever."

But Theodora let out her jubilant larking laugh. "The Master will. Doubtless your Mr. Conrad will. And so shall we—we mere amanuenses.—Wait, Lily, where are you off to? We agreed you would stay the night—"

Lilian flung herself from Theodora's touch. "It's been weeks since I had a proper visit with Mother," she called back—what foolishness, it was two in the morning!—and hurried down the stairs.

Theodora had frightened Lilian, but Theodora was, as it happened, altogether in her right mind. She was far from mad; she was consummately clever. Her stratagem was both ingenious and simple. And it was covert, designed to remain permanently undetected—this accounted for its originality. Also, it eschewed what has always been regarded as axiomatic: that immortality implies, and resides in, a name. Shakespeare is immortal, we say; and Archimedes, because his bath water spilled over, permitting him to dub the mess "physics." The Pyramids are rumored to owe their shape to Pythagoras and his hypotenuse. Shakespeare, Archimedes, Pythagoras, and any number of other luminaries (not forgetting James and Conrad) may all merit immortality in the ordinary sense—but Theodora's notion of everlastingness was more cunning than any such homage given to the longevity of a proper noun. What Theodora was after was distinctly radical: she wished to send into the future a nameless immutability, visible though invisible, smooth while bent, unchangeable yet altered, integrated even as it sought to be wholly alien. And it was to be secret. Nor could she accomplish it alone. It demanded a sharer, a double, a partner.

But meanwhile she had lost Lilian, and Lilian was indispensable for Theodora's plan. How to get her back? Four or five notes, wreathed in remorse and painted sunflowers (copied from one of those smeary foreign artists she incomprehensibly admired), went unanswered. It was a month before Lilian replied. Her tone was cool. Mr. Conrad, she explained, was keeping her exceedingly occupied; and her mother's spirits had sunk yet again, requiring Lilian's almost nightly attendance; and Mrs. Conrad had lately been particularly disagreeable. "I hope," the letter ended, "that in view of these increasing difficulties you will understand why I must discontinue our meetings, which by their nature distract me from my obligations and concerns."

Theodora was undiscouraged.

My dear Lilian [she wrote],

Of the "difficulties" you allude to, surely your relation to Mrs. Conrad continues as the most onerous. I believe I can, even at this removal, discern what you must bear. A great man's wife, should he have one—and unlike Mr. James, Mr. Conrad is very much a married man!—will too often be under the delusion that, by virtue of conjugal proximity, she can see into the heart of his genius. Yet how can this be? A shameful hubris! It is only you, the artist's true vessel, the sole brain to receive the force of creation in its first flooding, who can make this claim. A day may come—that day inevitably *will* come—when an imperious wife will publicly usurp your knowledge, your penetration, your having *inhabited* the work, and will profess to see and feel what you alone have seen and felt. What form this wrongful seizure will take, who can tell? In gossip to future biographers perhaps, in boastful letters (doubtless she already misleads Mr. Pinker), and, heaven forfend, even in a braggart's memoir from her own unskilled pen.

No, Lily, this cannot go forward. You must forestall such a devouring—it has the power to demean Mr. Conrad's art. You rightly speak of obligation and concern. *Here* must be your obligation and concern. Lily, come back to me! Together we will thwart these spousal depredations!

The response was quick:

Then you must make me a promise. You will no longer speak absurdly of the soul's afterlife—I hold with Mr. Conrad that we are tragic creatures destined to become dust. That is why his ambition is pure (it is the ambitiousness mortality confers), while Mrs. Conrad's is impure: it is, as you say, a lust to purloin, to burn with a stolen fire.—Secondly, though not secondarily, you will no longer press on me unfamiliar intimacies. If you keep to this agreement, I will consent to a resumption of our acquaintance.

How easily it was done! Theodora had won her back—wooed her, rather, through the bait of jealousy, that lowest of human passions. Lilian, Theodora concluded, was now sufficiently primed to collaborate—on the condition that Theodora would merely revise the footing of their connection. Easily, easily done! Lilian cannot be tempted by the sweet fruit of everlastingness? No matter: then she will be seduced by the bitter hope of undermining her persecutor. Lilian repudiates Theodora's kisses? Ah, but what transports are being granted elsewhere, and without the impediment of the other's reluctance!

In the weeks during which Lilian had absented herself, Henry James had received yet another eminent literary visitor: Mr. Leslie Stephen, accompanied by the younger of his two daughters. She had come to pay homage to the Master, who welcomed her charmingly, partly out of deference to her redoubtable father, a stern bearded figure with the bent back of a myopic scholar, but also because she had begun to acquire some respectable small notice of her own. At twenty-eight, she was already an accomplished critic. Theodora, watchful as she went on tidying the masses of papers surrounding her Machine,

took care to observe Miss Stephen in particular. She was impatient and nervous, and appeared to be irritated by her father,
who was enveloping their host in a burst of egotistical volubil-
ity. It was well known that Miss Stephen had a denigrating wit,
and that she belonged to a notorious cenacle of youthful writers
and artists, Fabians and freethinkers all, two or three of whom
Theodora had encountered in those dusky contentious heter-
odox cellars. Miss Stephen herself was said to be melancholic
and reclusive; even here, in this pleasant and spacious room,
she kept her distance from her father, roaming disconsolately
from the hearth to the window, where she took in with an
indifferent blink the Turkish embassy's rooftop, and again back
to the fire. Her troubled eyes were round and gray and judging,
her throat was bare of any ornament, and she wore her hair in a
softly sculpted chignon (a chignon as unlike Lilian's unreliable
falling-apart bun as a croissant is different from a dumpling), so
that in profile she had the look of a dreaming Aphrodite. An
unprompted indulgence drew Theodora to the clear silhouette
of that brow and nose and chin; but Miss Stephen's magnetism
was reserved and unconfessed.

That same night (Theodora learned this only long afterward)
Miss Stephen wrote in her diary: "Poor Mr. James eaten alive
by Father today, who harangued incessantly, evidently taking
the wrong side of the Conrad question. Miss Bosanquet rather
handsome, an overvigilant coxswain in white shirt-waist and
cinched blue skirt. For a loyal amanuensis she is not notably
submissive. A sapphist, I wager."

Easily, easily done. Soon enough, Theodora had no further
desire for Lilian's clandestine lips. She had Miss Stephen's. And
when Miss Stephen became, of all things, engaged to a penniless Jew, she had them still.

Lilian was safe; she *felt* safe. She had abandoned Theodora
and returned—it meant she had prevailed. She had warned
Theodora, and Theodora had yielded. There were no more
endearments, no more embraces, no more unwanted kisses.
The kisses especially disturbed: they called up shivery hallucinations, illicit longings, and always at the rim of these, the

threatening accusing glaring phantom of a scornful Jessie Conrad. It was a relief to be rid of them. And strange to say, Theodora in the relinquishment of these affectionate habits was as peacefully gratified as before, and even multiplied her smiles. With the kisses gone, so was that foolish talk of immortality, whatever Theodora had intended by it—it seemed to have nothing to do with heaven or angels.

Yet the plan was to go on precisely as it had first been conceived. It was only that they must now confront it through Lilian's eyes. "I have been too terribly selfish," Theodora said. "You were right to chastise me, Lilian. I have been forgetful of what you must be enduring—"

"It's not Mother I mind so much," Lilian said, mildly enough.

"Your mother's resentments are minor. Mrs. Conrad's are mammoth. She treats you as an appendage. A household tool, perhaps."

"She hates me," Lilian said.

"Then you will triumph in the end."

"In the end?"

"When our purpose is in place."

Cozening Lilian was becoming tedious. Theodora was restless: when *would* their purpose be in place? The beautiful task lay just ahead. She was eager to effect it, she had transformed its carapace to please her necessary confederate, and here was Lilian, dragging, dragging, perpetually in want of wheedling. It was difficult to be attentive: her innermost thoughts were dizzying, they were with Miss Stephen, who had begun to say Teddie, and Teddie had begun to say . . . but meanwhile Lilian was reflecting that Theodora no longer cared to call her Lily, though once or twice the old companionable syllables slipped out, broken or misspoken, so that Lilian believed she almost heard—it could not have been—something that sounded like . . . was it Ginny? Or was it Lily after all? Or *was* it Ginny? Or perhaps—but of course it must have been Geneva.

"That time in the hotel," Lilian joined in, "in Geneva, when Mr. Conrad had the gout again—"

Theodora stared. A lurking heat engorged her neck. The

dream is father to the word: good Lord, had she actually pronounced Miss Stephen's name aloud? No, not her name exactly . . .

"You remember, don't you, when he was wrestling with his anarchist story, three years ago or so, and Mrs. Conrad *would* insist on taking the children abroad, and the baby had the whooping cough, and Borys came down with a fever—"

"Geneva, yes," Theodora agreed, unbuttoning her collar— bloody hot or no, she must recover now—"you mention it so often. How Mrs. Conrad blundered."

"Interfered! Underfoot night and day with those sick boys, never permitting him to concentrate, despoiling his work—"

This, then, was the hour.

"And that is why," Theodora trumpeted, "it is imperative to defeat her. We are going to defeat her, Lilian," and at long last she defined her design.

Theodora's plot.

Plot? Should art be dismissed as a conniving? The will to change nature's given is the font of all creation. Even God, faced with *tohu vavohu*, welter and waste, formlessness and void, thought it suitable to introduce light and dark, day and night: the seamlessness of disparity. Or regard the mosaic maker, painstakingly choosing one tessera to set beside another, in a glorious pattern of heretofore unimagined juxtapositions—yet because the stones as they were found have been disarranged, shall he be despised as a violator? If Theodora's scheme is sinful, let Michelangelo be ashamed: he prevails on God to touch Adam's finger. Like twinned with unlike is beauty's shock. And beauty, as Theodora knows, is eternal.

"Now first," she began, "you must tell me Mr. Conrad's procedure exactly as it occurs each day."

"He dictates, I type," Lilian said.

"Of course. And when do you present him with a finished typescript?"

"Never immediately. Sometimes our sessions are very long. Mr. Conrad rushes on, he puts up his hand as if to seize an elusive word out of the air. And sometimes—well, it can happen that he misspeaks an English idiom. Which, I will confess, I silently correct. Often I must retype a day's work several times in order to have a fair copy."

"All that is similar to my own experience with Mr. James. Mr. James, however, is beyond correction."

"Mr. James was not born in Poland."

"But he was born in America, which makes his intimacy with the English language all the more remarkable. Then you believe you have Mr. Conrad's trust?"

"Fully. Completely. I am confident of this. It's only Mrs. Conrad—"

"Very well," Theodora broke in. "This is what you will do, Lilian. I am to give you a passage—some sentences, let us say, or a paragraph or two—this remains to be decided upon. It will be selected from a singular work Mr. James is currently engaged in, a kind of ghost story, about a double, a man appalled by the encroachment of a second self—"

But Lilian gasped, "Why should you give such a thing to me?"

"You must listen attentively, or you will fail to follow. What I propose is not overly intricate, but it demands an orderly patience. We cannot allow missteps, we must be scrupulous. As I say, you will take from me a passage from Mr. James—an exquisite passage, I assure you—and in return I will receive from you some small striking extract from whatever work it is that occupies Mr. Conrad at present."

"Theodora, what nonsense is this, why are you making sport—"

"Mr. James's story is called 'The Jolly Corner.' What name does Mr. Conrad give his?"

"He has settled finally on 'The Secret Sharer,' and though it looks to grow long, it is not to be a novel. A tale rather, an astonishing tale, also about a double, how can this be!—but what has one to do with the other?"

"When we are done, everything. And if you are fastidious, it will yield everything you desire. Please hear me out. After we have made the exchange, you will carefully embed Mr. James's fragment in some hospitable part of Mr. Conrad's final copy, and I will insert Mr. Conrad's into a suitable cleft in Mr. James's manuscript. Now do you see?"

"Do I see? What *should* I see? A confusion, a scramble! What is to be gained by such mischief? Mr. Conrad reads over very thoroughly whatever I show him, and the fair copy when it is ready for print most thoroughly of all. Any foreign matter, whatever its intent, he will instantly detect, he will certainly excise it—"

"He will detect nothing. He will excise nothing. He will not perceive it as foreign matter. Nor will Mr. James."

"Mr. Conrad not to recognize what is and is not his own voice? How can you say this? What is to prevent him from discerning so bizarre an intrusion?"

"A lack of suspicion, a lack of any expectation of the extraneous. Simply that—and something still more persuasive. The egoism of the artist. The greater the art, the greater the egoism—and the greater the assumptions of egoism. Mr. Conrad will read—he will admire—he will wonder at what he believes he has wrought—he will congratulate himself! Privately, in the way of the artist in contemplation of his art. And there it will rest, what you call foreign matter, foreign no more, absorbed, ingested, seamless—a kidnapped diamond to shine through the ages, and you and I, Lilian, will have set it there!"

Theodora blazed; she was all theater; it seemed to Lilian that her fevered look, her shamelessly unbuttoned blouse, her untamed zeal, were more terrible than when Mrs. Patrick Campbell had pretended to be Lady Macbeth—but Theodora was not pretending.

In her mother's flat wail Lilian asked, "And will you also take Mr. James for a dupe?"

"Certainly not. Self-belief is no deception. It is how the artist's mind assimilates and transforms, and who has witnessed these raptures more than we?"

"But what you want from me is a deception all the same. Why do you suppose I care to have any part in it?"

"Because you do care. It means your triumph. Can't you *see*, Lilian? Mrs. Conrad exalts herself—how many times have I heard you complain of this?"

"I complain only of her presumption."

"Precisely. Her presumption in thinking that she has right-ful possession of her husband's fecundity, that she is equal to its every motion, that she—she, a wife!—is the habitation of every word, and why? Because she sleeps in his bed. In his bed in the oblivion of night!—when it is you who in the light of day drink in the minutest vibrations of his spirit. What will Mrs. Conrad ever know of the kidnapped diamond? As long as you live, you will own this secret. If she demeans you, what will it matter? You have the hidden proof of her exclusion. Her exclusion! What deeper power than the power of covert knowledge? A victory, Lilian—see it, take it!"

Lilian was silent. Then "Ah," she murmured. And again, as if born for the first time into airy breath, "Ah."

Oh, easily, easily done! Lilian was satisfied, she was assuaged, she was enticed, she was caught; she was *in*. It was plain to Theodora that Miss Stephen . . . *Ginny* . . . could not have been won over so readily. Miss Stephen was not so pliant. Miss Stephen was prone to mockery—she was no one's confederate, she went her own way. Sometimes, she said, she could hear the birds sing in Greek.

And so Theodora's determined map, with its side roads and turnings, proceeded.

"How fortuitous," she told Lilian, "to find ourselves so very far advanced even before we have rightly begun. We could not be better placed. This image of a strange and threatening alter ego—that two such illustrious minds should seize on an iden-tical notion!"

"But Mr. Conrad's is a tale of the sea," Lilian demurred.

"That is why you must remember to keep clear of vistas—we cannot allow Mr. James's indoor characters to go wandering over Mr. Conrad's watery world. And the same with interi-ors: they must not fall into contradiction, a chimney-piece abutting a mast. As for names and dialogue, these too must be avoided—"

"If we are to omit all that," Lilian argued, "what remains to be extracted?"

The vexation of a dull counterpart. What would be the point of it all if the result were to fail of beauty, of artfulness?

"The heart, the lung, the blood and the brain!" Theodora shot out. "What we mean to search for are those ruthless invokings, those densest passages of psychological terror that can chill the bone. Pick out a charged exactitude, tease out of your man the root of his fertility—"

Theodora halted; she looked hard at Lilian: fearful dry celibate Lilian. How to arouse her to reckless nerve, to position her at the mouth of the beckoning labyrinth? To crank her imagination into life? She had been induced to favor the goal. She must now be induced to brave the dive.

"Lilian," Theodora dared, "I entreat you: squeeze out the very semen of the thing!"

Lilian neither blushed nor paled. "When we were first taken to see Warren's body, Mother and I," she said, "it was I who observed that the bullet, though applied to the head, had done exactly that. I have never forgotten the sight of it."

Theodora was chastened. "Then you are ready for our venture."

And still there were brambles and stiles on the way: the matter of timing, for one, impossible to predict or control. The synchronization vital to success. It was not a race, and even if it had been, it was scarcely likely that a pair of magisterial eminences would reach the finish line together. Now and again either Theodora or Lilian was obliged to temporize, and it happened once that Mr. Pinker received two notes only days apart, each puzzling over an untoward delay:

Dear Pinker,

Am being held up, though you should have the promised clutch of pages before too long. Miss Hallowes regretfully reports that her ribbon is fading toward illegibility. A fresh one awaits at the stationer's. In the meantime I am bursting with various damnations—

Yrs,
J. Conrad

My dear Pinker,

　　To attend most confidingly to your anxiety: Miss Bosanquet is indeed conscientiously aware of the exigencies of
Scribner et al. I rely on her own admirable impatience—she
assures me that she hastens, she drives on!

Yours faithfully,
Henry James

Nevertheless it is on an ordinary Thursday afternoon in
the late winter of 1910 that the illumined moment strikes. It
erupts with the miraculous yet altogether natural simultaneity
of petals in a flowerbed unfolding all at once. Or else (so Theodora conceives it) as an ingeniously skilled artisan will slide a
wedge of finely sanded wood into its neighboring groove to
effect an undetectable coupling. Mortise and tenon!—the fit
flawless, perfected, burnished. Or else (as Lilian, hesitant still,
yet elated, sees it): like two birds trading nests, noiselessly, delicately, each one instantly at home.

　　In Henry James's London rooms a small dazzling fragment
of "The Secret Sharer" flows, as if ordained, into the unsuspecting veins of "The Jolly Corner," and in Joseph Conrad's
study in a cottage in Kent the hot fluids of "The Jolly Corner"
run, uninhibited, into a sutured crevice in "The Secret Sharer."
There is no visible seam, no hair's-breadth fissure; below the
surface—submicroscopically, so to speak—the chemical amalgam causes no disturbance, molecule melds into molecule all
serenely. And meanwhile Mrs. Conrad goes on sniffing and
frowning in those leisured intervals when her husband and his
amanuensis sit smoking together—but Lilian, far from cower-
ing, only glows. And Theodora?—well, it makes up for fickle
Miss Stephen's recent defection that Theodora has, after all,
won more than an ephemeral kiss.

　　What has Theodora won? Exactly the thing she so resplend-
ently envisioned: two amanuenses, two negligible footnotes
overlooked by the most diligent scholarship, unsung by all the
future, leaving behind an immutable mark—an everlasting sign
that they lived, they felt, they acted! An immortality equal to
the unceasing presence of those prodigious peaks and craters

thrown off by some meaningless cataclysm of meteorites: but peaks and craters are careless nature's work, while Theodora and Lilian humanly, mindfully, with exacting intent, dictate the outcome of their desires. Lilian wills her hopeful fragile spite. Theodora commands her fingerprint, all unacknowledged, to be eternally engraven, as material and manifest as peak and crater. And so it is, and so it will be.

As for James and Conrad, in personal and literary character they are too unlike to sustain the early ardor of their long friendship. Though it has cooled, they are, if unwittingly, bonded forever: a fact in plain print, and in successive editions, that no biographer has yet been able to trace.

What is most extraordinary of all, however, is that Miss Bosanquet and Miss Hallowes, after the changelings were crucially implanted, never spoke another word to each other, nor did they ever meet again. It is probable that posterity, gullible as always, will suppose that they never met at all. But—truth to tell—posterity will have nothing in particular to remark of either one, there being no significant record extant.

NOTE: Among the historical actualities imagination dares to flout are club rules and death. Was Leslie Stephen in his grave nearly a decade before he makes his appearance here, and was no woman permitted to set foot in London's all-male Reform Club? Never mind, says Fiction; what fun, laughs Transgression; so what? mocks Dream.

ESSAYS

Transcending the Kafkaesque

HOW, AFTER ALL, does one dare, how can one presume? Franz Kafka, named for the fallen crown of a defunct empire, has himself metamorphosed into an empire of boundless discourse, an empire stretched out across a firmament of interpretation: myth, parable, allegory, clairvoyance, divination; theory upon thesis upon theophany; every conceivable incarnation of the sexual, the political, the psychological, the metaphysical. Another study of the life? Another particle in the deep void of a proliferating cosmos. How, then, does one dare to add so much as a single syllable, even in the secondary exhalation of a biography?

One dares because of the culprits. The culprits are two. One is "Kafkaesque," which buries the work. The other is "transcend," which buries the life. A scrupulous and capacious biography may own the power to drive away these belittlements, and Reiner Stach's mammoth three volumes (only the second and third have appeared in English so far) are superbly tempered for exorcism. With its echo of "grotesque," the ubiquitous term "Kafkaesque" has long been frozen into permanence, both in the dictionary and in the most commonplace vernacular. Comparative and allusive, it has by now escaped the body of work it is meant to evoke. To say that such and such a circumstance is Kafkaesque is to admit to the denigration of an imagination that has burned a hole in what we take to be modernism—even in what we take to be the ordinary fabric and intent of language. Nothing is "like" "The Hunger Artist." Nothing is "like" "The Metamorphosis." Whoever utters "Kafkaesque" has neither fathomed nor intuited nor felt the impress of Kafka's devisings. If there is one imperative that ought to accompany any biographical or critical approach, it is that Kafka is not to be mistaken for the Kafkaesque. The Kafkaesque is what

Kafka presumably "stands for"—an unearned and usurping explication. And from the very start, serious criticism has been overrun by the Kafkaesque, the lock that portends the key: homoeroticism for one maven, the father-son entanglement for another, the theological uncanny for yet another. Or else it is the slippery commotion of time; or of messianism; or of Thanatos as deliverance. The Kafkaesque, finally, is reductiveness posing as revelation.

The persistence of "transcend" is still more troublesome. What is it that Kafka is said to transcend? Every actual and factual aspect of the life he lived, everything that formed and informed him, that drew or repelled him, the time and the place, the family and the apartment and the office—and Prague itself, with its two languages and three populations fixed at the margins of a ruling sovereignty sprawled across disparate and conflicting nationalities. Kafka's fictions, free grains of being, seem to float, untethered and self-contained, above the heavy explicitness of a recognizable society and culture. And so a new and risen Kafka is born, cleansed of origins, unchained from the tensions, many of them nasty, of Prague's roiling German-Czech-Jewish brew, its ambient anti-Semitism and its utopian Zionism, its Jewish clubs and its literary stewpot of Max Brod, Oskar Baum, Franz Werfel, Otto Pick, Felix Weltsch, Hugo Bergmann, Ernst Weiss. In this understanding, Kafka is detached not from the claims of specificity—what is more strikingly particularized than a Kafka tale?—but from a certain designated specificity.

In an otherwise seamless introduction to Kafka's *Collected Stories*, John Updike takes up the theme of transcendence with particular bluntness: "Kafka, however unmistakable the ethnic source of his 'liveliness' and alienation, avoided Jewish parochialism, and his allegories of pained awareness take upon themselves the entire European—that is to say, predominantly Christian—malaise." As evidence, he notes that the Samsas in "The Metamorphosis" make the sign of the cross. Nothing could be more wrong-headed than this parched Protestant misapprehension of Mitteleuropa's tormented Jewish psyche. (Danilo Kiš, Isaac Babel, Elias Canetti, Walter Benjamin,

Gershom Scholem, Stefan Zweig, Josef Roth: from these wounded ghosts, a chorus of knowing laughter.) The idea of the parochial compels its opposite: what is not parochial must be universal. And if the parochial is deemed a low distraction from the preponderant social force—"that is to say, predominantly Christian"—then what is at work is no more than supercilious triumphalism. To belittle as parochial the cultural surround ("the ethnic source") that bred Kafka is to diminish and disfigure the man—to do to him what so many of Kafka's stories do to their hapless protagonists.

As biographer, Reiner Stach will have none of this. Nowhere in *The Decisive Years* nor in *The Years of Insight* does he impose on Kafka an all-encompassing formula. He offers no key, no code, no single-minded interpretive precept: the Kafkaesque is mercifully missing. Instead, he allows Kafka's searing introspections, as they emerge from the letters and diaries, to serve as self-defining clues. Kafka saw his stories not as a reader or critic will, but *from the inside*, as the visceral sensations of *writing*. "I am made of literature; I am nothing else and cannot be anything else," he announced to Felice Bauer, the woman he would never marry. It was a statement meant not so much metaphorically as bodily. At twenty-nine, on September 23, 1912, he exulted in his diary as an exhausted but victorious long-distance swimmer, on completing a marathon, might:

> The story, "The Judgment," I wrote during the night of the 22nd, from 10 P.M. to 6 A.M., in one sitting. I could hardly pull my legs out from under the desk; they had become stiff from sitting. The frightful exertion and pleasure of experiencing how the story developed right in front of me, as though I were moving forward through a stretch of water. Several times during the night I lugged my own weight on my back. How everything can be hazarded, how for everything, even for the strangest idea, a great fire is ready in which it expires and rises up again. . . . At 2 A.M. I looked at the clock for the last time. As the maid came through the front room in the morning, I was writing the last sentence. Turning off the lamp, the light of day. The

slight pains in my chest. The exhaustion that faded away in
the middle of the night. . . . Only in this way can writing be
done, only in a context like this, with a complete opening
of body and soul.

Stach will go no further than Kafka's own reflections and
admissions. In this restraint he follows Kafka himself: on no
account, he instructed the publisher of "The Metamorphosis,"
should the insect be pictured. He saw explication as intrusion,
and willful interpretation as a false carapace. A premonitory
authorial warning: he was already warding off the Kafkaesque.

In refusing the critic's temptation, Stach is freed as biographer. Open to him is the limitless web of the societal, the
political, the historical, the customary, the trivial; everything
material, explicit, contemporaneous—sometimes day by day,
on occasion even hour by hour; the trains and the telephones;
the offices and the office machines; the bureaucrats and their
litigations; the apartment and the family's noises. In brief:
the parochial, in all its dense particularity. The biographer
excavates, he does not transcend, and through this robustly
determined unearthing he rescues Kafka from the unearthli-
ness of his repute.

Foremost is the question of language. In Prague, Czechs
spoke Czech, Germans spoke German, Jews spoke German.
Kafka's ruminations on his relation to the language he was
born into are by now as familiar (or as overfamiliar) as his face
in the photographs, and equally revealing of shrouded pain.
Jews who wrote in German, he lamented, resembled trapped
beasts, neither at home in their native idiom nor alien to it.
They lived, moreover, with three impossibilities: "the impossibility of not writing, the impossibility of writing German,
the impossibility of writing differently." To which he added a
fourth, "the impossibility of writing."

Kafka's prose has been universally lauded as spare, somber,
comic, lucent, almost platonically pure; but many of those
who acclaim it are compelled to read through the art of the
translator. Shelley Frisch, Stach's heroic American translator,
movingly reproduces his intended breadth and pace and tone,

though now and again she is tempted to transmute the biographer's turns of phrase into popular local catchwords ("tickled pink," "thrown for a loop," "let off steam," "went to temple," "right off the bat," and many more). This is not altogether a failing, since it is Stach, not Kafka, whom these displaced Americanisms represent; but at the same time they serve to remind us that the biographer, whose *Muttersprache* is German, comes to Kafka's idiom with the deep linguistic affinities that only a native German, one who is also a literary writer, can assert. It is with such felt authority that Stach looks back at Kafka's writing—not to say how and what it is, but rather how and what it is not: "There were no empty phrases, no semantic impurities, no weak metaphors—even when he lay in the sand and wrote postcards." Yet there is another side to Stach's closeness to Kafka's rhetoric. When Kafka declared the impossibility of writing German, it was plainly not the overriding mastery of his language that was in doubt, but its ownership—not that German did not belong to him, but that he did not belong to it. German was unassailably at the root of his tongue; might he claim it societally, nationally, as a natural inheritance, as an innate entitlement? The culture that touched him at all points had a prevailing Jewish coloration. Family traditions, however casually observed, were in the air he breathed, no matter how removed he was from their expression. His most intimate literary friendships consisted entirely of writers of similar background; at least two, Max Brod and Hugo Bergmann, were seriously committed to Zionism. He studied Hebrew, earnestly if fitfully, at various periods of his life, and he attended Martin Buber's lectures on Zionism at the meetings of Bar Kochba, the Association of Jewish University Students. Unlike the disdainful Jewish burghers of Prague, who had long ago shed what they dismissed as an inferior *zhargón*, he was drawn to a troupe of Yiddish-speaking players from Poland and their lively but somewhat makeshift theater. He was a warm proponent of the work of Berlin's Jewish Home, which looked after the welfare and education of impoverished young immigrants from Eastern Europe. He read Heinrich Graetz's massive *History of the Jews*; he read *Der Jude*, the monthly founded by Buber; he read *Die*

Jüdische Rundschau, a Zionist weekly; he read *Selbstwahr*, yet another Zionist periodical, whose editor and all of its contributors he knew. He also read *Die Fackel*, Karl Kraus's scourging satiric journal.

If Kafka's profoundest conviction ("I am made of literature") kept its distance from these preoccupations and influences, he nevertheless felt their pressure in the way of an enveloping skin. His commanding conundrums, including the two opposing impossibilities—writing and not-writing—are almost suffocatingly knotted into Jewish insecurities. Zionism was one symptom of this powerful unease; and so was Kraus's repudiation of Zionism, and his furious advocacy of radically self-obscuring assimilation.

It is difficult to refrain from pondering how a biographer (and a biographer is inevitably also a historian) will confront these extremes of cultural tension. Every biography is, after all, a kind of autobiography: it reveals predispositions, parallels, hidden needs; or possibly an unacknowledged wish to take on the subject's persona, to become his secret sharer. The biographer's choice of subject is a confession of more than interest or attunement. The desire to live alongside another life, year by year, thought for thought, is what we mean by possession. And for Stach to be close, both as a given and as a fortuity, to Kafka's language can hardly reflect the full scope of his willed immersion. He must also come close to Jewish foreboding—a foreboding marinated in the political and tribal and linguistic complexities of Austria-Hungary at the turbulent crux of its demise. Much of Kafka's fiction—*The Trial*, *The Castle*, "In the Penal Colony"—has too often made of him a prognosticator, as if he could intuit, through some uncanny telescope, the depredations that were soon to blacken Europe in the middle of the twentieth century. But the times required no clairvoyance; Jewish disquiet was an immediacy. At fourteen, Kafka witnessed anti-Semitic rioting that had begun as an anti-German protest against the Habsburg government's denial of Czech language rights. At thirty-seven, three years before his death, and with *The Castle* still unwritten, he saw Prague's historic Altneu synagogue attacked and its Torah scrolls torched. "I've been spending every afternoon outside on the streets, wallowing in anti-Semitism," he recounted. "The other day I heard the Jews called *Prasivé plenemo* [mangy brood]. Isn't it natural to leave a place where one is so hated? . . . The heroism of staying on nevertheless is the heroism of cockroaches that cannot be exterminated even from the bathroom."

Post-Holocaust, all this must sting a susceptible German ear; note that Zyklon B, the genocidal gas of the extermination camps, was originally used as an insecticide. Yet there are reminders still more unsettling. Because a biography of Kafka will perforce include minor characters—his sisters Elli, Valli, and Ottla, for instance—it must finally arrive at Kafka's afterlife, the destiny he did not live long enough to suffer: that zone of ultimate impossibility wherein all other impossibilities became one with the impossibility of staying alive. Between 1941 and 1943, all three sisters perished, Elli and Valli in Chelmno, Ottla in Auschwitz. They hover over Kafka's biographies—this one, and all the rest—like torn and damaged Fates. Stach is never unaware of these points of connection; at first, uninvited, *sotto voce*, behind the scenes, in quiet recognition, they pierce the weave of his narrative. But by the time he attains his coda, Stach's watchful voicing of the fraught history of the Jews of central Europe during the passage of Kafka's life will have risen to a thunder.

And while a biographer may be willy-nilly a historian, and subliminally an autobiographer, he is, even more so, a species of novelist—of the nineteenth-century, loose-baggy-monster variety. He is in pursuit of the whole trajectory of a life, beginning, middle, end: chronology is king, postmodern fragmentation unwelcome, landscapes lavish, rooms and furnishings the same, nothing goes unnoticed. The biographer is a simulacrum, say, of George Eliot, who places her characters against the background of a society rendered both minutely and expansively, attending to ancestry, religion, economic standing, farming, banking, business, reading, travel, and more. Stach, in this vein, is doubtless the first to give so plentiful an account of the activities of the Prague Workers' Accident Insurance Company, the government agency where Kafka was employed

as a lawyer from 1908 until 1918, when advancing tuberculosis
forced his retirement. That he divided his day into office and
work—by declaring them antithetical—is itself a type of credo;
but Kafka's exalted literary image has too readily obscured the
press of the quotidian. What did Kafka *do*, what were his everyday responsibilities? Stach lifts the dry-as-dust veil:

> If an industrialist submitted an appeal, the office had to
> establish proof that the safety precautions of the firm in
> question were not up to the latest standards. But what were
> the latest standards? They could not be definitively stipulated
> with ordinances; they had to be continually reestablished, if
> possible by personal observation. Kafka, who already had
> legal expertise, quickly acquired the technical know-how;
> he attended courses and traveled through northern Bohe-
> mian industrial cities. Next to the swaying stacks of appeals
> on his huge office desk there was an array of journals on
> accident prevention . . . in the areas in which he special-
> ized—particularly the woodworking industry and quarries.

And so on and so on. An annual report, ostensibly submitted by
Kafka, is titled "Accident Prevention Rules for Wood Planing
Machines," and recommends the use of a cylindrical spindle.
It is accompanied by illustrations of mutilated hands. In the
wake of World War I, with its tens of thousands of maimed and
shell-shocked soldiers, he was to see far worse.

For Kafka, none of these lawyerly obligations, however
demanding, counted as work. No matter that his acumen and
skills were regularly rewarded with promotion by the pair of
bookish and obliging men who were his superiors, and though
he was deemed so valuable that they contrived to have him
exempted from military service, he felt depleted, and even
assaulted, by the very papers his own hand produced. Of this
necessarily official language he wrote bitterly, "I am still holding all of it in my mouth with revulsion and a feeling of shame,
as though it were raw flesh cut out of me (that is how much
effort it cost me) . . . everything in me is ready for lyrical work,
and a work of that kind would be a heavenly resolution and a

real coming alive for me, while here, in the office, because of such a wretched document I have to tear from a body capable of such happiness a piece of its flesh." And again, with the emphasis of despair: "*real hell is there in the office; I no longer fear any other.*" And yet another tightening of the vise: "For me it is a horrible double life from which there is probably no way out except insanity."

At two o'clock in the afternoon, at the close of the six tormenting hours in the office, he escaped to the family apartment, a noisy and crowded habitat that was less a refuge than a second entrapment. Seven persons occupied these cramped and untranquil rooms: the blustering bullying paterfamilias, the compliant mother, the three daughters, the discontented son yearning for privacy and quiet, and a live-in maid. Kafka's bedroom, the burning vortex of his nocturnal writing, lay between the parlor and his parents' room; it was a passageway for his father's comings and goings, early and late, trailing his bathrobe. And the apartment, like the office, had its own distinct raison d'être: it was the ground, the support, and the indispensable source of administrative personnel for the family shop, a successful fancy-goods emporium with numerous employees. Since both parents put in many hours there, and all family members were obliged to do the same, in this way the shop fed the apartment, and the apartment fed the shop. Hermann Kafka, the son of a *shochet*—a ritual butcher—had risen from a burdened childhood in a backward rural village to bourgeois respectability, and was impatient with any deviation from conventional expectations. Ottla, the youngest daughter, was attracted to the countryside and aspired to farming—a far cry from her duties in the shop. Franz was still another riddle. At the dinner table he confined himself to an ascetic diet of mainly fruits and nuts, masticating each mouthful thirty-two times, according to the nutritional tenets of Fletcherism. But his most controversial habit was sleeping in the afternoon after leaving the office: this was to secure a usable wakefulness for the sake of his work—his true work—in the apartment's welcome middle-of-the-night silence. Sleeping in the afternoon, during shop hours? To the business-minded father, this was incomprehensible; it was delinquent.

Kafka's delinquency became still more scandalous when he was recruited to take on the ownership and management of an asbestos factory, in partnership with the ambitious husband of his newly married sister Elli. Hermann Kafka approved of his son-in-law's entrepreneurial plans, but since family money was being dedicated to this enterprise, and the young man was an untried stranger, it was imperative that a blood relation contribute to the stability and probity of the business. At first Kafka attempted to fulfill a commitment he had never sought—the literature-besotted son as industrialist!—and grudgingly gave his afternoons to the factory, which meant sacrificing his nights. Despite his father's irritable proddings, he could not keep up even a pretense of interest (he was at this time far more absorbed in the precarious fortunes of the Yiddish players he had befriended), and at length the business failed. The record Kafka left of it is oblivious to product and profit-and-loss; and though conceivably he might have appraised the factory and its perilously superannuated machines through the eyes of the workers' accident official, it was instead the fevered midnight writer who observed "the girls in their absolutely unbearably dirty and untailored clothing, their hair unkempt, as though they had just got out of bed, their facial expressions set by the incessant noise of the transmission belts and by the separate machine that is automatic but unpredictable, stopping and starting. The girls," he went on,

> are not people—you don't say hello to them, you don't apol-
> ogize for bumping into them; when you call them over to
> do something, they do it but go right back to the machine;
> with a nod of the head you show them what to do; they
> stand there in petticoats; they are at the mercy of the pettiest
> power. . . . When six o'clock comes, however, and they call
> it out to one another, they untie their kerchiefs from around
> their necks and hair, dust themselves off with a brush that
> is passed around the room and is demanded by the ones
> that are impatient, they pull their skirts over their heads and
> wash their hands as well as they can, they are women, after
> all; . . . you can no longer bump into them, stare at them, or

ignore them; . . . and you do not know how to react when
one of them holds your winter coat for you to put on.

The kerchiefs, the skirts, the brush, the washing, the coat:
Walter Benjamin, in his discriminating musings on Kafka,
concludes that "the gesture remains the decisive thing."
"Each gesture," he writes, "is an event—one might even say,
a drama—in itself." And it is the factory girl's simple act of
helping with a coat that has the power to embarrass, perhaps
even to shame, the owner.

This drama of the minutely mundane was what Kafka
demanded of Felice Bauer; it was an inquisition of the hum-
drum, a third degree of her every movement and choice. He
wanted a description of her blouse, her room, her reading, her
sleeping; what her employment entailed; how she was occupied
when at leisure (she liked to go dancing, she practiced gym-
nastics). He wanted to claim and envelop her altogether. He
repeatedly asked for her photograph, and he repeatedly sent his
own. When in their accelerating daily—sometimes hourly—
correspondence she abandoned the formal *Sie* and addressed
him familiarly as *Du*, he fell into a trance of happiness.

Felice, a distant relation of Max Brod's visiting from Berlin,
was introduced to Kafka at the Brod family dinner table. It was,
apart from Brod's parents, a meeting of young people. Felice
was twenty-five, Max twenty-eight, Kafka twenty-nine. Stach
announces this unwittingly portentous occasion with a trumpet blast: "The history of human events, like intellectual and
literary history, highlights certain dates; these are engraved in
the cultural formation of future generations. . . . The evening
of August 13, 1912 . . . changed the face of German language
literature, of world literature." These grand phrases might have
been applied to the somewhat more modest purpose of Kafka's
presence that night: he and Brod had planned to look over
a collection of sketches that Brod had long been urging his
reluctant friend to agree to publish. The final decision about
the order of the pieces was consummated in a colloquy after
dinner, and what was to become Kafka's earliest publication,
Meditation, was at last ready to be sent off. From the point of

view of Kafka's biographers, though, what changed the face of world literature was not this small book by a little-known writer too perfectionist to release his work without lacerating self-doubt; it was the face of Felice Bauer. If not for the blizzard of revelatory letters that swept over her, enraptured and entreating to begin with, and then dismissive and retreating, Kafka's ponderings and sufferings during five crucially introspective years would have remained a vacuum: cries unheard, crises unrecorded.

Hers was a wholly ordinary face. Kafka, sitting across from the young woman from Berlin, at first mistook her for the maid. "Bony empty face," he later wrote, looking back at his initial impression, "displaying its emptiness openly. A bare throat. Her blouse tossed on. . . . A nose almost broken. Blond, somewhat stiff, unappealing hair, and a strong chin." He did not note the two black moles that are prominent in one of her photos, though absent in others, or, in nearly all of these, the bad teeth masked by closed lips. He learned that she worked for Parlograph, a firm selling dictation machines, having risen from typist to managerial status, and often traveling to trade fairs as company representative. If her looks and dress failed to attract him, her independence, reflected in her conversation, did. That she frequently read through the night impressed him. When she mentioned that she was studying Hebrew, he was captivated, and before the evening was over, the two of them were planning a journey to Palestine together—after which Kafka did not set eyes on her again for the next seven months. When he began to write to her, it was as a smitten and instantly possessive lover.

The Felice of Kafka's tumultuous letters was an imagined—a wished-for—figure. The actual Felice was an intelligent, practical, reasonable, efficient, problem-solving, generous woman who very soon recognized that she had been singled out by an uncommon rapture stirred by an uncommon nature. She was more than willing to respond, but every accommodating attempt resulted in a setback. He complained that she was not open enough; yet according to the standards and constraints of the proper middle-class background that defined her, how could she be? Her father was living apart from his family, her unmarried sister was suddenly pregnant, her brother had to be shipped off to America to escape reckless money entanglements. When these secret shames were finally disclosed, they were scarcely what put off Kafka; her habit of silence would bring him a deeper dismay. He had sent her an inscribed copy of *Meditation*, and though he appealed to her, piteously, for a comment ("Dearest, look, I want to have the feeling that you turn to me with everything; nothing, not the slightest thing should be left unsaid"), she never replied. Perhaps she could not: what was she to make of writing so enigmatic? She went to the theater, she read Ibsen; still, what was she to make of, say, "Trees," a story, if that is what it was, of four perplexing sentences? How was she to fathom such a thing?

> For we are like tree trunks in the snow. In appearance they
> lie sleekly and a little push should be enough to set them
> rolling. No, it can't be done, but they are firmly wedded to
> the ground. But see, even that is only appearance.

His passionate explanation—"I am made of literature and nothing else"—led to misunderstanding. Pragmatist that she was, she counseled moderation. And worse yet: it led to what she took to be understanding—she had begun to sense in him "seeds of greatness." And with all the sympathetic warmth of wishing to please him, she stumbled into a critical misjudgment (she offered to be close to him while he wrote) and lost him altogether. His shock at this innocent proposal turned into vehement resentment, bordering even on revulsion, as if she were intending to fleece him of his survival as a writer; and shock, resentment, revulsion culminated in one of his most wrenchingly monastic images of artistic self-entombment:

> Once you wrote that you wanted to sit by my side as I write;
> just keep in mind that I cannot write like that (even so I
> cannot write much), but in that case I would not be able
> to write at all. Writing means revealing oneself to excess,
> the utmost candor and surrender, in which a person would

feel he is losing himself in his interaction with other people and from which he will always shy away as long as he hasn't taken leave of his senses—because everyone wants to live as long as he is alive. . . . Anything that writing adopts from the surface of existence . . . is nothing, and caves in on itself at the moment that a truer feeling rattles this upper ground. That is why one cannot be alone enough when one is writing; that is why it cannot be quiet enough around one; the night is not night enough. . . . I have often thought that the best kind of life for me would be to stay in the innermost room of an extended locked cellar with my writing materials and a lamp. . . . What I would write! From what depths I would draw it up!

Here he was assuring the woman who trusted she would soon become his wife that the prospect of her coming near would threaten his capacity to live, and that rather than have her sit beside him, he would prefer to be immured underground. This ruthless detachment continued through two painful official engagements (the later embroiling him in the off-putting ritual of choosing the marital furniture and the conjugal apartment), until he had depleted Felice down to the very lees of her usable sustenance.

In the vista of Kafka's life, Felice is a promontory, partly because she occupied so large a tract of it, but also because of a simple bibliographical datum: she kept his letters. (He did not preserve hers.) She kept them through her marriage, and through her emigration to America in 1936, when escape from Nazi Germany became imperative, until her unremarked death in 1960 in a New York suburb. Beyond—or below—the promontory are the foothills, lesser outcroppings that reflect the configuration of the greater. Or put it that the letters to Felice expose the template, the very genome, of Kafka's character as it has revealed itself to biographers, and to Stach in particular; and by now they are seen to be *literature* as much as the canonical work itself. They underlie a binding continuum: from the diaries to the letters to Felice to the letters to Milena Jesenská to the letters to Max Brod to the prodigious one-hundred-page

letter to Kafka's father—and even to a single sketch, ink on
paper, drawn by Kafka. A stark black stick figure, stick elbows
bent, stick legs outstretched among stick legs of table and chair,
all of it spider-like. The spider's body—a human head—rests on
the table. It is an image of defeat, surrender, despair, submission.

Milena Jesenská came to Kafka as a translator; in every way
she was what Felice was not. Her eyes were as pale as Felice's,
but rounder, and her nose was round, and her chin, and her
mouth. Felice was a conformist: the furniture must be heavy
and ornate, signaling a settled and prosperous marriage. Milena
was a rebel, and to earn money in a lean time she was not above
carrying luggage for travelers in the Vienna train station. She
was a nimble writer and an ardent if contrarian spirit: "a living
fire," as Kafka described her to Brod. Her mother was long
dead, and her father, an eminent professor of dentistry, rec-
ognizing her exceptional gifts, sent her to an elite high school
for Czech girls, where the classics and modern languages were
taught and the arts were encouraged and cultivated. She and
a handful of likeminded classmates made it a habit to loiter
in Prague's literary cafés, where she encountered Ernst Pollak,
ten years her senior, whom she eventually married. From her
father's standpoint it was an insurrectionist act that estranged
him from his daughter. The professor was a Czech national-
ist, hostile to Germans, and especially averse to their Prague
subdivision, German-identified Jews. After futilely confining
Milena in a mental institution for some months, he dispatched
her and the social embarrassment of her Jewish husband to
Vienna—where, in a period of serious postwar scarcity, food
was even harder to come by than in Prague. Only yesterday the
capital of an empire, Vienna was now a weakened and impoverished outlier, despite its lively literary scene. It turned out to
be an uneasy match: Pollak was a persistent philanderer and a
dissatisfied writer manqué, impressively voluble in bookish circles but stymied on the page. It was he who introduced Milena
to Kafka's still sparse publications, which inspired her to render
"The Stoker" into Czech—the story that was to become the
opening chapter of *The Man Who Disappeared*, his abandoned
early novel. Kafka was admiring and gratified ("I find there is

constant powerful and decisive understanding," he told her), and
their correspondence began, rapidly turning intimate: Kafka's
second limitless outpouring of letters to a young woman who
kindled his longings and embodied his subterranean desires.

But if Felice had been a fabricated muse, as unresponsively
remote from his idée fixe as a muse ought not to be, Milena
was no muse at all. She provoked and importuned him from
a position of equality; she was perceptive and quick and blunt
and forward. Almost instantly she startled him: "Are you a
Jew?" And though he had rarely spoken to Felice of the dis-
quieting Jewish consciousness that perpetually dogged him (a
self-punishing sensitiveness he and Brod had in common), to
Milena he unburdened himself with a suicidal bitterness that
in one ferocious stroke reviled and mocked the choking anti-
Semitism he knew too well:

> I could sooner reproach you for having much too high an
> opinion of the Jews (me included) . . . at times I'd like to
> stuff them all, as Jews (me included) into, say, the drawer
> of the laundry chest, wait, open the drawer a little to see if
> they've all suffocated, and if not, shut the drawer again, and
> keep doing this until the end.

She had to put up with this; yet she summoned him, and he
came, and in the Vienna woods one afternoon they lived out an
idyll, the two of them lying on the forest floor, he with his head
on her half-exposed breast. Together they schemed how she
might leave Pollak; in the end she could not. He was himself
not free; he was at this time engaged to be married to Julie
Wohryzek, a young woman whom Hermann Kafka, threatening and berating, disapproved of as déclassé; unlike Felice, she
was not suitably respectable. Her father was a penniless cobbler
and the *shammes* of a synagogue—worse, she occasionally fell
into a low Yiddish phrase, and still worse, she had a "loose"
reputation. Kafka had met her at a boardinghouse passing for a
tuberculosis sanitorium; like him, she was there to convalesce.
When Milena swept in, he disposed of this inflamed but short-
lived attachment as no better than a dalliance, to be blown

away like a stray straw. A space, then, was cleared for Milena: a landscape wherein the intellectual could be joined to the erotic. She filled it with her certainties and uncertainties, her conviction too often erased by ambivalence. Kafka's uncertainties ran deeper, and his mode of retreat was well practiced: "We are living in misunderstandings; our questions are rendered worthless by our replies. Now we have to stop writing to one another and leave the future to the future." To Brod, Milena sent an epitaph to the marriage that both she and Kafka had evaded. "He always thinks that he himself is the guilty and weak one," she wrote. "And yet there is not another person in the world who has his colossal strength: that absolutely unalterable necessity for perfection, purity, and truth." Milena outlived Kafka by twenty years. In 1944, she was arrested for sheltering Jews and aiding their flight; she perished in Ravensbrück.

Despite three failed engagements, Kafka never married. Yet he was not without such confidential support; there were, in fact, three loyally solicitous persons who took on a wifely role: his sister Ottla, Max Brod, and, at the close of his life, Dora Diamant. Ottla and Kafka had, early on, an obstacle in common—Hermann Kafka and his resistance to their independence. The monstrous (in size and in force) *J'accuse* that the son addressed, though never delivered, to the father now stands as yet another canonical work. Ottla's more quiet eruption came through stubborn acts of autonomy; unlike Kafka, she left behind both the family apartment and her role in the family economy. Hermann Kafka might mock his Czech employees as "my paid enemies," but Ottla chose to marry a Czech. And when the domestic commotion became unsustainable for Kafka's work, she gave him the use of the little neighborhood hideaway she had privately acquired. When his tuberculosis began to advance, and he declined to be admitted to yet another sanitorium (there were many such recuperative sojourns), with wifely devotion she cared for him at the longed-for farm she finally secured in the remote village of Zürau, where Kafka felt uncommonly serene. "I live with Ottla in a good little marriage," he assured Brod.

Brod was Kafka's confidant and champion, first reader, and

also first listener: despite reticence and self-denigration, Kafka relished reading his work to friends. It was Brod who pushed Kafka to publish, pursuing skeptical editors on his behalf. "I personally consider Kafka (along with Gerhart Hauptmann and Hamsun) the greatest living writer!" he exclaimed to Martin Buber. "What I wouldn't do to make him more active!" Brod was himself energetic on many fronts: he turned out novels, plays, polemics, political broadsides; he ran to meetings for this cause and that; he labored to bridge the divide between Germans and Czechs; he promoted Czech writers and composers; and with Kafka (though not so diligently) he studied Hebrew. The two friends traveled to Weimar to visit Goethe's house, where each drew a sketch of the house and garden, and Kafka was all at once infatuated with the caretaker's young daughter.

But increasingly, Kafka's excursions away from Prague were solitary journeys to health resorts and tuberculosis sanitoriums; and inexorably in step with these, Stach's later chapters hurtle through harrowing episodes of fever, relentless coughing, days forcibly spent in bed, and finally, when the disease spread to the larynx, the threat of suffocation. Brod, always Kafka's anxious guardian, pressed him from the first to see the proper specialist and undertake the proper treatment. Kafka himself was oddly unperturbed: he believed that a psychosomatic element was the cause, and that, as he wrote to Ottla, "there is undoubtedly justice in this illness." As his condition worsened, he was compelled to give up his position at the Workers' Accident Insurance Company—which, like much of postwar Europe, was undergoing a political transformation. Habsburg officialdom was now replaced by Czech officialdom, in Munich swastikas were flying, and in Prague the decibels of anti-Semitism rang shriller. Hermann Kafka, uneasy in the company of his paid enemies, closed up his shop.

In the summer of 1923, Kafka—already seriously beginning to fail—entered into what can only be called a marriage, even if it had no official sanction and may never have been sexually consummated. It was his most daring personal commitment, and the only one untroubled by vacillation or doubts. Dora Diamant was twenty-five years old, the daughter of a rigidly observant Polish Hasidic family loyal to the dynastic rebbe of Ger. Though Zionism was frowned on as dangerously secular, Dora found her way to the writings of Theodor Herzl, broke from the constrictions of her background, and settled in Berlin. Here she worked with the children of the Jewish Home, the very institution Kafka had been so moved by in the past (and had pressed hard for Felice to support as a volunteer). Berlin was in chaos, reeling under strikes, riots, food shortages, and massive inflation. Despite every predictable discomfort and gravely diminishing funds, it was into this maelstrom that Kafka came to join Dora for one of the most tranquil intervals of his life. Half earnestly, half fancifully, they spoke of a future in Palestine, where, to make ends meet, together they would open a little restaurant. But the fevers continued to accelerate, and while Dora nursed him with singular tenderness, it became clear, especially under pressure from the family in Prague, that he was in urgent need of professional care. Another sanitorium followed, and then a hospital specializing in diseases of the larynx, always with Dora hovering protectively near. By now Kafka's suffering had intensified: unable to speak, he communicated on slips of paper; unable to swallow food, he was facing actual starvation, even as he struggled over proofs of "The Hunger Artist." At the last he pleaded for a lethal dose of morphine, warning—Kafka's deliberate paradox of the final paroxysm—that to be deprived of his death would count as murder. With Tolstoyan power, Stach carries us through these sorrowful cadences; the reader is left grieving.

Ottla; Hermann Kafka; Felice; Milena; Dora. They are, ultimately, no more than arresting figures in a biography. When the book is shut, their life-shaping influences evaporate. Not so Max Brod. He became—and remains—a lasting force in Kafka's posthumous destiny. In disobeying his friend's firm request to destroy the existing body of his unpublished manuscripts and to prevent further dissemination of those already in print, Brod assured the survival of the work of an unparalleled literary master. Solely because of this proprietary betrayal, *The Trial*, *The Castle*, and *Amerika* (Brod's title for *The Man Who Disappeared*) live on; had there been no Brod, there would be no

Kafka as we now read him. (And had Brod not fled German-occupied Prague for Tel Aviv in 1939, there would today not be a substantial cache of still unvetted manuscripts preserved in an Israeli national archive. It is from this trove that Stach's yet-to-be-published final volume will be drawn.) Savior though he was, Brod also manipulated whatever came into his hands. He invented titles for what was left untitled. He organized loose chapters into a sequence of his own devising. Having taken on the role of Kafka's authentic representative, he argued for what he believed to be the authoritative interpretation of Kafka's inmost meanings.

Stach ventures no such defining conviction. Instead, he ruminates and speculates, not as a zealously theorizing critic, but as a devoted literary sympathizer who has probed as far as is feasible into the concealments of Kafka's psyche. Often he stops to admit that "we cannot know." In contemplating the work, he tentatively supposes and experientially exposes. He eschews the false empyrean, and will never look to transcend the ground that both moored and unmoored his subject. In this honest and honorable biography there is no trace of the Kafkaesque; but in it you may find a crystal granule of the Kafka that was.

The Phantasmagoria of Bruno Schulz

THIRTY-FIVE YEARS AGO, Bruno Schulz, a fifty-year-old high-school art teacher in command of one of the most original literary imaginations of modern Europe, was gunned down by a Jew-hunting contingent of SS men in the streets of an insignificant provincial town in eastern Galicia. On the map of Poland the town hides itself from you; you have to search out the tiniest print to discover Drogobych. In this cramped crevice of a place Schulz too hid himself—though not from the Nazis. Urged on by a group of writers, the Polish underground devised a means of escape—false papers and a hiding place. Schulz chose to die unhidden in Drogobych. But even before the German storm, he had already chosen both to hide and to die there. He knew its streets, and their houses and shops, with a paralyzed intimacy. His environment and his family digested him. He was incapable of leaving home, of marrying, at first even of writing. On a drab salary, in a job he despised, he supported a small band of relatives, and though he visited Warsaw and Lvov, and once even went as far as Paris, he gave up larger places, minds, and lives for the sake of Drogobych—or, rather, for the sake of the gargoylish and astonishing map his imagination had learned to draw of an invisible Drogobych contrived entirely out of language.

In English there is virtually no biographical information to be had concerning Schulz. It is known that his final manuscript, a novel called "The Messiah," was carried for safekeeping to a friend; both friend and manuscript were swallowed up by the sacrificial fires of the Europe of 1942. All of Schulz's letters, and two-thirds of the very small body of his finished work—two novels, one novella—remain untranslated

Bruno Schulz, *The Street of Crocodiles* (Penguin Books, 1977). Published in *The New York Times Book Review*, February 13, 1977.

and, so far, inaccessible to American readers. It is a powerful omission. Think what our notion of the literature of the Dark Continent of Europe would be like if we had read our way so late into the century without the most renowned of the stories in *Red Cavalry*, or without "Gimpel the Fool," or without *The Metamorphosis*. A verbal landscape stripped of Babel or Singer or Kafka is unimaginable to us now, and it may turn out, in the wake of *The Street of Crocodiles*, that Schulz can stand naturally—or unnaturally—among those writers who break our eyes with torches, and end by demonstrating the remarkable uses of a purposeful dark.

In this dark the familiar looms freakish, and all of these— Babel as Cossack Jew, Singer purveying his imps and demiurges, Kafka with his measured and logical illogic—offer mutations, weird births, essences and occasions never before suspected. *The Street of Crocodiles*, at one with that mythic crew, is a transmogrified Drogobych: real town and real time and real tasks twisted and twisted until droplets of changed, even hateful, even hideous, beauty are squeezed out of bolts of cloth, ledgers, tailors' dummies, pet birds, a row of shops, a puppy, a servant girl. As in Kafka, the malevolent is deadpan; its loveliness of form is what we notice. At the heart of the malevolent—also the repugnant, the pitiless—crouches the father: Schulz's own father, since there is an inviolable autobiographical glaze that paints over every distortion. The father is a shopkeeper, the owner of a dry-goods store. He gets sick, gives up work, hangs around home, fiddles with his account books, grows morbid and sulky, has trouble with his bowels, bursts out into fits of rage. All this is novelist's material, and we are made to understand it in the usual way of novels.

But parallel with it, engorging it, is a running flame of amazing imagery—altogether exact and meticulous—that alters everything. The wallpaper becomes a "pullulating jungle . . . filled with whispers, lisping and hissing." Father "sitting clumsily on an enormous china chamberpot" turns into a prophet of "the terrible Demiurge," howling with "the divine anger of saintly men." Father shrinks, hides in closets, climbs the curtains and perches there like a baleful stuffed vulture, disappears "for many days into some distant corner of the house." Schulz's language is dense with disappearances, losses, metamorphoses. The dry-goods shop is flooded by a "cosmogony of cloth." Crowded streets become "an ultra-barrel of myth." The calendar takes on a thirteenth month. Rooms in houses are forgotten, misplaced. A bicycle ascends into the zodiac. Even death is somehow indefinite; a murk, a confusion. Father "could not merge with any reality and was therefore condemned to float eternally on the periphery of life, in half-real regions, on the margins of existence. He could not even earn an honest citizen's death." Father, alive, lectures on manikins: "There is no dead matter . . . lifelessness is only a disguise behind which hide unknown forms of life." A dog represents "the most essential secret of life, reduced to this simple, handy, toy-like form." Wallpapers become bored; furniture, "unstable, degenerate," breaks out into rashes. The maid rules the master with ominous and magisterial positions of her fingers—she points, waggles, tickles. She is a kind of proto-Nazi. Father takes up ornithology and hatches a condor like "an emaciated ascetic, a Buddhist lama," an idol, a mummy—it resembles father himself. (A fore-echo of Kosinski, another Pole obsessed by fearful birds.) Father loathes cockroaches, violently pursues them, and is transformed, undertaking at last their "ceremonial crawl."

> He lay on the floor naked, stained with black totem spots, the lines of his ribs heavily outlined, the fantastic structure of his anatomy visible through the skin; he lay on his face, in the grip of an obsession of loathing which dragged him into the abyss of its complex paths. He moved with the many-limbed, complicated movements of a strange ritual in which I recognized with horror an imitation of the ceremonial crawl of a cockroach.

In Kafka's myth, it is the powerless son who turns into a cockroach; here it is the father who has lost control. Everything is loosened; it is not that the center does not hold; there never *was* a center. "Reality is as thin as paper and betrays with all

its cracks its imitative character." "Our language has no definitions which would weigh, so to speak, the grade of reality."
Given these hints, it may be misleading to anticipate *The Street
of Crocodiles* with so "normal" a signal as *novel*: it is a thick string
of sights and sinuosities, a cascade of flashes, of extraordinary
movements—a succession of what television has taught us to
call "film clips," images in magnetic batches, registered storms,
each one shooting memories of itself into the lightnings of all
the others. What is being invented in the very drone of our
passive literary expectations is Religion—not the taming religion of theology and morality, but the brute splendors of rite,
gesture, phantasmagoric transfiguration, sacrifice, elevation,
degradation, mortification, repugnance, terror, cult. The religion of animism, in fact, where everything comes alive with an
unpredictable and spiteful spirit-force, where even living tissue
contains ghosts, where there is no pity.

Such metaphysical specters have their historical undersides.
Home shifts, its forms are unreliable, demons rule. Why should
these literary Jews of twentieth-century Slavic Europe—Babel,
whose language was Russian, two years younger than Schulz;
Kafka, who wrote in German, seven years older; Singer, a Yiddish writer, a dozen years younger; and finally (one is tempted
to enter the next generation) the American Kosinski—why
should these cultivated Slavic Jews run into the black crevices of
nihilism, animalism, hollow riddle? Why, indeed, should these
writers be the very ones almost to *invent* the literary signposts
of such crevices? Gogol came first, it is true; but it is the Slavic
Jews who have leaped into the fermenting vat. The homeless-
ness and ultimate pariahship felt by Schulz—an assimilated,
Polish-speaking Jew, not so much a Jew as a conscious Pole—in
the years before the fiery consummation of the Final Solution
may explain why the real Drogobych took on the symbolic
name Crocodile Street, and became the place where "nothing
ever succeeds . . . nothing can ever reach a definite conclusion."
But it did, in gunshot, on the streets of Drogobych in 1942.
"Over the whole area," Schulz writes of his visionary town,
"there floats the lazy licentious smell of sin."

The shock of Schulz's images brings us the authentic

bedevilment of the Europe we are heir to. Schulz's life was cut short. His work, a small packet, reminds us of father: "the small shroud of his body and the handful of nonsensical oddities." Some of the packet was lost in the human ash heap. As for the little that remains: let us set it beside Kafka and the others and see how it measures up for truthtelling.

What Helen Keller Saw

SUSPICION STALKS FAME; incredulity stalks great fame. At least three times—at ages eleven, twenty-three, and fifty-two—Helen Keller was assaulted by accusation, doubt, and overt disbelief. Though her luster had surpassed the stellar figures of generations, she was disparaged nearly as hotly as she was exalted. She was the butt of skeptics and the cynosure of idolators. Mark Twain compared her to Joan of Arc, and pronounced her "fellow to Caesar, Alexander, Napoleon, Homer, Shakespeare and the rest of the immortals." Her renown, he said, would endure a thousand years.

It has, so far, lasted more than a hundred, while steadily dimming. Fifty years ago, even twenty, nearly every ten-year-old knew who Helen Keller was. *The Story of My Life*, her youthful autobiography, was on the reading lists of most schools, and its author was popularly understood to be, if not the equal of Mark Twain's lavish exaggerations, a heroine of uncommon grace and courage, a sort of worldly saint. To admire her was an act of piety, and she herself, by virtue of the strenuous conquest of her limitations, was a living temple dedicated to the spirit of resurrection. Much of that worshipfulness has receded. Her name, if not entirely in eclipse, hardly elicits the awed recognition it once held. No one nowadays, without intending satire, would place her alongside Caesar and Napoleon; and in an era of earnest disabilities legislation, with wheelchair ramps on every street corner, who would think to charge a stone-blind, stone-deaf woman with faking her experience?

Yet as a child she was accused of plagiarism, and in maturity of "verbalism," illicitly substituting parroted words for first-hand perception. All this came about because she was at once liberated by language and in bondage to it, in a way few other human beings, even the blind and the deaf, can fathom. The merely blind have the window of their ears, the merely deaf listen through their eyes. For Helen Keller there was no partially ameliorating "merely." What she suffered was a totality of exclusion. Her early life was meted out in hints and inferences—she could still touch, taste, smell, and feel vibrations; but these were the very capacities that turned her into a wild creature, a kind of flailing animal in human form.

The illness that annihilated Helen Keller's sight and hearing, and left her mute, has never been diagnosed. In 1882, when she was four months short of two years, medical knowledge could assert only "acute congestion of the stomach and brain," though later speculation proposes meningitis or scarlet fever. Whatever the cause, the consequence was ferocity—tantrums, kicking, rages—but also an invented system of sixty simple signs, intimations of intelligence. The child could mimic what she could neither see nor hear: putting on a hat before a mirror, her father reading a newspaper with his glasses on. She could fold laundry and pick out her own things. Such quiet times were few. Frenzied, tempestuous, she was an uncontrollable barbarian. Having discovered the use of a key, she shut up her mother in a closet. She overturned her baby sister's cradle. Her wants were concrete, physical, impatient, helpless, and nearly always belligerent.

She was born in Tuscumbia, Alabama, fifteen years after the Civil War, when Confederate consciousness and mores were still inflamed. Her father, who had fought at Vicksburg, called himself a "gentleman farmer," and edited a small Democratic weekly until, thanks to political influence, he was appointed a United States marshal. He was a zealous hunter who loved his guns and his dogs. Money was usually short; there were escalating marital angers. His second wife, Helen's mother, was younger by twenty years, a spirited woman of intellect condemned to farmhouse toil. She had a strong literary side (Edward Everett Hale, the New Englander who wrote "The Man Without a Country," was a relative) and read seriously and searchingly. In Charles Dickens's *American Notes* she learned about Laura Bridgman, a deaf-blind country girl who was being educated at the Perkins Institution for the Blind, in Boston. Her savior was its director, Samuel Gridley Howe, humanitarian activist and husband of Julia Ward Howe, author of "The Battle Hymn of the Republic": New England idealism at its collective zenith.

Laura Bridgman was thirteen years old when Dickens met her, and was even more circumscribed than Helen Keller—she could neither smell nor taste. She was confined, he said, "in a marble cell, impervious to any ray of light, or particle of sound." But Laura Bridgman's cell could be only partly unlocked. She never mastered language beyond a handful of words unidiomatically strung together. Scientists and psychologists studied her almost zoologically, and her meticulously intricate lacework was widely admired and sold. She lived out her entire life in her room at the Perkins Institution; an 1885 photograph shows her expertly threading a needle with her tongue. She too had been a normal child, until scarlet fever ravaged her senses at the age of two.

News of Laura Bridgman ignited hope—she had been socialized into a semblance of personhood, while Helen remained a small savage—and hope led, eventually, to Alexander Graham Bell. By then the invention of the telephone was well behind him, and he was tenaciously committed to teaching the deaf to speak intelligibly. His wife was deaf; his mother had been deaf. When the six-year-old Helen was brought to him, he took her on his lap and instantly calmed her by letting her feel the vibrations of his pocket watch as it struck the hour. Her responsiveness did not register in her face; he described it as "chillingly empty." But he judged her educable, and advised her father to apply to Michael Anagnos, Howe's successor as director of the Perkins Institution, for a teacher to be sent to Tuscumbia.

Anagnos chose Anne Mansfield Sullivan, a former student at Perkins. "Mansfield" was her own embellishment; it had the sound of gentility. If the fabricated name was intended to confer an elevated status, it was because Annie Sullivan, born into penury, had no status at all. At five she contracted trachoma, a disease of the eye. Three years on, her mother died of tuberculosis and was buried in potter's field—after which her father, a drunkard prone to beating his children, deserted the family. The half-blind Annie and her small brother Jimmie, who had a tubercular hip, were tossed into the poorhouse at Tewksbury, Massachusetts, among syphilitic prostitutes and madmen. Jimmie did not survive the appalling inhumanity of the place, and decades later, recalling its "strangeness, grotesqueness and even terribleness," Annie Sullivan wrote, "I doubt if life or for that matter eternity is long enough to erase the terrors and ugly blots scored upon my mind during those dismal years from 8 to 14." She never spoke of them, not even to her intimates.

She was rescued from Tewksbury by a committee investigating its spreading notoriety, and was mercifully transferred to Perkins. There she learned Braille and the manual alphabet and came to know Laura Bridgman. At the Massachusetts Eye and Ear Infirmary she underwent two operations, which enabled her to read almost normally, though the condition of her eyes continued fragile and inconsistent over her lifetime. After six years she graduated from Perkins as class valedictorian; Anagnos recognized in her clear traces of "uncommon powers." His affectionate concern was nearly a flirtation (he had once teasingly caressed her arm), while she, orphaned and alone, had made certain to catch his notice and his love. When her days at Perkins were ended, what was to become of her? How was she to earn a living? Someone suggested that she might wash dishes or peddle needlework. "Sewing and crocheting are inventions of the devil," she sneered. "I'd rather break stones on the king's highway than hem a handkerchief."

She went to Tuscumbia instead. She was twenty years old and had no experience suitable for what she would encounter in the despairs and chaotic defeats of the Keller household. She had attempted to prepare herself by studying Laura Bridgman's training as it was recorded in the Perkins archives. Apart from this, she had no resources other than the manual alphabet that enlivened her fingers, and the steely history of her own character. The tyrannical child she had come to educate threw cutlery, pinched, grabbed food off dinner plates, sent chairs tumbling, shrieked, struggled. She was strong, beautiful but for one protruding eye, unsmiling, painfully untamed: virtually her first act on meeting the new teacher was to knock out one of her front teeth. The afflictions of the marble cell had become inflictions. Annie demanded that Helen be separated from her family; her father could not bear to see his ruined little daughter disciplined. The teacher and her recalcitrant pupil retreated to a cottage on the grounds of the main house, where Annie was to be sole authority.

What happened then and afterward she chronicled in letter after letter, to Anagnos and, more confidingly, to Mrs. Sophia Hopkins, the Perkins housemother who had given her shelter during school vacations. Mark Twain saw in Annie Sullivan a *writer*: "How she stands out in her letters!" he exclaimed. "Her brilliancy, penetration, originality, wisdom, character and the fine literary competencies of her pen—they are all there." Her observations, both of herself and of the developing child, are kin, in their humanity, particularity, and psychological acumen, to philosophical essays. Jubilantly, and with preternatural awareness, she set down the progress, almost hour by hour, of Helen Keller's disentombment, an exuberant deliverance far more remarkable than Laura Bridgman's frail and inarticulate release. Howe had taught the names of things by attaching to them labels written in raised type—but labels on spoons are not the same as self-generated thoughts. Annie Sullivan's method, insofar as she recognized it formally as a method, was pure freedom. Like any writer, she wrote and wrote and wrote, all day long. She wrote words, phrases, sentences, lines of poetry, descriptions of animals, trees, flowers, weather, skies, clouds, concepts: whatever lay before her or came usefully to mind. She wrote not on paper with a pen, but with her fingers, spelling rapidly into the child's alert palm. Helen, quick to imitate yet uncomprehending, was under a spell of curiosity (the pun itself reveals the manual alphabet as magical tool). Her teacher spelled into her hand; she spelled the same letters back, mimicking unknowable configurations. But it was not until the connection was effected between finger-wriggling and its referent—the cognitive key, the insight, the crisis of discovery—that what we call mind broke free.

This was, of course, the fabled incident at the well pump,

dramatized in film and (by now) collective memory, when Helen suddenly understood that the tactile pattern pecking at her hand was inescapably related to the gush of cold water spilling over it. "Somehow," the adult Helen Keller recollected, "the mystery of language was revealed to me." In the course of a single month, from Annie's arrival to her triumph in forcibly bridling the household despot, Helen had grown docile, eagerly willing, affectionate, and tirelessly intent on learning from moment to moment. Her intellect was fiercely engaged, and when language began to flood it, she rode on a salvational ark of words.

To Mrs. Hopkins Annie wrote ecstatically:

> Something within me tells me that I shall succeed beyond my wildest dreams. I know that [Helen] has remarkable powers, and I believe that I shall be able to develop and mould them. I cannot tell how I know these things. I had no idea a short time ago how to go to work; I was feeling about in the dark; but somehow I know now, and I know that I know. I cannot explain it; but when difficulties arise, I am not perplexed or doubtful. I know how to meet them; I seem to divine Helen's peculiar needs. . . .
>
> Already people are taking a deep interest in Helen. No one can see her without being impressed. She is no ordinary child, and people's interest in her education will be no ordinary interest. Therefore let us be exceedingly careful in what we say and write about her. . . . My beautiful Helen shall not be transformed into a prodigy if I can help it.

At this time Helen was not yet seven years old, and Annie was being paid twenty-five dollars a month.

The fanatical public scrutiny Helen Keller aroused far exceeded Annie's predictions. It was Michael Anagnos who first proclaimed her to be a miracle child—a young goddess. "History presents no case like hers," he exulted. "As soon as a slight crevice was opened in the outer wall of their twofold imprisonment, her mental faculties emerged full-armed from their living tomb as Pallas Athene from the head of Zeus."

And again: "She is the queen of precocious and brilliant children, Emersonian in temper, most exquisitely organized, with
intellectual sight of unsurpassed sharpness and infinite reach,
a true daughter of Mnemosyne. It is no exaggeration to say
that she is a personification of goodness and happiness." Annie,
the teacher of a flesh-and-blood earthly child, protested: "His
extravagant way of saying [these things] rubs me the wrong
way. The simple facts would be so much more convincing!"
But Anagnos's glorifications caught fire: one year after Annie
had begun spelling into her hand, Helen Keller was celebrated
in newspapers all over the world. When her dog was inadvertently shot, an avalanche of contributions poured in to replace
it; unprompted, she directed that the money be set aside for
the care of an impoverished deaf-blind boy at Perkins. At eight
she was taken to visit President Cleveland at the White House,
and in Boston was introduced to many of the luminaries of
the period: Oliver Wendell Holmes, John Greenleaf Whittier,
Edward Everett Hale, and Phillips Brooks (who addressed her
puzzlement over the nature of God). At nine, saluting him as
"Dear Poet," she wrote to Whittier:

> I thought you would be glad to hear that your beautiful
> poems make me very happy. Yesterday I read "In School
> Days" and "My Playmate," and I enjoyed them greatly.
> . . . It is very pleasant to live here in our beautiful world. I
> cannot see the lovely things with my eyes, but my mind can
> see them all, and so I am joyful all the day long.
>   When I walk out in my garden I cannot see the beautiful
> flowers, but I know that they are all around me; for is not
> the air sweet with their fragrance? I know too that the tiny
> lilybells are whispering pretty secrets to their companions
> else they would not look so happy. I love you very dearly,
> because you have taught me so many lovely things about
> flowers, birds, and people.

Her dependence on Annie for the assimilation of her immediate surroundings was nearly total—hands-on, as we would
say, and literally so—but through the raised letters of Braille she

could be altogether untethered: books coursed through her. In childhood she was captivated by *Little Lord Fauntleroy*, Frances Hodgson Burnett's story of a sunnily virtuous boy who melts a crusty old man's heart; it became a secret template of her own character as she hoped she might always manifest it—not sentimentally, but in full awareness of dread. She was not deaf to Caliban's wounded cry: "You taught me language, and my profit on't/ Is, I know how to curse." Helen Keller's profit was that she knew how to rejoice. In young adulthood, casting about for a faith bare of exclusiveness or harsh images, and given over to purifying idealism, she seized on Swedenborgian spiritualism. Annie had kept away from teaching any religion at all: she was a down-to-earth agnostic whom Tewksbury had cured of easy belief. When Helen's responsiveness to bitter social deprivation later took on a worldly strength, leading her to socialism, and even to unpopular Bolshevik sympathies, Annie would have no part of it, and worried that Helen had gone too far. Marx was not in Annie's canon. Homer, Virgil, Shakespeare, and Milton were: she had Helen reading *Paradise Lost* at twelve.

But Helen's formal schooling was widening beyond Annie's tutelage. With her teacher at her side, Helen spent a year at Perkins, and then entered the Wright-Humason School in New York, a fashionable academy for deaf girls; she was its single deaf-blind pupil. She also pleaded to be taught to speak like other people, and worked at it determinedly—but apart from Annie and a few others who were accustomed to her efforts, she could not be readily understood. Speech, even if imperfect, was not her only ambition: she intended to go to college. To prepare, she enrolled in the Cambridge School for Young Ladies, where she studied mathematics, German, French, Latin, and Greek and Roman history. In 1900 she was admitted to Radcliffe (then an "annex" to Harvard), still with Annie in attendance. Despite her necessary presence in every class, diligently spelling the lecture into Helen's hand, and hourly wearing out her troubled eyes as she transcribed text after text into the manual alphabet, no one thought of granting Annie a degree along with Helen. It was not uncommon for Annie Sullivan to play second fiddle to Helen Keller; the radiant miracle outshone the driven miracle worker. Not so for Mark Twain: he saw them as two halves of the same marvel. "It took the pair of you to make a complete and perfect whole," he said. Not everyone agreed. Annie was sometimes charged with being Helen's jailer, or harrier, or ventriloquist. During examinations at Radcliffe, she was not permitted to be in the building. For the rest, Helen relied on her own extraordinary memory and on Annie's lightning fingers. Luckily, a second helper, adept at the manual alphabet, soon turned up: he was John Macy, a twenty-five-year-old English instructor at Harvard, a writer and editor, a fervent socialist, and, eventually, Annie Sullivan's husband, eleven years her junior.

The money for all this schooling, and for the sustenance of the two young women (both enjoyed fine clothes and vigorous horseback riding), came in spurts from a handful of very rich men—among them John Spaulding, the Sugar King, and Henry Rogers, of Standard Oil. Helen charmed these wealthy eminences as she charmed everyone, while Annie more systematically cultivated their philanthropy. She herself was penniless, and the Kellers of Tuscumbia were financially useless. Shockingly, Helen's father had once threatened to put his little daughter on exhibit, in order to earn her keep. (Twenty years afterward, Helen took up his idea and went on the vaudeville circuit—she happily, Annie reluctantly—and even to Hollywood, where she starred in a silent movie, with the mythical Ulysses as her ectoplasmic boyfriend.)

At Radcliffe Helen became a writer. She also became a third party to Annie's difficult romance: whoever wanted Annie inevitably got Helen too. Drawn by twin literary passions like his own, Macy was more than willing, at least at first. Charles Townsend Copeland—Harvard's illustrious "Copey," a professor of rhetoric—had encouraged Helen (as she put it to him in a grateful letter) "to make my own observations and describe the experiences peculiarly my own. Henceforth I am resolved to be myself, to live my own life and write my own thoughts." Out of this came *The Story of My Life*, the autobiography of a twenty-one-year-old, published while she was still an undergraduate. It began as a series of sketches for the *Ladies' Home Journal*; the fee was three thousand dollars. John Macy described the laborious process:

> When she began work at her story, more than a year ago, she set up on the Braille machine about a hundred pages of what she called "material," consisting of detached episodes and notes put down as they came to her without definite order or coherent plan. Then came the task where one who has eyes to see must help her. Miss Sullivan and I read the disconnected passages, put them into chronological order, and counted the words to make sure the articles should be the right length. All this work we did with Miss Keller beside us, referring everything, especially matters of phrasing, to her for revision. . . .
>
> Her memory of what she had written was astonishing. She remembered whole passages, some of which she had not seen for many weeks, and could tell, before Miss Sullivan had spelled into her hand a half-dozen words of the paragraph under discussion, where they belonged and what sentences were necessary to make the connection clear.

This method of collaboration, essentially mechanical, continued throughout Helen Keller's professional writing life; yet within these constraints the design, the sensibility, the cadences were her own. She was a self-conscious stylist. Macy remarked that she had the courage of her metaphors—he meant that she sometimes let them carry her away—and Helen herself worried that her prose could now and then seem "periwigged." To the contemporary ear, many of her phrases are too much immersed in Victorian lace and striving uplift—but the contemporary ear has no entitlement, simply by being contemporary, to set itself up as judge: every period is marked by a prevailing voice. Helen Keller's earnestness is a kind of piety; she peers through the lens of a sublimely aspiring poetry. It is as if Tennyson and the Transcendentalists had together got hold of her typewriter. At the same time, she is turbulently embroiled in the whole human enterprise—except, tellingly, for irony. She has no "edge," and why should she? Irony is a radar that seeks out the dark side;

she had darkness enough. Her unfailing intuition was to go after the light. She flew toward it, as she herself said, in the hope of "clear and animated language." She knew what part of her mind was instinct and what part was information, and she was cautious about the difference; she was even suspicious, as she had good reason to be. "It is certain," she wrote, "that I cannot always distinguish my own thoughts from those I read, because what I read become the very substance and texture of my mind. . . . It seems to me that the great difficulty of writing is to make the language of the educated mind express our confused ideas, half feelings, half thoughts, where we are little more than bundles of instinctive tendencies." She, who had once been incarcerated in the id, did not require knowledge of Freud to instruct her in its inchoate presence.

The Story of My Life was first published in 1903, with Macy's ample introduction. He was able to write about Helen nearly as authoritatively as Annie, but also—in private—more skeptically: after his marriage to Annie, the three of them set up housekeeping in rural Wrentham, Massachusetts. Possibly not since the Brontës had so feverishly literary a crew lived under a single roof. Of this ultimately inharmonious trio, one, internationally famous for decades, was catapulted now into still greater renown by the recent appearance of her celebrated memoir. Macy, meanwhile, was discovering that he had married not a woman, a moody one at that, but the indispensable infrastructure of a public institution. As Helen's secondary amanuensis, he continued to be of use until the marriage collapsed. It foundered on his profligacy with money, on Annie's irritability—she fought him on his uncompromising socialism, which she disdained—and finally on his accelerating alcoholism.

Because Macy was known to have assisted Helen in the preparation of *The Story of My Life*, the insinuations of control that often assailed Annie now also landed on him. Helen's ideas, it was said, were really Macy's; he had transformed her into a "Marxist propagandist." It was true that she sympathized with his political bent, but his views had not shaped hers. As she had come independently to Swedenborgian idealism, so had she come to societal utopianism. The charge of expropriation, of both thought and idiom, was old, and dogged her at intervals during much of her early and middle life: she was a fraud, a puppet, a plagiarist. She was false coin. She was "a living lie."

She was eleven when these words were first hurled at her, spewed out by a wrathful Anagnos. Not long before, he had spoken of Helen in celestial terms. Now he denounced her as a malignant thief. What brought on this defection was a little story she had written, called "The Frost King," which she sent him as a birthday present. In the voice of a highly literary children's narrative, it recounts how the "frost fairies" cause the season's turning.

When the children saw the trees all aglow with brilliant colors they clapped their hands and shouted for joy, and immediately began to pick great bunches to take home. "The leaves are as lovely as flowers!" cried they, in their delight.

Anagnos—doubtless clapping his hands and shouting for joy—immediately began to publicize Helen's newest accomplishment. "The Frost King" appeared both in the Perkins alumni magazine and in another journal for the blind, which, following Anagnos, unhesitatingly named it "without parallel in the history of literature." But more than a parallel was at stake; the story was found to be nearly identical to "The Frost Fairies," by Margaret Canby, a writer of children's books. Anagnos was infuriated, and fled headlong from adulation and hyperbole to humiliation and enmity. Feeling personally betrayed and institutionally discredited, he arranged an inquisition for the terrified Helen, standing her alone in a room before a jury of eight Perkins officials and himself, all mercilessly cross-questioning her. Her mature recollection of Anagnos's "court of investigation" registers as pitiably as the ordeal itself:

Mr. Anagnos, who loved me tenderly, thinking that he had been deceived, turned a deaf ear to pleadings of love

and innocence. He believed, or at least suspected, that Miss
Sullivan and I had deliberately stolen the bright thoughts of
another and imposed them on him to win his admiration.
. . . As I lay in my bed that night, I wept as I hope few
children have wept. I felt so cold, I imagined that I should
die before morning, and the thought comforted me. I think
if this sorrow had come to me when I was older, it would
have broken my spirit beyond repairing.

She was defended by Alexander Graham Bell, and by Mark
Twain, who parodied the whole procedure with a thumping
hurrah for plagiarism, and disgust for the egotism of "these
solemn donkeys breaking a little child's heart with their ignorant damned rubbish! A gang of dull and hoary pirates piously
setting themselves the task of disciplining and purifying a
kitten that they think they've caught pilfering a chop!" Margaret Canby's tale had been spelled to Helen perhaps three years
before, and lay dormant in her prodigiously retentive memory;
she was entirely oblivious of reproducing phrases not her own.
The scandal Anagnos had precipitated left a lasting bruise. But
it was also the beginning of a psychological, even a metaphysical, clarification that Helen refined and ratified as she grew
older, when similar, if more subtle, suspicions cropped up in
the press, compelling her to interrogate the workings of her
mind. *The Story of My Life* was attacked in the *Nation* not for
plagiarism in the usual sense, but for the purloining of "things
beyond her powers of perception with the assurance of one who
has verified every word. . . . One resents the pages of secondhand description of natural objects." The reviewer blamed her
for the sin of vicariousness: "all her knowledge," he insisted, "is
hearsay knowledge."
It was almost a reprise of the Perkins tribunal: she was again
being confronted with the charge of inauthenticity. Anagnos's
rebuke—"Helen Keller is a living lie"—regularly resurfaced,
sometimes less harshly, sometimes as acerbically, in the form
of a neurologist's or a psychologist's assessment, or in the reser-
vations of reviewers. A French professor of literature, who was
himself blind, determined that she was "a dupe of words, and

her aesthetic enjoyment of most of the arts is a matter of auto-suggestion rather than perception." A *New Yorker* interviewer complained, "She talks bookishly. . . . To express her ideas, she falls back on the phrases she has learned from books, and uses words that sound stilted, poetical metaphors." A professor of neurology at Columbia University, after a series of tests, pooh-poohed the claim that her remaining senses might be in any way extraordinary—the acuity of her touch and smell, he concluded, was no different from that of other mortals. "That's a stab at my vanity," she joked.

But the cruelest appraisal of all came, in 1933, from Thomas Cutsforth, a blind psychologist. By this time Helen was fifty-three, and had published four additional autobiographical volumes. Cutsforth disparaged everything she had become. The wordless child she once was, he maintained, was closer to reality than what her teacher had made of her through the imposition of "word-mindedness." He objected to her use of images such as "a mist of green," "blue pools of dog violets," "soft clouds tumbling." All that, he protested, was "implied chicanery" and "a birthright sold for a mess of verbiage." He criticized

> the aims of the educational system in which she has been confined during her whole life. Literary expression has been the goal of her formal education. Fine writing, regardless of its meaningful content, has been the end toward which both she and her teacher have striven. . . . Her own experiential life was rapidly made secondary, and it was regarded as such by the victim. . . . Her teacher's ideals became her ideals, her teacher's likes became her likes, and whatever emotional activity her teacher experienced she experienced.

For Cutsforth—and not only for him—Helen Keller was the victim of language rather than its victorious master. She was no better than a copy; whatever was primary, and thereby genuine, had been stamped out. As for Annie, while here she was pilloried as the callous instrument of her pupil's victimization, elsewhere she was pitied as a woman cheated of her own life by having sacrificed it to serve another. Either Helen was Annie's slave, or Annie was Helen's.

Once again Helen had her faithful defenders. The philosopher Ernst Cassirer reflected that "a human being in the construction of his human world is not dependent upon the quality of his sense material." Even more trenchantly, a *New York Times* editor quoted Cicero: "When Democritus lost his sight he could not, to be sure, distinguish black from white; but all the same he could distinguish good from bad, just from unjust, honorable from disgraceful, expedient from inexpedient, great from small, and it was permitted him to live happily without seeing changes of color; it was not permissible to do so without true ideas."

But Helen did not depend on philosophers, ancient or modern, to make her case. She spoke for herself: she was nobody's puppet, her mind was her own, and she knew what she saw. Once, having been taken to the uppermost viewing platform of what was then the tallest building in the world, she defined her condition:

> I will concede that my guides saw a thousand things that escaped me from the top of the Empire State Building, but I am not envious. For imagination creates distances that reach to the end of the world. . . . There was the Hudson—more like the flash of a swordblade than a noble river. The little island of Manhattan, set like a jewel in its nest of rainbow waters, stared up into my face, and the solar system circled about my head!

Her rebuttal to word-mindedness, to vicariousness, to implied chicanery and the living lie, was inscribed deliberately and defiantly in her daring images of swordblade and rainbow waters. That they were derived was no reason for her to be deprived—why should she alone be starved of enchantment? The deaf-blind person, she wrote, "seizes every word of sight and hearing, because his sensations compel it. Light and color, of which he has no tactual evidence, he studies fearlessly,

believing that all humanly knowable truth is open to him."
She was not ashamed of talking bookishly: it meant a ready
access to the storehouse of history and literature. She disposed
of her critics with a dazzling apothegm: "The bulk of the
world's knowledge is an imaginary construction," and went
on to contend that history itself "is but a mode of imagining,
of making us see civilizations that no longer appear upon the
earth." Those who ridiculed her rapturous rendering of color
she dismissed as "spirit-vandals" who would force her "to bite
the dust of material things." Her idea of the subjective onlooker
was broader than that of physics, and while "red" may denote
an explicit and measurable wavelength in the visible spectrum,
in the mind it is flittingly fickle (and not only for the blind),
varying from the bluster of rage to the reticence of a blush:
physics cannot cage metaphor.

She saw, then, what she wished, or was blessed, to see, and
rightly named it imagination. In this she belongs to a wider class
than that narrow order of the tragically deaf-blind. Her class,
her tribe, hears what no healthy ear can catch, and sees what
no eye chart can quantify. Her common language was not with
the man who crushed a child for memorizing what the fairies
do, or with the carpers who scolded her for the crime of a
literary vocabulary. She was a member of the race of poets, the
Romantic kind; she was close cousin to those novelists who
write not only what they do not know, but what they cannot
possibly know.

And though she was early taken in hand by a writerly intelligence leading her purposefully to literature, it was hardly in
the power of the manual alphabet to pry out a writer who was
not already there. Laura Bridgman stuck to her lace making,
and with all her senses intact might have remained a needle-
woman. John Macy believed finally that between Helen and
Annie there was only one genius—his wife. Helen's intellect,
he asserted, was "stout and energetic, of solid endurance," able
to achieve through patience and toil, but void of real brilliance.
In the absence of Annie's inventiveness and direction, he
implied, Helen's efforts would show up as the lesser gifts they
were. This did not happen. Annie died, at seventy, in 1936, four

years after Macy; they had long been estranged. By then her always endangered eyesight had deteriorated; depressed, obese, cranky, and inconsolable, she had herself gone blind. Helen came under the care of her secretary, Polly Thomson, a Scotswoman who was both possessively loyal and dryly unliterary: the scenes she spelled into Helen's hand never matched Annie's quicksilver evocations.

But even as she mourned the loss of her teacher, Helen flourished. Annie was dead; only the near-at-hand are indispensable. With the assistance of Nella Henney, Annie Sullivan's biographer, she continued to publish journals and memoirs. She undertook grueling visits to Japan, India, Israel, Europe, Australia, everywhere championing the blind, the deaf, the dispossessed. She was indefatigable until her very last years, and died in 1968 weeks before her eighty-eighth birthday.

Yet the story of her life is not the good she did, the panegyrics she inspired, or the disputes (genuine or counterfeit? victim or victimizer?) that stormed around her. The most persuasive story of Helen Keller's life is what she said it was: "I observe, I feel, I think, I imagine."

She was an artist. She imagined.

"Blindness has no limiting effect on mental vision. My intellectual horizon is infinitely wide," she was impelled to argue again and again. "The universe it encircles is immeasurable." And like any writer making imagination's mysterious claims before the material-minded, she had cause enough to cry out, "Oh, the supercilious doubters!"

But it was not herself alone she was shielding from these skirmishes: she was a warrior in a wide and thorny conflict. Helen Keller, if we are presumptuous enough to reduce her so, can be taken to be a laboratory for empirical demonstration. Do we know only what we see, or do we see what we somehow already know? Are we more than the sum of our senses? Does a picture—whatever strikes the retina—engender thought, or does thought create the picture? Can there be subjectivity without an object to glance off from? Metaphysicians and other theorists have their differing notions, to which the ungraspable organism that is Helen Keller is a retort. She is not an advocate for one side or the other in the ancient debate concerning the nature of the real. She is not a philosophical or neurological or therapeutic topic. She stands for enigma, and against obtuseness; there lurks in her still the angry child who demanded to be understood, yet could not be deciphered. She refutes those who cannot perceive, or do not care to value, what is hidden from sensation.

Against whom does she rage, whom does she refute? The mockers of her generation and ours. The psychiatrist Bruno Bettelheim, for instance. "By pretending to have a full life," he warned in a 1990 essay, "by pretending that through touch she knew what a piece of sculpture, what flowers, what trees were like, that through the words of others she knew what the sky or clouds looked like, by pretending that she could hear music by feeling the vibrations of musical instruments," she fooled the world into thinking the "terribly handicapped are not suffering deeply every moment of their lives." Pretender, trickster: this is what the notion of therapy makes of "the words of others," which we more commonly term experience; heritage; literature. At best the therapist pities, at worst he sees delusion. Perhaps Helen Keller did suffer deeply. Then all the more honor to the flashing embossments of the artist's mask. Oddly, practitioners of psychology—whom one would least expect to be literalists—have been quickest to blame her for imposture. Let them blame Keats, too, for his delusionary "Heard melodies are sweet, but those unheard are sweeter," and for his phantom theme of negative capability, the poet's oarless casting about for the hallucinatory shadows of desire.

Helen Keller's lot, it turns out, was not unique. "We work in the dark," Henry James affirmed, on behalf of his own art, and so did she. It was the same dark. She knew her Wordsworth: "Visionary power/Attends the motions of the viewless winds/ Embodied in the mystery of word:/There, darkness makes abode." She fought the debunkers who, for the sake of a spurious honesty, would denude her of landscape and return her to the marble cell. She fought the iron pragmatists who meant to disinherit her, and everyone, of poetry. She fought the tin ears who took imagining to be mendacity. Her legacy, after all, is an epistemological marker of sorts: proof of the real existence of the mind's eye.

In one respect, though, she was incontrovertibly as fraudulent as the cynics charged. She had always been photographed in profile: this hid her disfigured left eye. In maturity she had both eyes surgically removed and replaced with glass—an expedient known only to those closest to her. Everywhere she went, her sparkling blue prosthetic eyes were admired for their living beauty and humane depth.

T. S. Eliot at 101

"The Man Who Suffers and the
Mind Which Creates"

THOMAS STEARNS ELIOT, poet and preëminent modernist, was born one hundred and one years ago.* His centennial in 1988 was suitably marked by commemorative reporting, literary celebrations in New York and London, and the publication of a couple of lavishly reviewed volumes: a new biography and a collection of the poet's youthful letters. Probably not much more could have been done to distinguish the occasion; still, there was something subdued and bloodless, even superannuated, about these memorial stirrings. They had the quality of a slightly tedious reunion of aging alumni, mostly spiritless by now, spurred to animation by old exultation recollected in tranquility. The only really fresh excitement took place in London, where representatives of the usually docile community of British Jews, including at least one prominent publisher, condemned Eliot for antisemitism and protested the public fuss. Elsewhere, the moment passed modestly, hardly noticed at all by the bookish young—who, whether absorbed by recondite theorizing in the academy, or scampering after newfangled writing careers, have long had their wagons hitched to other stars.

In the early Seventies it was still possible to uncover, here and there, a tenacious English department offering a vestigial graduate seminar given over to the study of Eliot. But by the close of the Eighties, only "The Love Song of J. Alfred Prufrock" appears to have survived the indifference of the schools—two or three pages in the anthologies, a fleeting assignment for high school seniors and college freshmen. "Prufrock," and "Prufrock" alone, is what the latest generations know—barely

---

* This essay was written in 1989.

know: not "The Hollow Men," not "La Figlia che Piange," not "Ash-Wednesday," not even *The Waste Land*. Never *Four Quartets*. And the mammoth prophetic presence of T. S. Eliot himself—that immortal sovereign rock—the latest generations do not know at all.

To anyone who was an undergraduate in the Forties and Fifties (and possibly even into the first years of the Sixties), all that is inconceivable—as if a part of the horizon had crumbled away. When, four decades ago, in a literary period that resembled eternity, T. S. Eliot won the Nobel Prize for literature, he seemed pure zenith, a colossus, nothing less than a permanent luminary fixed in the firmament like the sun and the moon—or like the New Criticism itself, the vanished movement Eliot once magisterially dominated. It was a time that, for the literary young, mixed authority with innovation: authority *was* innovation, an idea that reads now, in the wake of the anti-establishment Sixties, like the simplest contradiction. But modernism then was an absolute ruler—it had no effective intellectual competition and had routed all its predecessors; and it was modernism that famously carried the "new."

The new—as embodied in Eliot—was difficult, preoccupied by parody and pastiche, exactingly allusive and complex, saturated in manifold ironies and inflections, composed of "layers," and pointedly inaccessible to anybody expecting run-of-the-mill coherence. The doors to Eliot's poetry were not easily opened. His lines and themes were not readily understood. But the young who flung themselves through those portals were lured by unfamiliar enchantments and bound by pleasurable ribbons of ennui. "April is the cruel-lest month," Eliot's voice, with its sepulchral cadences, came spiralling out of 78 r.p.m. phonographs, "breeding / Lilacs out of the dead land, mixing / Memory and desire . . ." That toney British accent—flat, precise, steady, unemotive, surprisingly high-pitched, bleakly passive—coiled through awed English departments and worshipful dormitories, rooms where the walls had pin-up Picassos, and Pound and Eliot and *Ulysses* and Proust shouldered one another higgledy-piggledy in the rapt late-adolescent breast. The voice was, like the poet himself, nearly sacerdotal, impersonal, winding and winding across the country's campuses like a spool of blank robotic woe. "Shantih shantih shantih," "not with a bang but a whimper," "an old man in a dry month," "I shall wear the bottoms of my trousers rolled"—these were the devout chants of the literarily passionate in the Forties and Fifties, who in their own first verses piously copied Eliot's tone: its restraint, gravity, mystery; its invasive remoteness and immobilized disjointed despair.

There was rapture in that despair. Wordsworth's nostalgic cry over the start of the French Revolution—"Bliss was it in that dawn to be alive, / But to be young was very heaven!"—belongs no doubt to every new generation; youth's heaven lies in its quitting, or sometimes spiting, the past, with or without a historical crisis. And though Eliot's impress—the bliss he evoked—had little to do with political rupture, it was revolutionary enough in its own way. The young who gave homage to Eliot were engaged in a self-contradictory double maneuver: they were willingly authoritarian even as they jubilantly rebelled. On the one hand, taking on the puzzlements of modernism, they were out to tear down the Wordsworthian tradition itself, and on the other they were ready to fall on their knees to a god. A god, moreover, who despised free-thinking, democracy, and secularism: the very conditions of anti-authoritarianism.

How T. S. Eliot became that god—or, to put it less extravagantly, how he became a commanding literary figure who had no successful rivals and whose formulations were in fact revered—is almost as mysterious a proposition as how, in the flash of half a lifetime, an immutable majesty was dismantled, an immutable glory dissipated. It is almost impossible nowadays to imagine such authority accruing to a poet. No writer today—Nobel winner or no—holds it or can hold it. The four* most recent American Nobel laureates in literature—Czeslaw Milosz, Saul Bellow, Isaac Bashevis Singer, and Joseph Brodsky (three of whom, though citizens of long standing, do not write primarily in English)—are much honored, but they

* There is, of course, now a fifth: Toni Morrison.

are not looked to for manifestos or pronouncements, and their comments are not studied as if by a haruspex. They are as far from being cultural dictators as they are from filling football stadiums.

Eliot *did* once fill a football stadium. On April 30, 1956, fourteen thousand people came to hear him lecture on "The Frontiers of Criticism" at the University of Minnesota, in Minneapolis. By then he was solidly confirmed as "the Pope of Russell Square," as his London admirer Mary Trevelyan began to call him in 1949. It was a far-reaching papacy, effective even among students in the American Midwest; but if the young flocked to genuflect before the papal throne, it was not they who had enthroned Eliot, nor their teachers. In the Age of Criticism (as the donnish "little" magazines of the time dubbed the Forties and Fifties), Eliot was ceded power, and accorded veneration, by critics who were themselves minor luminaries. "He has a very penetrating influence, perhaps not unlike an east wind," wrote William Empson, one of whose titles, *Seven Types of Ambiguity*, became an academic catchphrase alongside Eliot's famous "objective correlative." R. P. Blackmur said of "Prufrock" that its "obscurity is like that of the womb"; Eliot's critical essays, he claimed, bear a "vital relation" to Aristotle's *Poetics*. Hugh Kenner's comparison is with still another monument: "Eliot's work, as he once noted of Shakespeare, is in important respects one continuous poem," and for Kenner the shape of Eliot's own monument turns out to be "the Arch which stands when the last marcher has left, and endures when the last centurion or sergeant-major is dust." F. R. Leavis, declaring Eliot "among the greatest poets of the English language," remarked that "to have gone seriously into the poetry is to have had a quickening insight into the nature of thought and language." And in Eliot's hands, F. O. Matthiessen explained, the use of the symbol can "create the illusion that it is giving expression to the very mystery of life."

These evocations of wind, womb, thought and language, the dust of the ages, the very mystery of life, not to mention the ghosts of Aristotle and Shakespeare: not since Dr. Johnson has a man of letters writing in English been received with so much adulation, or seemed so formidable—almost a marvel of nature itself—within his own society.

Nevertheless there was an occasional dissenter. As early as 1929, Edmund Wilson was complaining that he couldn't stomach Eliot's celebrated conversion to "classicism, royalism, and Anglo-Catholicism." While granting that Eliot's essays "will be read by everybody interested in literature," that Eliot "has now become the most important literary critic in the English-speaking world," and finally that "one can find no figure of comparable authority," it was exactly the force of this influence that made Wilson "fear that we must give up hope." For Wilson, the argument of Eliot's followers "that, because our society at the present time is badly off without religion, we should make an heroic effort to swallow medieval theology, seems . . . utterly futile as well as fundamentally dishonest." Twenty-five years later, when the American intellectual center had completed its shift from freelance literary work like Wilson's—and Eliot's—to the near-uniformity of university English departments, almost no one in those departments would dare to think such unfastidious thoughts about Eliot out loud. A glaze of orthodoxy (not too different from the preoccupation with deconstructive theory currently orthodox in English departments) settled over academe. Given the normal eagerness of succeeding literary generations to examine new sets of entrails, it was inevitable that so unbroken a dedication would in time falter and decline. But until that happened, decades on, Eliot studies were an unopposable ocean; an unstoppable torrent; a lava of libraries.

It may be embarrassing for us now to look back at that nearly universal obeisance to an autocratic, inhibited, depressed, rather narrow-minded and considerably bigoted fake Englishman—especially if we are old enough (as I surely am) to have been part of the wave of adoration. In his person, if not in his poetry, Eliot was, after all, false coinage. Born in St. Louis, he became indistinguishable (though not to shrewd native English eyes), in his dress, his manners, his loyalties, from a proper British Tory. Scion of undoctrinaire rationalist New England Unitarianism (his grandfather had moved from Boston to Missouri to found Washington University), he was possessed by guilty notions of sinfulness and martyrdom and by the monkish disciplines of asceticism, which he pursued in the unlikely embrace of the established English church. No doubt Eliot's extreme self-alterations should not be dismissed as ordinary humbug, particularly not on the religious side; there is a difference between impersonation and conversion. Still self-alteration so unalloyed suggests a hatred of the original design. And certainly Eliot condemned the optimism of democratic American meliorism; certainly he despised Unitarianism, centered less on personal salvation than on the social good; certainly he had contempt for Jews as marginal if not inimical to his notions of Christian community. But most of all, he came to loathe himself, a hollow man in a twilight kingdom.

In my undergraduate years, between seventeen and twenty-one, and long after as well, I had no inkling of any of this. The overt flaws—the handful of insults in the poetry—I swallowed down without protest. No one I knew protested—at any rate, no professor ever did. If Eliot included lines like "The rats are underneath the piles. / The jew [sic] is underneath the lot," if he had his Bleistein, "Chicago Semite Viennese," stare "from the protozoic slime" while elsewhere "The jew squats on the windowsill, the owner" and "Rachel *née* Rabinovitch / Tears at the grapes with murderous paws"—well, that, sadly, was the way of the world and to be expected, even in the most resplendent poet of the age. The sting of those phrases—the shock that sickened—passed, and the reader's heart pressed on to be stirred by other lines. What was Eliot to me? He was not the crack about "Money in furs," or "Spawned in some estaminet in Antwerp." No, Eliot was "The Lady is withdrawn / In a white gown, to contemplation, in a white gown" and "Then spoke the thunder / DA/ *Datta*: what have we given?" and "Afternoon grey and smoky, evening yellow and rose"; he was incantation, mournfulness, elegance; he was liquescence, he was staccato, he was quickstep and oar, the hushed moan and the sudden clap. He was lyric shudder and roseburst. He was, in brief, poetry incarnate; and poetry was what one lived for.

And he was something else beside. He was, to say it quickly, absolute art: high art, when art was at its most serious and
elitist. The knowledge of that particular splendour—priestly,
sacral, a golden cape for the initiate—has by now ebbed out of
the world, and many do not regret it. Literary high art turned
its back on egalitarianism and prized what is nowadays scorned
as "the canon": that body of anciently esteemed texts, most of
them difficult and aristocratic in origin, which has been designated Western culture. Modernism—and Eliot—teased the
canon, bruised it, and even sought to astonish it by mocking
and fragmenting it, and also by introducing Eastern infusions,
such as Eliot's phrases from the Upanishads in *The Waste Land*
and Pound's Chinese imitations. But all these shatterings, dis-
locations, and idiosyncratic juxtapositions of the old literary
legacies were never intended to abolish the honor in which
they were held, and only confirmed their centrality. Undoing
the canon is the work of a later time—of our own, in fact,
when universal assent to a central cultural standard is almost
everywhere decried. For the moderns, and for Eliot especially, the denial of permanently agreed-on masterworks—what
Matthew Arnold, in a currency now obsolete beyond imagining, called "touchstones"—would have been unthinkable.
What one learned from Eliot, whose poetry skittered toward
disintegration, was the power of consolidation: the understanding that literature could genuinely *reign*.

One learned also that a poem could actually be penetrated to
its marrow—which was not quite the same as comprehending
its meaning. In shunting aside or giving up certain goals of
ordinary reading, the New Criticism installed Eliot as both
teacher and subject. For instance, following Eliot, the New
Criticism would not allow a poem to be read in the light of
either biography or psychology. The poem was to be regarded
as a thing-in-itself; nothing environmental or causal, including
its own maker, was permitted to illuminate or explain it. In
that sense it was as impersonal as a jar or any other shapely artifact that must be judged purely by its externals. This objective
approach to a poem, deriving from Eliot's celebrated "objective correlative" formulation, did not dismiss emotion; rather,

it kept it at a distance, and precluded any speculation about the poet's own life, or any other likely influence on the poem. "The progress of an artist is a continual self-sacrifice, a continual extinction of personality," Eliot wrote in his landmark essay, "Tradition and the Individual Talent." "Emotion . . . has its life in the poem and not in the history of the poet." And, most memorably: "The more perfect the artist, the more completely separate in him will be the man who suffers and the mind which creates." This was a theory designed to prevent old-fashioned attempts to read private events into the lines on the page. Artistic inevitability, Eliot instructed, "lies in this complete adequacy of the external to the emotion" and suggested a series of externals that might supply the "exact equivalence" of any particular emotion: "a set of objects, a situation, a chain of events." Such correlatives—or "objective equivalences"—provided, he insisted, the "only way of expressing emotion in the form of art." The New Criticism took him at his word, and declined to admit any other way. Not that the aesthetic scheme behind Eliot's formulation was altogether new. Henry James, too, had demanded—"Dramatize, dramatize!"—that the work of art resist construing itself in public. When Eliot, in offering his objective correlative, stopped to speak of the "*données* of the problem"—*donnée* was one of James's pet Gallicisms—he was tipping off his source. No literary figure among James's contemporaries had paid any attention to this modernist dictum, often not even James himself. Emerging in far more abstruse language from Eliot, it became a papal bull. He was thirty-five at the time.

The method used in digging out the objective correlative had a Gallic name of its own: *explication de texte*. The sloughing off of what the New Criticism considered to be extraneous had the effect of freeing the poem utterly—freeing it for the otherwise undistracted mind of the reader, who was released from "psychology" and similar blind alleys in order to master the poem's components. The New Criticism held the view that a poem could indeed be mastered: this was an act of trust, as it were, between poem and reader. The poem could be relied on to yield itself up to the reader—if the reader, on the other side of the bargain, would agree to a minutely close "*explication*," phrase by phrase: a process far more meticulous than "interpretation" or the search for any identifiable meaning or definitive commentary. The search was rather for architecture and texture—or call it resonance and intricacy, the responsive web-work between the words. *Explication de texte*, as practiced by the New Critics and their graduate-student disciples, was something like watching an ant maneuver a bit of leaf. One notes first the fine veins in the leaf, then the light speckled along the veins, then the tiny glimmers charging off the ant's various surfaces, the movements of the ant's legs and other body parts, the lifting and balancing of the leaf, all the while scrupulously aware that ant and leaf, though separate structures, become—when linked in this way—a freshly imagined structure.

A generation or more was initiated into this concentrated scrutiny of a poem's structure and movement. High art in literature—which had earlier been approached through the impressionistic "appreciations" that commonly passed for critical reading before the New Criticism took hold—was seen to be indivisible from *explication de texte*. And though the reverence for high art that characterized the Eliot era is now antiquated—or dead—the close reading that was the hallmark of the New Critics has survived, and remains the sine qua non of all schools of literary theory. Currently it is even being applied to popular culture; hamburger advertisements and television sitcoms can be serious objects of up-to-date critical examination. Eliot was hugely attracted to popular culture as an innovative ingredient of pastiche—"Sweeney Agonistes," an unfinished verse drama, is saturated in it. But for Eliot and the New Critics, popular culture or "low taste" contributed to a literary technique; it would scarcely have served as a literary subject, or "text," in its own right. Elitism ruled. Art was expected to be strenuous, hard-earned, knotty. Eliot explicitly said so, and the New Critics faithfully concurred. "It is not a permanent necessity that poets should be interested in philosophy," Eliot wrote (though he himself had been a graduate student in philosophy at Harvard and Oxford, and had completed a thesis on F. H. Bradley, the British idealist). "We can only say that it appears likely that poets in our civilization, as it exists at present, must be *difficult*. Our civilization comprehends great variety and complexity, and this variety and complexity, playing upon a refined sensibility, must produce various and complex results. The poet must become more and more comprehensive, more allusive, more indirect, in order to force, to dislocate if necessary, language into his meaning."

He had another requirement as well, and that was a receptiveness to history. Complexity could be present only when historical consciousness prevailed. He favored history over novelty, and tradition over invention. While praising William Blake for "a remarkable and original sense of language and the music of language, and a gift of hallucinated vision," Eliot faulted him for his departures from the historical mainstream. "What his genius required, and what it sadly lacked, was a framework of accepted and traditional ideas which would have prevented him from indulging in a philosophy of his own." And he concluded, "The concentration resulting from a framework of mythology and theology and philosophy is one of the reasons why Dante is a classic, and Blake only a poet of genius." Genius was not enough for Eliot. A poet, he said in "Tradition and the Individual Talent," needs to be "directed by the past." The historical sense "compels a man to write not merely with his own generation in his bones, but with the feeling that the whole of the literature of Europe from Homer and within it the whole of the literature of his own country has a simultaneous existence and composes a simultaneous order."

A grand view; a view of grandeur; high art defined: so high that even the sublime Blake fails to meet its measure. It is all immensely elevated and noble—and, given the way many literary academics and critics think now, rare and alien. Aristocratic ideas of this kind, which some might call Eurocentric and obscurantist, no longer engage most literary intellectuals; nor did they, sixty years ago, engage Edmund Wilson. But they were dominant for decades, and in the reign of Eliot they were law. Like other postulates, they brought good news and bad news; and we know that my good news may well be your bad news. Probably the only legacy of the Eliot era that everyone can affirm as enduringly valuable is the passionate, yet also dis-interested, dissection of the text, a nuanced skill that no critical reader, taking whatever ideological stand, can do without. This exception aside, the rest is all disagreement. As I see it, what appeared important to me at twenty-one is still important; in some respects I admit to being arrested in the Age of Eliot, a permanent member of it, unregenerate. The etiolation of high art seems to me to be a major loss. I continue to suppose that some texts are worthier than other texts. The same with the diminishment of history and tradition: not to incorporate into an educable mind the origins and unifying principles of one's own civilization strikes me as a kind of cultural autolobotomy. Nor am I ready to relinquish Eliot's stunning declaration that the reason we know so much more than the dead writers knew is that "they are that which we know." As for that powerful central body of touchstone works, the discredited "canon," and Eliot's strong role in shaping it for his own and the following generation, it remains clear to me—as Susan Sontag remarked at the 1986 International PEN Convention—that literary genius is not an equal opportunity employer; I would not wish to drop Homer or Jane Austen or Kafka to make room for an Aleutian Islander of lesser gifts, however unrepresented her group may be on the college reading list.

In today's lexicon these are no doubt "conservative" notions, for which Eliot's influence can be at least partly blamed or—depending on your viewpoint—credited. In Eliot himself they have a darker side—the bad news. And the bad news is very bad. The gravity of high art led Eliot to envision a controlling and exclusionary society that could, presumably, supply the conditions to produce that art. These doctrinal tendencies, expressed in 1939 in a little book called *The Idea of a Christian Society*, took Eliot—on the eve of Nazi Germany's ascendancy over Europe—to the very lip of shutting out, through "radical changes," anyone he might consider ineligible for his "Com-munity of Christians." Lamenting "the intolerable position of those who try to lead a Christian life in a non-Christian world," he was indifferent to the position of those who would try to thrive as a cultural minority within his contemplated

Utopia. (This denigration of tolerance was hardly fresh. He had argued in a lecture six years before that he "had no objection to being called a bigot.") In the same volume, replying to a certain Miss Bower, who had frowned on "one of the main tenets of the Nazi creed—the relegation of women to the sphere of the kitchen, the children, and the church," Eliot protested "the implication that what is Nazi is wrong, and need not be discussed on its own merits." Nine years afterward, when the fight against Germany was won, he published *Notes Toward the Definition of Culture*, again proposing the hegemony of a common religious culture. Here he wrote—at a time when Hitler's ovens were just cooled and the shock of the Final Solution just dawning—that "the scattering of Jews amongst peoples holding the Christian faith may have been unfortunate both for these peoples and for the Jews themselves," because "the effect may have been to strengthen the illusion that there can be culture without religion." An extraordinary postwar comment. And in an Appendix, "The Unity of European Culture," a radio lecture broadcast to Germany in 1946, one year after the Reich was dismantled, with Europe in upheaval, the death camps exposed, and displaced persons everywhere, he made no mention at all of the German atrocities. The only reference to "barbarism" was hypothetical, a worried projection into a potentially barren future: "If Christianity goes, the whole of our culture goes," as if the best of European civilization (including the merciful tenets of Christianity) had not already been pulverized to ash throughout the previous decade. So much for where high art and traditional culture landed Eliot.

There is bad news, as it happens, even in the objective correlative. What was once accepted as an austere principle of poetics is suddenly decipherable as no more than a device to shield the poet from the raw shame of confession. Eliot is now unveiled as a confessional poet above all—one who was driven to confess, who *did* confess, whose subject was sin and guilt (his own), but who had no heart for the act of disclosure. That severe law of the impersonality of the poem—the masking technique purported to displace emotion from its crude source in the poet's real-life experience to its heightened incarnation in "a set of objects, a situation, a chain of events"—turns out to be motivated by something less august and more timorous than pure literary theory or a devotion to symbol. In the name of the objective correlative, Eliot had found a way to describe the wound without the embarrassment of divulging who held the knife. This was a conception far less immaculate than the practitioners of the New Criticism ever supposed; for thirty years or more Eliot's close readers remained innocent of—or discreet about—Eliot's private life. Perhaps some of them imagined that, like the other pope, he had none.

The assault on the masking power of the objective correlative—the breach in Eliot's protective wall—came about in the ordinary way: the biographies began. They began because time, which dissolves everything, at last dissolved awe. Although the number of critical examinations of Eliot, both book-length and in periodicals, is beyond counting, and although there are a handful of memoirs by people who were acquainted with him, the first true biography did not appear until a dozen years after his death. In 1977 Lyndall Gordon published *Eliot's Early Years*, an accomplished and informative study taking Eliot past his failed first marriage and through the composition of *The Waste Land*. Infiltrated by the familiar worshipfulness, the book is a tentative hybrid, part dense critical scrutiny and part cautious narrative—self-conscious about the latter, as if permission has not quite been granted by the author to herself. The constraints of awe are still there. Nevertheless the poetry is advanced in the light of Eliot's personal religious development, and these first illuminations are potent. In 1984 a second biography arrived, covering the life entire; by now awe has been fully dispatched. Peter Ackroyd's *T. S. Eliot: A Life* is thorough, bold, and relaxed about its boldness—even now and then a little acid. Not a debunking job by any means, but admirably straightforward. The effect is to bring Eliot down to recognizably human scale—disorienting to a reader trained to Eliot-adulation and ignorant until now of the nightmare of Eliot's youthful marriage and its devastating evolution. Four years on, Eliot's centenary saw the publication of *Eliot's New Life*, Lyndall Gordon's concluding volume, containing augmented portraits—in

the nature of discoveries—of two women Ackroyd had touched
on much less intensively; each had expected Eliot to marry her
after the death of his wife in a mental institution. Eliot was
callous to both. Eleven years following her first study, Gordon's
manner continues respectful and her matter comprehensive,
but the diffidence of the narrative chapters is gone. Eliot has
acquired fallibility, and Gordon is not afraid to startle herself,
or the long, encrusted history of deferential Eliot scholarship.
Volume Two is daring, strong, and psychologically brilliant.
Finally, 1988 also marked the issuance of a fat book of letters,
The Letters of T. S. Eliot, Vol. I: 1898–1922, from childhood to
age thirty-five (with more to come), edited by Eliot's widow,
Valerie Eliot, whom he married when she was thirty and he
sixty-eight.

"The man who suffers and the mind which creates"—these
inseparables, sundered long ago by Eliot himself, can now be
surgically united.

If Eliot hid his private terrors behind the hedge of his poetry,
the course of literary history took no notice of it. Adoration,
fame, and the Nobel Prize came to him neither in spite of nor
because of what he left out; his craft was in the way he left it
out. And he had always been reticent; he had always hidden
himself. It can even be argued that he went to live in England
in order to hide from his mother and father.

His mother, Charlotte Stearns Eliot, was a frustrated poet
who wrote religious verse and worked for the civic good. His
father, Henry Ware Eliot, was an affluent businessman who ran
a St. Louis brick-manufacturing company. Like any entrepreneur, he liked to see results. His father's father, an intellectual
admired by Dickens, was good at results—though not the conventional kind. He had left the family seat in blueblood Boston
to take the enlightenment of Unitarianism to the American
West; while he was at it he established a university. Both of
Eliot's parents were strong-willed. Both expected him to make
a success of himself. Both tended to diminish his independence.
Not that they wanted his success on any terms but his own—it
was early understood that this youngest of six siblings (four

sisters, one of whom was nineteen years older, and a brother almost a decade his senior) was unusually gifted. He was the sort of introspective child who is photographed playing the piano or reading a book or watching his girl cousins at croquet (while himself wearing a broad-brimmed straw hat and a frilly dress, unremarkable garb for upper-class nineteenth-century male tots). His mother wrote to the headmaster of his prep school to ensure that he would not be allowed to participate in sports. She wrote again to warn against the dangers of swimming in quarry ponds. She praised Eliot's schoolboy verse as better than her own, and guaranteed his unease. "I knew what her verses meant to her. We did not discuss the matter further," he admitted long afterward. At his Harvard commencement in 1910, the same year as the composition of "Portrait of a Lady" and a year before "Prufrock," he delivered the farewell ode in a style that may have been a secret parody of his mother's: "For the hour that is left us Fair Harvard, with thee, / Ere we face the importunate years . . ." His mother was sympathetic to his ambitions as a poet—too sympathetic: it was almost as if his ambitions were hers, or vice versa. His father took a brisk view of Eliot's graduate studies in philosophy: they were the ticket to a Harvard professorship, a recognizably respectable career.

But Eliot would not stay put. To the bewilderment of his parents—the thought of it gave his mother a "chill"—he ran off to Paris, partly to catch the atmosphere of Jules Laforgue, a French poet who had begun to influence him, and partly to sink into Europe. In Paris he was briefly attracted to Henri Bergson, whose lectures on philosophy he attended at the Collège de France, but then he came upon Charles Maurras; Maurras's ideas—*"classique, catholique, monarchique"*—stuck to him for life, and were transmuted in 1928 into his own "classicist, royalist, Anglo-Catholic." In 1910 the word "fascist" was not yet in fashion, but that is exactly what Maurras was: later on he joined the pro-Nazi Vichy regime, and went to jail for it after World War II. None of this dented Eliot's enduring admiration; *Hommage à Charles Maurras* was written as late as 1948. When Eliot first encountered him, Maurras was the founder of an anti-democratic organization called Action Française, which specialized in student riots and open assaults on free-thinkers and Jews. Eliot, an onlooker on one of these occasions, did not shrink from the violence. (Ackroyd notes that he "liked boxing matches also.")

After Paris he obediently returned to Harvard for three diligent years, doing some undergraduate teaching and working on his doctoral degree. One of his courses was with Bertrand Russell, visiting from England. Russell saw Eliot at twenty-five as a silent young dandy, impeccably turned out, but a stick without "vigour or life—or enthusiasm." (Only a year later, in England, the diffident dandy—by then a new husband—would move with his bride right into Russell's tiny flat.) During the remainder of the Harvard period, Eliot embarked on Sanskrit, read Hindu and Buddhist sacred texts, and tunneled into the investigations that would culminate in his dissertation, *Experience and the Objects of Knowledge in the Philosophy of F. H. Bradley*. Screened by this busy academic program, he was also writing poetry. When Harvard offered him a traveling scholarship, he set off for Europe, and never again came back to live in the country of his birth. It was the beginning of the impersonations that were to become transformations.

He had intended an extensive tour of the Continent, but, in August of 1914, when war broke out, he retreated to England and enrolled at Oxford, ostensibly to continue his studies in philosophy. Oxford seemed an obvious way station for a young man headed for a professorial career, and his parents, shuttling between St. Louis and their comfortable New England summer house, ineradicably American in their habits and point of view, could not have judged otherwise, or suspected a permanent transatlantic removal. But what Eliot was really after was London: the literary life of London, in the manner of Henry James's illustrious conquest of it three decades before. He was quiet, deceptively passive, always reserved, on the watch for opportunity. He met Ezra Pound almost immediately. Pound, a fellow expatriate, was three years older and had come to London five years earlier. He had already published five volumes of poetry. He was idiosyncratic, noisy, cranky, aggressive, repetitively and tediously humorous as well as perilously unpredictable, and he kept an eye out for ways to position himself at the center of whatever maelstrom was current or could be readily invented. By the time he and Eliot discovered each other, Pound had been through Imagism and was boosting Vorticism; he wanted to shepherd movements, organize souls, administer lives. He read a handful of Eliot's Harvard poems, including "Portrait of a Lady" and "Prufrock," and instantly anointed him as the real thing. To Harriet Monroe in Chicago, the editor of *Poetry*, then the most distinguished—and coveted—American journal of its kind, he trumpeted Eliot as the author of "the best poem I have yet had or seen from an American," and insisted that she publish "Prufrock." He swept around London introducing his new protégé and finding outlets for his poems in periodicals with names like *Others* and *BLAST* (a Vorticist effort printed on flamingo-pink paper and featuring eccentric typography).

Eliot felt encouraged enough by these successes to abandon both Oxford and Harvard, and took a job teaching in a boys' secondary school to support the poet he was now heartened to become. His mother, appalled by such recklessness, directed her shock not at Eliot but at his former teacher, Bertrand Russell (much as she had gone to the headmaster behind the teen-age Eliot's back to protest the risks of the quarry pond): "I hope Tom will be able to carry out his purpose of coming on in May to take his degree. The Ph.D. is becoming in America . . . almost an essential condition for an Academic position and promotion therein. The male teachers in our secondary schools are as a rule inferior to the women teachers, and they have little social position or distinction. I hope Tom will not undertake such work another year—it is like putting Pegasus in harness." Eliot's father, storming behind the scenes, was less impressed by Pegasus. The appeal to Russell concluded, "As for 'The *BLAST*,' Mr. Eliot remarked when he saw a copy he did not know there were enough lunatics in the world to support such a magazine."

Home, in short, was seething. Within an inch of his degree, the compliant son was suddenly growing prodigal. A bombardment of cables and letters followed. Even the war conspired against the prodigal's return; though Pound was already

preparing to fill Eliot's luggage with masses of Vorticist material for a projected show in New York, the danger of German
U-boats made a journey by sea unsafe. Russell cabled Eliot's
father not to urge him to sit for his exams "UNLESS IMMEDI-
ATE DEGREE IS WORTH RISKING LIFE." "I was not greatly
pleased with the language of Prof. Russell's telegram," Eliot's
father complained in a letter to Harvard. "Mrs. Eliot and I will
use every effort to induce my son to take his examinations later.
Doubtless his decision was much influenced by Prof. Russell."
Clearly the maternal plea to Russell had backfired. Meanwhile
Harvard itself, in the person of James H. Woods, Eliot's mentor
in the philosophy department, was importuning him; Woods
was tireless in offering an appointment. Eliot turned him
down. Three years on, the family campaign to lure him home
was unabated: the biggest gun of all was brought out—Charles
W. Eliot, eminent educational reformer, recently President
of Harvard, architect of the "five-foot shelf" of indispensable
classics, and Eliot's grandfather's third cousin once removed.
"I conceive that you have a real claim on my attention and
interest," he assured his wayward young relative.

It is, nevertheless, quite unintelligible to me how you or
any other young American scholar can forgo the privilege
of living in the genuine American atmosphere—a bright
atmosphere of freedom and hope. I have never lived long
in England—about six months in all—but I have never got
used to the manners and customs of any class in English
society, high, middle, or low. After a stay of two weeks or
two months in England it has been delightful for me to
escape . . .

Then, too, I have never been able to understand how any
American man of letters can forgo the privilege of being of
use primarily to Americans of the present and future generations, as Emerson, Bryant, Lowell, and Whittier were.
Literature seems to me highly climatic and national . . . You
mention in your letter the name of Henry James. I knew his
father well, and his brother William very well; and I had

some conversation with Henry at different times during his life. I have a vivid remembrance of a talk with him during his last visit to America. It seemed to me all along that his English residence for so many years contributed neither to the happy development of his art nor to his personal happiness.

. . . My last word is that if you wish to speak through your work to people of the "finest New England spirit" you had better not live much longer in the English atmosphere. The New England spirit has been nurtured in the American atmosphere.

What Eliot thought—three years before the publication of *The Waste Land*—of this tribal lecture, and particularly of its recommendation that he aspire to the mantle of the author of "Thanatopsis," one may cheerfully imagine. In any case it was too late, and had long been too late. The campaign was lost before the first parental shot. Eliot's tie to England was past revocation. While still at Oxford he was introduced to Vivien Haigh-Wood, a high-spirited, high-strung, artistic young woman, the daughter of a cultivated upper-class family; her father painted landscapes and portraits. Eliot, shy and apparently not yet relieved of his virginity, was attracted to her rather theatrical personality. Bertrand Russell sensed in her something brasher, perhaps rasher, than mere vivaciousness—he judged her light, vulgar, and adventurous. Eliot married her only weeks after they met. The marriage, he knew, was the seal on his determination to stay in England, the seal his parents could not break and against which they would be helpless. After the honeymoon, Russell (through pure chance Eliot had bumped into him on a London street) took the new couple in for six months, from July to Christmas—he had a closet-size spare room—and helped them out financially in other ways. He also launched Eliot as a reviewer by putting him in touch with the literary editor of the *New Statesman*, for whom Eliot now began to write intensively. Probably Russell's most useful service was his arranging for Eliot to be welcomed into the intellectual and literary circle around Lady Ottoline Morrell at Garsington, her country estate. Though invitations went to leading artists and writers, Garsington was not simply a salon: the Morrells were principled pacifists who provided farm work during the war for conscientious objectors. Here Eliot found Aldous Huxley, D. H. Lawrence, Lytton Strachey, Katherine Mansfield, the painter Mark Gertler, Clive Bell, and, eventually, Leonard and Virginia Woolf. Lady Ottoline complained at first that Eliot had no spontaneity, that he barely moved his lips when he spoke, and that his voice was "mandarin." But Russell had carried him—in his arms, as it were—into the inmost eye of the most sophisticated whorl of contemporary English letters. The American newcomer who had left Harvard on a student fellowship in 1914 was already, by the middle of 1915, at the core of the London literary milieu he had dreamed of. And with so many models around him, he was working on disposing of whatever remnants of St. Louis remained lodged in his mouth, and perfecting the manner and accent of a high-born Englishman. (If he was grateful to Russell for this happy early initiation into precisely the society he coveted, by 1931—in "Thoughts After Lambeth," an essay on the idea of a national English church—he was sneering, in italics, at Russell's "*gospel of happiness*.")

Meanwhile his parents required placating. A bright young man in his twenties had gone abroad to augment his studies; it was natural for him to come home within a reasonable time to get started on real life and his profession. Instead, he had made a precipitate marriage, intended to spend the rest of his days in a foreign country, and was teaching French and arithmetic in the equivalent of an American junior high school. Not surprisingly, the brick manufacturer and his piously versifying wife could not infer the sublime vocation of a poet from these evidences. Eliot hoped to persuade them. The marriage to Vivien took place on June 26, 1915; on June 28 Ezra Pound wrote a very long letter to Eliot's father. It was one of Eliot's mother's own devices—that of the surrogate pleader. As his mother had asked Russell to intervene with Eliot to return him to Harvard, so now Eliot was enlisting Pound to argue for London. The letter included much information about Pound's own situation, which could not have been reassuring, since—as Pound himself remarked—it was unlikely that the elder Eliot had ever heard of him. But he sweetened the case with respectable references to Edgar Lee Masters and Robert Browning, and was careful to add that Robert Frost, another American in London, had "done a book of New England eclogues." To the heartbroken father who had looked forward to a distinguished university career for his son, Pound said, "I am now much better off than if I had kept my professorship in Indiana"—empty comfort, considering it was Fair Harvard that was being mourned; what Pound had relinquished was Wabash College in a place called Crawfordsville. What could it have meant to Eliot's father that this twenty-nine-year-old contributor to the lunatic *BLAST* boasted of having "engineered a new school of verse now known in England, France and America," and insisted that "when I make a criticism of your son's work it is not an amateur criticism"? "As to his coming to London," Pound contended,

> anything else is a waste of time and energy. No one in London cares a hang what is written in America. After getting an American audience a man has to begin all over again here if he plans for an international hearing . . . The situation has been very well summed up in the sentence: "Henry James stayed in Paris and read Turgenev and Flaubert, Mr. Howells returned to America and read Henry James." . . . At any rate if T.S.E. is set on a literary career, this is the place to begin it and any other start would be very bad economy.

"I might add," he concluded, "that a literary man's income depends very much on how rigidly he insists on doing exactly what he himself wants to do. It depends on his connection, which he makes himself. It depends on the number of feuds that he takes on for the sake of his aesthetic beliefs. T.S.E. does not seem to be so pugnacious as I am and his course should be smoother and swifter."

The prediction held. The two-year eruption that was Vorticism waned, and so did Pound's local star; he moved on to

Paris—leaving London, as it would turn out, in Eliot's possession. Pound's letter to the elder Eliot was not all bluster: he may
have been a deft self-promoter, but he was also a promoter of
literary ideas, and in Eliot's work he saw those ideas made flesh.
The exuberance that sent Pound bustling through London to
place Eliot here and there was the enthusiasm of an inventor
whose thingamajig is just beginning to work in the world at
large, in the breakthrough spirit of Alexander Graham Bell's
"Mr. Watson, come here." In Pound's mind Eliot was Pound's
invention. Certainly the excisions he demanded in *The Waste
Land* radically "modernized" it in the direction of the objective correlative by keeping in the symbols and chopping out
context and narrative, maneuvering the poem toward greater
obliqueness and opacity. He also maneuvered Eliot. A determined literary man must go after his own "connection," he
had advised Eliot's father, but the boisterous Pound served the
reticent Eliot in a network of useful connections that Eliot
would not have been likely to make on his own—including
John Quinn, a New York literary philanthropist who became
his (unpaid) agent in America and shored him up from time to
time with generous money contributions.

Eliot was dependent on Pound's approval, or for a long
while behaved as if he was. It was Pound who dominated the
friendship, periodically shooting out instructions, information,
scalawag counsel and pontification. "I value his verse far higher
than that of any other living poet," Eliot told John Quinn in
1918. Gradually, over a span of years, there was a reversal of
authority and power. Eliot rose and Pound sank. Under the
pressure of his marriage (Vivien never held a job of any kind,
nor could she have, even if it had been expected of her), Eliot
ascended in the pragmatic world as well. He gave up teaching
secondary school—it required him to supervise sports—and
tried evening adult extension-course lecturing. The preparation was all-consuming and the remuneration paltry. Finally he
recognized—he was, after all, his father's son—that this was no
way to earn a living. A friend of Vivien's family recommended
him to Lloyds Bank, where he turned out to be very good at the
work—he had a position in the foreign department—and was

regularly praised and advanced. Eventually he joined Faber & Gwyer, the London publishing house (later Faber & Faber), and remained associated with it until the end of his life. And then it was Pound who came to Eliot with his manuscripts. Eliot published them, but his responses, which had once treated Pound's antics with answering foolery, became heavily businesslike and impatient. As founder and editor of a literary journal Vivien had named *The Criterion*, Eliot went on commissioning pieces from Pound, though he frequently attempted to impose coherence and discipline; occasionally he would reject something outright. In 1922 Pound had asserted that "Eliot's *Waste Land* is I think the justification of the 'movement,' of our modern experiment, since 1900," but by 1930 he was taunting Eliot for having "arrived at the supreme Eminence among English critics largely through disguising himself as a corpse." Admiration had cooled on both sides. Still, Eliot's loyalty remained fundamentally steadfast, even when he understood that Pound may have been approaching lunacy. After the Second World War, when Pound was a patient in St. Elizabeth's Federal Hospital for the Insane in Washington, D.C.—the United States government's alternative to jailing him for treason—Eliot signed petitions for his release and made sure to see him on visits to America. Eliot never publicly commented on the reason for Pound's incarceration: Pound had supported the Axis and had actively aided the enemy. On Italian radio, in Mussolini's employ, he had broadcast twice-weekly attacks on Roosevelt, Churchill, and the Jews (whom he vilified in the style of Goebbels).

Though in the long run the friendship altered and attenuated—especially as Eliot grew more implicated in his Christian commitment and Pound in his self-proclaimed paganism—Eliot learned much from Pound. He had already learned from Laforgue the technique of the ironically illuminated persona. The tone of youthful ennui, and the ageless though precocious recoil from the world of phenomena, were Eliot's own. To these qualities of negation Pound added others: indirection, fragmentation, suggestibility, the force of piebald and zigzag juxtaposition—what we have long recognized as the signs of modernism, that famous alchemy of less becoming more. But even as he was tearing down the conventional frame of art, Pound was instructing Eliot in how to frame a career: not that Eliot really needed Pound in either sphere. Poets and critics may fabricate "movements," but no one can invent the Zeitgeist, and it was the Zeitgeist that was promulgating modernism. Eliot may well have been headed there with or without Pound at the helm. That Pound considered Eliot a creature of his own manufacture—that he did in fact tinker with the design— hardly signifies, given that Eliot's art was anyhow likely to fall into the rumbling imperatives of its own time. As for Eliot's advancement into greater and greater reputation, even pushy Pound could not push a miracle into being. Still, it was evident early on that Pound's dictates were in full operation. "Now I am going to ask you to do something for me," Eliot informs his brother Henry in 1915,

> in case you are in Boston or New York this summer. These are suggestions of Ezra Pound's, who has a very shrewd head, and has taken a very great interest in my prospects. There will be people to be seen in Boston and New York, editors with whom I might have some chance . . . As you are likeliest to be in Boston, the first thing is the *Atlantic Monthly*. Now Pound considers it important, whenever possible, to secure introductions to editors from people of better social position than themselves,

and he goes on to propose that Isabella Stewart Gardner, an influential blueblood connection of his, be dragooned into sending a note to the editor of the *Atlantic* on Eliot's behalf. A few days later he is writing to Mrs. Gardner herself, announcing the imminent arrival of his brother, "in order that he may get your advice." To Henry he admits he has only a handful of poems to show, including "some rather second rate things," but anyhow he asks him to try for an opening at *Harper's*, *Century*, *Bookman*, and the *New Republic*. "Nothing needs to be done in Chicago, I believe."

Thus, Pound's training in chutzpah. Yet much of it was native to Eliot, picked up at the parental knee. Not for nothing

was he the offspring of a mother who was a model of the epis-
tolary maneuver, or of a father who demanded instant success.
He had been reared, in any event, as one of the lords of creation
in a conscious American aristocracy that believed in its superi-
or birthright—a Midwestern enclave of what Cousin Charles
Eliot had called "the finest New England spirit." In the alien
precincts of London, where his credentials were unknown or
immaterial, the top could not be so easily guaranteed; it would
have to be cajoled, manipulated, seduced, dared, commanded,
now and then dodged; it would have to be pressed hard, and
cunningly. All this Eliot saw for himself, and rapidly. Reserve
shored up cunning. It scarcely required Pound to teach him
how to calculate the main chance, or how to scheme to impose
his importance. He was actually better at it than Pound, because
infinitely silkier. Whereas Pound had one voice to assault the
barricades with—a cantankerous blast in nutty frontiersman
spelling ("You jess set and hev a quiet draw at youh cawn-
kob") that was likely to annoy, and was intended to shake you
up—Eliot had dozens of voices. His early letters—where he is
sedulously on the make—are a ventriloquist's handbook. To
Mrs. Gardner he purrs as one should to a prominent patroness
of the arts, with friendly dignity, in a courteously appreciative
tone, avoiding the appearance of pursuit. Addressing the irascibly playful Pound, he is irascibly playful, and falls into identical
orthographical jokiness. To his benefactor John Quinn he is
punctiliously—though never humbly—grateful, recording the
state of his literary barometer with a precision owed to the
chairman of the board; nor does he ever fail to ask after Quinn's
health. To his father he writes about money, to his mother
about underwear and overcoats. Before both of them, anxiety
and dutifulness prevail; he is eager to justify himself and to tot
up his triumphs. He means to show them how right he was in
choosing a London life; he is not a disappointment after all.
"I am staying in the bank," he reports (he had been offered
an editorship on a literary journal)—this alone will please his
father, but there is much more:

As it is, I occupy rather a privileged position. I am out of the intrigues and personal hatreds of journalism, and everyone respects me for working in a bank. My social position is quite as good as it would be as editor of a paper. I only write what I want to—now—and everyone knows that anything I do write is good. I can influence London opinion and English literature in a better way. I am known to be disinterested. Even through the *Egoist* I am getting to be looked up to by people who are far better known to the general public than I. There is a small and select public which regards me as the best living critic, as well as the best living poet, in England. I shall of course write for the *Ath.* [*The Athenaeum*] and keep my finger in it. I am much in sympathy with the editor, who is one of my most cordial admirers. With that and the *Egoist* and a young quarterly review which I am interested in, and which is glad to take anything I will give, I can have more than enough power to satisfy me. I really think that I have far more *influence* on English letters than any other American has ever had, unless it be Henry James. I know a great many people, but there are many more who would like to know me, and I can remain isolated and detached.

All this sounds very conceited, but I am sure it is true, and as there is no outsider from whom you would hear it, and America really knows very little of what goes on in London, I must say it myself. Because it will give you pleasure if you believe it, and it will help to explain my point of view.

This was surely the voice of a small boy making his case to his skeptical parents: *it will give you pleasure if you believe it.* He was thirty years old. The self-assurance—or call it, as others did, the arrogance—was genuine, and before his father and mother he was unashamed of speaking of the necessity of power. Such an aspiration was axiomatic among Eliots. What he had set himself to attain was the absolute pinnacle—a place inhabited by no one else, where he could "remain isolated and detached." Fate would give him his wish exactly and with a vengeance, though not quite yet. If he was puffing London to St. Louis, and representing himself there as "the best living critic, as well as the best living poet, in England," two months later he was telling Lytton Strachey that he regarded "London with disdain," and divided "mankind into supermen, termites, and wireworms. I am sojourning among the termites."

In all this there is a wonder and an enigma: the prodigy of Eliot's rocketlike climb from termite to superman. London (and New York and Boston) was swarming with young men on a course no different from Eliot's. He was not the only one with a hotly ambitious pen and an appetite for cultivating highly-placed people who might be useful to him. John Middleton Murry and Wyndham Lewis, for example, both of whom were in Eliot's immediate circle, were equally striving and polished, and though we still know their names, we know them more in the nature of footnotes than as the main text. All three were engaged in the same sort of essayistic empire-building in the little magazines, and at the same time. Lewis published Eliot in *BLAST*, Murry published him in the *Athenaeum*, and later Eliot, when he was editing the *Criterion*, published Lewis. Yet Eliot very quickly overshadowed the others. The disparity, it can be argued, was that Eliot was primarily a poet; or that Eliot's talent was more robust. But even if we believe, as most of us do, that genius of its own force will sooner or later leap commandingly out (Melville's and Dickinson's redemption from obscurity being our sacred paradigms), the riddle stands: why, for Eliot, so soon? His termite days were a brevity, a breath; he was superman in an instant. What was it that singled Eliot out to put him in the lead so astoundingly early? That he ferociously *willed* it means nothing. Nearly all beginning writers have a will for extreme fame; will, no matter how resilient, is usually no more efficacious in the marketplace than daydream.

If there is any answer to such questions—and there may not be—it may lie hidden in one of Eliot's most well-appointed impersonations: the voice he employed as essayist. That charm of intimacy and the easy giving of secrets that we like to associate with essayists—Montaigne, Lamb, Hazlitt, George Orwell, Virginia Woolf when the mood struck her—was not Eliot's. As in what is called the "familiar" essay, Eliot frequently said "I"—but it was an "I" set in ice cut from the celestial vault:

uninsistent yet incontestable, serenely sovereign. It seemed to take its power from erudition, and in part it did; but really it took it from some proud inner figuration or incarnation—as if Literature itself had been summoned to speak in its own voice:

> I am not considering whether the language of Dante or Shakespeare is superior, for I cannot admit the question: I readily affirm that the differences are such as make Dante easier for a foreigner. Dante's advantages are not due to greater genius, but to the fact that he wrote when Europe was still more or less one. And even had Chaucer or Villon been exact contemporaries of Dante, they would still have been farther, linguistically as well as geographically, from the center of Europe than Dante.

Who could talk back to that? Such sentences appear to derive from a source of knowledge—a congeries of assumptions—indistinguishable from majesty. In short, Eliot would not *permit* himself to be ignored, because it was not "himself" he was representing, but the very flower of European civilization. And there may have been another element contributing to the ready acceptance of his authority: as a foreigner, he was drawn to synthesizing and summarizing in a way that insiders, who take their context for granted, never do. He saw principles where the natives saw only phenomena. Besides, he had a clear model for focused ascent: Henry James. Knowing what he meant to become, he was immune to distraction or wrong turnings. "It is the final perfection, the consummation of an American," Eliot (in one of his most autobiographical dicta) wrote of James, "to become, not an Englishman, but a European—something which no born European, no person of any European nationality, can become."

So much for the larger trajectory. He had mapped out an unimpeded ideal destination. In the lesser geography of private life, however, there was an unforeseen impediment. Henry James had never married; Eliot had married Vivien. In 1915 she was twenty-seven, slender, lively, very pretty, with a wave in her hair and a pleasant mouth and chin. By 1919, Virginia

Woolf was describing her as "a washed out, elderly and worn looking little woman." She complained of illness from the very first, but otherwise there were few immediate hints of the devastation to come. She was absorbed in Eliot's career. He brought his newest work to her for criticism; she read proofs; she assisted in preparing the *Criterion*. She also did some writing of her own—short stories, and prose sketches that Eliot admired and published in the *Criterion*. She had energy enough at the start: there were excursions, dinners, visits to Garsington, dance halls, dance lessons, theater, opera; even a flirtation with Bertrand Russell that turned into a one-night stand. ("Hellish and loathsome," Russell called it.) A month after the wedding she told Russell that she had married Eliot because she thought she could "stimulate" him, but that it could not be done. She began to suffer from headaches, colitis, neuralgia, insomnia. "She is a person who lives on a knife edge," Russell said. Eliot himself often woke at night feeling sick. He was plagued by colds, flu, bronchial problems; he smoked too much and he consistently drank too much, though he held it well. Retreating from Vivien, he threw himself into the work at the bank and into developing his literary reputation. Vivien had nowhere to go but into resentment, ill-will, hysteria. In the mornings the bed linens were frequently bloody—she menstruated excessively, and became obsessed with washing the sheets. She washed them herself even when they stayed in hotels. Morphine was prescribed for her various symptoms; also bromides and ether (she swabbed her whole body with ether, so that she reeked of it), and mercilessly bizarre diets—a German doctor combined starvation with the injection of animal glands. She collapsed into one nervous illness after another. Eliot repeatedly sent her to the country to recuperate while he remained in town. When his mother, now an elderly widow, and one of his sisters came on a visit from America, Vivien was absent, and Eliot was obliged to manage the complications of hospitality on his own. Anxiety over Vivien crept into all his business and social correspondence: "my wife has been very ill"; "she is all right when she is lying down, but immediately she gets up is very faint"; "wretched today—another bad night"; "Have you ever been in such incessant and extreme pain that you felt your sanity going, and that you no longer knew reality from delusion? That's the way she is. The doctors have never seen so bad a case, and hold out no definite hope, and have so far done her no good. Meanwhile she is in screaming agony . . ."

She brought out in him all his responsibility, vigilance, conscientiousness, troubled concern; in brief, his virtue. Her condition bewildered him; nothing in his experience, and certainly nothing in his upbringing, had equipped him for it; her manifold sicknesses were unpredictable, and so was she. Her sanity was in fact going. Daily she made him consider and reconsider his conduct toward her, and her ironic, clever, assaultive, always embarrassing responses ran tumbling over his caution. He dreaded dinner parties in her company, and went alone or not at all. It became known that Eliot was ashamed of his wife. But he was also ashamed of his life. Little by little he attempted to live it without Vivien, or despite Vivien, or in the few loopholes left him by Vivien. She was in and out of sanitoria in England, France, and Switzerland; it was a relief to have her away. What had once been frightened solicitude was gradually transmuted into horror, and horror into self-preservation, and self-preservation into callousness, and callousness into a kind of moral brutality. She felt how, emotionally and spiritually, he was abandoning her to her ordeal. However imploringly she sought his attention, he was determined to shut her out; the more he shut her out, the more wildly, dramatically, and desperately she tried to recapture him. He was now a man hunted—and haunted—by a mad wife. He saw himself transmogrified into one of the hollow men of his own imagining, that scarecrow figure stuck together out of "rat's coat, crowskin, crossed staves":

> The eyes are not here
> There are no eyes here
> In this valley of dying stars
> In this hollow valley
> This broken jaw of our lost kingdoms

He carried this Golgothan self-portrait with him everywhere;

his lost kingdoms were in the stony looks he gave to the world. Virginia Woolf was struck by "the grim marble face . . . mouth twisted and shut; not a single line free and easy; all caught, pressed, inhibited." "Humiliation is the worst thing in life," he told her. Vivien had humiliated him. Torment and victimization—she of him, and he of her—had degraded him. Bouts of drink depleted him. At times his behavior was as strange as hers: he took to wearing pale green face powder, as if impersonating the sickly cast of death. Virginia Woolf thought he painted his lips. In 1933, after eighteen years of accelerating domestic misery, he finally broke loose: he went to America for a series of angry lectures (published later as *After Strange Gods: A Primer of Modern Heresy*) in which he attacked Pound, D. H. Lawrence, liberalism, and "free-thinking Jews," complaining that the United States had been "invaded by foreign races" who had "adulterated" its population. In London, meanwhile, a remorseful Vivien was refurbishing the flat for his homecoming; she even offered to join him overseas. In the black mood of his lectures her letter shocked him into a quick cruel plan. Writing from America, he directed his London solicitors to prepare separation documents and to deliver them to Vivien in his absence. When he arrived back in England, the deed was done. Vivien in disbelief continued to wait for him in the reupholstered flat. He moved instead into the shabby guest rooms of the parish house of St. Stephen's, an Anglican congregation with a high-church bent. There, subdued and alone among celibate priests, he spent the next half-dozen years in penance, suffering the very isolation and detachment he had once prized as the influential poet's reward.

Yet Vivien was in pursuit. Though he kept his lodgings secret from her, with fearful single-mindedness she attempted to hunt him down, turning up wherever there might be a chance of confronting him, hoping to cajole or argue or threaten him into resuming with her. He contrived to escape her time after time. By now he had left the bank for Faber; she would burst into the editorial offices without warning, weeping and pleading to be allowed to talk to him. One of the staff would give some excuse and Eliot would find a way of sneaking out of the building without detection. She carried a knife in her purse—it was her customary flamboyance—to alarm him; but it was a theater knife, made of rubber. She sent Christmas cards in the name of "Mr. and Mrs. T. S. Eliot," as if they were still together, and she advertised in *The Times* for him to return. She called herself sometimes Tiresias, and sometimes Daisy Miller, after the doomed Jamesian heroine. In a caricature of what she imagined would please him, she joined the newly formed British Union of Fascists. One day she actually caught him; she went up to him after a lecture, handed him books to sign as if they were strangers, and begged him to go home with her. He hid his recoil behind a polite "How do you do?" When she got wind of a scheme to commit her to a mental hospital, she fled briefly to Paris. In 1938 she was permanently institutionalized, whether by her mother or her brother, or by Eliot himself, no one knows; but Eliot had to have been consulted, at the very least. When her brother visited her in 1946, a year before her death, he reported that she seemed as sane as he was. She had tried on one occasion to run away; she was captured and brought back. She died in the asylum a decade after her commitment. Eliot never once went to see her.

Out of this brutalizing history of grieving and loss, of misalliance, misfortune, frantic confusion, and recurrent panic, Eliot drew the formulation of his dream of horror—that waste land where

> . . . *I Tiresias have foresuffered all*
> . . . *and walked among the lowest of the dead*
> *Here is no water but only rock* . . .
> *If there were only water amongst the rock*
> *Dead mountain mouth of carious teeth that cannot spit*
>
> . . . *blood shaking my heart*
> *The awful daring of a moment's surrender*
> *Which an age of prudence can never retract*
> *By this, and this only, we have existed*
> *Which is not to be found in our obituaries*
> *Or in memories draped by the beneficent spider*

> *Or under seals broken by the lean solicitor*
> *In our empty rooms*

He might have regarded his marriage and its trials as a regrettable accident of fallible youth—the awful daring of a moment's surrender—compounded by his initial sense of duty and loyalty. But he was shattered beyond such realism, and finally even beyond stoicism. He felt he had gazed too long on the Furies. The fiery brand he had plucked out of his private inferno seemed not to have been ignited in the ordinary world; it blackened him metaphysically, and had little to do with fractured expectations or the social difficulties of mental illness. What he knew himself to be was a sinner. The wretchedness he had endured was sin. Vivien had been abused—by doctors and their scattershot treatments, and by regimens Eliot could not have prevented. The truth was she had been drugged for years. And he had abused her himself, perhaps more horribly, by the withdrawal of simple human sympathy. It was she who had smothered his emotional faculties, but reciprocal humiliation had not earned reciprocal destinies. Vivien was confined. He was freed to increase his fame. Nevertheless—as if to compensate her—he lived like a man imprisoned; like a penitent; like a flagellant. He was consumed by ideas of sin and salvation, by self-loathing. The scourge that was Vivien had driven him to conversion: he entered Christianity seriously and desperately, like a soul literally in danger of damnation, or as though he believed he was already half-damned. The religiosity he undertook was a kind of brooding medieval monkishness: ascetic, turned altogether inward, to the sinful self. Its work was the work of personal redemption. In "Ash-Wednesday" he exposed the starting-point, the beginning of abnegation and confession:

> *Because these wings are no longer wings to fly*
> *But merely vans to beat the air*
> *The air which is now thoroughly small and dry*
> *Smaller and dryer than the will*
> *Teach us to care and not to care*
> *Teach us to sit still.*

And in a way he did learn to sit still. He was celibate. He was diligent and attentive in his office life while conducting an orderly if lonely domestic routine. He was at Mass every morning, and frequently went on retreat. During the night blitz of London in 1939, he served for a time as an air raid warden, often staying up till dawn. Then, to escape the exhausting bombings, like so many others he turned to commuting from the far suburbs, where he became the paying guest of a family of gentlewomen. In 1945, at the war's end, he made another unusual household arrangement, one that also had its spiritual side: he moved in with John Hayward, a gregarious wit and bookish extrovert whom disease had locked in a wheelchair. Eliot performed the necessary small personal tasks for his companion, wheeled him to the park on pleasant afternoons, and stood vigilantly behind his chair at the parties Hayward liked to preside over—Eliot reserved and silent under the burden of his secret wounds and his eminence, Hayward boisterous, funny, and monarchically at ease. In the evenings, behind the shut door of the darkest room at the back of the flat, Eliot recited the rosary, ate his supper from a tray, and limited himself to a single game of patience. This odd couple lived together for eleven years, until Eliot suddenly married his young secretary, Valerie Fletcher. She offered him the intelligent adoration of an infatuated reader who had been enchanted by his poetry and his fame since her teens; she had come to Faber & Faber with no other motive than to be near him. Vivien had died in 1947; the marriage to Valerie took place in 1957. After the long discipline of penance, he opened himself to capacious love for the first time. As he had known himself for a sinner, so now he knew himself for a happy man.

But the old reflex of recoil—and abandonment—appeared to have survived after all. From youth he had combined ingrained loyalty with the contrary habit of casting off the people who seemed likely to impede his freedom. He had fled over an ocean to separate himself from his demanding parents—though it was his lot ultimately to mimic them. He was absorbed by religion like his mother, and ended by writing, as she did, devotional poetry. Like his father, he was now a well-established businessman, indispensable to his firm and its most influential officer. (It developed that he copied his father even in trivia. The elder Eliot was given to playful doodlings of cats. The son—whose knack for cartooning exceeded the father's—wrote clever cat verses. These, in the form of the long-running Broadway musical, are nearly the whole sum of Eliot's current American renown: if today's undergraduates take spontaneous note of Eliot at all, it will be *Cats* on their tape cassettes, not *The Waste Land*.) Still, despite these evolving reversions, it was the lasting force of his repudiations that stung: his scorn for the family heritage of New England Unitarianism, his acquisition in 1927 of British citizenship. He had thrown off both the liberal faith of his fathers—he termed it a heresy—and their native pride of patriotism. He had shown early that he could sever what no longer suited. The selfless interval with John Hayward was cut off overnight: there is a story that Eliot called a taxi, told Hayward he was going off to be married, and walked out. After so prolonged a friendship—and a dependence—Hayward felt cruelly abandoned. He never recovered his spirit. Eliot was repeatedly capable of such calculated abruptness. His abandonment of Vivien—the acknowledged sin of his soul, the flaming pit of his exile and suffering—was echoed in less theological tones in his careless dismissal of Emily Hale and Mary Trevelyan, the wounded women whose loving attachment he had welcomed for years. When Vivien died, each one—Emily Hale in America and Mary Trevelyan close at hand in London—believed that Eliot would now marry her.

Miss Hale—as she was to her students—was a connection of the New England cousins; Eliot had known her since her girlhood. Their correspondence, with its webwork of common associations and sensibilities, flourished decade after decade—she was a gifted teacher of drama at various women's colleges and private schools for girls, with a modest but vivid acting talent of her own. Eliot's trips to America always included long renewing visits with her, and she in turn traveled to England over a series of summer vacations to be with him. One of their excursions was to the lavish silent gardens of Burnt Norton, the unoccupied country mansion of an earl. (That single afternoon of sunlight and roses was transformed by "a grace of sense, a white light still and moving," into the transcendent incantations of "Burnt Norton," the first of the *Quartets*.) In America she waited, in tranquil patience and steady exultation, for the marriage that was never to come: generations of her students were informed of her friendship with the greatest of living poets. Eliot found in her, at a distance, unbodied love, half-elusive nostalgia, the fragility of an ideal. When she threatened, at Vivien's death, to become a real-life encumbrance, he diluted their intimacy; but when he married Valerie Fletcher he sloughed Emily off altogether—rapidly and brutally. Stunned and demoralized—they had been friends for fifty years—she gave up teaching and spiralled into a breakdown. She spent the rest of her life in the hope that her importance to Eliot would not go unrecognized. Her enormous collection of his letters (more than a thousand) she donated to Princeton University, and—Eliot-haunted and Eliot-haunting—she asked him to return hers. He did not reply; he had apparently destroyed them. The "man I loved," she wrote to Princeton, "*I* think, did not respond as he should have to my long trust, friendship and love." She stipulated that the Princeton repository not be opened until 2019; she looked to her vindication then. Having been patient so long, she was willing to be patient even beyond the grave. Eliot may have bestowed his infirm old age on Miss Fletcher, but the future would see that he had loved Miss Hale in his prime.

As for Mary Trevelyan, she was a hearty pragmatist, a spunky activist, a bold managerial spirit. For nineteen years she was a prop against Eliot's depressions, a useful neighbor—she drove him all over in her car—and, to a degree, a confidante. From the beginning of Vivien's incarceration until his marriage to Valerie—i.e., from 1938 until 1957—Eliot and Mary were regularly together at plays, at parties, and, especially, at church. Their more private friendship centered on lunches and teas, domestic evenings cooking and listening to music in Mary's flat, her matter-of-fact solicitude through his illnesses and hypochondria. They made a point of mentioning each other in their separate devotions. Mary was at home in the pieties

Eliot had taken on—she came of distinguished High Anglican stock, the elite of government, letters, and the cloth, with a strong commitment to public service. Her father was a clergyman who erected and administered churches; the historian G. M. Trevelyan was a cousin; her relatives permeated Oxford and Cambridge. (Humphrey Carpenter, author of a remarkably fine biography of Ezra Pound—fittingly published in Eliot's centenary year—represents the newest generation of this family.)

With Mary, Eliot could unbutton. He felt familiar enough to indulge in outbursts of rage or contemptuous sarcasm, and to display the most withering side of his character, lashing out at the people he despised. Through it all she remained candid, humorous, and tolerant, though puzzled by his unpredictable fits of withdrawal from her, sometimes for three months at a time. He drew lines of conduct she was never permitted to cross: for instance, only once did he agree to their vacationing together, and that was when he needed her—and the convenience of her driving—to help entertain his sister, visiting from America. Mary was accommodating but never submissive. During the war she organized a rest hostel in Brussels for soldiers on leave from the front; in 1944 she nursed hundreds of the wounded. After the war she traveled all over Asia for UNESCO, and founded an international house in London for foreign students. Plainly she had nothing in common with the wistful and forbearing Miss Hale of Abbot Academy for girls. But her expectations were the same. When Vivien died, Mary proposed marriage to Eliot—twice. When he refused her the first time, he said he was incapable of marrying anyone at all; she thought this meant his guilt over Vivien. The second time, he told her about his long attachment to Emily Hale, and how he was a failure at love; she thought this meant psychological exhaustion. And then he married Valerie. Only eight days before the wedding—held secretly in the early morning at a church Eliot did not normally attend—he and Mary lunched together for hours; he disclosed nothing. On the day of the wedding she had a letter from him commemorating their friendship and declaring his love for Valerie. Mary sent back two notes, the earlier one to congratulate him, the second an unrestrained account of her shock. Eliot responded bitterly; putting an end to two decades of companionship.

But all this—the years of self-denial in the parish house, the wartime domesticity among decorous suburban ladies, the neighborly fellowship with John Hayward and Mary Trevelyan, the break with Hayward, the break with Emily Hale, the break with Mary Trevelyan, the joyous denouement with Valerie Fletcher—all this, however consecrated to quietism, however turbulent, was aftermath and postlude. The seizure that animated the poetry had already happened—the seizure was Vivien. Through Vivien he had learned to recognize the reality of sin in all its influences and phases; she was the turning wind of his spiritual storm. Vivien herself understood this with the canniness of a seer: "As to Tom's *mind*," she once said, "I am his mind." The abyss of that mind, and its effect on Eliot as it disintegrated, led him first through a vortex of flight, and then to tormented contemplation, and finally to the religious calm of "Burnt Norton":

> *Time present and time past*
> *Are both perhaps present in time future.*
> *And time future contained in time past.*

Time past marked the psychological anarchy of his youthful work, that vacuous ignorance of sin that had produced "Prufrock," "Gerontion," "The Hollow Men," *The Waste Land*. Not to acknowledge the real presence of sin is to be helpless in one's degradation. Consequently Prufrock is a wraith "pinned and wriggling on the wall," uncertain how to "spit out all the butt-ends of my days and ways"; Gerontion is "a dry brain in a dry season"; the hollow men "filled with straw" cannot falter through to the end of a prayer—"For Thine is / Life is / For Thine is the"; the voice of *The Waste Land*—"burning burning burning burning"—is unable to imagine prayer. And the chastening "future contained in time past" is almost surely the inferno that was Vivien: what else could that earlier hollowness have arrived at if not a retributive burning? The waste land—a dry season of naked endurance without God—had earned him the ordeal with Vivien; but the ordeal with Vivien was to serve both time past and time future. Time past: he would escape from the formless wastes of past metaphysical drift only because Vivien had jolted him into a sense of sin. And time future: only because she had jolted him into a sense of sin would he uncover the means to future absolution—the genuine avowal of himself as sinner. To the inferno of Vivien he owed clarification of what had been. To the inferno of Vivien he owed clarification of what might yet be. If Vivien was Eliot's mind, she had lodged Medusa there, and Medusa became both raging muse and purifying savior. She was the motive for exorcism, confession, and penitence. She gave him "Ash-Wednesday," a poem of supplication. She gave him *Four Quartets*, a subdued lyric of near-forgiveness, with long passages of serenely prosaic lines (occasionally burned out into the monotone of philosophic fatigue), recording the threshold of the shriven soul:

> . . . *music heard so deeply*
> *That it is not heard at all, but you are the music*
> *While the music lasts. These are only hints and guesses,*
> *Hints followed by guesses; and the rest*
> *Is prayer, observance, discipline, thought and action.*
> *The hint half guessed, the gift half understood, is*
> *Incarnation.*

What makes such "reading backward" possible, of course, is the biographies. (I have relied on Peter Ackroyd and Lyndall Gordon for much of the narrative of Eliot's life.) Knowledge of the life interprets—decodes—the poems: exactly what Eliot's theory of the objective correlative was designed to prevent. Occasionally the illuminations cast by reading backward provoke the uneasy effect of looking through a forbidden keyhole with a flashlight:

> *"My nerves are bad tonight. Yes, bad. Stay with me.*
> *"Speak to me. Why do you never speak? Speak.*

> *"What are you thinking of? What thinking? What?*
> *"I never know what you are thinking. Think."*
>
> I think we are in rats' alley
> Where the dead men lost their bones.

That, wailing out of a jagged interval in *The Waste Land*, can only be Vivien's hysteria, and Eliot's recoil from it. But it hardly requires such explicitness (and there is little else that is so clearly explicit) to recognize that his biographers have broken the code of Eliot's reticence—that programmatic reticence embodied in his doctrine of impersonality. The objective correlative was intended to direct the reader to a symbolic stand-in for the poet's personal suffering—not Vivien but Tiresias. Secret becomes metaphor. Eliot's biographers begin with the metaphor and unveil the secret. When the personal is exposed, the objective correlative is annihilated.

And yet the objective correlative has won out, after all, in a larger way. If *The Waste Land* can no longer hide its sources in Eliot's private malaise, it has formidably sufficed as an "objective equivalence" for the public malaise of generations. Its evocations of ruin, loss, lamentation, its "empty cisterns and exhausted wells," are broken sketches of the discontents that remain when the traditional props of civilization have failed: for some (unquestionably for Eliot), a world without God; for others, a world without so much as an illusion of intelligibility or restraint. In 1867, contemplating the Victorian crisis of faith, Matthew Arnold saw "a darkling plain . . . where ignorant armies clash by night," but in Eliot's echoing "arid plain" there is nothing so substantial as even a clash—only formlessness, "hooded hordes swarming," "falling towers"; hallucination succeeds hallucination, until all the crowns of civilization— "Jerusalem Athens Alexandria / Vienna London"—are understood to be "unreal."

In 1922 (a postwar time of mass unemployment, economic disintegration and political uncertainty), *The Waste Land* fell out upon its era as the shattered incarnation of dissolution, the very text and texture of modernism—modernism's consummate document and ode. In the almost seventy years since its first publication, it has taken on, as the great poems do (but not the very greatest), a bloom of triteness (as ripe truth can overmature into truism). It is no more "coherent" to its newest readers than it was to its astonished earliest readers, but it is much less difficult; tone and technique no longer startle. Post-Bomb, post-Holocaust, post-moonwalk, it may actually be too tame a poem to answer to the mindscape we now know more exhaustively than Eliot did. Professor Harry Levin, Harvard's eminent pioneer promulgator of Proust, Joyce, and Eliot, quipped a little while ago—not altogether playfully—that modernism "has become old-fashioned." *The Waste Land* is not yet an old-fashioned poem, and doubtless never will be. But it does not address with the same exigency the sons and daughters of those impassioned readers who ecstatically intoned it, three and four decades ago, in the belief that infiltration by those syllables was an aesthetic sacrament. Even for the aging generation of the formerly impassioned, something has gone out of the poem—not in *The Waste Land* proper, perhaps, but rather in that parallel work Eliot called "Notes on 'The Waste Land.'" This was the renowned mock-scholarly apparatus Eliot tacked on to the body of the poem, ostensibly to spell out its multiple allusions—a contrivance that once seemed very nearly a separate set of modernist stanzas: arbitrary, fragmented, dissonant, above all solemnly erudite. "The whole passage from Ovid," drones the sober professorial persona of the "Notes," "is of great anthropological interest." There follow nineteen lines of Latin verse. The procession of brilliantly variegated citations—Augustine, the Upanishads, Verlaine, Baudelaire, Hermann Hesse, Shakespeare, Tarot cards, the Grail legend— suggests (according to Professor Levin) that context was to Eliot what conceit was to the metaphysical poets. A fresh reading of the "Notes" admits to something else—the thumbed nose, that vein in Eliot of the practical joker, released through Macavity the Mystery Cat and in masses of unpublished bawdy verses (nowadays we might regard them as more racist than bawdy) starring "King Bolo's big black bassturd kween." In any case, whatever pose Eliot intended, no one can come to the "Notes" today with the old worshipful gravity. They seem drained of austerity—so emphatically serious that it is hard to take them seriously at all.

The same with the plays. With the exception of the first of the five, *Murder in the Cathedral*—a major devotional poem of orchestral breadth—the plays are all collapsed into curios. From our perspective, they are something worse than period pieces, since that is what they were—Edwardian drawing room dramas—when they were new. They hint at (or proclaim) a failure of Eliot's public ear. His aim was to write popular verse plays for the English stage—an aim worthy (though Eliot never had the hubris to say this) of Shakespeare. George Bernard Shaw had been content with prose—and the majestically cunning prose speeches in *Murder in the Cathedral* are reminiscent of nothing so much as Shaw's *Saint Joan*, including Shaw's preface to that play. The dialogue of enjambment that is the style and method of *The Cocktail Party*, *The Confidential Clerk*, and *The Elder Statesman*, never attains the sound of verse, much less poetry. That was precisely Eliot's hope: he considered *Murder in the Cathedral* too blatantly poetic, a "dead end." His goal was to bury the overt effects of poetry while drawing out of ordinary speech and almost ordinary situations a veil of transcendence— even, now and then, of mystical horror, as when (in *The Family Reunion*) the Furies suddenly appear, or when (in *The Cocktail Party*) a character we are meant to imagine as a saint and a martyr goes off to be a missionary among the "natives" and is eaten by ants. (Having first been crucified, it ought to be added. And though there are farcical moments throughout, the devouring anthill is not intended as one of them.) Nevertheless nothing transcendent manages to rise from any printed page of any of the last four plays—almost nothing suggestive of poetry, in fact, except an occasional "wisdom" patch in the semi-lyrical but largely prosy manner of the philosophical lines in *Four Quartets*. Possibly this is because the printed page is perforce bare of technical stagecraft, with its color and excitement. Yet—similarly unaccoutered—Shakespeare, Marlowe, and Shaw, in their greater and lesser written art, send out language with presence and power enough to equal absent actors, sets, lighting, costumes. Much of Eliot's dialogue, rather than achieving that simplicity of common speech he aspired to, plummets to the stilted, the pedestrian, the enervated:

> *Oh, Edward, when you were a little boy,*
> *I'm sure you were always getting yourself measured*
> *To prove how you had grown since the last holidays.*
> *You were always intensely concerned with yourself;*
> *And if other people grow, well, you want to grow too.*

Given only the text and nothing else, a reader of *The Cocktail Party*, say, will be perplexed by its extravagant performing history: in London and New York in the Fifties, it filled theaters and stunned audiences. Read now, these later plays are unmistakably dead, embalmed, dated beyond endurance—dated especially in the light of the vigorous Fifties, when the energetic spokesmen of the Angry Young Men were having their first dramatic hearing. As playwright, Eliot inexplicably eschewed or diluted or could not pull off his theory of demarcation between "the man who suffers and the mind which creates," so the plays are surprisingly confessional—the Furies harbor Vivien, a character is tormented by thinking he has killed his wife, Valerie turns up as a redemptive young woman piously named Monica, etc. Since Eliot's private life was not only closed but unguessed-at in those years, gossip could not have been the lure for theater-goers. The lure was, in part, skillful production: on the page, the Furies when they pop up seem as silly as the news of the hungry anthill, but their theatrical embodiment was electrifying. Fine performances and ingenious staging, though, were at bottom not what brought overflowing audiences to see Eliot's plays. They came because of the supremacy of Eliot's fame. They came because verse drama by T. S. Eliot was the most potent cultural vitamin of the age.

Inevitably we are returned to the issue (there is no escaping it at any point) of Eliot's renown. As a young man, he had hammered out the prestige of a critical reputation by means of essay after essay. By the time of the later plays he had become a world celebrity, an international feature story in newspapers and magazines. But neither the essays by themselves, nor (certainly) the plays—always excepting *Murder in the Cathedral*, which ought to count among the most lastingly resonant of the poems—could have won for Eliot his permanent place in English letters. The fame belongs to the poems. The rest, however much there might be of it, was spinoff. Yet the body of poems is amazingly small in the light of Eliot's towering repute. In 1958, for example, invited to Rome for an honorary degree, he was driven through streets mobbed with students roaring "*Viva* Eliot!" Mass adulation of this sort more often attaches to presidents and monarchs—or, nowadays, to rock stars. What did that roar rest on? Leaving aside the early Bolo ribaldry (which in any case never reached print), the fourteen cat verses, and the contents of a little posthumous collection called *Poems Written in Early Youth* (from ages sixteen to twenty-two), but not omitting two unfinished works—"Sweeney Agonistes" and "Coriolan"—Eliot's entire poetic oeuvre comes to no more than fifty-four poems. England, at least, is used to more abundant output from the poets it chooses to mark with the seal of permanence. My copy of Wordsworth's *Poetical Works* adds up to nine hundred and sixty-six pages of minuscule type, or approximately a thousand poems. The changes in the written culture between, say, the "Ode on Intimations of Immortality," published in 1807, and Eliot's *Waste Land*, published one hundred and fifteen years later, speak for themselves. Still, granting the impertinence of measuring by number, there remains something extraordinary—even uncanny—about the torrent of transoceanic adoration that, for Eliot, stemmed from fifty-four poems.

Eliot may have supposed himself a classicist, but really he is in the line of the Romantics: subjective, anguished, nostalgic, mystical, lyrical. The critic Harold Bloom's mild view is that he "does not derive from Dante and Donne, as he thought, but from Tennyson and Whitman"—a judgment that might have stung him. For Eliot to have believed himself an offspring of the cosmic Dante and the precision-worker Donne, and to end, if Professor Bloom is correct, as a descendant of the softer, lusher music of Tennyson, is no serious diminishment (Tennyson is permanent too)—though it is a diminishment. Lord Tennyson, the British Empire's laureate, may have seemed a weighty and universal voice to the Victorians. For us he is lighter and more parochial. It is in the nature of fame to undergo revision: Eliot appears now to be similarly receding into the parochial, even the sectarian (unlike the all-embracing Whitman, with whom he shares the gift of bel canto). His reach—once broad enough to incorporate the Upanishads—shrank to extend no farther than the neighborhood sacristy, and to a still smaller space: the closet of the self. His worship was local and exclusionary not simply in the limited sense that it expressed an astringent clerical bias, or that he observed the forms of a narrow segment of the Church of England—itself an island church, after all, though he did his best to link it with what he termed "the Universal Church of the World." What made Eliot's religiosity local and exclusive was that he confined it to his personal pain and bitterness: he allowed himself to become estranged from humanity. Feeling corrupt in himself, he saw corruption everywhere: "all times are corrupt," he wrote; and then again, "the whole of modern literature is corrupted by what I call Secularism." Demanding that faith—a particular credo—be recognized as the foundation of civilization, he went on to define civilization as extraneous to some of its highest Western manifestations—the principles of democracy, tolerance, and individualism. Despite his youthful study of Eastern religion and his poet's immersion in Hebrew scripture, he was finally unable to imagine that there might be rival structures of civilization not grounded in the doctrine of original sin, and yet intellectually and metaphysically exemplary. Even within the familial household of Christendom, he was quick to cry heretic. In any event, the style of his orthodoxy was, as Harry Levin put it, "a literary conception." As a would-be social theorist he had a backward longing for the medieval hegemony of cathedral spires—i.e., for a closed society. It was a ruefulness so poignant that it preoccupied much of the prose and seeped into the melancholy cadences of the poetry. As a modernist, Eliot was the last of the Romantics.

In the end he could not disengage the mind that created from the man who suffered; they were inseparable. But the

mind and the man—the genius and the sufferer—had contributed, in influence and authority, more than any other
mind and man (with the exception perhaps of Picasso) to the
formation of the most significant aesthetic movement of the
twentieth century. It was a movement so formidable that its
putative successor cannot shake off its effects and is obliged to
carry on its name; helplessly, we speak of the "postmodern."
Whether postmodernism is genuinely a successor, or merely
an updated variant of modernism itself, remains unresolved.
Yet whichever it turns out to be, we do know for certain that
we no longer live in the literary shadow of T. S. Eliot. "Mistah
Kurtz—he dead"—the celebrated epigraph Eliot lifted from
Conrad's *Heart of Darkness* and affixed to "The Hollow Men"—
applies: the heart has gone out of what once ruled. High art is
dead. The passion for inheritance is dead. Tradition is equated
with obscurantism. The wall that divided serious high culture
from the popular arts is breached; anything can count as "text."
Knowledge—saturated in historical memory—is displaced by
information, or memory without history: data. Allusiveness is
crosscultural in an informational and contemporary way (from,
say, beekeeping to film-making), not in the sense of connect-
ing the present with the past. The relation of poets to history
is that they can take it or leave it, and mostly they leave it,
whether in prosody or in the idea of the venerable. If it is true
that *The Waste Land* could not be written today because it is
too tame for the savagery we have since accumulated, there is
also a more compelling truth: because we seem content to live
without contemplation of our formal beginnings, a poem like
The Waste Land, mourning the loss of an integral tradition, is
for us inconceivable. For the modernists, the center notoriously
did not hold; for us (whatever *we* are), there is no recollection of
a center, and nothing to miss, let alone mourn.

Was it the ever-increasing rush to what Eliot called "Secularism" that knocked him off his pinnacle? Was it the vague
nihilism of "modern life" that deposed modernism's prophet?
Was Eliot shrugged off because his pessimistic longings were
ultimately judged to be beside the point? The answer may not
be as clearcut as any of that. The changes that occurred in the

forty years between the Nobel award in 1948 and Eliot's centennial in 1988 have still not been assimilated or even remotely understood. The Wordsworth of the "Ode to Duty" (composed the same year as "Intimations of Immortality") has more in common with the Eliot of *Four Quartets*—the differing idioms of the poetry aside—than Eliot has with Allen Ginsberg. And yet Ginsberg's "Howl," the single poem most representative of the break with Eliot, may owe as much, thematically, to *The Waste Land* as it does to the bardic Whitman, or to the opening of the era of anything-goes. Ginsberg belongs to the generation that knew Eliot as sanctified, and, despite every irruption into indiscipline, Eliot continues alive in Ginsberg's ear. For the rest, a look at the condition of most poetry in America today will disclose how far behind we have left Eliot. William Carlos Williams, a rival of Eliot's engaged in another vein of diction and committed to sharply contrasting aesthetic goals ("no ideas but in things"), said of the publication of *The Waste Land* that he "felt at once it had set me back twenty years," largely because of its European gravity of erudition. The newest generation in the line of descent from Williams, though hardly aware of its own ancestry, follows Williams in repudiating Eliot: music is not wanted, history is not wanted, idea is not wanted. Even literature is not much wanted. What *is* wanted is a sort of verbal snapshot: the quick impression, the short flat snippet that sounds cut from a sentence in a letter to a friend, the casual and scanty "revelation." As Eliot in his time spurned Milton's exalted epic line as too sublime for his need, so now Eliot's elegiac fragments appear too arcane, too aristocratic, and too difficult, for contemporary ambition. Ironic allusiveness—Eliot's inspired borrowing—is out of the question: there is nothing in stock to allude to. Now and then there are signs—critical complaints and boredom—that the school of pedestrian verse-making is nearly exhausted, and more and more there are poets who are venturing into the longer line, the denser stanza, a more intense if not a heightened diction.

But the chief elements of the Age of Eliot are no longer with us, and may never return: the belief that poetry can be redemptive, the conviction that history underlies poetry. Such

notions may still be intrinsic to the work of Joseph Brodsky and
Czeslaw Milosz—Europeans resident in America. Eliot was an
American resident in Europe. Even as he was exacting from
both poetry and life a perfected impersonation of the European
model, he was signing himself, in letters, *Metoikos*, the Greek
word for resident alien. He knew he was a contradiction. And it
may simply be that it is in the renunciatory grain of America to
resist the hierarchical and the traditional. Eliot's "high culture"
and its regnancy in and beyond the American university may
have been an unsuccessful transplant that "took" temporarily,
but in the end would be rejected by the formation of natural
tissue. Or, as Eliot himself predicted in the "Dry Salvages"
section of *Four Quartets*,

We had the experience but missed the meaning.

For the generation for whom Eliot was once a god (my own),
the truth is that we had the experience and were irradiated
by the meaning. Looking back over the last forty years, it is
now our unsparing obligation to disclaim the reactionary Eliot.
What we will probably go on missing forever is that golden
cape of our youth, the power and prestige of high art.

Who Owns Anne Frank?

IF ANNE FRANK had not perished in the criminal malevolence of Bergen-Belsen early in 1945, she would have marked her seventieth birthday at the brink of the twenty-first century. And even if she had not kept the extraordinary diary through which we know her, it is likely that we would number her among the famous of the twentieth—though perhaps not so dramatically as we do now. She was born to be a writer. At thirteen, she felt her power; at fifteen, she was in command of it. It is easy to imagine—had she been allowed to live—a long row of novels and essays spilling from her fluent and ripening pen. We can be certain (as certain as one can be of anything hypothetical) that her mature prose would today be noted for its wit and acuity, and almost as certain that the trajectory of her work would be closer to that of Nadine Gordimer, say, than that of Françoise Sagan. Put it that as an international literary presence she would be thick rather than thin. "I want to go on living even after my death!" she exclaimed in the spring of 1944.

This was more than an exaggerated adolescent flourish. She had already intuited what greatness in literature might mean, and she clearly sensed the force of what lay under her hand in the pages of her diary: a conscious literary record of frightened lives in daily peril; an explosive document aimed directly at the future. In her last months she was assiduously polishing phrases and editing passages with an eye to postwar publication. *Het Achterhuis*, as she called her manuscript—"the house behind," often translated as "the secret annex"—was hardly intended to be Anne Frank's last word; it was conceived as the forerunner work of a professional woman of letters.

Yet any projection of Anne Frank as a contemporary figure is an unholy speculation: it tampers with history, with reality, with deadly truth. "When I write," she confided, "I can shake

off all my cares. My sorrow disappears, my spirits are revived!"
But she could not shake off her capture and annihilation, and
there are no diary entries to register and memorialize the
snuffing of her spirit. Anne Frank was discovered, seized, and
deported; she and her mother and sister and millions of others
were extinguished in a program calculated to assure the cruelest and most demonically inventive human degradation. The
atrocities she endured were ruthlessly and purposefully devised,
from indexing by tattoo to systematic starvation to factory-
efficient murder. She was designated to be erased from the
living, to leave no grave, no sign, no physical trace of any kind.
Her fault—her crime—was having been born a Jew, and as such
she was classified among those who had no right to exist: not
as a subject people, not as an inferior breed, not even as usable
slaves. The military and civilian apparatus of an entire society
was organized to obliterate her as a contaminant, in the way of
a noxious and repellent insect. Zyklon B, the lethal fumigant
poured into the gas chambers, was, pointedly, a roach poison.

Anne Frank escaped gassing. One month before liberation,
not yet sixteen, she died of typhus fever, an acute infectious
disease carried by lice. The precise date of her death has never
been determined. She and her sister Margot were among 3,659
women transported by cattle car from Auschwitz to the merciless conditions of Bergen-Belsen, a barren tract of mud. In
a cold, wet autumn, they suffered through nights on flooded straw in overcrowded tents, without light, surrounded by
latrine ditches, until a violent hailstorm tore away what had
passed for shelter. Weakened by brutality, chaos, and hunger,
fifty thousand men and women—insufficiently clothed, tormented by lice—succumbed, many to the typhus epidemic.

Anne Frank's final diary entry, written on August 1, 1944,
ends introspectively—a meditation on a struggle for moral
transcendence set down in a mood of wistful gloom. It speaks
of "turning my heart inside out, the bad part on the outside
and the good part on the inside," and of "trying to find a way
to become what I'd like to be and what I could be if . . . if
only there were no other people in the world." Those curiously
self-subduing ellipses are the diarist's own; they are more than

merely a literary effect—they signify a child's muffled bleat against confinement, the last whimper of a prisoner in a cage. Her circumscribed world had a population of eleven—the three Dutch protectors who came and went, supplying the necessities of life, and the eight in hiding: the van Daans, their son Peter, Albert Dussel, and the four Franks. Five months earlier, on May 26, 1944, she had railed against the stress of living invisibly—a tension never relieved, she asserted, "not once in the two years we've been here. How much longer will this increasingly oppressive, unbearable weight press down on us?" And, several paragraphs on, "What will we do if we're ever . . . no, I mustn't write that down. But the question won't let itself be pushed to the back of my mind today; on the contrary, all the fear I've ever felt is looming before me in all its horror. . . . I've asked myself again and again whether it wouldn't have been better if we hadn't gone into hiding, if we were dead now and didn't have to go through this misery. . . . Let something happen soon. . . . Nothing can be more crushing than this anxiety. Let the end come, however cruel." And on April 11, 1944: "We are Jews in chains."

The diary is not a genial document, despite its author's often vividly satiric exposure of what she shrewdly saw as "the comical side of life in hiding." Its reputation for uplift is, to say it plainly, nonsensical. Anne Frank's written narrative, moreover, is not the story of Anne Frank, and never has been. That the diary is miraculous, a self-aware work of youthful genius, is not in question. Variety of pace and tone, insightful humor, insupportable suspense, adolescent love-pangs and disappointments, sexual curiosity, moments of terror, moments of elation, flights of idealism and prayer and psychological acumen—all these elements of mind and feeling and skill brilliantly enliven its pages. There is, besides, a startlingly precocious comprehension of the progress of the war on all fronts. The survival of the little group in hiding is crucially linked to the timing of the Allied invasion; overhead the bombers, roaring to their destinations, make the house quake. Sometimes the bombs fall terrifyingly close. All in all, the diary is a chronicle of trepidation, turmoil, alarm. Even its report of quieter periods of reading and study express the hush of imprisonment. Meals are boiled lettuce and rotted potatoes; flushing the single toilet is forbidden for ten hours at a time. There is shooting at night. Betrayal and arrest always threaten. Anxiety and immobility rule. It is a story of fear.

But the diary in itself, richly crammed though it is with incident and passion, cannot count as Anne Frank's story. A story may not be said to be a story if the end is missing. And because the end is missing, the story of Anne Frank in the fifty years since *The Diary of a Young Girl* was first published has been bowdlerized, distorted, transmuted, traduced, reduced; it has been infantilized, Americanized, homogenized, sentimentalized; falsified, kitschified, and, in fact, blatantly and arrogantly denied. Among the falsifiers and bowdlerizers have been dramatists and directors, translators and litigators, Anne Frank's own father, and even—or especially—the public, both readers and theatergoers, all over the world. A deeply truth-telling work has been turned into an instrument of partial truth, surrogate truth, or anti-truth. The pure has been made impure—sometimes in the name of the reverse. Almost every hand that has approached the diary with the well-meaning intention of publicizing it has contributed to the subversion of history.

The diary is taken to be a Holocaust document; that is overridingly what it is not. Nearly every edition—and there have been innumerable editions—is emblazoned with words like "a song to life," "a poignant delight in the infinite human spirit." Such characterizations rise up in the bitter perfume of mockery. A song to life? The diary is incomplete, truncated, broken off; or, rather, it is completed by Westerbork (the hellish transit camp in Holland from which Dutch Jews were deported), and by Auschwitz, and by the fatal winds of Bergen-Belsen. It is here, and not in the "secret annex," that the crimes we have come to call the Holocaust were enacted. Our entry into those crimes begins with columns of numbers: the meticulous lists of deportations, in handsome bookkeepers' handwriting, starkly set down in German "transport books." From these columns—headed, like goods for export, *"Ausgange-Transporte nach Osten"* (outgoing shipments to the east)—it is possible to learn that Anne Frank and the others were moved to Auschwitz on the night of September 6, 1944, in a collection of 1,019 *Stücke* (or "pieces," another commodities term). That same night, 549 persons were gassed, including one from the Frank group (the father of Peter van Daan), and every child under fifteen. Anne, at fifteen, and seventeen-year-old Margot were spared, apparently for labor. The end of October, from the twentieth to the twenty-eighth, saw the gassing of more than 6,000 human beings within two hours of their arrival, including a thousand boys eighteen and under. In December, 2,093 female prisoners perished, from starvation and exhaustion, in the women's camp; early in January, Edith Frank expired.

But Soviet forces were hurtling toward Auschwitz, and in November the order went out to conceal all evidences of gassing and to blow up the crematoria. Tens of thousands of inmates, debilitated and already near extinction, were driven out in bitter cold on death marches. Many were shot. In an evacuation that occurred either on October 28 or November 2, Anne and Margot were dispatched to Bergen-Belsen. Margot was the first to succumb. A survivor recalled that she fell dead to the ground from the wooden slab on which she lay, eaten by lice, and that Anne, heartbroken and skeletal, naked under a bit of rag, died a day or two later.

To come to the diary without having earlier assimilated Elie Wiesel's *Night* and Primo Levi's *The Drowned and the Saved* (to mention two accounts only), or the columns of figures in the transport books, is to allow oneself to stew in an implausible and ugly innocence. The litany of blurbs—"a lasting testimony to the indestructible nobility of the human spirit," "an everlasting source of courage and inspiration"—is no more substantial than any other display of self-delusion. The success—the triumph—of Bergen-Belsen was precisely that it blotted out the possibility of courage, that it proved to be a lasting testament to the human spirit's easy destructibility. "*Hier ist kein warum*," a guard at Auschwitz warned Primo Levi: here there is no "why," neither question nor answer, only the dark of unreason. Anne Frank's story, truthfully told, is unredeemed and unredeemable.

These are notions that are hard to swallow—so they have

not been swallowed. There are some, bored beyond toleration and callous enough to admit it, who are sick of hearing—yet again!—about depredations fifty years gone. "These old events," one of these fellows may complain, "can rake you over only so much. . . . If I'm going to be lashed, I might as well save my skin for more recent troubles in the world." (I quote from a private letter from a distinguished author.) This may be a popular, if mostly unexpressed, point of view, but it is not socially representative. The more common response respectfully discharges an obligation to pity: it is dutiful. Or it is sometimes less than dutiful. It is sometimes frivolous, or indifferent, or presumptuous. But what even the most exemplary sympathies are likely to evade is the implacable recognition that Auschwitz and Bergen-Belsen, however sacramentally prodded, can never yield light.

And the vehicle that has most powerfully accomplished this almost universal obtuseness is Anne Frank's diary. In celebrating Anne Frank's years in the secret annex, the nature and meaning of her death has been, in effect, forestalled. The diary's keen lens is helplessly opaque to the diarist's explicit doom—and this opacity, replicated in young readers in particular, has led to shamelessness.

It is the shamelessness of appropriation. Who owns Anne Frank? The children of the world, say the sentimentalists. A case in point, then, is the astonishing correspondence, published in 1995 under the title *Love, Otto*, between Cara Wilson, a Californian born in 1944, and Otto Frank, the father of Anne Frank. Wilson, then twelve-year-old Cara Weiss, was invited by Twentieth Century-Fox to audition for the part of Anne in a projected film version of the diary. "I didn't get the part," the middle-aged Wilson writes, "but by now I had found a whole new world. Anne Frank's diary, which I read and reread, spoke to me and my dilemmas, my anxieties, my secret passions. She felt the way I did. . . . I identified so strongly with this eloquent girl of my own age, that I now think I sort of became her in my own mind." And on what similarities does Wilson rest her acute sense of identification with a hunted child in hiding?

I was miserable being me. . . . I was on the brink of that awful abyss of teenagedom and I, too, needed someone to talk to. . . . (Ironically, Anne, too, expressed a longing for more attention from her father.) . . . Dad's whole life was a series of meetings. At home, he was too tired or too frustrated to unload on. I had something else in common with Anne. We both had to share with sisters who were prettier and smarter than we felt we were. . . . Despite the monumental difference in our situations, to this day I feel that Anne helped me get through the teens with a sense of inner focus. She spoke for me. She was strong for me. She had so much hope when I was ready to call it quits.

A sampling of Wilson's concerns as she matured appears in the interstices of her exchanges with Otto Frank—which, remarkably, date from 1959 until his death in 1980. For instance: "The year was 1968—etched in my mind. I can't ever forget it. Otis Redding was 'Sittin' on the Dock of the Bay' . . . while we hummed along to 'Hey Jude' by the Beatles." Or again: "What a year 1972 was! That was when I saw one of my all-time favorite movies, *Harold and Maude*, to the tune of Cat Stevens' incredible sound track. . . . I remember singing along to Don McLean's 'American Pie' and daydreaming to Roberta Flack's exquisite 'The First Time Ever I Saw Your Face,' " and so on. "In 1973–74," she reports, "I was wearing headbands, pukka-shell necklaces, and American Indian anything. Tattoos were a rage"—but enough. Tattoos were the rage, she neglects to recall, in Auschwitz; and of the Auschwitz survivor who was her patient correspondent for more than two decades, Wilson remarks: "Well, what choice did the poor man have? Whenever an attack of 'I-can't-take-this-any-longer' would hit me, I'd put it all into lengthy diatribes to my distant guru, Otto Frank."

That the designated guru replied, year after year, to embarrassing and shabby effusions like these may open a new pathway into our generally obscure understanding of the character of Otto Frank. His responses—from Basel, where he had settled with his second wife—were consistently attentive, formal, kindly. When Wilson gave birth, he sent her a musical toy, and he faithfully offered a personal word about her excitements as she supplied them: her baby sons, her dance lessons, her husband's work on commercials, her freelance writing. But his letters were also political and serious: it is good, he wrote in October 1970, to take "an active part in trying to abolish injustices and all sorts of grievances, but we cannot follow your views regarding the Black Panthers." And in December 1973, "As you can imagine, we were highly shocked about the unexpected attack of the Arabs on Israel on Yom Kippur and are now mourning with all those who lost their families." Presumably he knew something about losing a family. Wilson, insouciantly sliding past these faraway matters, was otherwise preoccupied, "finding our little guys sooo much fun."

The unabashed triflings of Cara Wilson—whose "identification" with Anne Frank can be duplicated by the thousand, though she may be more audacious than most—point to a conundrum. Never mind that the intellectual distance between Wilson and Anne Frank is immeasurable; not every self-conscious young girl will be a prodigy. Did Otto Frank not comprehend that Cara Wilson was deaf to everything the loss of his daughter represented? Did he not see, in Wilson's letters alone, how a denatured approach to the diary might serve to promote amnesia of what was rapidly turning into history? A protected domestic space, however threatened and endangered, can, from time to time, mimic ordinary life. The young who are encouraged to embrace the diary cannot always be expected to feel the difference between the mimicry and the threat. And (like Cara Wilson) most do not. Natalie Portman, then sixteen years old, who in December 1997 débuted as Anne Frank in the Broadway revival of the famous play based on the diary—a play that has itself influenced the way the diary is read—was reported to have concluded from her own reading that "it's funny, it's hopeful, and she's a happy person."

Otto Frank, it turns out, is complicit in this shallowly upbeat view. Again and again, in every conceivable context, he had it as his aim to emphasize "Anne's idealism," "Anne's spirit," almost never calling attention to how and why that idealism and spirit were smothered, and unfailingly generalizing the sources of hatred. If the child is father of the man—if childhood shapes future sensibility—then Otto Frank, despite his sufferings in Auschwitz, may have had less in common with his own daughter than he was ready to recognize. As the diary gained publication in country after country, its renown accelerating year by year, he spoke not merely about but for its author—and who, after all, would have a greater right? The surviving father stood in for the dead child, believing that his words would honestly represent hers. He was not entitled to such certainty: fatherhood does not confer surrogacy. His own childhood, in Frankfurt, Germany, was wholly unclouded. A banker's son, he lived untrammeled until the rise of the Nazi regime, when he was already forty-four. At nineteen, in order to acquire training in business, he went to New York with Nathan Straus, a fellow student who was heir to the Macy's department-store fortune. During the First World War, Frank was an officer in the German military, and in 1925 he married Edith Holländer, a manufacturer's daughter. Margot was born in 1926 and Anneliese Marie, called Anne, in 1929. His characteristically secular world view belonged to an era of quiet assimilation, or, more accurately, accommodation (which includes a modicum of deference), when German Jews had become, at least in their own minds, well integrated into German society. From birth, Otto Frank had breathed the free air of the affluent bourgeoisie.

Anne's childhood, in contrast, fell into shadows almost immediately. She was four when the German persecutions of Jews began, and from then until the anguished close of her days she lived as a refugee and a victim. In 1933 the family fled from Germany to Holland, where Frank had commercial connections, and where he founded and directed a spice and pectin business. By 1940 the Germans had occupied the Netherlands. In Amsterdam, Jewish children, Anne among them, were thrown out of the public-school system and made to wear the yellow star. At thirteen, on November 19, 1942, already in hiding, Anne Frank could write:

> In the evenings when it's dark, I often see long lines of good, innocent people accompanied by crying children, walking

on and on, ordered about by a handful of men who bully
and beat them until they nearly drop. No one is spared. The
sick, the elderly, children, babies, pregnant women—all are
marched to their death.

And earlier, on October 9, 1942, after hearing the report of an
escape from Westerbork:

> Our many Jewish friends and acquaintances are being taken
> away in droves. The Gestapo is treating them very roughly
> and transporting them in cattle cars to Westerbork. . . . The
> people get almost nothing to eat, much less to drink, as
> water is available only one hour a day, and there's only one
> toilet and sink for several thousand people. Men and women
> sleep in the same room, and women and children have their
> heads shaved. . . . If it's that bad in Holland, what must it
> be like in those faraway and uncivilized places where the
> Germans are sending them? We assume that most of them
> are being murdered. The English radio says they're being
> gassed.

Perhaps not even a father is justified in thinking he can dis-
till the "ideas" of this alert and sorrowing child, with scenes
such as these inscribed in her psyche, and with the desolations
of Auschwitz and Bergen-Belsen still ahead. His preference was
to accentuate what he called Anne's "optimistical view of life."
Yet the diary's most celebrated line (infamously celebrated, one
might add)—"I still believe, in spite of everything, that people
are truly good at heart"—has been torn out of its bed of thorns.
Two sentences later (and three weeks before she was seized
and shipped to Westerbork), the diarist sets down a vision of
darkness:

> I see the world being transformed into a wilderness, I hear
> the approaching thunder that, one day, will destroy us too,
> I feel the suffering of millions. . . . In the meantime, I must
> hold on to my ideals. Perhaps the day will come when I'll
> be able to realize them!

Because that day never came, both Miep Gies, the selflessly courageous woman who devoted herself to the sustenance of those in hiding, and Hannah Goslar, Anne's Jewish schoolmate and the last to hear her tremulous cries in Bergen-Belsen, objected to Otto Frank's emphasis on the diary's "truly good at heart" utterance. That single sentence has become, universally, Anne Frank's message, virtually her motto—whether or not such a credo could have survived the camps. But why should this sentence be taken as emblematic, and not, for example, another? "There's a destructive urge in people, the urge to rage, murder, and kill," Anne wrote on May 3, 1944, pondering the spread of guilt. These are words that do not soften, ameliorate, or give the lie to the pervasive horror of her time. Nor do they pull the wool over the eyes of history.

Otto Frank grew up with a social need to please his environment and not to offend it; it was the condition of entering the mainstream, a bargain German Jews negotiated with themselves. It was more dignified, and safer, to praise than to blame. Far better, then, in facing the larger postwar world the diary had opened to him, to speak of goodness rather than destruction: so much of that larger world had participated in the urge to rage. (The diary notes how Dutch anti-Semitism, "to our great sorrow and dismay," was increasing even as the Jews were being hauled away.) After the liberation of the camps, the heaps of emaciated corpses were accusation enough. Postwar sensibility hastened to migrate elsewhere, away from the cruel and the culpable. It was a tone and a mood that affected the diary's reception; it was a mood and a tone that, with cautious yet crucial excisions, the diary itself could be made to support. And so the diarist's dread came to be described as hope, her terror as courage, her prayers of despair as inspiring. And since the diary was now defined as a Holocaust document, the perception of the cataclysm itself was being subtly accommodated to expressions like "man's inhumanity to man," diluting and befogging specific historical events and their motives. "We must not flog the past," Frank insisted in 1969. His concrete response to the past was the establishment, in 1957, of the Anne Frank Foundation and its offshoot the International Youth Center, situated in the Amsterdam house where the diary was composed, to foster "as many contacts as possible between young people of different nationalities, races and religions"—a civilized and tender-hearted goal that nevertheless washed away into do-gooder abstraction the explicit urge to rage that had devoured his daughter.

But Otto Frank was merely an accessory to the transformation of the diary from one kind of witness to another kind: from the painfully revealing to the partially concealing. If Anne Frank has been made into what we nowadays call an "icon," it is because of the Pulitzer Prize-winning play derived from the diary—a play that rapidly achieved worldwide popularity, and framed the legend even the newest generation has come to believe in. Adapted by Albert Hackett and Frances Goodrich, a Hollywood husband-and-wife screenwriting team, the theatricalized version opened on Broadway in 1955, ten years after the ovens of Auschwitz had cooled; its portrayal of the "funny, hopeful, happy" Anne continues to reverberate, not only in how the diary is construed, but in how the Holocaust itself is understood. The play was a work born in controversy, and was destined to roil on and on in rancor and litigation. Its tangle of contending lawyers finally came to resemble nothing so much as the knotted imbroglio of Jarndyce vs. Jarndyce, the unending court case of *Bleak House*. "This scarecrow of a suit," as Dickens describes it, "has, in course of time, become so complicated, that no man alive knows what it means. . . . Innumerable children have been born into the cause; innumerable young people have married into it; old people have died out of it." Many of the chief figures in the protracted conflict over the Hacketts' play have by now died out of it, but the principal issues, far from fading away, have, after so many decades, intensified. And whatever the ramifications of these issues, whatever perspectives they illumine or defy, the central question stands fast: who owns Anne Frank?

The hero, or irritant (depending on which side of the controversy one favors), in the genesis of the diary's dramatization was Meyer Levin, a Chicago-born novelist of the social realist school, author of such fairly successful works as *The Old Bunch*,

Compulsion, and *The Settlers*. Levin began as a man of the left, though a strong anti-Stalinist: he was drawn to proletarian fiction (*Citizens*, about steel workers), and had gone to Spain in the thirties to report on the Civil War. In 1945, as a war correspondent attached to the Fourth Armored Division, he was among the first Americans to enter Buchenwald, Dachau, and Bergen-Belsen. What he saw there was ungraspable and unendurable. "As I groped in the first weeks, beginning to apprehend the monstrous shape of the story I would have to tell," he wrote, "I knew already that I would never penetrate its heart of bile, for the magnitude of the horror seemed beyond human register." The truest telling, he affirmed, would have to rise up out of the mouth of a victim.

His "obsession," as he afterward called it—partly in mockery of the opposition his later views evoked—had its beginning in those repeated scenes of piled-up bodies as he investigated camp after camp. From then on he could be said to carry the mark of Abel. He dedicated himself to helping the survivors get to Mandate Palestine, a goal that Britain had made illegal. In 1946, he reported from Tel Aviv on the uprising against British rule, and during the next two years he wrote and produced a pair of films on the struggles of the survivors to reach Palestine. In 1950 he published *In Search*, an examination of the effects of the European cataclysm on his experience and sensibility as an American Jew; Thomas Mann acclaimed it as "a human document of high order, written by a witness of our fantastic epoch whose gaze remained both clear and steady." Levin's intensifying focus on the Jewish condition in the twentieth century grew more and more heated, and when his wife, the novelist Tereska Torres, handed him the French edition of the diary (it had previously appeared only in Dutch), he felt he had found what he had thirsted after: a voice crying up from the ground, an authentic witness to the German onslaught.

He acted instantly. He sent Otto Frank a copy of *In Search* and offered his services as, in effect, an unofficial agent to secure British and American publication, asserting his distance from any financial gain; his interest, he said, was purely "one of sympathy." He saw in the diary the possibility of "a very touching play or film," and asked Frank's permission to explore the idea. Frank at first avoided reading Levin's book, saturated as it was in passions and commitments so foreign to his own susceptibilities; but he was not unfamiliar with Levin's preoccupations. He had seen and liked one of his films. He encouraged Levin to go ahead—though a dramatization, he observed, would perforce "be rather different from the real contents" of the diary. Hardly so, Levin protested: no compromise would be needed; all the diarist's thoughts could be preserved.

The "real contents" had already been altered by Frank himself, and understandably, given the propriety of his own background and of the times. The diary contained, here and there, intimate adolescent musings—talk of how contraceptives work, and explicit anatomical description: "In the upper part, between the outer labia, there's a fold of skin that, on second thought, looks like a kind of blister. That's the clitoris. Then come the inner labia. . . ." All this Frank edited out. He also omitted passages recording his daughter's angry resistance to her mother's nervous fussiness ("the most rotten person in the world"). Undoubtedly he better understood Edith Frank's protective tremors, and was unwilling to perpetuate a negative portrait. Beyond this, he deleted numerous expressions of religious faith, a direct reference to Yom Kippur, terrified reports of Germans seizing Jews in Amsterdam. It was prudence, prudishness, and perhaps his own diffidently acculturated temperament that had stimulated many of these tamperings. In 1991, eleven years after Frank's death, a "definitive edition" of the diary restored everything he had expurgated. But the image of Anne Frank as merry innocent and steadfast idealist—an image the play vividly promoted—was by then ineradicable.

A subsequent bowdlerization, in 1950, was still more programmatic, and crossed over even more seriously into the area of Levin's concern for uncompromised faithfulness. The German edition's translator, Anneliese Schütz, in order to mask or soft-pedal German culpability, went about methodically blurring every hostile reference to Germans and German. Anne's parodic list of house rules, for instance, includes "*Use of language*: It is necessary to speak softly at all times. Only the

language of civilized people may be spoken, thus no German."
The German translation reads: "*Alle Kultursprachen . . . aber lei-
se!*"—"all civilized languages . . . but softly!" "Heroism in war
or when confronting Germans" is dissolved into "heroism in
war and in the struggle against oppression." ("A book intended
after all for sale in Germany," Schütz explained, "cannot abuse
the Germans.") The diarist's honest cry, in the midst of a vast
persecution, that "there is no greater hostility in the world than
exists between Germans and Jews," became, in Schütz's version, "there is no greater hostility in the world than between
these Germans and Jews!" Frank agreed to the latter change
because, he said, it was what his daughter had really meant: she
"by no means measured all Germans by the same yardstick.
For, as she knew so well, even in those days we had many good
friends among the Germans." But this guarded accommoda-
tionist view is Otto Frank's own; it is nowhere in the diary.
Even more striking than Frank's readiness to accede to these
misrepresentations is the fact that for forty-one years (until a
more accurate translation appeared) no reader of the diary in
German had ever known an intact text.

In contemplating a dramatization and pledging no compromise—he would do it, he told Frank, "tenderly and with
the utmost fidelity"—Levin was clear about what he meant by
fidelity. In his eyes the diary was conscious testimony to Jewish
faith and suffering; and it was this, and this nearly alone, that
defined for him its psychological, historical, and metaphysical
genuineness, and its significance for the world. With these convictions foremost, Levin went in search of a theatrical producer.
At the same time he was unflagging in pressing for publication; but the work was meanwhile slowly gaining independent
notice. Janet Flanner, in her "Letter from Paris" in *The New
Yorker* of November 11, 1950, noted the French publication of
a book by "a precocious, talented little Frankfurt Jewess"—
apparently oblivious to the unpleasant echoes, post–Hitler, of
"Jewess." Sixteen English-language publishers on both sides of
the Atlantic had already rejected the diary when Levin succeeded in placing it with Valentine Mitchell, a London firm.
His negotiations with a Boston house were still incomplete

when Doubleday came forward to secure publication rights directly from Frank. Relations between Levin and Frank were, as usual, warm; Frank repeatedly thanked Levin for his efforts to further the fortunes of the diary, and Levin continued under the impression that Frank would support him as the playwright of choice.

If a single front-page review in the *New York Times Book Review* can rocket a book to instant sanctity, that is what Meyer Levin, in the spring of 1952, achieved for *Anne Frank: The Diary of a Young Girl*. It was an assignment he had avidly gone after. But Barbara Zimmerman (afterward Barbara Epstein, a founder of *The New York Review of Books*), the diary's young editor at Doubleday, had earlier recognized its potential as "a minor classic," and had enlisted Eleanor Roosevelt to supply an introduction. (According to Levin, it was ghostwritten by Zimmerman.) Levin now joined Zimmerman and Doubleday in the project of choosing a producer. Doubleday was to take over as Frank's official agent, with the stipulation that Levin would have an active hand in the adaptation. "I think I can honestly say," Levin wrote Frank, "that I am as well qualified as any other writer for this particular task." In a cable to Doubleday, Frank appeared to agree: "DESIRE LEVIN AS WRITER OR COLLABORATOR IN ANY TREATMENT TO GUARANTEE IDEA OF BOOK." The catch, it would develop, lurked in a perilous contingency: whose idea? Levin's? Frank's? The producer's? The director's? In any case, Doubleday was already sufficiently doubtful about Levin's ambiguous role: what if an interested producer decided on another playwright?

What happened next—an avalanche of furies and recriminations lasting years—has become the subject of a pair of arresting discussions of the Frank-Levin affair. And if "affair" suggests an event on the scale of the Dreyfus case, that is how Levin saw it: as an unjust stripping of his rightful position, with implications far beyond his personal predicament. *An Obsession with Anne Frank*, by Lawrence Graver, brought out by the University of California Press in 1995, is the first study to fashion a coherent narrative out of the welter of claims, counterclaims, letters, cables, petitions, polemics, and rumbling confusions that accompany any examination of the diary's journey to the stage. *The Stolen Legacy of Anne Frank*, by Ralph Melnick, published in 1997 by Yale University Press, is denser in detail and in sources than its predecessor, and more insistent in tone. Both are accomplished works of scholarship that converge on the facts and diverge in their conclusions. Graver is reticent with his sympathies; Melnick is Levin's undisguised advocate. Graver finds no villains. Melnick finds Lillian Hellman.

Always delicately respectful of Frank's dignity and rights—and mindful always of the older man's earlier travail—Levin had promised that he would step aside if a more prominent playwright, someone "world famous," should appear. Stubbornly and confidently, he went on toiling over his own version. As a novelist, he was under suspicion of being unable to write drama. (In after years, when he had grown deeply bitter, he listed, in retaliation, "Sartre, Gorky, Galsworthy, Steinbeck, Wilder!") Though there are many extant drafts of Levin's play, no definitive script is available; both publication and performance were proscribed by Frank's attorneys. A script staged without authorization by the Israel Soldiers' Theater in 1966 sometimes passes from hand to hand, and reads well: moving, theatrical, actable, professional. This later work was not, however, the script submitted in 1952 to Cheryl Crawford, one of a number of Broadway producers who rushed in with bids in the wake of the diary's acclaim. Crawford, an eminent co-founder of the Actors Studio, was initially encouraging to Levin, offering him first consideration and, if his script was not entirely satisfactory, the aid of a more experienced collaborator. Then—virtually overnight—she rejected his draft outright. Levin was bewildered and infuriated, and from then on became an intractable and indefatigable warrior on behalf of his play—and on behalf, he contended, of the diary's true meaning. In his *Times* review he had summed it up stirringly as the voice of "six million vanished Jewish souls."

Doubleday, meanwhile, sensing complications ahead, had withdrawn as Frank's theatrical agent, finding Levin's presence—injected by Frank—too intrusive, too maverick, too independent and entrepreneurial: fixed, they believed, only on his own interest, which was to stick to his insistence on the superiority of his work over all potential contenders. Frank, too, had begun—kindly, politely, and with tireless assurances of his gratitude to Levin—to move closer to Doubleday's cooler views, especially as urged by Barbara Zimmerman. She was twenty-four years old, the age Anne would have been, very intelligent and attentive. Adoring letters flowed back and forth between them, Frank addressing her as "little Barbara" and "dearest little one." On one occasion he gave her an antique gold pin. About Levin, Zimmerman finally concluded that he was "impossible to deal with in any terms, officially, legally, morally, personally"—a "compulsive neurotic . . . destroying both himself and Anne's play." (There was, of course, no such entity as "Anne's play.")

But what had caused Crawford to change her mind so precipitately? She had sent Levin's script for further consideration to Lillian Hellman, and to the producers Robert Whitehead and Kermit Bloomgarden. All were theater luminaries; all spurned Levin's work. Frank's confidence in Levin, already much diminished, failed altogether. Advised by Doubleday, he put his trust in the Broadway professionals, while Levin fought on alone. Famous names—Maxwell Anderson, John Van Druten, Carson McCullers—came and went. Crawford herself ultimately pulled out, fearing a lawsuit by Levin. In the end—in a plethora of complications, legal and emotional, and with the vigilant Levin still agitating loudly and publicly for the primacy of his work—Kermit Bloomgarden surfaced as producer and Garson Kanin as director. Hellman had recommended Bloomgarden; she had also recommended Frances Goodrich and Albert Hackett. The Hacketts had a long record of Hollywood hits, from *Father of the Bride* to *It's A Wonderful Life*, and they had successfully scripted a series of light-hearted musicals. Levin was appalled—had his sacred vision been pushed aside not for the awaited world-famous dramatist, but for a pair of frivolous screen drudges, mere "hired hands"?

The hired hands were earnest and reverent. They began at once to read up on European history, Judaism and Jewish practice; they consulted a rabbi. They corresponded eagerly with Frank, looking to satisfy his expectations. They traveled to Amsterdam and visited 263 Prinsengracht, the house on the canal where the Franks, the Van Daans, and Dussel had been hidden. They met Johannes Kleiman, who, together with Harry Kraler and Miep Gies, had taken over the management of Frank's business in order to conceal and protect him and his family in the house behind. Reacting to the Hacketts' lifelong remoteness from Jewish subject matter, Levin took out an ad in the New York *Post* attacking Bloomgarden and asking that his play be given a hearing. "My work," he wrote, "has been with the Jewish story. I tried to dramatize the Diary as Anne would have, in her own words. . . . I feel my work has earned the right to be judged by you, the public." "Ridiculous and laughable," said Bloomgarden. Appealing to the critic Brooks Atkinson, Levin complained—extravagantly, outrageously—that his play was being "killed by the same arbitrary disregard that brought an end to Anne and six million others." Frank stopped answering Levin's letters; many he returned unopened.

The Hacketts, too, in their earliest drafts, were devotedly "with the Jewish story." Grateful to Hellman for getting them the job, and crushed by Bloomgarden's acute dislike of their efforts so far, they flew to Martha's Vineyard weekend after weekend to receive advice from Hellman. "She was amazing," Goodrich crowed, happy to comply. Hellman's suggestions— and those of Bloomgarden and Kanin—were consistently in a direction opposite to Levin's. Wherever the diary touched on Anne's consciousness of Jewish fate or faith, they quietly erased the reference or changed its emphasis. Whatever was specific they made generic. The sexual tenderness between Anne and the young Peter van Daan was moved to the forefront. Comedy overwhelmed darkness. Anne became an all-American girl, an echo of the perky character in *Junior Miss*, a popular play of the previous decade. The Zionist aspirations of Margot, Anne's sister, disappeared. The one liturgical note, a Hanukkah ceremony, was absurdly defined by local contemporary habits ("eight days of presents"); a jolly jingle replaced the traditional "Rock of Ages," with its somber allusions to historic travail. (Kanin had insisted on something "spirited and gay," so as not to give "the wrong feeling entirely." "Hebrew," he added, "would simply alienate the audience.")

Astonishingly, the Nazified notion of "race" leaped out in a line attributed to Hellman and nowhere present in the diary. "We're not the only people that've had to suffer," says the Hacketts' Anne. "There've always been people that've had to . . . sometimes one race . . . sometimes another." This pallid speech, yawning with vagueness, was conspicuously opposed to the pivotal reflection it was designed to betray:

> In the eyes of the world, we're doomed, but if after all this suffering, there are still Jews left, the Jewish people will be held up as an example. Who knows, maybe our religion will teach the world and all the people in it about goodness, and that's the reason, the only reason, we have to suffer. . . . God has never deserted our people. Through the ages Jews have had to suffer, but through the ages they've gone on living, and the centuries of suffering have only made them stronger.

For Kanin, this kind of rumination was "an embarrassing piece of special pleading. . . . The fact that in this play the symbols of persecution and oppression are Jews is incidental, and Anne, in stating the argument so, reduces her magnificent stature." And so it went throughout. The particularized plight of Jews in hiding was vaporized into what Kanin called "the infinite." Reality—the diary's central condition—was "incidental." The passionately contemplative child, brooding on concrete evil, was made into an emblem of evasion. Her history had a habitation and a name; the infinite was nameless and nowhere.

For Levin, the source and first cause of these excisions was Lillian Hellman. Hellman, he believed, had "supervised" the Hacketts, and Hellman was fundamentally political and inflexibly doctrinaire. Her outlook lay at the root of a conspiracy. She was an impenitent Stalinist; she followed, he said, the Soviet line. Like the Soviets, she was anti-Zionist. And just as the Soviets had obliterated Jewish particularity at Babi Yar, the ravine where thousands of Jews, shot by the Germans, lay unnamed and effaced in their deaths, so Hellman had directed the Hacketts to blur the identity of the characters in the play. The sins of the Soviets and the sins of Hellman and her Broadway deputies were, in Levin's mind, identical. He set out to punish the man who had allowed all this to come to pass. Otto Frank had allied himself with the pundits of erasure; Otto Frank had stood aside when Levin's play was elbowed out of the way. What recourse remained for a man so affronted and injured? Meyer Levin sued Otto Frank. It was as if, someone observed, a suit were being brought against the father of Joan of Arc.

The bulky snarl of courtroom arguments resulted in small satisfaction for Levin: because the structure of the Hacketts' play was in some ways similar to his, the jury detected plagiarism; yet even this limited triumph foundered on the issue of damages. Levin sent out broadsides, collected signatures, summoned a committee of advocacy, lectured from pulpits, took out ads, rallied rabbis and writers (Norman Mailer among them). He published *The Obsession*, his grandly confessional "J'accuse," rehearsing, in skirmish after skirmish, his fight for the staging of his own adaptation. In return, furious charges flew at him: he was a redbaiter, a McCarthyite. The term "paranoid" began to circulate: why rant against the popularization and dilution that was Broadway's lifeblood? "I certainly have no wish to inflict depression on an audience," Kanin had argued. "I don't consider that a legitimate theatrical end." (So much for *Hamlet* and *King Lear*.)

Grateful for lightness, reviewers agreed. What they came away from was the liveliness of Susan Strasberg as a radiant Anne, and Joseph Schildkraut in the role of a wise and steadying Otto Frank, whom the actor engagingly resembled. "Anne is not going to her death; she is going to leave a dent on life, and let death take what's left," Walter Kerr, on a mystical note, wrote in the *Herald Tribune*. *Variety* seemed relieved that the play avoided "hating the Nazis, hating what they did to millions of innocent people," and instead left a "glowing, moving, frequently humorous" impression, with "just about everything one could wish for. It is not grim." The *Daily News* confirmed what Kanin had striven for: "not in any important sense a Jewish play. . . . Anne Frank is a Little Orphan Annie brought into vibrant life." Audiences laughed and were charmed; but they were also dazed and moved.

And audiences multiplied: the Hacketts' drama went all over the world, including Israel—where numbers of survivors were remaking their lives—and was everywhere successful. The play's reception in Germany was especially noteworthy. In an impressive and thoroughgoing essay entitled "Popularization and Memory," Alvin Rosenfeld, a professor of literature at Indiana University, recounts the development of the Anne Frank phenomenon in the country of her birth. "The theater reviews of the time," Rosenfeld reports, "tell of audiences sitting in stunned silence at the play and leaving the performance unable to speak or look one another in the eye." These were self-conscious and thin-skinned audiences; in the Germany of the fifties, theatergoers still belonged to the generation of the Nazi era. (On Broadway, Kanin had unblinkingly engaged Gusti Huber, of that same generation, to play Anne Frank's mother. As a member of the Nazi Actors Guild until Germany's defeat, Huber had early on disparaged "non-Aryan artists.") But the strange muteness in theaters all over Germany may have derived not so much from guilt or shame as from an all-encompassing compassion; or call it self-pity. "We see in Anne Frank's fate," a German drama critic offered, "our own fate—the tragedy of human existence per se." Hannah Arendt, philosopher and Hitler refugee, scorned such oceanic expressions: "cheap sentimentality at the expense of a great catastrophe," she wrote. And Bruno Bettelheim, a survivor of Dachau and Buchenwald, condemned the play's most touted line: "If all men are good, there was never an Auschwitz." A decade after the fall of Nazism, the spirited and sanitized young girl of the play became a vehicle of German communal identification—with the victim, not the persecutors—and, according to Rosenfeld, a continuing "symbol of moral and intellectual convenience." The Anne Frank whom thousands saw in seven openings in seven cities "spoke affirmatively about life and not accusingly about her torturers." No German in uniform appeared onstage.

"In a word," Rosenfeld concludes, "Anne Frank has become a ready-at-hand formula for easy forgiveness."

The mood of consolation lingers on, as Otto Frank meant it to—and not only in Germany, where, even after fifty years, the issue is touchiest. Sanctified and absolving, shorn of darkness, Anne Frank remains in all countries a revered and comforting figure in the contemporary mind. In Japan, because both diary and play mention first menstruation, "Anne Frank" is a code word among teenagers for getting one's period. In Argentina in the seventies, church publications began to link her with Roman Catholic martyrdom. "Commemoration," the French cultural critic Tsvetan Todorov explains, "is always the adaptation of memory to the needs of today."

But there is a note that drills deeper than commemoration: it goes to the idea of identification. To "identify with" is to become what one is not, to become what one is not is to usurp, to usurp is to own—and who, after all, in the half-century since Miep Gies retrieved the scattered pages of the diary, really owns Anne Frank? Who can speak for her? Her father, who, after reading the diary and confessing that he "did not know" her, went on to tell us what he thought she meant? Meyer Levin, who claimed to be her authentic voice—so much so that he dared to equate the dismissal of his work, however ignobly motivated, with Holocaust annihilation? Hellman, Bloomgarden, Kanin, whose interpretations clung to a collective ideology of human interchangeability? (In discounting the significance of the Jewish element, Kanin had asserted that "people have suffered because of being English, French, German, Italian, Ethiopian, Mohammedan, Negro, and so on"—as if this were not all the more reason to comprehend and particularize each history.) And what of Cara Wilson and "the children of the world," who have reduced the persecution of a people to the trials of adolescence?

All these appropriations, whether cheaply personal or densely ideological, whether seen as exalting or denigrating, have contributed to the conversion of Anne Frank into usable goods. There is no authorized version other than the diary itself, and even this has been brought into question by the

Holocaust-denial industry—in part a spinoff of the Anne Frank industry—which labels the diary a forgery. One charge is that Otto Frank wrote it himself, to make money. (Scurrilities like these necessitated the issuance, in 1986, of a Critical Edition by the Netherlands State Institute for War Documentation, including forensic evidence of handwriting and ink—a defensive hence sorrowful volume.)

No play can be judged wholly from what is on the page; a play has evocative powers beyond the words. Still, the Hacketts' work, read today, is very much a conventionally well-made Broadway product of the fifties, alternating comical beats with scenes of alarm, a love story with a theft, wisdom with buffoonery. The writing is skilled and mediocre, not unlike much of contemporary commercial theater. Yet this is the play that electrified audiences everywhere, that became a reverential if robot-like film, that—far more than the diary—invented the world's Anne Frank. Was it the play, or was it the times?

As the Second World War and the Holocaust recede for each new generation into distant fable, no different from tales, say, of Attila the Hun, Holocaust scholarship nevertheless accelerates prodigiously—survivor memoirs, oral histories, wave after wave of fresh documentation and analysis. Under the rubric "reception studies," Holocaust incidents and figures are being examined for how current cultural perceptions have affected them. And Steven Spielberg's *Schindler's List*, about a Nazi industrialist as the savior of hunted Jews, has left its transformative mark. (The security guard who uncovered the Swiss banks' culpability in appropriating survivors' assets is said to have been inspired by the Spielberg film.) Unsurprisingly, the 1997 revival of the Hacketts' dramatization entered an environment psychologically altered from that of its 1955 predecessor. The new version's adapter and director were far more scrupulous in keeping faith with the diary, and went out of their way to avoid stimulating all the old quarrelsome issues. Yet the later production, with its cautious and conscientious additions, leaves no trace; it is as if it never was. What continues in the public consciousness of Anne Frank is the unstoppable voice of the original play. It was always a voice of good will; it meant, as we say, well—and, financially, it certainly did well. But it was Broadway's style of good will, and that, at least for Meyer Levin, had the scent of ill. For him, and signally for Bloomgarden and Kanin, the most sensitive point—the focus of trouble—lay in the ancient dispute between the particular and the universal. All that was a distraction from the heart of the matter: in a drama about hiding, evil was hidden. History was transcended, ennobled, rarefied. And if any proof is needed that the puffery of false optimism remains uneffaced, only recall how the young lead of 1997, forty years after the furies of the Kanin-Bloomgarden-Levin conflict, saw her role as Anne: *it's funny, it's hopeful, and she's a happy person.*

Evisceration, an elegy for the murdered. Evisceration by blurb and stage, by shrewdness and naïveté, by cowardice and spirituality, by forgiveness and indifference, by success and money, by vanity and rage, by principle and passion, by surrogacy and affinity. Evisceration by fame, by shame, by blame. By uplift and transcendence. By usurpation.

On Friday, August 4, 1944, the day of the arrest, Miep Gies climbed the stairs to the hiding place and found it ransacked and wrecked. The beleaguered little band had been betrayed by an informer who was paid seven and a half guilders—about a dollar—for each person: sixty guilders for the lot. Miep Gies picked up what she recognized as Anne's papers and put them away, unread, in her desk drawer. There the diary lay untouched, until Otto Frank emerged alive from Auschwitz. "Had I read it," she said afterward, "I would have had to burn the diary because it would have been too dangerous for people about whom Anne had written." It was Miep Gies—the uncommon heroine of this story, a woman profoundly good, a failed savior—who succeeded in rescuing an irreplaceable masterwork. It may be shocking to think this (I am shocked as I think it), but one can imagine a still more salvational outcome; Anne Frank's diary burned, vanished, lost—saved from a world that made of it all things, some of them true, while floating lightly over the heavier truth of named and inhabited evil.

Isaac Babel and the Identity Question

Identity, at least, is prepared to ask questions.
—LEON WIESELTIER

A YEAR OR so before the Soviet Union imploded, S.'s mother, my first cousin—whose existence until then had been no more than a distant legend—telephoned from Moscow. "Save my child!" she cried, in immemorial tones. So when S. arrived in New York, I expected a terrified refugee on the run from the intolerable exactions of popular antisemitism; at that time the press was filled with such dire reports. For months, preparing for her rescue, I had been hurtling from one agency to another, in search of official information on political asylum.

But when S. finally turned up, in black tights, a miniskirt, and the reddest lipstick, it was clear she was indifferent to all that. She didn't want to be saved; what she wanted was an American holiday, a fresh set of boyfriends, and a leather coat. She had brought with her a sizable cosmetics case, amply stocked, and a vast, rattling plastic bag stuffed with hundreds of cheap tin Komsomol medals depicting Lenin as a boy. She was scornful of these; they were worthless, she said; she had paid pennies for the lot. Within two weeks S., a natural entrepreneur, had established romantic relations with the handsome young manager of the local sports store and had got him to set up a table at Christmas in his heaviest traffic location. She sold the tin Lenin medals for three dollars each, made three hundred dollars in a day, and bought the leather coat.

Of course she was a great curiosity. Her English was acutely original, her green eyes gave out ravishing ironic lightnings, her voice was as dark as Garbo's in *Ninotchka*, and none of us had ever seen an actual Soviet citizen up close before. She thought the telephone was bugged. She thought the supermarket was a public exhibition. Any show of household shoddiness—a lamp, say, that came apart—would elicit from her a comical crow: "Like in Soviet!" She was, emphatically, no atheist: she had an affinity for the occult, believed that God could speak in dreams (she owned a dream book, through which Jesus often walked), adored the churches of old Russia, and lamented their destruction by the Bolsheviks. On the subject of current anti-semitism she was mute; that was her mother's territory. Back in Moscow, her boyfriend, Gennadi, had picked her up in the subway *because* she was Jewish. He was in a hurry to marry her. "He want get out of Soviet," she explained.

At home she was a *Sportsdoktor*: she traveled with the Soviet teams, roughneck country boys, and daily tested their urine for steroids. (Was this to make sure her athletes were properly dosed?) She announced that *everybody* hated Gorbachev, only the gullible Americans liked him, he was a joke like all the others. A historically-minded friend approached S. with the earnest inquiry of an old-fashioned liberal idealist: "We all know, obviously, about the excesses of Stalinism," she said, "but what of the *beginning*? Wasn't Communism a truly beautiful hope at the start?" S. laughed her cynical laugh; she judged my friend profoundly stupid. "Communism," she scoffed, "what Communism? Naive! Fairy tale, always! No Communism, never! Naive!"

And leaving behind five devastated American-as-apple-pie boyfriends (and wearing her leather coat), S. returned to Moscow. She did not marry Gennadi. Her mother emigrated to Israel. The last I heard of S., she was in business in Sakhalin, buying and selling—and passing off as the real thing—ersatz paleolithic mammoth tusks.

Well, it is all over now—the Great Experiment, as the old brave voices used to call it—and S. is both symptom and proof of how thoroughly it is over. She represents the Soviet Union's final heave, its last generation. S. is the consummate New Soviet Man: the unfurled future of its seed. If there is an axiom here, it is that idealism squeezed into utopian channels will gener-ate a cynicism so profound that no inch of human life—not youth, not art, not work, not romance, not introspection—is left untainted. The S. I briefly knew trusted nothing; in her world there was nothing to trust. The primal Communist fairy tale had cast its spell: a baba yaga's birth-curse.

In college I read the Communist Manifesto, a rapture-bringing psalm. I ought to have read Isaac Babel's *Red Cavalry* stories—if only as a corrective companion-text. Or antidote. "But what of the beginning?" my friend had asked. S. answered better than any historian, but no one will answer more terrifyingly than Isaac Babel. If S. is the last generation of New Soviet Man, he is the first—the Manifesto's primordial manifestation.

That Babel favored the fall of the Czarist regime is no anomaly. He was a Jew from Odessa, the child of an enlightened family, hungry for a European education; he was subject to the *numerus clausus*, the Czarist quota that kept Jews as a class out of the universities, and Babel in particular out of the University of Odessa. As a very young writer, he put himself at risk when—to be near Maxim Gorky, his literary hero—he went to live illegally in St. Petersburg, a city outside the Pale of Settlement (the area to which Jews were restricted). What Jew would not have welcomed the demise of a hostile and obscurantist polity that, as late as 1911, tried Mendel Beiliss in a Russian court on a fantastic blood libel charge, and what Jew in a time of government-sanctioned pogroms would not have turned with relief to forces promising to topple the oppressors? In attaching himself to the Bolshevik cause, Babel may have been more zealous than many, but far from aberrant. If the choice were either Czar or Bolshevism, what Jew could choose Czar? (A third possibility, which scores of thousands sought, was escape to America.) But even if one were determined to throw one's lot in with the Revolution, what Jew would go riding with Cossacks?

In 1920 Isaac Babel went riding with Cossacks. It was the third year of the Civil War—Revolutionary Reds versus Czarist Whites; he was twenty-six. Babel was not new to the military. Two years earlier, during the First World War, he had been a volunteer—in the Czar's army—on the Romanian front, where he contracted malaria. In 1919 he fought with the Red Army to secure St. Petersburg against advancing government troops. And in 1920 he joined ROSTA, the Soviet wire service, as a war correspondent for the newspaper *Red Cavalryman*. Poland, newly independent, was pressing eastward, hoping to recover its eighteenth-century borders, while the Bolsheviks, moving west, were furiously promoting the Communist salvation of Polish peasants and workers. The Polish-Soviet War appeared to pit territory against ideology; in reality territory—or, more precisely, the conquest of impoverished villages and towns and their wretched inhabitants—was all that was at stake for either side. Though the Great War was over, the Allies, motivated by fear of the spread of Communism, went to the aid of Poland with equipment and volunteers. (Ultimately the Poles prevailed and the Bolsheviks retreated, between them despoiling whole populations.)

In an era of air battles, Babel was assigned to the First Cavalry Army, a Cossack division led by General Semyon Budyonny. The Cossack image—glinting sabers, pounding hooves—is indelibly fused with Czarist power, but the First Cavalry Army was, perversely, Bolshevik. Stalin was in command of the southern front—the region abutting Poland—and Budyonny was in league with Stalin. Ostensibly, then, Babel found himself among men sympathetic to Marxist doctrine; yet Red Cossacks were no different from White Cossacks: untamed riders, generally illiterate, boorish and brutish, suspicious of ideas of any kind, attracted only to horseflesh, rabid looting, and the quick satisfaction of hunger and lust. "This isn't a Marxist revolution," Babel privately noted; "it's a rebellion of Cossack wild men." Polish and Russian cavalrymen clashing in ditches while warplanes streaked overhead was no more incongruous than the raw sight of Isaac Babel—a writer who had already published short stories praised by Gorky—sleeping in mud with Cossacks.

Lionel Trilling, in a highly nuanced (though partially misinformed) landmark introduction to a 1955 edition of *The Collected Stories of Isaac Babel*—which included the *Red Cavalry* stories—speaks of "the joke of a Jew who is a member of a Cossack regiment." A joke, Trilling explains, because

traditionally the Cossack was the feared and hated enemy of the Jew. . . . The principle of his existence stood in total

> antithesis to the principle of the Jew's existence. The Jew
> conceived of his own ideal character as being intellectu-
> al, pacific, humane. The Cossack was physical, violent,
> without mind or manners . . . the natural and appropriate
> instrument of ruthless oppression.

Yet Trilling supplies another, more glamorous, portrait of the
Cossack, which he terms Tolstoyan: "He was the man as yet
untrammeled by civilization, direct, immediate, fierce. He was
the man of enviable simplicity, the man of the body—the man
who moved with speed and grace." In short, "our fantasy of the
noble savage." And he attributes this view to Babel.

As it turns out, Babel's tenure with Budyonny's men was
more tangled, and more intricately psychological, than Trilling—for whom the problem was tangled and psychological
enough—could have known or surmised. For one thing, Trilling mistakenly believed that Babel's job was that of a supply
officer—i.e., that he was actually a member of the regiment. But
as a correspondent for a news agency (which meant grinding
out propaganda), Babel's position among the troops was from
the start defined as an outsider's, Jew or no. He was there as a
writer. Worse, in the absence of other sources, Trilling fell into
a crucial—and surprisingly naive—second error: he supposed
that the "autobiographical" tales were, in fact, autobiographical.

Babel, Trilling inferred from Babel's stories, "was a Jew
of the ghetto" who "when he was nine years old had seen
his father kneeling before a Cossack captain." He compares
this (fictitious) event to Freud's contemplation of his father's
"having accepted in a pacific way the insult of having his new
fur cap knocked into the mud by a Gentile who shouted at
him, 'Jew, get off the pavement.'" "We might put it," Trilling
concludes, that Babel rode with Budyonny's troops because
he had witnessed his father's humiliation by "a Cossack on a
horse, who said, 'At your service,' and touched his fur cap with
his yellow-gloved hand and politely paid no heed to the mob
looting the Babel store."

There was no Babel store. This scene—the captain with the
yellow glove, the Jew pleading on his knees while the pogrom

rages—is culled from Babel's story "First Love." But it was reinforced for Trilling by a fragmentary memoir, published in 1924,
wherein Babel calls himself "the son of a Jewish shopkeeper."
The truth was that Babel was the son of the class enemy: a well-
off family. His father sold agricultural machinery and owned
a warehouse in a business section of Odessa where numerous
import-export firms were located. In the same memoir Babel
records that because he had no permit allowing him residence
in St. Petersburg, he hid out "in a cellar on Pushkin Street
which was the home of a tormented, drunken waiter." This
was pure fabrication: in actuality Babel was taken in by a highly
respectable engineer and his wife, with whom he was in correspondence. The first invention was to disavow a bourgeois
background in order to satisfy Communist dogma. The second
was a romantic imposture.

It did happen, nevertheless, that the young Babel was witness to a pogrom. He was in no way estranged from Jewish
suffering or sensibility, or, conversely, from the seductive
winds of contemporary Europe. Odessa was modern, bustling,
diverse, cosmopolitan; its very capaciousness stimulated a
certain worldliness and freedom of outlook. Jewish children
were required to study the traditional texts and commentaries,
but they were also sent to learn the violin. Babel was early on
infatuated with Maupassant and Flaubert, and wrote his first
stories in fluent literary French. In his native Russian he lashed
himself mercilessly to the discipline of an original style, the
credo of which was burnished brevity. At the time of his arrest
by the NKVD in 1939—he had failed to conform to Socialist
Realism—he was said to be at work on a Russian translation of
Sholem Aleichem.

Given these manifold intertwinings, it remains odd that
Trilling's phrase for Babel was "a Jew of the ghetto." Trilling
himself had characterized Babel's Odessa as "an eastern Mar-
seilles or Naples," observing that "in such cities the transient,
heterogeneous population dilutes the force of law and tradition,
for good as well as for bad." One may suspect that Trilling's
cultural imagination (and perhaps his psyche as well) was circumscribed by a kind of either/or: *either* worldly sophistication

or the ghetto; and that, in linking Jewish learning solely to the
ghetto, he could not conceive of its association with a broad and
complex civilization. This partial darkening of mind, it seems
to me, limits Trilling's understanding of Babel. An intellectual
who had mastered the essentials of rabbinic literature, Babel
was an educated Jew not "of the ghetto," but of the world. And
not "of both worlds," as the divisive expression has it, but of the
great and variegated map of human thought and experience.

Trilling, after all, in his own youth had judged the world to
be rigorously divided. In 1933, coming upon one of Hemingway's letters, he wrote in his notebook:

> [A] crazy letter, written when he was drunk—self-revealing,
> arrogant, scared, trivial, absurd; yet [I] felt from reading it
> how right such a man is compared to the "good minds" of my
> university life—how he will produce and mean something
> to the world . . . how his life which he could expose without
> dignity and which is anarchic and "childish" is a better life
> than anyone I know could live, and right for his job. And
> how far—far—far—I am going from being a writer.

Trilling envied but could not so much as dream himself into
becoming a version of Hemingway—rifle in one hand and pen
in the other, intellectual Jew taking on the strenuous life; how
much less, then, could he fathom Babel as Cossack. Looking
only to Jewish constriction, what Trilling vitally missed was
this: coiled in the bottommost pit of every driven writer is an
impersonator—protean, volatile, restless and relentless. Trilling
saw only stasis, or, rather, an unalterable consistency of identity:
either lucubrations or daring, never both. But Babel imagined
for himself an identity so fluid that, having lodged with his
civilized friend, the St. Petersburg engineer, it pleased him to
invent a tougher Babel consorting underground with a "tormented, drunken waiter." A drunken waiter would have been
adventure enough—but ah, that Dostoyevskian "tormented"!

"He loved to confuse and mystify people," his daughter
Nathalie wrote of him, after decades spent in search of his
character. Born in 1929, she lived with her mother in Paris,

where her father was a frequent, if raffish, visitor. In 1935 Babel was barred from leaving the Soviet Union, and never again saw his wife and child. Nathalie Babel was ten when Babel was arrested. In 1961 she went to look for traces of her father in Moscow, "where one can still meet people who loved him and continue to speak of him with nostalgia. There, thousands of miles from my own home in Paris, sitting in his living room, in his own chair, drinking from his glass, I felt utterly baffled. Though in a sense I had tracked him down, he still eluded me. The void remained."

In a laudatory reminiscence published in a Soviet literary magazine in 1964—a time when Babel's reputation was undergoing a modicum of "rehabilitation"—Georgy Munblit, a writer who had known Babel as well as anyone, spoke of "this sly, unfaithful, eternally evasive and mysterious Babel"; and though much of this elusiveness was caution in the face of Soviet restriction, a good part of it nevertheless had to do with the thrill of dissimulation and concealment. In a mid-Sixties Moscow speech at a meeting championing Babel's work, Ilya Ehrenburg—the literary Houdini who managed to survive every shift of Stalinlist whim—described Babel as liking to "play the fool and put on romantic airs. He liked to create an atmosphere of mystery about himself; he was secretive and never told anybody where he was going."

Other writers (all of whom had themselves escaped the purges) came forward with recollections of Babel's eccentricities in risky times: Babel as intrepid wanderer; as trickster, rapscallion, ironist; penniless, slippery, living on the edge, off the beaten track, down and out; seduced by the underlife of Paris, bars, whores, cab-drivers, jockeys—all this suggests Orwellian experiment and audacity. Babel relished Villon and Kipling, and was delighted to discover that Rimbaud too was an "adventurer." Amusing and mercurial, "he loved to play tricks on people," according to Lev Nikulin, who was at school with Babel and remembered him "as a bespectacled boy in a rather shabby school coat and a battered cap with a green band and badge depicting Mercury's staff."

Trilling, writing in 1955, had of course no access to

observations such as these; and we are as much in need now
as Trilling was of a valid biography of Babel. Yet it is clear
even from such small evidences and quicksilver portraits that
Babel's connection with the Cossacks was, if not inevitable,
more natural than not; and that Trilling's Freudian notion of
the humilated ghetto child could not have been more off the
mark. For Babel lamp-oil and fearlessness were not antithetical.
He was a man with the bit of recklessness between his teeth.
One might almost ask how a writer so given to disguises and
role-playing could not have put on a Cossack uniform.

"The Rebbe's Son," one of the *Red Cavalry* tales, is explicit
about this fusion of contemplative intellect and phsyical danger.
Ilya, the son of the Zhitomir Rebbe, "the last prince of the
dynasty," is a Red Army soldier killed in battle. The remnants
of his possessions are laid out before the narrator:

> Here everything was dumped together—the warrants of
> the agitator and the commemorative booklets of the Jewish
> poet. Portraits of Lenin and Maimonides lay side by side.
> Lenin's nodulous skull and the tarnished silk of the portraits
> of Maimonides. A strand of female hair had been placed in a
> book of the resolutions of the Sixth Party Congress, and in
> the margins of Communist leaflets swarmed crooked lines
> of ancient Hebrew verse. In a sad and meager rain they fell
> on me—pages of the Song of Songs and revolver cartridges.

Babel was himself drawn to the spaciousness and elasticity of
these unexpected combinations. They held no enigma for him.
But while the Rebbe's son was a kind of double patriot—loyal
to the God of Abraham, Isaac and Jacob, and loyal to a dream
of the betterment of Russia—Babel tended toward both theological and (soon enough) political skepticism. His *amor patriae*
was—passionately—for the Russian mother-tongue. Before the
Stalinist prison clanged shut in 1935, Babel might easily have
gone to live permanently in France, with his wife and daughter.
Yet much as he reveled in French literature and language, he
would not suffer exile from his native Russian. A family can be
replaced, or duplicated; but who can replace or duplicate the

syllables of Pushkin and Tolstoy? And, in fact (though his wife in Paris survived until 1957, and there was no divorce), Babel did take another wife in the Soviet Union, who gave birth to another daughter; a second family was possible. A second language was not. (Only consider what must be the intimate sorrows—even in the shelter of America, even after the demise of Communism—of Czeslaw Milosz, Joseph Brodksy, Norman Manea, and countless other less celebrated literary refugees.) By remaining in the Soviet Union, and refusing finally to bend his art to Soviet directives, Babel sacrificed his life to his language.

It was a language he did not allow to rest. He meant to put his spurs to it, and run it to unexampled leanness. He quoted Pushkin: "precision and brevity." "Superior craftsmanship," Babel told Munblit, "is the art of making your writing as unobtrusive as possible." Ehrenburg recalled a conversation in Madrid with Hemingway, who had just discovered Babel. "I find that Babel's style is even more concise that mine. . . . It shows what can be done," Hemingway marveled. "Even when you've got all the water out of them, you can still clot the curds a little more." Such idiosyncratic experiments in style were hardly congruent with official pressure to honour the ascent of socialism through prescriptive prose about the beauty of collective farming. Babel did not dissent from Party demands; instead he fell mainly into silence, writing in private and publishing almost nothing. His attempts at a play and a filmscript met convulsive Party criticism; the director of the film, an adaptation of a story by Turgenev, was forced into a public apology.

The *Red Cavalry* stories saw print, individually, before 1924. Soviet cultural policies in those years were not yet consolidated; it was a period of postrevolutionary leniency and ferment. Russian modernism was sprouting in the shape of formalism, acmeism, imagism, symbolism; an intellectual and artistic avant-garde flourished. Censorship, which had been endemic to the Czarist regime, was reintroduced in 1922, but the restraints were loose. Despite a program condemning elitism, the early Soviet leadership, comprising a number of intellectuals—Lenin, Bukharin, Trotsky—recognized that serious literature could not be wholly entrusted to the sensibilities of

Party bureaucrats. By 1924, then, Babel found himself not only famous, but eligible eventually for Soviet rewards: an apartment in Moscow, a dacha in the country, a car and chauffeur.

Yet he was increasingly called on to perform (and conform) by the blunter rulers of a darkening repression: why was he not writing in praise of New Soviet Man? Little by little a perilous mist gathered around Babel's person; though his privileges were not revoked (he was at his dacha on the day of his arrest), he began to take on a certain pariah status. When a leftist Congress for the Defense of Culture and Peace met in Paris, for example, Babel was deliberately omitted from the Soviet delegation, and was grudgingly allowed to attend only after the French organizers brought their protests to the Soviet Embassy.

Certain manuscripts he was careful not to expose to anyone. Among these was the remarkable journal he had kept, from June to September 1920, of the actions of Budyonny's First Cavalry Army in eastern Poland. Because it was missing from the papers seized by the secret police at the dacha and in his Moscow flat, the manuscript escaped destruction, and came clandestinely into the possession of Babel's (second) wife only in the 1950's. Ehrenburg was apparently the journal's first influential reader, though very likely he did not see it until the 1960's when he mentioned it publicly, and evidently spontaneously, in his rehabilitation speech:

> I have been comparing the diary of the Red Cavalry with the stories. He scarcely changed any names, the events are all practically the same, but everything is illuminated with a kind of wisdom. He is saying: this is how it was. This is how the people were—they did terrible things and they suffered, they played tricks on others and they died. He made his stories out of the facts and phrases hastily jotted down in his notebook.

It goes without saying that the flatness of this essentially evasive summary does almost no justice to an astonishing historical record set down with godlike prowess in a prose of frightening clarity. In Russia the complete text of the journal finally appeared in 1990. Yale University Press brings it to us now under the title *Isaac Babel: 1920 Diary*, in an electrifying translation, accompanied by a first-rate (and indispensable) introduction. (It ought to be added that an informative introduction can be found also in the Penguin *Collected Stories*; but the reader's dependence on such piecemeal discussions only underscores the irritating absence of a formal biography.) In 1975 Ardis Publishers, specialists in Russian studies, made available the first English translation of excerpts from the journal (*Isaac Babel: Forgotten Prose*). That such a manuscript existed had long been known in the Soviet Union, but there was plainly no chance of publication; Ehrenburg, in referring to it, was discreet about its contents.

The *Diary* may count, then, as a kind of secret document; certainly as a suppressed one. But it is "secret" in another sense as well. Though it served as raw material for the *Red Cavalry* stories, Babel himself, in transforming private notes into daring fiction, was less daring than he might have been. He was, in fact, circumspect and selective. One can move from the notes to the stories without surprise—or put it that the surprise is in the masterliness and shock of a ripe and radical style. Still, as Ehrenburg reported, "the events are all practically the same," and what is in the *Diary* is in the stories.

But one cannot begin with the stories and then move to the journal without the most acute recognition of what has been, substantively and for the most part, shut out of the fiction. And what has been shut out is the calamity (to say it in the most general way) of Jewish fate in Eastern Europe. The *Diary* records how the First Cavalry Army, and Babel with it, went storming through the little Jewish towns of Galicia, in Poland—towns that had endured the Great War, with many of their young men serving in the Polish army, only to be decimated by pogroms immediately afterward, at the hands of the Poles themselves. And immediately after *that*, the invasion of the Red Cossacks. The Yale edition of the *Diary* supplies maps showing the route of Budyonny's troops; the resonant names of these places, rendered half-romantic through the mystical tales of their legendary hasidic saints, rise up with the nauseous

familiarity of their deaths: Brody, Dubno, Zhitomir, Belz,
Chelm, Zamosc, etc. Only two decades after the Red Cossacks
stampeded through them, their Jewish populations fell prey to
the Germans and were destroyed. Riding and writing, writing
and riding, Babel saw it all: saw it like a seer. "Ill-fated Galicia,
ill-fated Jews," he wrote. "Can it be," he wrote, "that ours is
the century in which they perish?"

True: everything that is in the stories is in the *Diary*—priest,
painter, widow, guncart, soldier, prisoner; but the heart of
the *Diary* remains secreted in the *Diary*. When all is said and
done—and much is said and done in these blistering pages:
pillaged churches, ruined synagogues, wild Russians, beaten
Poles, mud, horses, hunger, looting, shooting—Babel's journal
is a Jewish lamentation: a thing the Soviet system could not tolerate, and Ehrenburg was too prudent to reveal. The merciless
minds that snuffed the identities of the murdered at Babi Yar
would hardly sanction Babel's whole and bloody truths.

Nor did Babel himself publicly sanction them. The *Red
Cavalry* narratives include six stories (out of thirty-five) that
touch on the suffering of Jews; the headlong *Diary* contains
scores. An act of authorial self-censorship, and not only because
Babel was determined to be guarded. Impersonation, or call
it reckless play, propelled him at all points. The *Diary* can
muse: "The Slavs—the manure of history?"—but Babel came
to the Cossacks disguised as a Slav, having assumed the name
K. L. Lyutov, the name he assigns also to his narrator. And in
the *Diary* itself, encountering terrified Polish Jews, he again
and again steers them away from the knowledge that rides in
his marrow, and fabricates deliberate Revolutionary fairy tales
(his word): he tells his trembling listeners how "everything's
changing for the better—my usual system—miraculous things
are happening in Russia—express trains, free food for children,
theaters, the International. They listen with delight and disbelief. I think—you'll have your diamond-studded sky, everything
and everyone will be turned upside down and inside out for the
umpteenth time, and [I] feel sorry for them."

"My usual system": perhaps it is kind to scatter false consolations among the doomed. Or else it is not kindness at all, merely

a writer's mischief or a rider's diversion—the tormented mice of Galicia entertained by a cat in Cossack dress. Sometimes he is recognized as a Jew (once by a child), and then he half-lies and explains that he has a Jewish mother. But mainly he is steadfast in the pretense of being Lyutov. And nervy: the *Diary* begins on June 3, in Zhitomir, and on July 12, one day before Babel's twenty-sixth birthday, he notes: "My first ride on horseback." In no time at all he is, at least on horseback, like all the others: a skilled and dauntless trooper. "The horse galloped well," he says on that first day. Enchanted, proud, he looks around at his companions: "red flags, a powerful, well-knit body of men, confident commanders, calm and experienced eyes of topknotted Cossack fighting men, dust, silence, order, brass band." But moments later the calm and experienced eyes are searching out plunder in the neat cottage of an immigrant Czech family, "all good people." "I took nothing, although I could have," the new horseman comments. "I'll never be a real Budyonny man."

The real Budyonny men are comely, striking, stalwart. Turning off a highway, Babel catches sight of "the brigades suddenly appear[ing], inexplicable beauty, an awesome force advancing." Another glimpse: "Night . . . horses are quietly snorting, they're all Kuban Cossacks here, they eat together, sleep together, a splendid silent comradeship . . . they sing songs that sound like church music in lusty voices, their devotion to horses, beside each man a little heap—saddle, bridle, ornamental saber, greatcoat, I sleep in the midst of them."

Babel is small, his glasses are small and round, he sets down secret sentences. And meanwhile his dispatches, propaganda screeches regularly published in *Red Cavalryman*, have a different tone: "Soldiers of the Red Army, finish them off! Beat down harder on the opening covers of their stinking graves!" And: "That is what they are like, our heroic nurses! Caps off to the nurses! Soldiers and commanders, show respect to the nurses!" (In the *Diary* the dubious propagandist writes satirically, "Opening of the Second Congress of the Third International, unification of the peoples finally realized, now all is clear . . . We shall advance into Europe and conquer the world.")

And always there is cruelty, and always there are the Jews.

"Most of the rabbis have been exterminated." "The Jewish cemetery . . . hundreds of years old, gravestones have toppled over . . . overgrown with grass, it has seen Khmelnitsky, now Budyonny . . . everything repeats itself, now that whole story—Poles, Cossacks, Jews—is repeating itself with stunning exactitude, the only new element is Communism." "They all say they're fighting for justice and they all loot." "Life is loathsome, murderers, it's unbearable, baseness and crime." "I ride along with them, begging the men not to massacre prisoners . . . I couldn't look at their faces, they bayoneted some, shot others, bodies covered by corpses, they strip one man while they're shooting another, groans, screams, death rattles." "We are destroyers . . . we move like a whirlwind, like a stream of lava, hated by everyone, life shatters, I am at a huge, never-ending service for the dead . . . the sad senselessness of my life."

The Jews: "The Poles ransacked the place, then the Cossacks." "Hatred for the Poles is unanimous. They have looted, tortured, branded the pharmacist with a red-hot iron, put needles under his nails, pulled out his hair, all because somebody shot at a Polish officer." "The Jews ask me to use my influence to save them from ruin, they are being robbed of food and goods . . . The cobbler had looked forward to Soviet rule—and what he sees are Jew-baiters and looters . . . Organized looting of a stationer's shop, the proprietor in tears, they tear up everything . . . When night comes the whole town will be looted—everybody knows it."

The Jews at the hands of the Poles: "A pogrom . . . a naked, barely breathing prophet of an old man, an old woman butchered, a child with fingers chopped off, many people still breathing, stench of blood, everything turned upside down, chaos, a mother sitting over her sabered son, an old woman lying twisted up like a pretzel, four people in one hovel, filth, blood under a black beard, just lying there in the blood."

The Jews at the hands of the Bolsheviks: "Our men non-chalantly walking around looting whenever possible, stripping mangled corpses. The hatred is the same, the Cossacks just the same, it's nonsense to think one army is different from another. The life of these little towns. There's no salvation. Everyone destroys them." "Our men were looting last night, tossed out the Torah scrolls in the synagogue and took the velvet covers for saddlecloths. The military commissar's dispatch rider examines phylacteries, wants to take the straps." The *Diary* mourns, "What a mighty and marvelous life of a nation existed here. The fate of Jewry."

And then: "I am an outsider." And again: "I don't belong, I'm all alone, we ride on . . . five minutes after our arrival the looting starts, women struggling, weeping and wailing, it's unbearable, I can't stand these never-ending horrors . . . [I] snatch a flatcake out of the hands of a peasant woman's little boy." He does this mechanically, and without compunction.

"How we eat," he explains. "Red troops arrive in a village, ransack the place, cook, stoves crackling all night, the householders' daughters have a hard time" (a comment we will know how to interpret). Babel grabs the child's flatcake—a snack on the fly, as it were—on August 3. On July 25, nine days earlier, he and a riding companion, Prishchepa, a loutish syphilitic illiterate, have burst into a pious Jewish house in a town called Demidovka. It is the Sabbath, when lighting a fire is forbidden; it is also the eve of the Ninth of Av, a somber fast day commemorating the destruction of the Temple in Jerusalem. Prishchepa demands fried potatoes. The dignified mother, a flock of daughters in white stockings, a scholarly son, are all petrified; on the Sabbath, they protest, they cannot dig potatoes, and besides, the fast begins at sundown. "Fucking Yids," Prishchepa yells; so the potatoes are dug, the fire to cook them is lit.

Babel, a witness to this anguish, says nothing. "I keep quiet, because I'm a Russian"—will Prishchepa discover that Lyutov is only another Yid? "We eat like oxen, fried potatoes and five tumblersful of coffee each. We sweat, they keep serving us, all this is terrible, I tell them fairy tales about Bolshevism." Night comes, the mother sits on the floor and sobs, the son chants the liturgy for the Ninth of Av—Jeremiah's Lamentations: "they eat dung, their maidens are ravished, their menfolk killed, Israel subjugated." Babel hears and understands every Hebrew word. "Demidovka, night, Cossacks," he sums it up, "all just as

ESSAYS

it was when the Temple was destroyed. I go out to sleep in the yard, stinking and damp."

And there he is, New Soviet Man: stinking, a sewer of fairy tales, an unbeliever—and all the same complicit. Nathalie Babel said of her father that nothing "could shatter his feeling that he belonged to Russia and that he had to share the fate of his countrymen. What in so many people would have produced only fear and terror, awakened in him a sense of duty and a kind of blind heroism." In the brutal light of the *Diary*—violation upon violation—it is hard not to resist this point of view. Despair and an abyss of cynicism do not readily accord with a sense of duty; and whether or not Babel's travels with the Cossacks—and with Bolshevism altogether—deserve to be termed heroic, he was anything but blind. He saw, he saw, and he saw.

It may be that the habit of impersonation, the habit of deception, the habit of the mask, will in the end lead a man to become what he impersonates. Or it may be that the force of "I am an outsider" overwhelms the secret gratification of having got rid of a fixed identity. In any case, the *Diary* tells no lies. These scenes in a journal, linked by commas quicker than human breath, run like rapids through a gorge—on one side the unrestraint of violent men, on the other the bleaker freedom of unbelonging. Each side is subversive of the other; and still they embrace the selfsame river.

To venture yet another image, Babel's *Diary* stands as a tragic masterwork of breakneck cinematic "dailies"—those raw, unedited rushes that expose the director to himself. If Trilling, who admitted to envy of the milder wilderness that was Hemingway, had read Babel's *Diary*—what then? And who, in our generation, should read the *Diary*? Novelists and poets, of course; specialists in Russian literature, obviously; American innocents who define the world of the Twenties by jazz, flappers, and Fitzgerald. And also: all those who protested Claude Lanzmann's film *Shoah* as unfair to the psyche of the Polish countryside; but, most of all, the cruelly ignorant children of the Left who still believe that the Marxist Utopia requires for its realization only a more favorable venue, and another go.

No one knows when or exactly how Babel perished. Some

suppose he was shot immediately after the NKVD picked him up and brought him to Moscow's Lyubanka prison, on May 16, 1939. Others place the date of his murder in 1941, following months of torture.* More than fifty years later, as if the writer were sending forth phantoms of his first and last furies, Babel's youthful *Diary* emerges. What it attests to above all is not simply that fairy tales can kill—who doesn't understand this?—but that Bolshevism was lethal in its very cradle.

Which is just what S., my ironical Muscovite cousin, found so pathetically funny when, laughing at our American stupidity, she went home to Communism's graveyard.

---

* But a letter from Robert Conquest, dated May 15, 1995, offers the following: "Babel's fate is in fact known. Arrested on 16 May 1939, he was subjected to three days and nights of intensive interrogation on 29–31 May, at the end of which he confessed. At various interrogations over the year he withdrew that part of his confession that incriminated other writers. At his secret trial on 26 January 1940, he pled not guilty on all counts. The main charges were of Trotskyism; espionage for Austria and France (the latter on behalf of André Malraux); and involvement in a terrorist plot against Stalin and Voroshilov by former NKVD chief Nikolai Yezhov, whose wife Babel knew. He was shot at 1:40 A.M. the next day."

Dostoyevsky's Unabomber

I.

SOON AFTER DAWN on a very cold winter morning in 1849, fifteen Russian criminals, in groups of three, were led before a firing squad. They were all insurgents against the despotism of Czar Nicholas I. They were mostly educated men, idealists in pursuit of a just society. They felt no remorse. Several were professed atheists. All were radicals. A priest carrying a cross and a Bible accompanied them. The first three were handed white gowns and shapeless caps and ordered to put these on; then they were tied to posts. The rest waited their turn. Each man in his own way prepared to die. The sun was beginning to brighten; the firing squad took aim. At just that moment there was a signal—a roll of drums—and the rifles were lowered. A galloping horseman announced a reprieve. Although the condemned were unaware of it, the execution was staged, and the reprieve was designed to demonstrate the merciful heart of the Czar. Instead of being shot, the criminals were to be transported in shackles to a Siberian penal colony.

One of the men went permanently mad. Another, fifteen years afterward, wrote *Crime and Punishment*, an impassioned assault on exactly the kind of radical faith that had brought its author to face the Czar's riflemen that day. It was a work almost in the nature of double jeopardy: as if Fyodor Dostoyevsky in middle age—a defender of the Czar, the enemy of revolutionary socialism—were convicting and punishing his younger self yet again for the theories the mature novelist had come to abhor.

2.

A NEW TYPE of crime is on the American mind—foreign, remote, metaphysical, even literary; and radically different from what we are used to. Street crime, drunken crime, drug-inspired crime, crimes of passion, greed, revenge, crimes against children, gangster crime, white-collar crime, break-ins, car thefts, holdups, shootings—these are familiar, and to a degree nearly expected. They shake us up without disorienting us. They belong to our civilization; they are the darker signals of home. "Our" crime has usually been local—the stalker, the burglar, the mugger lurking in a doorway. Even Jeffrey Dahmer, the cannibal sadist who kept boys' body parts in his kitchen refrigerator, is not so very anomalous in the context of what can happen in ordinary neighborhoods—a little girl imprisoned in an underground cage; children tormented, starved, beaten to death; newborns bludgeoned; battered women, slain wives, mutilated husbands. Domesticity gone awry.

All that is recognizable and homespun. What feels alien to America is the philosophical criminal of exceptional intelligence and humanitarian purpose who is driven to commit murder out of an uncompromising idealism. Such a type has always seemed a literary construct of a particular European political coloration (*The Secret Agent*, *The Princess Casamassima*), or else has hinted at ideologies so removed from tame Republicans and Democrats as to be literally outlandish. Then came the mysterious depredations of the Unabomber. Until the melodramatic publication of his manifesto in major newspapers, the Unabomber remained an unpredictable riddle, unfathomable, sans name or habitation. In garrulous print his credo revealed him to be a visionary. His dream was of a green and pleasant land liberated from the curse of technological proliferation. The technical élites were his targets: computer wizards like Professor David Gelernter of Yale, a thinker in pursuit of artificial intelligence. Maimed by a package bomb, Gelernter escaped death; others did not.

In the storm of interpretation that followed the Unabomber's public declaration of principles, he was often mistaken for

a kind of contemporary Luddite. This was a serious misno-
mer. The nineteenth-century Luddites were hand weavers
who rioted against the introduction of mechanical looms in
England's textile industry; they smashed the machines to protect their livelihoods. They were not out to kill, nor did they
promulgate romantic theories about the wholesome superiority
of hand looms. They were selfish, ruthlessly pragmatic, and
societally unreasonable. By contrast, Theodore Kaczynski—
the Unabomber—is above all a calculating social reasoner and
messianic utopian. His crimes, for which he was found guilty
as charged, were intended to restore us to cities and landscapes
clear of digital complexities; he meant to clean the American
slate of its accumulated technostructural smudges. At the same
time, we can acknowledge him to have been selfless and pure,
loyal and empathic, the sort of man who befriends, without con-
descension, an uneducated and impoverished Mexican laborer.
It is easy to think of the Unabomber, living out his principles
in his pollution-free mountain cabin, as a Thoreauvian philosopher of advanced environmentalism. The philosopher is
one with the murderer. The Napoleonic world-improver is one
with the humble hermit of the wilderness.

In the Unabomber, America has at last brought forth its
own Raskolnikov—the appealing, appalling, and disturbingly
visionary murderer of *Crime and Punishment*, Dostoyevsky's
masterwork of 1866. But the Unabomber is not the only
ideological criminal (though he may be the most intellectual)
to burst out of remoteness and fantasy onto unsuspecting native
grounds. It was a political conviction rooted in anti-government
ideas of liberty suppressed that fueled the deadly bombing of a
Federal building in Oklahoma City. God's will directed the
bombing of the World Trade Center, and the Muslim zealots who devised the means are world-improvers obedient to
the highest good; so are the bombers of abortion clinics. The
Weathermen of the sixties, who bombed banks and shot police
in order to release "Amerika" from the tyranny of a democratic polity, are close ideological cousins of the Russian nihilists
who agitated against Alexander II, the liberalizing Czar of a
century before. That celebrated nineteen-sixties mantra—to

make an omelet you need to break eggs—had its origin not in an affinity for violence, but in the mouth-watering lure of the humanitarian omelet. It was only the gastronomic image that was novel. In the Russian sixties, one hundred years earlier—in 1861, the very year Alexander II freed the serfs—a radical young critic named Dimitry Pisarev called for striking "right and left" and announced, "What resists the blow is worth keeping; what flies to pieces is rubbish." Here was the altruistic bomber's dogma, proclaimed in the pages of a literary journal—and long before *The New York Review of Books* published on its front cover a diagram of how to construct a Molotov cocktail.

Like the Unabomber, Raskolnikov is an intellectual who publishes a notorious essay expounding his ideas about men and society. Both are obscure loners. Both are alienated from a concerned and affectionate family. Both are tender toward outcasts and the needy. Both are élitists. Both are idealists. Both are murderers. Contemporary America, it seems, has finally caught up with czarist Russia's most argumentative novelist.

And in *Crime and Punishment* Dostoyevsky was feverishly pursuing an argument. It was an argument against the radicals who were dominant among Russian intellectuals in the eighteen-sixties, many of them espousing nihilist views. In the universities especially, revolutionary commotion was on the rise. Yet there was an incongruity in the timing of all these calls for violent subversion. St. Petersburg was no longer the seat of the old Czar of the repressive eighteen-forties, the tyrannical Nicholas I, against whose cruelties convulsive outrage might be justly presumed. Paradoxically, under that grim reign even the most fiery radicals were at heart gradualists who modeled their hopes on Western reformist ideas. By the incendiary sixties, the throne was held by Nicholas's moderate son and successor, whose numerous democratic initiatives looked to be nudging Russia toward something that might eventually resemble a constitutional monarchy. The younger revolutionary theorists would have none of it. It was incomplete; it was too slow. Liberalism, they roared, was the enemy of revolution, and would impede a more definitive razing of evil.

The first installments of *Crime and Punishment* had just begun to appear in *The Russian Messenger,* a Slavophile periodical, when a student revolutionary made an attempt on the life of the Czar as he was leaving the gardens of the Winter Palace to enter his carriage. The government responded with a draconian crackdown on the radicals. "You know," Dostoyevsky wrote cuttingly to his publisher in the wake of these events, "they are completely convinced that on a *tabula rasa* they will immediately construct a paradise." But he went on to sympathize with "our poor little defenseless boys and girls" and "their enthusiasm for the good and their purity of heart." So many "have become nihilists so purely, so unselfishly, in the name of honor, truth, and genuine usefulness! You know they are helpless against these stupidities, and take them for perfection." And though in the same letter he spoke of "the powerful, extraordinary, sacred union of the Czar with the people," he objected to the increase in repression. "But how can nihilism be fought without freedom of speech?" he asked.

This mixture of contempt for the radicals and solicitude for their misguided, perplexed, and perplexing humanity led to the fashioning of Raskolnikov. Pisarev striking right and left was one ingredient. Another was the appeal of self-sacrificial idealism. And a third was the literary mode through which Dostoyevsky combined and refined the tangled elements of passion, brutishness, monomaniacal principle, mental chaos, candor, mockery, fury, compassion, generosity—and two brutal ax-murders. All these contradictory elements course through Raskolnikov with nearly a Joycean effect; but if stream of consciousness flows mutely and uninterruptedly, assimilating the outer world into the inner, Raskolnikov's mind—and Dostoyevsky's method—is zigzag and bumpy, given to rebellious and unaccountable alterations of purpose. Raskolnikov is without restraint—not only as an angry character in a novel, but as a reflection of Dostoyevsky himself, who was out to expose the entire spectrum of radical thought engulfing the writers and thinkers of St. Petersburg.

This may be why Raskolnikov is made to rush dizzyingly from impulse to impulse, from kindliness to withdrawal to lashing out, and from one underlying motive to another—a disorderliness at war with his half-buried and equivocal conscience. Only at the start is he seen, briefly, to be deliberate and in control. Detached, reasoning it out, Raskolnikov robs and murders a pawnbroker whom he has come to loathe, an unpleasant and predatory old woman alone and helpless in her flat. He hammers her repeatedly with the heavy handle of an ax:

> Her thin hair, pale and streaked with gray, was thickly greased as usual, plaited into a ratty braid and tucked under a piece of horn comb that stuck up at the back of her head . . . he struck her again and yet again with all his strength, both times with the butt-end, both times on the crown of the head. Blood poured out as from an overturned glass.

Unexpectedly, the old woman's simple-minded sister just then enters the flat; she is disposed of even more horribly: "The blow landed directly on the skull, with the sharp edge, and immediately split the whole upper part of the forehead, almost to the crown."

The second slaying is an unforeseen by-product of the first. The first is the rational consequence of forethought. What is the nature—the thesis—of this forethought? Shortly before the murder, Raskolnikov overhears a student in a tavern speculating about the pawnbroker: she is "rich as a Jew," and has willed all her money to the Church. "A hundred, a thousand good deeds and undertakings . . . could be arranged and set going by the money that old woman has doomed to the monastery!" exclaims the student.

> Hundreds, maybe thousands of lives put right; dozens of families saved from destitution, from decay, from ruin, from depravity, from the venereal hospitals—all on her money. Kill her and take her money, so that afterwards with its help you can devote yourself to the service of all mankind and the common cause. . . . One death for hundreds of lives— it's simple arithmetic! And what does the life of this stupid,

consumptive, and wicked old crone mean in the general
balance? No more than the life of a louse, a cockroach.

Startled by this polemic, Raskolnikov admits to himself that
"*exactly the same thoughts* had just been conceived in his own
head"—though not as harmless theoretical bombast.

The theory in Raskolnikov's head—Benthamite utilitarianism, the greatest good for the greatest number, with its
calibrated notions of what is useful and what is expendable—
had been current for at least a decade among the Westernizing
majority of the Russian intelligentsia, especially the literati of
the capital. In supplying Bentham with an ax, Dostoyevsky
thought to carry out the intoxications of the utilitarian doctrine as far as its principles would go: brutality and bloodletting
would reveal the poisonous fruit of a political philosophy based
on reason alone.

A fiercely sardonic repudiation of that philosophy—some of
it in the vocabulary of contemporary American controversy—
is entrusted to Raskolnikov's affectionate and loyal comrade,
Razumikhin:

> It started with the views of the socialists. . . . Crime is a
> protest against the abnormality of the social set-up—that
> alone and nothing more, no other causes are admitted—
> but nothing! . . . With them one is always a "victim of the
> environment"—and nothing else! . . . If society itself is
> normally set up, all crimes will at once disappear, because
> there will be no reason for protesting. . . . Nature isn't taken
> into account, nature is driven out, nature is not supposed
> to be! . . . On the contrary, a social system, coming out of
> some mathematical head, will at once organize the whole
> of mankind and instantly make it righteous and sinless. . . .
> And it turns out in the end that they've reduced everything
> to mere brickwork and the layout of corridors and rooms in
> a phalanstery!

The phalanstery, a cooperative commune, was the brain-
child of Charles Fourier, who, along with the political theorist

Saint-Simon (and well before Marx), was an enduring influence on the Francophile Russian radical intelligentsia. But Razumikhin's outcry against the utopian socialists who idealize the life of the commune and fantasize universal harmony is no more than a satiric rap on the knuckles. Dostoyevsky is after a bloodier and more threatening vision—nihilism in its hideously perfected form. This is the ideological cloak he next throws over Raskolnikov; it is Raskolnikov's manifesto as it appears in his article. The "extraordinary man," Raskolnikov declaims, has the right to "step over certain obstacles" in order to fulfill a mission that is "salutary for the whole of mankind."

> In my opinion, if, as the result of certain combinations, Kepler's or Newton's discoveries could become known to people in no other way than by sacrificing the lives of one, or ten, or a hundred or more people who were hindering the discovery, or standing as an obstacle in its path, then Newton would have the right, and it would even be his duty . . . *to remove* those ten or a hundred people, in order to make his discoveries known to all mankind.

Every lawgiver or founder of a new idea, he goes on, has always been a criminal—"all of them to a man . . . from the fact alone that in giving a new law they thereby violated the old one . . . and they certainly did not stop at shedding blood either, if it happened that blood . . . could help them." Such extraordinary men—Lycurgus, Solon, Napoleon—call for "the destruction of the present in the name of the better," and will lead the world toward a new Jerusalem.

To which Razumikhin, recoiling, responds: "You do finally permit bloodshed *in all conscience*." And just here, in the turbulence of Razumikhin's revelation—and prefiguring Sakharov, Solzhenitsyn, and Sharansky—Dostoyevsky makes his case for the dismantling of the Soviet state half a century before the revolutionary convulsion that brought it into being.

3.

YET THE MAMMOTH irony of Dostoyevsky's life remains: the
writer who excoriated the radical theorists, who despised the
nihilist revolutionaries, who wrote novel after novel to defy
them, once belonged to their company.

It is easy to dislike him, and not because the spectacle of
a self-accusing apostate shocks. He ended as a Slavophile
religious believer; but in his twenties he was what he bitterly
came to scorn—a Westernizing Russian liberal. Nevertheless
a certain nasty consistency ruled. At all times he was bigoted and xenophobic: he had an irrational hatred of Germans
and Poles, and his novels are speckled with anti-Semitism. He
attacked Roman Catholicism as the temporal legacy of a pagan
empire, while extolling Russian Orthodoxy. He was an obsessive and deluded gambler scheming to strike it rich at the snap
of a finger: he played madly at the roulette tables of Europe,
and repeatedly reduced himself and his pregnant young second
wife to actual privation. Escaping debtors' prison in Russia, he
was compelled for years to wander homelessly and wretchedly
through Germany and Switzerland. In Wiesbaden he borrowed
fifty thalers from Turgenev and took ten years to repay him.
He held the rigidly exclusionary blood-and-soil tenet that the
future of civilization lay with Russia alone. He was seriously
superstitious and had a silly trust in omens and dreams. He was
irritable, sometimes volcanically so, and inordinately vain. And
if all these self-inflicted debilities of character were not ugly
enough, he suffered from a catastrophic innate debility: he was
subject, without warning, to horrifying epileptic seizures in a
period when there were no medical controls.

Though not quite without warning. Dostoyevsky's fits were
heralded by a curious surge of ecstasy—an "aura" indistinguishable from religious exaltation. He underwent his first seizure,
he reported, on Easter morning in 1865, when he was forty-four
years old: "Heaven had come down to earth and swallowed me.
I really grasped God and was penetrated by Him." But there
may have been unidentified earlier attacks, different in kind.
At the age of ten he experienced an auditory hallucination; he

thought he heard a voice cry "A wolf is on the loose!" and was comforted by a kindly serf who belonged to his father.

Later fits uniformly triggered the divine penumbra. He was well prepared for it. From childhood he had been saturated in a narrow household piety not unlike the unquestioning devoutness of the illiterate Russian peasant. Prayers were recited before icons; a clergyman came to give lessons. The Gospels were read, and the *Acta Martyrum*—the lives of the saints—with their peculiarly Russian emphasis on passive suffering. No Sunday or religious holiday went unobserved, on the day itself and at vespers the evening before. Rituals were punctiliously kept up. Dostoyevsky's father, a former army doctor on the staff of a hospital for the poor outside Moscow, frequently led his family on excursions to the great onion-domed Kremlin cathedrals, where religion and nationalism were inseparable. Every spring, Dostoyevsky's mother took the children on a pilgrimage to the Monastery of St. Sergey, sixty miles from Moscow, where they knelt among mobs of the faithful before an imposing silver reliquary said to contain the saint's miraculous remains. None of this was typical of the Russian gentry of the time. Neither Tolstoy nor Turgenev had such an upbringing. Joseph Frank, Dostoyevsky's superb and exhaustive biographer, explains why. "Most upper-class Russians," he recounts, "would have shared the attitude exemplified in Herzen's anecdote about his host at a dinner party who, when asked whether he was serving Lenten dishes out of personal conviction, replied that it was 'simply and solely for the sake of the servants.' "

There is speculation that Dostoyevsky's father may himself have had a mild form of epilepsy: he was gloomy, moody, and unpredictably explosive, a martinet who drank too much and imposed his will on everyone around him. In his youth he had completed his studies at a seminary for non-monastic clergy, a low caste, but went on instead to pursue medicine, and eventually elevated himself to the status of the minor nobility. His salary was insufficient and the family was not well off, despite the doctor's inheritance of a small and scrubby estate, along with its "baptized property"—the serfs attached to the land. When Dostoyevsky was sixteen, his father dispatched him and his older brother Mikhail, both of whom had literary ambitions, to the Academy of Military Engineers in St. Petersburg, in preparation for government careers. But the doctor's plan for his sons came to nothing. Less than two years later, in a season of drought, bad crops, and peasant resentment, Dostoyevsky was informed that his father had been found dead on the estate, presumably strangled by his serfs. Killings of this kind were not uncommon. In a famous letter to Gogol (the very letter that would ultimately send Dostoyevsky before the firing squad), the radical critic Vissarion Belinsky wrote that the Czar was "well aware of what landowners do with their peasants and how many throats of the former are cut every year by the latter."

Freed from engineering (and from a despotic father), Dostoyevsky went flying into the heart of St. Petersburg's literary life. It was the hugely influential Belinsky who catapulted him there. Dostoyevsky's first novel, *Poor Folk*—inspired by the social realism of Balzac, Victor Hugo, and George Sand, and published in 1846—was just the sort of fiction Belinsky was eager to promote. "Think of it," he cried, "it's the first attempt at a social novel we've had." Belinsky was a volatile man of movements—movements he usually set off himself. He was also quickly excitable: he had leaped from art-for-art's-sake to a kind of messianic socialism (with Jesus as chief socialist) to blatant atheism. In literature he espoused an ardent naturalism, and saw Dostoyevsky as its avatar. He instantly proclaimed the new writer to be a genius, made him famous overnight, and admitted him, at twenty-four, into St. Petersburg's most coveted intellectual circle, Belinsky's own "pléiade." Turgenev was already a member. The talk was socialist and fervent, touching on truth and justice, science and atheism, and, most heatedly, on the freeing of the serfs. Here Christianity was not much more than a historical metaphor, a view Dostoyevsky only briefly entered into; but he was fiery on the issue of human chattel.

Success went to his head. "Everywhere an unbelievable esteem, a passionate curiosity about me," he bragged to his brother. "Everyone considers me some sort of prodigy. . . . I am now almost drunk with my own glory." The pléiade responded to this posturing at first with annoyance and then with rough ribbing. Belinsky kept out of it, but Turgenev took off after the young prodigy with a scathing parody. Dostoyevsky walked out, humiliated and enraged, and never returned. "They are all scoundrels and eaten up with envy," he fumed. He soon gravitated to another socialist discussion group, which met on Friday nights at the home of Mikhail Petrashevsky, a twenty-six-year-old aristocrat. Petrashevsky had accumulated a massive library of political works forbidden by the censors, and was even less tolerant of Christianity than the pléiade: for him Jesus was "the well-known demagogue." To improve the miserable living conditions of the peasants on his land, Petrashevsky had a commodious communal dormitory built for them, with every amenity provided. They all moved in, and the next day burned down the master's paternalistic utopia. Undaunted, Petrashevsky continued to propagandize for his ideas: the end of serfdom and censorship, and the reform of the courts. His commitment was to gradualism, but certain more impatient members of the Petrashevsky circle quietly formed a secret society dedicated to an immediate and deeply perilous activism.

It was with these that Dostoyevsky aligned himself; he joined a scheme to print and disseminate the explosive manifesto in the form of the letter to Gogol, which Belinsky had composed a year or so earlier, protesting the enslavement of the peasants. Russia, Belinsky wrote, "presents the dire spectacle of a country where men traffic in men, without ever having the excuse so insidiously exploited by the American plantation owners who claim that the Negro is not a man." Dostoyevsky gave an impressive reading of this document at one of Petrashevsky's Friday nights. His audience erupted into an uproar; there were yells of "That's it! That's it!" A government spy, unrecognized, took notes, and at four in the morning Dostoyevsky's bedroom was invaded by the Czar's secret police. He was arrested as a revolutionary conspirator; he was twenty-seven years old.

Nicholas I took a malicious interest in the punishment for this crime against the state—the Czar *was* the state—and personally ordered the mock execution, the last-minute reprieve, the transport to Siberia. Dostoyevsky's sentence was originally eight years; he served four at forced labor in a prison camp at

Omsk and the rest in an army regiment. In Siberia, after his
release from the camp, he married for the first time—a tumultuous widow with worsening tuberculosis. His own affliction
worsened; seizure followed on seizure. For the remainder of his
life he would not be free of the anguish of fits. He feared he
would die while in their grip.

The moment of cataclysmic terror before the firing squad
never left him. He was not so much altered as strangely—almost
mystically—restored: restored to what he had felt as a child,
kneeling with his mother at the reliquary of St. Sergey. He
spoke circumspectly of "the regeneration of my convictions."
The only constant was his hatred of the institution of serfdom—but to hate serfdom was not to love peasants, and when
he began to live among peasant convicts (political prisoners
were not separated from the others), he found them degraded and savage, with a malignant hostility toward the gentry
thrown into their midst. The agonies of hard labor, the filth,
the chains, the enmity, the illicit drunkenness, his own nervous
disorders—all these assailed him, and he suffered in captivity
from a despondency nearly beyond endurance.

And then—in a metamorphosis akin to the Ancient Mari-
ner's sudden love for the repulsive creatures of the sea—he was
struck by what can only be called a conversion experience. In
the twisted and branded faces of the peasant convicts—men
much like those who may have murdered his father—he saw
a divine illumination; he saw the true Russia; he saw beauty;
he saw the kind-hearted serf who had consoled him when the
imaginary wolf pursued. Their instinctive piety was his. Their
soil-rootedness became a precept. He struggled to distinguish
between one criminal motive and another: from the viewpoint
of a serf, was a crime against a hardened master really a crime?
Under the tatters of barbarism, he perceived the image of God.

The collective routine of the stockade drove him further and
further from the socialist dream of communal living. "To be
alone is a normal need," he railed. "Otherwise, *in this enforced
communism one turns into a hater of mankind.*" And at the same
time he began to discover in the despised and brutalized lives of
the peasant convicts a shadow of the redemptive suffering that

is the Christian paradigm. More and more he inclined toward the traditional Orthodoxy of his upbringing. He fought doubt with passionate unreason: "If someone proved to me that Christ is outside the truth, then I should prefer to remain with Christ than with the truth." This set him against his old associates, both radicals and liberals. It set him against Petrashevsky and Belinsky, whose highest aspiration had been a constitutional republic in league with a visionary ethical socialism. It set him against illustrious literary moderates and Westernizers like Turgenev and Alexander Herzen. Emerging from his Siberian ordeal, he thundered against "the scurvy Russian liberalism propagated by good-for-nothings." Years later, when Belinsky was dead, Dostoyevsky was still sneering at "shitheads like the dung-beetle Belinsky," whom he would not forgive because "that man reviled Christ to me in the foulest language."

The culmination of these renunciations was a white-hot abomination of radicalism in all its forms—from the Western-influenced gentry-theorists of the eighteen-forties to the renegade *raskolniki* (dissenters) who burst into nihilism in the sixties, when student revolutionaries radicalized the universities. With his brother Mikhail, Dostoyevsky founded *Vremya* (*Time*), a literary-political periodical intended to combat the socialist radicals. Their immediate target was *The Contemporary*, an opposing polemical journal; it was in the arena of the monthlies that the ideological fires, under literary cover to distract the censors, smoldered. Though *Vremya* was a success, a misunderstanding led the censorship to close it down. Soon afterward, Dostoyevsky's wife died of consumption; then Mikhail collapsed and died. The grieving Dostoyevsky attempted to revive the magazine under another name, but in the absence of his brother's business management he fell into serious debt, went bankrupt, and in 1867 fled to the hated West to escape his creditors.

With him went Anna, the worshipful young stenographer to whom he had begun to dictate his work, and whom he shortly married. Four enforced years abroad took on the half-mad, hallucinatory frenzy of scenes in his own novels: he gambled and lost, gambled and wrote, pawned his wife's rings and gambled and lost and wrote. His work was appearing regularly in the reactionary *Russian Messenger*. Dostoyevsky had now altogether gone over to the other side. "All those trashy little liberals and progressives," he mocked, "find their greatest pleasure and satisfaction in criticizing Russia . . . everything of the slightest originality in Russia [is] hateful to them." It was on this issue that he broke with Turgenev, to whom words like "folk" and "glory" smelled of blood. Turgenev, for his part, thought Dostoyevsky insane. And yet it was Turgenev's *Fathers and Sons*, with its ambiguous portrait of a scoffing nihilist, that was Raskolnikov's sensational precursor.

Turgenev's novel was dedicated to Belinsky. Dostoyevsky broke with Belinsky, he broke with Turgenev, he broke with Petrashevsky, he broke with Herzen—not only because of their liberalism, but because he believed that they did not love Russia enough. To love Russia was to love the Czar and the debased peasant (who, debased by the Czar, also loved the Czar); it was to see human suffering as holy and the peasant as holy; it was to exalt the *obshchina*, the Russian village commune, while condemning the French philosophic cooperative; it was to love the Russian Church largely through the vilification of all other churches; it was to press for the love of God with a hateful ferocity.

Joseph Frank seems certain that Dostoyevsky's conversion "should not be seen as that of a strayed ex-believer returning to Christ," since he had "always remained in some sense a Christian." But the suggestion of a continuum of sensibility may be even stronger than that. After a plunge into the period's dominant cultural milieu, the son of an authoritarian father— authoritarian personally, religiously, nationally—returns to the father. It is common enough that an intellectual progression will lead to a recovery of the voices around the cradle.

In January of 1881, Dostoyevsky, now an honored literary eminence more celebrated than Turgenev, died of a hemorrhage of the throat. Two months later, Czar Alexander II—Russia's earnest liberalizer and liberator—was assassinated. From the last half of the nineteenth century until the Bolshevik defeat of the liberal Kerensky government in the second decade of the twentieth, revolution continued to overcome reform. In this guise—injury for the sake of an ideal—Raskolnikov lives on. For seventy years he was victorious in Russia. And even now, after the death of the Soviet Union, auguring no one knows what, his retributive figure roves the earth. If he is currently mute in Russia, he remains restive in Northern Ireland, and loud in the Middle East; he has migrated to America. He survives in the violence of humanitarian visionaries who would seize their utopias via ax, Molotov cocktail, or innocent-looking packages sent through the mail.

4.

RASKOLNIKOV AS MONSTER of ruination, reason's avenging angel: here speaks the ideologue Dostoyevsky, scourge of the radicals. But this single clangorous note will not hold. Dostoyevsky the novelist tends toward orchestration and multiplicity. Might there be other reasons for the murder of the old woman? Raskolnikov has already been supplied with messianic utilitarianism, a Western import, carried to its logical and lethal end. On second thought (Dostoyevsky's second thought), the killing may have a different and simpler source—family solidarity. A university dropout, unable to meet his tuition payments, Raskolnikov, alienated and desperate, has been guiltily taking money from his adoring mother and sister in the provinces. At home there is crisis: Dunya, his sister, has been expelled from her position as governess in the Svidrigailov household, where the debauched husband and father had been making lecherous advances. To elude disgrace and to ease her family's poverty—but chiefly to secure a backer for her brother's career—Dunya becomes engaged to a rich and contemptible St. Petersburg bureaucrat. In this version of Raskolnikov's intent, it is to save his sister from a self-sacrificial marriage that he robs the old woman and pounds her to death.

Dostoyevsky will hurry the stealing-for-sustenance thesis out of sight quickly enough. As a motive, it is too narrow for his larger purpose, and by the close of the novel it seems almost

forgotten, and surely marginal—not only because Raskolnikov
hides the stolen money and valuables and never touches them
again, but because such an obvious material reason is less shat-
tering than what Dostoyevsky will soon disclose. He will goad
Raskolnikov to a tempestuousness even past nihilism. Past
nihilism lies pure violence—violence for is own sake, without
the vindication of a superior future. The business of revolution
is only to demolish, the anarchist theorist and agitator Mikhail
Bakunin once declared. But in Raskolnikov's newest stand, not
even this extremist position is enough:

> Then I realized . . . that power is given only to the one who
> dares to reach down and take it. Here there is one thing, one
> thing only: one has only to dare! . . . I wanted to *dare*, and I
> killed . . . that's the whole reason! . . . I wanted to kill with-
> out casuistry . . . to kill for myself, for myself alone! I didn't
> want to lie about it even to myself! It was not to help my
> mother that I killed—nonsense! I did not kill so that, having
> obtained means and power, I could become a benefactor of
> mankind. Nonsense! . . . And it was not money above all
> that I wanted when I killed . . . I wanted to find out then,
> and find out quickly, whether I was a louse like all the rest,
> or a man? . . . Would I dare to reach down and take, or not?

A rapid shuttling of motives, one overtaking the other:
family reasons, societal reasons, altruism, utilitarianism, socialism, nihilism, Napoleonic raw domination. Generations of
readers have been mystified by this plethora of incitements and
explanations. Why so many? One critic, the Russian Formalist
Mikhail Bakhtin, analyzing Dostoyevsky's frequent ellipses
and the back-and-forth interior dialogue of characters disputing with themselves—each encompassing multiple points of
view—concludes that Dostoyevsky was the inventor of a new
"multi-voice" genre, which Bakhtin calls the "polyphonic
novel." Some simply assume that Dostoyevsky changed his
mind as he went along, and since he was unable to revise what
was already in print—the novel appeared in installments written against deadlines—he was compelled to stitch up the loose

ends afterward as best he could. (This sounds plausible enough; if true, it would leave most serious Dostoyevsky scholars of the last century with egg on their faces.)

A British academic, A. D. Nuttall, offers a psychiatric solution: Raskolnikov is in a state of self-hypnotic schizophrenia. Walter Kaufmann invokes existentialism, drawing Dostoyevsky into Nietzsche's and Kierkegaard's web. Freud speculates that Dostoyevsky expresses "sympathy by identification" with criminals as a result of an Oedipal revolt against his father. Harold Bloom, sailing over Raskolnikov's inconsistencies, sees in him an apocalyptic figure, "a powerful representative of the will demonized by its own strength." "The best of all murder stories," says Bloom, "*Crime and Punishment* seems to me beyond praise and beyond affection." For Vladimir Nabokov, on the other hand, the novel is beyond contempt; he knew even in his teens that it was "long-winded, terribly sentimental, and badly written." Dostoyevsky is "mediocre," and his "gallery of characters consists almost exclusively of neurotics and lunatics." As for Dostoyevsky's religion, it is a "special lurid brand of the Christian faith." "I am very eager to debunk Dostoyevsky," Nabokov assures us.

Is this a case of the blind men and the elephant? Or the novel as Rorschach test? There is something indeterminate in all these tumbling alternatives—in Raskolnikov's changing theories, in the critics' clashing responses. Still, all of them taken together make plain what it is that Dostoyevsky's novel turns out not to be. It is not, after all, a singlemindedly polemical tract fulminating against every nineteenth-century radical movement in sight—though parts may pass for that. It is not a detective thriller, despite its introduction of Porfiry, a crafty, nimble-tongued, penetratingly intuitive police investigator. It is not a social protest novel, even if it retains clear vestiges of an abandoned earlier work on alcoholism and poverty in the forlorn Marmeladovs, whom Raskolnikov befriends: drunken husband, unbalanced tubercular wife, daughter driven to prostitution.

And it is not even much of what it has often been praised for being: a "psychological" novel—notwithstanding a startling stab, now and then, into the marrow of a mind. George Eliot is what we mean, in literature, by psychological; among the moderns, Proust, Joyce, James. Dostoyevsky is not psychological in the sense of understanding and portraying familiar human nature. *Crime and Punishment* is in exile from human nature—like the deeply eccentric *Notes from Underground*, which precedes it by a year. The underground man, Raskolnikov's indispensable foreshadower, his very embryo, revels in the corrupt will to seek out extreme and horrible acts, which gladden him with their "shameful accursed sweetness." But Raskolnikov will in time feel suffocated by the mental anguish that dogs his crime. Suspicions close in on him; a room in a police station seems no bigger than a cupboard. And soon suffering criminality will put on the radiant robes of transcendence. Led by the saintly Sonya Marmeladova, who has turned harlot to support her destitute family, Raskolnikov looks at last to God. The nihilist, the insolent Napoleon, is all at once redeemed—implausibly, abruptly—by a single recitation from the Gospels, and goes off, docile and remorseful, to serve out his sentence in Siberia.

Nabokov gleefully derides Dostoyevsky's sentimental conventions: "I do not like this trick his characters have of 'sinning their way to Jesus.'" Ridiculing Raskolnikov's impetuous "spiritual regeneration," Nabokov concedes that "the love of a noble prostitute . . . did not seem as incredibly banal in 1866 . . . as it does now when noble prostitutes are apt to be received a little cynically." Yet the doctrine of redemption through suffering came to be the bulwark of Dostoyevsky's credo. He believed in spiritual salvation. He had been intimate with thieves and cutthroats; he had lived among criminals. He had himself been punished as a criminal. Even as he was writing *Crime and Punishment*, he was under the continuing surveillance of the secret police.

The secret police, however, are not this novel's secret. Neither are the ukases and explosives of that Czarist twilight. Murder and degradation; perversity, distortion, paralysis, abnormal excitation, lightning conversion; dive after dive into fits of madness (Raskolnikov, his mother, Svidrigailov, Katerina Marmeladova); a great imperial city wintry in tone, huddled, frozen in place, closeted, all in the heart of summertime—these are not the usual characteristics of a work dedicated to political repudiations. *Crime and Punishment* is something else, something beyond what Dostoyevsky may have plotted and what the scholars habitually attend to. Its strangeness is that of a galloping centaur pulling a droshky crowded with groaning souls; or else it is a kaleidoscopic phantasmagoria, confined, churning, stuttering. St. Petersburg itself has the enclosed yet chaotic quality of a perpetual dusk, a town of riverbank and sky, taverns, tiny apartments cut up into rented cabins and cells, mazy alleys, narrow stairways, drunks, beggars, peddlers, bedraggled students, street musicians, whores—all darkened and smudged, as if the whole of the city were buried in a cellar, or in hell.

This irresistible deformation of commonly predictable experience is what fires Dostoyevsky's genius. Nabokov dislikes that genius (I dislike it too) because its language is a wilderness and there are woeful pockets of obscurantist venom at its center. But in the end *Crime and Punishment* is anything but a manifesto. Citizenly rebuttal is far from its delirious art. In the fever of his imagining, it is not the radicals Dostoyevsky finally rebukes, but the Devil himself, the master of sin, an unconquerable principality pitted against God.

"Please, Stories Are Stories": Bernard Malamud

HART AND SCHAFFNER are dead; Marx, ringed round with laurels, has notoriously retired. But the firm itself was dissolved long ago, and it was Saul Bellow who, with a sartorial quip, snipped the stitches that had sewn three acclaimed and determinedly distinct American writers into the same suit of clothes, with its single label: "Jewish writer." In Bellow's parody, Bellow, Malamud, and Roth were the literary equivalent of the much-advertised men's wear company—but lighthearted as it was, the joke cut two ways: it was a declaration of imagination's independence of collective tailoring, and it laughingly struck out at the disgruntlement of those who, having themselves applied the label in pique, felt displaced by it.

Who were these upstarts, these "pushy intruders" (as Gore Vidal had it), who were ravishing readers and seizing public space? Surveying American publishing, Truman Capote railed that "the Jewish mafia has systematically frozen [Gentiles] out of the literary scene." In a 1968 essay, "On Not Being a Jew," Edward Hoagland complained that he was "being told in print and sometimes in person that I and my heritage lacked vitality . . . because I could find no ancestor who had hawked copper pots in a Polish shtetl." Katherine Anne Porter, describing herself as "in the direct, legitimate line" of the English language, accused Jewish writers of "trying to destroy it and all other living things they touch." More benignly, John Updike invented Bech, his own Jewish novelist, and joined what he appeared to regard as the dominant competition.

Yet it was not so much in response to these dubious preconceptions as it was to a rooted sense of their capacious American literary inheritance that all three unwillingly linked novelists were reluctant to be defined by the term "Jewish writer." "I am not a Jewish writer, I am a writer who is a Jew," Philip Roth announced in Jerusalem in 1963. And Bellow, pugnaciously in a 1988 lecture: "If the WASP aristocrats wanted to think of me as a Jewish poacher on their precious cultural estates then let them."

Bernard Malamud sorted out these contentious impulses far more circumspectly. "I am a writer," he said in an interview on his sixtieth birthday, "and a Jew, and I write for all men. A novelist has to, or he's built himself a cage. I write about Jews, when I write about Jews, because they set my imagination going. I know something about their history, the quality of their experience and belief. . . . The point I am making is that I was born in America and respond, in American life, to more than Jewish experience."

Though unexpressed, there lurks in all these concurring animadversions a fear of the stigma of the "parochial"—a charge never directed (and why not?) against Cather's prairie Bohemians, or the denizens of Updike's Brewer or Faulkner's Yoknapatawpha. Still, it is not through sober public rhetoric but in the wilder precincts of fiction that Malamud discloses his animating credo. It emerges in the clear voice of Levitansky, the antihero of "Man in the Drawer," a harried Soviet-Jewish writer whose work is barred from publication because it speaks human truths inimical to Stalinist policy. The American journalist who has worriedly befriended Levitansky asks whether he has submitted any Jewish stories, to which the writer retorts: "Please, stories are stories, they have not nationality. . . . When I write about Jews comes out stories, so I write about Jews." It is this unanchored drive to create tales, Malamud implies, that generates subject matter—the very opposite of Henry James's reliance on the story's "germ," the purloinings and devisings of the observed world. "Stories are stories" is Malamud's ticket to untrammeled writerly freedom. Except to Scheherazade, he owes no social debts.

Despite this purist manifesto, Malamud is in fact steeped everywhere in social debt; his aesthetic is instinct with the muted pulse of what used to be called moral seriousness, a notion gone out of fashion in American writing, where too often flippancy is mistaken for irony. Malamud, a virtuoso of darkest irony,

refuses the easy conventions of cynicism and its dry detachment. His stories know suffering, loneliness, lust, confinement,
defeat; and even when they are lighter, they tremble with subterranean fragility. Older readers who were familiar with the
novels and stories in the years of their earliest publication will
recall the wonderment they aroused, beginning with the fables
of *The Magic Barrel*, as each new tale disrupted every prevailing
literary expectation. The voice was unlike any other, haunted
by whispers of Hawthorne, Babel, Isak Dinesen, even Poe, and
at the same time uniquely possessed: a fingerprint of fire and
ash. It was as if Malamud were at work in a secret laboratory of
language, smelting a new poetics that infused the inflections of
one tongue into the music of another. His landscapes, nature's
and the mind's, are inimitable; the Malamudian sensibility, its
wounded openness to large feeling, has had no successors.

When the ambient culture changes, having moved toward
the brittleness of wisecrack and indifference, and the living
writer is no longer present, it can happen that a veil of forget-
fulness falls over the work. And then comes a literary crisis:
the recognition that a matchless civilizational note has been
muffled. A new generation, mostly unacquainted with the risks
of uncompromising and hard-edged compassion, deserves Malamud even more than the one that made up his contemporary
readership. The idea of a writer who is intent on judging the
world—hotly but quietly, and aslant, and through the subver-
sions of tragic paradox—is nowadays generally absent: who
is daring enough not to be cold-eyed? For Malamud, trivia
has no standing as trivial, everything counts, everything is at
stake—as in "The Jewbird," where a bossy crow-like intruder
named Schwartz invades a family, refuses birdseed in favor of
herring, and to ingratiate himself tutors the dull son. But the
father, sensing a rival for domination, is enraged, and this fanciful comedy ends in primal terror and murder. Pity leaves its
signature even in farce.

"The Jewbird" is one of thirty-six stories in the Library
of America's definitive three-volume publication (the third is
forthcoming) honoring Malamud's work on the hundredth
anniversary of his birth; six of these Malamud himself never

saw in print. Also included in the pair of volumes are five novels: *The Natural, The Assistant, A New Life, The Fixer*, and *Pictures of Fidelman*.

A New Life may be the most overlooked of Malamud's long fictions, perhaps because it has been mistaken for yet another academic novel. But the sheath is not the sword, and *A New Life* is as exquisite in its evocation of American transformation as Gatsby himself. Reversing the classic theme of the young-man-from-the-provinces, S. Levin, incipient wife stealer, "formerly a drunkard," is a refugee from the New York tenements who leaves behind the grit of urban roil to be absorbed by village ways. Cascadia, the unprepossessing northwestern college he joins as a low-ranking teacher, turns out to be precisely that: a provincial village of the kind we might read of in an English novel of rural life, with its petty hierarchies and spites and rivalries. Yet the local terrain—trees, flowers, green hills, pristine vistas—is intoxicating to the city dweller, and here Malamud, whose impoverished outer-borough warrens are uniformly grim, writes peerlessly, as nowhere else, of proliferating natural beauty. And in the vein of Huck Finn, who chooses damnation over the lies of conventional morality, he casts a redemptive radiance on the fraught flight of an adulterous woman and her fornicating lover. In its tormented, satiric, and startling underminings, *A New Life*—which, like *The Natural*, stands tonally apart from Malamud's other work—is one of those rare transfiguring American novels that turn wishing into destiny.

The Assistant and *The Fixer* are closer to the stories in their melancholy texture and feverish desperation. And as in the stories, a man's labor becomes his identity. Morris Bober tends a precarious grocery store, where his assistant hungers after love. The fixer, Yakov Bok, a worker in a brickyard, is unjustly imprisoned, walled in by an anti-Semitic blood-libel charge. Each person's fate pursues him: Fidelman in Rome, "a self-confessed failure as a painter," is stalked by the elusive Susskind, who covets Fidelman's suit. Leo Finkle, a rabbinical student, is hounded by Salzman the marriage broker. Alexander Levine, "a black Jew and an angel to boot," appears to Manischevitz, a tailor mired in suffering. Rosa, a maid in thrall to her lover, wheedles a pair of shoes out of the dignified professor whose rooms she cleans. Apparitions, stalkings, houndings, claims and demands: unbidden, duties and obligations fall on Malamud's characters with the power of commandments. The pursuer and the quarry are each other's double; through self-recognition, repugnance is conjured into acquiescence. In the shifting kaleidoscope of all these whirling tales, Malamud's quest is for renewal—freedom from the shackled self. Some have argued, not unpersuasively, that his humble Jews are stand-ins for universal suffering: in fiction as in life, living human beings ought not to be thrust into the annihilating perils of metaphor. Malamud easily escapes these transgressive erasures—the allegorical Jew, the Jew-as-symbol—through the blunt and earthy specificity of his ordinary Jews: census taker, shoemaker, bookseller, night school student, baker, egg candler, peddler, janitor, tailor (several), grocer (several, failing), taxi driver, actor, painter (failed), writer (several, failed). Wrenched into life by a master fabulist, they breathe, feel, yearn, struggle.

Then with all these believable Jews on hand, is Malamud a "parochial" writer, after all? Yes, blessedly so, as every sovereign imaginative artist is obliged to be, from Dickens to Nabokov to Flannery O'Connor to Malamud himself: each one the sole heir to a singular kingdom.

Mrs. Virginia Woolf:
A Madwoman and Her Nurse

NO RECENT BIOGRAPHY has been read more thirstily by readers
and writers of fiction than Quentin Bell's account of the life of
his aunt Virginia. Reviewing it, Elizabeth Hardwick speaks of
"the present exhaustion of Virginia Woolf," and compares the
idea of Bloomsbury—it "wearies"—to a pond run out of trout.
But for most American writers, bewildered by the instability
of what passes for culture and literature, envious of the English
sense of place and of being placed, conscious of separations that
yet lack the respectability of "schools" or even the interest of
alien perspectives, stuck mainly with the crudity of being either
For or Against Interpretation, the legend of Bloomsbury still
retains its inspiriting powers. Like any Golden Age, it promises
a mimetic future: some day again, says Bloomsbury of 1905,
there will be friends, there will be conversation, there will be
moods, and they will all again *really matter*, and fall naturally, in
the way of things that matter, into history.

Part of the special history of the Bloomsbury of mood is
pictorial—and this has nothing to do with the art critic Roger
Fry, or the painter Duncan Grant. It is not what the painters
painted or what the writers wrote about painting that hangs
on: it is the photographs, most of them no more official than
snapshots, of the side of a house, two people playing checkers
on an old kitchen chair set out in the yard, three friends and a
baby poking in the sand. The snapshots are all amateur. Goblets
of brightness wink on eaves, fences, trees, and wash out faces
in their dazzle; eyes are lost in blackened sockets. The hem of
a dress is likely to be all clarity, but the heads escape—under
hat brims, behind dogs, into mottled leaf-shade. And out of the

Quentin Bell, *Virginia Woolf: A Biography* (Harcourt Brace Jovanovich, 1972).
Book review published in *Commentary*, August 1973.

blur of those hopeless poses, cigarettes, hands on knees, hands over books, anxious little pups held up to the camera, walking sticks, long grotesque nose-shadows, lapels, outdoor chairs and tables, there rises up—no, leaks down—so much tension, so much ambition, so much fake casualness, so much heart-breaking attention to the momentariness of the moment. The people in the snapshots knew, in a way we do not, who they were. Bloomsbury was self-conscious in a way we are not. It sniffed at its own perceptions, even its own perceived posterity. Somewhere early in the course of her diaries, Virginia Woolf notes how difficult it would be for a biographer to understand her—how little biographers can know, she said—only from the evidence of her journals. Disbelieving in the probity of her own biography, she did not doubt that she would have her own biographer.

She did not doubt; she knew; they knew. Hatched from the last years of the reign of Victoria, Bloomsbury was still a world where things—if not people, then ideas—could be said to reign. Though old authority might be sneered at (or something worse even than a sneer—Virginia Woolf declared her certainty that she could not have become a writer had her father lived), though proprieties might be outrageously altered ("Semen?" asked Lytton Strachey, noticing a stain on Vanessa Bell's skirt one afternoon), though sex was accessible and often enough homoerotic, though freedom might be pro-claimed on Gordon Square, though livings were earned, there was nonetheless a spine of authority to support Bloomsbury: family, descent, class and community—the sense of having-in-common. Bloomsbury, after all, was an inheritance. Both E. M. Forster's and Virginia Woolf's people were associated with the liberal and intellectual Clapham Sect of the century before. Cambridge made a kind of cousinship—the staircase at Trinity that drew together Clive Bell, Saxon Sydney-Turner, and Virginia Woolf's brother Thoby Stephen was the real beginning of the gatherings at Gordon Square. Bloomsbury was pacifist and busy with gossip about what it always called "buggery," but it was not radical and it did not harbor rebels. Rebels want to make over; the Bloomsburyites reinforced themselves with their like. The staircase at Trinity went on and on for the rest of their lives, and even Virginia Woolf, thinking to make over the form of the novel, had to have each newly completed work ratified by Morgan Forster and sometimes Maynard Keynes before she could breathe at ease again. The authority of one's closest familiars is the unmistakable note of Bloomsbury. It was that sure voice she listened for. "Virginia Woolf was a Miss Stephen," Quentin Bell begins, in the same voice; it is an opening any outsider could have written, but not in that sharp cadence. He is not so much biographer as a later member of the circle—Virginia Woolf's sister's son, the child of Vanessa and Clive Bell. He knows, he does not doubt. It is the note of self-recognition; of confidence; of inheritance. Everything is in his grip.

And yet—as she predicted—Virginia Woolf's biographer fails her. He fails her, in fact, more mournfully than any outsider could. It is his grip that fails her. This is not only because, sticking mainly to those matters he has sure authority over, he has chosen to omit a literary discussion of the body of work itself. "I have found the work of the biographer sufficiently difficult without adventuring in other directions," he tells us, so that to speak of Quentin Bell's "sure authority" is not to insinuate that all his data are, perhaps, out of childhood memory or family reminiscence, or that he has not mined library after library, and collection after collection of unpublished papers. He is, after all, of the next generation, and the next generation is always in some fashion an outsider to the one before. But what *is* in his grip is something more precise, curiously, than merely data, which the most impersonal research can reliably throw up: it is that particular intimacy of perspective—of experience, really—which characterizes not family information, but family bias. Every house has its own special odor to the entering guest, however faint—it sticks to the inhabitants, it is in their chairs and in their clothes. The analogy of bias to scent is chiefly in one's unconsciousness of one's own. Bell's Woolf is about Virginia, but it has the smell of Vanessa's house. The Virginia Woolf that comes off these pages is a kind of emanation of a point of view, long settled, by now, into family feeling. Stephens, Pattles, Fishers—all the family lines—each has its distinct and legendary scent. The Stephens are bold, the Pattles are fair, the Fishers are self-righteous. And Virginia is mad.

She was the family's third case of insanity, all on the Stephen side. Leslie Stephen, Virginia Woolf's celebrated father—a man of letters whose career was marked not least by the circumstance that Henry James cherished him—was married twice, the second time to Julia Duckworth, a widow with children. Together they produced Vanessa and Virginia, Thoby and Adrian. A child of Leslie Stephen's first marriage, the younger of Virginia's two half-sisters, was born defective—it is not clear whether backward or truly insane—and was confined to an asylum, where she died old. Virginia's first cousin—the child of her father's brother—went mad while still a young man, having struck his head in an accident. But one wonders, in the retrograde and rather primitive way one contemplates families, whether there might not have been a Stephen "taint." In a family already accustomed to rumor of aberration, Virginia Woolf, in any case, was incontrovertibly mad. Her madness was distinguished, moreover, by a threatening periodicity: at any moment it could strike, disabling everyone around her. Vanessa had to leave her children and come running, nurses had to be hired, rest homes interviewed, transport accomplished. The disaster was ten times wider than its victim.

And just here is the defect in writing out of family authority. The odor is personal, hence partial. Proust says somewhere that the artist brings to the work his whole self, to his familiars only those aspects that accommodate them. The biographer close to his subject has the same difficulty; the aspect under which Quentin Bell chiefly views his aunt Virginia is not of accommodation but of a still narrower partiality: discommodity, the effect on family perspective of Virginia Woolf's terrible and recurrent insanity. It was no mere melancholia, or poetic mooning—as, reading Leonard Woolf's deliberately truncated edition of her diary, we used to guess. A claustrophilic though inspired (also self-inspiring) document, it made us resent the arbitrary "personal" omissions: was it the madness he was leaving out?

Certainly we wanted the madness too, supposing it to be the useful artistic sort: grotesque moods, quirks—epiphanies really. But it was not that; it was the usual thing people get put away for, an insanity characterized by incoherent howling and by violence. She clawed her attendants and had to be restrained; she would not touch food; she was suicidal. Ah, that cutting difference: not that she longed for death, as poets and writers sometimes do for melancholy's sake, but that she wanted, with the immediacy of a method, to be dead.

Bell's Woolf, then, is not about the Virginia Woolf of the diaries, essays, and novels—not, in the Proustian sense, about the writer's whole self. And surely this is not simply because literary criticism is evaded. Bell's Woolf is not about a writer, in fact; it is about the smell of a house. It is about a madwoman and her nurse.

The nurse was Leonard Woolf. Upon him Quentin Bell can impose no family aspects, rumors, characteristics, old experience, inherited style. He does not trail any known house-scent, like Stephens, Pattles, Fishers. Though he shared the Cambridge stairs—Thoby Stephen, Saxon Sydney-Turner, Clive Bell, Lytton Strachey, and Leonard Woolf together briefly formed the Midnight Society, a reading club that met on Saturday evenings in Clive Bell's rooms—he was not an inheritor of Cambridge. Cambridge was not natural to him, Bloomsbury was not natural to him, even England was not natural to him—not as an inheritance; he was a Jew. Quentin Bell has no "authority" over Leonard Woolf, as he has over his aunt; Leonard is nowhere in the biographer's grip.

The effect is unexpected. It is as if Virginia Woolf escapes—possessing her too selectively, the biographer lets her slip—but Leonard Woolf somehow stays to become himself. Which is to say, Bell's Virginia Woolf can be augmented by a thousand other sources—chiefly by her own work—but we learn as much about Leonard Woolf here as we are likely to know from any other source. And what we learn is a strange historical judgment, strange but unfragmented, of a convincing wholeness: that Leonard Woolf was a family sacrifice. Without him—Quentin Bell's clarity on this point is ineffaceable—Virginia

Woolf might have spent her life in a mental asylum. The elder
Stephens were dead, Thoby had died at twenty-six, Adrian
married a woman apparently indifferent to or incompatible
with the Bloomsburyites; it was Vanessa on whom the grimness
fell. Leonard Woolf—all this is blatant—got Vanessa off the
hook. He was, in fact, deceived: he had no inkling he was being
captured for a nurse.

> Neither Vanessa nor Adrian gave him a detailed and explicit
> account of Virginia's illnesses or told him how deadly seri-
> ous they might be. . . . Her insanity was clothed, like some
> other painful things in that family, in a jest. . . . Thus, in
> effect if not in intention, Leonard was allowed to think of
> Virginia's illnesses as something not desperately serious, and
> he was allowed to marry her without knowing how fearful
> a care such a union might be. In fairness to all parties it must
> be said that, even if Virginia's brother and sister had been
> as explicit and circumstantial as they ought to have been,
> Leonard would certainly not have been deflected from his
> purpose of marrying Virginia. . . . As it was, he learnt the
> hard way and one can only wonder, seeing how hard it was,
> and that he had for so long to endure the constant threat
> of her suicide, to exert constant vigilance, to exercise end-
> less persuasive tact at mealtimes and to suffer the perpetual
> alternations of hope and disappointment, that he too did
> not go mad.
>   In fact he nearly did, although he does not mention it.

"He does not mention it." There was in Leonard Woolf an
extraordinary silence, a containment allied to something like
concealment, and at the same time open to a methodical candor.
This is no paradox; candor is often the mode of the obtuse
person. It is of course perilous to think of Leonard Woolf as
obtuse: he was both activist and intellectual, worldly and introspective; his intelligence, traveling widely and serenely over
politics and literature, was reined in by a seriousness that makes
him the most responsible and conscientious figure among all
the Bloomsburyites. His seriousness was profound. It was what

turned a hand press "small enough to stand on a kitchen table" into the Hogarth Press, an important and innovative publishing house. It was what turned Leonard Woolf himself from a highly able agent of colonialism—at the age of twenty-four he was an official of the British ruling apparatus in Ceylon—into a convinced anti-imperialist and a fervent socialist. And it was what turned the Jew into an Englishman.

Not that Leonard Woolf is altogether without ambivalence on this question; indeed, the word "ambivalence" is his own. Soon after his marriage to Virginia Stephen, he was taken round on a tour of Stephen relations—among them Virginia's half-brother, Sir George Duckworth, in his large house in Dalingridge Place, and "Aunt Anny," who was Lady Ritchie, Thackeray's daughter, in St. George's Square. He suffered in these encounters from an "ambivalence in my attitude to the society which I found in Dalingridge Place and St. George's Square. I disliked its respectability and assumptions while envying and fearing its assurance and manners." And: "I was an outsider to this class, because, although I and my father before me belonged to the professional middle class, we had only recently struggled up into it from the stratum of Jewish shopkeepers. We had no roots in it." This looks like candor—"we had no roots"—but it is also remarkably insensible. Aware of his not belonging, he gives no evidence anywhere that the people he moved among were also aware of it. It is true that his own group of self-consciously agnostic Cambridge intellectuals apparently never mentioned it to his face. Thoby Stephen in a letter to Leonard in Ceylon is quick enough to speak of himself, mockingly, as a nonbelieving Christian—"it's no good being dainty with Christians and chapel's obviously rot"—but no one seems ever to have teased Leonard about his being an agnostic Jew. In the atmosphere of that society, perhaps, teasing would have too dangerously resembled baiting; levity about being a Christian was clearly not interchangeable with levity about being a Jew. Fair enough: it never is. But Virginia, replying to a letter in which Leonard implores her to love him, is oddly analytical: ". . . of course, I feel angry sometimes at the strength of your desire. Possibly, your being a Jew comes in also at this

point. You seem so foreign." Was he, like all those dark lubri-
cious peoples whose origins are remote from the moderating
North, too obscurely other? She corrects herself at once, with
a kind of apology: "And then I am fearfully unstable. I pass
from hot to cold in an instant, without any reason; except that
I believe sheer physical effort and exhaustion influence me."
The correction—the retraction—is weak, and fades off; what
remains is the blow: "You seem so foreign."

We do not know Leonard's response to this. Possibly he
made none. It would have been in keeping had he made
none. Foreignness disconcerted him—like Virginia he was at
moments disturbed by it and backed away—and if his own
origins were almost never mentioned to his face, his face was
nevertheless *there*, and so, in those striking old photographs,
were the faces of his grandparents. Leonard Woolf is bemused
in his autobiography by his paternal grandfather, "a large, stern,
black-haired, and black-whiskered, rabbinical Jew in a frock
coat." Again he speaks of this "look of stern rabbinical orthodoxy," and rather prefers the "round, pink face of an incredibly
old Dutch doll," which was the face of his Dutch-born maternal
grandmother—about whom he speculates that it was "possible
that she had a good deal of non-Jewish blood in her ancestry.
Some of her children and grandchildren were fair-haired and
facially very unlike the 'typical' Jew." Her husband, however,
was a different case: "No one could have mistaken him for
anything but a Jew. Although he wore coats and trousers,
hats and umbrellas, just like those of all the other gentlemen
in Addison Gardens, he looked to me as if he might have
stepped straight out of one of those old pictures of caftaned,
bearded Jews in a ghetto. . . ." Such Jews, he notes, were
equipped with "a fragment of spiritual steel, a particle of passive
and unconquerable resistance," but otherwise the character,
and certainly the history, of the Jews do not draw him. "My
father's father was a Jew," he writes, exempting himself by two
generations. "I have always felt in my bones and brain and heart
English and, more narrowly, a Londoner, but with a nostalgic love of the city and civilization of ancient Athens." He
recognizes that his "genes and chromosomes" are something

else; he is a "descendant" of "the world's official fugitives and scapegoats."

But a "descendant" is not the same as a member. A descendant shares an origin, but not necessarily a destiny. Writing in his eighties, Leonard Woolf recollects that as a schoolboy he was elected to an exclusive debating society under the thumb of G. K. Chesterton and his brother, and "in view of the subsequent violent anti-Semitism of the Chestertons" he finds this "amusing"; he reports that he was "surprised and flattered." Sixty-three years afterward he is still flattered. His description of the public school that flattered him shows it to be a detestable place, hostile to both intellect and feeling: "I got on quite well with the boys in my form or with whom I played cricket, football, and fives, but it would have been unsafe, practically impossible, to let them know what I really thought or felt about anything which seemed to me important." *Would have been unsafe*. It was a risk he did not take—unlike Morgan Forster, who, in the same situation in a similar school, allowed himself to be recognized as an intellectual and consequently to suffer as a schoolboy pariah. Leonard Woolf did not intend to take on the role of pariah, then or later. Perhaps it was cowardice; or perhaps it was the opposite, that "fragment of spiritual steel" he had inherited from the ghetto; or perhaps it was his sense of himself as exempt from the ghetto.

Certainly he always thought of himself as wholly an Englishman. In the spring of 1935 he and Virginia drove to Rome. "I was astonished then (I am astonished still)," Quentin Bell comments, "that Leonard chose to travel by way of Germany." They were on German soil three days; near Bonn they encountered a Nazi demonstration but were unharmed, and entered Italy safely. What prompted Leonard Woolf to go into Germany in the very hour Jews were being abused there? Did he expect Nazi street hoodlums to distinguish between an English Jewish face and a German Jewish face? He carried with him—it was not needed and in the event of street hoodlumism would anyhow have been useless—a protective letter from an official of the German embassy in London. More than that, he carried—in his "bones and brain and heart"—the designation of Englishman. It was a test, not of the inherited fragment of spiritual steel, but of the strength of his exemption from that heritage. If Quentin Bell is twice astonished, it may be because he calculated the risk more closely than Leonard; or else he is not quite so persuaded of the Englishness of Leonard Woolf as is Leonard Woolf.

And, superficially at least, it is difficult to be persuaded of it. One is drawn to Leonard's face much as he was drawn to his grandfather's face, and the conclusion is the same. What Leonard's eyes saw was what the eyes of the educated English classes saw. What Leonard felt on viewing his grandfather's face must have been precisely what Clive Bell and Thoby Stephen would have felt. There is an arresting snapshot—still another of those that make up the pictorial history of Bloomsbury—of Leonard Woolf and Adrian Stephen. They are both young men in their prime; the date is 1914. They are standing side by side before the high narrow Gothic-style windows of Asham House, the Sussex villa Leonard and Virginia Woolf owned for some years. They are dressed identically (vests, coats, ties) and positioned identically—feet apart, hands in pockets, shut lips gripping pipe or cigarette holder. Their shoes are lost in the weedy grass, and the sunlight masks their faces in identical skull-shadows. Both faces are serene, holding back amusement, indulgent of the photographer. And still it is not a picture of two cultivated Englishmen, or not only that. Adrian is incredibly tall and Vikinglike, with a forehead as broad and flat as a chimney tile; he looks like some blueblood American banker not long out of Princeton; his hair grows straight up like thick pale straw. Leonard's forehead is an attenuated wafer under a tender black forelock, his nose is nervous and frail, he seems younger and more vulnerable than his years (he was then thirty-four) and as recognizably intellectual as—well, how does one put the contrast? Following Leonard, one ought to dare to put it with the clarity of a certain cultural bluntness: he looks like a student at the yeshiva. Leonard has the unmistakable face of a Jew. Like his grandfather—and, again like him, despite his costume— Leonard Woolf might have stepped out of one of those pictures of caftaned Jews in the ghetto.

The observation may be obvious and boring but it is not insignificant, if only because it is derived from Leonard himself; it is his own lesson. What can be learned from it is not merely that he was himself conscious of all that curious contrast, but that his fellows could not have been indifferent to it. In a 1968 review of the penultimate volume of Leonard Woolf's memoirs, Dan Jacobson wonders, "Did his being a Jew never affect . . . his career or social life in the several years he spent as a colonial officer in Ceylon, his only companions during that time being other colonial civil servants—not in general the most enlightened, tolerant, or tactful of British social groups? Did it not arise in the political work he carried out later in England, especially during the rise of Nazism?" On all these matters Leonard is mute; he does not mention it. Not so Virginia. "He's a penniless Jew," she wrote in a letter to a friend announcing her marriage, and we know that if she had married a poor man of her own set she would not have called him a penniless Englishman. She called Leonard a Jew not to identify or explain him, but because, quite simply, that is how she saw him; it was herself she was explaining. And if she wrote light-heartedly, making a joke of marriage without inheritance, it was also a joke in general about unaccoutered Jews—from her point of view, Leonard had neither inheritance nor heritage. He was—like the Hogarth Press later on—self-created.

Of course, in thinking about Leonard Woolf, one is plainly not interested in the question of the acculturated Jew (". . . nearly all Jews are both proud and ashamed of being Jews," Leonard writes—a model of the type); it is not on the mark. What *is* to the point is the attitude of the class Leonard aspired to join. "Virginia for her part," Quentin Bell notes—and it is unnecessary to remind oneself that he is her nephew—

> had to meet the Woolf family. It was a daunting experience. Leonard himself was sufficiently Jewish to seem to her disquietingly foreign; but in him the trait was qualified. He had become so very much a citizen of her world. . . . But Leonard's widowed mother, a matriarchal figure living with her large family in Colinette Road, Putney, seemed very

alien to Virginia. No place could have been less like home than her future mother-in-law's house.

And how did the Woolfs regard her? Did they perceive that she thought their furniture hideous? Did she seem to them a haughty goy thinking herself too good for the family of their brilliant son? I am afraid that they probably did.

[Here follows an account of Virginia's response—aloof and truculent—upon learning the character of the dietary laws, which Mrs. Woolf observed.]

Virginia was ready to allow that Mrs. Woolf had some very good qualities, but her heart must have sunk as she considered what large opportunities she would have for discovering them.

"Work and love and Jews in Putney take it out of me," she wrote, and it was certainly true.

This aspect of Virginia Stephen's marriage to Leonard Woolf is usually passed over in silence. I have rehearsed it here at such length not to emphasize it for its own sake—there is nothing novel about upper-class English distaste for Jews—but to make a point about Leonard. He is commonly depicted as, in public, a saintly socialist, and, in private, a saintly husband. He was probably both; but he also knew, like any percipient young man in love with a certain segment of society, how to seize vantage ground. As a schoolboy he was no doubt sincerely exhilarated by the playing field, but he hid his intellectual exhilarations to make it look as if the playing field were all there was to esteem; it was a way, after all, of buying esteem for himself. And though he was afterward no doubt sincerely in love with Virginia Stephen (surely a woman less intelligent would not have satisfied him), it would be a mistake to suppose that Virginia herself—even given her brilliance, her splendid head on its splendid neck, the radiance of her first appearance in Thoby's rooms in Cambridge wearing a white dress and round hat and carrying a parasol, astonishing him, Leonard says, as when "in a picture gallery you suddenly come face to face with a great Rembrandt or Velasquez"—it would be ingenuous, not to say credulous, to think that Virginia alone was all there was to adore. Whether Leonard Woolf fell in love with a young woman of beauty and intellect, or more narrowly with a Stephen of beauty and intellect, will always be a formidable, and a necessary, question.

It is a question that, it seems to me, touches acutely on Leonard Woolf in his profoundly dedicated role as nurse. He was dedicated partly because he was earnestly efficient at everything, and also because he loved his wife, and also because he was a realist who could reconcile himself to any unlooked-for disaster. He came to the situation of Virginia's health determinedly and unquestioningly, much as, years later, when the German bombings had begun, he joined up with the Local Defence Volunteers: it was what had to be done. But in the case of Virginia more than merely courage was at issue; his "background" had equipped him well to be Virginia Stephen's nurse. When things were going badly he could take on the burden of all those small code-jottings in his diary—"V.n.w.," "b.n.," "V.sl.h."—and all the crises "Virginia not well," "bad night," "Virginia slight headache" horrendously implied, for the simple reason that it was worth it to him. It was worth it because she was a genius; it was worth it because she was a Stephen.

The power and allure of the Stephen world lay not in its distance from the Jews of Putney—Bloomsbury was anyhow hardly likely to notice the Jews of Putney, and if Virginia did notice, and was even brought to tea there, it was through the abnormal caprice of a freakish fate—but in its illustriousness. Virginia was an illustrious young woman: had she had no gift of her own, the luster of her father's situation, and of the great circle of the aristocracy of intellect into which she was born, would have marked her life. It was additionally marked by her double fortune of genius and insanity, and though her primary fortune—the circle into which she was born—attracted, in the most natural way, other members of that circle, the biting and always original quality of her mind put the less vivid of them off. Her madness was not public knowledge, but her intellect could not be hidden. Her tongue had a fearful and cutting brilliance. "I was surprised to find how friendly she made herself appear," said Walter Lamb, another of Thoby

Stephen's Cambridge friends, amazed on one occasion to have been undevoured. He courted her for a time, pallidly, asking frightened questions: "Do you want to have children and love in the normal way?"—as if he expected nothing usual from Virginia Stephen. "I wish," she wrote to Lytton Strachey, after reporting Lamb's visits, "that earth would open her womb and let some new creature out." The courtship was brief and ended in boredom. Lamb's offer was one of at least four proposals of marriage from differing sources; Strachey himself had tendered her one. Since he preferred stableboys to women, a fact they both understood very well, it was a strange mistake. Sydney Waterlow, still another Cambridge name, was a suitor; she regarded him as "amiable." Hilton Young, a childhood friend—cast, says Quentin Bell, from a "smooth and well-proportioned mould"—might have been an appropriate match, mixing politics with poetry and gaining a peerage; he was merely "admirable." Meanwhile, Virginia was thoughtfully flirting with her sister's husband. At twenty-nine, despite all these attentions, she was depressed at being still unmarried; she was despondent, as she would be for the rest of her life, over her childlessness. Not one of those triflings had turned to infatuation, on either side.

It was fortunate. There was lacking, in all these very intelligent men, and indeed in their type in general, the kind of sexual seriousness that is usually disparaged as uxoriousness. It was a trait that Leonard invincibly possessed and that Clive Bell despised as "provincial and puritanical, an enemy to all that was charming and amusing in life." Clive was occupied by a long-standing affair and lived apart from Vanessa, who, at various times, lived with Roger Fry and with Duncan Grant—who was (so closely was this group tied) Lytton Strachey's cousin, and who may have been (so Quentin Bell allows us to conjecture) the father of Quentin's sister, Angelica. Vanessa typed and distributed copies of Lytton Strachey's indecent verse; once at a party she did a topless dance; it was legendary that she had at another party fornicated with Maynard Keynes "coram publico"—the whole room looking on. It may have been in honor of these last two occasions that Virginia Woolf, according to Quentin

Bell, pronounced human nature to have been "changed in or about December 1910."

It was not a change Leonard Woolf approved of. Four years after this crucial date in human history he published a novel critical of "unnatural cultured persons" given to "wild exaggerated talk" and frivolous behavior; it was clearly an assault on Vanessa and Clive Bell and their circle. The novel, called *The Wise Virgins*, was about *not* marrying Virginia. Instead the hero is forced to marry a Putney girl, and lives unhappily ever after—only because, having been infected with Bloomsbury's licentious notions, he has carelessly gotten her with child. The fictional Leonard loses the heroine who represents Virginia, and is doomed to the drabness of Putney; in the one act he both deplores Bloomsbury and laments his deprivation of it. The real Leonard tried to pick his way between these soul-cracking contradictions. He meant to have the high excitement of Bloomsbury—and certainly "frivolity" contributed to Bloomsbury's dash and éclat—without the frivolity itself. He meant to be master of the full brilliant breadth of all that worldliness, and at the same time of the more sober and limiting range of his native seriousness.

That he coveted the one while requiring the other was—certainly in her biographer's eyes—the salvation of Virginia. No one else in that milieu could have survived—surely not as husband—her illnesses. Roger Fry, for instance, put his own mad wife away and went to live with Vanessa. As for Lamb, Waterlow, Young—viewed in the light of what Virginia Woolf's insanity extracted from her caretaker, their possibilities wither. Of all her potential husbands, only Leonard Woolf emerged as fit. And the opposite too can be said: of Bloomsbury's potential wives, only Virginia emerged as fit for Leonard. He was fit for her because her madness, especially in combination with her innovative genius, demanded the most grave, minutely persevering and attentive service. She was fit for him not simply because she represented Bloomsbury in its most resplendent flowering of originality and luminousness; so, after all, did Vanessa, an accomplished painter active with other painters in the revolutionary vitality of the Post-Impressionists. But just as

no marriage could survive Vanessa for long, so Leonard married to Vanessa would not have survived Bloomsbury for long.
What Leonard needed in Virginia was not so much her genius
as her madness. It made possible for him the exercise of the one
thing Bloomsbury had no use for: uxoriousness. It allowed him
the totality of his seriousness unchecked. It *used* his seriousness,
it gave it legitimate occupation, it made it both necessary and
awesome. And it made *her* serious. Without the omnipresent
threat of disintegration, freed from the oppression of continuous vigil against breakdown, what might Virginia's life have
been? The flirtation with Clive hints at it: she might have lived,
at least outwardly, like Vanessa. It was his wife's insanity, in
short, that made tenable the permanent—the secure—presence
in Bloomsbury of Leonard himself. Her madness fed his genius
for responsibility; it became for him a corridor of access to her
genius. The spirit of Bloomsbury was not Leonard's, his temperament was against it—Bloomsbury could have done without
him. So could a sane Virginia.

The whole question of Virginia's sexuality now came into
Leonard's hands. And here too he was curiously ambivalent.
The honeymoon was not a success; they consulted Vanessa, Vanessa the sexual creature—when had she had her first
orgasm? Vanessa could not remember. "No doubt," she reflected, "I sympathised with such things if I didn't have them from
the time I was 2." "Why do you think people make such a
fuss about marriage & copulation?" Virginia was writing just
then; ". . . certainly I find the climax immensely exaggerated."
Vanessa and Leonard put their heads together over it. Vanessa
said she believed Virginia "never had understood or sympathised with sexual passion in men"; this news, she thought,
"consoled" Leonard. For further consolation the two of them
rehearsed (and this was before England had become properly
aware of Freud) Virginia's childhood trauma inflicted by her
elder half-brother George Duckworth, who had, under cover
of big-brotherly affection, repeatedly entered the nursery at
night for intimate fondlings, the nature of which Virginia then
hardly comprehended; she knew only that he frightened her
and that she despised him. Apparently this explanation satisfied

Leonard—the "consolation" worked—if rather too quickly; the ability to adjust speedily to disappointment is a good and useful trait in a colonial officer, less so in a husband. It does not contradict the uxorious temperament, however, and certainly not the nursing enterprise: a wife who is seen to be frigid as well as mad is simply taken for that much sicker. But too ready a reconcilement to bad news is also a kind of abandonment, and Leonard seems very early to have relinquished, or allowed Virginia to relinquish, the sexual gratifications of marriage. All the stranger since he repeatedly speaks of himself as "lustful." And he is not known to have had so much as a dalliance during his marriage.

On the other hand, Quentin Bell suggests—a little coyly, as if only blamelessly hinting—that Virginia Woolf's erotic direction was perhaps toward women rather than men. The "perhaps" is crucial: the index to the first volume lists "passion for Madge Vaughan," "passion for Violet Dickinson," but the corresponding textual passages are all projections from the most ordinary sort of data. Madge Vaughan was a cousin by marriage whom Virginia knew from the age of seven; at sixteen she adored her still, and once stood in the house paralyzed by rapture, thinking, "Madge is here; at this moment she is actually under this roof"—an emotion, she once said, that she never equaled afterward. Many emotions at sixteen are never equaled afterward. Of Virginia's intense letter-writing to Violet Dickinson—a friend of her dead half-sister—Quentin Bell says: ". . . it is clear to the modern reader, though it was not at all clear to Virginia, that she was in love and that her love was returned." What is even clearer is that it is possible to be too "modern," if that is what enables one to read a sensual character into every exuberant or sympathetic friendship between women. Vita Sackville-West, of course, whom Virginia Woolf knew when both writers were already celebrated, was an established sapphist, and was plainly in pursuit of Virginia. Virginia, she wrote, "dislikes the quality of masculinity," but that was the view of one with a vested interest in believing it. As for Virginia, she "felt," according to her biographer, "as a lover feels—she desponded when she fancied herself neglected, despaired when

Vita was away, waited anxiously for letters, needed Vita's company and lived in that strange mixture of elation and despair which lovers—and one would have supposed only lovers—can experience." But all this is Quentin Bell. Virginia herself, reporting a three-day visit from Sackville-West, appears erotically detached: "These Sapphists *love* women; friendship is never untinged with amorosity. . . . I like her and being with her and the splendour—she shines in the grocer's shop . . . with a candle lit radiance." She acknowledged what she readily called Vita's "glamour," but the phrase "these Sapphists" is too mocking to be lover's language. And she was quick to criticize Vita (who was married to Harold Nicolson) as a mother: ". . . she is a little cold and off-hand with her boys." Virginia Woolf's biographer nevertheless supposes—he admits all this is conjecture—"some caressing, some bedding together." Still, in the heart of this love, if it was love, was the ultimate withdrawal: "In brain and insight," Virginia remarked in her diary, "she is not as highly organised as I am." Vita was splendid but "not reflective." She wrote "with a pen of brass." And: "I have no enormous opinion of her poetry." Considering all of which, Quentin Bell notes persuasively that "she could not really love without feeling that she was in the presence of a superior intellect." Sackville-West, for her part, insisted that not only did Virginia not like the quality of masculinity, but also the "possessiveness and love of domination in men."

Yet Leonard Woolf dominated Virginia Woolf overwhelmingly—nor did she resist—not so much because his braininess impressed her (his straightforwardly thumping writing style must have claimed her loyalty more than her admiration), but because he possessed her in the manner of—it must be said again—a strong-minded nurse with obsessive jurisdiction over a willful patient. The issue of Virginia Woolf's tentative or potential lesbianism becomes reduced, at this point, to the merest footnote of possibility. Sackville-West called her "inviolable"; and the fact is she was conventionally married, and had conventional expectations of marriage. She wanted children. For a wedding present Violet Dickinson sent her a cradle. "My baby shall sleep in [it]," she said at thirty. But it stood empty, and she felt, all her life, the ache of the irretrievable. "I don't like the physicalness of having children of my own," she wrote at forty-five, recording how "the little creatures"—Vanessa's children—"moved my infinitely sentimental throat." But then, with a lurch of candor: "I can dramatise myself a parent, it is true. And perhaps I have killed the feeling instinctively; or perhaps nature does." Two years after declaring the feeling killed, during a dinner party full of worldly conversation with the Webbs and assorted eminences, she found herself thinking: "L. and myself . . . the pathos, the symbolical quality of the childless couple."

The feeling was not killed; it had a remarkable durability. There is no record of her response to the original decision not to have children. That decision was Leonard's, and it was "medical." He consulted three or four people variously qualified, including Vanessa's doctor and the nurse who ran the home to which Virginia was sent when most dangerously disturbed (and to whom, according to Bell, Leonard ascribed "an unconscious but violent homosexual passion for Virginia"—which would, one imagines, make one wonder about the disinterestedness of her advice). Leonard also requested the opinion of Dr. George Savage, Virginia's regular physician, whom he disliked, and was heartily urged to have babies; soon after we find him no longer in consultation with Dr. Savage. Bell tells us that "in the end Leonard decided and persuaded Virginia to agree that, although they both wanted children, it would be too dangerous for her to have them." The "too dangerous" is left unexplained; we do not even know Leonard's ostensible reason. Did he think she could not withstand pregnancy and delivery? She was neither especially frail nor without energy, and was a zealous walker, eight miles at a time, over both London and countryside; she hefted piles of books and packed them for the Hogarth Press; she had no organic impediments. Did he believe she could not have borne the duties of rearing? But in that class there was no household without its nanny (Vanessa had two), and just as she never had to do a housekeeping chore (she never laid a fire, or made a bed, or washed a sock), she need not have been obliged to take physical care of a child. Did he, then, fear an

inherited trait—diseased offspring? Or did he intend to protect
the phantom child from distress by preventing its birth into a
baleful household? Or did he mean, out of some curious notion
of intellectual purity, not to divide the strength of Virginia's
available sanity, to preserve her undistracted for her art?

Whatever the reason, and to spare her—or himself—what
pains we can only guess at, she was in this second instance
released from "normality." Normality is catch-as-catch-can.
Leonard, in his deliberateness, in his responsibility, was more
serious than that, and surrendered her to a program of omissions.
She would be spared the tribulations both of the conjugal bed
and of childbed. She need not learn ease in the one; she need
not, no, must not, venture into the other. In forbidding Virginia maternity, Leonard abandoned her to an unparalleled and
unslakable envy. Her diary again and again records the pangs
she felt after visits with Vanessa's little sons—pangs, defenses,
justifications: she suffered. Nor was it a social suffering—she
did not feel deprived of children because she was expected
to. The name "Virginia Woolf" very soon acquired the same
resonance for her contemporaries ("this celebrity business is
quite chronic," she wrote) as it has for us—after which she was
expected to be only Virginia Woolf. She learned, after a while,
to be only that (which did not, however, prevent her from being
an adored and delightful aunt), and to mock at Vanessa's moth-
ering, and to call it obsessive and excessive. She suffered the
envy of the childless for the fruitful, precisely this, and nothing
societally imposed; and she even learned to transmute maternal
envy into a more manageable variety—literary begrudging.
This was directed at Vanessa's second son, Julian Bell, killed in
the Spanish Civil War, toward whose literary ambitions Virginia Woolf was always ungenerous, together with Leonard; a
collection of Julian's essays, prepared after his death, Leonard
dubbed "Vanessa's necrophily." Vanessa-envy moved on into
the second generation. It was at bottom a rivalry of creature-
liness, in which Virginia was always the loser. Vanessa was on
the side of "normality," the placid mother of three, enjoying all
the traditional bourgeois consolations; she was often referred to
as a madonna; and at the same time she was a thorough-going

bohemian. Virginia was anything but placid, yet lived a sober sensible domestic life in a marriage stable beyond imagining, with no trace of bohemianism. Vanessa the bohemian madonna had the best of both hearth-life and free life. Virginia was barred from both.

Without the authoritative domestic role maternity would have supplied, with no one in the household dependent on her (for years she quarreled with her maid on equal or inferior terms), and finding herself always—as potential patient—in submission, Virginia Woolf was by degrees nudged into a position of severe dependency. It took odd forms: Leonard not only prescribed milk at eleven in the morning, but also topics for conversation in the evening. Lytton Strachey's sister-in-law recalls how among friends Leonard would work up the "backbone" of a subject "and then be happy to let [Virginia] ornament it if she wanted to." And he gave her pocket money every week. Her niece Angelica reports that "Leonard kept Virginia on very short purse-strings," which she exercised through the pleasures of buying "coloured string and sealing-wax, notebooks and pencils." When she came to the end of writing a book, she trembled until Leonard read it and gave his approval. William Plomer remembers how Leonard would grow alarmed if, watching Virginia closely, he saw her laugh a little too convulsively. And once she absentmindedly began to flick bits of meat off her dinner plate; Leonard hushed the company and led her away.*

—All of which has given Leonard his reputation for saintliness. A saint who successively secures acquiescence to frigidity, childlessness, dependency? Perhaps; probably; of course. These are, after all, conventual vows—celibacy, barrenness, obedience. But Leonard Woolf was a socialist, not an ascetic; he had a practical political intelligence; he was the author of books called *Empire and Commerce in Africa* and *Socialism and Co-operation*; he ran the Hogarth Press like a good businessman; at the same time he edited a monthly periodical, *The International Review*; he was literary editor of *The Nation*. He had exactly the kind

* Joan Russell Noble, ed., *Recollections of Virginia Woolf by Her Contemporaries* (William Morrow & Company, Inc., 1972).

of commonsensical temperament that scorns, and is repelled by, religious excess. And of Virginia he made a shrine; of himself, a monk. On the day of her death Virginia walked out of the house down to the river Ouse and drowned herself; not for nothing was that house called Monk's House. The letter she left for Leonard was like almost every other suicide note, horribly banal, not a writer's letter at all, and rich with guilt—"I feel certain I am going mad again. I feel we can't go through another of those terrible times. . . . I can't go on spoiling your life any longer." To Vanessa she wrote, "All I want to say is that Leonard has been so astonishingly good, every day, always; I can't imagine that anyone could have done more for me than he has. . . . I feel he has so much to do that he will go on, better without me. . . ."

Saints make guilt—especially when they impose monkish values; there is nothing new in that. And it was the monk as well as her madness she was fleeing when she walked into the Ouse, though it was the saint she praised. "I don't think two people could have been happier than we have been," the note to Leonard ended. A tragic happiness—such a thing is possible: cheerful invalids are a commonplace, and occasionally one hears of happy inmates. A saintly monk, a monkish nurse? All can be taken together, and all are true together. But the drive toward monkishness was in Leonard. What was natural for himself he prescribed for Virginia, and to one end only: to prevent her ongoing nervous crises from reaching their extreme state; to keep her sane. And to keep her sane was, ultimately, to keep her writing. It is reasonable to imagine that without Leonard Woolf there would have been very little of that corpus the name Virginia Woolf calls to mind—there would have been no *Mrs. Dalloway*, no *To the Lighthouse*, no *The Waves*, no *Common Reader*. And it may be that even the word Bloomsbury—the redolence, the signal—would not have survived, since she was its center. "She would not have been the symbol" of Bloomsbury, T. S. Eliot said, "if she had not been the maintainer of it." For Bloomsbury as an intellectual "period" to have escaped oblivion, there had to be at least one major literary voice to carry it beyond datedness. That voice was hers.

The effort to keep her sane was mammoth. Why did Leonard think it was worth it? The question, put here for the second time, remains callous but inevitable. Surely it would have been relieving at last (and perhaps to both of them) to let her slide away into those rantings, delusions, hallucinations; she might or might not have returned on her own. It is even possible that the nursing was incidental, and that she recovered each time because she still had the capacity to recover. But often enough Leonard—who knew the early symptoms intimately—was able to prevent her from going under; each pulling-back from that brink of dementia gained her another few months of literary work. Again and again he pulled her back. It required cajolery, cunning, mastery, agility, suspiciousness, patience, spoon-feeding, and an over-whelming sensitiveness to every flicker of her mood. Obviously it drained him; obviously he must have been tempted now and then to let it all go and give up. Almost anyone else would have. Why did he not? Again the answer must be manifold. Because she was his wife; because she was the beloved one to whom he had written during their courtship, "You don't know what a wave of happiness comes over me when I see you smile";* because his conscience obliged him to; because she suffered; because—this before much else—it was in his nature to succor suffering. And also: because of her gift; because of her genius; for the sake of literature; because she was unique. And because she had been a Miss Stephen; because she was Thoby Stephen's sister; because she was a daughter of Leslie Stephen; because she was, like Leonard's vision of Cambridge itself, "compounded of . . . the atmosphere of long years of history and great traditions and famous names [and] a profoundly civilized life"; because she was Bloomsbury; because she was England.

For her sake, for art's sake, for his own sake. Perhaps above all for his own sake. In her he had married a kind of escutcheon; she represented the finest grain of the finest stratum in England. What he shored up against disintegration was the life

---

* From an unpublished letter in the Berg Collection. Quoted in *The New York Times*, June 14, 1973.

he had gained—a birthright he paid for by spooning porridge between Virginia Woolf's resisting lips.

Proust is right to tell us to go to a writer's books, not to his loyalties. Wherever Leonard Woolf is, there Virginia Woolf is not. The more Leonard recedes or is not present, the more Virginia appears in force. Consequently Quentin Bell's biography—the subversive strength of which is Leonard—demands an antidote. The antidote is, of course, in the form of a reminder—that Virginia Woolf was a woman of letters as well as a patient; that she did not always succumb but instead could be an original fantasist and fashioner of an unaccustomed way of seeing; that the dependency coincided with a vigorous intellectual autonomy; that together with the natural subordination of the incapacitated she possessed the secret confidence of the innovator.

Seen through Leonard's eyes, she is, in effect, always on the verge of lunacy. "I am quite sure," he tells us in his autobiography, "that Virginia's genius was closely connected with what manifested itself as mental instability and insanity. The creative imagination in her novels, her ability to 'leave the ground' in conversation, and the voluble delusions of the breakdown all came from the same place in her mind—she 'stumbled after her own voice' and followed 'the voices that fly ahead.'" At the same time her refusal to eat was associated with guilt—she talked of her "faults"—and Leonard insists that "she remained all through her illness, even when most insane, terribly sane in three-quarters of her mind. The point is that her insanity was in her premises, in her beliefs. She believed, for instance, that she was not ill. . . ."

Seen through the books, she is never "ill," never lunatic. Whether it was mental instability or a clear-sighted program of experiment in the shape of the novel that unhinged her prose from the conventional margins that had gone before is a question not worth speculating over. Leonard said that when mad she heard the birds sing in Greek. The novels are not like that: it is not the data that are altered, but the sequence of things. When Virginia Woolf assaulted the "old" fiction in her famous

Mr. Bennett and Mrs. Brown, she thought she was recommending getting rid of the habit of data; she thought this was to be her fictive platform. But when she grappled with her own inventions, she introduced as much data as possible and strained to express it all under the pressure of a tremendous simultaneity. What she was getting rid of was consecutiveness; precisely the habit of premises. If clinging to premises was the sanity of her insanity, then the intent of her fiction was not an extension of her madness, as Leonard claimed, but its calculated opposite. The poetry of her prose may have been like the elusive poetry of her dementia, but its steadfast design was not. "The design," she wrote of *Mrs. Dalloway*, "is so queer and so masterful"; elated, she saw ahead. She was an artist; she schemed, and not through random contractions or inflations of madness, but through the usual methods of art: inspired intellection, the breaking down of expectation into luminous segments of shock.

A simpler way of saying all this is that what she achieved as a stylist cannot really be explained through linking it with madness. The diaries give glimpses of rationalized prefigurations; a letter from Vanessa suggests moths, which metamorphosed into *The Moths*, which became *The Waves*. She knew her destination months before she arrived; she was in control of her work, she did what she meant to do. If the novels are too imaginatively astonishing to be persuasive on this point, the essays will convince. They are read too little, and not one of them is conceptually stale, or worn in any other way. In them the birds do not sing in Greek either, but the Greek—the sign of a masterly nineteenth-century literary education—shows like a spine. In the essays the control of brilliant minutiae is total—historical and literary figures, the particulars of biography, society, nationality, geography. She is a courier for the past. In Volume III of the *Collected Essays*, for instance, the range is from Chaucer through Montaigne through some Elizabethans major and minor, through Swift and Sterne and Lord Chesterfield, Fanny Burney and Cowper. She was interested also in the lives of women, especially writers. She studies Sara Coleridge, the poet's daughter; Harriette Wilson, the mistress of the Earl of Craven; Dr. Johnson's Mrs. Thrale; and Dorothy Osborne, a talented

letter-writer of the seventeenth century. The language and
scope of the essays astound. If they are "impressionistic," they
are not self-indulgent; they put history before sensibility. When
they are ironic, it is the kind of irony that enlarges the discrim-
inatory faculty and does not serve the cynical temper. They
mean to interpret other lives by the annihilation of the crack
of time: they are after what the novels are after, a compression
of then and now into the simultaneity of a singular recognition and a single comprehension. They mean to make every
generation, and every instant, contemporaneous with
every other generation and instant. And yet—it does not contradict—they are, taken all together, the English Essay incarnate.

The autonomous authority of the fiction, the more public
authority of the essays, are the antidotes to Bell's Woolf, to
Leonard's Virginia. But there is a third antidote implicit in the
whole of the work, and in the drive behind the work, and that
is Virginia Woolf's feminism. It ought to be said at once that it
was what can now be called "classical" feminism. The latter-
day choice of Virginia Woolf, on the style of Sylvia Plath, as a
current women's-movement avatar is inapposite and mistaken.
Classical feminism is inimical to certain developing strands of
"liberation." Where feminism repudiates the conceit of the
"gentler sex," liberation has come to reaffirm it. Where feminism asserts a claim on the larger world, liberation shifts to
separatism. Where feminism scoffs at the plaint of "sisters under
the skin," and maintains individuality of condition and temperament, liberation reinstates sisterhood and sameness. Where
feminism shuns self-preoccupation, liberation experiments
with self-examination, both psychic and medical. Classical
feminism as represented by Virginia Woolf meant one thing
only: access to the great world of thinking, being, and doing.
The notion of "male" and "female" states of intellect and feeling, hence of prose, ultimately of culture, would have been the
occasion of a satiric turn for Virginia Woolf; so would the idea
of a politics of sex. Clive Bell reports that she licked envelopes
once or twice for the Adult Suffrage League, but that she "made
merciless fun of the flag-waving fanaticism" of the activists.
She was not political—or, perhaps, just political enough, as

when Chekhov notes that "writers should engage themselves
in politics only enough to protect themselves from politics."
Though one of her themes was women in history (several of her
themes, rather; she took her women one by one, not as a race,
species, or nation), presumably she would have mocked at the
invention of a "history of women"—what she cared for, as *A
Room of One's Own* both lucidly and passionately lays out, was
access to a unitary culture. Indeed, *Orlando* is the metaphorical
expression of this idea. History as a record of division or exclusion was precisely what she set herself against: the Cambridge
of her youth kept women out, and all her life she preserved her
resentment by pronouncing herself undereducated. She studied
at home, Greek with Janet Case, literature and mathematics
with her father, and as a result was left to count on her fingers
forever—but for people who grow up counting on their fingers,
even a Cambridge education cannot do much. Nevertheless
she despised what nowadays is termed "affirmative action,"
granting places in institutions as a kind of group reparation;
she thought it offensive to her own earned prestige, and once
took revenge on the notion. In 1935 Forster, a member of the
Committee of the London Library, informed her that a debate
was under way concerning the admission of women members.
No women were admitted. Six years later Virginia Woolf was
invited to serve; she said she would not be a "sop"—she ought
to have been invited years earlier, on the same terms as Forster,
as a writer; not in 1941, when she was already fifty-nine, as a
woman.

Nor will she do as martyr. Although Cambridge was closed
to her, literary journalism was not; although she complains of
being chased off an Oxbridge lawn forbidden to the feet of
women, no one ever chased her off a page. Almost immediately
she began to write for the *Times Literary Supplement* and for
Cornhill; she was then twenty-two. She was, of course, Leslie
Stephen's daughter, and it is doubtful whether any other young
writer, male or female, could have started off so auspiciously:
still, we speak here not of "connections" but of experience. At
about the same time she was summoned to teach at Morley,
a workers' college for men and women. One of her reports

survives, and Quentin Bell includes it as an appendix. "My four women," she writes, "can hear eight lectures on the French Revolution if they wish to continue their historical learning"—and these were working-class women, in 1905. By 1928, women had the vote, and full access to universities, the liberal professions, and the civil service. As for Virginia Woolf, in both instances, as writer and teacher, she was solicited—and this cannot be, after all, only because she was Leslie Stephen's daughter. She could use on the spot only her own gifts, not the rumor of her father's. Once she determined to ignore what Bell calls the "matrimonial market" of upper-class partying, into which for a time her half-brother George dragooned her, she was freed to her profession. It was not true then, it is not true now, that a sublime and serious pen can be circumscribed.

Virginia Woolf was a practitioner of her profession from an early age; she was not deprived of an education, rather of a particular college; she grew rich and distinguished; she developed her art on her own line, according to her own sensibilities, and was acclaimed for it; though insane, she was never incarcerated. She was an elitist, and must be understood as such. What she suffered from, aside from the abysses of depression which characterized her disease, was not anything like the condition of martyrdom—unless language has become so flaccid that being on occasion patronized begins to equal death for the sake of an ideal. What she suffered from really was only the minor inflammations of the literary temperament. And she was not often patronized: her fame encouraged her to patronize others. She could be unkind, she could be spiteful, she could envy—her friendship with Katherine Mansfield was always unsure, being founded on rivalry. Mansfield and her husband, the journalist John Middleton Murry, "work in my flesh," Virginia Woolf wrote, "after the manner of the jigger insect. It's annoying, indeed degrading, to have these bitternesses." She was bitter also about James Joyce; she thought him, says Bell, guilty of "atrocities." Her diary speaks of "the damned egotistical self; which ruins Joyce," and she saw *Ulysses* as "insistent, raw, striking and ultimately nauseating." But she knew Joyce to be moving in the same direction as herself; it was a race that,

despite her certainty of his faults, he might win. By the time of
her death she must have understood that he *had* won. Still, to be
outrun in fame is no martyrdom. And her own fame was and
is in no danger, though, unlike Joyce, she is not taken as a fact
of nature. Virginia Woolf's reputation in the thirty and more
years since her death deepens; she becomes easier to read,
more complex to consider.

To Charlotte Brontë, born sixty-six years before Virginia
Woolf, Robert Southey, then Poet Laureate, had written, "Literature cannot be the business of a woman's life, and it ought
not to be." No one addressed Virginia Woolf of Bloomsbury
in this fashion; she was sought out by disciples, editors, litter-
ateurs; in the end Oxford and Cambridge asked her to lecture
before their women's colleges. If the issue of martyrdom is
inappropriate (implying as it does that a woman who commits
suicide is by definition a martyr), what of heroism? Virginia
Woolf's death was or was not heroic, depending on one's view
of suicide by drowning. The case for Leonard's heroism is more
clear-cut: a saint is noble on behalf of others, a hero on behalf of
himself. But if Virginia Woolf is to be seen as a heroine, it must
be in those modes outside the manner of her death and even the
manner of her life as a patient in the house.

If she is to be seen as a heroine, it must be in the conjuring of
yet another of those Bloomsbury photographs—this time one
that does not exist. The picture is of a woman sitting in an old
chair holding a writing board; the point of her pen touches a
half-filled page. To gaze at her bibliography is, in a way, to
conjure this picture that does not exist—hour after hour, year
after year, a life's accumulation of stupendous visionary toil.
A writer's heroism is in the act of writing; not in the finished
work, but in the work as it goes.

Vanessa's son gives us no heroine: only this stubborn and
sometimes querulous self-starving madwoman, with so stoic,
so heroic, a male nurse. And when she runs away from him
to swallow the Ouse, the heroism of both of them comes to
an end.

The Lastingness of Saul Bellow

HOW EASY IT IS, and plausible, to regard a collection of letters spanning youth and old age as an approximation of autobiography: the procession of denizens who inhabit a life, the bit players with their entrances and exits, the faithful chronology of incidents—all turn up reliably in either form, whether dated and posted or backward-looking. Yet autobiography, even when ostensibly steeped in candor, tends toward reconsideration—if not revisionary paperings-over, then late perspectives and second thoughts. Whereas letters (but here let us specify a *writer's* letters) are appetite and urgency, unmediated seizures of impulse and desire torn from the fraught and living moment. And letters—sorted, indexed, bound—are themselves a paradox: hotly alive, they claim death as a requisite. Rare and anomalous is the publisher who would prefer the correspondence of the quick, however celebrated, to the letters of the dead: the death of a writer who answers his mail, especially one possessed of a powerful fame, lengthens and amplifies the body of work.

Even so, death disports with writers more cruelly than with the rest of humankind. The grave can hardly make more mute those who were voiceless when alive—dust to dust, muteness to muteness. But the silence that dogs the established writer's noisy obituary, with its boisterous shock and busy regret, is more profound than any other. Oblivion comes more cuttingly to the writer whose presence has been *felt*, argued over, championed, disparaged—the writer who is seen to be what Lionel Trilling calls a Figure. *Lionel Trilling?* Consider: who at this hour (apart from some professorial specialist currying his "field") is reading Mary McCarthy, James T. Farrell, John Berryman, Allan Bloom, Irving Howe, Alfred Kazin, Edmund Wilson, Anne Sexton, Alice Adams, Robert Lowell, Grace

Paley, Owen Barfield, Stanley Elkin, Robert Penn Warren, Norman Mailer, Leslie Fiedler, R. P. Blackmur, Paul Goodman, Susan Sontag, Lillian Hellman, John Crowe Ransom, Stephen Spender, Daniel Fuchs, Hugh Kenner, Seymour Krim, J. F. Powers, Allen Ginsberg, Philip Rahv, Jack Richardson, John Auerbach, Harvey Swados—or Trilling himself? These names of the dead—a good number of them past luminaries, a few (Lillian Hellman, say) worthy of being forgotten—do not come randomly. They all have their fleeting turn in Saul Bellow's letters, whether vituperatively, casually, or approvingly (though scarcely ever indifferently). It is safe to say that most are nowadays not much in demand either at your local library or on Amazon, and safer yet to surmise that many have little chance of outlasting even the first third of the twenty-first century; several have barely outlasted the twentieth. Nearly all have been overtaken by newer writers lately grown familiar, vernal aspirants who crowd the horizon with their addictive clamor.

And even as these contemporary importunings swamp our perception, what can already be clearly discerned rising from this swelling armada of the twice-buried is a single exemption: Bellow. Among all the literary tumults and public roilings of the recently Famous, he alone courts lastingness, he alone escapes eclipse. To state this so bluntly is not so much a declaration as it is an inquiry. Only see how speedily the grave works its mufflings and comedowns—Ginsberg, mum; Mailer, dumb as stone. In the tracings of unassailable art, high or low, they leave improbable spoor: the poet no poet but minstrel and mountebank, the would-be immortal novelist undone by the politicized harlequin he became. Gradually they decay into symptom and artifact—documents of a receding social history—while the vestigial rustlings surrounding their names testify to nothing more memorable than outdated literary tinsel.

But Bellow stays, and why? Language—the acclaimed style—cannot be the whole of it, though its energetic capaciousness captures and capsizes American English with an amplitude and verve not heard since Whitman, and never before in prose. The mandarin-poolroom link, elevated riffs married to street vernacular, has become Bellow's signature, and attracts lovestruck imitators. Yet brilliant flourishes alone, even when embedded in galloping ambition, will not make a second Bellow. (A second Bellow? Not for a hundred years!) There is instead something else, beyond the heated braininess and lavish command of ideas: call it *feeling*. In this bountiful volume of letters, the writer's last brief words, set down fourteen months before his death, should all at once break open the hidden-in-plain-sight code that reveals why Bellow stays:

> [My parents] needed all the help they could get. They were forever asking, "What does the man say?" and I would translate for them into heavy-footed English. The old people were as ignorant of English as they were of Canadian French. We often stopped before a display of children's shoes. My mother coveted for me a pair of patent-leather sandals with an *elegantissimo* strap. I finally got them—I rubbed them with butter to preserve the leather. This is when I was six or seven years old. . . . Amazing how it all boils down to a pair of patent-leather sandals.

It all boils down to a pair of patent-leather sandals. A dying old man's sentimental nostalgia, a fruitlessly self-indulgent yearning for a mother lost too soon? No; or not only. What we are hearing also is the culmination of a theory of pastness—and pastness means passage. In nine sentences, an annotated history of an immigrant family, where it settled, how it struggled, how it aspired; and a hint of the future novelist's moral aesthetic, the determination to preserve. As with the family, so with the family of man. Bellow, who as a graduate student studied anthropology, as a writer pursues the history of civilized thought—an inquisitiveness directed to the way experience (Augie) turns into a quest for philosophy (Henderson, Sammler, Herzog), sometimes via a scalding bath of comedy.

The letters are all zest and craving and demand—so many journeys, so many cities, so many liaisons, so many courtings, so many marriages and partings, so many spasms of rage, so many victories and downers, so many blue or frenetic melancholias and grievances; but cumulatively they add up to a rich montage of knowing, speckled now and again with laughter, that most metaphysical of emotions. And always, pulsing below the hungry race, the loyalty to pastness. Well into Bellow's old age, Chicago's Tuley High School held an emblematic place in his psyche. Tuley was where the excitations of intellectual ambition first encountered their kin in the formidably intelligent children of mostly working-class immigrant Jews, boys and girls drenched in ferocious bookishness and utopian politics, unselfconsciously asserting ownership of American culture at a time when it was most vigorously dominated by WASPs. Nathan Gould, Louis Lasco, Oscar Tarcov, David Peltz, Stuart Brent, Herbert Passin, Abe Kaufman, Hymen Slate, Louis Sidran, Rosalyn Tureck, Zita Cogan, Yetta Barshevsky, Sam Freifeld, and especially Isaac Rosenfeld—Bellow kept up with a surprising number of these witnesses to his early ardors, and mourned acutely when the dying of old friends began. In a letter to Nathan Gould in 1981, the Nobel five years behind him, he fell into elegy:

> I attended the Tuley reunion and it was a depressing affair—
> elderly people nostalgic for youth and the Depression years.
> There seemed nothing for them (for us) to do but turn into
> middle-class Americans with the same phrases and thoughts
> from the same sources. Some came from far away . . . and
> some were crippled and required wheeling. . . . [One] who
> seemed well preserved turned out to have a heredity disor-
> der affecting his memory so that he was groping, while we
> talked, and his new wife was deeply uneasy. . . . But my
> closest friends were Oscar and Isaac, dead for many years.
> In every decade I try to think what they might have been
> had they lived.

He ended with a tribute to "the old days." If as "a sort of public man" he didn't retain the old affections, he said, "I would feel alienated from my own history, *false*."

Fifteen years later, at a memorial service for Yetta Barshevsky, who had been Tuley's class orator and radical firebrand, elegy burst into exuberant reminiscence. After reciting Yetta's street

address of seven decades before (and his own, "right around the
corner"), after dismissing her "spectacularly handsome" mother
as an unregenerate Stalinist and describing her carpenter father's
"jalopy . . . filled with saws and sawdust," he appended a tour
de force of recollection:

> I even came to know Yetta's grandfather, whom I often
> saw at the synagogue when I came to say Kaddish for my
> mother. He was an extremely, primitively orthodox short
> bent man with a beard that seemed to rush out of him and
> muffled his face. He wore a bowler hat and elastic-sided
> boots. The old women, it seems, were wildly radical com-
> munist sympathizers. The grandfathers were the pious ones.

Passages like these, with their sociohistorical notation and
their indelible optical prowess—rushing beard, elastic-sided
boots!—can easily be found reverberating in any of Bellow's
stories and novels. And even in the very first letter in this
collection, a clowning response to Yetta's having jilted him in
favor of one Nathan Goldstein, Bellow at seventeen was already
a conscious writer—antic, teasing, showing off, pumping adolescent brio and witty pastiche. He *felt* what he was; he was
sure of what he had. Like Henry James and T. S. Eliot, those
confident conquistadors of London who were his precursors
in early self-knowledge, Bellow claimed recognition before he
was in a position to have earned it. But London was an insular
village vulnerable to conquest, and America was a continent.
What could be accomplished gracefully, if cattily, in Virginia
Woolf's Tavistock Square required boldness in Chicago.

In 1932, Bellow is a teenage boy writing to a teenage girl;
five years on, as subeditor of an obscure Trotskyist journal, he
addresses James T. Farrell in the worldly tones of a seasoned
colleague—though at twenty-two he has so far published
only occasional pieces. "It is peculiar," Bellow instructs Farrell, who had become his mentor, "how the Stalinites have
lost central discipline by spreading themselves through liberal
groups. . . . [Sydney] Harris thinks nothing of assassinating a
scruple or knifing a principle if thereby he can profit." This

fierce disparagement—the skewering of a now nearly forgotten journalist in that antediluvian period when "Trotskyist"
and "Stalinite" were warring bywords—only intensified as
Bellow aged into viewpoints adversarial to his youthful radicalism. In 1986, summing up for Karl Shapiro his impressions
of an international writers' congress in New York sponsored
by PEN, he dismissed a clutch of contemporary notables:
"Mailer," he reported, "mostly wanted a huge media event—
that's what he calls living. . . . It boggled my mind to see
how greedy the radicals were for excitement 'radical-style.'
I'm speaking of big-time subversives like Ginsberg, Nadine
Gordimer, Grace Paley, Doctorow, and other representatives
of affluent revolution." One can marvel at how the polemical
voice of the mature Bellow is scarcely changed (despite the
change of politics) from that of the self-assured and strenuously
contentious young man of fifty years before—yet even more
striking is how Bellow in his twenties is ready to pit his taste
and his talent against anyone, however more established. To
be famous and forceful at seventy is one thing; to believe in
one's fame before it has evolved is a kind of magical faith. It
was an authority—no, an authenticity—that carried him far.
He had no intention (so the letters reveal) of wasting time as
a novitiate pursuing deferential cultivation of influential eminences. His approach was that of an instant equal. His successful
candidacy (and third try) for a Guggenheim fellowship elicit-
ed support from Farrell, Edmund Wilson, and Robert Penn
Warren. He had already been in friendly correspondence with
all three, and was intimate enough with Warren to know him
as "Red."

Still earlier, he had quickly formed a connection with Philip
Rahv of *Partisan Review*, the most imperially prestigious literary
magnet of the Forties. For the young Bellow, publication failed
to satisfy if it fell short of widening both courage and opportunity. James Henle of Vanguard Press, who in 1944 brought out
Dangling Man, Bellow's first published novel—later followed
by *The Victim*—was soon jettisoned. To Henry Volkening, his
agent, Bellow spoke of "swollen feelings," and to Henle he
wrote sourly:

I know you will accuse me again of putting off the philosopher's robe and of being too impatient, and that you will
repeat that before I have published five or six books I can't
expect to live by writing. But as I write slowly I will be
forty before my fifth book is ready and I don't think it is
unreasonable of me to expect that the most should be made
of what I do produce. When I see my chances for uninterrupted work going down the drain I can't help protesting
the injustice of it. This year I have been ill and teaching
leaves me no energy for writing. [Bellow at this time was
assistant professor of English at the University of Minnesota.] . . . I see next year and the next and the one after that
fribbled away at the university. My grievance is a legitimate
one, I think. I don't want to be a commercial writer or to be
taken up with money. I have never discussed money matters
with you in four years, except for the letter I wrote you last
spring about [*The Victim*]. You were annoyed with me. . . .
But now the book is out, it hasn't been badly received and
already it seems to be going the way of *Dangling Man*.

The letter was not sent. But the break with Henle was carried out; it stood for more than ambition, more than a writer's
nervous self-advocacy. It was clairvoyance, it was a heralding,
it spoke for the cause of imagination untrammeled. Already
it bristled with the thickening future. His second novel only
just published, Bellow was numbering the long row of still-
to-be-written novels ahead. The unsent letter was not about
money—it was about freedom, it was about becoming. Even
more, it was about knowing. Bellow knew what he knew, and
like some youthfully anointed evangelist, he wanted what he
knew to be known. The flight from Henle was the beginning
of a credo.

And what was that credo? An impulse running through
many of the letters discloses it: it was, plainly and unaffectedly,
how to *see*; meaning, at bottom, how a novelist must think.
For decades it has been common wisdom—common because
Bellow himself made it so—that *Dangling Man* and *The Victim*,
the pair of novels preceding *The Adventures of Augie March*, were

too "Flaubertian," too controlled, pinched by the orderliness of European modernist constraint, while *Augie* was an extravagant release into the impetuous comedic buoyancy of a manifold America. Of *The Victim*, Bellow was moved to write:

> Compared to what is published nowadays between boards, it is an accomplishment. By my own standards, however, it is promissory. It took hold of my mind and imagination very deeply but I know that I somehow failed to write it *freely*, with all the stops out from beginning to end. . . . And I must admit that in spite of the great amount of energy I brought to the book at certain times, I was at others, for some reason, content to fall back on lesser resources. . . . But there is a certain diffidence about me . . . that prevents me from going all out. . . . I assemble the dynamite but I am not ready to touch off the fuse. Why? Because I am working toward something and have not arrived. . . . I wanted to write before I had the maturity to write as "high" as I wished and so I had a very arduous and painful apprenticeship and am still undergoing it.

Or so he declared in January 1948. But by April he was disputing this unforgiving verdict, complaining of "a rather disagreeable letter from Kurt [Wolff] about *The Victim*. I didn't mind his criticisms of specific things but I disliked extremely his telling me 'you aren't there *yet*.' " *The Victim*, he went on, "is a powerful book. . . . There aren't many recent books that come close to it and I can't take seriously any opinion that doesn't begin by acknowledging that." Adding more than sixty years of reappraisal to Bellow's spare three months, we can argue even more effectively against the notion of apprenticeship. There is by now no getting away from it: the earlier novels need not, should not, be overshadowed or diminished by *Augie*. It is not too daring to venture that if *Augie*—grand gusts of vitality notwithstanding—had never come into being, Bellow would still have been Bellow: the mind, the wit, the word, the reach; the perplexity and the delirium of the human animal. There are whole pages in *Dangling Man* that might have been torn out of

Seize the Day. There are rolling tracts of dialogue in *The Victim* with telling affinities to *Ravelstein*. The familiar metaphysical cunning is everywhere. From the start, Bellow wrote "high." And the key to writing high, said this most intellectual of novelists, is to force intellect into hiding, to trick the explicit into vanishing into the implicit.

To Leslie Fiedler, who accused him of "misology"—hatred of argument and reason—he recited his unwavering principle of elasticity:

> I think positions *emerge* in a work of art, and you seem to think they're imposed. It makes small difference what the artist says he thinks, and a "prepared" attitude is an invitation to disaster. . . . I only complain that intelligence has become so naked.

And to Josephine Herbst:

> If you think *Seize the Day* is good, I'm satisfied that I'm doing all right. It's hard for me to know, because so much of the time I'm deaf, dumb and blind, the slave of unknown masters.

To John Berryman:

> All the formal properties have to be cracked and the simplicities released.

To Ruth Miller, who had sent him her essay on Ralph Ellison's *Invisible Man*:

> Your explication is too dense, too detailed. . . . Perhaps it is too much like laboratory analysis. . . . You see, you have left out the literary side of the matter almost entirely, and that, to my mind, is a mistake. I myself distinguish between the parts of the novel that were *written* and those that were constructed as part of the argument; they are not alike in quality . . . your interest is in Opinion rather than Creation.

To the Guggenheim Foundation, in support of Bernard Malamud's application for a fellowship:

> Imagination has been steadily losing prestige in American life, it seems to me, for a long time. I am speaking of the poetic imagination. Inferior kinds of imagination have prospered, but the poetic has less credit than ever before. Perhaps that is because there is less room than ever for the personal, the spacious, unanxious and free, for the unprepared, unorganized, and spontaneous elements from which poetic imagination springs.

To Louis Gallo, while working on *Herzog*:

> You'll find the book I'm writing now less "tender," "tolerant," etc. When a writer has such feelings, however, it's his business to lead them all into the hottest fire. He must expose them to the most destructive opposites he can find and, if he wishes to be tender, confront the murderer's face. The converse, however, is equally true, for writers who believe there is a Sargasso of vomit into which we must drift are obliged to confront beauty. To deny that, you would have to deny your instincts as a writer.

To Robert Penn Warren:

> Augie was very difficult for me in the last half. I suppose I succumbed to the dreadful thing I warn everyone against— seriousness. . . . My slogan was "Easily or not at all," but I forgot it. Too much of a temptation to speak the last word.

To Susan Glassman:

> Somehow I've managed to do exactly what I like. There are certain philosophers (Samuel Butler, if he is one) who say we really do get what we want. Question: Can we bear it when we get it? That's the question that's the beginning of religion.

To Richard Stern:

No amount of assertion will make an ounce of art.

But he did assert his *idea* of art—he asserted his instincts, his intuitions—and he did do exactly what he liked, at least in everything he wrote, and he really did get what he wanted, if not sooner, then later. His sovereignty as a writer was, so to say, *built in.* And for every statement of credo-instruction, especially when directed to other writers, he appended generous tributes. When he was stirred to criticism, he almost always began with self-criticism, taking on himself the very flaw he had fingered in the other. There might be an occasional exception, most particularly if the object of scrutiny was a fellow novelist publicly acknowledged to be on his own team. With such confirmed colleagues he pulled no punches: he wrote scathingly to Philip Roth, disparaging *I Married a Communist* and lecturing him on Stalin's Western loyalists and "hatred of one's own country." He was merciless toward Malamud's *A New Life*: "all the middle-class platitudes of love and liberalism . . . mean and humorless." Nevertheless there was personal warmth and varying degrees of literary admiration for his confederates in the triumvirate he parodied as "Hart, Schaffner and Marx," a quip that has survived the decades. What reluctantly united all three—Bellow, Roth, Malamud—was a concept imposed on them by the celebrity-sloganeering of the journalists: "American Jewish writers." But the link was both superficial and specious: each invented his own mythos and imagined his own republic of letters. It was not the complexity of heritage Bellow was resisting in his tailor-made mockery, but its reduction to a narrowing palliative, nowadays fashionably termed "identity." In a memorial tribute to Malamud, Bellow reiterated his ties to the old atmospherics of origins, while introducing a still greater claim:

> We were cats of the same breed. The sons of Eastern European immigrant Jews, we had gone early into the streets of our respective cities, were Americanized by schools,

newspapers, subways, streetcars, sandlots. Melting Pot children, we had assumed the American program to be the real
thing: no barriers to the freest and fullest American choices.
Of course we understood that it was no simple civics-course
matter. We knew too much about the slums, we had assimilated too much dark history in our mothers' kitchens to
be radiant optimists . . . it was admiration, it was love that
drew us to the dazzling company of the great masters, all of
them belonging to the Protestant Majority—some of them
explicitly anti-Semitic. . . . But one could not submit to
control by such prejudices. My own view was that in religion the Christians had lived with us, had lived in the Bible
of the Jews, but when the Jews wished to live in Western
history with them they were refused. As if that history was
not, by now, also ours.

These words (brilliantly included among the letters) were
recited on Bellow's behalf under the dim chandeliers of the
meeting room of the American Academy of Arts and Letters,
where the members' chairs bore brass plaques inscribed with
such storied names as Henry Adams, Owen Wister, Hamlin
Garland, Edwin Markham, and other venerable representatives
of Bellow's capitalized Majority. And when, not yet out of
their teens, he and Isaac Rosenfeld dissolved the solemn ironies
of Eliot's "Love Song of J. Alfred Prufrock" into a hilarious-
ly lampooning Yiddish ditty, it may have marked the signal
moment when writers born Jewish and awakened into America
would refuse to be refused by Western history.

Bellow's capacity for what might (in quick march) be
called Jewish intelligence summoned deeps far beyond where
the journalists could follow: the literary talent that rose up,
in puzzling if impressive flocks, out of what appeared to be a
low immigrant culture. Bellow was distinctive in transcending—transgressing against—the archetype of the coarse and
unlettered ghetto greenhorn. The greenhorns in their humble
trades were aware that they were carriers of a moral civilization. ("You are too intelligent for this," Herzog protests to his
vaporously overtheorizing friend Shapiro. "Your father had

rich blood. He peddled apples.") Though he had repeatedly declared himself, as an American, free to choose according to will or desire, Bellow also chose not to be disaffected. He was in possession of an inherited literacy that few novelists of Jewish background, writers of or close to his generation, could match, however sophisticated otherwise they might be. His range spanned an inclusive continuum; as his eulogy for Malamud insisted, Western learning and literature had also to mean Jewish learning and literature. He was at home in biblical Hebrew, was initiated into the liturgy from early childhood, and read and spoke (always with relish) a supple Yiddish. In the letters he will now and again slide into a Yiddish word or phrase for its pungent or familial aptness where English might pale. It was Bellow who, with Irving Howe and the Yiddish poet Eliezer Greenberg standing by, translated I. B. Singer's "Gimpel the Fool," in effect creating, in a matter of hours, a modernist American writer out of what had passed, mistakenly, for an old-fashioned Yiddish storyteller. What other "American Jewish writer" could have pulled off this feat? Or would have been willing to set aside the mask of fiction to pursue—his personal viewpoint plain to see—the political culture of Israel, as Bellow did in *To Jerusalem and Back*, a book-length essay composed at the crux of churning contention? (Decades old and read today, it remains, in its candor and credibility, shatteringly up-to-date.) And finally—we are compelled to come to this—there is the strangely misunderstood question of Bellow and the Holocaust.

In a letter dated July 19, 1987, he wrote:

It's perfectly true that "Jewish writers in America" (a repulsive category!) missed what should have been for them the central event of their time, the destruction of European Jewry. We (I speak of Jews now and not merely writers) should have reckoned more fully, more deeply with it. . . . I was too busy becoming a novelist to take note of what was happening in the Forties. I was involved with "literature" and given over to preoccupations with art, with language, with my struggle on the American scene, with the claims for recognition of my talent or, like my pals at the *Partisan Review*, with modernism, Marxism, New Criticism, with Eliot, Yeats, Proust, etc.—with anything except the terrible events in Poland. Growing slowly aware of this unspeakable evasion I didn't even know how to begin to admit it into my inner life. Not a particle of this can be denied. And can I really say—can anyone say—what was to be done, how this "thing" ought to have been met? Since the late Forties I have been brooding about it and sometimes I imagine I *can* see something. But what brooding may amount to is probably insignificant. I can't even begin to say what responsibility any of us may bear in such a matter, a crime so vast that it brings all Being into Judgment.

If there appears to be a contradiction in this arresting statement, it is hardly to the point. "I was too busy becoming a novelist to take note of what was happening in the Forties" may in fact clash with "Since the late Forties I have been brooding about it," but it is the closing phrase that calls reality into question—the known reality of "the terrible events in Poland." Bellow was made fully aware of these events earlier than most, and with a close-up precision unbefogged by such grand metaphorical abstractions as "a crime so vast that it brings all Being into Judgment." The writer who could explicitly describe the particular texture of an old man's boots glimpsed seventy years before here fades into the elusiveness of high declamation. Yet a single much-overlooked biographical datum may dispute these assertions of overriding literary distraction. In 1948, three years after the defeat of Germany and the appalling revelations of the death camps, Bellow and Anita Goshkin, the social worker who became his first wife, went with their small son Gregory to live in Paris; a Guggenheim grant made the move possible. Bellow settled in to work on a new novel, caught up in the convivial cadres of literary Americans drawn to postwar Paris, while Anita found a job with the Joint Distribution Committee. Here we must pause to take this in. The Joint, as it was called, was a privately funded American effort to salvage the broken lives of the remnant of Holocaust survivors; Anita was perforce immersed daily in freshly accumulating news of "the terrible events in Poland." Are we to believe that the wife never imparted to the husband what she learned and witnessed and felt every day, or that, detached, he took no notice of it?

But if we may not conjecture what a wife privately recounts to a husband—even one so alert to the historically momentous—the letters themselves, with their multiple sharp retrospections, are testimony enough. In 1978, writing to the twenty-something Leon Wieseltier ("I found I could tell you things"), Bellow responded to a pair of articles Wieseltier had sent him on the philosophic origins of Hannah Arendt's post-Holocaust thinking. "That superior Krautess," as Bellow dubbed her, had notoriously charged the European Jewish leadership with collaboration in the administration of the Nazi ghettos and deportations. "She could often think clearly," Bellow tells Wieseltier, "but to think simply was altogether beyond her, and her imaginative faculty was stunted." He goes on to cite the "simple facts":

> I once asked Alexander Donat, author of *The Holocaust Kingdom*, how it was that the Jews went down so quickly in Poland. He said something like this: "After three days in the ghetto, unable to wash and shave, without clean clothing, deprived of food, all utilities and municipal services cut off, your toilet habits humiliatingly disrupted, you are demoralized, confused, subject to panic. A life of austere discipline would have made it possible to keep my head, but how many civilized people had such a life?" Such simple facts— had Hannah had the imagination to see them—would have vitiated her theories.

Arendt may have been a respectable if not wholly respected adversary, but the treasonous Ezra Pound was likely the most poisonous figure by whom Bellow judged both "the terrible events in Poland" and the writers who declined to face them. In 1982, addressing Robert Boyers's commiseration with what Boyers termed an "uncharitable" review of *The Dean's December* by the critic Hugh Kenner, Bellow fulminated against Kenner's "having come out openly in his Eliot-Pound anti-Semitic regalia" in defense of Pound. Infamous for his wartime broadcasts from Mussolini's Italy—tirade after tirade on Jews and "usury"—Pound had nevertheless attracted faithful literary champions. "It was that the poet's convictions could be separated from his poetry," Bellow argued. "It was thus possible to segregate the glory from the shame. Then you took possession of the glory in the name of 'culture' and kept the malignancies as a pet." A quarter of a century before, in 1956, in the most coldly furious confrontation to be found here, Bellow had already accused William Faulkner of heartlessly overlooking Pound's malevolence. As head of a presidentially appointed committee of writers "to promote pro-American values abroad," Faulkner had asked Bellow to sign on to a recommendation for Pound's release from his confinement in a hospital for the insane; though deemed a traitor, he had been spared prison. With uncommon bitterness, Bellow retorted:

> Pound advocated in his poems and in his broadcasts enmity to the Jews and preached hatred and murder. Do you mean to ask me to join you in honoring a man who called for the destruction of my kinsmen? I can take no part in such a thing even if it makes effective propaganda abroad, which I doubt. Europeans will take it instead as a symptom of reaction. In France, Pound would have been shot. Free him because he is a poet? Why, better poets than he were exterminated perhaps.
>
> Shall we say nothing in their behalf? America has dealt mercifully with Pound in sparing his life. To release him is a feeble and foolish idea. It would identify this program in the eyes of the world with Hitler and Himmler and Mussolini and genocide. . . . What staggers me is that you and Mr. [John] Steinbeck who have dealt for so many years in words should fail to understand the import of Ezra Pound's plain and brutal statements about the "kikes" leading the "goy" to slaughter. Is this—from *The Pisan Cantos*—the stuff of poetry? It is a call to murder. . . . The whole world conspires to ignore what has happened, the giant wars, the colossal

hatreds, the unimaginable murders, the destruction of the
very image of man. And we—"a representative group of
American writers"—is this what we come out for, too?

In light of this uncompromising cri de coeur, and of similar
mordant reflections in the novels and stories (covertly in *The
Victim* and boldly elsewhere), how are we to regard Bellow's "I
was too busy becoming a novelist" apologia? A false note: there
was, in fact, no "unspeakable evasion"; rather, an enduring recognition of acid shame and remorse. *And can I really say—can
anyone say—what was to be done?* Clearly, and from the first, he
saw and he knew.

Now it may be imagined—or even insisted—that too much
is being made of all this, that the emphasis here is dispropor-
tionate, and that there are other dimensions, more conspicuous
and profuse, which can more readily define Bellow as writer.
Or it can be said, justifiably, that he openly denigrated anything resembling special pleading—after all, hadn't he brushed
off as "a repulsive category" the phrase "Jewish writers in
America"? And what was this dismissal if not a repudiation of
a vulgarizing tendency to bypass the art in order to laud the
artist as a kind of ethnic cheerleader—much as young Jewish
baseball fans are encouraged to look to Hank Greenberg for
prideful self-validation. Besides, he had long ago put himself
on record as freewheeling, unfettered, unprescribed, liberated
from direction or coercion. In words that will not be found in
the correspondence (they derive from the essays, those publicly
personal letters to readers), Bellow wrote, "I would not allow
myself to become the product of an *environment*"—flaunting
willful italics. And though he never failed to refresh his law
of the unleashed life, it rang now with a decisive coda: "In
my generation, the children of immigrants *became* American.
An effort was required. One made oneself, freestyle. . . . I was
already an American, and I was also a Jew. I had an American
outlook, superadded to a Jewish consciousness." To Faulkner's
indifference he could speak—powerfully, inexorably—of "my
kinsmen." And to history the same.

Say, then, that he was, as he intended to be, free, unstinting in what he chose to love or mourn or recoil from. The letters tell us whom and how he loved. He loved his sons. He loved John Berryman, John Cheever, Ralph Ellison, Martin Amis. He loved Alfred Kazin (whom he mostly disliked). He loved, to the end, Janis Bellow and their little daughter, Naomi Rose. He loved, even in death, Isaac Rosenfeld, the tumultuously inspired intimate of his youth (who nastily destroyed a hoard of his old friend's letters). He revered—but not always—thought, civilization, and what he named "the very image of man," all of which could be undone. He believed in outcry, and trusted the truth of his own. He was adept at witticism and outright laughter. He was serious in invoking whatever particle of eternity he meant by soul, that old, old inkling he was fearless in calling up from contemporary disgrace.

Like the novels and stories, the letters in their proliferation and spontaneity unveil the life—those sinews of it amenable to utterance—almost to its final breath. What happened soon afterward came to something less. On September 21, 2005, five months after Bellow's death, a celebratory symposium was convened at the 92nd Street Y in New York. The participants included British writers Ian McEwan, Martin Amis, and the critic James Wood, the first two having flown from London for the occasion; William Kennedy and Jeffrey Eugenides completed the panel. Each spoke movingly in turn: joyfully reverential, heartfelt, intermittently (and charmingly) anecdotal, adoring—a density of love. There was mention of modernism, fictional digression, character, childhood, Chicago, crowded tenements, the immigrant poor. Riffing in homage, Amis delivered an imitation of Bellow's laugh, the delight and self-delight of it, the lifted chin, the head thrown back. But all this was a departure from the culminating sentiment—it *was* a sentiment, a susceptibility, a rapturous indulgence—that captivated and dominated these writerly temperaments. Wood: "I judge all modern prose by his. . . . The prose comes before and it comes afterward." Amis: "His sentences and his prose were a force of nature." McEwan: "The phrase or sentence has become part of our mental furniture. . . . Sentences like these are all you need to know about Saul Bellow." And so on. Understandable,

plainly: superb novelists, stellar craftsmen, each one mesmerized by Bellow's unparalleled combinations.

Yet, despite these plenitudes, Saul Bellow was missing on
that platform and in that auditorium teeming with admirers—as
much missing there as, clothed in living flesh, he is an insistent
presence in the letters. It was as if a committee of professional
jewelers, loupes in place, had met to sift through heaps of gems
strewn scattershot on a velvet scarf—the splendor and flash and
glitter of opal and ruby and emerald, the word, the phrase, the
sentence, the marvelous juxtapositions, the sublime clashes of
style, the precious trove of verbal touchstones!

It was not enough. It was an abundant truth that diminished
even as it aggrandized. A mammoth absence opened its jaws—
where was the century, the century that Bellow's reality-stung
inquisitiveness traversed almost in its entirety, from Trotsky
to Wilhelm Reich to Rudolf Steiner; where was the raw and
raucously shifting society he knocked about in, undermined,
reveled in, and sometimes reviled? Where was his imagined
Africa, where were the philosophies he devoured, where were
the evanescent infatuations he pursued, where was the clamor
of history, and the defiant angers, and the burning lamentations
for the beloved dead, the broken heart for Isaac Rosenfeld,
whose writer's envy blazed, and for the father and brothers
whose belittlements never left off hurting? And where, during
that long tribute-laden afternoon in New York, was America
itself?

Among the soon-to-be-forgotten novelists of our time, Saul
Bellow stays on. Surely it is for the kaleidoscopic astonishments
of his sentences that he lasts. But not only.

A Drug Store Eden

IN 1929 MY PARENTS sold their drug store in Yorkville—a neighborhood comprising Manhattan's East Eighties—and bought a pharmacy in Pelham Bay, in the northeast corner of the Bronx. It was a move from dense city to almost country. Pelham Bay was at the very end of a relatively new stretch of elevated train track that extended from the subway of the true city all the way out to the small-town feel of little houses and a single row of local shops: shoemaker's, greens store, grocery, drug store, bait store. There was even a miniature five-and-ten where you could buy pots, housedresses, and thick lisle stockings for winter. Three stops down the line was the more populous Westchester Square, with its bank and post office, which old-timers still called "the village"—Pelham Bay had once lain outside the city limits, in Westchester County.

This lost little finger of the borough was named for the broad but mild body of water that rippled across Long Island Sound to a blurry opposite shore. All the paths of Pelham Bay Park led down to a narrow beach of rough pebbles, and all the surrounding streets led, sooner or later, to the park, wild and generally deserted. Along many of these streets there were empty lots that resembled meadows, overgrown with Queen Anne's lace and waist-high weeds glistening with what the children termed "snake spit"; poison ivy crowded between the toes of clumps of sky-tall oaks. The snake spit was a sort of bubbly botanical excretion, but there were real snakes in those lots, with luminescent skins, brownish-greenish, crisscrossed with white lines. There were real meadows, too: acres of downhill grasses, in the middle of which you might suddenly come on a set of rusty old swings—wooden slats on chains—or a broken red-brick wall left over from some ruined and forgotten Westchester estate.

The Park View Pharmacy—the drug store my parents

bought—stood on the corner of Colonial Avenue, between Continental and Burr: Burr for Aaron Burr, the Vice President who killed Alexander Hamilton in a duel. The neighborhood had a somewhat bloodthirsty Revolutionary flavor. Not far away you could still visit Spy Oak, the venerable tree on which captured Redcoats had once been hanged; and now and then Revolutionary bullets were churned up a foot or so beneath the front lawn of the old O'Keefe house, directly across the street from the Park View Pharmacy. George Washington had watered his horses, it was believed, in the ancient sheds beyond Ye Olde Homestead, a local tavern that, well after Prohibition, was still referred to as the "speak-easy." All the same, there were no Daughters of the American Revolution here: instead, Pelham Bay was populated by the children of German, Irish, Swedish, Scottish, and Italian immigrants, and by a handful of the original immigrants themselves. The greenhorn Italians, from Naples and Sicily, kept goats and pigs in their back yards, and pigeons on their roofs. Pelham Bay's single Communist— you could tell from the election results that there was such a rare bird—was the Scotsman who lived around the corner, though only my parents knew this. They were privy to the neighborhood's opinions, ailments, and family secrets.

In those years a drug store seemed one of the world's permanent institutions. Who could have imagined that it would one day vanish into an aisle in the supermarket, or re-emerge as a kind of supermarket itself? What passes for a pharmacy nowadays is all open shelves and ceiling racks of brilliant white neon suggesting perpetual indoor sunshine. The Park View, by contrast, was a dark cavern lined with polished wood cabinets rubbed nearly black and equipped with sliding glass doors and mirrored backs. The counters were heaped with towering ziggurats of lotions, potions, and packets, and under them ran glassed-in showcases of the same sober wood. There was a post office (designated a "substation") that sold penny postcards and stamps and money orders. The prescription area was in the rear, closed off from view: here were scores of labeled drawers of all sizes, and rows of oddly shaped brown bottles. In one of those drawers traditional rock candy was stored, in two flavors, plain and maple, dangling on long strings. And finally there was the prescription desk itself, a sloping lecternlike affair on which the current prescription ledger always lay, like some sacred text.

There was also a soda fountain. A pull at a long black handle spurted out carbonated water; a push at a tiny silver spout drew out curly drifts of whipped cream. The air in this part of the drug store was steamy with a deep coffee fragrance, and on wintry Friday afternoons the librarians from the Traveling Library, a green truck that arrived once a week, would linger, sipping and gossiping on the high-backed fountain chairs, or else at the little glass-topped tables nearby, with their small three-cornered seats. Everything was fashioned of the same burnished chocolate-colored wood; but the fountain counters were heavy marble. Above the prescription area, sovereign over all, rose a symbolic pair of pharmacy globes, one filled with red fluid, the other with blue. My father's diploma, class of 1917, was mounted on a wall; next to it hung a picture of the graduates. There was my very young father, with his round pale eyes and widow's peak—a fleck in a mass of black gowns.

Some time around 1937, my mother said to my father, "Willie, if we don't do it now, we'll never do it."

It was the trough of the Great Depression. In the comics, Pete the Tramp was swiping freshly baked pies set out to cool on windowsills; and in real life, tramps (as the homeless were then called) were turning up in the Park View nearly every day. Sometimes they were city drunks—"Bowery bums"—who had fallen asleep on the subway downtown and had ended up in Pelham Bay. Sometimes they were exhausted Midwesterners who had been riding the rails, and had rolled off into the obscuring cattails of the Baychester marsh. But always my father sat them down at the fountain and fed them a sandwich and soup. They smelled bad, these penniless tramps, and their eyes were red and rheumy; often they were very polite. They never left without a meal and a nickel for carfare.

No one was worse off than the tramps, or more desolate than the family who lived in an old freight car on the way to Westchester Square; but no one escaped the Depression. It stalked the country, it stalked Pelham Bay, it stalked the Park View. Drugstore hours were famously long—monstrously long: seven days a week the Park View opened at nine a.m. and closed at two the next morning. My mother scurried from counter to counter, tended the fountain, unpacked cartons, climbed ladders; her varicose veins oozed through their strappings. My father patiently ground powders, and folded the white dust into translucent paper squares with elegantly efficient motions. The drug store was, besides, a public resource: my father bandaged cuts, took specks out of strangers' eyes, and once removed a fishhook from a man's cheek—though he sent him off to the hospital, on the other side of the Bronx, immediately afterward. My quiet father had cronies and clients, grim women and voluble men who flooded his understanding ears with the stories of their sufferings, of flesh or psyche. My father murmured and comforted, and later my parents would whisper sadly about who had "the big C," or, with an ominous gleam, they would smile over a geezer certain to have a heart attack: the geezer would be newly married to a sweet young thing. (And usually they were right about the heart attack.)

Yet no matter how hard they toiled, they were always in peril. There were notes to pay off; they had bought the Park View from a pharmacist named Robbins, and every month, relentlessly, a note came due. They never fell behind, and never missed a payment (and, in fact, were eventually awarded a certificate attesting to this feat); but the effort—the unremitting pressure, the endless anxiety—ground them down. "The note, the note," I would hear, a refrain that shadowed my childhood, though I had no notion of what it meant.

What it meant was that the Depression, which had already crushed so many, was about to crush my mother and father: suddenly their troubles intensified. The Park View was housed in a building owned by a catlike woman my parents habitually referred to, whether out of familiarity or resentment, only as Tessie. The pharmacy's lease was soon to expire, and at this moment, in the cruelest hour of the Depression, Tessie chose to raise the rent. Her tiger's eyes narrowed to slits: no appeal could soften her.

It was because of those adamant tiger's eyes that my mother said, "Willie, if we don't do it now, we'll never do it."

My mother was aflame with ambition, emotion, struggle. My father was reticent, and far more resigned to the world as given. Once, when the days of the Traveling Library were over, and a real library had been constructed at Westchester Square— you reached it by trolley—I came home elated, carrying a pair of books I had found side by side. One was called *My Mother Is a Violent Woman*; the other was *My Father Is a Timid Man*. These seemed a comic revelation of my parents' temperaments. My mother was all heat and enthusiasm. My father was all logic and reserve. My mother, unrestrained, could have run an empire of drug stores. My father was satisfied with one.

Together they decided to do something revolutionary; something virtually impossible in those raw and merciless times. One street over—past McCardle's sun-baked gas station, where there was always a Model-T Ford with its hood open for repair, and past the gloomy bait store, ruled over by Mr. Isaacs, a dour and reclusive veteran of the Spanish-American War who sat reading military histories all day under a mastless sailboat suspended from the ceiling—lay an empty lot in the shape of an elongated lozenge. My parents' daring plan—for young people without means it was beyond daring—was to buy that lot and build on it, from scratch, a brand-new Park View Pharmacy.

They might as well have been dreaming of taking off in Buck Rogers' twenty-fifth-century rocket ship. The cost of the lot was a stratospheric $13,500, unchanged from the Boom of 1928, just before the national wretchedness descended; and that figure was only for the land. After that would come the digging of a foundation and the construction of a building. What was needed was a miracle.

One sad winter afternoon my mother was standing on a ladder, concentrating on setting out some newly arrived drug items on a high shelf. (Although a typical drug store stocked several thousand articles, the Park View's unit-by-unit inventory was never ample. At the end of every week I would hear my father's melodious, impecunious chant on the telephone, ordering goods from the jobber: "A sixth of a dozen, a twelfth of a dozen . . .") A stranger wearing a brown fedora and a long overcoat entered, looked around, and appeared not at all interested in making a purchase; instead he went wandering from case to case, picking things up and putting them down again, trying to be inconspicuous, asking an occasional question or two, all the while scrupulously observing my diligent and tireless parents. The stranger turned out to be a mortgage officer from the American Bible Society, and what he saw, he explained afterward, was a conscientious application of the work ethic; so it was the American Bible Society that supplied the financial foundation of my parents' Eden, the new Park View. They had entertained an angel unawares.

The actual foundation, the one to be dug out of the ground, ran into instant trouble. An unemployed civil engineer named Levinson presided over the excavation; he was unemployed partly because the Depression had dried up much of the job market, but mostly because engineering firms in those years were notorious for their unwillingness to hire Jews. Poor Levinson! The vast hole in the earth that was to become the Park View's cellar filled up overnight with water; the bay was near, and the water table was higher than the hapless Levinson had expected. The work halted. Along came Finnegan and rescued Levinson: Finnegan the plumber, who for a painful fee of fifty dollars (somehow squeezed out of Levinson's mainly empty pockets) pumped out the flood.

After the Park View's exultant move in 1939, the shell of Tessie's old place on Colonial Avenue remained vacant for years. No one took it over; the plate-glass windows grew murkier and murkier. Dead moths were heaped in decaying mounds on the inner sills. Tessie had lost more than the heartless increase she had demanded, and more than the monthly rent the renewed lease would have brought: there was something ignominious and luckless—tramplike—about that fly-specked empty space, now dimmer than ever. But within its freshly risen walls, the Park View Redux gleamed. Overhead, fluorescent tubes—an indoor innovation—shed a steady white glow, and a big square skylight poured down shifting shafts of brilliance. Familiar objects appeared clarified in the new light: the chocolate-colored fixtures, arranged in unaccustomed configurations, were all at once thrillingly revivified. Nothing from the original Park View had been left behind—everything was just the same, yet zanily out of order: the two crystal urns with their magical red and blue fluids suggestive of alchemy; the entire stock of syrups, pills, tablets, powders, pastes, capsules; tubes and bottles by the hundreds; all the contents of all the drawers and cases; the fountain with its marble top; the prescription desk and its sacrosanct ledger; the stacks of invaluable cigar boxes stuffed with masses of expired prescriptions; the locked and well-guarded narcotics cabinet; the post office, and the safe in which the post office receipts were kept. Even the great, weighty, monosyllabically blunt hanging sign—"DRUGS"—had been brought over and rehung, and it too looked different now. In the summer heat it dropped its black rectangular shadow over Mr. Isaacs' already shadowy headquarters, where vials of live worms were crowded side by side with vials of nails and screws.

At around this time my mother's youngest brother, my uncle Rubin, had come to stay with us—no one knew for how long—in our little house on Saint Paul Avenue, a short walk from the Park View. Five of us lived in that house: my parents, my grandmother, my brother and I. Rubin, who was called Ruby, was now the sixth. He was a bachelor and something of a family enigma. He was both bitter and cheerful; effervescence would give way to lassitude. He taught me how to draw babies and bunnies, and could draw anything himself; he wrote ingenious comic jingles, which he illustrated as adroitly, it struck me, as Edward Lear; he cooked up mouth-watering corn fritters, and designed fruit salads in the shape of ravishing unearthly blossoms. When now and then it fell to him to put me to bed, he always sang the same heartbreaking lullaby: "Sometimes I fee-eel like a motherless child, a long, long way-ay from ho-ome," in a deep and sweet quaver. In those days he was mostly jobless; on occasion he would crank up his Tin Lizzie and drive out to upper Westchester to prune trees. Once he was stopped at a police roadblock, under suspicion of being the Lindbergh baby kidnapper—the back seat of his messy old Ford was strewn with ropes, hooks, and my discarded baby bottles.

Ruby had been disappointed in love, and was somehow a disappointment to everyone around him. When he was melancholy or resentful, the melancholy was irritable and the resentment acrid. As a very young man he had been single-minded in a way none of his immigrant relations, or the snobbish mother of the girlfriend who had been coerced into jilting him, could understand or sympathize with. In Czarist Russia's restricted Pale of Settlement, a pharmacist was the highest vocation a Jew could attain to. In a family of pharmacists, Ruby wanted to be a farmer. Against opposition, he had gone off to the National Farm School in New Jersey—one of several Jewish agricultural projects sponsored by the German philanthropist Baron Maurice de Hirsch. Ruby was always dreaming up one sort of horticultural improvement or another, and sometimes took me with him to visit a certain Dr. McClain, at the Bronx Botanical Gardens, whom he was trying to interest in one of his inventions. He was kindly received, but nothing came of it. Despite his energy and originality, all of Ruby's hopes and strivings collapsed in futility.

All the same, he left an enduring mark on the Park View. It was a certain circle of stones—a mark more distinctive than his deserted bachelor's headstone in an overgrown cemetery on Staten Island.

Ruby assisted in the move from Tessie's place to the new location. His presence was fortuitous—but his ingenuity, it would soon develop, was benison from the goddess Flora. The Park View occupied all the width but not the entire depth of the lot on which it was built. It had, of course, a welcoming front door, through which customers passed; but there was also a back door, past a little aisle adjoining the prescription room in the rear of the store, and well out of sight. When you walked out this back door, you were confronted by an untamed patch of weeds and stones, some of them as thick as boulders. At the very end of it lay a large flat rock, in the center of which someone had scratched a mysterious X. The X, it turned out, was a surveyor's mark; it had been there long before my parents bought the lot. It meant that the property extended to that X and no farther.

I was no stranger either to the lot or its big rock. It was where the neighborhood children played—a sparse group in that sparsely populated place. Sometimes the rock was a pirate ship; sometimes it was a pretty room in a pretty house; in January it held a snow fort. But early one summer evening, when the red ball of the sun was very low, a little girl named Theresa, whose hair was as red as the sun's red ball, discovered the surveyor's X and warned me against stamping on it. If you stamp on a cross, she said, the devil's helpers climb right out from inside the earth and grab you and take you away to be tortured. "I don't believe that," I said, and stamped on the X as hard as I could. Instantly Theresa sent out a terrified shriek; chased by the red-gold zigzag of her hair, she fled. I stood there abandoned—suppose it was true? In the silence all around, the wavering green weeds seemed taller than ever before.

Looking out from the back door at those same high weeds stretching from the new red brick of the Park View's rear wall all the way to the flat rock and its X, my mother, like Theresa, saw hallucinatory shapes rising out of the ground. But it was not the devil's minions she imagined streaming upward; it was their very opposite—a vision of celestial growths and fragrances, brilliant botanical hues, golden pears and yellow sunflower-faces, fruitful vines and dreaming gourds. She imagined an enchanted garden. She imagined a secret Eden.

Ruby was angry at my mother; he was angry at everyone but me: I was too young to be held responsible for his lost loves and aspirations. But he could not be separated from his love of fecund dirt. Dirt—the brown dirt of the earth—inspired him; the feel and smell of dirt uplifted him; he took an artist's pleasure in the soil and all its generative properties. And though he claimed to scorn my mother, he became the subaltern of her passion. Like some wizard commander of the stones—they were scattered everywhere in a wild jumble—he swept them into orderliness. A pack of stones was marshaled into a low wall. Five stones were transformed into a perfect set of stairs. Seven stones surrounded what was to become a flower bed. Stones were borders, stones were pathways, stones—placed just so—were natural sculptures.

And finally Ruby commanded the stones to settle in a circle in the very center of the lot. Inside the circle there was to be a green serenity of grass, invaded only by the blunders of violets and wandering buttercups. Outside the circle the earth would be a fructifying engine. It was a dreamer's circle, like the moon or the sun; or a fairy ring; or a mystical small Stonehenge, miniaturized by a spell.

The back yard was cleared, but it was not yet a garden. Like a merman combing a mermaid's weedy hair, my uncle Ruby had unraveled primeval tangles and brambles. He had set up two tall metal poles to accommodate a rough canvas hammock, with a wire strung from the top of one pole to the other. Over this wire a rain-faded old shop-awning had been flung, so that the hammock became a tent or cave or darkened den. A backyard hammock! I had encountered such things only in storybooks.

And then my uncle was gone. German tanks were biting into Europe. Weeping, my grandmother pounded her breast with her fist: the British White Paper of 1939 had declared that ships packed with Jewish refugees would be barred from the beaches of Haifa and Tel Aviv and returned to a Nazi doom. In P.S. 71, our neighborhood school, the boys were drawing cannons and warplanes; the girls were drawing figure skaters in tutus; both boys and girls were drawing the Trylon and the Perisphere. The Trylon was a three-sided obelisk. The Perisphere was a shining globe. They were already as sublimely legendary as the Taj Mahal. The official colors of the 1939 World's Fair were orange and blue—everyone knew this; everyone had ridden in noiselessly moving armchairs into the Fair's World of Tomorrow, where the cloverleaf highways of the impossibly futuristic nineteen-sixties materialized among inconceivable suburbs. In the magical lanes of Flushing you could watch yourself grin on a television screen as round and small as the mouth of a teacup. My grandmother, in that frail year of her dying, was taken to see the Palestine Pavilion, with its flickering films of Jewish pioneers.

Ruby was drafted before the garden could be dug. He sent a photograph of himself in Army uniform, and a muffled recording of his voice, all songs and jolly jingles, from a honky-tonk arcade in an unnamed Caribbean town.

So it was left to my mother to dig the garden. I have no inkling of when or how. I lived inside the hammock all that time, under the awning, enclosed; I read and read. Sometimes, for a treat, I would be given two nickels for carfare and a pair of quarters, and then I would climb the double staircase to the train and go all the way to Fifty-ninth Street: you could enter Bloomingdale's directly from the subway, without ever glimpsing daylight. I would run up the steps to the book department on the mezzanine, moon over the Nancy Drew series in an agony of choosing (*The Mystery of Larkspur Lane*, *The Mystery of the Whispering Statue*, each for fifty cents), and run down to the subway again, with my lucky treasure. An hour and a half later, I would be back in the hammock, under the awning, while the afternoon sun broiled on. But such a trip was rare. Mostly the books came from the Traveling Library; inside my hammock-cave the melting glue of new bindings sent out a blissful redolence. And now my mother would emerge from the back door of the Park View, carrying—because it was so hot under the awning—half a cantaloupe, with a hillock of vanilla ice cream in its scooped-out center. (Have I ever been so safe, so happy, since? Has consciousness ever felt so steady, so unimperiled, so immortal?)

Across the ocean, synagogues were being torched, refugees were in flight. On American movie screens Ginger Rogers and Fred Astaire whirled in and out of the March of Time's grim newsreels—Chamberlain with his defeatist umbrella, the Sudetenland devoured, Poland invaded. Meanwhile my mother's garden grew. The wild raw field Ruby had regimented was ripening now into a luxuriant and powerful fertility: all around my uncle's talismanic ring of stones the ground swelled with thick savory smells. Corn tassels hung down over the shut greenleaf lids of pearly young cobs. Fat tomatoes reddened on sticks. The bumpy scalps of cucumbers poked up. And flowers! First, as tall as the hammock poles, a flock of hunchbacked sunflowers, their heads too weighty for their shoulders—huge heavy heads of seeds, and a ruff of yellow petals. At their feet, rows of zinnias and marigolds, with tiny violets and the weedy pink buds of clover sidling between.

Now and then a praying mantis—a stiffly marching fake leaf—would rub its skinny forelegs together and stare at you with two stern black dots. And butterflies! These were mostly white and mothlike; but sometimes a great black-veined monarch would alight on a stone, in perfect stillness. Year by year the shade of a trio of pear trees widened and deepened.

Did it rain? It must have rained—it must have thundered—in those successive summers of my mother's garden; but I remember a perpetual sunlight, hot and honeyed, and the airless boil under the awning, and the heart-piercing scalliony odor of library glue (so explicit that I can this minute re-create it in my very tear ducts, as a kind of mourning); and the fear of bees.

Though I was mostly alone there, I was never lonely in the garden. But on the other side of the door, inside the Park View, an unfamiliar churning had begun—a raucous teeming, the world turning on its hinge. In the aftermath of Pearl Harbor, there were all at once jobs for nearly everyone, and money to spend in any cranny of wartime leisure. The Depression was receding. On weekends the subway spilled out mobs of city picnickers into the green fields of Pelham Bay Park, bringing a tentative prosperity to the neighborhood—especially on Sundays. I dreaded and hated this new Sunday frenzy, when the Park View seemed less a pharmacy than a carnival stand, and my own isolation grew bleak. Open shelves sprouted in the aisles, laden with anomalous racks of sunglasses, ice coolers, tubes of mosquito repellent and suntan lotion, paper cups, colorful towers of hats—sailors' and fishermen's caps, celluloid visors, straw topis and sombreros, headgear of every conceivable shape. Thirsty picnickers stood three deep at the fountain, clamoring for ice-cream cones or sodas. The low, serious drug-store voices that accompanied the Park View's weekday decorum were swept away by revolving laughing crowds—carnival crowds. And at the close of these frenetic summer Sundays, my parents would anxiously count up the cash register in the worn night of their exhaustion, and I would hear their joyful disbelief: unimaginable riches, almost seventy-five dollars in a single day!

Then, when the safe was locked up, and the long cords of the fluorescent lights pulled, they would drift in the dimness into the garden, to breathe the cool fragrance. At this starry hour the katydids were screaming in chorus, and fireflies bleeped like errant semaphores. In the enigmatic dark, my mother and father, with their heads together in silhouette, looked just then as I pictured them looking on the Albany night boat, on June 19, 1921, their wedding day. There was a serial photo from that long-ago time I often gazed at—a strip taken in an automatic-photo booth in fabled, faraway Albany. It showed them leaning close, my young father quizzical, my young mother trying to smile, or else trying not to; the corners of her lips wandered toward one loveliness or the other. They had brought back a honeymoon souvenir: three sandstone monkeys joined at the elbows: see no evil, hear no evil, speak no evil. And now, in their struggling forties, standing in Ruby's circle of stones, they breathed in the night smells of the garden, onion grass and honeysuckle, and felt their private triumph. Seventy-five dollars in eighteen hours!

No one knew the garden was there. It was utterly hidden. You could not see it, or suspect it, inside the Park View, and because it was nested in a wilderness of empty lots all around, it was altogether invisible from any surrounding street. It was a small secluded paradise.

And what vegetable chargings, what ferocities of growth, the turbulent earth pushed out! Buzzings and dapplings. Birds dipping their beaks in an orgy of seed-lust. It was as if the ground itself were crying peace, peace; and the war began. In Europe the German death factories were pumping out smoke and human ash from a poisoned orchard of chimneys. In Pelham Bay, among bees and white-wing flutterings, the sweet brown dirt pumped ears of corn.

Nearly all the drug stores—of the old kind—are gone, in Pelham Bay and elsewhere. The Park View Pharmacy lives only in a secret Eden behind my eyes. Gone are Bernardini, Pressman, Weiss, the rival druggists on the way to Westchester Square. They all, like my father, rolled suppositories on glass slabs and ground powders with brass pestles. My mother's garden has returned to its beginning: a wild patch, though enclosed now by brick house after brick house. The houses have high stoops; they are city houses. The meadows are striped with highways. Spy Oak gave up its many ghosts long ago.

But under a matting of decayed pear pits and thriving ragweed back of what used to be the Park View, Ruby's circle of stones stands frozen. The earth, I suppose, has covered them over; as—far off in Staten Island—it covers my dreaming mother, my father, my grandmother, my resourceful and embittered farmer uncle.

Washington Square, 1946

> . . . this portion of New York appears to many
> persons the most delectable. It has a kind of
> established repose which is not of frequent
> occurrence in other quarters of the long, shrill
> city; it has a riper, richer, more honorable look
> than any of the upper ramifications of the great
> longitudinal thoroughfare—the look of having
> had something of a social history.
> —HENRY JAMES, *Washington Square*

I FIRST CAME down to Washington Square on a colorless February morning in 1946. I was seventeen and a half years old and was carrying my lunch in a brown paper bag, just as I had carried it to high school only a month before. It was—I thought it was—the opening day of spring term at Washington Square College, my initiation into my freshman year at New York University. All I knew of N.Y.U. then was that my science-minded brother had gone there; he had written from the Army that I ought to go there too. With master-of-ceremonies zest he described the Browsing Room on the second floor of the Main Building as a paradisal chamber whose bookish loungers leafed languidly through magazines and exchanged high-principled witticisms between classes. It had the sound of a carpeted Olympian club in Oliver Wendell Holmes's Boston, Hub of the Universe, strewn with leather chairs and delectable old copies of *The Yellow Book*.

On that day I had never heard of Oliver Wendell Holmes or *The Yellow Book*, and Washington Square was a faraway bower where wounded birds fell out of trees. My brother had once brought home from Washington Square Park a baby sparrow with a broken leg, to be nurtured back to flight. It died instead,

Published as "The First Day of School: Washington Square 1946," *Harper's*, September 1985.

emitting in its last hours melancholy faint cheeps, and leaving behind a dense recognition of the minute explicitness of mortality. All the same, in the February grayness Washington Square had the allure of the celestial unknown. A sparrow might die, but my own life was luminously new: I felt my youth like a nimbus.

Which dissolves into the dun gauze of a low and sullen city sky. And here I am flying out of the Lexington Avenue subway at Astor Place, just a few yards from Wanamaker's, here I am turning the corner past a secondhand bookstore and a union hall; already late, I begin walking very fast toward the park. The air is smoky with New York winter grit, and on clogged Broadway a mob of trucks shifts squawking gears. But there, just ahead, crisscrossed by paths under high branches, is Washington Square; and on a single sidewalk, three clear omens; or call them riddles, intricate and redolent. These I will disclose in a moment, but before that you must push open the heavy brass-and-glass doors of the Main Building, and come with me, at a hard and panting pace, into the lobby of Washington Square College on the earliest morning of the freshman year.

On the left, a bank of elevators. Straight ahead, a long burnished corridor, spooky as a lit tunnel. And empty, all empty. I can hear my solitary footsteps reverberate, as in a radio mystery drama: they lead me up a short staircase into a big dark ghost-town cafeteria. My brother's letter, along with an account of the physics and chemistry laboratories (I will never see them), has already explained that this place is called Commons—and here my heart will learn to shake with the merciless newness of life. But not today; today there is nothing. Tables and chairs squat in dead silhouette. I race back through a silent maze of halls and stairways to the brass-and-glass doors—there stands a lonely guard. From the pocket of my coat I retrieve a scrap with a classroom number on it and ask the way. The guard announces in a sly croak that the first day of school is not yet; come back tomorrow, he says.

A dumb bad joke: I'm humiliated. I've journeyed the whole way down from the end of the line—Pelham Bay, in the northeast Bronx—to find myself in desolation, all because of a muddle: Tuesday isn't Wednesday. The nimbus of expectation fades off. The lunch bag in my fist takes on a greasy sadness. I'm not ready to dive back into the subway—I'll have a look around.

Across the street from the Main Building, the three omens. First, a pretzel man with a cart. He's wearing a sweater, a cap that keeps him faceless—he's nothing but the shadows of his creases—and wool gloves with the fingertips cut off. He never moves; he might as well be made of papier-mâché, set up and left out in the open since spring. There are now almost no pretzels for sale, and this gives me a chance to inspect the construction of his bare pretzel poles. The pretzels are hooked over a column of gray cardboard cylinders, themselves looped around a stick, the way horseshoes drop around a post. The cardboard cylinders are the insides of toilet paper rolls.

The pretzel man is rooted between a Chock Full o' Nuts (that's the second omen) and a newsstand (that's the third).

The Chock Full: the doors are like fans, whirling remnants of conversation. *She will marry him. She will not marry him.* Fragrance of coffee and hot chocolate. *We can prove that the senses are partial and unreliable vehicles of information, but who is to say that reason is not equally the product of human limitation?* Powdered doughnut sugar on their lips.

Attached to a candy store, the newsstand. Copies of *Partisan Review*: the table of the gods. Jean Stafford, Mary McCarthy, Elizabeth Hardwick, Irving Howe, Delmore Schwartz, Alfred Kazin, Clement Greenberg, Stephen Spender, William Phillips, John Berryman, Saul Bellow, Philip Rahv, Richard Chase, Randall Jarrell, Simone de Beauvoir, Karl Shapiro, George Orwell! I don't know a single one of these names, but I feel their small conflagration flaming in the gray street: the succulent hotness of their promise. I mean to penetrate every one of them. Since all the money I have is my subway fare—two nickels—I don't buy a copy (the price of *Partisan* in 1946 is fifty cents); I pass on.

I pass on to the row of houses on the north side of the Square. Henry James was born in one of these, but I don't know that either. Still, they are plainly old, though no longer aristocratic:

haughty last-century shabbies with shut eyelids, built of rosy-ripe respectable brick, down on their luck. Across the park bulks Judson Church, with its squat squarish bell tower; by the end of the week I will be languishing at the margins of a basketball game in its basement, forlorn in my blue left-over-from-high-school gym suit and mooning over Emily Dickinson:

> There's a certain Slant of light,
> Winter Afternoons—
> That oppresses, like the Heft
> Of Cathedral Tunes—

There is more I don't know. I don't know that W. H. Auden lives just down *there*, and might at any moment be seen striding toward home under his tall rumpled hunch; I don't know that Marianne Moore is only up the block, her doffed tricorn resting on her bedroom dresser. It's Greenwich Village—I know *that*—no more than twenty years after Edna St. Vincent Millay has sent the music of her name (her best, perhaps her only, poem) into these bohemian streets: bohemia, the honey pot of poets.

On that first day in the tea-leafed cup of the town I am ignorant, ignorant! But the three riddle-omens are soon to erupt, and all of them together will illumine Washington Square.

Begin with the benches in the Park. Here, side by side with students and their loose-leafs, lean or lie the shadows of the pretzel man, his creased ghosts or doubles: all those pitiables, half-women and half-men, neither awake nor asleep, the discountable, the repudiated, the unseen. No more notice is taken of any of them than of a scudding fragment of newspaper in the path. Even then, even so long ago, the benches of Washington Square are pimpled with this hell-tossed crew, these Mad Margarets and Cokey Joes, these volcanic coughers, shakers, groaners, tremblers, droolers, blasphemers, these public urinators with vomitous breath and rusted teeth-stumps, dead-eyed and self-abandoned, dragging their makeshift junkyard shoes, their buttonless layers of raggedy ratfur. The pretzel man with his toilet paper rolls conjures and spews them all—he is a loftier brother to these citizens of the lower pox, he is guardian of the garden of the jettisoned. They rattle along all the seams of Washington Square. They are the pickled City, the true and universal City-below-Cities, the wolfish vinegar-Babylon that dogs the spittled skirts of bohemia. The toilet paper rolls are the temple-columns of this sacred grove.

Next, the whirling doors of Chock Full o' Nuts. Here is the marketplace of Washington Square, its bazaar, its roiling gossip parlor, its matchmaker's office and arena—the outermost wing, so to speak, evolved from the Commons. On a day like today, when the Commons is closed, the Chock Full is thronged with extra power, a cello making up for a missing viola. Until now, the fire of my vitals has been for the imperious tragedians of the *Aeneid*; I have lived in the narrow throat of poetry. Another year or so of this oblivion, until at last I am hammer-struck with the shock of Europe's skull, the bled planet of death camp and war. Eleanor Roosevelt has not yet written her famous column announcing the discovery of Anne Frank's diary. The term "cold war" is new. The Commons, like the college itself, is overcrowded, veterans in their pragmatic thirties mingling with the reluctant dreamy young. And the Commons is convulsed with politics: a march to the docks is organized, no one knows by whom, to protest the arrival of Walter Gieseking, the German musician who flourished among Nazis. The Communists—two or three readily recognizable cantankerous zealots—stomp through with their daily leaflets and sneers. There is even a Monarchist, a small poker-faced rectangle of a man with secretive tireless eyes who, when approached for his views, always demands, in perfect Bronx tones, the restoration of his king. The engaged girls—how many of them there seem to be!—flash their rings and tangle their ankles in their long New Look skirts. There is no feminism and no feminists; I am, I think, the only one. The Commons is a tide: it washes up the cold war, it washes up the engaged girls' rings, it washes up the several philosophers and the numerous poets. The philosophers are all Existentialists; the poets are all influenced by "The Waste Land." When the Commons overflows, the engaged girls cross the street to show their rings at the Chock Full.

Call it density, call it intensity, call it continuity: call it, finally, society. The Commons belongs to the satirists. Here, one
afternoon, is Alfred Chester, holding up a hair, a single strand,
before a crowd. (He will one day write stories and novels. He
will die young.) "What is that hair?" I innocently ask, having
come late on the scene. "A pubic hair," he replies, and I feel as
Virginia Woolf did when she declared human nature to have
"changed in or about December 1910"—soon after her sister
Vanessa explained away a spot on her dress as "semen."

In or about February 1946 human nature does not change; it
keeps on. On my bedroom wall I tack—cut out from *Life* magazine—the wildest Picasso I can find: a face that is also a belly.
Mr. George E. Mutch, a lyrical young English teacher twenty-
seven years old, writes on the blackboard: "When lilacs last in
the dooryard bloom'd," and "Bare, ruined choirs, where late
the sweet birds sang," and "A green thought in a green shade";
he tells us to burn, like Pater, with a hard, gemlike flame.
Another English teacher—his name is Emerson—compares
Walt Whitman to a plumber; next year he will shoot himself in
a wood. The initial letters of Washington Square College are
a device to recall three of the Seven Deadly Sins: Wantonness,
Sloth, Covetousness. In Commons they argue the efficacy of
the orgone box. Eda Lou Walton, sprightly as a bird, knows all
the Village bards, and is a Village bard herself. Sidney Hook is
an intellectual rumble in the logical middle distance. Homer
Watt, chairman of the English Department, is the very soul
who, in a far-off time of bewitchment, hired Thomas Wolfe.

And so, in February 1946, I make my first purchase of a
"real" book—which is to say, not for the classroom. It is displayed in the window of the secondhand bookstore between the
Astor Place subway station and the union hall, and for weeks I
have been coveting it: *Of Time and the River*. I am transfigured;
I am pierced through with rapture; skipping gym, I sit among
morning mists on a windy bench a foot from the stench of Mad
Margaret, sinking into that cascading syrup: "Man's youth is a
wonderful thing: It is so full of anguish and of magic and he
never comes to know it as it is, until it is gone from him forever.
. . . And what is the essence of that strange and bitter miracle

of life which we feel so poignantly, so unutterably, with such a bitter pain and joy, when we are young?" Thomas Wolfe, lost, and by the wind grieved, ghost, come back again! In Washington Square I am appareled in the "numb exultant secrecies of fog, fog-numb air filled with solemn joy of nameless and impending prophecy, an ancient yellow light, the old smoke-ochre of the morning. . . ."

The smoke-ochre of the morning. Ah, you who have flung Thomas Wolfe, along with your strange and magical youth, onto the ash heap of juvenilia and excess, myself among you, isn't this a lovely phrase still? It rises out of the old pavements of Washington Square as delicately colored as an eggshell.

The veterans in their pragmatic thirties are nailed to Need; they have families and futures to attend to. When Mr. George E. Mutch exhorts them to burn with a hard, gemlike flame, and writes across the blackboard the line that reveals his own name,

> The world is too much with us; late and soon,
> Getting and spending, we lay waste our powers,

one of the veterans heckles, "What about getting a Buick, what about spending a buck?" Chester, at sixteen, is a whole year younger than I; he has transparent eyes and a rosebud mouth, and is in love with a poet named Diana. He has already found his way to the Village bars, and keeps in his wallet Truman Capote's secret telephone number. We tie our scarves tight against the cold and walk up and down Fourth Avenue, winding in and out of the rows of secondhand bookshops crammed one against the other. The proprietors sit reading their wares and never look up. The books in all their thousands smell sleepily of cellar. Our envy of them is speckled with longing; our longing is sick with envy. We are the sorrowful literary young.

Every day, month after month, I hang around the newsstand near the candy store, drilling through the enigmatic pages of *Partisan Review*. I still haven't bought a copy; I still can't understand a word. I don't know what "cold war" means. Who is Trotsky? I haven't read *Ulysses*; my adolescent phantoms are rowing in the ablative absolute with *pius* Aeneas. I'm in my mind's cradle, veiled by the exultant secrecies of fog.

Washington Square will wake me. In a lecture room in the Main Building, Dylan Thomas will cry his webwork syllables. Afterward he'll warm himself at the White Horse Tavern. Across the corridor I will see Sidney Hook plain. I will read the Bhagavad Gita and Catullus and Lessing, and, in Hebrew, a novel eerily called *Whither?* It will be years and years before I am smart enough, worldly enough, to read Alfred Kazin and Mary McCarthy.

In the spring, all of worldly Washington Square will wake up to the luster of little green leaves.

She: Portrait of the Essay
as a Warm Body

AN ESSAY IS a thing of the imagination. If there is information in an essay, it is by-the-by, and if there is an opinion in it, you need not trust it for the long run. A genuine essay has no educational, polemical, or sociopolitical use; it is the movement of a free mind at play. Though it is written in prose, it is closer in kind to poetry than to any other form. Like a poem, a genuine essay is made out of language and character and mood and temperament and pluck and chance.

And if I speak of a genuine essay, it is because fakes abound. Here the old-fashioned term poetaster may apply, if only obliquely. As the poetaster is to the poet—a lesser aspirant—so the article is to the essay: a look-alike knockoff guaranteed not to wear well. An article is gossip. An essay is reflection and insight. An article has the temporary advantage of social heat—what's hot out there right now. An essay's heat is interior. An article is timely, topical, engaged in the issues and personalities of the moment; it is likely to be stale within the month. In five years it will have acquired the quaint aura of a rotary phone. An article is Siamese-twinned to its date of birth. An essay defies its date of birth, and ours too. (A necessary caveat: some genuine essays are popularly called "articles"—but this is no more than an idle, though persistent, habit of speech. What's in a name? The ephemeral is the ephemeral. The enduring is the enduring.)

A small historical experiment. Who are the classical essayists that come at once to mind? Montaigne, obviously. Among the nineteenth-century English masters, the long row of Hazlitt, Lamb, De Quincey, Stevenson, Carlyle, Ruskin, Newman, Arnold, Harriet Martineau. Of the Americans, Emerson. It may be argued that nowadays these are read only by specialists and literature majors, and by the latter only when they are compelled to. However accurate the claim, it is irrelevant to the experiment, which has to do with beginnings and their disclosures. Here, then, are some introductory passages:

> One of the pleasantest things in the world is going a journey; but I like to go by myself. I can enjoy society in a room; but out of doors, nature is company enough for me. I am then never less alone than when alone.
> —William Hazlitt, "On Going a Journey"

> To go into solitude, a man needs to retire as much from his chamber as from society. I am not solitary whilst I read and write, though nobody is with me. But if a man would be alone, let him look at the stars.
> —Ralph Waldo Emerson, "Nature"

> I have often been asked how I first came to be a regular opium eater; and have suffered, very unjustly, in the opinion of my acquaintance, from being reputed to have brought upon myself all the sufferings which I shall have to record, by a long course of indulgence in this practice purely for the sake of creating an artificial state of pleasurable excitement. This, however, is a misrepresentation of my case.
> —Thomas De Quincey, "Confessions of an
>   English Opium Eater"

> The human species, according to the best theory I can form of it, is composed of two distinct races, the men who borrow, and the men who lend.
> —Charles Lamb, "The Two Races of Men"

> I saw two hareems in the East; and it would be wrong to pass them over in an account of my travels; though the subject is as little agreeable as any I can have to treat, I cannot now think of the two mornings thus employed without a heaviness of heart greater than I have ever brought away

from Deaf and Dumb Schools, Lunatic Asylums, or even Prisons.
          —Harriet Martineau, "From Eastern Life"

The future of poetry is immense, because in poetry, where it is worthy of its high destinies, our race, as time goes on, will find an ever and surer stay. There is not a creed which is not shaken, not an accredited dogma which is not shown to be questionable, not a received tradition which does not threaten to dissolve. . . . But for poetry the idea is everything; the rest is a world of illusion, of divine illusion.
          —Matthew Arnold, "The Study of Poetry"

The changes wrought by death are in themselves so sharp and final, and so terrible and melancholy in their consequences, that the thing stands alone in man's experience, and has no parallel upon earth. It outdoes all other accidents because it is the last of them. Sometimes it leaps suddenly upon its victims, like a Thug; sometimes it lays a regular siege and creeps upon their citadel during a score of years. And when the business is done, there is a sore havoc made in other people's lives, and a pin knocked out by which many subsidiary friendships hung together.
          —Robert Louis Stevenson, "Aes Triplex"

It is recorded of some people, as of Alexander the Great, that their sweat, in consequence of some rare and extraordinary constitution, emitted a sweet odor, the cause of which Plutarch and others investigated. But the nature of most bodies is the opposite, and at their best they are free from smell. Even the purest breath has nothing more excellent than to be without offensive odor, like that of very healthy children.
          —Michel de Montaigne, "Of Smells"

What might such a little anthology of beginnings reveal? First, that language differs from one era to the next: there are touches of archaism here, if only in punctuation and cadence.

Second, that splendid minds may contradict each other (out-doors, Hazlitt never feels alone; Emerson urges the opposite). Third, that the theme of an essay can be anything under the sun, however trivial (the smell of sweat) or crushing (the thought that we must die). Fourth, that the essay is a consist-ently recognizable and venerable—or call it ancient—form. In English: Addison and Steele in the eighteenth century, Bacon and Browne in the seventeenth, Lyly in the sixteenth, Bede in the eighth. And what of the biblical Koheleth—Ecclesiastes—who may be the oldest essayist reflecting on one of the oldest subjects: world-weariness?

So the essay is ancient and various: but this is a commonplace. There is something else, and it is more striking yet—the essay's power. By "power" I mean precisely the capacity to do what force always does: coerce assent. Never mind that the shape and inclination of any essay is against coercion or suasion, or that the essay neither proposes nor purposes to get you to think like its author—at least not overtly. If an essay has a "motive," it is linked more to happenstance and opportunity than to the driven will. A genuine essay is not a doctrinaire tract or a prop-aganda effort or a broadside. Thomas Paine's "Common Sense" and Emile Zola's "J'accuse" are heroic landmark writings; but to call them essays, though they may resemble the form, is to misunderstand. The essay is not meant for the barricades; it is a stroll through someone's mazy mind. Yet this is not to say that there has never been an essayist morally intent on making an argument, however obliquely—George Orwell is a case in point. At the end of the day, the essay turns out to be a force for agreement. It co-opts agreement; it courts agreement; it seduces agreement. For the brief hour we give to it, we are sure to fall into surrender and conviction. And this will occur even if we are intrinsically roused to resistance.

To illustrate: I may not be persuaded by Emersonianism as an ideology, but Emerson—his voice, his language, his music—persuades me. When we look for superlatives, not for nothing do we speak of "commanding" or "compelling" prose. If I am a skeptical rationalist or an advanced biochemist, I may regard (or discard) the idea of the soul as no better than a puff of warm vapor. But here is Emerson on the soul: "when it breathes through [man's] intellect, it is genius; when it breathes through his will, it is virtue; when it flows through his affection, it is love." And then—well, I am in thrall, I am possessed; I believe.

The novel has its own claims on surrender. It suspends our participation in the society we ordinarily live in, so that—for the time we are reading—we forget it utterly. But the essay does not allow us to forget our usual sensations and opinions; it does something even more potent: it makes us deny them. The authority of a masterly essayist—the authority of sublime language and intimate observation—is absolute. When I am with Hazlitt, I know no greater companion than nature. When I am with Emerson, I know no greater solitude than nature.

And what is most odd about the essay's power to lure us into its lair is how it goes about this work. We feel it when a political journalist comes after us with a point of view—we feel it the way the cat is wary of the dog. A polemic is a herald, complete with feathered hat and trumpet. A tract can be a trap. Certain magazine articles have the scent of so-much-per-word. What is indisputable is that all of these are more or less in the position of a lepidopterist with his net: they mean to catch and skewer. They are focused on prey—i.e., us. The genuine essay, in contrast, never thinks of us; the genuine essay may be the most self-centered (the politer word would be subjective) arena for human thought ever devised.

Or else, though still not having you and me in mind (unless as an exemplum of common folly), it is not self-centered at all. When I was a child, I discovered in the public library a book that enchanted me then, and the idea of which has enchanted me for life. I have no recollection either of the title or of the writer—and anyhow very young readers rarely take note of authors; stories are simply and magically *there*. The characters included, as I remember them, three or four children and a delightful relation who is a storyteller, and the scheme was this: each child calls out a story-element—most often an object—and the storyteller gathers up whatever is supplied (blue boots, a river, a fairy, a pencil box) and makes out of these random, unlikely, and disparate offerings a tale both logical

and surprising. An essay, it seems to me, may be similarly constructed—if so deliberate a term applies. The essayist, let us
say, unexpectedly stumbles over a pair of old blue boots in a
corner of the garage, and this reminds her of when she last wore
them—twenty years ago, on a trip to Paris, where on the banks
of the Seine she stopped to watch an old fellow sketching, with
a box of colored pencils at his side. The pencil wiggling over
his sheet is a grayish pink, which reflects the threads of sunset
pulling westward in the sky, like the reins of a fairy cart . . . and
so on. The mind meanders, slipping from one impression to
another, from reality to memory to dreamscape and back again.

In the same way Montaigne, in our sample, when contemplating the unpleasantness of sweat, ends with the pure breath
of children. Or Stevenson, starting out with mortality, speaks
first of ambush, then of war, and finally of a displaced pin. No
one is freer than the essayist—free to leap out in any direction,
to hop from thought to thought, to begin with the finish and
finish with the middle, or to eschew beginning and end and
keep only a middle. The marvel of it is that out of this apparent
causelessness, out of this scattering of idiosyncratic seeing and
telling, a coherent world is made. It is coherent because, after
all, an essayist must be an artist, and every artist, whatever the
means, arrives at a sound and singular imaginative frame—or
call it, on a minor scale, a cosmogony.

And it is into this frame, this work of art, that we tumble
like tar babies, and are held fast. What holds us there?
The authority of a voice, yes; the pleasure—sometimes the
anxiety—of a new idea, an untried angle, a snatch of reminiscence, bliss displayed or shock conveyed. An essay can be
the product of intellect or memory, lightheartedness or gloom,
well-being or disgruntlement. But always there is a certain qui-
etude, on occasion a kind of detachment. Rage and revenge, I
think, belong to fiction. The essay is cooler than that. Because
it so often engages in acts of memory, and despite its gladder
or more antic incarnations, the essay is by and large a serene
or melancholic form. It mimics that low electric hum, sometimes rising to resemble actual speech, that all human beings
carry inside their heads—a vibration, garrulous if somewhat

indistinct, that never leaves us while we wake. It is the hum of perpetual noticing: the configuration of someone's eyelid or tooth, the veins on a hand, a wisp of string caught on a twig, some words your fourth-grade teacher said, so long ago, about the rain, the look of an awning, a sidewalk, a bit of cheese left on a plate. All day long this inescapable hum drums on, recalling one thing and another, and pointing out this and this and this. Legend has it that Titus, emperor of Rome, went mad because of the buzzing of a gnat that made her home in his ear; and presumably the gnat, flying out into the great world and then returning to her nest, whispered what she had seen and felt and learned there. But an essayist is more resourceful than an emperor, and can be relieved of this interior noise, if only for the time it takes to record its murmurings. To seize the hum and set it down for others to hear is the essayist's genius.

It is a genius bound to leisure, and even to luxury, if luxury is measured in hours. The essay's limits can be found in its own reflective nature. Poems have been wrested from the inferno of catastrophe or war, and battlefield letters too: these are the spontaneous bursts and burnings that danger excites. But the meditative temperateness of an essay requires a desk and a chair, a musing and a mooning, a connection to a civilized surround; even when the subject itself is a wilderness of lions and tigers, mulling is the way of it. An essay is a fireside thing, not a con-flagration or a safari.

This may be why, when we ask who the essayists are, it turns out—though novelists may now and then write essays—that true essayists rarely write novels. Essayists are a species of metaphysician: they are inquisitive—also analytic—about the least grain of being. Novelists go about the strenuous business of marrying and burying their people, or else they send them to sea, or to Africa, or (at the least) out of town. Essayists in their stillness ponder love and death. It is probably an illusion that men are essayists more often than women (especially since women's essays have in the past frequently assumed the form of unpublished correspondence). And here I should, I suppose, add a note about maleness and femaleness as a literary issue—what is popularly termed "gender," as if men and women were

French or German tables and sofas. I *should* add such a note; it is the fashion, or, rather, the current expectation or obligation— but there is nothing to say about any of it. Essays are written by men. Essays are written by women. That is the long and the short of it. John Updike, in a genially confident discourse on maleness ("The Disposable Rocket"), takes the view—though he admits to admixture—that the "male sense of space must differ from that of the female, who has such an interesting, active, and significant inner space. The space that interests men is outer." Except, let it be observed, when men write essays: since it is only inner space—interesting, active, significant— that can conceive and nourish the contemplative essay. The "ideal female body," Updike adds, "curves around the centers of repose," and no phrase could better describe the shape of the ideal essay—yet women are no fitter as essayists than men. In promoting the felt salience of sex, Updike nevertheless drives home an essayist's point. Essays, unlike novels, emerge from the sensations of the self. Fiction creeps into foreign bodies; the novelist can inhabit not only a sex not his own, but also beetles and noses and hunger artists and nomads and beasts; while the essay is, as we say, personal.

And here is an irony. Though I have been intent on distin- guishing the marrow of the essay from the marrow of fiction, I confess I have been trying all along, in a subliminal way, to speak of the essay as if it—or she—were a character in a novel or a play: moody, fickle, given on a whim to changing her clothes, or the subject; sometimes obstinate, with a mind of her own; or hazy and light; never predictable. I mean for her to be dressed—and addressed—as we would Becky Sharp, or Ophelia, or Elizabeth Bennet, or Mrs. Ramsay, or Mrs. Wilcox, or even Hester Prynne. Put it that it is pointless to say (as I have done repeatedly, disliking it every moment) "the essay," "an essay." The essay—an essay—is not an abstraction; she may have recognizable contours, but she is highly colored and individuated; she is not a type. She is too fluid, too elusive, to be a category. She may be bold, she may be diffident, she may rely on beauty, or on cleverness, on eros or exotica. Whatever her story, she is the protagonist, the secret self's personification.

When we knock on her door, she opens to us, she is a presence in the doorway, she leads us from room to room; then why should we not call her "she"? She may be privately indifferent to us, but she is anything but unwelcoming. Above all, she is not a hidden principle or a thesis or a construct: she is *there*, a living voice. She takes us in.

Bibliographical Note

STORIES

"The Coast of New Zealand". Periodical: *New Yorker*, June 14, 2021. Book: *Antiquities and Other Stories*, Knopf, 2022. Copyright © 2021, 2022 by Cynthia Ozick. *Antiquities and Other Stories*, Weidenfeld & Nicolson, 2022. Copyright © Cynthia Ozick 2022. With permission of Weidenfeld & Nicolson, an imprint of The Orion Publishing Group Ltd, an Hachette UK Company.

"The Biographer's Hat". Periodical: *New Yorker*, March 7, 2022. Copyright © 2022, 2025 by Cynthia Ozick. With permission of Melanie Jackson Agency, LLC. Copyright © Cynthia Ozick. Reproduced by permission of the author c/o Rogers, Coleridge & White Ltd, 20 Powis Mews, London W11.

"Sin". Periodical: *American Scholar*, September 3, 2019. Book: *Antiquities and Other Stories*, Knopf, 2022. Copyright © 2019, 2022 by Cynthia Ozick. *Antiquities and Other Stories*, Weidenfeld & Nicolson, 2022. Copyright © Cynthia Ozick 2022. With permission of Weidenfeld & Nicolson, an imprint of The Orion Publishing Group Ltd, an Hachette UK Company.

"A Mercenary". Periodical: *American Review* 23, October 1975. Book: *Bloodshed and Three Novellas*, Knopf, 1976. Copyright © 1975, 1976 by Cynthia Ozick. With permission of Melanie Jackson Agency, LLC. *Bloodshed and Three Novellas*, Secker & Warburg, 1976. *Cynthia Ozick: Collected Stories*, Weidenfeld & Nicolson, 2006. Copyright © Cynthia Ozick 2006. With permission of Weidenfeld & Nicolson, an imprint of The Orion Publishing Group Ltd, an Hachette UK Company.

"Virility". Periodical: *Anon.*, February 1971. Book: *The Pagan Rabbi and Other Stories*, Knopf, 1971. Copyright © 1971 by Cynthia Ozick. With permission of Melanie Jackson Agency, LLC. *The Pagan Rabbi and Other Stories*, Secker & Warburg, 1972. *Cynthia Ozick: Collected Stories*, Weidenfeld & Nicolson, 2006. Copyright © Cynthia Ozick 2006. With permission of Weidenfeld & Nicolson, an imprint of The Orion Publishing Group Ltd, an Hachette UK Company.

"Bloodshed". Periodical: *Esquire*, January 1976. Book: *Bloodshed and Three Novellas*, Knopf, 1976. Copyright © 1976 by Cynthia Ozick. With permission of Melanie Jackson Agency, LLC. *Bloodshed and Three Novellas*,

Secker & Warburg, 1976. *Cynthia Ozick: Collected Stories*, Weidenfeld & Nicolson, 2006. Copyright © Cynthia Ozick 2006. With permission of Weidenfeld & Nicolson, an imprint of The Orion Publishing Group Ltd, an Hachette UK Company.

"Shots". Periodical: *Quest/77*, 1, July–August 1977. Book: *Levitation: Five Fictions*, Knopf, 1982. Copyright © 1977, 1982 by Cynthia Ozick. With permission of Melanie Jackson Agency, LLC. *Levitation: Five Fictions*, Secker & Warburg, 1982. *Cynthia Ozick: Collected Stories*, Weidenfeld & Nicolson, 2006. Copyright © Cynthia Ozick 2006. With permission of Weidenfeld & Nicolson, an imprint of The Orion Publishing Group Ltd, an Hachette UK Company.

"Usurpation (Other People's Stories)". Periodical: *Esquire*, May 1974. Book: *Bloodshed and Three Novellas*, Knopf, 1976. Copyright © 1974, 1976 by Cynthia Ozick. With permission of Melanie Jackson Agency, LLC. *Bloodshed and Three Novellas*, Secker & Warburg, 1976. *Cynthia Ozick: Collected Stories*, Weidenfeld & Nicolson, 2006. Copyright © Cynthia Ozick 2006. With permission of Weidenfeld & Nicolson, an imprint of The Orion Publishing Group Ltd, an Hachette UK Company.

"Levitation". Periodical: *Partisan Review* 46:3, 1979. Book: *Levitation: Five Fictions*, Knopf, 1982. Copyright © 1979, 1982 by Cynthia Ozick. With permission of Melanie Jackson Agency, LLC. *Levitation: Five Fictions*, Secker & Warburg, 1982. *Cynthia Ozick: Collected Stories*, Weidenfeld & Nicolson, 2006. Copyright © Cynthia Ozick 2006. With permission of Weidenfeld & Nicolson, an imprint of The Orion Publishing Group Ltd, an Hachette UK Company.

"The Bloodline of the Alkanas". Periodical: *Harper's*, February 2013. Book: *Antiquities and Other Stories*, Knopf, 2022. Copyright © 2013, 2022 by Cynthia Ozick. *Antiquities and Other Stories*, Weidenfeld & Nicolson, 2022. Copyright Cynthia Ozick 2022. With permission of Weidenfeld & Nicolson, an imprint of The Orion Publishing Group Ltd, an Hachette UK Company.

"The Story of My Family". Periodical: *Commentary*, March 2024. Copyright © 2024, 2025 by Cynthia Ozick. With permission of Melanie Jackson Agency, LLC. Copyright © Cynthia Ozick. Reproduced by permission of the author c/o Rogers, Coleridge & White Ltd, 20 Powis Mews, London W11 1JN.

"Actors". Periodical: *New Yorker*, October 5, 1998. Book: *Dictation: A Quartet*, Houghton Mifflin Company, 2008. Copyright © 2008 by Cynthia Ozick. Used by permission of HarperCollins Publishers. *Cynthia Ozick: Collected Stories*, Weidenfeld & Nicolson, 2006. Copyright © Cynthia Ozick 2006. With permission of Weidenfeld & Nicolson, an imprint of The Orion Publishing Group Ltd, an Hachette UK Company.

"At Fumicaro". Periodical: *New Yorker*, July 29, 1984. Book: *Dictation: A Quartet*, Houghton Mifflin Company, 2008. Copyright © 2008 by Cynthia Ozick. Used by permission of HarperCollins Publishers. *Cynthia Ozick: Collected Stories*, Weidenfeld & Nicolson, 2006. Copyright © Cynthia Ozick 2006. With permission of Weidenfeld & Nicolson, an imprint of The Orion Publishing Group Ltd, an Hachette UK Company.

"A Hebrew Sibyl". Periodical: *Granta*, November 13, 2014 (UK). Book: *Antiquities and Other Stories*, Knopf, 2022. Copyright © 2014, 2022 by Cynthia Ozick. *Antiquities and Other Stories*, Weidenfeld & Nicolson, 2022. Copyright © Cynthia Ozick 2022. With permission of Weidenfeld & Nicolson, an imprint of The Orion Publishing Group Ltd, an Hachette UK Company.

"What Happened to the Baby?". Periodical: *Atlantic*, August 1, 2006. Book: *Dictation: A Quartet*, Houghton Mifflin Company, 2008. Copyright © 2008 by Cynthia Ozick. Used by permission of HarperCollins Publishers. *Cynthia Ozick: Collected Stories*, Weidenfeld & Nicolson, 2006. Copyright © Cynthia Ozick 2006. With permission of Weidenfeld & Nicolson, an imprint of The Orion Publishing Group Ltd, an Hachette UK Company.

"The Conversion of the Jews". Periodical: *Harper's*, May 2023. Copyright © 2023, 2025 by Cynthia Ozick. With permission of Melanie Jackson Agency, LLC. Copyright © Cynthia Ozick. Reproduced by permission of the author c/o Rogers, Coleridge & White Ltd, 20 Powis Mews, London W11 1JN.

"Dictation". Periodical: *The Conradian* 32, no. 2, 2007 (UK). Book: *Dictation: A Quartet*, Houghton Mifflin Company, 2008. Copyright © 2008 by Cynthia Ozick. Used by permission of HarperCollins Publishers. *Cynthia Ozick: Collected Stories*, Weidenfeld & Nicolson, 2006. Copyright © Cynthia Ozick 2006. With permission of Weidenfeld & Nicolson, an imprint of The Orion Publishing Group Ltd, an Hachette UK Company.

ESSAYS

"Transcending the Kafkaesque". Periodical: *New Republic*, April 11, 2014. Book: *Critics, Monsters, Fanatics, and Other Literary Essays*, Houghton Mifflin Harcourt, 2016. Copyright © 2016 by Cynthia Ozick. Used by permission of HarperCollins Publishers. Cynthia Ozick, *Letters of Intent: Selected Essays*, ed. David Miller, Atlantic Books, 2017. Copyright © 2017 Cynthia Ozick. With permission of Atlantic Books Ltd.

"The Phantasmagoria of Bruno Schulz". Periodical: *New York Times Book Review*, February 13, 1977. Book: *Art & Ardor*, Knopf, 1983. Copyright 1977, 1983 by Cynthia Ozick. With permission of Melanie Jackson Agency, LLC. *What Henry James Knew and Other Essays on Writers*,

Jonathan Cape, 1993. Cynthia Ozick, *Letters of Intent: Selected Essays*, ed. David Miller, Atlantic Books, 2017. Copyright © 2017 Cynthia Ozick. With permission of Atlantic Books Ltd.

"What Helen Keller Saw". Periodical: *New Yorker*, June 8, 2003. Book: *The Din in the Head*, Houghton Mifflin Company, 2006. Copyright © 2006 by Cynthia Ozick. Used by permission of HarperCollins Publishers. Cynthia Ozick, *Letters of Intent: Selected Essays*, ed. David Miller, Atlantic Books, 2017. Copyright © 2017 Cynthia Ozick. With permission of Atlantic Books Ltd.

"T. S. Eliot at 101". Periodical: *New Yorker*, November 20, 1989. Book: *Fame & Folly*, Knopf, 1996. Copyright © 1989, 1996 by Cynthia Ozick. *What Henry James Knew and Other Essays on Writers*, Jonathan Cape, 1993. Cynthia Ozick, *Letters of Intent: Selected Essays*, ed. David Miller, Atlantic Books, 2017. Copyright © 2017 Cynthia Ozick. With permission of Atlantic Books Ltd.

"Who Owns Anne Frank?". Periodical: *New Yorker*, October 6, 1997. Book: *Quarrel & Quandary*, Knopf, 2000. Copyright © 1997, 2000 by Cynthia Ozick. Cynthia Ozick, *Letters of Intent: Selected Essays*, ed. David Miller, Atlantic Books, 2017. Copyright © 2017 Cynthia Ozick. With permission of Atlantic Books Ltd.

"Isaac Babel and the Identity Question". Periodical: *New Republic*, May 8, 1995. Book: *Fame & Folly*, Knopf, 1996. Copyright © 1995, 1996 by Cynthia Ozick. *Portrait of the Artist as a Bad Character and Other Essays on Writing*, Pimlico, 1996. Cynthia Ozick, *Letters of Intent: Selected Essays*, ed. David Miller, Atlantic Books, 2017. Copyright © 2017 Cynthia Ozick. With permission of Atlantic Books Ltd.

"Dostoyevsky's Unabomber". Periodical: *New Yorker*, February 16, 1997. Book: *Quarrel & Quandary*, Knopf, 2000. Copyright © 1997, 2000 by Cynthia Ozick. Cynthia Ozick, *Letters of Intent: Selected Essays*, ed. David Miller, Atlantic Books, 2017. Copyright © 2017 Cynthia Ozick. With permission of Atlantic Books Ltd.

" 'Please, Stories Are Stories': Bernard Malamud". Periodical: *New York Times Book Review*, May 2014. Book: *Critics, Monsters, Fanatics, and Other Literary Essays*, Houghton Mifflin Harcourt, 2016. Copyright © 2016 by Cynthia Ozick. Used by permission of HarperCollins Publishers. Cynthia Ozick, *Letters of Intent: Selected Essays*, ed. David Miller, Atlantic Books, 2017. Copyright © 2017 Cynthia Ozick. With permission of Atlantic Books Ltd.

"Mrs. Virginia Woolf: A Madwoman and her Nurse". Periodical: *Commentary*, August 1, 1973. Book: *Art & Ardor*, Knopf, 1983. Copyright 1973, 1983 by Cynthia Ozick. With permission of Melanie Jackson Agency, LLC. *What Henry James Knew and Other Essays on Writers*, Jonathan Cape,

1993. Cynthia Ozick, *Letters of Intent: Selected Essays*, ed. David Miller, Atlantic Books, 2017. Copyright © 2017 Cynthia Ozick. With permission of Atlantic Books Ltd.

"The Lastingness of Saul Bellow". Periodical: *New Republic*, February 10, 2011. Book: *Critics, Monsters, Fanatics, and Other Literary Essays*, Houghton Mifflin Harcourt 2016. Copyright © 2016 by Cynthia Ozick. Used by permission of HarperCollins Publishers. Cynthia Ozick, *Letters of Intent: Selected Essays*, ed. David Miller, Atlantic Books, 2017. Copyright © 2017 Cynthia Ozick. With permission of Atlantic Books Ltd.

"A Drug Store Eden". Periodical: *New Yorker*, September 8, 1996. Book: *Quarrel & Quandary*, Knopf, 2000. Copyright © 1996, 2000 by Cynthia Ozick. Cynthia Ozick, *Letters of Intent: Selected Essays*, ed. David Miller, Atlantic Books, 2017. Copyright © 2017 Cynthia Ozick. With permission of Atlantic Books Ltd.

"Washington Square, 1946". Periodical: *Harper's*, September 1985. Book: *Metaphor & Memory*, Knopf, 1989. Copyright © 1985, 1989 by Cynthia Ozick. *Portrait of the Artist as a Bad Character and Other Essays on Writing*, Pimlico, 1996. Cynthia Ozick, *Letters of Intent: Selected Essays*, ed. David Miller, Atlantic Books, 2017. Copyright © 2017 Cynthia Ozick. With permission of Atlantic Books Ltd.

"She: Portrait of the Essay as a Warm Body". Periodical: *Atlantic*, September 1998. Book: *Quarrel & Quandary*, Knopf, 2000. Copyright © 1998, 2000 by Cynthia Ozick. Copyright © Cynthia Ozick. Reproduced by permission of the author c/o Rogers, Coleridge & White Ltd, 20 Powis Mews, London W11 1JN.

Grateful acknowledgment is made for permission to reprint previously published material: Excerpts from *The Waste Land*, "Burbank with a Baedeker: Bleistein with a Cigar," "Gerontion," "Sweeney Among the Nightingales," and "Ash-Wednesday" from *Collected Poems 1909–1962* by T. S. Eliot, copyright © 1936 by Harcourt Brace & Company, copyright © 1963, 1964 by T. S. Eliot; excerpts from "Burnt Norton" and "The Dry Salvages" from *Four Quartets* by T. S. Eliot, copyright © 1943 by T. S. Eliot, copyright renewed 1971 by Esme Valerie Eliot. Rights outside the United States administered by Faber and Faber Limited, London, from *The Complete Poems and Plays of T. S. Eliot*. Excerpts of three letters from *The Letters of T. S. Eliot, 1898–1922*, Volume One, edited by Valerie Eliot, copyright © 1988 by SET Copyrights Limited. Rights outside the United States administered by Faber and Faber Limited, London. Reprinted by permission of Harcourt Brace & Company and Faber and Faber Limited. Excerpts from *Isaac Babel: 1920 Diary*, edited by Carol J. Avins, translated by H. T. Willetts (New Haven: Yale University Press, 1995). Reprinted by permission of Yale University Press.